MW01284985

Digital Marketing: Foundations and Strategy

Fifth Edition

Debra Zahay, PhD, MM, JD
Professor of Marketing, Department of Marketing, Operations and Analytics
St. Edward's University, Austin, Texas

Lauren Labrecque, PhD, MA
Associate Professor and Area Coordinator, Marketing
University of Rhode Island, Kingston, Rhode Island

Brooke Reavey, PhD, MS
Associate Professor of Marketing
Dominican University, River Forest, Illinois

Mary Lou Roberts, PhD
Professor Emeritus of Management and Marketing
University of Massachusetts, Boston

 Cengage

Australia • Brazil • Canada • Mexico • Singapore • United Kingdom • United States

Digital Marketing: Foundations and Strategy, **5th Edition**

Debra Zahay, Lauren Labrecque, Brooke Reavey, Mary Lou Roberts

SVP, Product: Cheryl Costantini

VP, Product: Thais Alencar

Portfolio Product Director: Joe Sabatino

Portfolio Product Manager: Heather Thompson

Learning Designer: Danae Kesel

Content Manager: Anupam Bose, MPS Limited

Content Manager: Samantha Enders

Digital Project Manager: Jessica Ivanovic

VP, Product Marketing: Jason Sakos

Content Acquisition Analyst: Erin McCullough

Production Service: MPS Limited

Designer: Chris Doughman

Cover Image Source: DrAfter123/DigitalVision Vectors/Getty Images

Copyright © 2024 Cengage Learning, Inc. ALL RIGHTS RESERVED.

No part of this work covered by the copyright herein may be reproduced or distributed in any form or by any means, except as permitted by U.S. copyright law, without the prior written permission of the copyright owner.

Unless otherwise noted, all content is Copyright © Cengage Learning, Inc.

Previous Editions: © 2018, © 2013, © 2007

For product information and technology assistance, contact us at
**Cengage Customer & Sales Support, 1-800-354-9706
or support.cengage.com.**

For permission to use material from this text or product, submit all requests online at **www.copyright.com.**

Library of Congress Control Number: 2023906757

ISBN: 978-0-357-72073-8

Cengage
200 Pier 4 Boulevard
Boston, MA 02210
USA

Cengage is a leading provider of customized learning solutions. Our employees reside in nearly 40 different countries and serve digital learners in 165 countries around the world. Find your local representative at **www.cengage.com**.

To learn more about Cengage platforms and services, register or access your online learning solution, or purchase materials for your course, visit **www.cengage.com**.

Printed at CLDPC, USA, 11-24

Dedication

The fifth edition is written to honor the memory of the late Mary Lou Roberts, whose dedication to the field of teaching direct and interactive and digital marketing inspired us all. Her mentorship will be greatly missed by this team and by her former students everywhere.

DZ/LL/BR

Contents

Preface

Introduction

Since *Digital Marketing: Foundations and Strategy* (previously titled *Internet Marketing: Integrating Online and Offline Strategies*) was first published in 2003, the internet has continued to undergo rapid and often disruptive change. The internet is now a worldwide communications and transactions channel that serves billions of people. Mobile has become the driving force in the development of what is now the digital space with many, especially in developing countries, having internet access only through mobile devices. Artificial intelligence is helping create ways to facilitate content creation and also aid in discovering search intent. Today, most marketers' focus is on digital marketing, implying a seamless integration of web and mobile with the goal of fostering engagement. That integration requires a focus on seamless customer experience on the internet, in the mobile space and in traditional channels of communications and transactions.

In addition, the explosive growth of digital has created a growing number of interesting and challenging jobs in the field and the book has taken a variety of approaches to informing students about the nature of jobs and offering useful preparation for them. So while this book focuses on digital marketing efforts, it continues to pay homage to the underlying network that binds us together for more than marketing communications channels, but also for the complex value-adding processes that support organizational prosperity and growth.

An outgrowth of digital change is the continuation of the eBook format of the fifth edition and the revision of the material on the MindTap learning platform. A welcome change is the return of the physical book format in four colors as an option as well. This additional format will ensure that the material can be accessible to all students.

In the midst of all the changes, adopters will find familiar and useful constructs. The strategy paradigm used in the book is based on customer acquisition, lead conversion, customer retention, and growing customer value. This framework is explained in the context of the direct marketing foundations of digital marketing. All these subjects are given extensive treatment either in a specific chapter or integrated into discussions of tools and techniques that are most appropriate for executing the particular strategy. Other useful strategic frameworks such as the Service-Dominant Logic and value creation have been retained and new ones have been added in burgeoning fields like search, mobile and social media marketing.

Strategy considerations are accompanied by in-depth coverage of the ever-increasing array of technologies, tools and services that support marketing program execution. The emphasis, however, is on marketing strategy and execution, not on technology for technology's sake. While keeping the focus on strategy students are introduced to and offered practical experience in using digital tools as an asset to their current or prospective jobs in digital marketing.

Search is where most consumers start the purchasing process on the web and search engine marketing that incorporates both optimization for organic search and pay-per-click is essential. Email remains a key part of the marketing programs of B2C, B2B, as well as nonprofit marketers, even as consumers continue to migrate to social media, mobile communications, and text messaging. Display advertising for branding and for direct response is undergoing a renaissance as new formats become available to better engage the viewer. Social media marketing is even more of an essential strategy element with paid social advertising growing in importance. And ever-present is mobile, with a growth rate that outstrips all others in every aspect of digital marketing.

The only constant in the digital space is change that often disrupts entire industries as Uber and Airbnb have done in the transportation and travel industries. Whether we call it waves of business change, stages of technology change, or the fourth wave of industrial revolution, marketers must be agile and resilient to deal with ongoing change.

Unifying Themes

This book is uniquely positioned to take advantage of the innovation and disruptive change that is inherent in the digital ecosystem. Digital marketing is only effective if strategies and messages are integrated across media. That viewpoint is pervasive throughout this book; digital marketing is considered in the context of overall marketing strategy executed in multiple channels. Throughout, examples show the integrated use of online, mobile and offline channels by B2C and B2B to achieve business and marketing objectives. This book also recognizes the internet as the global phenomenon it truly is. Coverage of global issues is integrated into the appropriate subject areas. Global data are presented when appropriate, and examples of programs in various countries are seamlessly woven into content coverage. Where, the stage of digital development, regulations, or culture affects digital marketing activities, they are treated separately and specifically.

It is impossible to understand digital marketing without having a layperson's appreciation of the technology that makes it possible. Technology also is covered in the context of the marketing activities affected by it, not as a separate issue. Complex technological subjects are explained in a manner that can be successfully grasped by those with only introductory or user-level familiarity with computer technology. At the same time, students are encouraged to gain experience in use of technology-driven marketing tools, both to increase their knowledge and to improve their job prospects in this dynamic environment. Many useful tips as to how they can obtain this knowledge are included in the Instructor's Manual, which was written by the authors themselves.

The overall emphasis, however, is rigorously strategic as it discusses the planning, development, execution, and evaluation of marketing campaigns across multiple channels. At every stage, conceptual frameworks are presented to aid student understanding of complex topics.

New and Updated in This Edition

The fifth edition of *Internet Marketing: Integrating Online and Offline Strategies in a Digital Environment* has been completely rewritten and renamed *Digital Marketing: Foundations and Strategy* so as to incorporate the changing digital ecosystem faced by marketers. Former chapters 1 and 4 form a new Chapter 1, which lays down strategic foundations while recognizing the direct marketing roots of digital marketing entitled *The Digital Marketing Landscape and Foundations.* Chapters 6 and 16 from the fourth edition form a new chapter, *Supporting the Digital Customer Journey,* focused on both the customer journey and the customer experience. These chapters were consolidated to allow room for the course to be taught over a 15-or 16-week semester with room for a digital marketing project at the end. To help instructors teach the class in this manner, a new appendix outlines how to incorporate a project into a digital marketing class, either as a semester-long effort or in the context of shorter sections and activities. Research in digital marketing education indicates that while simulations can be helpful, there is no substitute for working with a real-life client. Instructors are encouraged to give their students this experience if time permits.

Importantly, the passing of Dr. Roberts necessitated two new co-authors, Dr. Lauren Labreque and Dr. Brooke Reavey. These scholars are actively involved in teaching and researching in the area of digital marketing and have extensive classroom experience and social media marketing presences. Their contributions have greatly strengthened this edition.

The book is divided into three sections of approximately equal length which will facilitate learning:

1. **Part I: Building the Foundations of Digital Marketing**

   This section introduces the topic in the context of underlying strategy, creating value, and the impact of disruptive change. The first chapter takes material from the prior chapters 1 and 4 and creates a new chapter that acknowledges the direct marketing roots of digital marketing but places them in a strategic context. It introduces a new definition of digital marketing from Dr. Zahay as "the use of any digital technology to facilitate the marketing process, with the end goal of customer interaction, engagement, and measurement." The section contains chapters on the value chain, evolving business models, the customer journey, and measurement. A reconfigured Chapter 4 (a combined version of old chapters 6 and 16) presents the digital customer journey in both B2C and B2B and gives the reader an early understanding of the essential topic of the Customer Experience (CX).

2. **Part II: Creating Visibility and Attracting Customers**

   This section focuses on those tools which are most likely to create visibility and draw the customer to a company's digital presence (website and mobile). In addition to sound web and mobile design, search (both paid and organic), social media, and display advertising play their role in attracting the customers. Social media marketing has been moved to this section to highlight its increased role in attracting customers to a brand. This section focuses on strategies to create effective and engaging social media campaigns. These chapters have been updated to include discussions of current data privacy issues around the use of third-party cookies and highlights challenges for marketers as new legislation is introduced around consumer data protection. Dr. Labrecque has contributed some new insights to these chapters from her own experiences in running online businesses.

3. **Part III: Maintaining and Strengthening Relationships**

   As with the rest of the text, the chapters in this section have been completely updated. The theme of strengthening and maintaining relationships means that this section focuses on email, content marketing, B2B Demand Generation, and Customer Relationship Management (CRM). B2B Demand Generation has evolved into Account Based Management (ABM) and that chapter relates that change as well as the role of the new buying group concept. The chapter on social and regulatory issues that was in this last section in the fourth edition has been eliminated and the issues have been embedded in the text. There were several reasons for this change. One, the chapter was often skipped because of the fact that there were more chapters than weeks in the semester, so students did not get the content. Two, the content changes so rapidly in the legal field relating to digital marketing these days that instead of covering many topics the authors decided to cover a few, important topics in-depth and to do that within the chapters.

Throughout this text, there is emphasis on student engagement. Discussion questions (answered in the Instructor's Manual) can provide endless opportunities to challenge student thinking on Digital Marketing. The instructor PowerPoint® slides offer additional interactive opportunities in each chapter.

Instructor Resources

Additional instructor resources for this product are available online. Instructor assets include an Instructor's Manual, Educator's Guide, PowerPoint® slides, and a test bank powered by Cognero®. Sign up or sign in at **www.cengage.com** to search for and access this product and its online resources.

MindTap

Today's leading online learning platform, MindTap for *Digital Marketing: Foundations and Strategy*, 5th edition, gives you complete control of your course to craft a personalized, engaging learning experience that challenges students, builds confidence and elevates performance.

MindTap introduces students to core concepts from the beginning of your course using a simplified learning path that progresses from understanding to application and delivers access to eBooks, study tools, interactive media, auto-graded assessments and performance analytics.

Use MindTap for *Digital Marketing: Foundations and Strategy*, 5th edition, as-is, or personalize it to meet your specific course needs. You can also easily integrate MindTap into your Learning Management System (LMS).

Acknowledgments

Reviewers of both the first and second editions contributed materially to the original soundness and readability of the book. Subsequent academic users of editions three and four and practitioners alike have made informal contributions that have been helpful throughout.

We are especially grateful to the many firms in the digital space that have provided content that is essential to a working understanding of digital marketing.

This information has contributed immeasurably to keeping the book relevant and timely.

There are many people involved in publishing a book.

We express our appreciation to the content team at Cengage and to production contractors who have brought the book to completion. The authors are particularly indebted to students and numerous guest lecturers in Digital Marketing and Social Media Marketing courses for introducing them to issues and developments they would never have otherwise recognized.

Debra Zahay wishes to acknowledge the support of her husband, Edward Blatz, and her mother, Joyce Zahay, and her late father, Albert Zahay, and their unswerving belief in her. She also is indebted to the insightful comments and contributions of her colleagues-at St. Edward's University, in particular Dr. Juli James, and to former students and the insights from her current students.

Lauren Labrecque wishes to thank her husband, Garret Warr, and their children, Nikola and Luca, for their unwavering love and support. Without them, this journey would not only have been impossible but also meaningless. She also would like to acknowledge her parents for their support and encouragement to pursue an academic career, as well as the students who inspire her to keep teaching.

Brooke Reavey wishes to thank her husband, Carl Urness, for his unwavering support and efforts to keep their kids, Isaac and Silas, entertained while she scrolled through (seemingly) endless pages on the internet while writing. She would also like to thank her mother for stoking the fire of her love for writing. She also wishes to thank her dog Jethro for being the best writing companion because he was always keen for a walk or a cuddle when she needed it. Finally, she thanks her go-to web developer, Ezra Silverman, for answering all of her technical questions about web programming and AI advances.

About the Authors

Debra Zahay is full, tenured professor of marketing and former department chair of in the Department of Marketing, Operations and Analytics at St. Edward's University in Austin, Texas. She oversaw the inclusion of digital marketing and analytics in the undergraduate curriculum and the development of a Master's Degree program in Digital Marketing and Analytics, where she served as program director. She holds her Doctorate from the University of Illinois in Urbana-Champaign, her Master of Management from Northwestern University in Evanston, Illinois, her Juris Doctor from Loyola University in Chicago, Illinois, and her undergraduate degree from Washington University in St. Louis, Missouri.

Dr. Zahay researches how firms can facilitate customer relationships, particularly using customer information. She also teaches and researches leading-edge pedagogy for teaching digital marketing. She has published extensively in marketing journals in the United States and Europe. She was selected as a Fulbright Specialist in 2023. She is on the editorial board of the Journal of Marketing Analytics as well as that of Industrial Marketing Management and the Journal of Marketing Education. She was the Editor-in-Chief of the Journal of Research in Interactive Marketing from 2012 to 2017, guiding the explosive growth in influence of that journal. She is the co-author of another Cengage Text, *Social Media Marketing: A Strategic Approach*, third edition, and solo author of the second edition of *Digital Marketing Management: A Handbook for the Current (or Future) CEO* by Business Expert Press, LLC.

Lauren Labrecque is an associate professor of marketing and area coordinator at the University of Rhode Island. Her primary research interests include digital marketing and the impact of emerging technology on marketing (including blockchain, digital empowerment, consumer privacy, and parasocial interactions) and sensory marketing (focus on color). Her research has been published in peer-reviewed academic journals including *Journal of Marketing*, *Journal of Marketing Research*, *Journal of the Academy of Marketing Science*, *Journal of Consumer Psychology*, *Journal of Interactive Marketing*, *Journal of Retailing*, *Journal of Advertising*, *Journal of Business Research*, *Psychology & Marketing*, and others. She serves as an associate editor for the *Journal of Interactive Marketing* and *Journal of Business Research* and is an editorial review board member for *Psychology &*

Marketing. Dr. Labrecque completed her Ph.D. in Marketing (Business Administration) from the University of Massachusetts, Amherst, in 2010, and her Master's Degree in Digital Media Studies from the University of Denver in 2003.

Brooke Reavey is an associate professor of marketing in the Brennan School of Business at Dominican University. She is a Fulbright Scholar, serving as a Senior Scholar in Bucharest, Romania from 2017–2018. She holds her doctorate in Marketing (Business Administration) from Drexel University, her Master's Degree in Marketing Research from Temple University, and was a dual major in Marketing and Psychology as an undergraduate at La Salle University. Dr. Reavey's academic work focuses on the intersection between digital marketing and market research, particularly when it comes to data democratization. Her work has been published in scholarly outlets such as the *International Journal of Advertising*, *Journal of Marketing Education*, and *Marketing Education Review*, among others. She is an active speaker and volunteers with the Insights Association, the largest marketing research and analytics association in the US, at the national and chapter levels. She also volunteers in the digital marketing and insights special interest group (SIG) for the American Marketing Association's Chicago chapter.

Mary Lou Roberts was a tenured professor of marketing at the University of Massachusetts, Boston, and held a number of administrative positions there including Director of Development. She passed in early 2020, leaving a gap in the field of teaching digital and internet marketing. During her retirement, she taught internet marketing and social media marketing to a global cadre of students at the Harvard University Extension School. She had a Ph.D. in marketing from the University of Michigan. She was the senior author of *Direct Marketing Management*, 2nd edition, which was a classic in its field and did much to professionalize the field of direct marketing and make it a separate discipline taught by academics. She had published extensively in marketing journals in the United States and Europe. Dr. Roberts was a frequent presenter on programs of both professional and academic marketing organizations and consulted and provided planning services and management training programs for a wide variety of corporations and nonprofit organizations. She was an active member of many professional organizations and had served on a number of their boards.

Part I | Building the Foundations of Digital Marketing

Chapter 1

The Digital Marketing Landscape and Foundations

Learning Objectives

By the time you complete this chapter, you will be able to:

1. Define digital marketing from a dynamic perspective.

2. List the elements of direct marketing.

3. List the elements of the internet which make it a direct response medium.

4. List the generic marketing objectives that form the basis for digital marketing strategies.

5. Define the critical strategy elements of direct marketing.

6. Describe the implications of disruptive change on digital marketing.

7. List the waves of change and relevant technologies.

8. Compare the concepts of digital disruption and digital transformation.

9. List the major trends in the use of digital marketing.

Most of you who are reading this book do not remember a world without the internet. Many of the rest of us cannot imagine what we ever did without it. These facts are remarkable, given the relatively short history of the network we now call the internet.

There are some wonderful accounts of the development of the internet, including one by the people directly responsible for it.[1] Those people are still active in the industry. That's true because—impossible as it seems—the internet officially celebrated its 30th birthday on August 23, 2021. That is the anniversary of the date on which, in 1991, the internet was opened to the public after years of development at the particle physics research laboratory CERN in Switzerland. Why is that such a milestone date? Tim Berners-Lee says,

> Had the technology been proprietary, and in my total control, it would probably not have taken off. The decision to make the web an open system was necessary for it to be universal. You can't propose that something be a universal space and at the same time keep control of it.[2]

That attitude set the standard for the World Wide Web that still rules today, although not without challenge at times. We will discuss later the implications of technology evolution. However, for a capsule summary of the early days of the web, it is important to note that the internet was originally a communications network for individuals, and commercial activity was not allowed. Consequently, the interest of marketers is focused on the years since 1991 when commercial traffic was first officially permitted on the internet.[3]

How Internet Marketing Has Evolved Into Digital Marketing

The major developments of the internet prior to the early 1990s were primarily technical in nature, building infrastructure and creating communications protocols. Early web browsers required extensive technical knowledge and it was not until the creation of browsers with graphical interfaces, including Netscape, that the general public became interested in the internet. Web portals Yahoo!, Lycos, and AOL gained early popularity. eBay and Amazon were among the earliest to recognize the potential of ecommerce. Myspace and Napster also achieved early popularity but most of these sites are now a mere shadow of their former selves. Starting in the early 2000s with iTunes, Facebook, YouTube, and others, we begin to see sites that are part of our daily lives.

Why so much change in the powerhouses of the industry in such a short time? In a word—search. Google became the leading search engine in the early 2000s because it was easy to use and gave useful results. As more and more internet users turned to search as their entry point to the web, there was less need for portals, whether a "walled garden" like AOL or an open portal like Yahoo! The portals were eclipsed, and Google and its smaller competitors thrived.

As the internet became more pervasive in marketing, the terminology used evolved from internet to digital marketing. Digital Marketing can be defined as using any digital technology to facilitate the marketing process, with the end goal of customer interaction, engagement, and measurement.[4,5] So digital marketing encompasses the process of engaging the customer and measuring the results of that engagement. The digital technology most often used to foster engagement and interaction is the internet.

digital marketing
using any digital technology to facilitate the marketing process, with the end goal of customer interaction, engagement, and measurement.

The Direct Marketing Roots of Digital Marketing

This definition of digital marketing owes its origins to the direct marketing roots of the internet. According to the DMA (formerly the Direct Marketing Association and then the Data and Marketing Association and now part of the umbrella organization ANA), direct marketing requires the following:

- An organized and planned system of contacts
- Using a variety of media
- Seeking to produce a lead or an order
- Developing and maintaining a database
- Measurable in cost and results
- Expandable with confidence

Thus, any system that is based on data analysis, has a clear objective, and is measurable can be considered direct marketing or direct response. In the past, it was only direct marketers who had access to data and who could truly measure results. So, a direct marketer, like Land's End, would send a catalog, see if the customer responded, and then send another catalog or offer based on the data. Now, many marketing channels and many types of marketers have access to data, resulting in the evolution of data-driven marketing versus direct marketing. The emphasis on data in digital marketing will become even more important as third-party data usage (data collected by companies that do not have a direct relationship to a particular firm's customers) diminishes and firms rely more on first-party data from their own websites and customer data repositories to reach their customers. This definition of digital marketing also incorporates the critical concepts of response mechanisms and engagement. It is a holistic and dynamic definition, rather than a static one, and adaptable to the changing environment of digital marketing.

third-party data
data collected by companies that do not have a direct relationship to a particular firm's customers.

first-party data
data from a company's own websites and customer data repositories.

The Internet as a Direct Response Medium

If there is a question about whether the internet can function as a direct response channel, think about Amazon and all it knows about its customers through its data collection and analysis. If someone buys a book for left-handed golfers, they are sure to be shown other products for left-handed individuals through the process known as *collaborative filtering*. Amazon's vast store of data on its customers makes it easier to target customers and get them to purchase again. This targeting is done via the internet as a direct response mechanism, without traditional forms of direct response such as mail, phone fax, or direct response television. In fact, many say the internet is the ultimate direct response medium. Why? Certainly, digital marketers use it as an interactive channel, allowing for a two-way dialog between marketers and prospective customers using direct response techniques or social media. It is also a sales channel, with ecommerce growing at a rapid rate from the early days of the internet to the present. The internet is also a powerful branding medium, as we discuss in various chapters.

interactive
presenting choices based on user actions and allowing for response.

The internet presents powerful opportunities to the shrewd marketer. From the consumer's perspective, it permits a seamless purchase process. From the marketer's perspective, the internet allows fine-tuning of marketing programs in ways previously unimaginable. There are four important characteristics—call them the "four Is"—that describe how digital marketing efforts are powerfully affected by the capabilities of the internet (see Figure 1.1).

The internet, more than any other current medium, allows *interactivity*. In direct response mode, marketers can initiate two-way communications with prospective customers by sending offers to them and tracking their responses or by initiating direct communications by way of surveys, chat rooms, or other internet-enabled techniques. Interactivity allows for marketing to become a true conversation. Marketers listen to the customer and present choices based on that feedback, changing offers and communications based on an ongoing dialog.

information
data that has been processed into more useful forms using techniques that range from simple summary formats to complex statistical routines.

All marketing activities on the web also have the potential to be information driven. Every move a website visitor makes, every action taken—from sending an email query to

Figure 1.1　The Four Is of Internet Marketing

nteractive
nformation-driven
mmediate
nvolving

purchasing a product—is a potential piece of data for the marketing database that drives targeted promotional activities. The internet fosters *immediacy* in a variety of ways. Marketers can reply directly to customer queries using human agents or automated systems. The internet makes it cost-efficient to construct offers that appeal to a specific market segment or to make offers that are seasonal or that are triggered by a particular event, say the NCAA basketball finals. Internet promotions can also be *involving*. Marketers are increasingly using streaming video, games, and other types of rich media in internet advertising to attract and involve prospective customers, also known as engagement. A good direct response offer incites prospects to take action—either to request information or to make a purchase on the spot.

data
raw, unprocessed facts and numbers. Raw data differs from the process of data mining, where analytic processes and specialized analytic tools are used to extract meaning from large data sets.

Generic Direct Marketing Strategies[6]

It is difficult to do successful internet marketing without understanding the basics of direct marketing. Essentially, these above-mentioned capabilities of the internet drive the four types of direct marketing strategies, which are acquisition, conversion, retention, and value growth. These strategies in turn parallel a basic customer lifecycle and are used extensively in digital marketing (see Figure 1.2). This figure is just one example of a customer lifecycle, and students will find other examples in the workplace.

Practically speaking, first, a customer must be attracted to the brand. This state represents a trial of a product or a service. In the *acquisition* stage, the customer has been attracted to the brand, made a single purchase, or perhaps engaged in free use as a result of a sample or a demonstration but is not yet committed to the brand. The second stage is conversion, so-called because, in this step, the prospect changes status and *converts* to a customer. More generally a marketing conversion can also be thought of as the customer taking a desired action, such as downloading a whitepaper, signing up for a webinar or, indeed, making a first purchase. This stage may require one to three purchases or enough to form a habitual purchasing pattern. The goal of the first two stages is retention, in which the customer continues to make purchases, a situation we might call behavioral loyalty. Even better, in this stage, the customer begins to exhibit loyalty in an attitudinal sense, which may result in behaviors ranging from rejecting competing offers to recommending the product to others. Finally, we continue to nurture the relationship and *grow the value* the customer represents for the brand. Marketers do this in a variety of ways, including increased engagement. Loyalty at this stage can deepen and transform into becoming a strong brand advocate.

conversion
when the customer takes an action desired by the marketer, such as a first purchase or signing up to receive more product information.

retention
when the customer continues to make purchases.

Each of the basic strategies requires a different type of effort on the part of the marketer. *Acquisition* is roughly equivalent to the awareness stage of general advertising

Figure 1.2 The Basic Direct Response Strategies

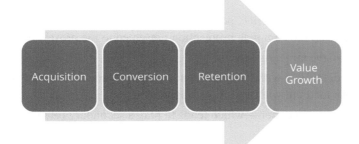

with an action component added. The step is focused on a conscious attempt to get the attention of the prospective customer through media placement and creative execution and interest them in completing a desired action, such as making a purchase, signing up for a newsletter, or another specific request. Direct marketers often add an incentive to clinch product trial. We discuss customer acquisition on the internet in detail throughout this text.

The *conversion* step means getting the onetime purchaser to convert to being a customer or taking another desired action. Product and service satisfaction is critical to achieving this goal. Customer contact, through media ranging from personal selling to newsletters, is often useful. Sequential incentives have also been used with good results. For example, a bank that wanted its customers to make more deposits at ATMs sent them a series of three checks, each of which could be used only with a series of ATM deposits. The first check was for $5, the second was for $3, and the third was for $1. The incentives were not only sequential but decreased in value as the presumed habit formation was taking place. It is hard to prove habit formation, but in this case, it seems reasonable to assume that many customers, after three successful deposits, recognized that it is safe to make deposits through ATMs. This was a sensible, low-cost conversion program aimed at achieving a worthwhile business goal. Its only visible drawback was that the bank did not make good use of its customer database. It sent the checks to customers who regularly made ATM deposits as well as to those who never deposited through an ATM! We discuss conversion marketing in Chapter 13.

After conversion, it is important to retain customers in order to create the highest possible customer lifetime value (CLV). Sometimes called lifetime customer values or LCV, CLV is the monetary value of the customer over time and is used to prioritize customers and to develop targeted marketing strategies for particular customer segments. *Retention* is most often the result of adding value to the customer purchase, user experience, and superior customer service. A planned program of customer contact, carried out at appropriate points in the purchase cycle, can also be a useful component of retention programs. We discuss retention in detail in Chapter 4.

After the customer is on board, we want them to continue to purchase, but also to foster *growth* in terms of not only their overall purchases but also their commitment to our brand and product. In the *growth* stage, we might involve the customer in our product line through engagement in social media, such as the sharing of the brand. HubSpot says that the goal in this stage is to "delight" the customer and continue to interact with them.[7]

customer lifetime value
the monetary value of a customer over time.

Critical Strategy Elements of Direct Marketing

In addition to generic direct marketing strategies, the marketing mix that supports direct marketing programs uses slightly different terminology from the four Ps of traditional marketing. They are as follows:

- The offer—product, price, positioning, and any other product-related elements that make up the complete proposition presented to the prospective customer
- The list—the targeting vehicle
- The media used—with the understanding that any medium can be a direct response medium with the proper implementation
- The creative execution—which tends to play a secondary role in this action-oriented context
- The service and support—long recognized as a key element in this environment where the shopping experience and many sensory stimuli are not present.

These elements are all required to implement any direct response program. It is, however, especially important to understand the role of the offer in developing internet marketing strategies. An offer typically answers the questions of What, By When, and Why. The customer should clearly understand what is required, by what time deadline and why. A good offer would be something like, "Free Shipping if ordering by midnight." The company wants the customer to order (what) by midnight (when) to get free shipping (why). Having a good list is generally considered to be the next most important of the critical strategy elements, and ties into having a strong database to support direct and digital marketing programs.

Disruptive Change

On the internet, disruptive change is ongoing. Businesses must maintain an innovation culture that has customer centricity at its heart and is guided by sound vision and strategy. No firm can practice business as usual. Change is a constant, making transformation a way of life, not an end goal.

Author Kevin Maney describes Yahoo! as the past of technology leaders and Amazon as the future. Apple is the present, on a huge run since the introduction of the iPhone in 2007, but not having found a category-changing product like it for the future. Amazon revolutionized internet storage with Amazon Web Services cloud-based storage, which we will discuss in detail in Chapter 2. It seems well on its way to disrupting another industry sector if it successfully harnesses artificial intelligence (AI) for use by its Echo home connectivity device. Maney describes it as "the front-end technology that will let us talk to a watch or car or loo ["bathroom" in U.S. English] and make sure the device will understand who we each are, what we want, and how to get it done."[8] Alexa is the voice-activated software assistant (conversational interface[9]) that works with the Echo device or from a smartphone or tablet app.[10] It's too soon to say that the technology will ultimately be everywhere, but Hyundai, BMW, Ford, and Lincoln have all incorporated voice-activated Echo technology to do everything from starting the car to setting its internal temperature.[11]

artificial intelligence (AI)
the ability of a computer to mimic human behaviors.

Incremental change happens in technology on a daily basis. Every few years a wave of change—such as the introduction of the smartphone—occurs that disrupts the industry. Figure 1.3 illustrates how change has been a constant since the early days of the internet. Once the network was established and approved for commercial use, what we now know as digital marketing expanded rapidly.

The Waves of Internet Change

The company Digital Leadership lays out their perspective on technology development in Figure 1.4. The graphic illustrates that we have moved from an agrarian culture to one based on information. The final wave, which we are in now, is one in which there is an increasing focus on technology, including virtualization and AI. Interestingly, there is also a desire to balance nature and technology and reach for sustainability. A more specific technology timeline with specifics of the commercialization of the internet is included in Figure 1.5. That means the potential for disruptive change is still present, as we will discuss in the next section.

Do you remember when personal computers were not connected to the internet? Again, many of you probably do not. However, many of the rest of us remember the frustrations of learning to use word processors, dumb terminals for access to a mainframe computer, and personal computers themselves. Connectivity to the internet and between our devices is now taken for granted. The history of the dramatic changes in the digital revolution is outlined in Figure 1.5, which illustrates everything from the sending of the first email, the launch of social media platforms, and the modern world where technology is transforming every aspect of our lives.

Figure 1.3 **Highlights of Early Internet Development** Source: http://www.livinginternet.com/i/ii_summary.htm

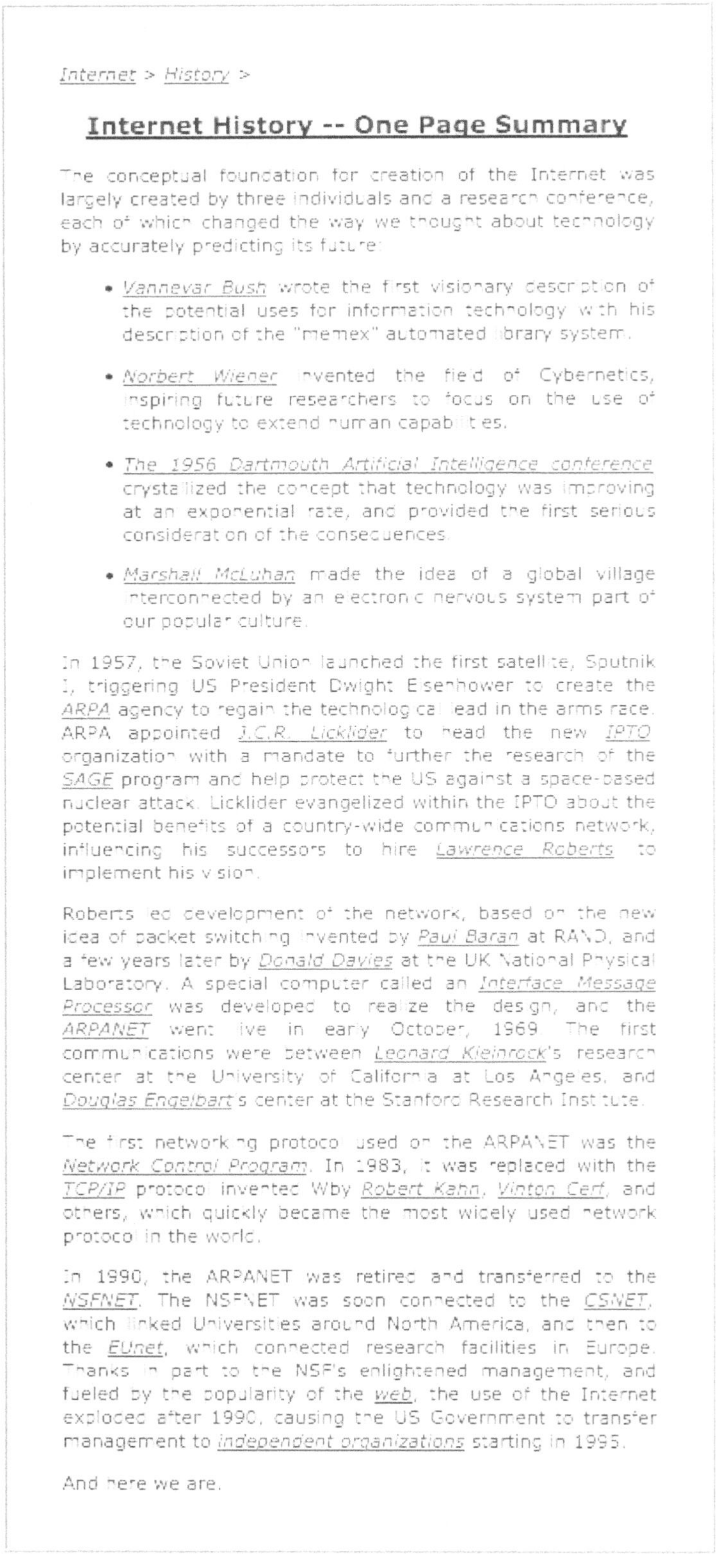

Internet > *History* >

Internet History -- One Page Summary

The conceptual foundation for creation of the Internet was largely created by three individuals and a research conference, each of which changed the way we thought about technology by accurately predicting its future:

- *Vannevar Bush* wrote the first visionary description of the potential uses for information technology with his description of the "memex" automated library system.

- *Norbert Wiener* invented the field of Cybernetics, inspiring future researchers to focus on the use of technology to extend human capabilities.

- *The 1956 Dartmouth Artificial Intelligence conference* crystallized the concept that technology was improving at an exponential rate, and provided the first serious consideration of the consequences.

- *Marshall McLuhan* made the idea of a global village interconnected by an electronic nervous system part of our popular culture.

In 1957, the Soviet Union launched the first satellite, Sputnik I, triggering US President Dwight Eisenhower to create the *ARPA* agency to regain the technological lead in the arms race. ARPA appointed *J.C.R. Licklider* to head the new *IPTO* organization with a mandate to further the research of the *SAGE* program and help protect the US against a space-based nuclear attack. Licklider evangelized within the IPTO about the potential benefits of a country-wide communications network, influencing his successors to hire *Lawrence Roberts* to implement his vision.

Roberts led development of the network, based on the new idea of packet switching invented by *Paul Baran* at RAND, and a few years later by *Donald Davies* at the UK National Physical Laboratory. A special computer called an *Interface Message Processor* was developed to realize the design, and the *ARPANET* went live in early October, 1969. The first communications were between *Leonard Kleinrock*'s research center at the University of California at Los Angeles, and *Douglas Engelbart*'s center at the Stanford Research Institute.

The first networking protocol used on the ARPANET was the *Network Control Program*. In 1983, it was replaced with the *TCP/IP* protocol invented Wby *Robert Kahn*, *Vinton Cerf*, and others, which quickly became the most widely used network protocol in the world.

In 1990, the ARPANET was retired and transferred to the *NSFNET*. The NSFNET was soon connected to the *CSNET*, which linked Universities around North America, and then to the *EUnet*, which connected research facilities in Europe. Thanks in part to the NSF's enlightened management, and fueled by the popularity of the *web*, the use of the Internet exploded after 1990, causing the US Government to transfer management to *independent organizations* starting in 1995.

And here we are.

Figure 1.4   **The Four Waves of Industrial Revolution** Source: https://digitalleadership.com/blog/four-waves-of-economic-development/

	Cradle of Humanity	1st Wave Agrian Culture		2nd Wave Industrial Culture		3rd Wave Information Culture	4th Wave Integrated (?)
Era	Pre-agrarian period	Early societies	Industry 1.0 (1st Industrial Revolution)	Industry 2.0 (2nd Industrial Revolution)	Industry 3.0 (1st Information Revolution)	Industry 4.0 (2nd Information Revolution)	Information 3.0
Innovation	Appearance of Homo sapiens	Agriculture	Mechanization	Electrification	Automation & Globalization	Digitalization	Smartification (merging AI/balance between individualism and collectivism)
Timescale	Roughly 3.4 million years	8,000 BCE	From 1765	From 1870	From 1969	From 2011	From 202x - 203x
Location of value creation	Dispersed	Village & countryside	Mechanized towns and cities	Industrial regions	Global production networks	Global value chains	Dispersed (virtual & decentralized)
Philosophical foundation	Animism and a belief in a holistic merging of humans and nature	Belief in god, holistic circular world view, possession of land and people and patriarchy	Belief in infinite growth. Rational, linear world view			Belief in infinite growth and a rational, linear world view leads to "Post Humanism" & "Singularity 2.0" theories	Belief in universal connectedness. Leads to holistic, systemic, circular world view & to "Earth 5.0" theories
Culture	Nomadic culture of extended families and tribes	Sedentary culture of peasants with patriarchal, feudalistic exploitation hierarchies	Division of labor leads to exploitation of labor and capital by owners	National industrial culture with a focus on dominating global politics through industrial strength	Globalized industrial culture with a focus on economic growth & consumption	Information culture with a more decentralized focus on economic growth & consumption	Smart Society, newly found focus on true sustainability
Technological inventions	The invention of tools, control of fire	Irrigation techniques, domestication of animals, the discovery of the number zero, enabeling mathematical thinking	Steam power, water power, division of labor increases efficiency, mechanization leads to start of mass production	Electricity, telegraph, telephone, light bulb, internal combustion engine, railroads, assembly line, standardized mass production	Electronics, semiconductors, computers, telecommunications, automated production, mass customization, Internet, connectivity	Digitalization, machine learning, robotics, Internet of Things (IoT), autonomous vehicles, 3D printing, virtual & augmented reality, wearables, nanotech, biotech, energy storage, digital	Expanding frontiers: quantum computing, increasing synergies among synthetic biology, nanotechnology, 3D & 4D printing, robotics, cognitive systems & the advent of artificial intelligence, collective intelligence & yet to emerge technologies that accelerate the rate of acceleration itself
Exemplary innivations or new capabilities	› Upright walk › Control of fire › Flint blades › Speech	› Axe 6,000 BCE › Wheel 4,000 BCE › Writing 3,300 BC › Printing press 1,440 CE	› First mechanical loom 1784 › Large-scale production of chemicals	› First assembly line 1870 › Ford Model 'T' 1908	› First programmable logic controller in manufacturing 1969 › First mobile phone 1979	› Smart factory › Cloud computing › Bitcoin 2009	Virtualisation of all aspects of life, digital money, lights out business processes, highly automated manufacturing, self-managed supply chains, selfdriving cars
Transformational change	Living in small tribes	Settling in villages & towns	Substitution of labor by capital, process stability & speed, industrially manufactured goods, start of the machine age	› Start of "mass production" › Division of labor ("Taylorism") › Process flow & throughout	› Start of "mass customization" information distribution › Business Process Reengineering › Process quality & 'Lean'	Access to education, global integration, digital industry, digital transformation, intangible goods	Deep, multi-level cooperation between humans & machines. New found conciousness on human level & artificial level (?) then Singularity 2.0
Who leads?	Tribal leaders	Religious leaders, aristocracy/ monarchs, warlords	Entrepreneurs, tradesmen	Directors	Management	Leadership (non-hierarchical)	Collegial leadership with 'growth hierarchies' not, exploitation hierarchies'
Primary axis of improvement	Surviving in nature	Dominating nature	Power	Speed	Memory	Interconnectedness	› Artificial Intelligence › Operating in accordance with nature-systemic circular thinking
Ability	Physical capability				Mental capability		Wholeness
Who is empowered?	People		Corporations			People	Balance between people & nature?
Global population	50,000	1 million	100 million	1 billion	3.5 billion	7.7 billion	
Sustainability/waste share	Permanent/no waste	Permanent/no waste	Long-term/5%	Long-term/10%	Mid-term/25%	Short-term/45%	(Hopefully) again long-term / 5% - circular economy
Human focus	Survival	Control	Efficiency	Scalability	Consumption	Digitalization	Human universal integration through smartification, purpose, sustainability

Figure 1.5 **A Brief History of the Digital Revolution** Source: https://pbs.twimg.com/media/DDfAtTAXcAA_xaf.jpg.

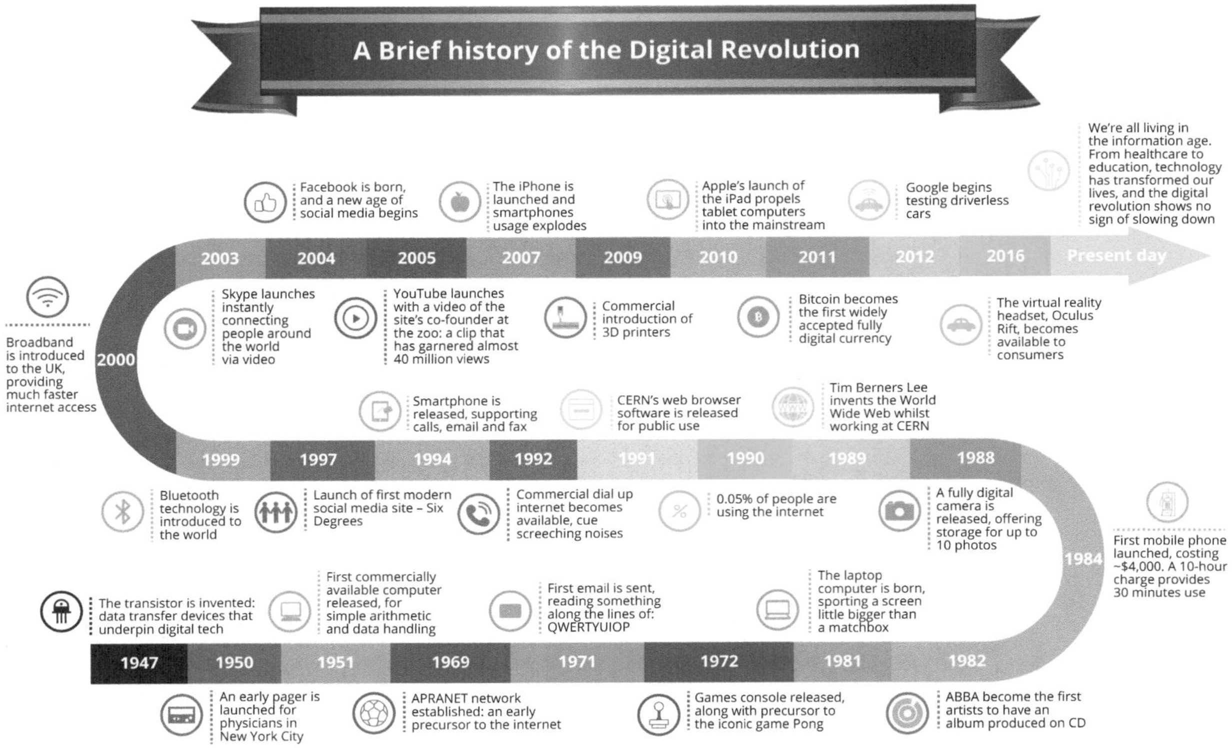

While the technology waves in Figure 1.4 are accepted and discussed in the technology industry, there are other perspectives. One writer describes it as the Fourth Industrial Revolution. He says:

> The possibilities of billions of people connected by mobile devices, with unprecedented processing power, storage capacity, and access to knowledge, are unlimited. And these possibilities will be multiplied by emerging technology breakthroughs in the fields such as AI, robotics, the Internet of Things, autonomous vehicles, 3-D printing, nanotechnology, biotechnology, materials science, energy storage, and quantum computing.[12]

Some of these issues are more in the manufacturing realm but most will over time be relevant to marketing. AI and virtual reality (VR) are of prime importance to marketers at present as you will see later in this chapter and other chapters. The Internet of Things (IoT) is upon us, and the vast quantity of data it will produce intrigues marketers as we will discuss later in this chapter. The point is that the fourth wave, with all its disruptive technology, is already upon us. Marketers, and the businesses they work for, must ride the wave or the wave will wipe them out. Let's discuss the two disruptive technologies that have the most current impact on marketing before going on to the broader topic of digital disruption.

virtual reality (VR)
simulation of a three-dimensional image or environment with which the user can interact by using special equipment.

Important Acronyms—IoT and AI/VR

The final wave of digital business is what is often called the Internet of Everything. The more often-heard term at the moment is the Internet of Things. What is the difference? Here are careful definitions for both:

Internet of Everything (IoE)
increasing the value of network connections by creating richer experiences.

> The Internet of Everything (IoE) "is bringing together people, process, data, and things to make networked connections more relevant and valuable than ever before—turning information into actions that create

new capabilities, richer experiences, and unprecedented economic opportunity for businesses, individuals, and countries. (Cisco 2013)"

The Internet of Things (IoT) is the network of physical objects accessed through the internet. These objects contain embedded technology to interact with internal states or the external environment.

The post further explains:

> The IoE with four pillars—people, process, data, and things—builds on top of the IoT with one pillar—things. In addition, IoE further advances the power of the internet to improve business and industry outcomes and ultimately make people's lives better by adding to the progress of IoT.[13]

In other words, the IoE is a broader concept with more far-reaching implications. You can see a considerable similarity between this definition and the discussion of digital strategy that concludes this chapter. It is a strategy concept, not purely a marketing one. Examples range from simple ones such as using telemedicine to meet with patients to more complex applications that use technology to predict customer preferences.[14]

The IoT, however, is a prime concern of marketers at the moment. It pervades many of our products and is already beginning to produce a tremendous volume of data for marketing purposes. Consequently, the IoT is our focus here.

Postscapes is a research firm that follows the evolution of the IoT. It says there are three elements—sensors, connectivity, and people and processes—that make up the IoT. They are shown in Figures 1.6a, b, and c.

Internet of Things (IoT)
network of physical objects embedded with electronics that allow the objects to collect and transfer data.

Figure 1.6a Sensors in IoT Source: https://image.slidesharecdn.com/uniten-june21-v1-160621070721/95/slide-6-1024.jpg

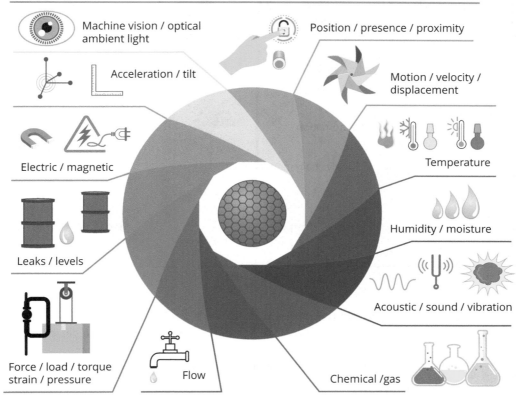

Figure 1.6b **Connectivity in the IoT** Source: https://image.slidesharecdn.com/uniten-june21-v1-160621070721/95/slide-7-1024.jpg

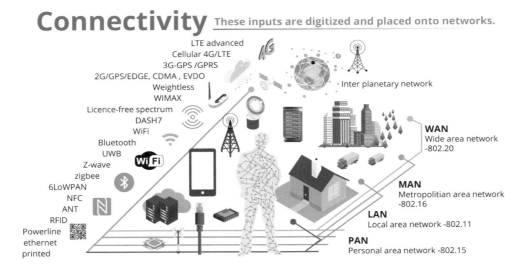

Figure 1.6c **What Is Connected: People and Processes** Source: https://image4.slideserve.com/7552783/source-http-postscapes -com-what-exactly2-l.jpg

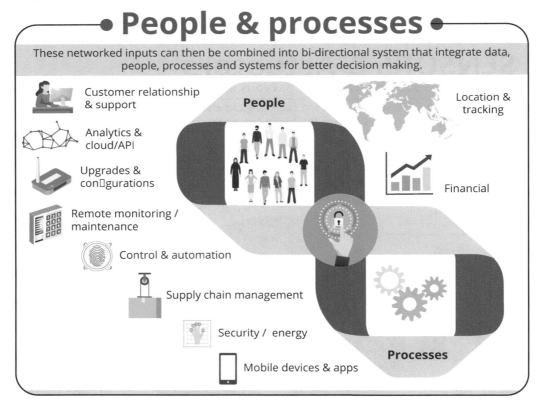

Sensors can measure changes in states like temperature, light, flow, and sound as seen in Figure 1.6a. In a smart home, for instance, sensors can detect water on the basement floor and notifies the owner via a smartphone app that there is a potential problem. The app allows the owner to unlock the door for a plumber who can correct the leaking pipe.

Smart cities can embed sensors in parking spaces so drivers with the appropriate app can locate vacant spaces with their smartphone or in-car connectivity.[15]

In an industrial setting, sensors can monitor various aspects of the contents of large vessels in real-time for process control, detect leaks of liquids or gases from tanks or pipelines, and much more.[16]

Connectivity is the essential link in the IoT (Figure 1.6b). Sensors are embedded in houses, cars, cities, and more. Many technologies are available to connect the data from the sensors to the appropriate network. That makes connectivity essentially a technology issue, but the implications are profound.

Take healthcare as just one example. The millions of elderly or frail consumers living alone can use in-home monitoring services to report events like falls and smoke in the house to the appropriate responder. They can connect with physicians who can monitor them remotely, saving trips into the office. A smart medication dispenser can tell them whether they've taken medication or not. Hospitals can use equipment like smart beds to reduce demands on staff time. They can use smart storage (Chapter 2) to streamline inventory and reduce the risk of errors. The potential is so great that Microsoft has developed a specialized set of Azure Cloud applications to serve the healthcare industry.[17,18]

People and their support processes are the ultimate beneficiaries of the IoT, as Figure 1.6c suggests. This chart shows people connected with customer services and their financial institutions, for example. Businesses can be connected with their supply chains (Chapter 2) and with transport fleets for remote diagnostics and maintenance. Both individuals and businesses use mobile devices and apps and both can take advantage of upgrades to their devices and monitoring of their energy and security systems.

Another way of thinking about it is that people and their data-producing devices are being connected with systems and other devices that can deliver services and generally make their lives easier and more productive.[19]

The IoT is still in its early days. The opportunities and potential in this market are huge. As *Business Insider* predicted that 2020 was the point where the IoT changed every aspect of our lives from the connected home, to consumer ecommerce applications, and more. Since then, the impact of the IoT has been felt in every sector of the economy.[20] While there are currently 11.57 billion devices installed worldwide, the prediction is a staggering 25.4 billion by 2030.[21]

One example of the IoT is the Walt Disney Magic Band. Disney has invested a substantial amount of money in Radio-Frequency IDentification (RFID) technology (discussed in the context of the supply chain in Chapter 2) in colorful bands that customers at Disney World can use for everything from catching the airport shuttle bus, to ordering food, reserving fast passes for rides, and through to paying for purchases. Each band has an embedded RFID transmitter that sends data to the RFID readers placed throughout the park and resort. The bands not only make it easier to get around the park but also provide valuable information to Disney about customer habits through the data transmitted. This data will later be used by Disney to help improve the customer experience. The latest version, Magic Band+, will allow customers to participate in VR and interactive experiences such as becoming a bounty hunter in the Star Wars area or interacting with characters.[22]

The next wave of technology features AI, VR, and something called MR. These technologies are interrelated:

- VR involves the embedding of graphics into actual settings. Some form of physical reality is incorporated into the experience. As this is written, students can view the Yosemite National Park experience with no special equipment on a virtual tour page, moving to whichever section of the park they desire.[23]

Radio-Frequency IDentification (RFID)
technology that allows the identification of tagged goods from a distance with no intervention by human operation.

Typically, VR settings include a headset or head-mounted display to immerse the user in the experience.

augmented reality (AR)
an enhanced version of reality created by superimposing computer-generated images on top of the user's view of the real world.

- Augmented reality (AR) is the technology that takes a person's view of the real world and adds digital information or data on top of it. The physical reality is extended and enriched. It is usually delivered through a wearable device with sensors such as Google Glass. Augmented reality can take place anywhere, whereas VR is usually in a secure setting, such as the home. One of the most powerful experiences in VR is Birdly, which gives an immersive feeling of flying. The feeling is not produced via a joystick, but rather through the participant's body movements. Participants don a VR headset and by moving and flapping their arms, these consumers fulfill a long-desired human aspiration of being able to fly like birds. Their experience is complete with a headwind simulator, and audio and visual impacts. Expect more of these types of experiences with even more sophisticated interfaces, as the technology matures.[24]

mixed reality
combining the real and virtual worlds to produce a new environment in which objects can interact and humans can interact with them.

- Mixed reality is a combination of the two in a way that is supposed to be more flexible than either. According to *Recode*, the viewer sees the real world like AR, and at the same time sees believable virtual objects. This is all anchored to a point in space making it seem real to the viewer. *Recode* gives an example of how it works with the Microsoft HoloLens:

> To borrow an example from Microsoft's presentation at the gaming trade show E3, you might be looking at an ordinary table, but see an interactive virtual world from the video game Minecraft sitting on top of it. As you walk around, the virtual landscape holds its position, and when you lean in close, it gets closer in the way a real object would.[25]

Each of these technologies seems to have potential applications that impact marketers, from games to advertising to the delivery of enhanced messages. It is a relatively new wave and like the IoT, there are many opportunities and possibilities.

There are more ways that technology is disrupting the landscape of digital business and we will cover two more important ones in a later section. First, however, we should look at the nature and consequences of digital disruption and transformation itself.

Digital Disruption and Digital Transformation

First, what do we mean when we talk about digital disruption and digital transformation? Are they the same? They are, in fact, both part of the same technology-driven phenomenon, but they have different implications. Straightforward definitions are as follows:

digital disruption
change caused by digital technologies that disrupts ways of thinking and acting.

- Digital disruption is the change that occurs when new digital technologies and business models affect the value proposition of existing goods and services.[26]

value proposition
a description of the customer value delivered to a specific target market.

Later in the text, we define a value proposition as the articulated value delivered by the firm to a specific, targeted customer segment. Companies need to create a compelling value proposition to survive in the marketplace. Netflix, for example, has disrupted the movie offerings of broadcast TV channels. Who would not rather have whatever movie they want available whenever they want it on whatever device they choose to use at the moment? That's a big improvement over a take-it-when-we-choose-to-offer-it, fixed movie schedule served up by broadcast channels (more formally called the "linear model" in the trade). On-demand mitigated the pain of the fixed schedule to some extent, but Netflix offers choice, convenience, and personalization that has made it the preferred option for

221 million subscribers as of late 2021.[27] What the TV channels offer just can't compete with the broad range of the Netflix product and service offering. This clearly articulated value proposition has given rise to many competitors in this space.

Digital transformation is the profound and accelerating transformation of business activities, processes, competencies, and models to fully leverage the changes and opportunities of digital technologies and their impact across society in a strategic and prioritized way.[28] Put even more simply, "Digital is the application of information and technology to raise human performance."[29]

So, if Netflix is disrupting the entertainment industry, their competitors from movie theaters to broadcast TV will fight back by transforming themselves, right? Companies usually are quick to sense the disruption, but slow to find a good way to deal with it. The infrastructure of the movie industry, all those theaters in all those locations, makes it hard for them to change. The TV networks also have infrastructure, employees, and organizational culture that make swift and decisive action difficult, even if they were sure of what would work.

CBS has made a signature effort to join the streaming ecosystem with its All Access offering. It offers on-demand access to CBS series with minimal ads and ad-free access to classic series. It offers many of its televised sports events via live streaming, but sometimes licensing restrictions prevent offering events like the NFL games on CBS Sports. It is available on mobile devices and computers and with Roku players, Chromecast, and Apple TV.[30] Rebranded as Paramount+ streaming, the service now includes material that is not only compelling for some sports fans, but also involves streaming television shows, movies, and family content on your television, phone, and other devices (limit three at a time). Most streaming services don't release subscriber figures, but the service appeared to have more than 100 thousand subscribers in early 2016 and CBS predicted 8 million subscribers to its All Access and Showtime streaming services by 2020. This prediction was quite shy of the mark as by 2022, Viacom CBS (rebranded as Paramount) had 56 million subscribers worldwide in the fourth quarter of 2021.[31] Streaming services like HBO and Amazon Prime releases have grown, but it appears that none comes close to Netflix's 221 million.[32] It's hard playing catch-up, and digital transformation is, indeed, hard work.

It is probably more fun to be a disrupter, and some companies in addition to Netflix have disrupted their industries more than once.

Engaging in Digital Transformation

Didier Bonnet and George Westerman surveyed over 1,300 executives in more than 750 global organizations. They found all moving forward on digital transformation but at varying speeds and with varying success. While only 38 percent of them considered their business digitally mature, the researchers confirmed that the more digitally mature the enterprise was, the better its operating results. The researchers identified the building blocks of digital transformation capabilities and were able to group them into five business fundamentals—customer experience, operations, business models, employee experience, and digital platforms. These five business fundamentals and the associated building blocks can be seen in Figure 1.7 and are each discussed in turn below:

- Customer experience will be described throughout this book as the unchallenged competitive battlefield of today and the foreseeable future. Customer experience issues affect all channels, all tools, and everything the marketer does. In order to create a successful customer experience, marketers must have customer knowledge gained from analytics (Chapter 5) and a social understanding of their lifestyles (Chapter 9 and more) to design a better experience. Top-line revenue growth requires digital selling and satisfying

digital transformation
the rapid change in business activities and operations caused by digital disruption.

Figure 1.7 The Building Blocks of Digital Transformation Source: http://sloanreview.mit.edu/article/the-nine-elements-of
-digital-transformation/

The new Elements of Digital Capability

The updated framework places more emphasis on employee experience and business model innovation, as well as on the digital platform, which powers the other elements and, when structured and managed well, enables further innovation.

Business Model		
Digital enhancements		
Information-based service extensions		
Multisided platform businesses		
Customer Experience	**Operations**	**Employee Experience**
Experience design	Core process automation	Augmentation
Customer intelligence	Connected and dynamic operations	Future-readying
Emotional engagement	Data-driven decision-making	Flexforcing
Digital Platform		
Core		
Externally facing		
Data		

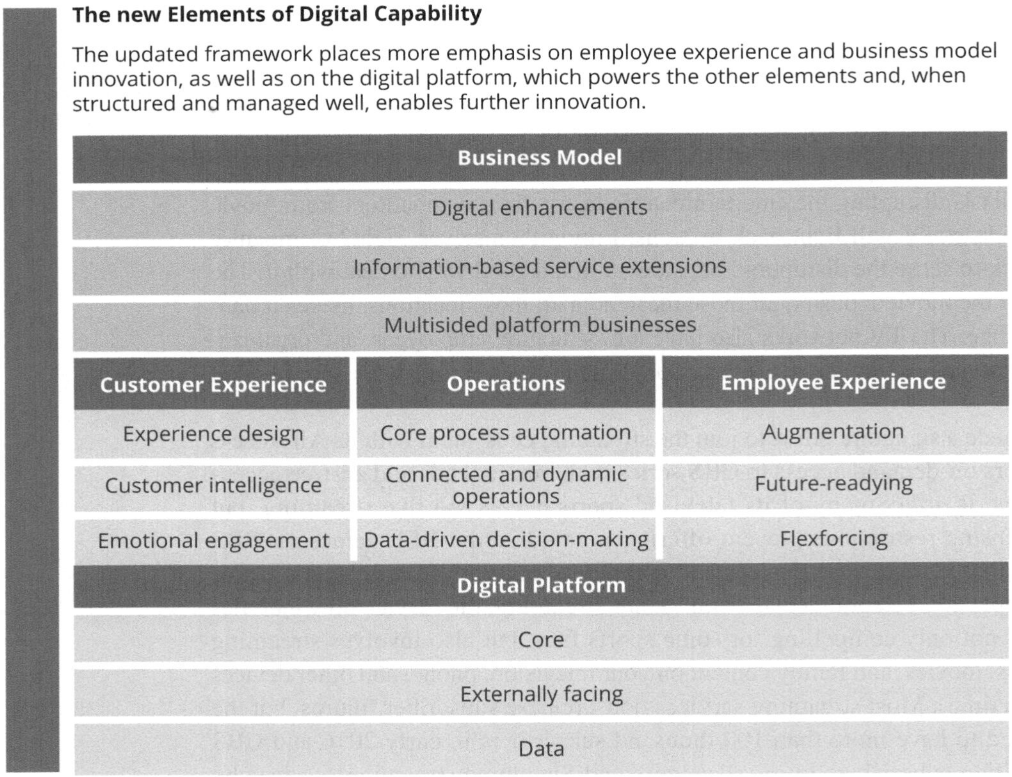

customer processes backed by predictive marketing and an understanding of how to emotionally engage the customer. Customer experience is the focus of Chapter 4, where the emphasis is on all customer touchpoints throughout the multichannel customer journey.

- The building blocks of operations—core process automation, connected and dynamic processes, and data-driven decision-making—are management topics but marketers will be affected by them in many ways. One example is the automated programmatic ad buying discussed in Chapter 10.

- Changing business models and the value propositions that are one component of them are the highly visible outcomes of digital transformation. Chapter 3 explicitly covers business models old and new and gives many examples. Throughout the book, we use examples taken from all over the world to stress that global marketing is an essential part of digital marketing, not a separate topic.

- The employee experience can be transformed through augmentation, i.e., training employees for the future, and providing multi-skill training so they can be deployed where the company needs them. Companies also need to consider using contingent ("gig") workers to fill in the employment gaps.

- Digital platforms have become part of our economy and are therefore critical to digital transformation. An organization that depends on cloud computing for its success first needs a core platform that is agile and can be the foundation for sound operations. While the operational platform is what external customers and suppliers see, the final element of the digital platform is a data platform that can process structured and unstructured data and can be used to build and test algorithms to improve the customer experience.

Achieving Digital Maturity

Accomplishing the transformation, described in Figure 1.7, is clearly a major process, involving all parts of the business. Brian Solis at Altimeter has distilled the process into six stages (Figure 1.8). In the previous section, we pointed out that digital disruption is ongoing, and no business can afford "business as usual" in the face of change of this magnitude. The process continues through several stages of experimentation that become progressively more formalized and strategic. When there is sufficient confidence in the process, it converges into a central team that is charged with overseeing the process throughout the business. The final stage is crucial—the end result of a transformation process is a firm that is innovative and adaptive, one that is agile enough to adapt to ongoing change. As the figure says, "change is constant." There is no more "business as usual." It is often said that digital transformation is a journey, not a destination. Constant adaptation to change is what that statement implies.

   We will end this chapter with a discussion of digital strategy and a case example of a business that seems well-launched on the road to constant innovation. In the next section, we illustrate the need for constant innovation and adaptation with a discussion of two interrelated technologies and the imminent disruption they foreshadow in marketing across all industries.

AI and Cloud Computing—Salesforce and North Face

As a technology, AI is by no means new. Throughout the ages, mankind has fantasized about investing inanimate objects with intelligence, creating god-like creatures with superhuman

Figure 1.8   **The Road to Digital Maturity** Source: https://www.prophet.com/pdf/the-six-stages-of-digital-transformation/?redirectedfrom=gatedpage

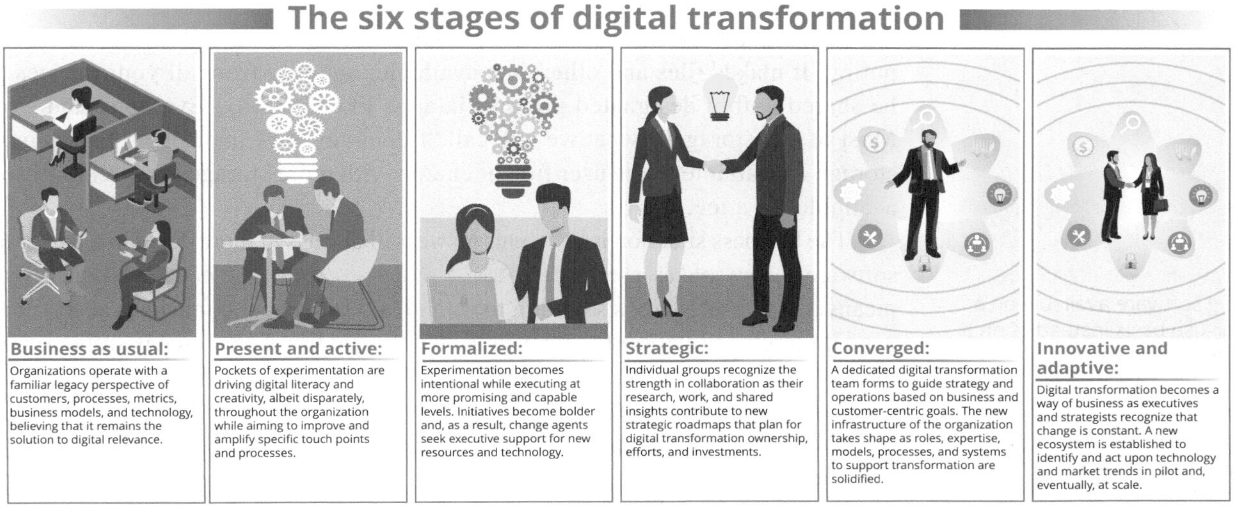

The six stages of digital transformation

Business as usual:
Organizations operate with a familiar legacy perspective of customers, processes, metrics, business models, and technology, believing that it remains the solution to digital relevance.

Present and active:
Pockets of experimentation are driving digital literacy and creativity, albeit disparately, throughout the organization while aiming to improve and amplify specific touch points and processes.

Formalized:
Experimentation becomes intentional while executing at more promising and capable levels. Initiatives become bolder and, as a result, change agents seek executive support for new resources and technology.

Strategic:
Individual groups recognize the strength in collaboration as their research, work, and shared insights contribute to new strategic roadmaps that plan for digital transformation ownership, efforts, and investments.

Converged:
A dedicated digital transformation team forms to guide strategy and operations based on business and customer-centric goals. The new infrastructure of the organization takes shape as roles, expertise, models, processes, and systems to support transformation are solidified.

Innovative and adaptive:
Digital transformation becomes a way of business as executives and strategists recognize that change is constant. A new ecosystem is established to identify and act upon technology and market trends in pilot and, eventually, at scale.

intelligence, or even creating intelligent machines. The field of computer science known as AI, however, can be traced to a conference at Dartmouth College in 1956 at which the term artificial intelligence was first used.

Almost seven decades later there is still no commonly accepted definition of AI.[33] The *Oxford English Dictionary* has one that is useful for general purposes:

> AI is a sub-field of computer science. Its goal is to enable the development of computers that are able to do things normally done by people—in particular, things associated with people acting intelligently.[34]

We have already highlighted one application of AI in Section 1-1—Amazon's effort to embed AI into its Echo home connectivity device. In that paragraph, there was also mention of cloud-based computing, another technology that is essential to the current wave of transformation. Cloud-based computing is a simple-sounding technology with a profound impact. *PC* magazine explains it in nontechnical terms:

cloud computing
using a network of remote servers hosted on the internet, not a local server or computer hard drive, to store data and programs and to process data.

> In the simplest terms, cloud computing means storing and accessing data and programs over the internet instead of your computer's hard drive. The cloud is just a metaphor for the internet.[35]

For individual users, that means accessing programs and data, not on the computer hard drive or even on a network but accessing them through the internet. As individuals, most of us already use many cloud services, perhaps without knowing it. Some examples are as follows:

- Microsoft Office may be resident on the computer itself, but it now includes OneDrive, storage in the cloud. There is also Office Online in which the most popular applications are accessed over the internet.
- Google Drive offers cloud storage that can be used by various applications like Google Docs and Google Sheets. It is accessible by mobile devices like smartphones and tablets.
- Apple offers iCloud that both stores data and syncs it across devices, including Windows devices once the app is installed. Ever wonder how the Find iPhone app works? It's in the cloud!
- Amazon's Cloud Drive is mainly for things purchased from Amazon—music and books, for example.

PC magazine points out that synchronization is an essential feature of cloud computing. It makes files and other data available, not only from all your devices, but to be shared within designated groups via apps like Dropbox, Evernote, and Notion.[36] Most of this storage is what we will call "freemium," in Chapter 3. A basic amount of storage is available to the user free of charge with more storage and premium services available for a fee.

The business situation is different. As we will discuss in more detail in Chapter 3, most software is now sold as a service (Software as a Service, (SaaS)), not as a product. This term means that the software is stored in the cloud and subscriber companies access it as they need it for a fee. Relationship management software firm Salesforce is sitting squarely at the intersection between the cloud and AI and its continued growth is a testament to the success of this business model.

Software as a Service (SaaS)
making software available on a fee-for-use basis instead of on a license or purchase basis.

customer relationship management (CRM)
(or customer relationship marketing) the process of managing and tracking customer relationships across channels.

Salesforce first disrupted the market for customer relationship management (CRM) software with its founding in 1999. CRM or marketing is the process of managing and tracking customer relationships across channels. The process is so complex that many vendors appeared to create software to manage and track the status of such things as offers to the customer and their corresponding actions or responses. Until Salesforce appeared, the makers of CRM software believed, rightly so, that numerous marketing and sales functions had to be integrated in order to make CRM work—customer service had to have access to marketing's customer database, for example. The result was huge integrated software systems that took months to install and were riddled with both coding and data issues. The results were budget overruns, lack of ROI, and the occasional epic fail. Salesforce entered the market with a modular system. After the customer database was plugged into the software, the customer service module could be added. It could be tested and debugged and then could demonstrate that it was meeting objectives—performance, monetary, or otherwise—before moving on to another module. This was a disruption felt throughout the specific industry sector and noted by others.

From the beginning, Salesforce offered distribution of its software over the internet as an option. That required an ever-growing IT infrastructure to serve its many customers on its own cloud platform. It has long been self-described as a "cloud computing company." That is itself a second disruption because cloud computing is still new to many businesses today.

Over the years, Salesforce has partnered with other cloud services firms like Microsoft and Amazon Web Services (AWS). In early 2016 Salesforce announced AWS as its preferred public cloud partner while promising to continue the development of its own infrastructure.[37] That development can be considered a disruption because of the shift of emphasis away from internal, owned infrastructure to cloud infrastructure. It also indicates how well-established AWS has become in the field of cloud services.

The announcement in the fall of 2016 of Salesforce Einstein is an example of a genuinely disruptive product. Salesforce Einstein integrates AI across the Salesforce product line. *Forbes* described it this way:

> Einstein will integrate AI into almost all of Salesforce's products, injecting predictive suggestions and insights into service, marketing, and sales, as well as its newest efforts in collaboration and commerce. As such, [CEO Marc] Benioff tells his executives, Einstein won't just slot in as another "cloud" for them to sell. Instead, Einstein will serve as a new nerve system across the entire business. "We are going to catch our competitors by surprise."

Einstein has out-of-the-box AI capabilities that allow firms to prioritize leads and maximize pipeline opportunities by automating functions previously done by hand. Automated data capture also frees up the sales force's time to focus on customer interaction.[38] Salesforce Einstein is a large undertaking, affecting all of its offerings to customers. However, AI-enabled products may not always be so large in scope, especially in the B2C marketplace. A post on the Cloud Tech site says:

> The future of AI isn't about one giant super-intelligence. Instead, it's about many small, dedicated agents that know you intimately and work on your behalf to improve your everyday life. That could be helping you shop, get to work, or even find a partner. Each is focused on a discrete task, and each gets better over time and adapts to your needs as they evolve.

At roughly the same time Einstein was introduced into the B2B market, retailer North Face announced an app that uses AI to help shoppers choose the best clothing to meet their needs. It is powered by IBM's Watson, which IBM describes as "a technology platform that uses natural language processing and machine learning from large amounts

unstructured data
data that has no predetermined models or is not organized in a predefined way. Unstructured data are often heavily text but not necessarily all text.

of unstructured data."[39] In this case, the unstructured data includes the features of the outdoor clothing items that North Face sell.

The app has another notable feature in that it is browser-based. That means the user does not have to install it; the app can be used from any computer, smartphone, or tablet connected to the internet. That is possible because North Face has a responsive website, a subject we will cover in Chapter 6.

Both of these examples highlight not only how much technology is changing but also the myriad of ways in which technology may be employed to make our lives easier and more interesting in years to come. They also point out that not even the largest and most innovative companies can do it alone. Salesforce has chosen to use the cloud computing services of AWS in tandem with its own platform. North Face used the personal shopping assistant already developed by IBM to power its clothing app. Collaborations and partnerships between companies, even ones that may be competitors in other aspects of their businesses, are already the norm in the digital economy.

This is all happening in the context of continued growth and change in the internet and the mobile web. We end the chapter with a brief profile of the status and change in who, how many, and for what purposes people access the internet and the mobile web.

A Profile of Digital Users

The statistics quoted here and throughout the book are mostly taken from free public sources, although some might require a login profile. In some instances, publishers have made paid content available to us and we are grateful for that. For you, however, it means that sources like this are available to you.

One thing you should keep in mind as you look at these data sources is that they are broad and, as such, of limited use to marketing practitioners. While it is helpful to have a broad grasp of the aspects of the digital ecosystem at the beginning, working marketers need data about specific market segments, products, geographical areas, and so forth. Much of this data is also available free of charge, although it is true that the finer the detail, the more likely the data is going to be behind a paid subscription wall. As you pursue your study of digital marketing, it behooves students to become acquainted with these resources and others you will find by searching on the web. University libraries usually have a wealth of information, including the ability to download data and reports from Statista.com, one of the sources in this chapter. If you can't access a particular resource listed here, check your university library website.

Internet and Mobile Trends

It is generally necessary to separate statistics about the fixed internet from those that apply to the mobile web. The technology is distinctly different, but that is not the reason. Mobile use has spread more quickly in Europe and in developing countries than it has in the United States, and therefore the United States is not always a good indicator of status. Neither is any other single country a good indicator, for that matter—that is among the reasons that marketers need specific, not broad, data.

In 2016 about 40 percent of the world population had an internet connection, up from less than 1 percent in 1995. The internet reached its first billion users in 2005, its second billion in 2010, and its third billion in 2014.[40] In 2022, there were five billion internet users worldwide, or 63 percent of the world's population. Of this total, 4.65 billion were social media users (see Figure 1.9). That is fast growth by any standard, and the growth rate for technological innovations has accelerated over the past few decades.

Figure 1.9 **Global Digital Population, April 2022** Source: https://www .statista.com/statistics/617136/digital-population-worldwide/WHO USES DIGITAL, FOR WHAT?

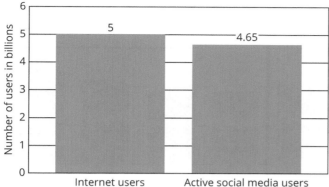

By contrast, the United Nations says that by 1990 there were 11 million mobile subscribers, rising to 2.2 billion in 2005.[41] Statista estimates that in 2025 there will be about seven and a half billion mobile users worldwide.[42] The prediction is also that global mobile web usage for internet and social media access will be increasing over time. What these numbers do not say directly is that mobile will be the only connection for much of the world's population.

Of global internet users, most are active on social media and are using their mobile devices for internet and social media access.

Shifting closer to home in March 2022, Statista put the percentage of internet users in the United States at just over 90 percent, a slight increase from the 89 percent reported in 2016.[43] It means that in terms of basic use, there is little room for growth among the adult population. The adults who want to use the internet are most likely already using it. It also means that some demographic descriptors are no longer meaningful in distinguishing internet users from the general population.

Typically, studies find no significant differences in internet usage between men and women or by ethnicity—White, African American, and Hispanic—or by community type—urban, suburban, or rural. What we tend to find is the differences between age groups, with young adults 18–29 being more likely to be internet users than older age groups. In terms of educational level, adults with some college or one college degree or more were more likely to use the internet, while the higher the income level, the more likely that segment was to use the internet.[44] You are probably saying that there is no real news here and you are correct. However, it does show the continuing democratization of the internet, although some differences persist.

The generational differences highlighted above suggest that not all internet users are using it for the same activities or with the same intensity. With that in mind, let's first look at consumer use and then at business use, with most of the data coming from the United States.

Consumer Trends

It is also not news that first the internet, and now mobile, have fundamentally changed the way people consume media. The big losers have been traditional broadcasters and, especially, print media. The traditional media are being forced to invent new business models, as we will discuss in Chapter 3, and the new models are digital. While Figure 1.10b shows that the total time spent with digital media is increasing, time spent on personal computers actually increased a bit during the early period of the COVID-19 pandemic, as consumers spent more time at home. The two categories that are big winners are mobile and other connected devices like tablets and game players. At over 12 hours each day

Figure 1.10a   Daily Time Spent with Selected Media in the United States from 2nd quarter 2015 to 1st Quarter 2020 (in minutes). Source: https://www.statista.com/statistics/246698/daily-time-spent-with-tv-in-the-us-by-type-of-use/

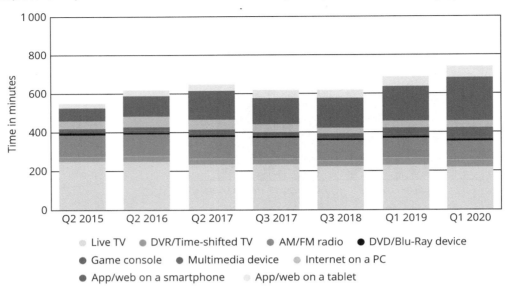

spent attending to one medium or the other—one screen or the other—we consumers are about out of available time!

The data by media type in Figure 1.10a covers differences in what consumers do on desktop, 5 percent of their media time, and on mobile, 30 percent of their time. Overall, users are spending almost 45 percent of their time on the internet. While these data suggest that users are still spending time with live TV, these data don't indicate the level at which they might be multitasking, i.e., checking email while watching television.

Figure 1.10b helps us to understand these trends by showing the dramatic shift in usage from traditional to digital media over the last decade. This trend, already evident, was only accelerated by the COVID-19 pandemic, as most consumers spent a significant

Figure 1.10b   Time Spent per day with Digital versus Traditional Media in the United States from 2011 to 2022 (in minutes). Source: https://www.statista.com/statistics/565628/time-spent-digital-traditional-media-usa/

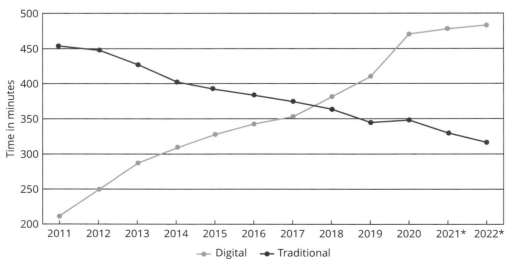

amount of time at home, and many relied on online shopping and delivery services. In addition, the work shifted remotely, leading to more time at home and more opportunities to interact online. In fact, Figure 1.11 illustrates that the online shopping trend is not confined to younger generations. Baby Boomers, who hold most of the wealth in the United States, have caught up and now 90 percent of them are shopping online. Increasingly, this shopping is done on mobile devices, with 29 percent of consumers reporting having shopped on mobile devices (see Figure 1.12). More online shopping is still done from desktop, with more chatting and gaming occurring on the smartphone, but the mobile and tablet numbers are significant.[45] The trend toward online shopping on mobile devices will continue as consumers feel more comfortable with the process and the underlying security of their data on mobile devices.

Fortune suggests that the growth in online buying is affecting the operating results of at least the largest U.S. retailers and recommends that they act more aggressively to meet the internet and mobile challenge. Despite that trend, access to the web is not even across all market segments. In the early days of the web, we described the "digital divide" as separating high- from low-income consumers in terms of access to the internet. While mobile technology has brought internet access to many low-income users, many low-income users may still be behind in the quality of their access to the web and awareness and use of collaborative services such as home- and ride-sharing and crowdfunding.[46]

A study from the Joan Ganz Cooney Center at Sesame Workshop found that there is a new aspect to the modern digital divide:

> Lower-income families in the United States have near-universal access to the internet and some kind of digital device, but they are often at a disadvantage when it comes to the quality and consistency of their connections, especially when they are limited to mobile devices such as smartphones.... "Not all connectivity is created equal, and not all devices provide the same kinds of online experiences," the report reads. "Many families face limitations in the form of service cutoffs, slow service, older technology, or difficulty using equipment because too many people are sharing devices."[47]

Figure 1.11   Percentage Share of Consumers in the United States that Shopped In-store and Online in the Past 12 Months in 2021 by Generation. Source: https://www.statista.com/statistics/1230474/share-of-us-consumers-that-shopped-online-and-offline-by-generation/

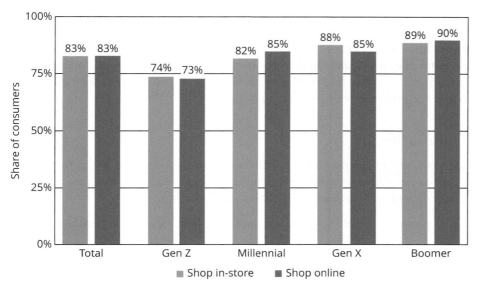

Figure 1.12 Leading Smartphone Activities Done at least Once per Week among Users in the United States as of April 2021. Source: https://www.statista.com/statistics/202535/activities-conducted-while-using-internet-on-smartphone/

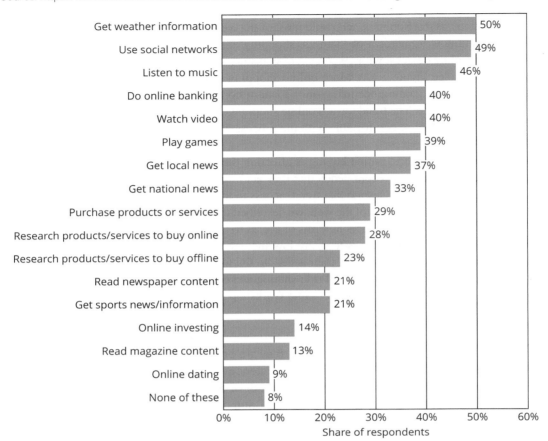

Another significant trend to note in internet usage is the move to video platforms and streaming video. As noted in Figure 1.13, streaming video and music account for over 40 percent of the time spent by internet users in the United States, and this trend is mirrored worldwide. The movement to video has implications for marketers as well as employers as they seek to communicate effectively with their target audiences and their workforces. If we add all the applications of video, including work and personal socializing, internet users are spending about 50 percent of their time in the video environment. These data account for the explosive use of YouTube and other video streaming platforms, such as the previously mentioned Netflix. If this is true in the United States, it is also true in other areas of the world, except more focused on mobile devices because mobile access is the norm.

Business Trends

Amid the constant change brought on by digital disruption, all the things that marketers do can be boiled down into four underlying marketing objectives, which are derived from the four direct response objectives as shown in Figure 1.2:

1. Customer acquisition—marketers must reach out to acquire new customers from their current market segments and to add new segments when the time is right. Customer acquisition is more costly than customer retention, but without a continuing stream of new customers, it is unlikely that growth targets can be met.

Figure 1.13 Most Popular Weekly Online Activities for Internet Users in the United States as of January 2022, by Time Spent (in hours). Source: https://www.statista .com/statistics/1292983/weekly-time-spent-us-users-online-activities/

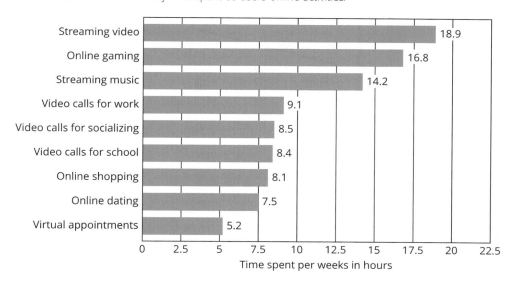

2. Customer conversion (sales)—actually achieving purchases by new customers is key to marketing success. Conversion can be defined in other ways as we will discuss in Chapters 12 and 13, but sales are the ultimate goal.

3. Customer retention—it is cheaper to retain an existing customer than to acquire a new one. It makes customer retention a priority for marketers, and it is the subject of Chapters 4 and 14.

4. Customer value growth—customers who remain loyal over time are likely to purchase more than other classes of customers. It is the job of marketers to facilitate the growth in customer value, as we have discussed earlier in this chapter.

Digital plays a key role in all four activities and the way marketers spend their money reflects that. Figure 1.14 is from the quarterly CMO/Duke University survey of marketing executives.[48] It shows that analytics investments are even more important to marketers than in previous years. Given the direct marketing roots of the internet and its ability to measure results, it was only a matter of time before analytics dominated the thoughts of marketers. Marketers will continue to invest in data analytics, marketing technology, and

Figure 1.14 Outcomes Emphasized by Marketers in 2021 Source: https://cmosurvey.org/wp-content/uploads/2022/02 /The_CMO_Survey-Highlights_and_Insights_Report-February_2022.pdf

Investment	% Reporting Yes	% Change Since Feb-21
Data analytics	77.5%	+37.2%
Optimizing of company website	74.0%	+0.3%
Digital media and search	70.9%	+9.1%
Marketing technology systems or platforms	69.8%	+29.7%
Direct digital marketing (e.g., email)	68.2%	+19.0%
Online experimentation and/or A/B testing	47.3%	+4.2%
Managing privacy issues	35.3%	+23.9%
Machine learning and automation	26.4%	+29.4%
Improving our app	24.4%	NA*

 Insights

Although investments in digital marketing have increased across the board, data-related activities experienced the largest growth. Data analytics, in particular, grew 37.2% from 56.5% of companies investing in February 2021 to 77.5% of companies investing today. Larger companies are investing the most in data analytics, with 91.9% of companies with more then 10K+ employees making the investment. With data collection and purchasing becoming more complex, companies are increasing their investments in capabilities to analyze, store/manage, and automate their data. MarTech stacks are becoming more complex by the minute and companies are investing in the technologies necessary to keep up.

Figure 1.15a Global Advertising Revenue Forecast in Billions in U.S. Dollars. Source: https://www.statista.com /study/42540/digital-advertising-report/

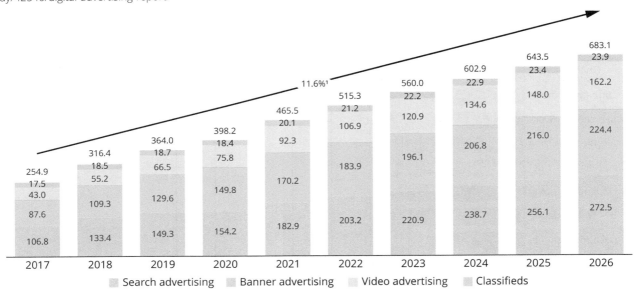

Search advertising   Banner advertising   Video advertising   Classifieds

automation. In addition, privacy is an increasing concern among consumers and, hence, is of prime concern to marketers.

The CMO survey paints a picture of strong growth in digital marketing activities driven by the increase in the use of the internet and digitally disruptive technologies. There are opportunities in this landscape for both brands and marketers themselves. In fact, companies now report that 57.1 percent of their marketing budget is spent on digital marketing. The survey also reflects market statistics that show all traditional media advertising except TV showing slight growth or decline while digital advertising continues to increase.

Figures 1.15a and b show digital advertising trends. Advertising is the key channel for customer acquisition and plays a role both in brand development and customer value growth.

Figure 1.15b Growth of Digital Advertising Revenue in the United States from 2020 to 2022. Source: Statista "Growth of digital advertising revenue in the United States from 2020 to 2022, by format," https://www.statista.com/statistics/288615/growth-of -digital-ad-spend-in-the-us-by-format/.

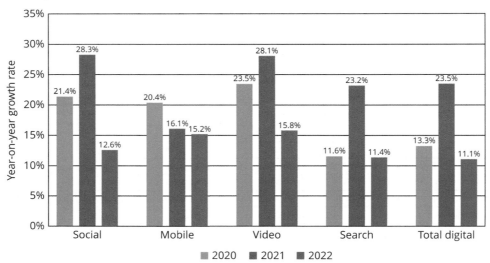

Paid search is predicted to continue to be the largest digital advertising category by 2026, showing steady growth. Display (banner) and video advertising are predicted to both show growth and are predicted to be steady. As is consistent with the viewing habits noted above, video advertising has grown by the highest percentages since 2020, followed closely by mobile and social.

Sales are, of course, the ultimate responsibility and goal of marketers. The movement of advertising dollars away from traditional to digital media reflects the growth of ecommerce and will be covered in subsequent chapters.

While retail ecommerce sales continue to be strong (Figure 1.16a) B2B ecommerce is also a strong player overall. Many students do not realize that much of ecommerce takes place on private business platforms that cannot be accessed by the public. This topic will be discussed further in Chapter 13, which focuses on B2B markets. In addition, as Figure 1.16b illustrates, there is no longer a question about whether the mobile channel can deliver sales. Mobile sales in the United States, which were negligible in 2013, are expected to total $728 billion in 2026, which will make mobile equal to ecommerce sales overall. Remember that in developing countries, more customers access the mobile web than the fixed internet, so U.S. figures understate the global reality.

As a way to reach both consumer and business customers, and then to convert them to customers, digital has demonstrated its clout. In the process, it has created some large and powerful enterprises around the world.

Some of the businesses listed in Figure 1.17, especially the top four, are the usual suspects—Amazon, Apple, Google, and Facebook (Meta). Did you expect to see any Chinese companies also dominating the top ten? There are still a number of firms—Airbnb is a Western example—that are still privately held and therefore not yet showing up in this list of public companies. The digital ecosystem is still in a state of flux and this list will change as public offerings, mergers, and consolidations occur. One thing to note also is the power of the top four companies in the marketplace. These companies remain vulnerable to charges of wielding monopoly power and may be the subject of future action by the federal government.

Figure 1.16a   **Retail Ecommerce Sales Worldwide, 2019–2025 in Trillions** Sources: https://www.emarketer.com/content/worldwide-e-commerce-continues-double-digit-growth-following-pandemic-push-online; eMarketer, August 2021

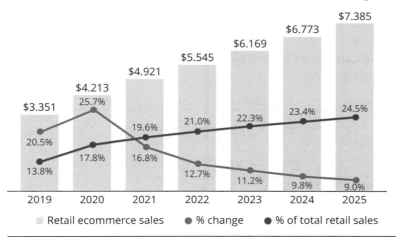

Note: Includes products or services ordered using the internet, regardless of the method of payment or fulfillment; excludes travel and event tickets, payments such as bill pay, taxes, or money transfers, food services and drinking place sales, gambling, and other vice goods sales

Figure 1.16b Retail Mcommerce Sales in the United States, 2019–2025 in Billions Sources: eMarketer, May 2021

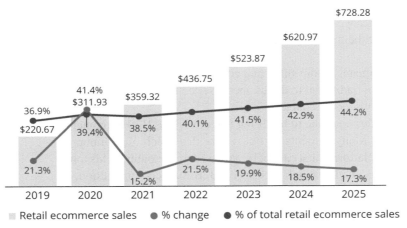

■ Retail ecommerce sales ● % change ● % of total retail ecommerce sales

Note: Includes products or services ordered using the internet via mobile devices, regardless of the method of payment or fulfillment; includes sales on tablets; excludes travel and event tickets, payments such as bill pay, taxes, or money transfers, food services and drinking place sales, gambling, and other vice goods sales

Drivers of Digital Transformation

The outline of digital transformation is becoming clear even though it is in its early days. For one thing, digital transformation is more than just the adoption of digital technologies; digital transformation means embedding technologies in an organization to facilitate fundamental change. It requires a strategy that focuses on business transformation, not just improvement at the margins. It requires leaders that understand the value of digital to the future of the organization. Most importantly, it is strategy, not technology that leads to digital transformation. The more digitally mature an organization, the more likely they are to have a clearly developed digital strategy.[49] As we discussed in a previous section, achieving digital maturity is a process, more a journey than a destination because the end goal is to be constantly innovating to fend off competition and take advantage of opportunities.

Figure 1.17 Leading Online Companies Ranked by Revenue, 2017–2021 Source: https://www.statista.com /statistics/277123/internet-companies-revenue/

Characteristic	2017	2018	2019	2020	2021
Amazon.com	177.87	232.89	280.52	386.06	469.82
Apple	229.23	265.6	260.17	274.52	365.82
Google	109.65	136.22	160.74	181.69	256.74
Alibaba	22.99	56.15	71.99	109.48	134.57
Meta (formerly Facebook Inc.)	40.65	55.84	70.7	85.97	117.93
Tencent	21.9	45.56	54.08	73.88	87.85
Netflix	11.69	55.84	20.16	25	26.7
PayPal	13.09	15.45	17.77	21.45	25.37
Baidu	13.03	14.88	15.43	16.41	19.54
eBay	8.01	8.65	7.43	8.89	10.42

It means taking advantage of digital technologies to improve human performance, leading to the achievement of business goals.[50]

Starting with strategy means following a process similar to that in Figure 1.18. The first step is to define the business value of the digital transformation and to put changing the culture first. Only then should a firm map out technology. Starting in a small way, seeking out partners and refining with feedback are other ways to ensure a scaleable digital transformation. This process is consistent with Dr. Zahay's own research on creating competitive technology through data applications. Her research showed that having a strong leadership role and clearly defined mission and vision drove the differences in using customer information well.[51,52] The adage "It's not what you do, it's just how you do it" holds true in digital marketing transformation as well.

For example, one company that started developing a strategy to lead its digital transformation has been Domino's Pizza. Had you invested $1,000 in Domino's in 2011 it would be worth approximately 23 times that today. That is because the company has continued to strategically transform itself, starting with the perception of the brand. It improved the quality of its pizza and digitally transformed the supply chain for sourcing its ingredients. The result of these efforts was a better-tasting pizza. With a solid product to market, Domino's digitally transformed its ordering and delivery processes. The innovative "Pizza Tracker" allowed customers to monitor the progress of their delivery. The "Anywhere" capability allows for ordering not just on mobile and desktop devices but through Amazon Echo, Facebook, Twitter, and a variety of other choices. This focus on digital transformation made it easy for the company to pivot to car-side, contactless delivery during the early part of the COVID-19 pandemic in 2020. The company continues to innovate based on its strategy of delivering a quality product in a timely manner any way the customer wishes to order.[53] This type of process is surely a sign of things to come as more companies begin on the path of digital transformation.

Figure 1.18   **Digital Transformation Strategy** Source: "Digital Transformation Strategy: Framework, Tips & Examples" https://digitalleadership.com/blog/organizational-development-full-guide/

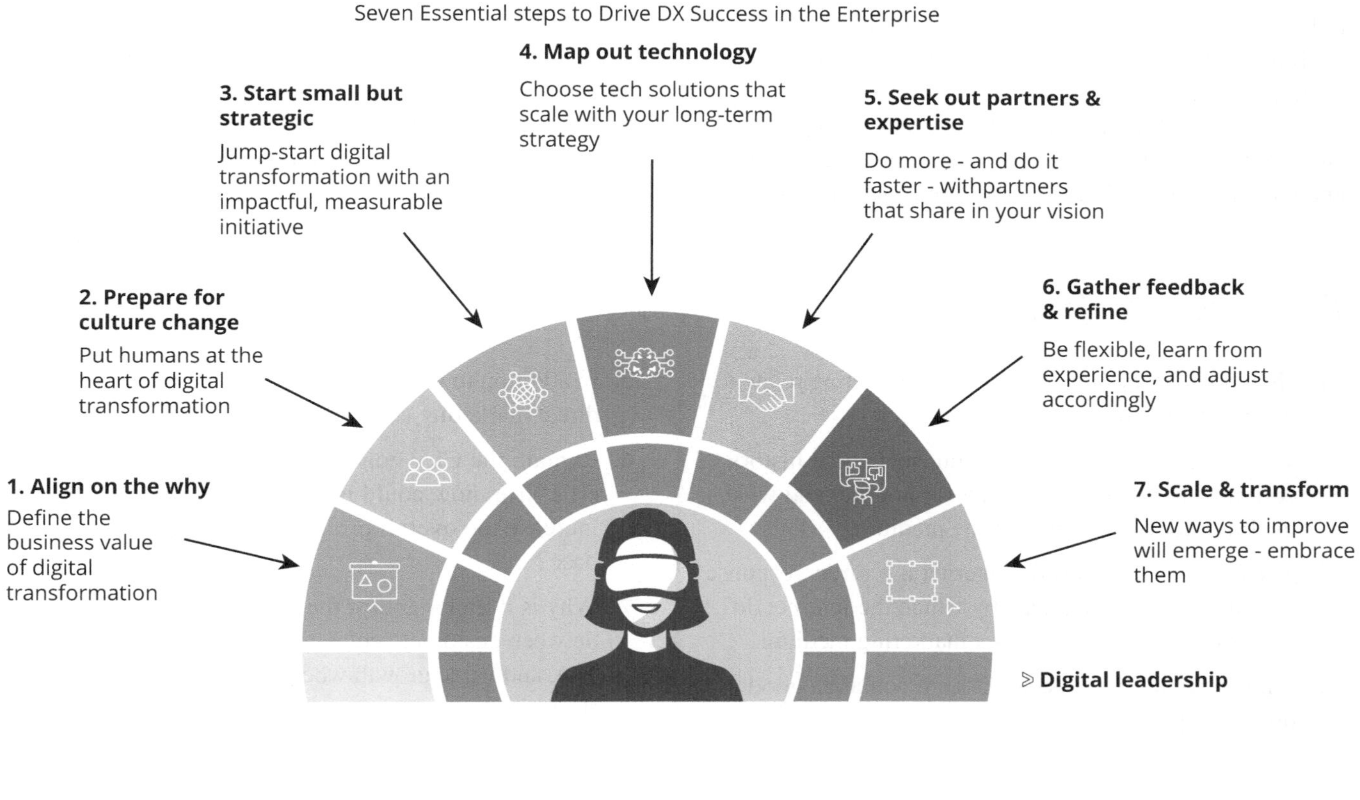

Seven Essential steps to Drive DX Success in the Enterprise

3. Start small but strategic
Jump-start digital transformation with an impactful, measurable initiative

4. Map out technology
Choose tech solutions that scale with your long-term strategy

5. Seek out partners & expertise
Do more - and do it faster - withpartners that share in your vision

2. Prepare for culture change
Put humans at the heart of digital transformation

6. Gather feedback & refine
Be flexible, learn from experience, and adjust accordingly

1. Align on the why
Define the business value of digital transformation

7. Scale & transform
New ways to improve will emerge - embrace them

▷ **Digital leadership**

Summary

Over the past three decades, the internet has grown from an esoteric network serving only a limited audience to an integral part of life for billions of people around the globe. It has been joined by the mobile web, which reaches even more people and is experiencing an even greater growth rate. Companies like Amazon, Google, and Salesforce are creatures of the internet itself. Old-economy companies like General Electric and IBM have integrated the internet into every aspect of their businesses in order to continue to thrive. In doing so, companies have developed digital marketing competencies. This focus involves using many aspects of the direct marketing foundations of the internet, such as interactivity and customer databases, to engage the customer and measure results. The emphasis on engagement and measurement is what led to the widespread adoption of the term digital marketing to describe the focus of this text. The generic direct response strategies from the internet's direct marketing roots provide a good framework for analyzing the success of digital marketing efforts across the customer lifecycle.

The digital marketer of today must be aware that the pace of change is not slowing. Digital disruption is all around us, disrupting business models and operations alike. It forces businesses—large and small, old and new—to undergo digital transformation or perish. Digital transformation is an activity that must engage the entire business in a strategic and ongoing process. Companies like Amazon, IBM, and Salesforce continue to disrupt their industries. Others, like Domino's Pizza, are taking advantage of technology and new business approaches to better serve their customers. Few companies, however, have yet to attain digital maturity.

Digital transformation must focus on providing excellent customer experience as well as on streamlining operations and reducing costs. Marketers must take the lead in creating satisfying customer experiences and be active participants in identifying needed changes in business models. Firms will continue to be impacted by technology that changes the way all parts of their businesses operate. In this chapter, we have also highlighted the importance of the IoT, virtual and augmented reality, AI, and cloud computing. These are among the technology drivers of change that are still in the early stages of disruption.

Marketers take advantage of the fixed internet and mobile web in various ways to perform the four basic marketing activities—customer acquisition, conversion, retention, and customer value growth. Various online and offline tools and techniques come into play at various points in the customer journey.

This chapter provides a snapshot at one point in time of the internet and mobile web and the people and companies that use them. The picture it portrays is one of rapid growth and evolution in the ways in which both people and businesses use digital. Change is universal in the digital ecosystem and any snapshot is quickly outdated. This evolutionary process requires that digital marketers understand sources of information that are relevant to their specific business and/or marketing function and to track that information, usually using the web itself.

This text is premised on the need to understand how technology-driven marketing works and how it can be integrated with traditional channels and activities in order to achieve marketing success. Understanding digital marketing is and will continue to be something of a moving target. At the same time that we wrestle with understanding complex, technology-driven activities, it is important to remember that good marketing puts strategy formulation first, then places the customer front and center, and focuses on excellent customer experiences at all customer touchpoints.

Discussion Questions

1. How does the definition of digital marketing relate to its origins in direct marketing?

2. The origins of the internet are unusual in the history of commercial media. What makes it unusual and what qualities does that impart to the medium?

3. The text lists the ways the internet is a direct response medium. List the elements by which the internet differs from direct response as a marketing medium.

4. Find an email or online ad. Does it contain a good offer? Why or why not?

5. In addition to the offer, what are the elements of a direct marketing strategy?

6. Explain the CLV concept. Thinking about a specific firm, how could it use the concept of CLV to increase the overall profitability of its customer base?

7. Why is it important for the marketer to distinguish between customer acquisition, conversion, retention, and value growth when developing marketing strategies?

8. What are the current characteristics of how consumers and businesses operate on the Internet?

9. What are some changes in your own life and that of your family that you can reasonably expect from the IoT?

10. Why is the mobile web a separate entity from the fixed internet? Why is it important that marketers track developments in mobile as well as in the internet?

11. What is the meaning of digital disruption? And of digital transformation?

12. How should businesses go about attaining digital maturity? What is the final outcome state that marks a digitally mature business?

13. Technology is at the center of all digital transformation. Why or why not?

14. Do you agree that Domino's Pizza is not a pizza company? Why or why not?

Endnotes

1. "A Brief History of the Internet," Internet Society, September 22, 2022, http://www.internetsociety.org/internet/what-internet/history-internet/brief-history-internet.

2. Anu Passary, "Happy 25th Birthday World Wide Web and Thank You Tim Berners-Lee," *Tech Times*, August 23, 2016, http://www.techtimes.com/articles/174759/20160823/happy-25th-birthday-world-wide-web-and-thank-you-tim-berners-lee.htm.

3. Martin Bryant, "20 Years Ago Today, the World Wide Web Was Born - TNW Insider," *TNW/Insider*, March 3, 2016, https://thenextweb.com/news/20-years-ago-today-the-world-wide-web-opened-to-the-public.

4. Debra Zahay, "Advancing Research in Digital and Social Media Marketing," *Journal of Marketing Theory and Practice* 29, no. 1 (February 2021): 125–139, https://doi.org/10.1080/10696679.2021.1882865.

5. Debra L. Zahay, *Digital Marketing Management: A Handbook for the Current (or Future) CEO* (New York, NY: Business Expert Press, 2020).

6. Mary Lou Roberts and Paul D. Berger, *Direct Marketing Management* (Upper Saddle River, NJ: Prentice Hall, 1999).

7. HubSpot, "What Is Inbound Marketing?," HubSpot, accessed December 15, 2022, http://www.hubspot.com/inbound-marketing.

8. Kevin Maney, "Yahoo, Apple, Amazon: Categories Past, Present and Future," LinkedIn, March 8, 2018, https://www.linkedin.com/pulse/yahoo-apple-amazon-categories-past-present-future-kevin-maney.

9. Tim O'Reilly, "What Would Alexa Do?," *O'Reilly Media*, August 19, 2016, https://www.oreilly.com/radar/what-would-alexa-do/.

10. Pablo Luna, "Pablo Luna," *The USB Port*, August 23, 2017, http://theusbport.com/amazon-will-open-bmw-doors-with-personal-assistant-alexa/12860.

11. Engadget, "Ford and Lincoln Owners Can Personalize Their Alexa Commands," *Autoblog*, April 9, 2022, https://www.autoblog.com/2022/04/09/alexa-ford-lincoln-personalize-commands/.

12. "The Fourth Industrial Revolution: What It Means and How to Respond," World Economic Forum, accessed December 15, 2022, https://www.weforum.org/agenda/2016/01/the-fourth-industrial-revolution-what-it-means-and-how-to-respond/.

13. Ahmed Banafa, "The Internet of Everything (IOE)," OpenMind, August 1, 2018, https://www.bbvaopenmind.com/en/the-internet-of-everything-ioe/.

14. Vijay Kanade, "What Is the Internet of Everything? Meaning, Examples, and Uses," *Spiceworks*, August 26, 2022, https://www.spiceworks.com/tech/iot/articles/what-is-internet-of-everthing/.

15. Patrick Thibodeau, "Explained: The Abcs of the Internet of Things," *Computerworld* (May 6, 2014), https://www.computerworld.com/article/2488872/emerging-technology-explained-the-abcs-of-the-internet-of-things.html.

16. Bill Lydon, "Automation.com," accessed December 15, 2022, http://www.automation.com/automation-news/article/sensors-are-fundamental-to-industrial-iot.

17. Andrew, Meola, "Internet of Things in Healthcare: Information Technology in Health," *Insider* (August 29, 2016), https://www.insider.com/internet-of-things-in-healthcare-2016-8.

18. "Azure for Healthcare-Healthcare Solutions: Microsoft Azure," *Azure for Healthcare-Healthcare Solutions | Microsoft Azure*, accessed December 15, 2022, https://azure.microsoft.com/en-us/solutions/industries /healthcare/#overview.

19. "Internet of Everything in the Public Sector - PPT Video Online Download," SlidePlayer, accessed December 15, 2022, http://slideplayer.com/slide/4240580/.

20. Insider Intelligence, "Here's How the Internet of Things Will Explode by 2020," *Business Insider*, accessed December 15, 2022, https://www.businessinsider.com/iot-ecosystem-internet-of-things-forecasts-and-business -opportunities-2016-4-28.

21. Lionel Sujay Vailshery, "IOT Connected Devices Worldwide 2019–2030," *Statista*, November 22, 2022, https:// www.statista.com/statistics/1183457/iot-connected-devices-worldwide/.

22. Cliff Kuang, "Disney's $1 Billion Bet on a Magical Wristband," *Wired* (Conde Nast, March 10, 2015), https:// www.wired.com/2015/03/disney-magicband/.

23. "Virtual Tour Directory," Virtual Yosemite, October 23, 2022, https://www.virtualyosemite.org/virtual-tour -directory/.

24. "Birdly VR," Birdly VR | The Ultimate Dream of Flying, accessed December 15, 2022, https://birdlyvr.com/.

25. Eric Johnson, "What Are the Differences between Virtual, Augmented and Mixed Reality?" "www.recode .net," accessed December 15, 2022, https://www.recode.net/2015/7/27/11615046/whats-the-difference-between -virtual-augmented-and-mixed-reality.

26. Linda Tucci, "What Is Digital Disruption? Definition from Whatis.com," CIO (*TechTarget*, July 31, 2019), https://www.techtarget.com/searchcio/definition/digital-disruption.

27. VB Staff, "Netflix Shares How It Grew to 81 Million Monthly Subscribers: Secrets of a Subscription Model (Webinar)," *VentureBeat* (April 21, 2016), http://venturebeat.com/2016/04/21/netflix-shares-how-it-grew -to-81-million-monthly-subscribers-secrets-of-a-subscription-model-webinar/.

28. "What Is Digital Business Transformation? The Essential Guide to DX," i, August 14, 2022, http://www.i -scoop.eu/digital-transformation/.

29. George Westerman, "The Nine Elements of Digital Transformation," *MIT Sloan Management Review*, January 7, 2014, http://sloanreview.mit.edu/article/the-nine-elements-of-digital-transformation/.

30. "CBS All Access Review," *PCMAG*, accessed December 15, 2022, https://www.pcmag.com/reviews/cbs-all -access.

31. Julia Stoll, "Global Paramount Subscriber Number 2022," *Statista*, November 4, 2022, https://www .statista.com/statistics/1047393/cbs-all-access-subscribers-us/#:~:text=As%20of%20the%20fourth%20 quarter,quarter%20of%20the%20previous%20year.

32. Todd Spangler, "Netflix Falls Short of Q4 Subscriber Target, Stock Tumbles on Weak Forecast," *Variety* (January 26, 2022), https://variety.com/2022/digital/news/netflix-q4-2021-earnings-subscribers -1235158494/.

33. Kris Hammond, "What Is Artificial Intelligence?," *Computerworld* (April 10, 2015), https://www.computerworld .com/article/2906336/what-is-artificial-intelligence.html.

34. "The Home of Language Data," *Oxford Languages*, accessed December 15, 2022, http://www.oxforddictionaries .com/us/definition/american_english/artificial-intelligence.

35. Eric Griffith, "What Is Cloud Computing?," *PCMAG* (February 15, 2022), https://www.pcmag.com/how-to /what-is-cloud-computing.

36. Matt Asay, "Salesforce's Data Centre Team 'Fought' AWS Cloud Outsourcing," *The Register* (June 7, 2016), http://www.theregister.co.uk/2016/06/03/salesforce_aws_microsoft_platform_wars/.

37. Alex Konrad, "Nonstop Benioff: Inside the Master Networker's Audacious Plan to Disrupt Salesforce—and the World," *Forbes* (August 24, 2016), http://www.forbes.com/sites/alexkonrad/2016/08/24 /nonstop-benioff-inside-the-audacious-plan-to-disrupt-salesforce-and-the-world/#7d636c215747.

38. "Salesforce Einstein Basics," Unit | *Salesforce Trailhead*, accessed December 15, 2022, https://trailhead .salesforce.com/content/learn/modules/get_smart_einstein_feat/get_smart_einstein_feat_basics.

39. Matt Marshall, "The North Face to Launch Insanely Smart Watson-Powered Mobile Shopping App next Month," *VentureBeat* (March 4, 2016), http://venturebeat.com/2016/03/04/the-north-face-to -launch-insanely-smart-watson-powered-shopping-app-next-month/.

40. Justas Gaubys, "How Many People Use the Internet in 2022? [February 2022 Update]," *Oberlo*, accessed December 15, 2022, https://www.oberlo.com/statistics/how-many-people-use-internet.
41. The Mobile Economy, November 29, 2022, http://www.gsma.com/mobileeconomy/.
42. S. O'Dea, "Forecast Number of Mobile Users Worldwide 2020-2025," *Statista*, July 12, 2021, https://www.statista.com/statistics/218984/number-of-global-mobile-users-since-2010/.
43. "Topic: Internet Usage in the United States," *Statista*, accessed December 15, 2022, https://www.statista.com/topics/2237/internet-usage-in-the-united-states/#dossierKeyfigures.
44. "Internet/Broadband Fact Sheet," *Pew Research Center: Internet, Science & Tech*, November 16, 2022, http://www.pewinternet.org/data-trend/internet-use/latest-stats/.
45. Vayola Jocelyn and Lodovica Biagi, "Smartphone vs. PC in the U.S. 2018 Report," *Statista*, accessed December 15, 2022, https://www.statista.com/study/57580/smartphone-vs-pc/.
46. Chris O'Brien, "The Sharing Economy Is Creating a New Digital Divide, Says Pew Study," *VentureBeat* (May 19, 2016), http://venturebeat.com/2016/05/19/pew-study-says-explosion-of-sharing-and-collaborative-services-is-creating-new-digital-divide/.
47. Benjamin Herold, "Mobile-Only Internet Access Presents Hurdles for Families, Survey Finds," Education Week (July 26, 2022), https://www.edweek.org/technology/mobile-only-internet-access-presents-hurdles-for-families-survey-finds/2016/02.
48. "Home," The CMO Survey, December 7, 2021, https://cmosurvey.org/.
49. Doug Palmer, Gerald C. Kane, "Strategy, Not Technology, Drives Digital Transformation," *MIT Sloan Management Review*, July 14, 2015, http://sloanreview.mit.edu/projects/strategy-drives-digital-transformation/.
50. Accenture, "Digital Transformation L Accenture," *Accenture* (November 20, 2022), https://www.accenture.com/us-en/insights/digital-transformation-index.
51. Debra Zahay and Abbie Griffin, "Customer Learning Processes, Strategy Selection, and Performance in Business-to-Business Service Firms*," *Decision Sciences* 35, no. 2 (2004): 169–203, https://doi.org/10.1111/j.00117315.2004.02338.x.
52. James W. Peltier, Debra Zahay, and Donald R. Lehmann, "Organizational Learning and CRM Success: A Model for Linking Organizational Practices, Customer Data Quality, and Performance," *Journal of Interactive Marketing* 27, no. 1 (2013): 1–13, https://doi.org/10.1016/j.intmar.2012.05.001.
53. Shikhar Goel, "Domino's Is Not a Pizza Delivery Company. What It Is Then?" *The Strategy Story*, April 9, 2021, https://thestrategystory.com/2020/07/11/dominos-digital-transformation.

Chapter 2

The Supply Chain Becomes a Value Ecosystem

Learning Objectives

By the time you complete this chapter, you will be able to:

1 Identify the impact of digital transformation on supply chains.

2 Explain the role of information in first, integrating the value chain and later, making it virtual.

3 Explain the concept that all goods are services and outline its relationship to the value ecosystem.

4 Identify the major ways the platform-based economy can deliver value.

5 List the major technologies that are enabling value chains and ecosystems at present.

6 Define the macro trends that will influence the supply chain's future.

Digital disruption is occurring throughout business processes. The transformation of channels of distribution has been ongoing for several decades, focusing on cost reduction and speeding goods and services to market. In recent years the focus has broadened to customer-facing activities. Digital transformation that matches supply to the demands of individual customers is no longer optional; it is becoming a necessity. According to Professor William Verdini, "Businesses don't compete, supply chains compete."[1]

channels of distribution
intermediaries through which products and information about transactions move in the course of a single exchange.

supply chain
the downstream portion of the value chain, the channel from suppliers to producers.

value ecosystem
connecting brands and their customers and business partners in a direct, non-linear fashion.

value chain
an integrated supply chain in which transactions are conducted electronically.

value
essentially the usefulness (economic utility) of the product less its price; also known as customer value or customer perceived value.

The Impact of Digital Transformation on Supply Chains

There was a time when channels of distribution described simple movements of goods or services through a series of intermediaries who performed a variety of business functions in the process of transporting them from manufacturer to customer. That is the linear supply chain portrayed in Figure 2.1a. Reaching the value ecosystem illustrated in Figure 2.1b is often a lengthy process.

It begins with a supply chain in which value is added at various points in the distribution process. That is the so-called value chain.

Michael Porter popularized the concept of the value chain in the early 1980s. His familiar graphic, which identifies the primary activities of inbound logistics, operations, outbound logistics, marketing and sales, and service, and recognizes the support activities of infrastructure, human resources, technology, and procurement, provides a useful basis for understanding *how the enterprise produces* value *for its customers*.

Unfortunately for our ease of understanding, in the last two decades the term has widely been used in a different way. In the context of the automation of business processes and later the internet, the term "value chain" has come to mean the *seamless, end-to-end integration of activities throughout the channel of distribution*. In essence, this value chain concept incorporates two familiar business processes—the supply chain and the channel of distribution. Companies have moved first to integrate the supplier-facing side of their

Figure 2.1 Supply Chains Evolve into Value Webs From Linear Supply Chain to Value Ecosystem Source: https://www2.deloitte.com/us/en/insights/focus/business-trends/2015/supply-chains-to-value-webs-business-trends.html

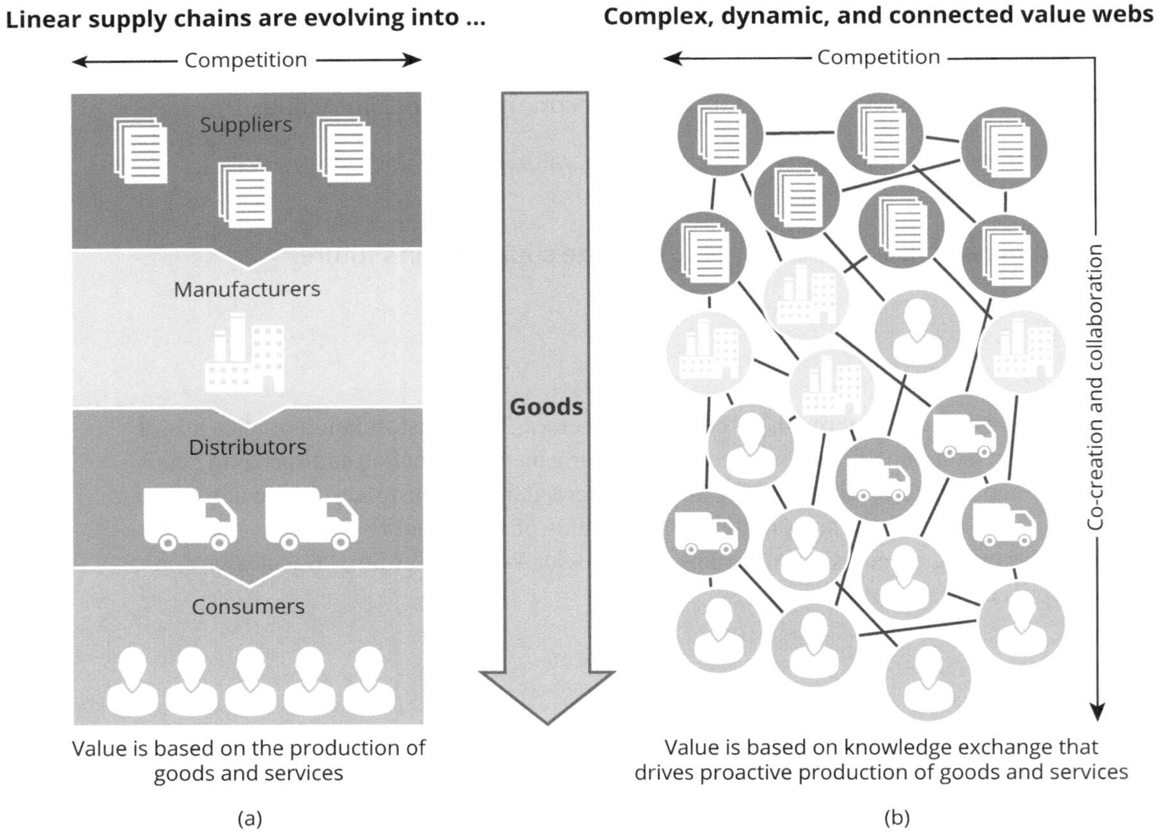

Linear supply chains are evolving into ...

Complex, dynamic, and connected value webs

Value is based on the production of goods and services

(a)

Value is based on knowledge exchange that drives proactive production of goods and services

(b)

channels—the supply chain. They have been slower to integrate on the customer-facing side, the channel of distribution. When they have, they have reaped significant benefits.

Otis Elevator, a business unit of United Technologies Corp., describes itself as "The world's leading manufacturer and service provider of elevators, escalators, and moving walkways."[2] Otis has been integrating with customer infrastructure for many years. In 1988 it introduced the first Remote Elevator Monitoring (REM) system. REM is a diagnostic system that monitors the performance of Otis elevators and other brands with which Otis has service contracts. It monitors both the usage level and individual systems within the elevator. The system schedules regular maintenance calls based on the level of usage. If it detects a problem, it reports the condition to a 24-hour communications center, which determines the severity of the problem, prioritizes service calls, and dispatches a repair person with the required tools and parts.

According to Otis, the system identifies most problems before they occur, minimizing elevator downtime. By analyzing each of the hundreds of systems in an elevator, the company also maintains them so that the number of service calls is minimized and performance is optimized. Reports covering both scheduled and REM-based service calls are available to the customer online.[3] Remote monitoring also illustrates how value can be added by improving product performance and thereby improving customer service, and lowering customer costs.

Other developments at Otis illustrate both the "greening of the supply chain" (ecological sustainability) and their continued attention to customer concerns and needs. Their GeN2 Switch product is an elevator that does not need the usual machine room full of equipment. It is described as "plug and go," just like other appliances that use available 220-volt energy, saving on installation costs. The movement of the GeN2 elevator generates energy, storing the excess in "accumulators." This technology not only saves energy costs but also allows for continued operation of the elevator in the event of power failure.[4] Elevator technology can be customized to fit customer needs in other ways. A sustainable housing development in Reze, France, contains an elevator that derives 80 percent of its power from solar panels on the roof of the building.[5] Localization is also part of Otis's strategy. To support the "Make in India" initiative it is adding to its manufacturing capacity in Bengaluru, India. This plant produces the GeN2 Switch elevator for the Indian market, which is the second largest elevator market in the world behind China. An elevator that is not affected by power outages is seen as especially desirable by Indian builders.[6] However, Otis has not been immune to recent developments in the supply chain, including the impact of inflationary pressures on raw materials. While its agility allows it to prepare and buy ahead and use computer chips that are more readily available, raw materials prices continue to increase, causing upward price pressure.[7]

There is no doubt that sophisticated digital and energy technologies are key to integrated systems such as this advanced elevator. The question becomes, "how do some firms manage to use technology well to please customers and reduce costs while many still do not?" McKinsey, the global consulting firm, has found there are factors that point the way to successful digitization of business processes. Their success factors are as follows:

- Define the precise outcome to be achieved. They give as an example a bank that digitized its mortgage application and approval process. In so doing they cut the cost of each new mortgage by 70 percent while reducing the time for preliminary approval of the mortgage from days to just a minute.
- Create a seamless, end-to-end customer experience. This takes the cooperation of every part of the business that is part of a customer touchpoint.
- Build an in-house team that has the skills and commitment to advance the digitization process over the long term. McKinsey points out that digitization skills are in short supply in today's workforce.

- Move quickly. End-to-end processes can take years to configure and install, incurring costs but providing no payback. Like CRM systems, to be discussed in Chapter 14, projects that develop modular components that can be installed and begin to show positive outcomes in a year or less have two advantages. First, they are more likely to work than larger, more complex systems. Second, they are much more likely to generate support among management, board members, and other stakeholders.

- Do not follow the traditional roll-out process. Digitized systems are often resisted by work units in the current organization. For instance, the mortgage officers in the bank may not trust the digitized system and may continue to review mortgage applications manually, negating all the benefits of the system. It may take a new mortgage unit to prove the worth of the digital process and integrate it into the existing workflows in the bank.[8]

Providing customers with the intuitive, immediate, and seamlessly gratifying experience they expect does not stop here for many firms, however. There are many ways in which supply chains can improve business function and delight the customer. As we look at examples, it is necessary to first look at a few supply chain basics.

While it seems clear that the linear supply chain is a relic of the past, we need to look at the origins of today's more complex value chains and supply ecosystems to understand the basic functions and management issues.

Essentials of the Supply Chain

A supply chain maps the physical movement of goods from initial production through assembly through the distribution process to the customer in the same way but with more detail than the supply chain in Figure 2.1. Whatever the degree of complexity, there are a set of processes that are involved in managing the supply chain (Table 2.1). As you look at the processes, which have an operations management flavor, keep in mind that a single enterprise like Nike has hundreds of suppliers whose activities must be coordinated.

Because supply chain management is such a complex task, enterprises can realize large cost savings from integrating and improving it, with best-in-class companies spending

Table 2.1   Supply Chain Management Processes Source: Rajendra K. Srivastava, Tasadduq A. Shervani, and Liam Fahey, "Marketing, Business Processes, and Shareholder Value: An Organizationally Embedded View of Marketing Activities and the Discipline of Marketing," *Journal of Marketing*, 1999, 170.

1.	Selecting and qualifying desired suppliers
2.	Establishing and managing inbound logistics
3.	Designing and managing internal logistics
4.	Establishing and managing outbound logistics
5.	Designing workflow in product-solution assembly
6.	Running batch manufacturing
7.	Acquiring, installing, and maintaining process technology
8.	Order processing, pricing, billing, rebates, and terms
9.	Managing (multiple) channels
10.	Managing customer services such as installation and maintenance to enable product use

5–6 percent less of their total revenue on supply chain costs than their median industry counterparts. They can also realize major improvements in process elements ranging from inventory (25–60 percent improvement) to overall productivity (10–16 percent improvement).[9] The classic example of a tightly integrated value chain is Dell Computer, which we will discuss later in the chapter. Zara, the European clothing chain, provides an example of combining customer information with supply chain integration to succeed in the ever-changing world of fashion.

Zara—Fast Fashion

Zara, a division of Spanish conglomerate Inditex Group, had over 3,000 retail stores in more than 96 countries in early 2020 as well as growing online sales. With an estimated brand value of €14.7 billion in 2020,[10] Zara continues to capture the attention of businesses and investors as well as fashionistas around the globe.

Zara's success comes from two key drivers. First is its fashion appeal. Zara commits to only 50–60 percent of items by the beginning of the season. That leaves them with about 50 percent of the season's inventory to be produced during the season itself. Customer trends are constantly monitored. Store employees using handheld devices roam the stores, asking customers what they like, do not like, and are looking for but don't find. That information is transmitted to the design team at headquarters, which immediately begins to sketch new items. At the end of each day, store managers provide sales reports to headquarters, giving constant updates on what merchandise is and is not selling. Stores receive shipments of new merchandise twice a week, keeping stock fresh at all times.

The second driver is the ability of Zara's supply chain to produce new items and get them into stores in just two weeks. Competitive fashion chains like Swedish-based H&M and Chicos in the United States often take as much as six months to spot a trend and react to it by producing more of desired items and disposing of unpopular ones. By that time the selling season is over. As a result of its speed to market, Zara can sell 85 percent of its stock at full price while the fashion industry averages only 60–70 percent.

How has Zara designed a supply chain that supplies desired merchandise so quickly and so effectively? First, it owns many of its own production facilities, making about 40 percent of its own fabric in highly automated factories in Spain. It also makes about 60 percent of the garments it sells. Most are produced in small workshops throughout Spain and Portugal instead of being outsourced to lower-cost-of-labor countries. Inventory reaches stores quickly, by truck in Europe and by air in more distant locations.[11] Their marketing effort includes a website that is carefully localized for the various countries in which it operates and what presents as a single Facebook page with over 30 million fans globally.[12]

The importance of supply chain excellence in the fashion industry is well recognized. Two surprising things describe the situation in the years since Zara was founded in 1974:

1. Zara's business model has changed little since then.
2. Competing fashion chains like Gap, H&M, and Abercrombie and Fitch have not been able to emulate the fast fashion model.

That does not mean that Zara does not keep up with other developments, however. Their website is carefully localized for the many countries they serve with some exceptions. For instance, their Chinese online presence is operated on a Chinese platform. The complexity of Zara's merchandising delayed their move into online sales until 2011. In 2014, online represented only 3 percent of Zara's total sales, but by 2021 had reached over 25 percent of sales.[13,14] Zara survived the worst part of the pandemic and is thriving, in part due to expanding ecommerce sales. In addition to the ability to pick up online orders in stores, as early as 2018 Zara developed a series of "click and collect" sites separate from its typically crowded stores. These innovations in online fulfillment have helped the company bounce back to pre-pandemic sales levels fasters than its competitors.

Zara[15] has had a global Facebook page from the early days of brand pages. Customers from all over the world could be seen asking for a particular pair of shoes to become available in their stores, complaining about the quality of a piece of merchandise, or even reporting a fraudulent Zara Facebook page. The operators of the Facebook page appeared to be responding within one day and providing clear and useful information.

Zara is active on other social media platforms but it seems to let its customers do a great deal of the talking—and the photographing and the sharing. According to one observer, the young consumers who are the heart of Zara's market are purchasing experiences, not just clothing. They want to parade it on Instagram and Snapchat. The fast fashion at Zara, along with the trendy but cheap fashion at Forever 21, meet young consumers' needs for a large number of images to be shared. "Their entire life, if it's not shareable, it didn't happen," Marcie Merriman, Generation Z expert and executive director of growth strategy and retail innovation at Ernst & Young, said to Business of Fashion. "Experiences define them much more than the products that they buy."[16] That kind of customer engagement may be an even more difficult standard to reach than a hyper-efficient supply chain, challenging as that is! Another challenge for Zara is sustainability. Zara's business model is based on abandoning items of clothing once they are not fashionable rather than seeking enduring styles. The company has recently published a list of sustainability goals, including reducing waste in landfills.[17]

The Virtual Value Chain

In order to create optimal value, a company must examine the entire supply chain, from initial production to final consumption, in order to understand where costs are incurred in the process. Consultants at Bain & Company liken it to a Swahili game called Jenga. In this game, each player must remove as many blocks as possible from a tower, using them to build additional structures, all without causing the original structure to come crashing down. This seems an apt analogy.

They identify four key factors in this effort:

- Information search costs
- Transaction costs
- Fragmentation of the customer marketplace
- Standardization of products

Together information and transaction costs typically account for over 40 percent of total costs. Economists characterize these costs as "friction" in channels of distribution and they offer ripe targets for cost reduction in value chains.[18] Integrated value chains represent an important step in managing both the supply facing and the customer-facing sides of the business. Dell's integrated value chain operates extensively in the internet space, and hence it is sometimes referred to as a virtual value chain.

virtual value chain
an integrated value chain that operates exclusively on the internet.

Dell's Direct Model

Dell Computers is one of the classic examples of creating a value chain in the internet space, one that is not a series of links but a network of interconnected enterprises, both supplier and customer. Like Zara, this aspect of Dell's business model has changed little from its early days. Before Dell's direct model became a force in the industry, personal computers had important issues in all four of the categories established by Bain and listed above. Search and transaction costs were high, especially for the small business or individual customer. The fragmented market ranged from the individual customer buying a single unit to the very large corporation which might purchase several hundred computers each month. Even very large customers tended to settle for a standard product because it was cheaper to buy in a large, standardized lot, until Dell. In its early years, Dell enjoyed great success as a result of its build-to-order model which featured a streamlined supply chain (Figures 2.2a and b) and careful financial control of manufacturing and distribution operations. Touting Dell's success in 2004, *Fast Company* magazine stated that "Dell has replaced inventory with information, and that has helped turn it into one of the fastest, most hyper-efficient organizations on the planet."[19]

Dell also uses information to create customer value. One primary mechanism for doing this is its Premier Pages. They were one of the first to provide each business customer, from a Fortune 500 enterprise to a small local business, its own secure page

Figure 2.2   (a) Traditional Computer Manufacturer and (b) Dell

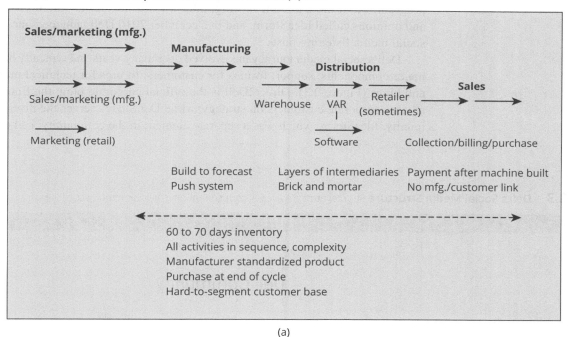

(a)

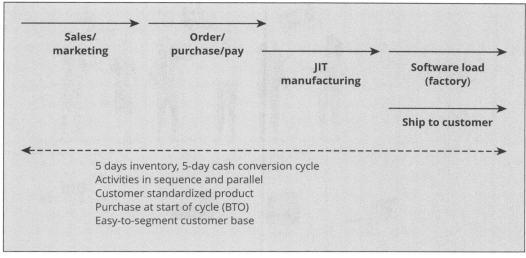

(b)

on the Dell site. This includes the products that have been approved for purchase by the firm and support information for those specific products. Products not approved for purchase are not even seen, making life easier for the purchasing department. In addition, employees with purchasing authority can simply log on and make their purchases without going through purchasing, saving time for both. Dell also wins because purchases are driven to the website, where transactions are cheaper. This service is feasible for even a small business because Dell's telephone representatives have easy-to-use templates that allow them to set up a page by simply entering information provided by the customer over the phone.

Dell's success has sometimes been uneven, however. Beginning in about 2005 Dell suffered a number of issues. The company that prided itself on customer service ignored the complaints of a customer who was a well-known blogger[20] until it became a media firestorm.[21] The next year a Dell laptop exploded in flames while sitting alone on a conference table. The event transfixed the internet.[22] In response to the customer care issues, Dell established the first elements of its social media program. First, the Direct2Dell blog, later a wiki-like site to solicit customer ideas and opinions called IdeaStorm, and in December 2010 Dell launched one of the early social media listening posts.[23]

Dell's social media journey has evolved over many years and typically has had three major components: support forums for customers, forums for technical professionals, and blogs (Figure 2.3). Direct2Dell is the official corporate blog, the Enterprise blog advises corporate customers on strategy, while DellShares serves the investment community. IdeaStorm, which was a separate element in the community, had over 24,000

Figure 2.3 **Dell's Social Media Structure** Source: https://www.dell.com/community/Dell-Community/ct-p/English

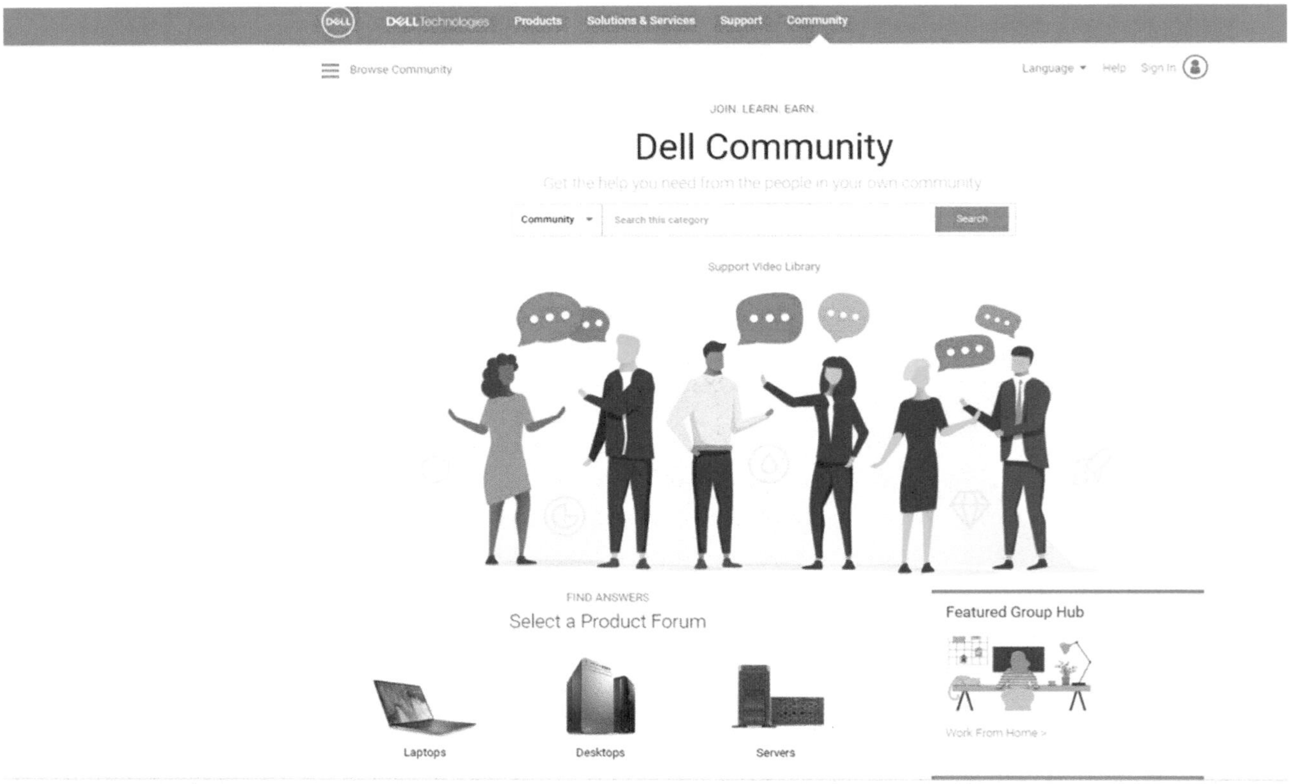

Source: Dell, Inc

ideas submitted in early 2016 and had implemented 549 of those ideas. While the IdeaStorm concept has been abandoned, Dell also listens and communicates with customers on a number of social media platforms, and its own community, shown in Figure 2.3. Dell's Director of Social Media and Community has said that the social media program focuses on building trust through engagement and integrity, using available online and offline channels of communication, co-creation with customers and employees, and in-depth employee training.[24] These are all activities that have the potential to create value for customers. In fact, not only does the team field thousands of posts each week from all over the world, the @DellCares support through social media has been linked to over $265,000 in weekly revenue. This result is achieved by meeting the customers where they are and addressing their concerns immediately. They have served Dell in good stead[25] through market disruption, economic turmoil, and the privatization of the company in 2013.[26]

One important change is a greater reliance on channels of distribution at the expense of its direct model.[27] Dell has also signaled greater emphasis on developing new markets in areas like digital services instead of relying primarily on continued streamlining of its value chain for cost-effectiveness. The emphasis on new markets signals a focus on revenue generation in addition to cost reduction.[28] That shift requires a relentless focus on creating value for the customer.

Benefits of an Integrated Value Chain

In the internet economy customer value has taken on a special meaning. The quality of products is still unquestionably important. However, the stark truth is that many companies have mastered the art of product quality. Companies have spent much of the last 10 to 20 years learning to produce products at or near the six-sigma level of quality (no more than 3.4 defects per million according to the American Society for Quality). That kind of quality has become expected and even standard in many applications. This level of quality is a necessary, but no longer sufficient, competency in businesses of all kinds.

It is customary to point out that customers want performance, reliability, speed, and convenience, both in products and in the distribution of those products. That is true, but leading marketing academic researchers Vargo and Lusch, searching for a way to integrate the subdisciplines of product marketing and services marketing, take that reasoning a step further. Their concept, dubbed Service-Dominant Logic, is nothing less than a new paradigm for marketing itself and has occasioned much discussion. They (Vargo and Lusch) state that:

> the service-centered dominant logic represents a reoriented philosophy that is applicable to all marketing offerings, including those that involve tangible output (goods) in the process of service provision.[29,30]

Are all goods—tangible and intangible—actually services? While that may sound like a revolutionary idea, advertisers have long known that they must sell product benefits, not product features. For the most part, people do not purchase products just to possess them; they purchase them to derive benefits of some sort, even if the benefit itself is something intangible like "status."

Vargo and Lusch have continued to update concepts and terminology associated with their logic. Their 2016 update contains several axioms that are especially relevant to value chains:

- Resources that create results, including knowledge and skills, are the fundamental basis of strategic benefit.
- Value is co-created by multiple actors of which the customer, or beneficiary, is always one.

six-sigma
quality management technique that results in near-perfect products; technically, results that fall within six standard deviations from the mean of a normal distribution.

Service-Dominant Logic
the idea that service is the basis of all economic exchange making all firms service providers and all products essentially services.

Figure 2.4 **The Narrative and Process of S-D Logic** Source: https://experts.arizona
.edu/en/publications/institutions-and-axioms-an-extension-and-update-of-service-domina

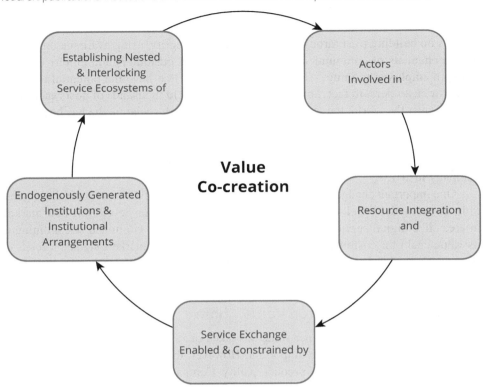

- A service-centered view is inherently beneficiary-oriented and relational.
- The beneficiary is the unique determiner of value.

In their view, "the narrative of value co-creation is developing into one of resource-integrating, reciprocal-service-providing actors cocreating value through holistic, meaning-laden experiences in nested and overlapping service ecosystems, governed and evaluated through their institutional arrangements."[31] Figure 2.4 illustrates the concept.

In this illustration of Service-Dominant Logic, the authors use both "networks" and "ecosystem" but the word linear is not used. The actors include traditional supply chain members as well as customers, all of whom may assume different roles at various times. The actors provide resources and integrate them through collaboration with one another. The services are exchanged using the processes of facilitating institutions. All of this results in an integrated service ecosystem which has, as its major purpose, the co-creation of value.[32]

Notice that customers are key to this co-creation of value; it is, after all, what they are seeking. A key task of any actor in the ecosystem is to create value. Articulating a value proposition is the first step in creating value and it is an integral part of business models. We will discuss value propositions in Chapter 3.

Next Step—the Digital Value Ecosystem

Nike's customized shoes and apparel blazed a digital trail that other brands have struggled to emulate. Nike established a new software division[33], Nike Fuel, which provides an excellent illustration of the concept of collaborating to co-create value. Nike Fuel Lab was established in 2014 to build a fitness ecosystem using the Nike Fuel platform. Previously, Nike had participated alone in the fitness tracking market with its fitness tracking hardware.[34] It signaled the end of that strategy in 2014 when it announced that it was discontinuing its FuelBand tracking devices to concentrate on software.[35] As of 2018, athletes can still track their runs but can do so on the Nike Run Club App, Nike Training Club App, and the Apple Watch[36] as part of the broader Nike Sports Research Lab (NSRL).[37]

These three applications above are a good example of the platform economy as discussed below. The Nike Run Club App connects athletes with coaches and other runners and collects statistics on individual performance. Figure 2.5 illustrates how the app creates statistics for a user on a typical morning run. The Training Club App also connects athletes with trainers and is focused on wellness and mindfulness. The partnership with Apple Watch allows for the collection of data and the constant display of feedback during the run. This collaboration means that other developers have access to the platform to develop meaningful feedback for the running community.

Echoing the ideas of Service-Dominant Logic, Accenture says that companies must move to an as-a-service ecosystem model even though that model may cannibalize existing products or services. They say that ecosystems require:

- Co-creation. The most valuable members of the company's workforce may no longer work for the company. In a service-dominant world, the workforce is a mélange of talent from different ecosystem players coming together to redefine value based on customer desires.

- Innovation. These practices are no longer an afterthought, but rather a process driver. Fifty-three percent of organizations indicate they are using an open innovation program with customers, suppliers, or partners.

- Interdependence and dynamic roles. A good ecosystem redefines the landscape within which new solutions are developed and consumed.

- Adaptive environments. Allowing entities to respond more rapidly to disruption is key in the digitally disruptive environment in which companies operate today.

- Governance. The service ecosystem model requires creating rules of engagement for communication, collaboration, and innovation.[38]

co-creation
bringing business entities or businesses and their customers together to create mutually valuable outcomes.

They assert that successful ecosystems will benefit companies in a number of ways. They will:

- Master digital relationships with customers to bring together talent—reassessing channel players and roles to foster collaboration.

Figure 2.5   **Nike Run Club App** Source: www.capgemini-consulting.com

- Ease adoption. Smart players will reduce risks to enable starting small and scaling fast, creating successful programs within their platform.
- Simplify the buying experience, obsessing over outcomes and solution benefits. Righting the ship means capitalizing on the indirect sales channel via an as-a-service platform you create fueled by an ecosystem of rivals and friendlies.

They conclude by asserting that, "Ecosystem as a service, done correctly, is the growth engine of the future and the battlefield on which all players now find themselves." Remember that we started this chapter with the quote, "Businesses don't compete, supply chains compete." Is it now becoming clear why that is the case?

The Platform Economy

One of the recent developments has been the concentration of ecommerce and value chain activities on major platforms. This trend has given rise to the term "Platform Economy." Although the term platform is used in many ways, in this context, platform means "an organization that uses digital and other emerging technologies to create value by facilitating connections between two or more groups of users."[39] Key to their success has been the explosion of networked devices, such as PCs, tablets, and smartphones, and the internet and cloud computing. So powerful has been the "network effect" that drives these major platforms that they have come to dominate their categories.

Platforms tend to be grouped into categories in terms of how they deliver value as follows:

1. Exchange (or commerce), i.e., Amazon, Alibaba
2. Service, i.e., Airbnb, Uber
3. Content: i.e., YouTube, Netflix
4. Software, i.e., Apple iOS, Google Android
5. Social, Facebook, Instagram
6. Investment, i.e., Priceline, Kayak, Open Table

The companies listed here, most of which are publicly owned, have been able to dominate digital marketing through their superior ability to connect consumers with markets, such as Amazon and Alibaba in the ecommerce field. Accenture sees the companies that are driving the platform economy as those tending to be less heavily invested in assets and more heavily invested in technology to connect consumers to each other, to brands, and to desired content.[40] Echoing the concept of the value ecosystem, these firms tend to rely less on traditional linear value chains and more on a continuous feedback loop connecting developers, publishers, content owners, retailers and service providers with consumers. With the platform-based value chain and its ability to process information, value creation is now two-way and continuous. It is not only that companies are relying on the major platform players listed above to create value. Firms are working on their own custom value networks, as described in this chapter, that have a substantial impact on the supply chain.

Technologies that Enable Value Chains and Ecosystems

Technology and the information flows it produces have been an integral part of supply chains for decades. The platform economy simply allows for a smoother flow of information and an enhanced ability to create value in many areas, including the supply chain. Exhibit 2.1 describes the most important of basic supply chain technologies. In recent years older

> ## Exhibit 2.1 Formative Technologies for Supply Chains
>
> ### EDI (electronic data interchange)
>
> EDI replaced the paper forms that had facilitated channels of distribution for hundreds of years. It offered speed, fewer content errors, and dramatically lower processing costs. However, EDI systems were large and cumbersome and the cost was out of the reach of most small businesses.
>
> ### ERP (enterprise resource planning)
>
> ERP software allowed firms to integrate all business activities across the enterprise. All these activities, for example,
>
> accounting and human resources, had previously run separately, and developing workflows to make them operate seamlessly as a single system has been a huge task. This is true even though ERP software is modular and can be installed one or a few activity modules at a time.
>
> ### RFID (radio frequency identification) Technology
>
> RFID technology is not new. It was used by the British in World War II to identify friendly aircraft. An RFID system begins with a tag which contains a chip with a unique identifying code. As the product moves along the supply chain, its movements are recorded and sent to a tracking database.

applications such as EDI (Electronic Data Interchange) and ERP (Enterprise Resource Planning) have been superseded by other software technologies that are easier to use and often less costly. Some technologies are having a resurgence. For example, RFID technology is still in use in numerous supply chain applications.

There are a number of newer technologies that are integral to the development and functioning of integrated value chains and ecosystems. They are as follows:

- Software-as-a-Service (SaaS)
- Cloud computing
- Smart devices
- Mobile apps

Software-as-a-Service (SaaS)

Over the last few years SaaS has become ubiquitous. All kinds of software—from filing your income tax return to major enterprise applications—are available for a user fee. The definition provided by TechTarget is straightforward. "Software-as-a-Service (SaaS) is a software distribution model in which applications are hosted by a vendor or service provider and made available to customers over a network, typically the internet."[41] Arguably the best known application of SaaS in marketing has been Salesforce CRM, which will be discussed in Chapter 14.

The fact is that supply chain applications are moving into the cloud. That shift effectively makes them SaaS. The movement has been slowed by the fact that most supply chain management (SCM) systems are part of legacy ERP systems, many of which are highly customized. The overall market for supply chain software applications is growing rapidly, however, as large enterprises begin to replace their legacy systems and small firms find new SaaS applications time- and cost-effective. Gartner says that cloud-based supply chain software revenues grew 17 percent in 2014.[42] While growth is slowing a bit, the firm iCrowd Research says the market is expected to continue to grow at 11 percent a year and to exceed $8.61 billion by 2027.[43]

Amazon Web Services is a good example of this transition. Just a few years ago, if a business wanted to run on Amazon software it was necessary to download the appropriate apps. Now Amazon's description is, "Amazon Web Services (AWS) is a secure cloud services platform, offering computer power, database storage, content delivery and other functionality to help businesses scale and grow…. From data warehousing to deployment

EDI (Electronic Data Interchange) general term used to describe the digitizing of business information like orders and invoices so that they may be communicated electronically between suppliers and customers.

ERP (Enterprise Resource Planning) implementation of processes and software that integrates all aspects of the business from manufacturing, resource planning. and scheduling through service functions like human resources.

tools, directories to content delivery, over 50 services are available in just a few mouse clicks with AWS."[44] On the same page is a "Get Started for Free" offer with some services being offered free for as long as a year.

A search of AWS identifies 17 supply chain management software offerings ranging from OpenERP, which it describes as a pre-configured, ready-to-run ERP and CRM service that connects various business processes to Sustainable Supply Chain, which enables optimal use of natural resources. One solution offered as SaaS is Retail Cloudhouse. Amazon says this business intelligence solution will allow the retail store to:

- Redesign the customer experience by analyzing customer interaction across multiple business channels.
- Reinvigorate operational excellence by streamlining retail store operations.
- Reimagine growth by streamlining the supply chain leading to right time, right place merchandising inventory.[45]

It is touted as simple and easy to use. Pricing is a monthly fee per user, which is commonplace for SaaS solutions.

Cloud Computing

The AWS example shows that it is almost impossible to separate SaaS products from the cloud computing platform today. Offering access via the cloud is simply the easiest way to make the software solutions available.

One industry expert points out that the transition to cloud computing from traditional supply chain management systems is still in the early stages. While it can be challenging to transition from a legacy system to a cloud-based one, he lists benefits that make it worthwhile. Cloud systems are more scalable than installed software, can be up and running quickly, make it easy to connect new trading partners, provide the ability to connect everyone in the supply chain, and more.[46]

Accenture has a nice way to cut through the technological complexities of cloud computing for the supply chain. It says that cloud computing "is the engine that makes supply chains talk to one another."[47] Pfizer has been reaping the benefits of cloud computing in its supply chain since 2012 and provides a good example of both the benefits and some of the difficulties.

Jim Cafone, VP of supply network services, calls it a virtual supply chain and says it allows Pfizer to respond quickly to both market pressures and unexpected events that might otherwise disrupt their complex supply chain. The market in which Pfizer competes is made up of two distinct segments with different issues and needs—the patented drug market and the generic drug market.

The market for drugs that are still under patent production requires responsiveness and flexibility as well as inventory to meet immediate customer needs. That means delivery strategies that can offer specialized services like temperature-controlled compartments and next-day air shipping. Speed and accuracy are the major concerns, not cost. The generic market, on the other hand, is highly cost sensitive. Logistics must focus on inventory management, efficiency, and optimized logistics that favor less costly shipping alternatives, even ocean shipping.[48]

The complexity of Pfizer's supply chain is intimidating. Pfizer has more than 24,000 SKUs and 200 contract manufacturer partners, and activities in more than 175 countries[49] Before the cloud integration, each of the supply chain partners had its own IT system separate from Pfizer's ERP system.

Instead of asking suppliers to implement Pfizer's existing system, Pfizer decided that a cloud-based approach that created a virtual supply chain, built in cooperation with its partners, would be more practical. All parties were required to adopt a common communications platform so they could easily send and receive information from Pfizer. Each supplier became a node on a virtual supply chain. The technology has many components but there are two key suppliers, GT Nexus and Unyson Logistics.[50] AWS provides the cloud computing platform.[51]

Just because the cloud-based system was expected to be cheaper, faster, and much easier to install did not mean that all suppliers greeted the concept with enthusiasm. "Not all Pfizer's partners were happy with the plan to start with," Mr. Cafone says. "There were certain providers that just didn't understand this whole world of cloud, and didn't understand this world of device agnostic, and there were certain ones that didn't necessarily like it, but they decided that they wanted to build it with us and go along with us and our software partner."[52]

The project, which took about 18 months to complete, has created a number of specific benefits for Pfizer. When partners join or leave the system they can be plugged in or out easily without disrupting the entire network. The system gives Pfizer a complete view of its shipments in parts of the world where they had previously not been able to track their products. When something unexpected happens they can find out immediately how the product and the shipment have been affected and where the product is located.[53]

At Pfizer, cloud computing now also supports other business functions. For instance, it uses cloud-based platforms in its global research and development operations. One application is a system that handles clinical trial data in partnership with research organizations Parexel and ICON as they run clinical studies. The research firms run the trials and Pfizer analyzes the data. These and other research and development activities also take place in the AWS cloud.[54]

Pfizer uses the term "device agnostic" as an important descriptor of their network. That characteristic has become even more important as the Internet of Things (IoT) has entered many aspects of daily life.

Pfizer continues to innovate and in 2022 received a Garner Supply Chain Award for its innovations in distributing the COVID-19 vaccine.[55]

> "A total of 195 vials are packed in a pizza-box-like tray. Up to five trays can be added into each shipper, and dry ice is added to keep the almost 6,000 vials of product at minus 75 degrees Celsius for 10 days. Shipments were traditionally monitored through sensors that store data and need a readout at their destination. This process, which can be cumbersome and reactive, was unlikely to work for COVID-19 vaccine distribution."

The award-winning system used GPRS (general packet radio service), a type of mobile technology, to track the vaccine's location, temperature, and humidity in real time and provide alerts if metrics were not within range.

The IoT Begins to Impact the Supply Chain

The IoT will eventually have a huge impact on supply chains. As digital devices are embedded in more products, an incredible amount of big data will be produced. Supply chains will be directly affected by some of these devices, smart storage, for example, and indirectly by products that include embedded devices, consumer wearables, for example. The data that results from the use of those products will lead to greater customer intimacy and should produce benefits for customers as well as for the makers of the products.

embedded devices
a device, often a microchip, that becomes part of another device, rendering various services, often doing so without human intervention.

Smart Storage Using RFID

Healthcare in general and hospitals, in particular, are a good example of an environment in which supply chain efficiencies and careful inventory management are critical to both the cost of operations and the quality of patient care. In some cases, individual items, a cardiac pacemaker, for instance, are quite expensive. Enter the smart storage cabinet. Each item of inventory carries an RFID tag. The storage cabinets shown in Figure 2.6a constantly monitor inventory at the item level. When a member of the medical team removes an item the inventory is immediately adjusted. Upon reaching the operating room a bar code attached to the patient is scanned and the item is attached to the record of that patient. The cabinet monitors and reports the inventory levels and can automatically order the replacement items. If the device specified by the physician is not on hand, other cabinets in the network of nearby hospitals can be searched to locate the appropriate device. The cabinets produce a great deal of data for analysis of everything from patient outcomes to inventory costs.

RFID tags are physical devices that can be attached to everything from the metal storage cabinets shown in Figure 2.6a to the cow being tagged as shown in Figure 2.6b. There was a time when only a cow valued at several thousand dollars was considered eligible for an RFID tag with its chip. Now chip technology has become so cheap that marketers can tag individual items of merchandise, not just shipping pallets. Embedded chips have many other applications. Prof. Roberts's dog has an embedded microchip. Does your dog or cat have one?

Figure 2.6a　Smart Storage in a Hospital Environment Source: www.theferrarigroup.com

Figure 2.6b　Cow with Canadian Cattle Identification Program-compliant RFID Tag Source: Canadian Cattle Identification Agency

Apparel with Embedded Devices

A number of firms, including Nike, are producing apparel with embedded sensors used for tracking purposes. Among the well-known are the Apple Watch and Fitbit athletic tracking devices and shirts that collect data from daily athletic activity and display it in various ways. Many of the products are designed for athletic and physical fitness activities, but the applications for medical tracking are obvious. Some are quite sophisticated.

One application of these types of technologies is a pair of leggings designed by researchers at King's College in London (Figure 2.7). This application measures muscle fatigue which previously could only be done in a lab by experienced personnel. The MIT Technology Review explains that the technology involves embroidering "an ordinary pair of runners' leggings with electrodes and circuitry that connect to a portable Arduino microprocessor. This product then collects and analyzes the electrical stimulation data. This circuitry is double-stitched in a zigzag pattern to allow for stretching. And the entire device is powered by a 7.5-volt rechargeable battery."[56] The post adds that the embroidered pattern and the stretch of the leggings automatically places the electrodes where they are needed, eliminating the need for a professional to position them. This makes the product both cheaper and easier to use. It can help athletes understand how their muscles are tiring and thus avoid injury. In time it may produce data that helps design better biomechanical prostheses.[57]

The upscale fashion chain Burberry has used RFID technology for its products since 2012.[58] It allows the company to check stock and quality control. In certain stores, the technology links to display screens that will produce bespoke content specific to certain products. Although Burberry says it is not collecting individual customer information with the tags, consumers do have the ability to ask that the tags be removed.

These are only a few examples of hundreds of how the IoT is going to impact various elements of the supply chain.

Figure 2.7 Leggings with Technology Embroidered On Source: www.technologyreview.com

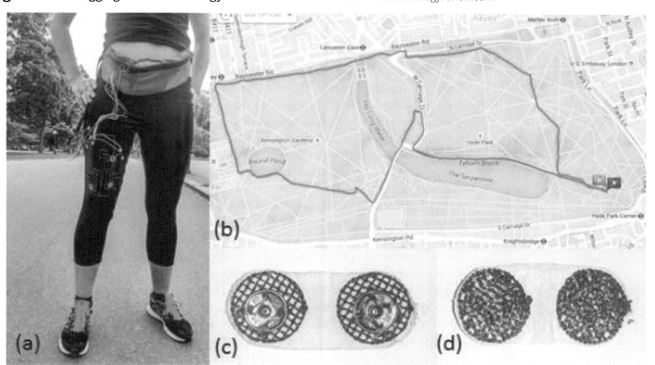

Mobile Apps

The use of mobile devices and apps in various inventory and logistics is commonplace. It is hard to walk around a large mass merchandise outlet without seeing an employee or supplier using a device to track inventory. The principle applies to many other supply chain activities. Some of the supply chain apps are made by firms that are familiar to consumers; some are B2B supply chain specialists. Most are smartphone apps, although a few require a handheld device. A few of the many apps in use today are as follows:

- Logistics by Logistics Management. This is a comprehensive app that can track drivers, vehicles, shipments, and clients.
- WEBFLEET by TomTom (now owned by Bridgestone). This fleet management app tracks a mobile workforce.
- ServiceMax based on the SalesForce.com platform. This app offers much of the salesforce functionality including order management, call center monitoring, salesforce optimization, social media monitoring, and much more.
- GasBuddy by Cheap Gas Buddy. Used by consumers and fleet operators alike, this app locates the cheapest gas in the area.[59]
- Route Plan Form by Motorola. This app for Motorola Solutions Devices develops route plans and provides details as well as storing driver and vehicle data and can capture signatures.
- Delivery Confirmation w/GPS by iPhone. This app stores relevant package data and captures delivery signatures with GPS location.[60]

Mobile apps are revolutionizing SCM just as they are revolutionizing all facets of consumer life. As you can see, some of the same apps work in both B2C and B2B markets while others are specially developed to meet business needs.

What Comes Next for the Supply Chain?

The easy answer to that question is "continuing digital disruption." Certainly, the COVID-19 pandemic has challenged supply chains around the world. A study from KPMG calls the goal a demand-driven supply chain that should look like the graphic in Figure 2.8. It is important to note that the graphic separates physical materials flows from information flows. Information needs to flow from consumer sources to all members of the supply chain immediately. Think of Zara and the speed with which it follows fashion trends. Materials flows are unlikely to be as swift although the importance of direct relationships with suppliers and the resulting cost and time savings have been stressed throughout this chapter. This graphic implies that information about both demand and supply should be accessible to all other members of the network. That is the all-important visibility feature of virtual supply networks.

As firms work toward supply networks and ecosystems that are driven by customer demand, the technologies we have discussed in this chapter will continue to impact their design and functioning. Software provided in the cloud, embedded devices, and mobile apps will all have important places in new supply ecosystems.

Another macro trend we have not yet discussed in this chapter but that is covered in Chapter 1 is artificial intelligence (AI). AI is a term that has been used and abused over the years. Many developers today seem to prefer some variant of "machine learning systems." IBM's Watson introduces himself: "Hello. My name is Watson. I am a cognitive system who can understand, reason, and learn. I work with humans around the world."[61] IBM explains by saying: "IBM Watson is a technology platform that uses natural language processing and machine learning to reveal insights from large amounts of unstructured data."[62]

demand-driven supply
a supply chain that operates in response to demand signals from customers.

Figure 2.8 Physical and Information Flows in an Integrated Supply Ecosystem

Source: https://www.kpmg.com/US/en/IssuesAndInsights/ArticlesPublications/Documents/demand-driven-supply-chains.pdf

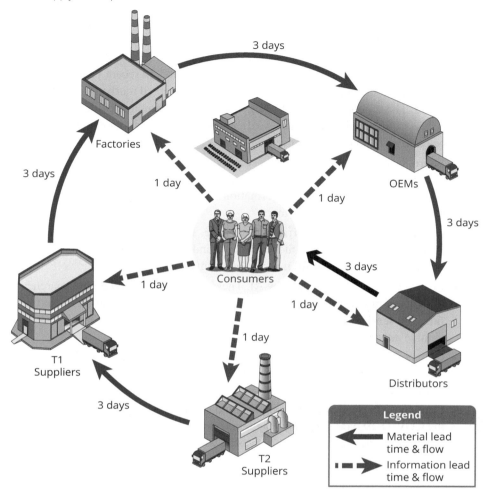

There are already examples of AI use in supply chains. Dell and other technology firms use control towers, a term borrowed from NASA, to collect and analyze data from across the supply chain. Many tools are used for the analytics. For instance, Dell's parts division has a control tower that uses predictive analysis, to be discussed in Chapter 4, to forecast when and how the weather is going to disrupt the supply chain. That enables them to have plans ready to meet weather emergencies when and where they occur.[63]

Another set of control towers uses business process management (BPM) software to support their service delivery supply chain. Dell says these control towers "provide visibility and process flows to parts, people, call center activity, and their technology resolution experts."[64] This kind of visibility allows them to meet their service level agreements. Those agreements with large enterprise customers provide for same-day, four-hour, or even two-hour guaranteed response times. The software can also do things like scan orders to see that the set of components ordered may not be the correct configuration or be technically correct in some other fashion. An analysis team does a variety of statistical tests on the data, looking at things like historical trends and deviations from expected service levels to detect patterns which the software can be programmed to detect and respond to in real time. No, the machine is not doing all the learning just yet, but systems that are this responsive can provide a huge competitive advantage.[65]

business process management (BPM)
a systematic attempt to make business processes more efficient.

Some other developments you can expect to see in supply ecosystems in the coming years include the following:

- Service chains becoming more important than product chains. Service chains refer to the process by which after-sale service is delivered. This kind of service is a major customer satisfier and a potential source of strong and consistent revenue. We will discuss processes for successfully delivering after-sale service in Chapter 4.[66]

- Putting more emphasis on the "base of the pyramid." In recent years this phrase has come to mean the millions of people in underserved markets around the world. These people represent a huge market, for example, people who have no access to financial services in Brazil, but products and supply chains will have to be configured to meet their needs.

- Micro-segmentation of markets becoming increasingly possible. Whether it is custom running shoes for the individual consumer at Nike or segments with only a few firms in B2B markets, information will allow supply chains to respond to the needs of individual customers.[67]

- Predictive forecasting occurring in real time. This includes abilities to predict customer demand, identify niche markets, and inform the development of products and services that fulfill marketplace demands.

- Electronic markets optimized by AI. These markets will provide transparency in terms of price, speed, and product features. They will be web-based and link financial services and manufacturing to networks that provide a significant competitive advantage.

- Collaborative IT infrastructures linking all parties in the network. Smarter software will lead to data-driven, agile solutions to customer demands and supply chain issues.[68]

- Continued challenges with supply chain disruption due to the aftereffects of the COVID-19 pandemic. The pandemic exposed weaknesses in supply chains. Interdependency meant that there was a "whiplash" effect down the supply chain when shortages appeared on the other end.[69]

Emerging supply chains will supply four key benefits in the future. They will provide speed in the movement of both physical products and information. They will scale easily through the use of plug-and-play software components. They will become smarter over time. They will be inexorably connected to every node in the ecosystem of customers and suppliers and be able to respond swiftly to disruptive change.

Finally, having accomplished all of this, they will provide a significant competitive advantage to firms who are diligent in creating smart, fast, demand-driven supply networks.

Summary

The supply chain of the past cannot meet the requirements of the digital economy. Neither can a "one size fits all" product that is pushed through channels using conventional marketing promotional and pricing techniques. In some cases, such as configuring internal and external networks, the final product is inherently a custom proposition. In others, prospering in a competitive marketplace requires using a set of products to meet customer needs in an individualized manner. Marketers are required to achieve these outcomes in a changing business environment that has recently increased emphasis on a green supply chain. They will have to address the supply chain vulnerabilities exposed by the COVID-19 pandemic and its aftermath.

The traditional linear supply chain has evolved into a value ecosystem made up of interconnected relationships and platforms. Each member contributes its core capability, and the final product is delivered to the customer as a single strong and recognizable brand, one that offers excellent customer experience throughout the process. This development represents a revolution in business organization and management that few enterprises have yet fully achieved. As examples throughout this chapter have emphasized, it is an achievement that can be years in the making.

One way of looking at the process is through the lens of service-centered dominant logic—the marketing concept that says all products deliver services and the job of the enterprise is to create value propositions.

None of this is easy. It is likely to require reengineering of existing business processes and major projects to integrate internal systems and to communicate across organizational boundaries with both suppliers and customers. Existing technologies like EDI, ERP, and RFID will be part of this process. Newer technologies like SaaS, cloud computing, embedded smart devices, and mobile apps are part of the digital transformation. Sometimes they are disruptive as in the case of SaaS which has virtually replaced the purchase of software. Sometimes they will require new skill sets as is the case with mobile apps.

The activities required to create value chains, transform them into value ecosystems, and finally create the demand-driven supply network of the future, are many and complex. They require changes on both the supplier-facing and the customer-facing sides of the business. Some firms that are far advanced in their supply chain transformation focus relentlessly on customer experience. This increases the competitive requirements for all firms.

Discussion Questions

1. Differentiate between four key concepts—supply chain, value chain, integrated value chain, and supply ecosystem.

2. Find a company that is using a strategic approach to the supply chain and outline how they are doing so.

3. Do you agree with the concept that all goods are essentially services? Why or why not?

4. What is the platform economy and how does it relate to the value chain?

5. What are the business practices used by Zara that have made it responsive to customer needs and successful financially in the B2C market?

6. What about Dell in the B2B market? What business practices have made it successful?

7. Which newer technologies are being used in developing integrated supply chains?

8. What are the advantages of newer technologies over the original supply chain technologies of EDI and ERP?

9. RFID is the oldest of the technologies discussed in the context of supply chains. Why do you think it is still in use when other early technologies are being superseded by other, more modern, choices?

10. Discuss one trend that you believe will be especially important in future supply chain evolution.

Endnotes

1. Stephen DeAngelis, "Supply Chain Management: Is It Still the next Big Thing? - Enterra Solutions," Enterra Solutions - Better Decisions, Automatically, March 3, 2013, https://enterrasolutions.com/blog/supply-chain-management-is-it-still-the-next-big-thing/.

2. "Otis Elevator Company," Otis Elevator Company, accessed December 15, 2022, http://www.otisworldwide.com/.

3. "Remote Elevator Monitoring - Files.otis.com," accessed December 15, 2022, https://files.otis.com/documents/256045/11655845/REM5.0_FACTSHEET_WHQ_EN_0118_FINAL.pdf/.

4. "With the Power of - Otis.com," accessed December 15, 2022, https://www.otis.com/documents/256045/35422495/Brochure+-+GeN2+Switch+-+EN_CH.pdf.

5. Marc Howe, "The Latest Groundbreaking Vertical Transit Innovations – Architecture. Construction. Engineering. Property," *Architecture Construction Engineering Property*, December 8, 2015, https://sourceable.net/latest-groundbreaking-vertical-transit-innovations/.

6. DH News Service, "Otis Aims to Increase Localisation Content," *Deccan Herald* (February 10, 2015), http://www.deccanherald.com/content/459012/otis-aims-increase-localisation-content.html.

7. Nina Trentmann, "Elevator Maker Otis Faces Pushback from Suppliers on Prices," *The Wall Street Journal* (Dow Jones & Company, July 27, 2021), https://www.wsj.com/articles/elevator-maker-otis-faces-pushback-from-suppliers-on-prices-11627422297.

8. Shahar Markovitch and Paul Willmott, "Accelerating the Digitization of Business Processes," *McKinsey & Company* (February 13, 2020), http://www.mckinsey.com/business-functions/business-technology/our-insights/accelerating-the-digitization-of-business-processes.

9. Scott Stephens, "Supply Chain Council & Supply Chain Operations Reference (SCOR) Model Overview," Power Point Presentation, May 2000, https://www.-supply-chain.org.

10. "Zara | Company Overview & News," *Forbes*, accessed December 15, 2022, http://www.forbes.com/companies/zara/.

11. "Zara Supply Chain Analysis-the Secret Behind Zara's Retail Success," June 25, 2018, https://www.tradegecko.com/blog/supply-chain-management/zara-supply-chain-its-secret-to-retail-success

12. https://www.facebook.com/Zara

13. https://www.modernretail.co/retailers/how-fast-fashion-retailer-zara-recovered-to-surpass-pre-pandemic-sales/#:~:text=In%202018%2C%20Inditex%20said%20that,came%20from%20e%2Dcommerce%20orders.https://www.modernretail.co/retailers/how-fast-fashion-retailer-zara-recovered-to-surpass-pre-pandemic-sales/#:~:text=In%202018%2C%20Inditex%20said%20that,came%20from%20e%2Dcommerce%20orders.

14. Stephen Burgen, "Zara Owner's Online Sales Jump 42% to €553m," *The Guardian* (November 19, 2014), https://www.theguardian.com/business/2014/nov/19/zara-owner-online-sales-553m-inditex.Stephen Burgen, "Zara owner's online sales jump 42% to €553m," November 19, 2014, https://www.theguardian.com/business/2014/nov/19/zara-owner-online-sales-553m-inditex

15. Lukas Peters, "E-Commerce Net Sales of Zara.com from 2014 to 2022," *Statista* (October 14, 2022), https://www.statista.com/forecasts/1218316/zara-revenue-development-ecommercedb.

16. Mallory Schlossberg, "Instagram and Pinterest Are Killing Gap, Abercrombie, & J. Crew," *Business Insider* (February 14, 2016), http://www.businessinsider.com/social-media-is-killing-traditional-retailers-2016-2

17. Lily, "How Sustainable Is Zara?," *Eco*, April 12, 2022, https://www.eco-stylist.com/how-sustainable-is-zara/.

18. Bob Bechek and Chris Zook, "The Jenga Phenomenon: How Ecommerce Is Reassembling Industry," *Brain*, September 5, 2018, https://www.bain.com/insights/the-jenga-phenomenon-how-ecommerce-is-reassembling-industry/.

19. Bill Breen, "Living in Dell Time – Fast Company," November 1, 2004, https://www.fastcompany.com/51967/living-dell-time

20. Jeff Jarvis, "Dear Mr. Dell," *BuzzMachine*, August 17, 2005, http://www.buzzmachine.com/2005/08/17/dear-mr-dell/

21. Jeff Jarvis, "Posts About," *BuzzMachine*, September 17, 2013, https://buzzmachine.com/tag/dell/.

22. Charlie White, "Dell Laptop Explodes in Flames," Gizmodo (June 21, 2006), https://gizmodo.com/dell-laptop-explodes-in-flames-182257.

23. "Dell Social Media Listening & Command Center Tour - 11/8/2011," YouTube (YouTube, December 8, 2011), https://www.youtube.com/watch?v=qj59qQXN_KY&t=15s.

24. Liz Bullock, "How Dell is Using Social Media to Deepen Relationships and Build Trust," Share and Discover Knowledge on SlideShare, April 19, 2013, https://www.slideshare.net/dellsocialmedia/how-dell-is-using-social-media-to-deepen-relationships-and-build-trust

25. https://hackernoon.com/dells-social-media-customer-support-is-actually-really-good-p32137nk?source=rss

26. Dell US, "Fiscal Year 2015 State of the Business," Dell, accessed December 15, 2022, https://www.dell.com/learn/us/en/vn/secure/state-of-the-business-lbo.

27. Maria Deutscher, "After Privatization, Michael Dell's Vision for an End-to-End Vendor Is Finally Coming Together: #DellWorld," SiliconANGLE, November 10, 2014, https://siliconangle.com/2014/11/11/after-privatization-michael-dells-vision-for-an-end-to-end-vendor-is-finally-coming-together-dellworld/.

28. Dana Cimilluca, Don Clark, and Robert McMillan, "EMC Takeover Marks Return of Michael Dell," (Dow Jones & Company), October 13, 2015, http://www.wsj.com/articles/dell-to-buy-emc-for-67-billion-1444649012

29. Stephen L. Vargo and Robert F. Lusch, "Evolving Toward a New Dominant Logic for Marketing," *Journal of Marketing*, Vol. 68 (January 2004): 1–17.

30. Stephen L. Vargo and Robert F. Lusch, "Service-Dominant Logic, Reactions, Reflections and Refinements," *Journal of Marketing Theory*, Vol 6, no. 3 (2006): 281–288.

31. Stephen L. Vargo and Robert F. Lusch, "Institutions and Axioms: An Extension and Update of Service -Dominant Logic," *Academy of Marketing Science*, 2015, https://arizona.pure.elsevier.com/en/publications /institutions-and-axioms-an-extension-and-update-of-service-domina

32. Ibid.

33. Rae Witte, "How Nike Innovates for Everyday Athletes," *TechCrunch*, October 26, 2021, https://techcrunch .com/2021/10/26/nike-sport-research-lab-lebron-james-innovation-center/.

34. Kevin Tofel, "Nike+ Moves from App to Platform with Four New Device Partners," Old GigaOm, March 6, 2015, https://gigaom.com/2015/03/06/nike-moves-from-app-to-platform-with-four-new-device-partners/

35. Nick Statt, "Exclusive: Nike Fires Majority of FuelBand team, will Stop Making Wearable Hardware," CNET (CNET, April 18, 2014), http://www.cnet.com/news/nike-fires-fuelband-engineers-will-stop-making-wearable -hardware

36. Rachel Kraus, "How Covid - and the Nike Run Club App - Turned Me into a Mindful Runner," Mashable (Mashable, March 1, 2022), https://mashable.com/review/nike-run-club-headspace-mindful-running.

37. "Get Help," Nike, accessed February 17, 2023, https://www.nike.com/help/a/why-cant-i-sync.

38. "Communication & Technology's New Battleground: Business Ecosystem vs. Business Ecosystem," 2016, https://www.accenture.com/us-en/insight-business-ecosystem-new-battleground?c=glb_acnemalert_10002919 &n=emc_1215&emc=21091589:emc-021516

39. "The Platform Economy - the Conference Board," accessed February 17, 2023, https://www.conference-board. org/publications/the-platform-economy.

40. "Trend 3 Platform Economy: Technology-Driven Business Model Innovation. . . ," accessed February 17, 2023, https://www.giz.de/expertise/downloads/Accenture_Platform-Economy-Technology-Vision-2016.pdf.

41. Wesley Chai and Kathleen Casey, "What Is SAAS (Software as a Service)? Everything You Need to Know," Cloud Computing (TechTarget, October 24, 2022), https://www.techtarget.com/searchcloudcomputing /definition/Software-as-a-Service

42. Josh Bond, "Top 20 Supply Chain Management Software Suppliers, 2015," Recently Filed RSS, accessed December 15, 2022, http://www.mmh.com/article/top_20_supply_chain_management_software_suppliers_2015.

43. "Cloud Supply Chain Management Market Size Analysed to Grow at a CAGR of 11.1% during the Forecast 2022-2027," iCrowdResearch, March 11, 2022, https://www.icrowdresearch.com/2022/03/11/cloud-supply -chain-management-market-size-analysed-to-grow-at-a-cagr-of-11-1-during-the-forecast-2022-2027/.

44. Amazon. (n.d.). Cloud computing with AWS. AWS. Retrieved April 16, 2022, from https://aws.amazon.com /what-is-aws/

45. Patrick J. Catania and Nancy Keefer, "The Marketplace," Amazon (Board of Trade, 1987), https://aws.amazon .com/marketplace/pp/B0089HDOI6/ref=srh_res_product_title?ie=UTF8&sr=0-10&qid=1456859148823.

46. Anthony Clervi, "Cloud Computing Is Transforming Supply Chain Management," *Supply and Demand Chain Executive*, August 27, 2020, http://www.sdcexec.com/article/12125647/cloud-computing-is-transforming -supply-chain-management.

47. Accenture, "Supply Chain Management in the Cloud," 2014, https://www.accenture.com/t20150523T022449 __w__/us-en/_acnmedia/Accenture/Conversion-Assets/DotCom/Documents/Global/PDF/Dualpub_1/Accenture -Supply-Chain-Management-in-the-Cloud.pdf

48. Max Garland, "How Pfizer Transformed Its Supply Chain to Deliver Vaccines at Lightspeed," *Supply Chain Dive*, September 21, 2021, https://www.supplychaindive.com/news/pfizer-jim-cafone-covid-vaccine -manufacturing-distribution-cscmp/606867/.

49. SupplyChainBrain, "Pfizer Builds Breakthrough App for Global Visibility of Its Supply Chain," *Supply Chain Brain* (December 26, 2018), https://www.supplychainbrain.com/articles/29161-pfizer-builds-breakthrough-app-for -global-visibility-of-its-supply-chain.

50. Anthony Clervi, "Cloud Computing Is Transforming Supply Chain Management," *Supply and Demand Chain Executive*, August 27, 2020, http://www.sdcexec.com/article/12125647/cloud-computing-is-transforming-supply -chain-management.

51. "Solutions," Amazon (National Council on Vocational Education, 1991), https://aws.amazon.com/solutions/case-studies/pfizer/.

52. Paul Taylor, "Pfizer Moves Supply Chain to Cloud," Subscribe to read | *The Financial Times,* accessed February 17, 2023, http://www.ft.com/intl/cms/s/0/1608e5d6-fc59-11e1-ac0f-00144feabdc0.html#axzz42t7nRXXx.

53. Anthony Clervi, "Cloud Computing Is Transforming Supply Chain Management," *Supply and Demand Chain Executive*, August 27, 2020, http://www.sdcexec.com/article/12125647/cloud-computing-is-transforming-supply-chain-management.

54. Billy MacInnes, "How Cloud Is Finding Its Place in the Pharmaceutical Industry," *IT PRO* (February 18, 2014), http://www.cloudpro.co.uk/cloud-essentials/public-cloud/3813/how-cloud-is-finding-its-place-in-the-pharmaceutical-industry.

55. "Emtemp.gcom.cloud," accessed February 17, 2023, https://emtemp.gcom.cloud/ngw/globalassets/en/supply-chain/documents/trends/2022_supply-chain-award-winner_customer-patient-innovation.pdf.

56. Emerging Technology from the arXiv, "Future Wearables: Intelligent Leggings Measure Muscle Fatigue in Runners," *MIT Technology Review* (April 2, 2020), https://www.technologyreview.com/s/600908/future-wearables-intelligent-leggings-measure-muscle-fatigue-in-runners/.

57. Anthony Clervi, "Cloud Computing Is Transforming Supply Chain Management," *Supply and Demand Chain Executive*, August 27, 2020, http://www.sdcexec.com/article/12125647/cloud-computing-is-transforming-supply-chain-management.

58. "Privacy Policy," Burberry, accessed February 17, 2023, https://us.burberry.com/legal-cookies/privacy-policy/.

59. Kate Granger, "10 Supply Chain and Inventory Management Apps," 10 Supply Chain and Inventory Management Apps, September 28, 2022, http://www.eazystock.com/blog/2015/06/04/8-amazing-logistics-supply-chain-mobile-applications/.

60. Canvas Solutions Inc., "Mobile Business Apps and Forms on Android, IPad, IPhone," GoCanvas, accessed December 15, 2022, http://www.gocanvas.com/mobile-forms-apps/48-Transportation-Warehousing/show_category.

61. "IBM Watson," IBM, accessed December 15, 2022, http://www.ibm.com/cognitive/outthink/stories/sciencefact/.

62. "About Watson," IBM, accessed December 15, 2022, https://www.ibm.com/watson/about.

63. James A. Cooke, "Control Towers Provide a Return on Risk Management Investments," *CSCMPs Supply Chain Quarterly RSS* (May 4, 2020), https://www.supplychainquarterly.com/articles/886-control-towers-provide-a-return-on-risk-management-investments.

64. Steve Banker, "Dell Uses Artificial Intelligence at Global Command Centers," Logistics Viewpoints, November 19, 2012, https://logisticsviewpoints.com/2012/11/19/dell-uses-artificial-intelligence-at-global-command-centers/.

65. "About Watson," IBM, accessed December 15, 2022, https://www.ibm.com/watson/about.

66. Christos Voudouris, "Service Chain Management: Technology Innovation for the Service Business" (Berlin: Springer, 2008).

67. Sumantra Sengupta, "10 Supply Chain Trends for the next 10 Years - Supply Chain 24/7," 10 Supply Chain Trends for the Next 10 Years - Supply Chain 24/7, accessed December 15, 2022, http://www.supplychain247.com/article/10_supply_chain_trends_for_the_next_10_years.

68. James Canton, "The Future of Collaborative Supply Chains and Global Business," Dr. James Canton | Institute for Global Futures | Keynotes, Forecasts & Strategy, 2011, http://www.globalfuturist.com/dr-james-canton/insights-and-future-forecasts/future-of-collaborative-supply-chains.html

69. Chowdhury P; Paul SK; Kaisar S; Moktadir MA; "COVID-19 Pandemic Related Supply Chain Studies: A Systematic Review," *Transportation Research. Part E, Logistics and Transportation Review* (U.S. National Library of Medicine), accessed February 17, 2023, https://pubmed.ncbi.nlm.nih.gov/33613082/.

Chapter 3

Business Models and Strategies

Learning Objectives

By the time you complete this chapter, you will be able to:

1 Describe what a business model is.

2 Discuss how business models can change over time.

3 Explain the importance of a value proposition.

4 Discuss the differences between pipe and platform models.

5 Describe different business models.

6 Explain how the Business Model Canvas can be used in the creation of a business model.

7 Discuss how new technologies are changing digital marketing.

Digital disruption is present throughout the economy as we discussed in Chapter 1. Our examination of value chains made it clear that organizations that existed prior to the advent of the internet (traditional retailers and manufacturers) have been taking advantage of the opportunities the internet presents just as pure-play internet firms have. They may, however, do so in different ways. A set of business models has emerged to meld the best of the offline world with the digital world.

In this chapter, we continue our discussion of value creation and explain how it is part of a business model. We discuss some basic business models and new technologies affecting business models.

Understanding Business Models

Business models are a source of much discussion, from mainstream television shows like Shark Tank to academic journals. Yet, there still seems to be no commonly accepted definition of the term "business model." An article in the *Harvard Business Review* traces the concept back to Peter Drucker in a 1994 article. It discussed the importance of defining what a business will and will not do and "assumptions about what a business gets paid for," but never used the term business model.[1] Later Prof. Joan Magretta

business models
the processes by which a business creates value, provides value to its customers, and captures value in the form of profits.

defined the business model in terms of the value chain with a supply-facing side and a customer side. She says "Part one includes all the activities associated with making something: designing it, purchasing raw materials, manufacturing, and so on. Part two includes all the activities associated with selling something: finding and reaching customers, transacting a sale, distributing the product, or delivering the service." Professor Alex Osterwalder regards a business model as a set of assumptions about how major business activities will be carried out. He developed a template that allows organizations to customize their own business models called the Business Model Canvas, which we will discuss later in the chapter. Among marketers, Professor Michael Rappa's definition is one of the most often quoted: A "business model is the method of doing business by which a company can sustain itself—that is, generate revenue. The business model spells out how a company makes money by specifying where it is positioned in the value chain."[2]

Lastly, a more detailed definition is set forth by Professors Ethriraj, Guler, and Singh. They define a "business model" as "a unique configuration of elements comprising the organization's goals, strategies, processes, technologies, and structure, conceived to create value for the customers and thus compete successfully in a particular market." They note that a business model describes the core value proposition, sources and methods of revenue generation, the costs involved in generating the revenue, and the plan and trajectory of growth.[3]

value proposition
a description of the customer value delivered to a specific target market.

In other words, a business model specifies how an organization makes money, essentially how an entity sustains itself in the economy. Sites of all kinds earn revenue from transactions. Websites may support themselves by generating advertising revenue, while others may sell products ranging from clothing to computers or services that vary from employment listings to credit cards. Some sites sell their own products or services, or they may be affiliates of large ecommerce sites such as Amazon.com or Target.com or operate using an auction system, like eBay. Sites may also be community-based or ask for donations to survive, such as Wikipedia. However, they are all achieving revenue from transactions with their audience. The many ways in which they do this is the subject of the business models discussion.

Functions of Business Models

Professors Henry Chesbrough and Richard Rosenbloom explain that the functions of a business model are to:

- Articulate the value proposition, that is, the value created for users by the offering based on the technology.
- Identify a market segment, that is, the users to whom the offering is useful and for what purpose.
- Define the structure of the value chain within the firm required to create and distribute the offering.
- Estimate the cost structure and profit potential of producing the offering, given the value proposition and the value chain structure chosen.
- Describe the position of the firm with the value network linking suppliers and customers, including identification of potential partners and competitors.
- Formulate the competitive strategy by which the innovating firm will gain and hold a competitive advantage over rivals.

It is important to note that *a business model and a business plan are two distinctly different entities*. A business model is a conceptual description that may have been given a name like "advertising-supported." A business plan is a detailed document that is prepared for strategic guidance and to aid in the acquisition of resources, either internal or external. There is some similarity between the two, but they are not synonymous. Recognizing this issue, Chesbrough and Rosenbloom go on to specify the differences between a business model and a strategy as follows:

- A business model focuses on creating value for the customer and delivering that value to the customer to a clearly defined market segment.
- It focuses on creating business value that can be translated into value for shareholders.
- It requires that managers use technical inputs to create economic results in a context of technological and market uncertainty.[4]

Chesbrough and Rosenbloom's final point puts the business model concept firmly in the arena of business innovation including internet-based businesses. It also reinforces the focus on value creation by the firm as a key element of a business model. A bad business model or failure to execute the model effectively can often lead to failure. Failures often result from a myriad of business model and execution mistakes, but in the end, if a business does not have a product people want at a price they are willing to pay, no business model in the world will save it.

Evolving Business Models—IBM, GE, and Amazon

There are many fascinating examples of businesses that have changed their models, sometimes more than once to accommodate changes in technology, the market, or both. IBM is often celebrated as a prime example of an agile business. Over the years it has morphed from a manufacturer of business machines—to a maker of computers—to a global technology services company. It is now in the process of transforming into a cognitive solutions and cloud platforms company and has been an early adopter of blockchain. Among other things, that implies a big investment in machine learning and artificial intelligence.[5] Case histories from researchers at Stanford University give detail on its business model changes over the years:[6]

> GE is another example of transformational change. When Jeff Immelt became the CEO of GE in 2001 it was a classic 20th-century conglomerate making everything from aircraft engines to refrigerators and marketing services including financial and entertainment. Now Immelt describes it as "the world's biggest infrastructure technology company."

He continues:

> Today, everything we sell is surrounded by sensors and produces data. The data fundamentally is going to be modeled and turned into performance, outcomes. . . . So when I talk about the "Industrial internet," it's about capturing data off of machines, turning it back into valuable insight for our customers and that's going to be worth trillions of dollars in the economy, and I think it's going to transform GE.[7]

Massive as the transformations have been for IBM and GE, they were both founded in the physical economy and forced to adapt to the digital economy. Amazon was founded in 1994 as an ecommerce business that sold books. The vision of Jeff Bezos to be the online place "where people can come to find and discover anything they might want to buy online"[8] was dismissed as hubris by many observers. But the business held to the vision and for many years placed investment over profits. Figure 3.1 displays a timeline of major changes in the business since its founding.

Figure 3.1 Timeline of Major Developments at Amazon Source: modified from https://www.officetimeline.com/blog/amazon-history-timeline.

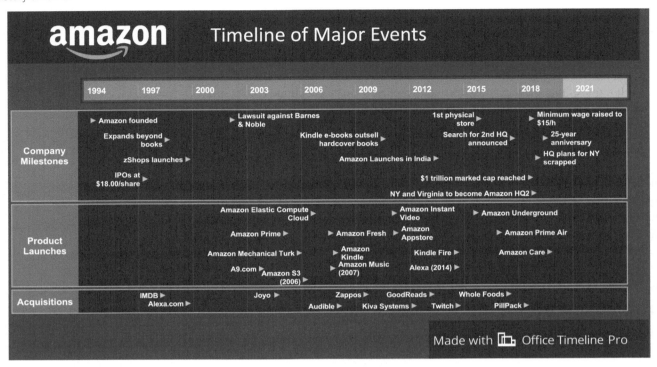

ecommerce
buying and selling goods and services online.

Amazon's business model has many working parts. In ecommerce alone it has:

- Direct sales of merchandise from Amazon Vendors and Amazon-owned brands (such as Amazon Basics).
- Sales from merchants (third party sellers) who list products for sale on Amazon, pay to advertise on Amazon, pay a commission to Amazon for each sale, and optionally pay Amazon to store and ship inventory through its Fulfillment by Amazon (FBA) program.

It also has subscription-based ecommerce activities:

subscription
a business model that delivers products, services, and content for a set fee.

- Amazon Prime, which reached over 200 million subscribers worldwide with 147 million U.S. subscribers in 2020.[9] Prime offers services such as free same-day or two-day delivery.
- Kindle Unlimited offers an unlimited number of ebooks for a monthly subscription fee.
- Amazon Prime Video, which delivers subscription-based digital content (channels) through third party streaming movies and television (such as HBO, Paramount+) and also offers select free content to Prime subscribers, some of which is produced by Amazon.
- Amazon Music, which offers a subscription to streaming music services.
- Audible (acquired by Amazon in 2008 for about $300 million) which offers access to audiobooks.
- It also has fee-based cloud computing services, such as AWS (Amazon Web Services) discussed in Chapter 2.

How was Amazon able to build all these activities and various business models under one roof? A number of key factors include:

- It focused on customer satisfaction.

- It focused on innovation both to provide satisfaction and to lower costs.

- It recognized technology as a core competency.

- It promoted a "culture of metrics" in which all activities are measured and data-driven improvements are made.

- The metrics culture also drove it to engage in experiments to improve its offerings.

- It constantly reevaluated its business model and makes changes or develops new approaches as required.[10,11]

The Value Proposition

The term value proposition has come to mean the value delivered by the firm to a specific, targeted customer segment. A value proposition is a promise of the value to be delivered, communicated, and acknowledged and encompasses customer beliefs about how value (benefit) will be delivered, experienced, and acquired.[12] Figure 3.2 outlines what a value proposition is and the steps in creating and articulating one. The process shown makes it clear that customer data is one vital step on the road to developing and articulating a good value proposition. It also emphasizes that a value proposition is not an advertising slogan or a positioning statement; it is a core element of the brand or business strategy.

From the rather simple concept, marketers can study the drivers of value in a particular market. Professors Osterwalder and Pigneur developed a simple framework that is useful in that process (see Figure 3.3). It combines consideration of the needs of the target customer, which define the nature of the value desired, with an understanding of the enterprise's core capabilities, which determines the value that can be delivered. Data can be obtained and used to understand both target customers and organizational capabilities, making developing a value proposition an information-driven marketing activity. Their Value Proposition Canvas takes a segment-by-segment approach, creating a value proposition for each customer segment.

There are many explanations of how to use the canvas and examples of its use and some modified versions. Figure 3.4a is one of these. It uses slightly different terminology, perhaps more B2C than B2B terms, but the process is the same. Figure 3.4b illustrates the Value Proposition Canvas for Tesla. In this case, the benefits, features, and experience are an electric vehicle manufacturer (note, while Tesla offers other products and services such as battery storage, solar roofs, and solar panels, the focus of this Value Proposition Canvas is on electric vehicles for which it is most known for).

Tesla Motors was established in 2003 by Martin Eberhard and Marc Tarpenning and it was named after the inventor Nikola Tesla, whose numerous technological innovations helped fuel many modern inventions. Nikola Tesla is best known for inventing alternating current, induction motors, radio, and magnifying transmitters to wireless transmit power, among others.[13] Current CEO Elon Musk joined the company by making a substantial investment in 2004 and has served as CEO since 2008.[14] As highlighted in the Value Proposition Canvas in Figure 3.4b, when understanding the potential target audience for an electric vehicle, Tesla realizes that the job-to-be-done is not only to commute; being able to convey an image of success and be unique from others are

Figure 3.2   **How to Create a Value Proposition** Source: http://blog.hubspot.com/marketing /write-value-proposition#sm.0000002to08kmvcpyv7vlb6v649jq.

Figure 3.3   The Value Proposition Canvas based on Osterwalder and Pigneur Source: https://designabetterbusiness.com /wp-content/uploads/2017/10/dbb_Value_Proposition_Canvas-1170x827.jpg.

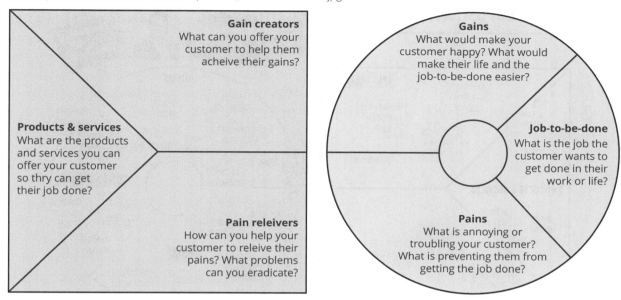

also important social aspects for this segment. Some of the pains related to electric cars are the lack of charging stations and the slowness of charging stations, which may inhibit adoption, but these pains are relieved through Tesla's push for extensive charging networks with lightning-fast superchargers.

While a strong value proposition is essential to business model success, there are other aspects of successful business models. Before we describe some of those models, however, there is an overarching classification we need to understand. In Chapter 1 we mentioned the concept of a platform economy. That becomes more logical in the context of a platform as one type of business model.

Figure 3.4a   A Revised Value Proposition Canvas Source: https://www.peterjthomson .com/wp-content/uploads/2013/11/Value-proposition-canvas-600x4501.jpg.

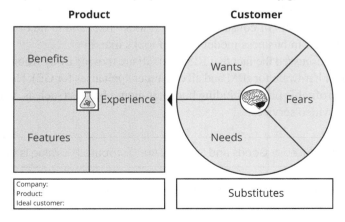

Figure 3.4b   **The Value Proposition for Tesla** Source: Business Model Foundry Inc.

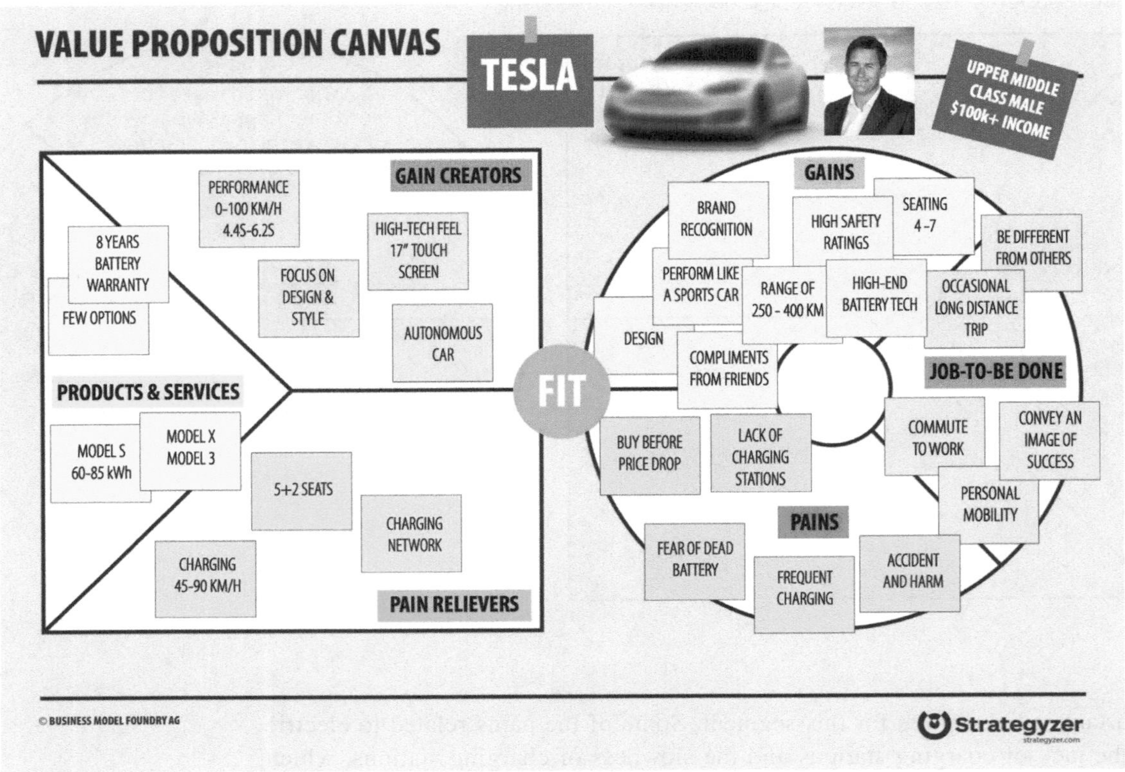

Types of Business Models

In recent years a consensus has emerged in the small and somewhat rarified group of business model enthusiasts that includes venture capitalists who fund new businesses. While the subject may seem a bit esoteric, the implications are highly practical. To simplify, all business models can be divided into two overarching types—pipes and platforms.

The Pipe Model

The pipe model describes traditional businesses of all kinds and still includes most of the major manufacturers of consumer goods. It looks like, and in fact is, the channel of distribution model. In business model terms it looks like this:

Earlier we discussed the fact that IBM and GE are moving away from their traditional pipes (computer hardware for IBM and all consumer appliances for GE). However, Amazon still has very profitable pipes including books, in-house brands (such as Amazon Basics), and streaming video services.

> Value Is Produced > Goods and Services Are Distributed > Value Is Consumed

Even more telling is the fact that there are internet-based businesses that are built on the pipe model. Zappos, now owned by Amazon, is an example of a successful online retailer that thrives on reselling the products of many manufacturers. Zappos owes its success to fanatical customer service, not to unique merchandise. Most distributors of content are also pipes. Netflix is an example of one that has enjoyed great success.

pipe
business model where businesses create value by controlling a linear series of activities—(the classic value-chain mode). The inputs at one end of the chain undergo a series of steps that transform them into a finished product to create value. Value is produced upstream and consumed downstream.

platform
a business model where businesses create value by facilitating interactions between external producers and consumers.

For some time, analysts have argued about whether Netflix is a "dumb pipe."[15] That is a term taken from discussions of data transmission on the internet—simply moving bits and bytes around without knowing what they are, much less adding value. That describes a product with no differentiation and therefore no pricing power. It is why you will not see Internet Service Providers as an identifiable business model in the table in the next section. It was not a profitable model and carriers have either diversified (Comcast), disappeared (France Telecomm's Mintel communications terminal, which was ubiquitous in France before the advent of the internet), or struggled to find a model that gets them out of the commodity trap (AOL). Trying to avoid that trap appears to be the reason Verizon acquired Yahoo!

Figure 3.5 lists the main differences between the pipe and platform models. Notice that in the pipe model products are prespecified, with or without detailed knowledge of customer needs. In the platform model, users and producers not only interact with one another but often have dual roles. An interactive network connects all the roles. One company can be a user of a software tool, for example, at the same time it produces business CRM software with transactions for both SaaS products taking place on the platform. "On the platform" usually translates to "in the cloud" as we discussed in Chapter 2.

The Platform Model

The competing type of model is the platform. There are two types of platforms—two-sided and multisided. A two-sided model connects two groups—consumer credit card users and retail merchants as one example, and organizations of health care providers and patients as another. The two-sided platform differs from the pipe in that network effects occur in the platform. *HBR* describes the difference by saying that in the pipe model all cost is on the left (value creation) and all revenue is on the right (value consumption). In the two-sided platform, the two sides interact with each other. Platform models facilitate connections and interactions across a large number of participants—this is where their value lies, and the value of the platform grows with increased connections and usage. For example, a credit card has more value to the user when more merchants accept it. The size of the network affects the value produced by it. Patients may choose a healthcare organization based on the number and perceived expertise of the providers. A social network gains value through the number of users and their frequency of use.

Platform interactions can be short-term transactions (like connecting buyers and sellers) or they can build longer-term relationships (like establishing connections in learning

Figure 3.5   **Differences between Pipe and Platform Models** Source: http://www
.slideshare.net/itcocchi/pres-7jan014-short.

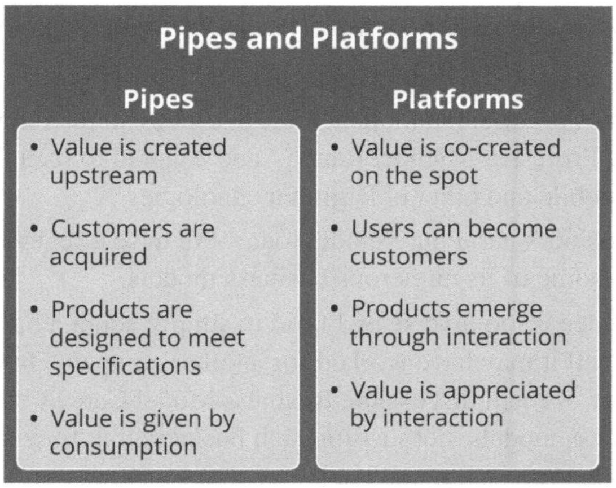

Pipes and Platforms

Pipes	Platforms
• Value is created upstream	• Value is co-created on the spot
• Customers are acquired	• Users can become customers
• Products are designed to meet specifications	• Products emerge through interaction
• Value is given by consumption	• Value is appreciated by interaction

Figure 3.6   **An Example of a Typical Transaction on a Platform Model**

Source: https://blog.hubspot.com/marketing/platform.

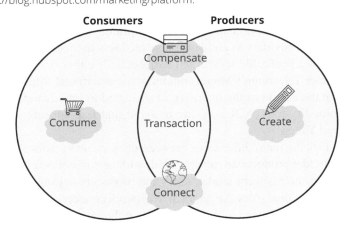

communities or social networks). The role of the platform business is to provide rules and structure that encourage transactions and allow the platform to scale, unleashing network effects.

Etsy is a simple example of a platform model. The Etsy platform focuses on connecting consumers looking to purchase handmade goods (buyers) with other consumers or small businesses that make their own products (sellers). The platform itself offers no goods or services to the end consumer but facilitates transactions within this maker-oriented community. Etsy's is ultimately dependent on its ability to attract both makers and buyers to interact with one another. Etsy generates revenue by taking a portion of each sale made on the platform and through other services, like advertising. Figure 3.6 provides an example of a transaction on a platform model.

While most platforms are two-sided, there are other multisided platforms that genuinely have more than two sides. For instance, Google's Android platform connects smartphone makers, software developers, and users, and customers who obtain Android apps from the Google Play Store, so its model is three-sided. However, Google's rival, Apple, makes its own devices, so it only needs to connect with customers and developers, again using the App Store to facilitate transactions with both—a two-sided model. These models represent fundamentally different strategic decisions by businesses operating in the same market.

Identifying Basic Business Models

Now that we have a better understanding of what a business model is, it is time to look at some basic models. Following are three caveats as we do so:

1. There is no commonly accepted set of models. Additionally, authors have given different names to the same model. Table 3.1 gives an overview of models suggested by Professor Michael Rappa[16] and adapted to include new models enabled by mobile and other emerging technologies.

2. Almost no business has a pure model today. We have already discussed Amazon and some of its numerous business models.

3. The marketplace is too diverse and fluid to simply adopt a basic model, no matter how well it may have worked for another company. In the final section of this chapter, we will discuss the Business Model Canvas which generates custom business models, not just for each business, but for each segment of the business's target market.

Table 3.1 is a listing of the basic types of business models. The list of models is not comprehensive although it does include most of the best-known models. The discussion of the models listed and the examples used are intended to stimulate thinking, not to provide a comprehensive catalog of business models. Some of the models existed and even thrived before the internet became a ubiquitous element of our lives, while other models owe their success to the existence of the internet.

Digital Business Models

When traditional "old economy" firms first established websites, most assumed that the business model that worked in the physical world could simply be duplicated in the digital ecosystem. For some that was true. For others, it was highly problematic. Table 3.1 lists several models that have made the transition from the physical world to the internet as well as new models developed with the advent of digital technologies.

Advertising Model: Delivering Awareness and Opportunities to Potential Customers

Advertising quickly found its way online in the early 1990s after the passing of the National Information Infrastructure Act of 1993 (which required the National Science Foundation to open public access to applications that had only previously been available to universities, libraries, and government).[17] The first online advertisement appeared on October 27, 1994, forever transforming both the advertising world and the internet. The first ad (see Figure 3.7) was a small banner ad with the words "Have you ever clicked your mouse right here? You will" sponsored by AT&T on Wired Magazine's Hotwired

Table 3.1   **Digital Business Models**

Business Model	Short Description	Examples
Advertising Model	Delivers ads to customer segments	Google (Alphabet), Facebook (Meta), LinkedIn, Amazon Advertising
Brokerage Model	Brings buyers & Sellers together	eBay, Etsy, Poshmark, Alibaba, Faire
Infomediary Model	Provides 3rd party data to business	Business.com, Upromise
Merchant Model (ecommerce)	Provides various goods and services for sale	Amazon.com, Walmart.com, Bulk Apothecary
Manufacturer (Direct) Model	Provides direct sale of own manufactured products	Dell Computers, Billie Razors
Affiliate Model	Earns incentives for bringing qualified buyers (typically gets % or flat fee commissions)	Amazon Associates, Target Partners Program, Advertise Purple, CJ Affiliate
Community / Crowdsourcing Model	Connecting individuals and groups	Threadless, Wikipedia, Reddit, Craigslist, GoFundMe
Subscription Model	Delivers services and content for a fee	Netflix, Salesforce, Spotify, Canva, Shopify
Utility Model	Provides services or content based on use (pay-as-you-go)	AWS, Ethereum, Shutterstock
Freemium Model	Offers free basic service with paid add-ons	Mobile apps, such as Pokémon Go, Candy Crush, LinkedIn, Spotify, Pandora

Figure 3.7 **The First Online Ad** Source: https://www.wired.com/2010/10/1027hotwired -banner-ads/

website. AT&T reportedly paid $30,000 for the ad which remained at the top of the website for three months.[18] Unlike modern ads, the first online ads lacked sophistication as they were often static and not targeted, resembling a simple extension of the traditional broadcast advertising model. Just about any type of content on a website, in an email, or on an app can be monetized through advertising in the form of overt banner ads or covert sponsored content, often referred to as "native advertising," (ads that appear to be part of the content and not a separate ad).

native advertising
paid media in which content follows the form and function of the site on which it is placed, not traditional advertising formats.

Many sites today still use advertising models to generate revenue. Some do so exclusively (such as personal blogs and niche-content websites), while others may supplement advertising models with other models such as affiliate or subscription. For example, news sites like the *New York Times* offer ad space for companies but also rely on subscriptions to supplement ad revenue.

Brokerage Model: Bringing Buyers and Sellers Together

brokers
a business model that brings buyers and sellers together to exchange goods and services, often in exchange for a fee or commission.

Brokers are market creators. Their function is to bring buyers and sellers together to facilitate transactions. Usually, but not always, a broker charges a fee or commission for each transaction it enables. For instance, eBay currently charges a small fee to list items for sale and then charges a percentage of the sale price (ranging from 0.5 to 15 percent) plus a small additional fee when the items sell[19], while Craigslist charges no fees for a basic listing.

Alibaba's marketplace, which is based in China but has a worldwide reach, operates much of its business on the brokerage model.[20] In addition to its B2C side, AliExpress, Alibaba is the largest B2B marketplace where it acts as a broker. Other large B2B marketplaces serve specialized needs—TradeIndia provides a global marketplace that fosters Indian overseas trade while TradeKey serves the electronics market globally. In all these cases the transaction mechanism is primarily brokerage.[21] Other examples abound in many different industries.

Infomediary Model: Gathering and Distributing Useful Data

infomediaries
intermediaries in channels of distribution that specialize in the capture, analysis, application, and distribution of information.

Some firms function as infomediaries (information intermediaries) assisting buyers and/or sellers to understand a given market. Infomediaries have always been important to direct marketers and many of those active today began as list brokers for the direct marketing industry. An infomediary on the web is a site that gathers and organizes large amounts of data and acts as an intermediary between those who want the information and those who supply the information.[22] The term is used broadly to cover virtually any third party that manages and distributes data on the internet.

InfoUSALeads is an example of one infomediary that smoothly transitioned from the direct mail era into the digital era. As such, it offers a variety of both physical address mailing lists and email lists. It also offers list enhancement services that add data to the basic list address to give marketers a better picture of each list member and therefore a better ability to target their messages. These firms are often called list brokers because they use the brokerage transactions model.

Websites that offer sources of information (such as whitepapers, infographics, and other reports), with free access after a user registers with the site or provides other information, are also infomediaries. The valuable data is gained by making registration or information disclosure a condition for viewing or downloading the information. These companies use the registration data to make sales attempts to potentially acquire new clients or offer the data to third parties. Data about consumers and their consumption habits are valuable, especially when that information can be carefully analyzed and used to target marketing campaigns.

Review sites follow an infomediary model where consumers are freely giving their data to be used on the site. There are many examples of these across the internet, from broad review sites like consumerreports.com (which offers reviews on over 9,000 products and services) to more focused review sites like yelp.com (which focuses on reviews of local businesses like restaurants, physical stores, and other service providers) to hyper-focused review sites like healthgrades.com (which offers ratings and reviews for doctors).

Incentive marketing (or loyalty marketing) sites such as MyPoints gather consumer data through purchases and surveys. Upromise, another example of such a site, offers a cautionary tale when it comes to covertly collecting consumer data. The company, which offers savings opportunities that are tied to a college fund, learned this the hard way, not once, but twice. As noted in the Federal Trade Commission (FTC) complaint, Upromise offered consumers its "TurboSaver Toolbar" as part of their service which was designed to highlight and identify Upromise partner companies in search results. Consumers used the toolbar to identify these partner companies for which they received rewards for each purchase. But, "unbeknownst to consumers, however, the TurboSaver Toolbar also collected certain user data– including usernames, passwords, and credit card information."[23] For failing to adequately disclose the collection and use of user data, Upromise was fined $500,000 by the FTC.[24]

Merchant Model: Providing Goods and Services

Online merchants are retailers or wholesalers of goods and services. We discussed the multiple examples of the ecommerce (merchant) model as part of Amazon's operations earlier in the chapter. Many firms have enjoyed success as single-line online retailers, as opposed to those like Amazon or Walmart which offer a huge assortment.

merchant
models consist of retailers or wholesalers that offer goods and services online

Zappos has already been mentioned as a limited-line merchant. It diversified from its original shoes-only offering to include clothing and accessories and still offers a deep assortment of footwear for the whole family. Other businesses following a merchant model include retailers like Nordstrom, Saks 5th Avenue, and Toy Whiz. Each of these businesses offers an assortment of brands under one site. While at first glance you may think this sounds similar to a brokerage model, the difference is that the goods and services offered under the merchant model all come from the same business (i.e., Nordstrom acquires the goods from vendor brand and then stores and ships the goods to the customer). In a brokerage model, the goods and services are not acquired and shipped directly from the business (i.e., Etsy doesn't actually acquire and ship the goods you buy, they are sent by a third party individual or business; Etsy just facilitates the transaction). Amazon fits under both models since it acquires goods directly from brand vendors, stores the goods, and ships them. These items are noted as "shipped and sold by Amazon". Amazon also allows third parties to list and sell on its marketplace. These are known as 3PLs (third party sellers). For these transactions, goods are marked as "sold and shipped by" the third party seller's name. Amazon also offers 3PL merchants to have access to their FBA shipping services, but even when shipped by FBA, the transactions are still brokerage since Amazon is not acquiring the goods for sale (only facilitating the transaction and the shipping).

Manufacturer Direct Model: Reaching Buyers Directly

manufacturer direct model
bypassing intermediaries such as wholesalers and manufacturers' reps in the channel of distribution; direct from manufacturer to customer.

The operations of the manufacturer direct model were discussed extensively in Chapter 2 where both Zara (Section 2-2a1) and Dell (Section 2-2b1) were used as examples.

Many software developers sell directly to their customers. Salesforce was mentioned in Chapter 2 as an example of software-as-a-service, which some people consider a business model on its own. As we discussed in our Amazon example (Section 2-5a), SaaS involves making software available to users from the cloud, usually charging them on a usage basis. That also qualifies as the utility model.

utility
business model that delivers services or content on a metered or "pay-as-you-go" basis.

Utility Model: Delivering Services or Content "Pay-as-You-Go"

The utility model, also referred to as an "on-demand model" or "metered usage model" is based on a "pay-as-you-go" approach. Unlike subscription services, metered services are based on actual usage rates. Traditionally, metering has been used for essential services such as electricity and water. Some phone and internet plans follow a utility model. Amazon Web Services (AWS) follows a utility model where businesses pay for individual cloud services.[25] You only pay for the services you consume, and once you stop using them you no longer pay. This approach allows businesses to adapt based on needs.

Ethereum
is a public blockchain widely used to create and run applications.

Ethereum (mentioned in more detail later in this chapter) also follows a utility model. Transactions made on the Ethereum blockchain require computational resources to execute; therefore, every transaction on the Ethereum blockchain is charged a fee to run. These fees are referred to as "gas" and fluctuate based on supply and demand. These "gas" fees are paid to miners who use their computing power to validate blockchain transactions (i.e., those running the computations).[26]

blockchain
is a shared, immutable ledger that facilitates the process of recording transactions and tracking assets in a business network.

gas
the fee required to conduct a transaction on Ethereum. These fees are paid to miners who use their computing power to validate blockchain transactions (i.e., those running the computations).

Subscription Model: Delivering Services and Content for a Set Fee

subscription
a business model that delivers services and content for a fee model that delivers services and content for a fee.

The subscription model has been popular since long before the internet. Newspapers, of course, are a prime example, as are magazines. Using the subscription model for content is popular among internet-era businesses as well. Digital content providers, such as Netflix and the Wall Street Journal, offer subscription-based services where users pay a monthly fee for access to content. Many television broadcasters have developed their own streaming services in response to "cord-cutting" trends. (Cord-cutting refers to the cancellation of traditional cable or satellite services in favor of digital streaming services.)[27]

While there are abundant examples of services that follow this model, the subscription model is not unknown on the product side of the marketplace. A number of products are sold on an automatic replenishment basis. Amazon seems to want to offer subscriptions to everything through its "subscribe and save" program. However, few have disrupted their industry like the Dollar Shave Club has. Dollar Shave Club's offer is simple. The customer selects the blade type from three quality levels priced at various tiers (currently $3, $6, or $9 per month). The club provides a free handle with the initial purchase and replacement blades are shipped each month so the customer always has a supply. There are no fees, no term of commitment, and the user can cancel at any time.[28]

Its success has upended the razor/razor blade industry which one writer says "has long been built on convincing people they need more and more blinged-out blades at higher and higher prices." Another adds that the success of Dollar Shave Club "shows that no company is safe from the creative destruction brought by technological change." Challenging market leader Gillette didn't require massive factories and a far-flung distribution network. It took the internet and the global economy.[29] When Unilever bought the company for about

$1 billion in 2016 Unilever CEO Paul Portman described it as an "innovative and disruptive brand with a cult-like following of diverse and highly engaged users."

Consumable products, such as makeup, skincare, cleaners, and toiletries, tend to work well with the subscription model as these types of items need to be replenished and this can be easily predicted based on usage frequency. Another successful example of a company that found success through the subscription model is the Honest Company. Co-founded by Jessica Alba, the Honest Company's mission was to offer nontoxic household staples to parents through a simple subscription model. In an interview, Alba notes that the subscription was at the heart of her idea: "What are the things that all parents need? Diapers and wipes, for sure. And then a mix of cleaning and personal care products. Wouldn't it be great if you could pick five things and get them delivered through a monthly subscription?"[30] Businesses offering subscription boxes are another notable example. Businesses following this model provide curated products or activities that are mailed to users on a monthly (or other time-bound) schedule.

Affiliate Model: Incentives for Bringing Qualified Buyers

Affiliate models are an example of an offline model flourishing online. The floral industry is a good example. Teleflora has been in existence since 1934 when telegraph was the preferred channel for quick communications. As a privately held company, its growth is hard to chart, but it currently has tens of thousands of affiliates around the world. It offers same-day and international delivery of flower arrangements. In its early days, it telegraphed, later telephoned, orders to affiliates. Support was primarily by mail, where information about new flower arrangements and promotions was shared with affiliates. The company now has a strong internet infrastructure to support its affiliates.

CJ Affiliate is an affiliate platform originally called Commission Junction. It boasts a large network of affiliates who are looking to connect with businesses to promote their products and services to their audiences. Businesses set up the payment terms, primarily CPA, a pay-for-performance revenue model in which payment is contingent on the completion of a visitor's behavior, which could be a sale or a request for more information or other actions specified by the retailer. Publisher affiliates can be anyone who owns a website or has a social media presence and wants to generate more traffic from the sites of brands that partner with CJ Affiliate. Publishers are also offered a variety of ad creation and tracking services and the pay-per-call option as well as CPA.[31,32] In many ways, this is a brokerage model, but affiliate marketers operate in a specialized manner. The affiliate model introduces another player in the channel— whereas the brokerage model connects buyers and sellers with a payment made by the seller for facilitating the transaction, the affiliate site links the affiliates (who earn commissions) with buyers and sellers. In this model both the affiliate (person sending the traffic) and the affiliate site (site facilitating the relationship between the affiliate and seller) get revenue from the transaction.

Lastly, no mention of affiliate marketing would be complete without Amazon. The Amazon Associates program offers links to products listed on Amazon, banner ads, and the ability to create an online store. Other retailers have begun to offer similar programs, such as Target's Partners Program (https://partners.target.com/).

affiliate
offers incentives to partner websites, wherein a website agrees to post a link (through an ad or other content) to a transactional site in return for a commission on sales made as a direct result of the link.

Community / Crowdfunding Model

The internet is based on network principles, which means the ability to connect not only nodes and computers on the internet but also individual internet users to each other. From the beginning, the internet saw the ability to connect virtually based on common levels of expertise and interests. Initially, these connections were in chat rooms and forums, and then through community-based websites, building the foundations for the rise of social media.

community model
a type of business model that utilizes the network effects of the internet to connect like-minded individuals and groups.

The community model relies on groups of people with shared interests, which could be anything from obtaining recipes for nutritious meals—to supporting cancer sufferers—to advocating for a political or community issue—to developing open-source software or content. These models rely on the internet or mobile apps for their very existence. Before the internet, communication was either one-to-one (e.g., personal communications) or one-to-many (e.g., commercial advertising). The web made possible many-to-many communications, which are the backbone of the community model.

Wikipedia is a prime example of a community model. The community creates and maintains the not-for-profit site, allowing community members to contribute new content and edit existing content. Arguably, Wikipedia would not exist without its community. Reddit and Quora are other examples of such sites where community members share information through discussion forums and question solicitation. Many community models like these rely on other models, such as the advertising model, to generate revenue, but the community is the key underlying component that creates value for users.

crowdfunding
a type of community model that is used to obtain needed resources, including financing, by soliciting from a community instead of traditional funding sources.

Crowdfunding sites rely on the community model to help businesses find funding from the community instead of traditional funding sources. Sites like Kickstarter allow businesses to solicit donations to support new projects (products, services, creative works). Project creators set a donation goal and deadline and only get to keep donation funds if it meets or exceeds the funding goal by the deadline. Donors often get rewards (ranging from a "thank you" note to the actual product or service). Oftentimes project creators add special rewards that are unlockable when certain goals are met. For instance, a company making T-shirts may offer new colors after meeting a certain monetary goal and may reward donors when these goals are met. These elements incentivize community backers to donate more and also spread word of mouth to their friends, families, and community. How does Kickstarter make money? This is mainly done by taking a small percentage of the donations, which means that the site follows a broker model in terms of its revenue generation.

Similar to crowdfunding, fundraising sites like GoFundMe solicit donations from individuals to help support not-for-profit companies or even other consumers. Fundraising has always been about relationships—existing relationships like a graduate to their alma mater or personal relationships developed by fund-raisers with wealthy individuals who have an affinity for their cause. Fundraising organizations were quick to realize that digital tools like email and social media could help nurture relationships. They also recognized the ability of websites to convey information to supporters and reach potential new donors.

Review sites also rely on a community model for success. One such site is TripAdvisor. TripAdvisor was founded in 2000, four years before Yelp! democratized the restaurant review business. Founder and CEO Stephen Kauferre recalls that the concept of open user reviews was frightening to the hotel industry at that time. The original business model was to license a database of travel information to consumer-facing sites. Online travel services like Expedia and Orbitz recognized the value of the concept but never got around to licensing the product for their own use. Consequently, the founding team **pivoted** the model to a traveler-facing site, one that earned its revenue from booking referrals. At that time a button was added that allows travelers to submit their own reviews and growth exploded.[33]

pivot
a quick change from one business model to another. It is usually applied to start-ups that can make rapid model changes that may be impossible for entrenched business models of large enterprises.

In a 2016 post on the TripAdvisor blog Kaufman says he believes in the power of its community, saying:

> "The TripAdvisor travel community has fundamentally changed the way we travel. Our community's voice has done more to improve service standards than professional reviews ever could. And eight out of ten business owners agree. Our community has helped small businesses all over the globe reach a global audience; to grow and succeed based on the quality of their product and the service they offer, not the size of their budgets or the savviness of their marketing efforts."[34]

Freemium Model: Offers Free Basic Service with Paid Add-ons

The freemium model also represents a time-honored practice in the physical world and on the internet. Freemium models offer free trials or limited usage which can be expanded for a fee. Freemium models are widespread in B2B markets for both SaaS and apps. Many services and mobile apps follow freemium models to allow users to try out the service before committing to purchase it, especially when there are multiple competing services. This strategy puts a premium on designing services and apps that are easy to use.

Freemium models may be paired with advertising-supported models. Good examples of this pairing can be seen in the realm of streaming music and video where services like Spotify, Pandora, Hulu, and YouTube offer free access to movies and music with the option to upgrade to ad-free versions. Free users may receive 15- or 30-second advertisements between songs or videos, while paid users have no ads. Services like Pandora may limit how often freemium users can skip songs and allow more options for paid subscribers. In addition to advertising, these services may offer lower-quality video or sound to freemium users, while paid users get access to higher quality. In addition, premium subscribers receive additional services like on-demand access, the ability to download music and movies for offline listening, and others.

The Dropbox file-sharing app also follows a freemium model with a pricing structure that is typical for apps that serve B2B as well as B2C customers. The free version offers less storage space and fewer options for sharing with other Dropbox users. Both businesses and individual users can upgrade to increase storage space and business users can get additional management and collaboration tools with a paid upgrade.[35]

Many mobile games also follow a freemium model where users can gain access to a select number of levels unless they pay to open up additional levels. Games may also be free to play but offer users the ability to pay for in-game items, or additional "lives" or plays. For example, Pokémon Go, an augmented reality mobile game developed in 2016 by Niantic, allows free gameplay, but users have the option to convert real money to "Poké Coins" which can be used in the game to buy items to use in the game, additional storage space, and tickets to events (see Figure 3.8). According to Statista, "in 2021 Pokémon GO in-app purchase revenues surpassed 904 million U.S. dollars worldwide. It was the mobile app's second-most profitable year since launching in 2016, when it netted approximately 588.77 million U.S. dollars."[36]

Figure 3.8   Pokémon Go Augmented Reality https://www.gamespot.com/amp-articles/pokemon-go-is-getting-a-better-ar-mode/1100-6455762/

Matthew Corley/Shutterstock.com

Business Models in Action

KANU

Remember that Table 3.1 is not an exhaustive listing of business models. Also, remember that not all businesses follow one model. Many businesses follow customized solutions that integrate multiple models to achieve success. One such business is KANU, highlighted in Figures 3.9 and 3.10.

First-year business students at the University of Rhode Island, Ben Grossman and Andrew Bikash, observed that their peers fell into two groups: those with an ambition to be in business and those that used business to help fund their education. They noted that for the latter, choices are few for a college student with generally inflexible schedules, while the other segment of students, those with an entrepreneurial spirit, will launch ventures with most slowly fading into nothing more than abandoned ideas. Ben and Andrew fell into both groups. They looked for an application to offer goods and services wanted by fellow students and found that none existed. Seeing this opportunity, they created KANU.

KANU is a safe, virtual marketplace that empowers college students to develop and launch venture ideas on campus, earn money, and gain entrepreneurial experience. KANU has helped universities inspire, educate, and engage their student communities in the classroom, in university-based incubators, and with the campus community at large.

KANU's value proposition is simple. It is the first experiential learning tool that allows students to launch a business on campus. Students are provided with the freedom to learn, build, test, launch, and connect with consumers on a state-of-the-art system, monitored by professors through an educator portal. Academics can customize the use of the platform to follow critical curriculum objectives.

KANU supports and structures the student's learning experience, creating an actual business beyond the pitch. KANU allows students to create a safe, campus-based venture, motivating them to earn additional money to help defer college costs while developing business knowledge and thinking skills in an authentic business environment. As a result, students learn by doing while making campus communities stronger.

Figure 3.9   **KANU** Source: Kanu

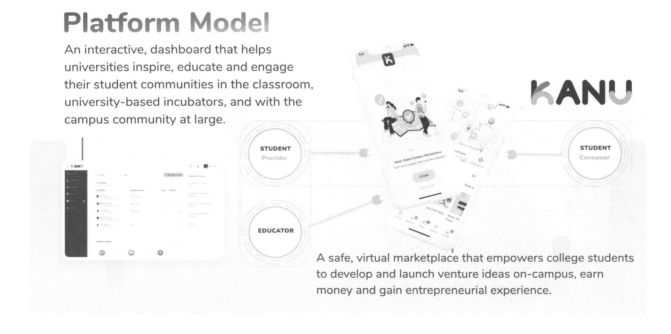

Figure 3.10 **The KANU Mobile App** Source: Kanu

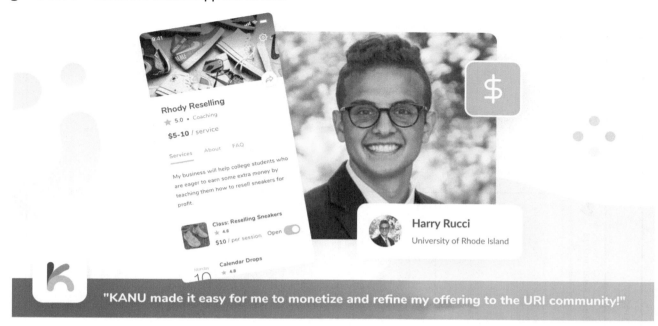

Students aren't KANU's only customers—the platform also delivers the opportunity for educators to use it as a powerful educational tool, adding value to universities and their faculty. Professors can analyze student businesses through the lens of an educational tool that enacts business curricula with hands-on entrepreneurial learning, motivating students both inside and outside the classroom. KANU offers supportive tools and a dashboard that allows an intuitive launch and development of a student-owned business. The dashboard covers interactive key performance indicators (KPIs), allowing educators to assess students in real-time with classroom leaderboards, customizable badges, and student self-assessment reports. KANU provides a campus-wide, peer-to-peer marketplace accessible to all students as consumers or providers. The mobile application offers payment processing, appointment scheduling, automated notifications, and an in-app messenger.

At its core, KANU relies on a *community business model*. The network of users is integral to its success and adoption. Student entrepreneurs set up their businesses on KANU, while other students use KANU when looking for a service or product. KANU also uses a *freemium model* for revenue generation. Students can sign up for a free basic account and can upgrade for more features. Additionally, KANU uses an *advertising model* to generate revenue through in-feed ads. Lastly, KANU follows a *brokerage model* as they charge a small transaction fee for facilitating transactions between the student business owners and their customers. As you can see, KANU cleverly combines multiple business models to create a unique offering. We next discuss how one tool, the Business Model Canvas, can be used to do just this—create a unique model to fit their needs.

Using the Business Model Canvas

Now it is time to put it all together and to understand how this approach allows the entrepreneur or evolving business to customize a unique model, not simply to blindly pick a model from Table 3.1. The Business Model Canvas (see Figure 3.11) approach is based on understanding the basic elements of a business model that can be applied in a traditional business setting or, even more importantly, in a disruptive one. As Alexander Osterwalder and Yves Pigneur write in their crowdsourced book Business Model Generation: "Disruptive new business models are emblematic of our generation. Yet they remain poorly understood, even as they transform competitive landscapes across industries." A business

Figure 3.11 The Business Model Canvas Source: https://en.wikipedia.org/wiki/Business_Model_Canvas#/media/File:Business_Model_Canvas.png

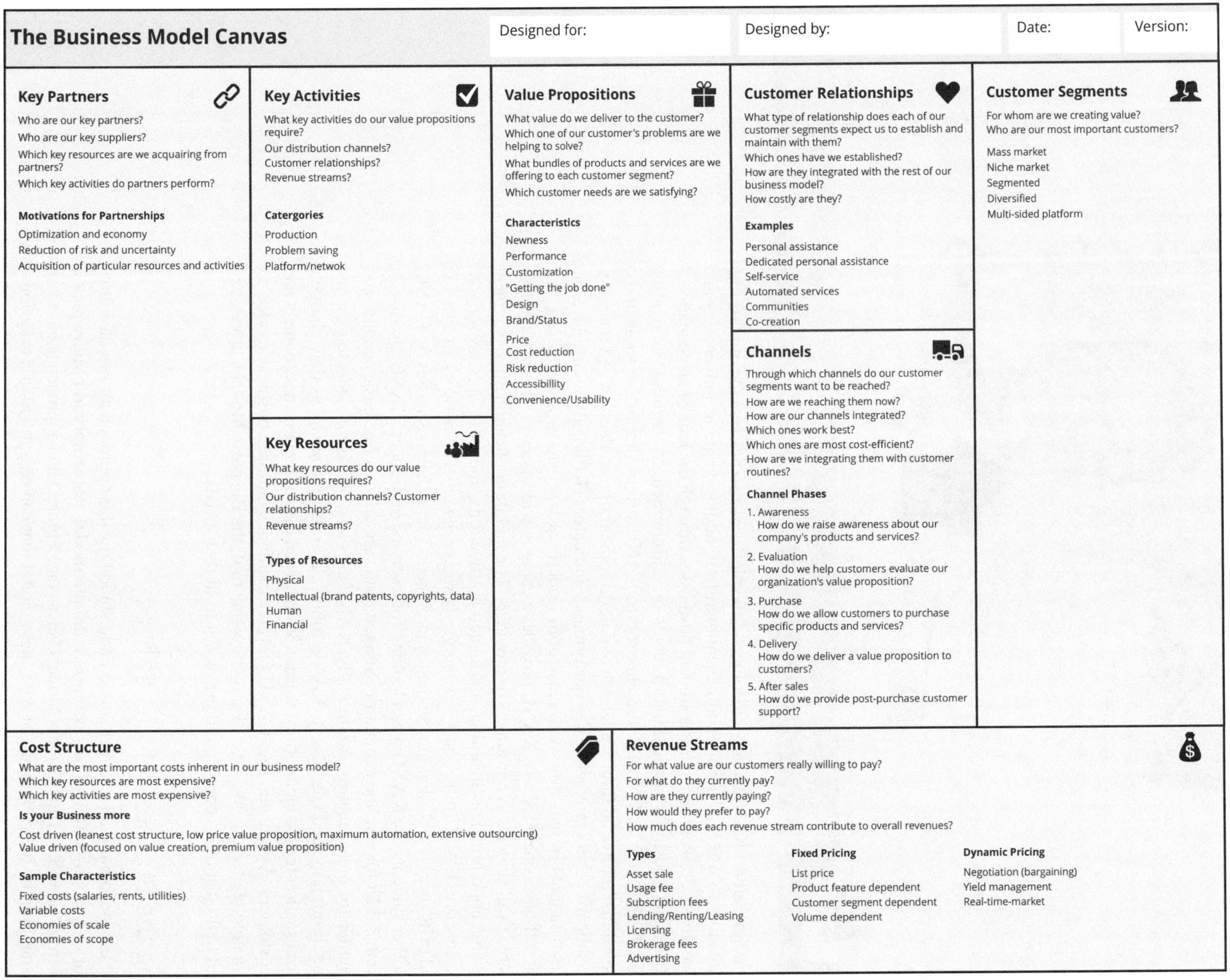

The Business Model Canvas

Designed for: Designed by: Date: Version:

Key Partners

Who are our key partners?
Who are our key suppliers?
Which key resources are we acquairing from partners?
Which key activities do partners perform?

Motivations for Partnerships

Optimization and economy
Reduction of risk and uncertainty
Acquisition of particular resources and activities

Key Activities

What key activities do our value propositions require?
Our distribution channels?
Customer relationships?
Revenue streams?

Categories

Production
Problem saving
Platform/netwok

Key Resources

What key resources do our value propositions requires?
Our distribution channels? Customer relationships?
Revenue streams?

Types of Resources

Physical
Intellectual (brand patents, copyrights, data)
Human
Financial

Value Propositions

What value do we deliver to the customer?
Which one of our customer's problems are we helping to solve?
What bundles of products and services are we offering to each customer segment?
Which customer needs are we satisfying?

Characteristics

Newness
Performance
Customization
"Getting the job done"
Design
Brand/Status
Price
Cost reduction
Risk reduction
Accessibility
Convenience/Usability

Customer Relationships

What type of relationship does each of our customer segments expect us to establish and maintain with them?
Which ones have we established?
How are they integrated with the rest of our business model?
How costly are they?

Examples

Personal assistance
Dedicated personal assistance
Self-service
Automated services
Communities
Co-creation

Channels

Through which channels do our customer segments want to be reached?
How are we reaching them now?
How are our channels integrated?
Which ones work best?
Which ones are most cost-efficient?
How are we integrating them with customer routines?

Channel Phases

1. Awareness
   How do we raise awareness about our company's products and services?
2. Evaluation
   How do we help customers evaluate our organization's value proposition?
3. Purchase
   How do we allow customers to purchase specific products and services?
4. Delivery
   How do we deliver a value proposition to customers?
5. After sales
   How do we provide post-purchase customer support?

Customer Segments

For whom are we creating value?
Who are our most important customers?

Mass market
Niche market
Segmented
Diversified
Multi-sided platform

Cost Structure

What are the most important costs inherent in our business model?
Which key resources are most expensive?
Which key activities are most expensive?

Is your Business more

Cost driven (leanest cost structure, low price value proposition, maximum automation, extensive outsourcing)
Value driven (focused on value creation, premium value proposition)

Sample Characteristics

Fixed costs (salaries, rents, utilities)
Variable costs
Economies of scale
Economies of scope

Revenue Streams

For what value are our customers really willing to pay?
For what do they currently pay?
How are they currently paying?
How would they prefer to pay?
How much does each revenue stream contribute to overall revenues?

Types	Fixed Pricing	Dynamic Pricing
Asset sale	List price	Negotiation (bargaining)
Usage fee	Product feature dependent	Yield management
Subscription fees	Customer segment dependent	Real-time-market
Lending/Renting/Leasing	Volume dependent	
Licensing		
Brokerage fees		
Advertising		

model describes the rationale of how an organization creates, delivers, and captures value. And a disruptive business model is one where a non-traditional industry player enters the mix and threatens to disrupt the status quo.[37]

The canvas has nine elements, each of which is necessary but not sufficient alone to describe a business model. The canvas is a visual chart with elements describing the following nine elements: (1) value propositions, (2) customer relationships, (3) customer segments, (4) channels, (5) revenue streams, (6) key activities, (7) key resources, (8) key partners, and (9) cost structure.

You can use the Business Model Canvas to analyze existing business models. The canvas can be used to create a business model for a start-up business or to help an existing firm evolve its business model to one more in keeping with the times.

It is a powerful tool, and you are encouraged to get some experience with its use.

Business Models Evolve with New Technologies

While new technologies, like augmented reality (AR), virtual reality (VR), and blockchain, play an immense role in developing new business opportunities and advancing existing businesses, they are not themselves new business models. VR is not new, but there is a recent renewed interest in this technology. Unlike AR, where computer-generated visuals are overlayed on top of real-world visuals, VR offers a fully virtual experience. A computer-generated environment is created with the use of special headsets or helmets, making the user feel fully immersed in the computer-constructed reality. Marketers are exploring new ways to use VR.[38] For example, Lowes created a virtual environment where customers could learn new home improvement skills.[39] They tested to see how this experience impacted customer recall and found that customers who learned the skill through the VR training had 36 percent better recall than those who watched a YouTube video demonstrating the same skill.

AR does not rely on the use of headsets but instead uses the video capabilities of computers or mobile devices. Retailers have explored how to use AR in interesting ways, such as developing smart mirrors and dressing rooms that would allow customers to virtually try on clothing.[40] Advertisers have experimented with AR for several years. For instance, an AR Pepsi Max ad in London (Figure 3.12) used a bus stop window to make users experience

Figure 3.12 **Pepsi Max Augmented Reality Ad** Alfred Maskeroni/Adweek

blockchain
a shared, immutable ledger that facilitates the process of recording transactions and tracking assets.

Bitcoin
the first cryptocurrency.

cryptocurrency
a decentralized digital currency that utilizes blockchain technology.

a tiger seeming to come straight at them, a tentacle monster trying to grab passers-by, alien spaceships flying overhead, and other highly unlikely but engaging stunts. The ad was part of Pepsi's #LiveForNowcampaign, although the purpose of this ad seems to be more attention-grabbing than conveying an advertising message.

Blockchain technology is changing the business landscape and in doing so has created new opportunities. It is the technological basis for Web 3.0, the next evolution of the internet. What is blockchain? First, it's important to note that blockchain is not Bitcoin. Bitcoin is a cryptocurrency, a virtual currency that utilizes blockchain technology. Bitcoin was first introduced to the world on October 31, 2008 in a whitepaper titled "Bitcoin: A Peer-to-Peer Electronic Cash System" by Satoshi Nakamoto, which outlined Bitcoin and the concept of blockchain technology.[41] Most people believe that Satoshi Nakamoto is a fictitious name and his real identity is unknown at the time of writing. A blockchain is a shared, immutable (unchangeable) ledger that records transactions and tracks assets. These assets can be intangible (copyright, intellectual property, patents, etc.) or tangible (land, coffee, cars, etc.) allowing for virtually anything to be tracked and traded on a blockchain network. Figure 3.13 provides an overview of how blockchains work.

Blockchains create immutable records, meaning no one can tamper with or change the transaction after it's been recorded on the shared ledger. This is because the ledger is public and can be verified. If it is found that a transaction record had an error, then it is necessary to add a new transaction to fix the error and both the original transaction and second transaction are visible. This transparency reduces risk and the need for trust. In essence, the blockchain allows for the creation of a shared truth. No one person can alter the record and any "mistakes" or inaccurate information can be seen by anyone since every transaction is recorded on the decentralized blockchain ledger. In a non-blockchain world, often participants in business relationships maintain their own set of records which makes it possible for any party to intentionally falsify their records.

Furthermore, blockchains are decentralized, meaning no one person or entity controls the platform. Sites like Facebook and banks are examples of centralized platforms. Here the entity (or a few people within the entity) have power while users are left with little or no input. This is important in many instances since users (who have little to no power) are often providing immense value as content creators and community members. For instance, social media platforms derive value from the content (writing, video, music, etc.) that users generate, which is often monetized through advertising. While some social media platforms offer revenue for content creators (e.g., YouTube), others do not (e.g., Facebook, Instagram). This decentralization is at the heart of the next phase of the internet, Web 3.0.

Additionally, privacy concerns abound with centralized platforms as users have little to no control over how their data is used. This includes information on actions they take on the sites (including likes and content consumption) that is then sold to third parties or used for advertising targeting. The centralized nature and power imbalance is why many platforms are able to monetize users' data without sharing revenue. The old saying, "if it's free, then you're the product" is the basis for revenue generation for many Web 2.0 companies. Additionally, the centralized storage model for user data creates a single point of attack where unauthorized individuals can gain access to large amounts of user data. This has resulted in numerous data breaches; therefore, users are becoming more concerned about having to trust platforms with their data. A decentralized internet fueled by blockchain technology has the potential to elevate many of these concerns.

Ethereum
a decentralized blockchain with smart contract functionality. Ether is the native cryptocurrency of the platform.

decentralized applications (dApps)
Applications, such as smart contracts, that are developed on blockchains.

Blockchains can be used for more than just cryptocurrencies—they can also be used to build decentralized applications. Ethereum is an example of a decentralized, open-source public blockchain. It was conceived by programmer Vitalik Buterin in 2013, and many decentralized applications (dApps) have been developed for it. Ether (ETH) is the native cryptocurrency of the platform, which is used to pay fees for running applications.

Figure 3.13　A Look at Blockchain Technology Source: https://www.pwc.com/us/en /industries/financial-services/fintech/bitcoin-blockchain-cryptocurrency.html

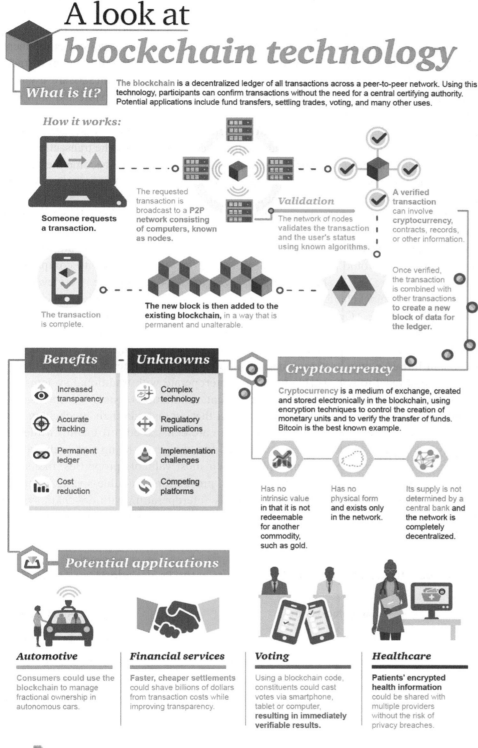

smart contracts

sets of rules that are written and stored on the blockchain that are automatically executed once the defined conditions in the contract are met.

Blockchains allow for the creation of smart contracts. Essentially, smart contracts are sets of rules that are written and stored on the blockchain. They are automatically executed once the defined conditions in the contract are met. Since these contracts can be created and executed on the blockchain without the need for human intervention, they are beneficial in terms of increased speed, reduced cost, and increased trust. As described by the cryptocurrency exchange, Gemini, "Smart contracts are one of the key components of many blockchain-based ecosystems and an especially important element of many application-focused blockchains like Ethereum. These digital contracts are trustless, autonomous, decentralized, and transparent—and are usually irreversible and unmodifiable once deployed. Smart contract advantages include reducing—or even removing—the need for intermediaries and contract enforcement in an agreement or transaction. That's because, with a smart contract, the code defines the mechanisms of the transaction and is the final arbiter of the terms. For this reason, smart contracts have become the building blocks of an entire ecosystem of decentralized applications (dApps) and represent a major focal point of blockchain development in general."[42]

One issue with smart contracts is that these transactions occur solely on the blockchain, however, some contracts need access to "off-chain" data. For instance, if a smart contract was executed to purchase 420 shares of Tesla stock upon some conditions being met, the contract would need to get the current price of Tesla stock to complete this task. This is where oracles become essential (Figure 3.14 provides an overview of how oracles connect blockchains to realworld data). As noted by Chainlink Labs creator of the Chainlink oracle, "Oracles provide a way for the decentralized Web 3.0 ecosystem to access existing data sources, legacy systems, and advanced computations. Decentralized oracle networks enable the creation of hybrid smart contracts, where on-chain code and off-chain infrastructure are combined to support advanced decentralized applications (dApps) that react to real-world events and interoperate with traditional systems. The blockchain oracle problem outlines a fundamental limitation of smart contracts—they cannot naturally interact with systems or data that are outside their blockchain environment. Resources external to the blockchain are considered 'off-chain,' while data already stored on the blockchain is considered 'on-chain.' By being purposely isolated from external systems, blockchains obtain their most valuable properties, like strong consensus on the validity of user transactions, prevention of double-spending attacks, and mitigation of network downtime. Securely interoperating with off-chain systems from a blockchain requires an additional piece of infrastructure known as an 'oracle' to bridge the two environments."[43]

oracles

facilitate secure communication between blockchains and off-chain systems (e.g., data providers, IoT devices, payment systems, web APIs, e-signature systems, and other blockchains).

Figure 3.14　Blockchain Oracles Connect Blockchains to Inputs and Outputs in the Real World Source: https://chain
.link/education/blockchain-oracles

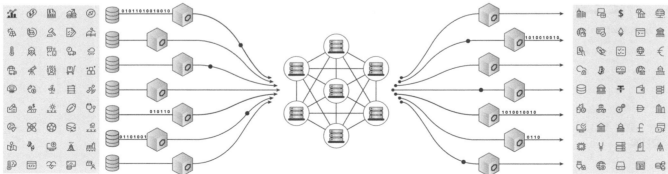

Any Input　　　　　**Any Blockchain**　　　　　**Any Output**

There are many uses for blockchains ranging from pure cryptocurrency (like Bitcoin, Litecoin, and Dogecoin), to smart contracts, to financial services (such as banking and trading). Other uses include gaming and the creation of non-fungible tokens (NFTs). In terms of the supply chain, blockchain can be used to track the origins of items such as food, gemstones, and other precious commodities. Ensuring food freshness and that farmers get fair wages for their products (such as coffee) is another application currently being deployed. In 2018 Walmart partnered with IBM to use blockchain for supply chain monitoring of lettuce and spinach in response to food-borne illness outbreaks. Typically, when such food-borne illness outbreaks occur, it can take days or even weeks, to find the source, but Walmart found that it can be reduced to seconds with blockchain tracking.[44] Documenting land ownership is another real-world application[45] and there is even hope that blockchain technology can be used to help the fashion industry become more sustainable through information transparency.[46]

Lastly, no discussion of blockchain technology's uses in marketing is complete without the mention of NFTs. NFTs are digital assets, like artwork, music, or other digital goods, that are created on the Ethereum blockchain and can't be replicated since they have unique identification codes. Many brands started becoming interested in NFTs around 2021 as part of their marketing mix and have gained the attention of fashion brands such as Gucci and Dolce & Gabbana and food brands such as Taco Bell, Coca-Cola, and McDonald's, among others. Brands have used NFTs as part of limited edition collectibles as a way to gain buzz and also build brand loyalty.[47]

non-fungible tokens (NFTs)
original digital assets, like artwork, music, or other digital goods, that are created using blockchain.

Summary

Business models are how enterprises are configured to create value for customers and to deliver that value profitably in the physical or digital world. A business model is a conceptual description of the business. Business models on the internet have been given a set of names, although there is no commonly accepted set of names or classifications of types of business models.

The emphasis on the value proposition, however, is characteristic of all discussions of business models. The drivers of value are customer wants and needs. It is up to the business to uncover the relevant wants and needs and design products and services that meet those needs and fit with its core expertise. This is a customer-centric, not a product-centric, approach. It is captured in the Value Proposition Canvas.

There are many commonly accepted business models, and we discuss key examples of each. Most of them can be found in both B2C and B2B marketspaces and are also used by nonprofits and governmental agencies. A key point of this discussion is that many businesses now have hybrid models or multiple models. There are few examples of pure models in practice. The same is true of revenue streams that support each model. Few businesses today prosper without multiple revenue streams.

The complexity and ever-changing nature of the world we live in suggest that adopting a basic business model in its entirety may not work well for most businesses. Enter the Business Model Canvas. The canvas sections the business model into nine parts, all of which must be present and each of which can be customized to the needs of a particular business concept.

The evolution of business models in the digital era continues. It is likely that different models may achieve prominence at different periods of time and possible that entirely new models may emerge as the digital space matures and new technologies like AR, VR, and blockchain become widely used.

Discussion Questions

1. Why is the concept of the business model important? In what ways is it useful?

2. What is the single reason that most new businesses fail?

3. Why is it sometimes necessary for existing firms to evolve their business model or for start-ups to pivot theirs?

4. How does the value proposition impact a firm's approach to the creation of new products and new marketing strategies?

5. Can a company have more than one business model?

6. How do business models evolve?

7. What is the difference between pipe-type business models and platform-type models?

8. Would you start a business today driven by the advertising-supported model?

9. Do you agree with the statement that the community/crowdsourcing model is likely to become even more prominent in the future?

10. What is blockchain and how can it be used by businesses?

11. What does it mean to be decentralized?

12. What is the meaning of the term "disruptive business model?" Give an example of a business model that you believe is genuinely disruptive and explain why.

Endnotes

1. Andrea Ovans, "What Is a Business Model?," *Harvard Business Review*, October 12, 2022, https://hbr.org/2015/01/what-is-a-business-model.

2. Professor Michael Rappa, "Business Models on the Web: Professor Michael Rappa," Business Models on the Web | Professor Michael Rappa, accessed December 7, 2022, http://digitalenterprise.org/models/models.html.

3. Sendil Ethiraj, Sendil, Isin Guler, and Harbir Singh, "The impact of Internet and electronic technologies on firms and its implications for competitive advantage." *The Wharton School. Research*

4. Henry Chesbrough and Richard S. Rosenbloom, "The Role of the Business Model in Capturing Value from Innovation: Evidence from Xerox Corporations's Technology Spin-Off Companies," *Industrial and Corporate Change*, Volume 11, Number 3, 2002, 533–534.

5. Margaret Visnji, "IBM Strategic Imperatives vs Traditional It Business Growth," *Revenues & Profits*, February 21, 2019, http://revenuesandprofits.com/ibm-strategic-imperatives-vs-traditional-business-growth/.

6. Michael Copeland, "The Difference between AI, Machine Learning, and Deep Learning?," NVIDIA Blog, July 17, 2021, https://blogs.nvidia.com/blog/2016/07/29/whats-difference-artificial-intelligence-machine-learning-deep-learning-ai/.

7. Henry Blodget, "CEO Jeff Immelt on Transforming Ge - Reflections on Winning the Race, Digitizing Manufacturing, and Leading 311,000 People into a New Age," *Business Insider*, accessed December 7, 2022, https://www.businessinsider.com/interview-with-ge-ceo-jeff-immelt-on-transforming-ge-2015-12.

8. Linton Weeks, "Can Amazon's Jeff Bezos Save Planet Earth?," *NPR* (January 8, 2014), https://www.npr.org/sections/theprotojournalist/2014/01/08/260457752/can-jeff-bezos-save-planet-earth.

9. David Curry, "Amazon Statistics (2022)," Business of Apps, August 11, 2022, https://www.businessofapps.com/data/amazon-statistics/.

10. "7 Surprising Things to Know about the Amazon Business Model," Digital Spark Marketing, July 10, 2021, http://digitalsparkmarketing.com/amazon-business-model/.

11. Dave Chaffey, "Amazon Marketing Strategy Business Case Study," *Smart Insights*, May 25, 2022, http://www.smartinsights.com/digital-marketing-strategy/online-business-revenue-models/amazon-case-study/.

12. Payne, Adrian, Pennie Frow, and Andreas Eggert, "The Customer Value Proposition: Evolution, Development, and Application in Marketing," *Journal of the Academy of Marketing Science* 45, no. 4 (2017): 467–489.

13. "Nikola Tesla Inventions," Tesla Science Center at Wardenclyffe, November 10, 2020, https://teslasciencecenter.org/nikola-tesla-inventions

14. Eric Reed, "History of Tesla: Timeline and Facts," *TheStreet* (February 4, 2020), https://www.thestreet.com /technology/history-of-tesla-15088992.

15. Melissa Lee, "Netflix a 'Dumb Pipe?,'" *CNBC* (October 13, 2015), https://www.cnbc.com/video/2015/10/13 /netflix-a-dumb-pipe.html.

16. Professor Michael Rappa, "Business Models on the Web: Professor Michael Rappa," Business Models on the Web | Professor Michael Rappa, accessed December 7, 2022, http://digitalenterprise.org/models/models.html.

17. "National Information Infrastructure Act of 1993 (1993 - H.R. 1757)," GovTrack.us, accessed December 7, 2022, https://www.govtrack.us/congress/bills/103/hr1757.

18. Karla Hesterberg, "A Brief History of Online Advertising," *HubSpot Blog* (November 29, 2021), https://blog .hubspot.com/marketing/history-of-online-advertising.

19. "Selling Fees," eBay, accessed December 7, 2022, https://www.ebay.com/help/selling/fees-credits-invoices /selling-fees?id=4822.

20. The Investopedia Team, "Amazon's vs. Alibaba's Business Models: What's the Difference?," *Investopedia* (November 10, 2022), http://www.investopedia.com/articles/investing/061215/difference-between-amazon-and -alibabas-business-models.asp.

21. "Top 10 B2B Websites in World. List of Trade Portal & Marketplaces for Exporters, Importers," Ads2020. Marketing, January 25, 2022, https://ads2020.marketing/top-10-b2b-marketplaces-in-world#Top_10 _Worldwide_B2B_Trade_Marketplaces_for_Exporters_Importers_Suppliers_Manufacturers_and_Traders _in_2022.

22. Webopedia Staff, "What Is Infomediary?," *Webopedia*, May 24, 2021, https://www.webopedia.com/definitions /infomediary/.

23. Cynthia J. Larose, Wynter Deagle, "More Broken Privacy Promises from Upromise: Key Takeaways from Upromise's Latest Settlement with the FTC," Mintz, accessed December 7, 2022, https://www.mintz.com /insights-center/viewpoints/2017-03-20-more-broken-privacy-promises-upromise-key-takeaways-upromises.

24. Cynthia J. Larose, Wynter Deagle, "More Broken Privacy Promises from Upromise: Key Takeaways from Upromise's Latest Settlement with the FTC," Mintz, accessed December 7, 2022, https://www.mintz.com /insights-center/viewpoints/2017-03-20-more-broken-privacy-promises-upromise-key-takeaways-upromises.

25. "AWS Pricing," Amazon, accessed December 7, 2022, https://aws.amazon.com/pricing/.

26. "Gas and Fees," ethereum.org, accessed December 7, 2022, https://ethereum.org/en/developers/docs/gas/.

27. Stephen Silver, "The Cord-Cutting Trend Continues to Rise," The National Interest (The Center for the National Interest, February 10, 2022), https://nationalinterest.org/blog/buzz/cord-cutting-trend-continues-rise-200482.

28. Dollar shave club, accessed December 7, 2022, https://www.dollarshaveclub.com/get-started/how-it-works.

29. The Week Staff, "Dollar Shave Club's Retail Disruption," *The Week* (*The Week*, August 7, 2016), http://theweek.com/articles/641015/dollar-shave-clubs-retail-disruption.

30. Lindsay Blakely, "How Jessica Alba Proved Her Doubters Wrong | Inc.com," accessed December 7, 2022, https://www.inc.com/magazine/201411/lindsay-blakely/how-jessica-alba-proved-her-doubters-were-wrong.html.

31. "Same Day Local Flower Delivery," Teleflora, accessed December 7, 2022, http://www.teleflora.com/.

32. Mahesh Mohan, "The 21 Best Affiliate Programs & Networks for Anyone and Everyone," @maheshone, June 5, 2021, http://www.minterest.org/best-affiliate-programs-and-networks/.

33. "Crowdsourcing," Wikipedia (Wikimedia Foundation, November 30, 2022), https://en.wikipedia.org/wiki /Crowdsourcing.

34. Kyle Alspach, "TripAdvisor at 15," accessed December 7, 2022, http://bostinno.streetwise.co/2015/01/31 /tripadvisor-trip-ceo-stephen-kaufer-on-the-travel-planning-sites-first-15-years/.

35. "Compare All Dropbox Plans - Dropbox," Dropbox, accessed December 7, 2022, https://www.dropbox.com /plans.

36. J. Clement, "Pokémon Go Revenue Worldwide 2022," *Statista*, August 30, 2022, https://www.statista.com /statistics/882474/pokemon-go-all-time-player-spending-countries/.

37. Matthew E. May, "The 9 Elements of an Ironclad Business Model," *Business Class: Trends and Insights | American Express*, accessed December 7, 2022, https://www.americanexpress.com/us/small-business /openforum/articles/the-9-elements-of-an-ironclad-business-model/.

38. Braden Becker, "7 VR Marketing Examples to Inspire You in 2022," *HubSpot Blog* (September 16, 2022), https://blog.hubspot.com/marketing/vr-marketing-examples.

39. "Holoroom How To," Lowe's Innovation Labs, accessed December 7, 2022, https://www.lowesinnovationlabs .com/projects/holoroom-how-to.

40. Alexey Chalimov, "Augmented Reality in Retail: Benefits and Use Cases of AR Retail Apps," Eastern Peak - Technology Consulting & Development Company, October 20, 2021, https://easternpeak.com/blog/bringing -augmented-reality-to-your-retail-app/.

41. Satoshi Nakamoto, "Bitcoin: A Peer-to-Peer Electronic Cash System," accessed December 7, 2022, https://www.bitcoin.com/bitcoin.pdf.

42. "Real World Examples of Smart Contracts," *Gemini*, accessed December 7, 2022, https://www.gemini.com /cryptopedia/smart-contract-examples-smart-contract-use-cases#section-smart-contract-use-cases-in-finance

43. "What Is a Blockchain Oracle?" accessed December 7, 2022, https://chain.link/education/blockchain-oracles.

44. "Walmart Case Study," Hyperledger Foundation, accessed December 7, 2022, https://www.hyperledger.org /learn/publications/walmart-case-study.

45. Professor Richard Rogers, "Blockchain-Based Property Registries May Help Lift Poor People out of Poverty," GovTech (GovTech, April 30, 2021), https://www.govtech.com/computing/blockchain-based-property -registries-may-help-lift-poor-people-out-of-poverty.html.

46. "Blockchain Basics: Utilizing Blockchain to Improve Sustainable Supply Chains in Fashion," Strategic Direction (Emerald Publishing Limited, May 28, 2021), https://www.emerald.com/insight/content/doi/10.1108 /SD-03-2021-0028/full/html.

47. Breanna Jacobs, "10 Examples of Brands Leading the Way with NFTs," accessed September 9, 2022, https://blog.socialmediastrategiessummit.com/brands-using-nfts/

Chapter 4

Supporting the Digital Customer Journey

Learning Objectives

By the time you complete this chapter you will be able to:

1 Explain what the customer journey means and the impact of the digital age upon it.

2 Explain what customer experience (CX) is.

3 Explain the importance of customer service in B2C and B2B markets.

4 Explain the role of omnichannel in the digital age.

5 Relate the role of customer service to business customer service goals.

The way customers approach making a purchase has changed. This trend has increased the importance of customer experience (CX) at each step. We will discuss those two important and interconnected topics in this chapter. Before we do so, however, we need to look at customers themselves—who they are and how they use the internet—keeping in mind the discussions of social media usage in chapters 8 and 9.

The Customer Journey in the Digital Age

Over the past decade it has become clear that marketers must rethink their model of the consumer decision process. It has typically been portrayed as a linear process, often as a funnel as in Figure 4.1a and other chapters in this book. The message of the funnel is that customers begin with a set of brands in mind and, over several stages of consideration, narrow the set down to a single brand for purchase. The implication that this takes place in an orderly, linear set of steps does not hold true in the digital age.

Instead, the terms customer journey or "customer decision journey" have come into widespread use. Like any journey, the customer's route to a purchasing decision can experience stops and starts, wrong turns, and progress that often appears to be anything but linear. That is the result of changes in customers themselves, changes in the environment (like more brands to consider), and the disruptive

customer experience (CX)
cumulative customer experiences across multiple touchpoints and in multiple channels over time

customer journey
a process or sequence that a customer goes through to access or use an offering of a company

Figure 4.1a The Purchase Funnel Source: http://www.forbes.com/sites/gregsatell/2015/10/12/marketers-need-to-drastically-rethink-the-customer-decision-journey/#f21bd073f285

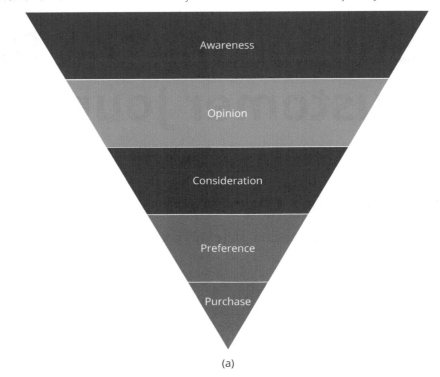

(a)

changes in media we have just discussed. Actual customer journeys can be complex as we will discuss later in this section. However, Figure 4.1b is a good portrayal of the basic concept.

Figure 4.1b The Journey Source: http://www.forbes.com/sites/gregsatell/2015/10/12/marketers-need-to-drastically-rethink-the-customer-decision-journey/#f21bd073f285

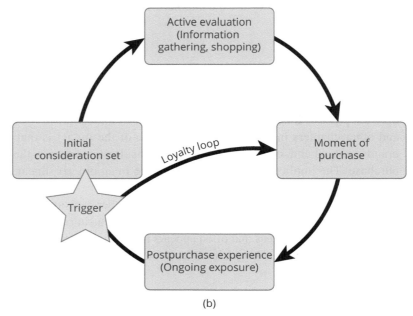

(b)

The term "customer journey" itself commonly refers to a process or sequence that a customer goes through to access or use an offering of a company (Følstad & Kvale, 2018b).[1] The customer journey, prepurchase, purchase, and post-purchase, take place along many dimensions. Tueanrat, Papagiannidis, and Alamanos (2021) define these dimensions as follows[2]:

Customer Response

How customers perceive what is occurring in the service environment and the network and processes that make up that environment.

Co-Creation

How involved customers are in providing feedback and creating new product enhancements, and the mechanism by which this is accomplished.

Service Satisfaction, Failure, and Recovery

The process of service mapping, service failure and recovery, and their effects on customer satisfaction.

Channels

How customers react along various channels and how the firm manages those interactions.

Technology

How technology is used along various touchpoints and how adaptive customers are to new technologies.

To illustrate these points, Figure 4.2 shows a theoretical example of a customer journey to make the simple purchase of a taco. The search for food might begin online with "best tacos Austin" as a search term. The search might result in a list of taco restaurants, leading the consumer to explore online reviews. This might then lead the consumer to consult what friends are saying on social media and in the offline environment. The consumer might then cycle back to reviews or even go back to the beginning

Figure 4.2   **The Complex Journey Toward a Simple Purchase** Source: Cengage Graphic

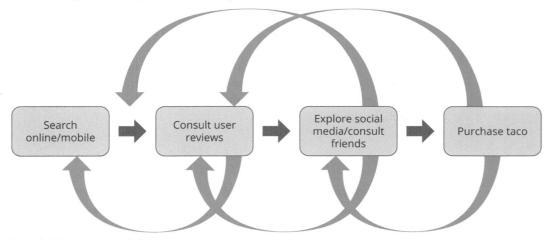

Search: "Best tacos austin"

of the search process before finally making a decision. Once that decision has been made, the consumer might write a review or return to social media to continue the dialogue about that particular purchase with the company and other users. Along this hypothetical journey, the customer is creating a perception of the product, interacting across various channels through technology, experiencing the service aspect of the purchase, and ultimately engaging in the co-creation process of the product or brand itself. What seems like a simple purchase is actually a complex series of interactions involving multiple technologies and interaction channels. This figure primarily illustrates the prepurchase decision, but more of the customer journey occurs during purchase as well as the post-purchase experience.

Much of the consumer decision journey as portrayed in Figures 4.1b and 4.2 is familiar to marketing students. In Figure 4.2, the journey begins with a trigger, perhaps the recognition of a need. Then the consumer considers an initial set of brands based on brand perceptions and recent exposure to various "touchpoints". These key touchpoints might include:

- Search engine visits—consumer searches online for information about retailers, products, and brands.
- Social media visits—consumer might consult social media influencers or see what friends are saying about a particular brand on social media.
- Retailer visits—consumers like to visit retail stores to actually see and experience the product and to get more information. Mobile phones are often a source of information while visiting a retailer.
- Brand visits—direct visits to brand and manufacturer sites appear to be decreasing as search uncovers brand information. Information is also available on large retail sites like Amazon or Target, which many shoppers use as a price and review check either before or after visiting a retail store.
- Review site or app visits—some shoppers make additional checks through third-party reference sites, often using their mobile apps.

In addition, consumers are becoming sensitive to obstacles or bumps in the road to their purchase decision, known as friction points, and expect retailers to eliminate them. They are responding well to personalization which can create an ROI of 20 times each dollar spent. Customers are also more concerned with trust and privacy issues and expect more resiliency from retailers as they themselves become more tech-savvy.[3]

At any point in the journey, the consumer may loop back and repeat an activity. After visiting one or more brand sites, the customer may decide to revisit the retailer (or visit another retailer) to reconsider one or more brands. Alternatively, the customer may skip a step. For example, the customer may forego a retail visit if they are familiar with the product category or the brand.

Active evaluation is going on during all this time. If the decision is made to purchase, a brand is chosen at the moment of purchase. The loyalty loop (See Figure 4.1b) begins when the consumer experiences the product and builds expectations for the next purchase situation.[4]

The Consumer Decision Journey

The description of the decision journey should sound familiar. It is similar to the way that we have always described the linear purchase process. It is the presence of the loyalty loop that causes marketers to look at the ongoing journey in a way that is different from a process with a beginning and an end. Research indicates that consumers are constantly reevaluating the product as a result of both their experience of using the product and the thousands of product- and brand-related messages they are exposed to during the period of using the product. The loyalty loop can be thought of as having three components as consumers experience the product and consume communications from peers as well as marketers. The loyalty stages are:

- Enjoy the use of the product.
- Become an advocate for the brand.
- Bond with the brand through satisfactory use and service experience and ongoing relevant and personalized content.

In other words, marketers have to develop and distribute content, not just for the purchase process but also for the loyalty process. That effort requires a large and detailed set of data about the individual consumer.

Figure 4.3 shows another decision journey map. In this case, it is for a business trip. Note the extensive use of apps along the way to facilitate the journey, starting with finding the airline to booking transportation and hotel. There is so much involved that there are now apps that incorporate every stage of the journey, including filing corporate expense reports. What additional stages might be added if it were a map for a family vacation? There would probably be a number of entertainment decisions to add if it were for a family trip. Companies often outline customer decision journey maps such as this one. In this map, there are a number of stages, each one of which seems to require a separate website or app. The company can analyze this journey to perhaps provide an opportunity to streamline the CX.

The point is that marketers first need to understand the consumer decision journey. Then they need to look at every stage in the journey for marketing opportunities.

The B2B Decision Journey

The illustration of the journey in B2B markets in Figure 4.4 is conceptual, and it helps to understand the mapping process in either B2B or B2C markets. Notice that it is divided into just three stages—awareness, consideration, and purchase. Each stage, however, has multiple possible actions. In the awareness stage, for example, the potential buyer can search, make discoveries, and share them. Notice also that the

Figure 4.3   **A Customer Decision Journey** Source: https://www.forrester.com/blogs/category/customer-experience/

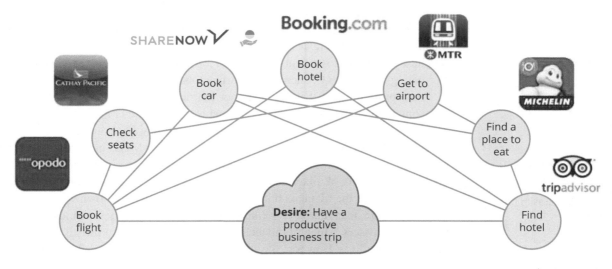

Figure 4.4 Conceptual Business Decision Journey Map Source: http://heidicohen.com/2015-b2b-purchase-decision-process/

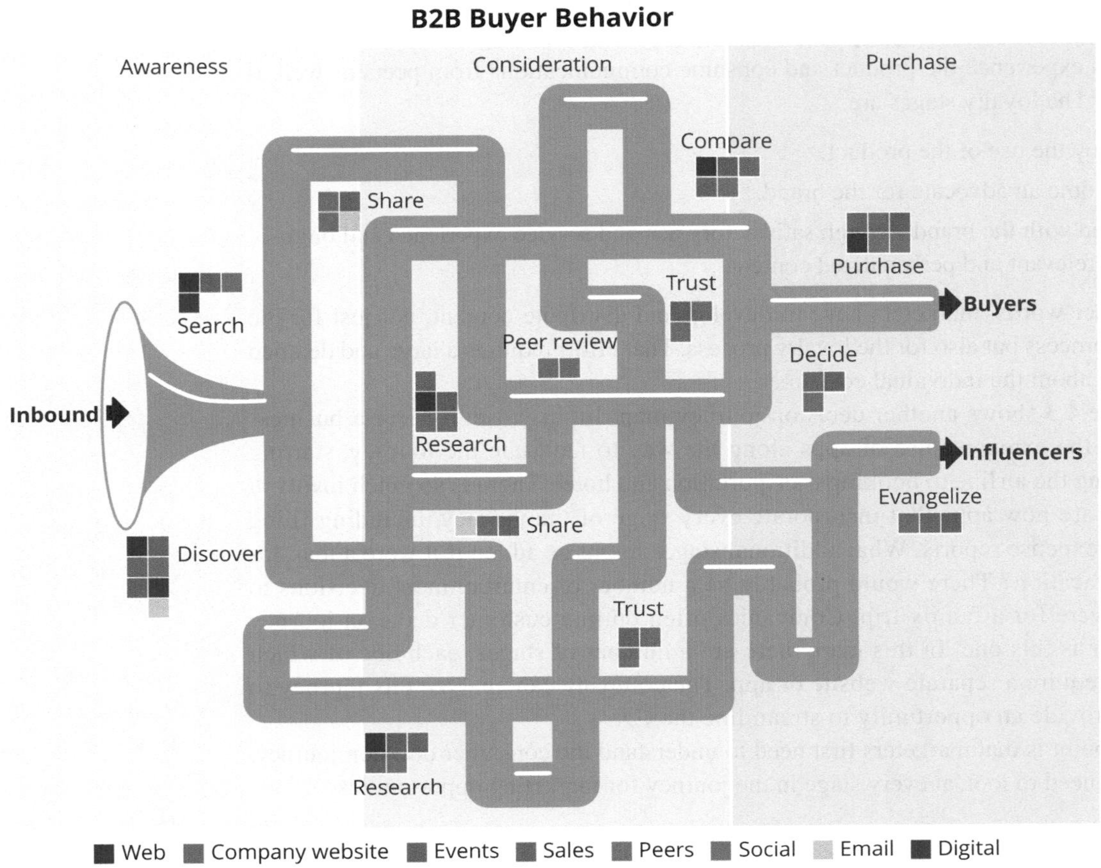

B2B Buyer Behavior

map has many turns, forward loops, and backward loops. It looks a bit like a bowl of noodles, but it captures the multiple activities that buyers can engage in and the almost infinite number of paths they can take.

The conceptual map of the consumer journey in Figure 4.1b is much simpler. However, when considering the discussion of consumer journeys, there might be other touchpoints, and there is likely to be much looping back and skipping forward. It is clear that the consumer journey can also be quite complex.

The point of this comparison is that both concepts represent a useful starting point, but the marketer needs to create a journey map that is specific to the product (e.g., travel) and purchase situation or segment (e.g., family). A level of specificity and detail is essential to creating a seamless CX across all journey touchpoints.

Accepting the fact that the customer journey can be complex and that it can vary from one individual to another, it is reasonable to ask whether marketers can respond at a granular level that corresponds to the customer's journey stage and their behaviors at that time. The answer is yes and no. While Facebook (now Meta) has used a dynamic pixel (a small bit of code) in the past to track the customer experience and Google has used cookies, the Facebook pixel has gone away and has been replaced by the Meta pixel[5]. Being able to use the Meta pixel information from a company's own website is important because, in the near future, it is likely that third-party cookies will also be gone from most web browsers. Much of the technology to replace these efforts is new and requires programming efforts. However, the ability to "retarget" customers in their purchase journey

pixel/pixel tag
a small bit of code in the form of a one-pixel transparent GIF that is added to the pages of a website allowing sites to track visitor activity.

will remain. The customer journey is complex and may require reminding customers about their intended purchase decision through retargeted ads, texts, or emails.

Creating a Satisfying CX in the Digital Age

What then is this "satisfying CX" that is the focus of marketers? Harvard Business Review has a simple but powerful definition. They say CX can only be understood as the customer's *"cumulative experiences across multiple touchpoints and in multiple channels over time."*[6] This simple definition echoes the definition of Lemon and Verhoef, that "the customer experience is a multidimensional construct focusing on a customer's cognitive, emotional, behavioral, sensorial, and social responses to a firm's offerings during the customer's entire purchase journey."[7] In other words, what characterizes the customer experience is the customer's various responses to interactions from the firm over the entire purchase journey.

There are wonderful examples of great CXs from many brands. Nike has long been a master of what is called experiential marketing with its "Nike by You" custom shoe experience. Customers can create their own pair of shoes by choosing various options in terms of style, color, and design and have them shipped to their homes. Levi's has created pop-up kiosks where customers can try on their jeans before purchasing. Knowing what a difficult process trying on jeans can be, this resource made it easier to bring the experience directly to customers. Levi's has expanded that concept into 'experiential stores' or NextGen stores. These stores curate their inventory using local customer data, offering the products most likely to be purchased by the customer base serviced by that particular store and also offering a tailoring service and larger fitting rooms. Store and curbside pickup, in-store personal shopping appointments, in-store digital tools, and contactless returns also add to the customer experience. It is clear that the modern retail customer experience will depend on good service, easy checkout, and great store design, as well as a seamless experience between customer channels that is facilitated by digital technology.[8]

> **experiential marketing**
> promotional activity that helps consumers understand a product by having direct contact with it

Event marketing, like Levi's pop-up kiosks, does a wonderful job of creating buzz around exciting CX. And it is part—but not all—of overall CX. There is general agreement that CX is the customer's perception of the brand that results from *all interactions with the brand over all touchpoints*. It is not the result of any single event or experience, no matter how satisfying (or perhaps even unsatisfying). It is not the result of interaction with a single touchpoint. It is the result of cumulative interactions over time.

> **event marketing**
> a themed activity that promotes a product, business, or cause

Good CX also results from more than one type of perception. CX expert Bruce Temkin says its components are function, how well the product performs, and accessibility—how easy it is to use and derive the benefits from (Figure 4.5). The final component is emotion, the feelings that result from experiencing the product. Considering what is needed in a resilient brand framework, there is agreement that experience is the key to a sustainable brand, and emotion is a key component.

One company that has consistently been rated high in customer service among online retailers is Amazon. Amazon Web Services (AWS) is one example of how Amazon is constantly exploring new technology to enhance its business and make the CX better. The company's highly automated distribution centers are essential to swift order fulfillment that enhances the experience. Amazon has been at the top of CX award categories year after year. How do they do it? The firm is obsessive in its focus on customer satisfaction and CX, and that obsession shows up in everything from its customer service to its many types of personalization to make shopping more convenient and enjoyable. Amazon makes mobile work for its customers for both search and purchase. Jeff Bezos is often quoted as saying, "If you make customers unhappy in the physical world, they might each tell six friends. If you make customers unhappy on the internet, they can each tell 6,000." He notes that it works the other way too. According to Bezos, "word of mouth is becoming more powerful. If you offer a great service, people find out."[9]

Figure 4.5   The Three Components of CX Source: https://experiencematters.wordpress
.com/2011/02/28/nokia-needs-more-design-less-engineering/

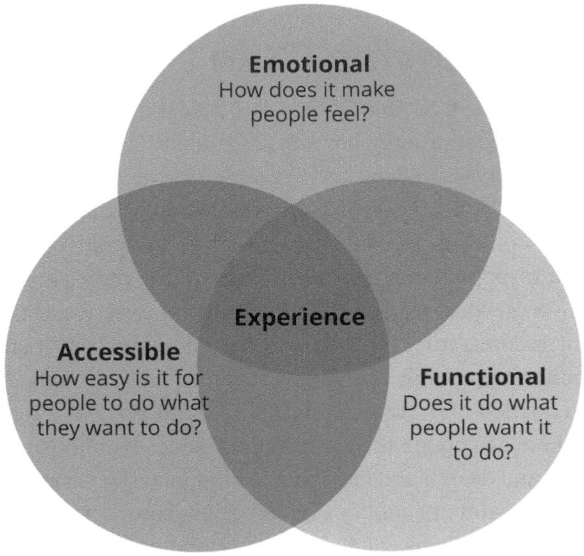

Emotional
How does it make
people feel?

Experience

Accessible
How easy is it for
people to do what
they want to do?

Functional
Does it do what
people want it
to do?

It is also important to note in this context that customer satisfaction scores have been plummeting, according to the American Customer Satisfaction Index (ACSI) as shown in Figure 4.6. Undoubtedly exacerbated by the recent COVID-19 global pandemic, which ensured supply chain and labor shortage issues, scores had actually been declining before the global pandemic.[10] As the ACSI website indicates, "From 2010 to 2019, about 70% of the companies tracked by ACSI had declining or flat customer satisfaction scores. Since then, American customers have become even more dissatisfied. As of the fourth quarter 2021, almost 80% of the companies have now failed to increase the satisfaction of their customers since 2010." The satisfaction decline continued into 2022.

Figure 4.6   American Customer Satisfaction Scores Decline Source: https://www
.theacsi.org/

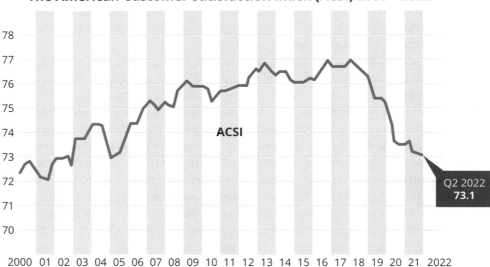

The American Customer Satisfaction Index (ACSI) 2000 – 2022

ACSI

Q2 2022
73.1

2000 01 02 03 04 05 06 07 08 09 10 11 12 13 14 15 16 17 18 19 20 21 2022

Another way to measure customer satisfaction and the effectiveness of the Customer Experience is the Net Promoter Score (NPS), which asks how likely a consumer would be to recommend the business (brand) to a friend or colleague. It was designed by Fred Reichheld of Bain and Company to be a simple measure of customer satisfaction. You might have encountered a simple one-question survey at the end of a purchase experience, and that question was most likely based on the NPS concept. It must be considered with other measures but can be useful in assessing the effectiveness of digital customer service efforts.

In spite of their efforts, companies are spending a lot of time and effort on customer satisfaction but not getting results. So what is the key to a successful customer experience and how can companies reverse this trend? In the end, experts and successful managers alike agree that while data analytics and technology are important, it is all about the employees.

Net Promoter Score (NPS) customer satisfaction score calculated based on a single question, "How likely is it that you would recommend <brand> to a friend or colleague".

CX—It's All About People

Wegmans is a relatively small family-run grocery chain that has been at or near the top of the grocery industry rankings for several years.[11] What makes it so special? "They were the first grocer to work from the customer's point of view," one food writer said.[12]

Instead of simply displaying aisles of packaged products that shoppers might buy, McCauley explains, Wegmans made grocery into a theater—not just with specialty food stations but also by preparing food in front of customers. Wegmans understood that, to a younger generation, "shopping" didn't mean filling your cart with canned peas, it meant hanging out, learning about food, and eating it.

"Wegmans was prescient," McCauley said. "They were aware of what millennials wanted before the millennials even got there."[13]

Customers and food experts agree that the European food hall-style layout, product quality, in-store dining, selection of prepared foods, and reasonable prices all make Wegmans appealing. However, the real secret sauce is their employees.

KMPG says about Wegmans and its CEO Danny Wegman:

> At Wegmans, there is no rule book for its employees. Staff are allowed to make their own decisions, with the only rule being that no customer is allowed to leave unhappy. CEO Wegman believes in giving employees training and experience, then trusting them to deliver the product and service experiences that are expected. It's a formula that works for both staff and customers. The company regularly ranks at the top of Fortune's "100 Best Places to Work For," as staff feel they are trusted to have control over decisions.[14]

That results in "almost *'telepathic levels of service'* where the staff anticipate what the customers might need before the customer is even aware."[15] In addition to loyal and responsive staff, Jack Ma, co-founder of Alibaba, suggests that today's retailing (the "new retail") requires new technology and that algorithms are playing a significant role in the customer experience by improving productivity.[16] This data must be used intelligently. For example, Wegman's takes data from its loyalty program to produce customized recommendations for its shoppers and to create a true 1:1 customer experience. Many companies are using technologies like chatbots to relieve the case burden on their service reps. If an automated response is not available, the customer's question can then be seamlessly transferred to a live agent for a response that can answer the customer's question or concern.[17] Both people and technology are key to creating a positive customer experience and creating loyalty.

There is another important example of the use of many customer-pleasing characteristics of the Ritz-Carlton experience. Just looking at online reviews for the hotel chain will unearth a number of stories like the one that follows. The Ritz-Carlton, owned by Marriott Corporation, has long been famous for superb customer service, delivered in a luxury environment by employees who are not highly paid but who are empowered to do their best for customers. Even at the Ritz-Carlton, though, the saga of Joshie the giraffe is outstanding.

After a family vacation at the Ritz-Carlton in Amelia Island, Florida, the young son's beloved stuffed giraffe went missing. He was inconsolable and found it hard to sleep without his Joshie. The parents, of course, reported the toy missing and were delighted when the resort found it in the laundry, having suffered no damage. Joshie was returned, complete with pictures of his vacation—lounging by the pool, driving a golf cart, and several others that were chronicled on Huffington Post.[18]

We wish we could tell you that the little boy slept peacefully ever after with his stuffed giraffe by his side, but that's not the case. Four years later the boy left the giraffe at another hotel in another city. Despite the best efforts of the hotel staff and the boy's mother, the toy was never found. Since the same model was no longer being made, the toy was replaced, if such a thing is possible, with a smaller giraffe named Tucker. Not long after this incident, the family returned to the Amelia Island Ritz-Carlton only to find that the staff remembered Joshie and were saddened over his recent disappearance. The staff presented the little boy with another giraffe, Jeffie—a long-lost cousin of Joshie's. Apparently, Tucker and Jeffie now co-exist happily in their new home. In addition, the Ritz-Carlton has another wonderful CX story to tell its employees in their never-ending quest for excellent customer service that creates memorable CX.[19]

Ritz-Carlton has moved forward to embrace digital technology to augment its well-known, personal customer service. The use of mobile technology for check-in and ordering things like extra towels in the room helps to smooth the guest's path and remove any additional "pain points."

The Overriding Importance of CX in the Customer Journey

Both B2B and B2C companies consider CX a more durable competitive advantage. Considering the challenges we have discussed in this chapter, it is hard not to agree that truly satisfying CX takes time and effort to achieve. Given its basis in engaged, motivated employees, it is hard for competitors to emulate.

Acxiom Corporation has dubbed 2023 the "Year of Customer Experience." CX has been at or near the top of marketing trend lists for many years, steadily increasing in importance. What makes 2023 especially important is that with the impending demise of cookies, companies will need to rely more on their own data (known as first-party data as noted in Chapter 1) and knowledge of their customers to create meaningful interactions.[20] IBM had a good summary of what it takes to provide an excellent CX. Their criteria were:

- Understanding what customers want, perhaps before they even know it themselves. (That is a special skill at Wegmans.)
- Identifying the perfect moment. (That is hard enough to do in person. It is even more difficult when the contact is made through some kind of technology.)
- Adding customer sentiment (positive or negative) (think Joshie the giraffe) and emotional response (think the Nike+ member receiving a pair of state-of-the-art custom athletic shoes) to the mix.
- Using data, analytics, and predictive models to create personalized communications that impact the purchasing decision.
- Being able to bring all marketing capabilities to bear across any touchpoint in real time.[21]

customer sentiment
customer response to in their journey that is measured as positive, negative, or neutral.

Others describe this process as putting the right content into the right context. By that, they mean getting it to the customer at the right time, in the right setting, and over the right communication channel.[22,23,24] This kind of omnichannel response is difficult and will be discussed later in this chapter.

While it is clear that most companies recognize the importance of CX, it is equally clear that the majority are not succeeding in creating excellent omnichannel CX. The numbers differ slightly from one study to another,[25,26,27] but the message of underperforming CX efforts is clear. These same studies find that companies with leading-edge CX programs outperform their competitors.

If CX is indeed the competitive battlefield of 2023 and beyond, companies need to focus their efforts on CX programs that result in customer satisfaction in order to achieve a truly sustainable competitive advantage.

omnichannel
a strategy that delivers personalized and consistent customer experience across multiple channels.

The Importance of Customer Service and Satisfaction

The Impact of Improved Customer Service

Earlier this chapter discussed the declining customer satisfaction scores in the United States. While customer satisfaction is important in assessing the customer experience and the customer journey, there is also ample evidence that good customer service is important to customer satisfaction and retention. There is equally strong evidence that poor customer service hurts a business's bottom line. As Figure 4.7 illustrates, the cost of poor customer service and the failure to resolve issues costs companies their customers and affects the bottom line.

Figure 4.7   **The Financial Impact of Customer Service Problems** Source: "Linking Measures of Customer Satisfaction, Value, and Loyalty to Financial Performance," White Paper Series, 5(3). p. 2, 2004.

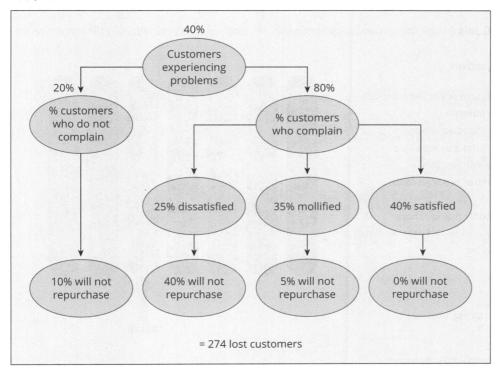

In fact, the Northridge group estimates that 54 percent of those receiving poor customer service will try a new brand, 51 percent would try another company and spend more money to receive excellent customer service, and 27 percent of customers will stop doing business with a company if they receive poor customer service. In addition, six of ten customers will tell others about a bad customer service experience.[28] Think about your own experience. If you have a great airline flight, do you tell your friends about it? Probably not. However, as Jeff Bezos has noted in a quotation earlier in this chapter, if you experience flight delays or other problems you are probably going to be broadcasting your experience on social media to all of your friends, followers, and their contacts. These numbers can add up quickly and negatively impact a brand's image.

What Are Firms' Customer Service Goals?

While all businesses have similar customer service goals to some degree, there are interesting differences. Retail scores much higher on customer retention and increasing sales from current customers as business goals. B2C consumer goods companies score higher on maintaining competitive position and especially on brand differentiation. B2B industries tend to empathize increasing sales from current customers and on converting prospects into customers. Both retail and B2B, where employees have direct contact with customers, focus on improving customer satisfaction. All these goals are important; none are easy to achieve (See Figure 4.8).

The knowledge needed to improve customer service is available; it is the business will that is often lacking.

Why Is Providing Excellent Customer Service So Difficult?

Providing an excellent customer service experience is becoming more difficult as time goes on. Technological change is part of the reason. The other part is the changing expectations of customers. Specific reasons include:

- The growing dominance of mobile. This book will further discuss the rise of mobile around the world, not only for communications but also for information

Figure 4.8 **Customer Service Goals** Source: https://www.oracle.com/webfolder/s/delivery_production/docs/FY15h1/doc9/Forbes -Report-Final-Web.pdf

Customer Service Business Objectives

	All respondents	Communications and telecome	Consumer goods and Manufacturing, process	Financial services and insurance	Retail	Technology	Wholesale distribution and Manufacturing, discrete
Retain existing customers and reduce customer turnover	53%	55%	55%	57%	65%	48%	44%
Increase sales from existing customers	40%	33%	43%	30%	61%	43%	43%
Convert more prospects/visitors into customers	35%	47%	28%	34%	30%	28%	39%
Maintain competitive position and/or market share	31%	29%	38%	26%	30%	38%	26%
Differentiate our brand from our competitors	30%	38%	38%	29%	28%	33%	21%
Produce more with less effort and/or reduced costs	25%	22%	28%	19%	13%	18%	36%
Improve employee satisfaction	24%	17%	18%	29%	28%	20%	28%
Improve competitive position and/or market share	23%	21%	25%	30%	17%	33%	20%
Improve number of customer advocates or brand ambassadors	19%	10%	10%	25%	15%	20%	25%
Improve products or service offering	19%	28%	18%	17%	11%	23%	18%

Retail

Key
- All respondents
- Communications and telecome
- Consumer goods and Manufacturing, process
- Financial services and insurance
- Retail
- Technology
- Wholesale distribution and Manufacturing, discrete

acquisition and increasingly for purchasing. It means that customers can ask for support from anywhere at any time. That demand puts a heavy burden on marketers for responsiveness.

- Customer expectations are high. Customers expect quick resolution of their issues in a single pleasant and productive service encounter. Many marketers simply are not set up to provide that level of service.

- Increase in self-service and crowd-based interactions. All customers have high expectations. Millennials and those younger prefer to have those expectations for immediacy and resolution satisfied by self-service. We all know that many marketers try for satisfactory self-service experiences, but many fall short.[29]

- Omnichannel *customer service is essential.* Customers may start shopping in one channel, switch to another channel for a final purchase, and request service in still another. One provider of omnichannel services says, "The number of customer service channels, including virtual agents, screen sharing, SMS, social media, and click-to-chat, has created unprecedented choice from a brand and customer perspective but creates significant challenges in terms of providing a truly integrated brand experience." Their research found that 73 percent of online shoppers think brands are making more effort in terms of omnichannel purchasing than omnichannel customer service. Even more, 78 percent say the brand's reputation for customer service is important when they are considering a purchase.[30]

In addition, the cost of providing service through various channels can differ significantly as shown in Table 4.1.

It probably comes as no surprise that the cost of live telephone support is the highest of all channels, with those served by a skilled technician the most expensive of all. Web-enabled services are less expensive even though they require a live agent. These channels offer more opportunities to sequence and prioritize contacts and for agents to multitask. Social media and email are significantly less expensive than the other channels. This information does not mean companies should automatically move to less expensive channels. Companies need to weigh the cost of providing service against the results that will be gained, always keeping the customer and customer satisfaction in mind.

In the face of all the challenges presented by consumer demands and differing channel costs, however, some companies are providing excellent customer service.

Who Are the Customer Service Champions?

Since 2010, media firm 24/7 Wall Street has partnered with Zogby Analytics each year to find out who those firms are. Table 4.2 shows the top firms, based on the number of "excellent"

Table 4.1 Cost of Customer Contact by Channel Source: https://www.textline.com/blog/dollars-and-sense-the-math-behind-support-communication-channels.

Customer Service Channel	Approx. Cost Per Contact
Call center technical support	$6 to 12 and higher
Live Chat	$5 and higher per contact
Text	.25 to $5
Email response	$1 and higher
Social Media	$1 and higher per interaction

Table 4.2 **Customer Service Hall of Fame—2020** Source: https://zogbyanalytics.com
/news/957-customer-service-hall-of-shame-fame

Rank	Company	% Excellence Score
1	Amazon	(88/12)
2	FedEx	(82/18)
3	Bed Bath and Beyond	(81/19)
4–7	Apple	(80/20)
4–7	Uber	(80/20)
4–7	AutoZone	(80/20)
4–7	Barnes and Noble	(80/20)
8–14	Google	(79/21)
8–14	YouTube	(79/21)
8–14	Netflix	(79/21)
8–14	UPS	(79/21)
8–14	Hilton	(79/21)
8–14	Chick-fil-A	(79/21)
8–14	Trader Joe's	(79/21)

responses received in their customer service ranking for 2020. Table 4.3 also shows the firms
that had the lowest rankings based on the number of "poor" responses received.

Several things stand out in the list of the best customer service providers. First is that
many of them reappear on the list year after year. Amazon has headed the list for several
years, while Apple and UPS are consistent repeaters. Mass merchandisers, fast food restaurants, and B2B firms are noticeably absent.

The list of worst customer service providers illustrates some of the same features.
Internet and Cable providers seem to be represented disproportionately on the list—Comcast

Table 4.3 **Customer Service Hall of Shame—2020**

Rank	Company	% Poor Score
1	DISH Network	(56/44)
2–3	Wells Fargo	(59/41)
2–3	DIRECTV	(59/41)
4	Spectrum	(60/40)
5	Sprint Nextel	(61/39)
6	AT&T U-verse	(62/38)
7	Super 8	(63/37)
8–9	Comcast	(64/36)
8–9	Days Inn	(64/36)
10	United Airlines	(65/35)

has been on list for six straight years. In fact, six of the ten worst providers are cable, satellite, or wireless companies.[31]

Prof. Praveen Kopalle provides some insights on the results for USA Today. While employee satisfaction is important in creating positive interactions with customers, he also points to the nature of various industries, with tech companies having to work very hard to keep demanding customers satisfied and food chains having to use customer service to compete with mass merchandisers who have lower prices. The product is also important, as in the cable and wireless industries where customers are notoriously fickle.[32]

What Do Consumers Want?

While developing a customer service strategy, it is important to focus on what customers really want. Data from the 2020 Customer Rage study sponsored by the University of Arizona sheds light on key issues. They found that:

- Sixty-six percent of households experienced a product or service problem in the last 12 months.
- More than half of complainants indicated that they get NOTHING when they complain.
- Rage is shared widely, with 14 percent of complainants sharing their experiences on social media an average of 16 times per year.
- Customers go elsewhere. Only one in eight less-than-satisfied customers will recommend the company at fault.[33]

Adding more detail to the description of what consumers want, The Harvard Business School found that they want resolution on the first contact. When they received that level of customer care, their willingness to continue purchasing (92 percent), to recommend (86 percent), and to spread positive WOM (88 percent) are all very high. The author asserts that it is not the number of customer service channels that is the issue, it is having channels that are perceived as convenient and that render quality service.[34]

A study by the Northridge group reiterates that speed of problem resolution is important to consumers (See Figure 4.9). The question of which channels and how many to offer continues to be a vexing one for companies. For one thing, channels differ in their ability to satisfy. Phone and online chat are the fastest channels for problem resolution and are most likely to solve issues within an hour. Note that both of those channels give access to

Figure 4.9 Phone and Online Chat are the Fastest Channels to Resolve Issues Source: https://www.northridgegroup.com /wp-content/uploads/2022/03/2021-State-of-Customer-Service-Experience-Report_The-Northridge-Group-Inc_.pdf

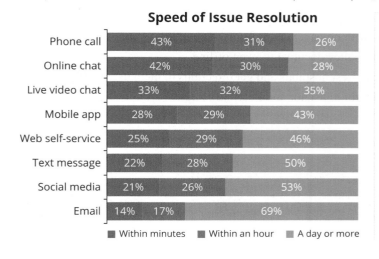

Speed of Issue Resolution

Channel	Within minutes	Within an hour	A day or more
Phone call	43%	31%	26%
Online chat	42%	30%	28%
Live video chat	33%	32%	35%
Mobile app	28%	29%	43%
Web self-service	25%	29%	46%
Text message	22%	28%	50%
Social media	21%	26%	53%
Email	14%	17%	69%

■ Within minutes ■ Within an hour ■ A day or more

Customers have the highest expectations of channels that provide human support. The number of customers reporting phone and online chat as the fastest channels for issue resolution increased 5–7% points since 2019.

Northridge Insight

The speed of online chat offers the opportunity to shift volume to channels that provide businesses higher productivity at a lower cost to serve.

a live agent. Self-service, email, and social media do not score as high. Many consumers say they want self-service channels and only turn to other channels when self-service does not satisfy them. While the preference for digital channels is increasing, particularly with labor shortages, forty-two percent of consumers still turn to the phone to resolve issues. These data indicate that while consumers are open to self-service channels, those options still need some improvements.

Remember that this is broad consumer data. If a firm's audience is made up of tech professionals, they might place greater emphasis on self-service. If the market is millennials or younger, the firm might explore what it takes to use social media customer service so that it satisfies them. Senior citizens might prefer phone and email channels.

The Evolution of Customer Service Strategy

The internet is not only a key reason why the expectations of both B2C and B2B customers are rising but also can be a way in which their expectations can be met cost-effectively. Figure 4.10 suggests an evolution in the way customer service is delivered that has the potential to improve service without increasing the cost of providing it. It involves, first, moving away from total reliance on *live service*, in-store service, and via telephone call centers, to *customer service provided on the internet*, either with or without direct human intervention. Whether live customer service is used or service over the web is the norm, notice that the first two stages are essentially reactive. The customer must ask; only then service will be forthcoming and then only if a customer service rep is available to provide the service.

Self-service is the next step and many customers are enthusiastic proponents. The reason may be that self-service is available on demand 24/7. Much attention has been given in recent years to customer self-service using *mobile apps*, but there are not a great many examples of companies doing mobile customer service, in the sense of resolving problems, and doing it well. An exception is the Allianz insurance company. The firm had a robust call center operation supporting customers of its travel insurance with medical information at home and abroad. In 2013, it introduced a free mobile app called TravelSmart based on its database of 2,000 hospitals in 129 countries, each accessible with one-touch dialing. The app allows users to manage travel insurance on their phones, access benefits, and contact customer service.

The app also includes a drug database with internationally recognized names for common drugs and first aid terms translated into 17 languages. There are emergency services numbers for 217 countries, which were also reached by one-touch dialing. The app also streamed travel news from USA Today.[35]

The company followed in 2014 with a more specialized Allianz MyHealth app. According to the company, features of the app include:

- First app that can photograph invoices for submission of international medical claims—with no paper claim forms to complete.
- Access to policy documents, even offline.
- Find the closest hospitals and get directions to them using GPS.
- Medical term translator and Pharmacy Aid.[36]

call centers
a department within an organization that handles telephone sales and/or service.

Figure 4.10   Customer Service Evolution

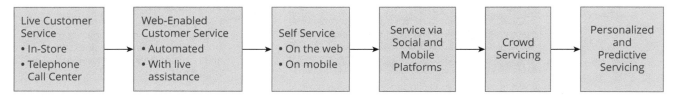

One year later BusinessWire reported that the app had been downloaded over 60,000 times and had been used to file more than 100,000 member insurance claims. Susan Landers, Head of Market Management at Allianz Worldwide Care said that its success had exceeded all expectations. In just one year, digital claims submissions had overtaken traditional snail mail submissions.

> "With a globally mobile client base, accustomed to operating in a digital landscape, it was a natural step for Allianz Worldwide Care to enhance its service offering for members. The early response to the MyHealth app is a clear demonstration of the demand for digital services and we will continue to provide even greater value and convenience to our clients through this exciting medium."[37]

The company has kept its word and has even expanded into markets like China.

The Allianz experience supports the results of a McKinsey study (Figure 4.11) that found digital customer service channels providing 33 percent more satisfaction than traditional channels alone, with combinations of digital and traditional channels scoring the next highest.

If both what consumers do and what they say in reply to a survey supports the transition to digital customer service, what are the other options? Customer service via *social media* is another option. Companies, including Dell, have long used elements of social media in dealing with customers, in some cases including customer problem resolution. Most companies, however, have been slow to jump on the bandwagon of digital customer service on social media. For one thing, expectations of customer service on social media platforms are high. Customer expectations can be summed up in two words— *accuracy and speed*—and not in any particular order. Both are essential. Typically, about 50 percent of users expect a response on social media in less than three hours,[38] which can be a tough metric to meet.

Figure 4.11   Digital Customer Service Channels Produce Highest Customer Satisfaction Source: https://www.mckinsey .com/capabilities/growth-marketing-and-sales/our-insights/why-companies-should-care-about-ecare.

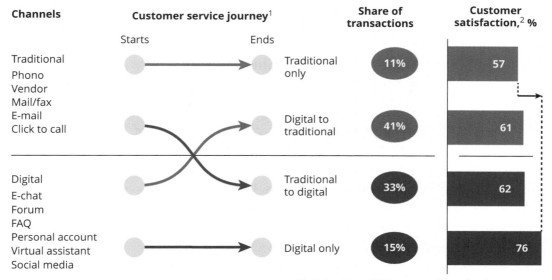

Exhibit

The more digital the journey, the higher the satisfaction.

Digital only = +33% over traditional only

[1]Telecom example, Western Europe; 4 service journey were identified based on an analysis of 11 touchpoints spanning traditional and digital channels. Fpr traditional-to-digital journeys (and vice versa), the first channel switch was used to allocate the journet.

[2]Respondents who ranked their satisfaction in the top 3 on a 7-point scale, where 7= most stisfied.

If customer service on social media has so much potential, and if it is directly linked to corporate profits, why do so many companies ignore it? There are two simple answers—it is not easy and it requires a significant investment of time and money. The response time of the fastest airline responders on Twitter, ranges from just over 4 minutes (JetBlue) to over an hour (United), quite a large discrepancy (See Table 4.4).

The social media customer service odyssey of JetBlue airlines has taken many years to reach the state of social media maturity that leads to its award-winning response quality and time, which we discuss in detail in the text *Social Media Marketing*.[39]

The bottom line? Social media customer service can and does work well, but it is neither easy, quick, nor cheap. It takes commitment and patience on the part of management to make it happen.

The next stage in Figure 4.10 is called *crowd servicing*. It is a social activity, but it is considered a separate stage because it represents a separate business model—Peer-to-peer (P2P) instead of B2B or B2C. It is not, however, a new customer service and support activity. For almost a decade we have called it a community, and there have been many successful examples of support communities.

There are a number of branded consumer communities. On the consumer side, craft and hobby firm Fiskars has a vibrant community of customers supporting one another in their crafting activities.[40] B2C marketers, such as IBM Developer, have been successful in creating communities whereby their customers answer each other's technical questions.

In addition to sites like Dell's Direct2Dell technologies blog, Cisco has a long-standing and highly effective set of over 20 forums, many managed by customers, which provide technical support to their users. (Cisco's customer support activities are also discussed in detail in *Social Media Marketing*.[41]) In fact, you would be hard-pressed to find a major tech firm today that did not have customer support communities of some kind.[42]

predictive analytics
using data, statistical algorithms, and machine-learning techniques to predict the likelihood of future outcomes or behaviors.

The highest level of customer service, at least as we can see it now, is to be able to genuinely *personalize customer service and/or to be able to predict customer need* and to deliver service in anticipation of that need. This has come to be called predictive analytics. One industry expert describes it as follows:

> *Predictive analytics is data mining technology that uses your customer data to automatically build a predictive model specialized for your business. This process learns from your organization's collective experience by leveraging your existing logs of customer purchases, behavior, and demographics.*[43]

Table 4.4 Airlines' Twitter Response Times

Short and tweet
Airlines with the fastest response to customers' tweets
Airlines with the fastest response times for North America[44]:
1. JetBlue — 4 minutes, 50 seconds
2. Virgin America — 4 minutes, 56 seconds
3. Alaska Air — 5 minutes, 10 seconds
4. Southwest Airlines — 6 minutes, 36 seconds
5. Air Canada — 9 minutes
6. WestJet — 10 minutes, 47 seconds
7. Spirit Airlines — 14 minutes, 15 seconds
8. American Air— 20 minutes, 19 seconds
9. Delta — 31 minutes, 4 seconds
10. United — 1 hour, 34 minutes

There are examples of predictive models in operation, mostly in e-commerce at this point. What about customer service? As this author searches for information on the omnichannel experience, chatbots pop up offering to answer questions on this topic or provide a referral to someone in sales or service who can answer the question.

There are several levels of analytics support for customer service. One is simple items of data like what page on the website is the customer currently looking at and whether we have resolved problems like this before and if so, how. It requires predictive models to be able to push relevant content to a visitor *before they ask*, anticipate when a particular customer on the website will call an agent, or predict the number of current customers who will call an agent. Each of these actions can make the corporate call center more efficient and less costly to run. These models can then provide a hyper-personalized customer experience and anticipation of customer service needs. The results of each interaction can be tracked to improve the model.[45]

Looking at live chat interactions, another type of model attempts to answer the question of whether the chat session successfully resolved the problem or if the customer will be calling back again within 24 hours. This model uses AI and machine learning to predict the emotional state of the customer. The objectives are to resolve the problem with the first contact and to understand which customers are unhappy and might abandon the brand if not given additional support. A human can make these judgments by looking at the transcript of a chat session but that is labor intensive and unlikely to happen in time to intervene if the problem resolution was not satisfactory. This is an example of substituting analytics for the judgment of the best human operators.[46]

It seems obvious that with a multitude of channels and technology solutions that aim to make them more effective and more efficient, making the decisions that lead to successful omnichannel customer service is difficult.

Omnichannel in the Digital Age: How to Make It Work

First, a definition of omnichannel customer service business may be in order. This definition covers the scope well:

> "businesses that have a formal strategy in place to deliver personalized and consistent customer experiences across multiple channels (e.g., phone, social media, web, mobile, and email) and devices (in-store, laptop, and smartphone)."[47]

While there is no doubt that this kind of omnichannel service is essential in today's marketplace, how does a company get there? There are a number of questions that need to be answered along that journey:

1. What channels do our customers want to use? A company has data on what channels their customers use for customer service, but what about the broader question of what channels they like to use in their everyday lives? What channels do they want to use for customer service? There is no real answer but to ask them, in a simple, straightforward way.

2. Which of these channels do we do well? Which of the ones we do not do well can we omit from the strategy? Customers want choice, but not all channels have to be, or perhaps should be, offered.

3. Are we using the appropriate self-service channels for our customers? Do the self-service tools provide a good experience to customers? Are the self-service tools such as a knowledge base that customers can access integrated with the call center so a customer can seamlessly move from one to the other?

4. Have we given the call center agents all the tools they need to do their jobs well, from the most effective call technology, to access to customer records, and to knowledge bases?

5. Have we made the experience a seamless whole, one in which customers are not subjected to long delays and to having to provide the same information over and over again?

6. Is some level of service available on all devices 24/7?

7. Are we getting consistently better at resolving issues on the first contact?[48]

Frank Pettinato, SVP and General Manager of Consumer Connexions of customer care company Telerx, summed it up: "We are moving to 24/7, like the news networks. Consumers are now expecting to be able to contact their brands anytime, anywhere, through any channel. Customers will always benefit from the powerful tools we can use to provide self-service because they can get a quick answer. That's not going to mitigate and solve all problems. With self-service tools such as FAQs and interactive voice response, our hope is that we can quickly answer simple questions for customers. But as questions become more complex, we do need to engage consumers via phone, email, chat, SMS/texting, or social media to make sure that we're responding to those detailed questions." He also says that millennials are expecting two-way communication via social media.[49]

Options for channels and tools are many and can be perplexing. Two customer service successes make some of the issues clearer.

The Evolution to Omnichannel at Eddie Bauer

Eddie Bauer established his retail store in 1920 in Seattle. An avid sportsman, he called his store Eddie Bauer's Sports Shop. By 1922, the store had a formal customer service creed with a delightfully old-fashioned tone and a ground-breaking guarantee policy. The company's stated creed is as follows: To give such outstanding quality, value, service, and guarantee that we may be worthy of high esteem. In addition, the company states that every item we sell will give complete satisfaction or may be returned for a full refund.[50]

This philosophy served Eddie Bauer well when he began a mail-order catalog in 1945. Successful mail-order retailers have always understood that since lacking an in-store experience can have important social dimensions, top-quality customer service was essential to mail-order success.

After Eddie Bauer's retirement in 1968, growth accelerated with the opening of new stores and the addition of specialty catalogs. The first international catalog was launched in Germany in 1993 followed by three stores and a catalog in Japan in 1994. There are now 370 stores worldwide. During the Christmas season of 2014, the company opened a pop-up store in New York City that featured a Twitter vending machine activated by @eddiebauer and #liveyouradventure. This was a centerpiece of the brand's return to its outdoor adventure heritage.

pop-up store (or pop-up shop) a temporary retail store. May also include a pop-up kiosk.

The company's 1996 website was one of the early entrants into the retail category and is now mobile-friendly. The website is easy-to-use with catalog quick order and store locator features that emphasize the multichannel nature of Eddie Bauer's business. The customer service page, which is accessible from every other page on the site, lists many self-help options, including order status and history (which allow customers to track their orders), delivery information, easy returns, size charts with instructions for measuring for a correct fit, gift certificates, watch repair, and monogramming services. It offers a number for 24-hour phone service as well as email and snail mail support.

Eddie Bauer is active on all the usual social media platforms—Facebook, YouTube, Twitter, Pinterest, Instagram, and TikTok. On Pinterest, it has a number of boards that feature products for specific activities. Its Instagram posts carry out the "Live Your Adventure" theme (#LiveYourAdventure) with adventure travel shots from around the globe. That is also the content strategy followed by its blog, which is accessible from its web page as Stories under the Guidepost tab. The blog features adventure content and ecology-related posts that have little or no direct product reference.

The same is true of the mobile app introduced in 2014. When introduced, it offered access to nine different activities at more than 10,000 locations in the United States. After answering questions about where the customers are, what they want to do, what skill level they have, how long they have, and how much they want to spend, the app presents a detailed guide to locations that match their requirements. It includes maps with directions, current weather conditions, and other information to make the trip safe and enjoyable. Each site features a star rating provided by outdoor experts. "With more and more people looking for an outdoor adventure to enjoy, whether it be in their own backyard or even for a few hours while traveling for work, they can now pull out their iPhone and with our app, easily find what they are looking for,"[51] PR Manager Molly McWhinnie said.

Continuing its progress to satisfying customer experience in early 2016, Eddie Bauer signed as a client with predictive analytics firm First Insight. Fashion is a business that has always succeeded as a result of the instinct and creativity of fashion designers and fashion buyers. Predictive analysis promises to help the company offer new products that have a high probability of success. In this case, the firm collects data from online customers over a two- to three-day period and feeds it into its analytic models. The firm says that results are 50–100 percent more accurate than in-store testing, can analyze more products, and are delivered with greater speed.[52]

The company has continued to focus on the customer experience and the customer journey. It recently engaged in a full website redesign project with a focus on the customer experience.[53] The company also has expanded its efforts to create more relevant content on social media channels and thereby increase engagement. Focusing on sustainability, rograms like the (Re)adventure allow customers to purchase like-new items or rent them to extend their life and keep them out of landfills. These service options are promoted on the website.

How Can Businesses Achieve Customer Service Goals?

The Eddie Bauer story illustrates several important points. First, never underestimate the importance of knowing your consumer. When self-service does not satisfy, the importance of good customer service representatives cannot be overstated. In order to create a good customer service team, reps must be hired with care, motivated, carefully trained and updated, and rewarded for success. Whether it is a field service force, an inside call center, or some combination of both, personnel issues are another major management task.

It is also important to keep in mind that technology is ever-changing and customer service operations must keep abreast of current trends. The next big thing in customer service may be the IoT and the data that is being provided by connected products (See Chapter 2). In both consumer and business markets, connected devices will monitor themselves and give forewarning of failure so preemptive service can be offered. Devices will also trigger suggestions about products and activities to customers.

Data from a wide variety of sources will drive customer service strategies. If companies can understand what customers are likely to do next, they can be ready with solutions and offers that fulfill customer needs.

Above all, interactions need to be easy, resolve problems on the first contact, and provide a practical and emotionally satisfying experience that generates loyalty and additional purchases. In the end, it is the simple but monumentally challenging goal of digital customer service.[54]

Summary

In this digital environment, the customer journey—both B2C and B2B—has changed. It is no longer a linear progression through a few identifiable stages. The customer journey is a process with stops, starts, feedback loops to earlier stages, and a variety of information sources other than the information provided by the brand or product itself. Marketers must make the effort to track customers throughout their journeys and to communicate with them in the context of their current journey stage.

Experiential marketing using techniques like marketing events has long been part of the marketer's toolkit. While important, these tools fall short of the concept of customer experience, which is made up of all interactions with the brand over all touchpoints over time. Customer experience is about people as well as technology, although technology can assist the marketer to understand and serve the customer.

Customer experience should be the focal point of marketing efforts. Providing excellent customer experience is not always easy, especially for the multichannel merchant. It is, however, essential because it is the competitive battlefield today and for the future.

Everyone—marketers and customers alike—agrees that excellent customer service is the key to customer retention, which in turn is the key to profitability. Unfortunately, seemingly everyone can report instances of poor customer service. Companies experience billions of dollars in lost sales each year as a result of poor customer service. These losses suggest that customer service is a business function that should not be overlooked.

Providing superior customer service is an important part of a CX strategy. Data from various sources emphasize that service is important to both customer loyalty and profits in B2C and B2B markets. The data also point out that customer service is a multifaceted construct that includes not only service recovery but also issues like timely delivery and provision of information that makes it easier for customers to use the product. Customers have shown a willingness to switch brands when customer service does not meet their expectations.

Anecdotal evidence helps us appreciate the complexity of the customer service issue and the necessity of a process of continuous improvement in order to develop and maintain excellent customer service. The process should include both making sure that business systems work and implementing technology to deliver service when appropriate. The examples in this chapter also stress the key role of both technological and organizational factors, such as training and supporting its people, in creating a successful customer service system for companies like Ritz-Carlton. Other companies rank high on the list of satisfaction through superior use of technology. For Amazon, in particular, its high customer service ratings translate to loyalty as measured by willingness to sign up for additional products or services. Developing the longer-term customer relationship seems to create superior customer satisfaction results to those of the telecommunications companies, who typically measure loyalty by the number of lost customers, called "churn," in the media industry.

Improving customer service is an information-driven activity. It requires segmenting and profiling customers, identifying and targeting high-value segments, developing differentiated service programs for different customer segments, and giving all segments seamlessly satisfying experiences appropriate to their values. Following this regimen is difficult for B2C marketers. It appears to be even more difficult for B2B marketers, few of whom rank high in customer service and satisfaction surveys.

In order to make customer service cost-effective, technology must be part of the equation. The level of customer satisfaction differs between different channels, with email ranking high and social media low. Perhaps that is because few companies appear to have the discipline to do social media customer service well. Customer communities are a time-honored channel for customer service, especially in the tech sector. Mobile apps are emerging as a potential customer service channel that offers convenience to both the customer and the business. Whatever channels are used; digital channels increasingly rank high in customer satisfaction. Marketers must make careful trade-offs between what customers need and the technology solutions they offer.

Analytics will also be part of the customer service equation. Predictive analysis can enable the brand to have a service available before the customer even knows he or she needs it.

Offering superb customer service and targeting customer segments with the appropriate level of service are both essential to marketing success in the global internet economy. The ability to deliver exceptional customer service as part of seamless CX has the potential to produce a sustainable competitive advantage that no other strategic marketing variable can match.

Discussion Questions

1. Explain your understanding of the term "customer experience."

2. True/False. A linear representation of the customer journey—whether B2C or B2B—represents the situation in the digital age. Why or why not?

3. Have you booked travel through a single site that was able to meet most of your requirements? Do you think this has improved the CX over what you see in Figure 4.3?

4. Is experiential marketing different from customer experience? If so, explain how.

5. Do you have any personal customer experiences that parallel Joshie at the Ritz-Carlton? If you cannot think of one, think about why it is hard to think of a customer experience that truly delighted you.

6. Why is it difficult to create a good customer experience in an omnichannel world?

7. Reference is made to exceptional customer service as the basis for sustainable competitive advantage. Do you agree with this perspective? Why or why not?

8. Moving all service delivery to the web, where customers can access it when they need it, is the most important aspect of building a successful customer service program. Do you agree or disagree? Why?

9. What channels do consumers find the most satisfactory/unsatisfactory at present?

10. Can you identify industries or specific businesses for which mobile customer service apps seem especially desirable?

11. Can you find other examples of companies that are actively using social networks for customer service?

12. How does customer service on social networks differ from customer service provided by communities?

13. How can predictive analysis improve the effectiveness of customer service?

14. Why is an omnichannel customer service strategy considered a necessity by many customer service experts?

15. Think about the organizational issues and the impact on the delivery of exceptional customer service. Have you encountered any customer service instances in which people in the same organization seemed to be giving you different information or advice? Why do you think this happened?

Endnotes

1. Asbjørn Følstad, and Knut Kvale, Customer Journeys: A Systematic Literature Review, *Journal of Service Theory and Practice* 28(2) (2018b): 196-227. https://doi.org/10.1108/jstp-11-2014-0261.

2. Yanika Tueanrat, Savvas Papagiannidis, and Eleftherios Alamanos, "Going on A Journey: A Review of the Customer Journey Literature," *Journal of Business Research* 125 (2021): 336-353, https://doi.org/10.1016/j.jbusres.2020.12.028.

3. "5 Ways The Shopper Journey Is Changing," accessed December 15, 2022, https://blog.luthresearch.com/ways-the-shopper-journey-is-changing.

4. Annmarie Hanlon, "Customer Journey Models <McKinsey Model & Race Framework>," *Smart Insights*, November 19, 2021, https://www.smartinsights.com/marketing-planning/marketing-models/mckinseys-consumer-decision-journey/.

5. Meta Business Help Center, "How to Set Up and Install a Meta Pixel," https://www.facebook.com/business/help/952192354843755?id=1205376682832142

6. Alex Rawson, Duncan Ewan, and Conor Jones, "The Truth About Customer Experience," *Harvard Business Review*, August 18, 2014, https://hbr.org/2013/09/the-truth-about-customer-experience.

7. Katherine N. Lemon, and Peter C. Verhoef, (2016). Understanding the Customer Experience throughout the Customer Journey, *Journal of Marketing: AMA/MSI Special Issue.* 80 (November 2016): 69-96. 1547-7185 (electronic) 69 DOI: 10.1509/jm.15.0420.

8. "Inside Levi's New 'Nextgen' Retail Store | Vogue Business," accessed December 15, 2022, https://www.voguebusiness.com/consumers/levis-doubles-down-on-dtc-launches-experiential-nextgen-stores-in-the-us.

9. Zarina de Ruiter, "3 Lessons from Amazon's Jeff Bezos to Improve Your Customer Experience Strategy," CX Network, October 28, 2022, https://www.cxnetwork.com/cx-experience/articles/article-customer-experience-lessons-from-amazon-jeff-bezos.

10. The American Customer Satisfaction Index, December 13, 2022, https://www.theacsi.org/.

11. "Supermarkets," The American Customer Satisfaction Index, June 20, 2022, https://www.theacsi.org/industries/retail/supermarkets/.

12. Robert Klara, "Why Do so Many People Go Crazy for Wegmans?," *Adweek* (February 12, 2016), https://www.adweek.com/brand-marketing/why-do-so-many-people-go-crazy-wegmans-169396/.

13. Ibid.

14. Customer domain, accessed December 15, 2022, http://www.nunwood.com/?portfolio=8-wegmans-us-customer-experience-excellence-report-2015.

15. Jeanne Bliss, "Is Your Trusting Cup Half Full or Half Empty?," WordofMouth.org, January 10, 2013, https://wordofmouth.org/blog/is-your-trusting-cup-half-full-or-half-empty/.

16. EcommerceStrategyChina.com, "The New Retail Concept Raised by Jack Ma," The New Retail Concept Raised by Jack Ma, accessed December 15, 2022, https://www.ecommercestrategychina.com/column/what-jack-mas-new-retail-looks-like.

17. Clint Fontanella, "10 Chatbots That Will Revolutionize Your Customer Service," *HubSpot Blog* (March 4, 2022), https://blog.hubspot.com/service/customer-service-bots.

18. Team CXP Asia, "Masterful Customer Experience: The Tale of Joshie the Giraffe," June 3, 2020, https://cxp.asia/2020/05/29/masterful-customer-experience-the-tale-of-joshie-the-giraffe/.

19. Mitra Sorrells, "Q&A: Ritz-Carlton Founder Horst Schulze on Tech's Role in Luxury Hotels," *PhocusWire* (September 3, 2019), https://www.phocuswire.com/q-and-a-ritz-carlton-founder-horst-schulze.

20. Chad Engelgau, "2023 Marketing Trends – The Year of Customer Experience," Acxiom, January 4, 2023, https://www.acxiom.com/blog/.

21. "10 Key Marketing Trends for 2016 - Silverpop <PDF> - Free Online Publishing," *AuthorZilla*, accessed January 3, 2023, https://authorzilla.com/r0v0/10-key-marketing-trends-for-2016-silverpop.html.

22. Phil Schraeder, "Going beyond 'Right Consumer, Right Time, Right Place,'" MarTech, August 23, 2021, https://martech.org/going-beyond-right-consumer-right-time-right-place/.

23. Erik Lindecrantz, Madeleine Tjon Pian Gi, and Stefano Zerbi, "Personalizing the Customer Experience: Driving Differentiation in Retail," McKinsey Company (April 28, 2020), https://www.mckinsey.com/industries/retail/our-insights/personalizing-the-customer-experience-driving-differentiation-in-retail.

24. Lynn Hunsaker, "Customer Experience for the Future – Key #1: Context Is King," Experience Leadership, February 2, 2022, https://clearaction.com/customer-experience-for-the-future-context-is-king/.

25. "What Is Omnichannel CX and How Does It Benefit Your Business," loginradius Blog, accessed December 16, 2022, https://blog.loginradius.com/growth/what-is-omnichannel-cx/.

26. Bruce Temkin, Moira Dorsey, and Talia Quaadgras, "The State of CX Management, 2021," XM Institute, August 5, 2022, https://www.xminstitute.com/research/state-cx-management-2021/.

27. "Lessons from the Leading Edge of Customer Experience Management - SAS," accessed December 16, 2022, https://www.sas.com/content/dam/SAS/en_us/doc/whitepaper2/hbr-leading-edge-customer-experience-mgmt-107061.pdf.

28. Northridge Thought Leader, "The Cost of Poor Customer Service <Infographic>," The Northridge Group, November 11, 2019, https://www.northridgegroup.com/blog/the-cost-of-poor-customer-service-infographic/.

29. Help Scout, "The Future of Customer Service: 10 Trends to Watch - Help Scout," Help Scout: Shared Inbox, Help Center, & Live Chat Software, June 20, 2022, https://www.helpscout.com/helpu/future-of-customer-support/.

30. "The Omnichannel Customer Service Gap - d16cvnquvjw7pr.Cloudfront.net," accessed December 16, 2022, https://d16cvnquvjw7pr.cloudfront.net/resources/whitepapers/Omnichannel-Customer-Service-Gap.pdf.

31. Written by Zogby, "Customer Service Hall of Shame/Fame," Zogby Analytics - Home, accessed December 16, 2022, https://www.zogbyanalytics.com/news/957-customer-service-hall-of-shame-fame.

32. Michael B. Sauter, Thomas C. Frohlich, and Sam Stebbins, "2015's Customer Service Hall of Fame," *USA Today* (Gannett Satellite Information Network, August 2, 2015), https://www.usatoday.com/story/money /business/2015/07/24/24-7-wall-st-customer-service-hall-fame/30599943/.

33. "2020 National Customer Rage Study," Customer Care Measurement & Consulting (CCMC), November 15, 2022, https://www.customercaremc.com/insights/national-customer-rage-study/2020-national-customer-rage-study/.

34. Cynthia Grimm, "When to Offer Fewer Customer Service Channels," *Harvard Business Review*, September 3, 2020, https://hbr.org/2015/05/when-to-offer-fewer-customer-service-channels.

35. Allianz Global Assistance USA, "Allianz Global Assistance Releases Upgraded TravelSmart Mobile App," Allianz Global Assistance Releases Upgraded TravelSmart Mobile App, June 26, 2018, https://www.prnewswire.com/news -releases/allianz-global-assistance-releases-upgraded-travelsmart-mobile-app-300568876.html.

36. "Allianz Worldwide Care Introduces the Fastest and Easiest Way to Submit International Medical Claims," *Business Wire*, August 19, 2014, https://www.businesswire.com/news/home/20140819005413/en/Allianz -Worldwide-Care-Introduces-the-Fastest-and-Easiest-Way-to-Submit-International-Medical-Claims.

37. "One Year On, Allianz Worldwide Care's MyHealth App Hits 100,000 Member Claim Submissions," October 15, 2015, Business Wire, https://www.businesswire.com/news/home/20151015006185/en /One-Year-on-Allianz-Worldwide-Care%E2%80%99s-MyHealth-App-Hits-100000-Member -Claim-Submissions.

38. "Social Media Customer Service," Khoros, accessed December 16, 2022, https://khoros.com/blog/social-media -customer-service-stats.

39. Debra L. Zahay et al., "Social Media Marketing: A Strategic Approach" (Singapore: Cengage Learning Asia Pte Ltd, 2023).

40. "Fiskateers Case Study: How a Social Community Became a Veritable Sales Force – What's next Blog," BL Ochman RSS, accessed December 16, 2022, https://www.whatsnextblog.com/fiskateers_how_a_social _community_became_a_veritable_sales_force/.

41. Zahay, Debra, Mary Lou Roberts, Janna Parker, Melissa S. Barker, and Donald I. Barker. Chapter 2 in *Social Media Marketing: A Strategic Approach,* 3rd ed., (Boston, MA, Cengage Learning, 2023).

42. Harold, Franny. "4 Examples of Great Online Communities and What Makes Them Work," Khoros, accessed December 16, 2022, https://khoros.com/blog/great-online-communities.

43. R. Scott Raynovich, "The Future of Customer Service: Predictive, Personalized " Machine Learning Times," Machine Learning Times, accessed December 16, 2022, https://www.predictiveanalyticsworld.com /machinelearningtimes/future-customer-service-predictive-personalized/3383/.

44. Bill Hethcock, "These Airlines Respond to Your Twitter Rants and Raves the Fastest," Dallas Business Journal, accessed Jan 11, 2018, https://www.bizjournals.com/dallas/news/2018/01/11/these-airlines-respond-to-your -twitter-rants-and.html.

45. Surya Ranjan Pandita, "4 Ways in Which Data Analytics Can Improve Customer Service," ClicData, September 30, 2022, https://www.clicdata.com/blog/ways-data-analytics-improve-customer-service/.

46. Micah Solomon, "Omnichannel Customer Experience: Expert Systems, 360 Degree Views and Ai," *Forbes* (May 4, 2015), https://www.forbes.com/sites/micahsolomon/2015/04/08/omnichannel -customer-experience-how-a-360-degree-view-of-customer-care-can-help/?sh=1d1de9ebb764.

47. Omer Minkara, "Executive Summary: Four Steps to Smart Omni-Channel Customer Service," p. 3, March 2016, https://www.verint.com/Assets/resources/resource-types/analyst-documents/aberdeen_12038-kb -omnichannel.pdf.

48. Jacob Firuta, "6 Things You Need to Know about Multi Channel Customer Service," Success by LiveChat, accessed December 16, 2022, https://www.livechat.com/success/multi-channel-customer-service/.

49. Forbes Insights, "Modern Customer Service," 19, 2015, http://images.forbes.com/forbesinsights/StudyPDFs /Oracle-ModernCustomerService-Report.pdf.

50. "Eddie Bauer Help Center," accessed December 16, 2022, https://www.eddiebauer.com/service/help?a=Return -Policy---id--07PyLfheTSijq4wK8-ajxg&campid=SHQ+Lapsed+Purchaser.

51. Rachel Lerman, "Eddie Bauer's foray into mobile lets you build an adventure," *Bizjournals.com*, August 8, 2014, https://www.bizjournals.com/albany/morning_call/2014/08/eddie-bauers-foray-into-mobile-lets-you -build-an.html.

52. Arthur Zaczkiewicz, "Eddie Bauer, Caleres Ink Partnership Deals with First Insight," *WWD*, January 13, 2016, https://wwd.com/business-news/technology/eddie-bauer-first-insight-deal-10313140/.

53. Steve Nicholas, "Eddie Bauer's Conversion Keeps on Climbing with Customer Hijacking Prevention," Namogoo, July 27, 2021, https://www.namogoo.com/resources/case-study/eddie-bauers-conversion-keeps-on -climbing-with-customer-hijacking-prevention/.

54. Help Scout, "The Future of Customer Service: 10 Trends to Watch - Help Scout," Help Scout: Shared Inbox, Help Center, & Live Chat Software, June 20, 2022, https://www.helpscout.com/helpu/future-of-customer -support/.

Chapter 5

Measuring and Evaluating Digital Marketing Programs

Learning Objectives

By the time you complete this chapter, you will be able to:

1 Discuss the various marketing metrics that are available for websites, mobile apps, social media, and video campaigns.

2 Summarize the process of website performance.

3 Define the key traffic, audience, campaign metrics, and the purpose of each.

4 Discuss the importance of Google Analytics and segmenting visitor activity.

5 Identify the differences between web metrics and key performance indicators (KPIs).

Like everything else in the digital space, the role of data and metrics has been rapidly evolving. Chapter 4 discussed customer data and the importance it plays in guiding strategy and digital marketing programs. Throughout the book, we have emphasized the importance of the insights data can produce in making marketing effective. However, the process is not automatic; the correct metrics must be selected, analyzed, and practical insights derived from them. Digital marketers subscribe to the Quality Management maxim that "What gets measured gets managed."

Producing insights from customer data has always been a difficult process. Four trends have upped the bar even further.

1. The amount of data is increasing rapidly, in numbers that are too big to comprehend. EMC predicted that there would be 44 zettabytes (ZB) (a zettabyte is computed as 2^{70} bytes, or 1 sextillion) of data produced by 2020.[1] However, because of the COVID-19 pandemic, more people were "forced" online so that they could work from home and as of 2021, there is an estimated 94 zb thanks to the increase in the internet of things (IoT) devices.[2]

Zettabytes (ZB)
another iteration of byte; this is multiplication by the 7th power of 1,000 or 10^{21}.

2. A phenomenon called "data democratization" or "data under glass" has occurred. Infor, a data management company, describes this as "the process of expanding business information and the tools to analyze it out to a much broader audience than traditionally has had access. In most companies, the IT department has long been the gatekeeper of business intelligence (BI) and analytical tools, not because of a desire to control information but out of necessity."[3]

That means data and the necessary analytic tools are available to small businesses as well as to all corporate employees who need to use it. In the process, data *per se* has become less of a competitive advantage—every business has it and tools to use it are available.[4]

3. By all accounts there are too few data scientists to deal with the massive amounts of data produced and hoarded by businesses.

4. The analytical skills of managers are improving, but they cannot keep up with the increasing volume and sophistication of data analytics. That implies that they are often making business decisions on the basis of information they do not completely understand.[5]

The *Harvard Business Review* adds:

a. Data comes from a variety of sources (e.g., website, social media) in a variety of formats and it is difficult to integrate into a single database that can be analyzed.

b. Unstructured data can have limits to its use. It is best to first use new data for old purposes to understand how it can and cannot be useful.

c. Correlation does not imply causation. Run field experiments to understand causality. It is often a mistake to try to infer causality from correlations.

d. Managers tend to underestimate the amount of skilled human judgment that is needed to make data useful. Someone has to understand what customers really want in order to produce insights that work.[6]

Marketing is responsible for the use of a large swath of business data. This data is essential to proving that marketing expenditures are worthwhile. Demonstrating the effectiveness of marketing expenditures turns out to be another difficult task.

Demonstrating Marketing Effectiveness Through Metrics

From the beginning of this book, we have discussed the important role that customer information plays in all aspects of digital marketing. Not all digital marketing functions are created equal, however, when it comes to being able to demonstrate ROI and the importance of ROI data in securing marketing budgets.

Figure 5.1a shows marketers' evaluations of their ability to measure ROI from various channels, with social media and video leading the way. At the bottom are a variety of functions including streaming audio, native advertising, and podcasts. According to the CMO survey, on average, marketing acquisition budgets are about 15 percent larger than retention budgets.[7] It's easier to count the noses of new customers than to determine whether a customer doesn't repurchase or leaves. Marketers and their IT counterparts are investing into data analytics quite heavily as there are more

Figure 5.1a   How Well Can Marketers Measure ROI from Digital Channels?
Source: https://www.insiderintelligence.com/content/brands-confidence-measuring-roi

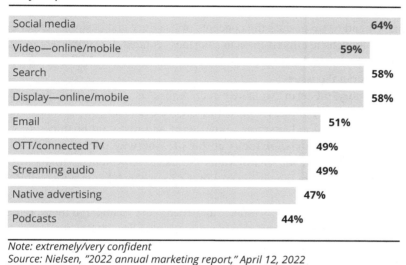

Brand marketers worldwide who are confident in their company's ability to measure ROI for paid media channels, by media, Jan 2022

% of respondents

Social media	64%
Video—online/mobile	59%
Search	58%
Display—online/mobile	58%
Email	51%
OTT/connected TV	49%
Streaming audio	49%
Native advertising	47%
Podcasts	44%

Note: extremely/very confident
Source: Nielsen, "2022 annual marketing report," April 12, 2022

ways to measure the metrics of newly acquired customers with marketing technology (MarTech) (Figure 5.1b).

We will break this task down into several distinct types of evaluation—website effectiveness, traffic and audience data, and campaign effectiveness on the internet and the mobile web. These metrics will be organized according to the stages of the customer journey.

Figure 5.1b   How Important Is ROI to Securing Marketing Budgets? Source: https://cmosurvey.org/wp-content/uploads
/2022/02/The_CMO_Survey-Highlights_and_Insights_Report-February_2022.pdf

Data analytics investments skyrocket to top priority, with digital marketing investments increasing across the board

What investments did your company make to improve the performance of your digital marketing activities over the last year?

Investment	% Reporting Yes	% Change Since Feb-21
Data analytics	77.5%	+37.2%
Optimizing of company website	74.0%	+0.3%
Digital media and search	70.9%	+9.1%
Marketing technology systems or platforms	69.8%	+29.7%
Direct digital marketing (e.g., email)	68.2%	+19.0%
Online experimentation and/or A/B testing	47.3%	+4.2%
Managing privacy issues	35.3%	+23.9%
Machine learning and automation	26.4%	+29.4%
Improving our app	24.4%	NA*

 Insights

Although investments in digital marketing have increased across the board, data-related activities experienced the largest growth. Data analytics, in particular, grew 37.2% from 56.5% of companies investing in February 2021 to 77.5% of companies investing today. Larger companies are investing the most in data analytics, with 91.9% of companies with more then 10K+ employees making the investment. With data collection and purchasing becoming more complex, companies are increasing their investments in capabilities to analyze, store/manage, and automate their data. MarTech stacks are becoming more complex by the minute and companies are investing in the technologies necessary to keep up.

Then we will look more briefly at evaluating the effectiveness of social media and video efforts. Those metrics are organized according to a model of social media effectiveness. Throughout all of this runs the basic theme of setting measurable objectives, choosing the right metrics, and analyzing them to gain insights that will improve future programs.

Ways to Evaluate Website Effectiveness

In Chapters 4 and 6, we discuss the concepts of usability and customer experience, both of which lead to website effectiveness in a business context. It is important to take a high-level view of that term, because it can have different but equally important meanings. Figure 5.2 lays out the issue.

Unfortunately, the term "website effectiveness" is strategically appropriate when used in three different ways, as shown in Figure 5.2. The first one is *site usability*, which is essential to good customer experience and resultant business success. This usability is the way *the visitor* looks at the site, the way they gauge its ease of use and its value to them. If the visitor finds the usage experience satisfactory, the site has a greater chance of being successful in the long run. That is why usability testing is so important.

The second perspective is "traffic," "audience," and "campaign measurement"—the terms used to describe metrics that provide effectiveness data vital to marketing programs. We will discuss those measurement techniques in detail in this chapter because they are measures of business performance.

The third perspective is that of *site performance*. This is the data that site technicians need to gauge and improve site performance. Even though it is the responsibility of the technical side of the web team, marketers should be familiar with the basic approaches, which we will cover along with other metrics.

Enterprise Metrics for Evaluating Websites

Site metrics fall into two basic categories—measures of business performance and measures of site performance. These business effectiveness measures provide data by which marketers can judge the success of marketing programs both on and off

Figure 5.2 **Perspectives on Website Effectiveness** Source: © Cengage Learning 2013

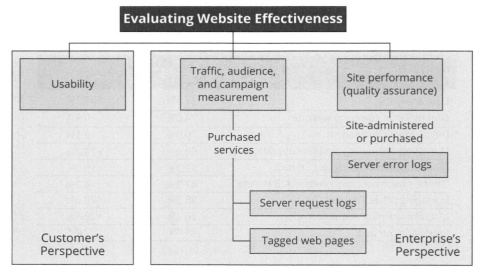

Table 5.1   Examples of Data-driven Companies Source: https://unscrambl.com /blog/data-driven-companies-examples/

McDonald's (MCD): In 2019, MCD paid $300 million USD for the firm Dynamic Yield to help them sort through all of their 68 million purchases made per day, around the globe. MCD is encouraging app usage to increase personalization for each consumer. They are also analyzing purchases as they relate to the time of day, weather, and local events.

Netflix: This firm is often viewed as being on the cutting-edge of data pioneering. By analyzing 30 million videos played, 4 million subscriber ratings, and 3 million searches, they were able to determine what makes a blockbuster new series. In doing so, they created shows such as the reboot of "Arrested Development" and "House of Cards," both of which are blockbusters in their own right.

Coca-Cola: With over 108 million followers on Facebook, 2.8 million on Instagram, and 225k on TikTok, Coca-Cola wanted to see how they could better serve their followers by creating more personalized ad experiences. They analyzed the when, where, and how their followers mention them on social media platforms and then personalized their ad experiences based on the findings. The results helped increase click-throughs that drive their followers to their website.

---

the website. They are key to managing internet marketing activities and demonstrating return on investment (ROI) on those activities. See Table 5.1 for example of data driven companies.

There are many other metrics available to and used by digital-first companies. These examples highlight just some of the metrics and the direct impact they have on business decisions. It also suggests the importance of integrated metrics solutions that can provide views of not only the website but also internet and mobile advertising, email campaigns, and related online activities like keyword searches.

Business effectiveness measures are vital to marketing managers. We will devote the majority of this chapter to discussing the source, nature, and use of detailed business effectiveness measures, discussing first websites on the internet and mobile web, mobile app, social media, and video metrics. If the firm has a separate mobile site, the metrics will be much the same as those accessed through a desktop website. App metrics, however, are different and will be discussed later in the chapter.

First, however, let us take a brief look at measures of website performance. Measures of site performance give directions to the technicians who maintain the site. In the words of the website development process, this means tuning the site to maintain and improve the manner in which it functions. While the performance measures are not the job of marketing, smooth site performance is essential to Customer Experience (CX) and marketing managers should be attentive to them.

Website Performance

The "Old" Way- Loading from a Single Physical Server

Figure 5.3 shows a report of the performance of a single web page—the page itself—and each file on it. This is the "old" way of doing things and the way that many websites still operate if they have not migrated to cloud computing. Timing starts from the time the URL (www.alertsite.com in this example) is translated into the IP (Internet Protocol)

IP (Internet Protocol) address a number assigned to each device that uses the internet.

Figure 5.3   Sample Web Page Performance Report—The "Old" Way, When Content Is Pulled from a Single Server Source: Cengage

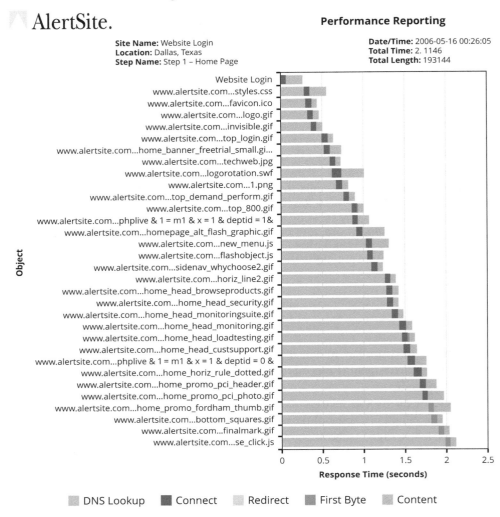

DNS (Domain Name System)
a database in which human readable domain names are located and translated into Internet Protocol (IP) addresses. The internet's DNS is similar to a phone book and manages the mapping between domain names and IP addresses (numbers).

hit
any file, including a graphic, that is requested from a server.

address which in turn triggers the DNS (Domain Name System) lookup on the legend at the bottom of the chart. The more detailed printed report (not shown) indicated that it required 0.0024 seconds to look up the IP address on the network. Then the page starts loading, file by file. Each file loaded is measured as a hit. Please note that "hit" is a slightly outdated term, though people still use it. The more updated term is "page views." For each file, the web administrator can see how many seconds it took to connect with the file, how long it took for the first byte of information to load, and how long it took for content to load. Notice that many of the files are graphics—.gifs or .jpegs—and do not have significant text content. It took 1.3902 seconds for the page to load completely, which would be acceptable to most users. Reports like this are available in real-time, that is, the web administrator can call up a status report for any page or many other elements of web functionality at any time.

Website performance data is essential to the web technicians whose job it is to make sure the site functions at an optimal level. Marketers should also be concerned about the smooth functioning of the site because it has direct impact on their customers.

The "New" Way- Cloud Hosting Increases Web Performance

Web performance, bounce rates, and load times are statistics that digital marketers and IT departments investigate regularly. As cloud computing has become more popular, the time required for a page to load has decreased. This is because the user does not have to pull the files directly from a single server (or computer) where the content is stored. Unlike traditional hosting, cloud hosting solutions are not deployed on a single server. Instead, the website or application is housed on a network of connected virtual and physical cloud servers, ensuring greater flexibility and decreased load times. Since the data is in the "cloud" the user can connect to the content faster, which decreases bounce rates. When a platform has migrated from a traditional hosting server to the cloud, the webpage performance increases because the requesting device (i.e., your phone, laptop) does not have to travel as far a distance to receive the information. The "old" way of having data saved on a single physical server required that the data traveled the hundreds or thousands of miles to access the server where the data was housed. Website performance is akin to daily housekeeping for digital marketers. It is necessary but not particularly exciting. The real excitement occurs when there are digital, social media, and mobile promotional campaigns to monitor.

Page Load Times and Bounce Rates

One statistic that websites continue to monitor is the page load time. The faster a page loads, the more likely the visitor is to stay on the page. The inverse is also true. The longer a page takes to load, the more likely the visitor is to exit the page. See Figure 5.4 below that depicts load time and likelihood for a consumer to "bounce" or exit the page.

Figure 5.4   **Page Load Time and Rate of Bounce Rate** Source: https://websitesetup.org/news/website-load-time-statistics/

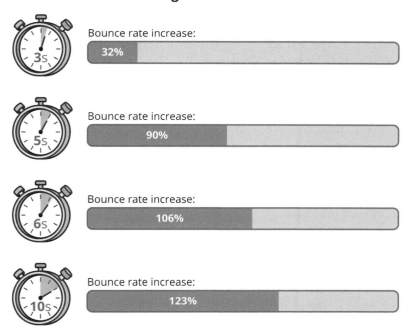

The Effect of Page Load Time From 1s to...

Bounce rate increase:
3s — 32%

Bounce rate increase:
5s — 90%

Bounce rate increase:
6s — 106%

Bounce rate increase:
10s — 123%

Table 5.2 Seven Factors that Influence Website Load Time Source: https://websitesetup.org/news/website-load-time-statistics/

Many elements affect page load time. The time it will take for your page to load depends on not only your internet connection and browser, but also your web hosting service, file types, and more.

Internet connection: The type of internet connection you have and the speed of that connection can directly affect the time it takes for a page to load—even if that page is well-optimized.

Web hosting service and uptime: The web hosting company you choose can have a huge impact on your website's load time. If your host server is slow, your whole website will be slow. When looking for a web hosting service, look for one with an uptime of 99.5 percent or greater.

Browser: The browser your customers use can also affect page speed. Older versions of browsers may have difficulty loading larger image files and code. Make sure you are always on the latest version of your favorite browser.

Large file types (i.e., images and video): Generally, the larger the file size the more difficult it will be to load. This is typically seen with images, video, and animation. It's essential to take the time to properly optimize and compress these larger files as much as possible.

Plugins: While plugins (like WordPress or Shopify plugins) are a great way to add functionality to a website, having too many can hurt your page load time. If you do choose to use a plugin, make sure it's optimized or built to improve page load time. If not, you risk slowing your site down.

Heavy CSS and JavaScript: Your website is comprised of JavaScript and CSS files. If these files are not optimized properly, they can slow down your website.

Cache clearance: The computer you or your customers use can also have an impact on page speed. The cache on your computer stores information from the various websites you visit, making it easier for those websites to load once you visit them again. However, if you clear your cache often, you'll notice these websites load slower.

In Figure 5.4, we can see the load times for a webpage when it's being housed on a cloud hosting platform. The same operations occur in the "new" versus the "old" way, but the distance to gather the data has decreased. For instance, let's assume you are located in Chicago and are trying to view a website for Game Stop. The Game Stop Headquarters is located in Grapevine, TX. So, the "old" way of websites would require that your browser contact the server in Grapevine, TX—about 1000 miles away from Chicago—so that you could interact with the data on your screen. However, with cloud computing, the firms that own the cloud servers (i.e., Microsoft Azure, Amazon's AWS) have multiple servers all over the world that house the information that your company uploads, so a visitor is able to access the content from the closest server to them. This decreases the time to load the webpage, decreases bounce rates, and increases page performance. According to the folks at websitesetup.org, there are seven factors that influence page load times. Please see Table 5.2 for the factors that influence website load time.

Collecting Website Traffic, Audience, and Campaign Data

Before we address the actual metrics there are two important issues to consider. First is the issue of quantitative versus qualitative data. Second is the discussion of tagging and cookies since these aspects of technology are crucial to campaign tracking.

The Issue of Quantitative Versus Qualitative Data

Data is basic to all marketing research as well as to metrics. Numerical data has benefits, especially in terms of model development like predictive targeting models. Qualitative, or nonnumeric, data has the potential benefit of producing an understanding of buyer motives and perceptions. Table 5.3 shows basic types of both quantitative and qualitative data. Topics like why people buy (buyer motivations-qualitative) and customer product use (quantitative) are familiar from marketing research. Traffic reporting is a class of metrics specific to the internet. The principle of counting quantitatively versus probing for understanding still applies. The web is awash with quantitative data as we will discuss in this chapter. Qualitative data can be collected online as well as offline using tools such as virtual focus groups and panel reporting.

While the distinction between the two types of data is clear, it is not now, nor has it ever really been, a choice between one type of data and the other. Anmol Rajpurohit from data science firm KDnuggets says that as Customer Experience Management becomes the paramount concern of CMOs, "there is an increasing need for holistic understanding of customer experience across the complete sale cycle. This can be achieved only through deploying qualitative analytics and integrating it with quantitative analytics to provide 360-degree data analysis."[8] This should not be taken as a recommendation for which comes first—qualitative or quantitative. There are good arguments for doing qualitative first to understand the questions for quantitative research. There are equally good arguments, especially among digital marketers who already have a trove of quantitative data, for following quantitative data with qualitative in order to unlock deeper meanings.

Although the argument for using both kinds of data for a thorough understanding of the customer is hard to refute, the data collected on the web itself is primarily quantitative and it is the main focus of this chapter. Social media and specialized data collection tools, however, do bring qualitative data into play and will be discussed later in the chapter. For the moment, however, we stay with quantitative data and a discussion of tags and how they are employed to collect user data.

Tagged Web Pages

Tags have been mentioned in a number of chapters, among them the discussion of following customers through their purchase journey in Chapter 4. The terms tags, pixels, and beacons are synonymous and do not represent a new technology; they have been in use since the beginning of the commercial internet. Tags and tagged web pages seem to be the most used terms today.

Table 5.3   **Basic Types of Data** Based on: https://blog.kissmetrics.com/qualitative-quantitative-analytics/

Quantitative	Qualitative
Traffic reporting	Why people buy
Customer product use	Perception of brand value proposition
Customer activities in various stages of the purchase journey	How customers talk about the product

Table 5.4 Examples of Data Made Available by Tagged Web Pages

Source: Adapted from http://ems.eos.nasa.gov/NI82/UnicaNetInsight821PageTagGuide.pdf.

Information About the Visitor (often called "Dimensions" in the metrics literature)	Metrics Produced for the Marketer
<ul><li>Page</li><li>Entry page</li><li>Exit page</li><li>Referrer</li><li>Browser</li><li>Platform</li><li>Geographic data (Country, City, Time zone, Organization, etc.)</li><li>Date</li><li>Time</li><li>Day of the week</li></ul>	<ul><li>Number of visitors</li><li>Number of views</li><li>Number of visits</li><li>Number of new visitors</li><li>Number of repeat visitors</li><li>Total time online</li><li>Average viewing time</li><li>Average visit duration</li><li>Views per visit</li></ul>

Tagged web pages
a technique in which a snippet of code is included on a web page that tracks data about users' activity on the web page. As an example, Google Analytics, uses JavaScript to track a visitor's activity across a website.

cookies
a few lines of code that a website or advertising network places on a user's computer to store data about the user's activities on the site. Cookies can be classified as either first-party or third-party depending on how they are used.

first-party cookies
small text file stored in the user's browser that are created by a website when a user visits. First-party cookies are designed only to be used by the website that created them (not shared across websites).

third-party cookies
use embedded references that point to other websites that share cookie information across websites.

A tag, then, is a few lines of code that are placed on each page of the site that is to be tracked. Tagged web pages allow marketers to track visitors as they move from one page of the site to another. It also allows tracking events that occur on the page, like changing a piece of data in a form or selecting an item from a drop-down menu.[9]

Table 5.4 gives an example of the visitor data that can be captured using tagged pages, and the resulting metrics that are made available to marketers. The metrics aggregate the data from many visitors into information that marketers need.

In order to capture the data, a cookie must be set on the user's computer. The two technologies—tags and cookies—work together to collect detailed information about visitor activity. Cookies themselves have become controversial as discussed throughout the book.

Cookies can also be set to retrieve personal information or not, which are controlled by the privacy options the user has selected (i.e., Accept Cookies).

Minus all the technical issues—and there are many—the concept is a simple one. The concept is portrayed in Figure 5.5. The first-party cookie—set on each visit or on first visit if a persistent cookie—stores data that makes the user experience easier like remembering user names and passwords for sites where the user has registered. The tags on web pages allow the capture of user behavior and its attribution to the individual—identified or anonymous. Third-party cookies are embedded on the page

Figure 5.5 Interaction between Cookie, Tagged Web Page, and Metrics Platform Source: © Cengage Learning 2013

as either a pixel or tag and they generally share data with advertising aggregators. The advertising aggregators then take the information that they gathered and show the consumer relevant advertisements. For instance, if a consumer abandons a cart, the consumer is likely to see an ad for their abandoned item "following" them around on multiple webpages. This is due to third-party cookies sharing information with the advertising aggregator who then launch a re-target campaign on the consumer to draw them back to the website.

Data are transmitted to the metrics platform, which stores enterprise customer data and maintains it for the sole use of that client and perhaps for purposes of model construction by the vendor. There is no movement of personal identifiable information (PII) data between clients of a metrics service; that would be an egregious violation of client trust. Site metrics are aggregated from individual-level data and reported to the client according to the client's instructions.

Marketers need to have a basic understanding of tagging and other methods used to collect traffic and audience data, but their primary job is to select the metrics that can accurately evaluate the effectiveness of the website and marketing campaigns. Let us turn now to a discussion of the metrics that are available.

First vs. third-party cookies will be discussed in more depth in Chapter 10. Please note that for decades advertisers have relied on third-party cookies for tracking and targeting users. However, after responding to public outcry regarding privacy concerns and privacy laws (i.e., GDPR in Europe and CCPA in California), digital advertisers are being phased out from using third-party cookies to collect data about their user. Mozilla (Firefox) and Apple (Safari) stopped using third-party cookies in 2019, and in January 2020, Google announced plans to eliminate third-party cookies. Google postponed its plans saying that it will now start phasing out third-party cookies starting in 2024, leaving advertisers with a bit more time to find a solution. Potential alternatives include a Universal ID that users have control over, more focus on contextual advertising, and increased first-party data collection. The key to keep in mind is that the reliance will be on first-party data collection—whether it's surveys, first-party cookies, or more direct interaction with the consumer via email, chatbots, text messages, etc.

Measuring Website Traffic, Audiences, and Campaigns

Many of these terms show their origins in traditional advertising, while others are unique to the web. The definitions that follow are generally accepted within the industry.

Traffic: measures simply document website activity. Some of the key traffic metrics are as follows:

- *Impressions*: the number of times a webpage is requested by a browser.
- Page views or deliveries: the number of times a web page is requested. Although you often see page views reported, they must be viewed with caution because it does not mean that a user viewed the entire page. Many sites use the Ajax technology to load multiple items on a page before the user requests them. Think of a retail ecommerce page with thumbnails that can be clicked on to get a larger image and text description. The entire page is loaded when the user requests it, although the user may choose to view none, all, or some of the full-size product images. What matters is which of the products are viewed, not the page view itself.[10] The various metrics platforms can handle this issue, but it requires special attention by the web administrator.

page views
an instance of a webpage being loaded (or reloaded) in a browser; generally measured as a page being delivered to the visitor.

sessions
group interactions that a user has with your website that occur within a specific time frame. For example, a single user session can contain viewing multiple pages on a website or other events within the site, such as social actions or ecommerce transactions. Many analytics programs also offer a pages-per-session metric, which captures the average number of pages viewed during a session. Sessions are time-based (e.g., expire after 30 minutes of inactivity, such as with Google Analytics).

- Sessions: the amount of activity on a site during a specified period of time. A single user can open multiple sessions. Sessions by the same user can occur on the same day or across multiple days, weeks, or months.
- *Click-throughs*: the number of times any link is clicked.

Audience measures provide data about the people who visit the site. Key audience metrics include:

- Visitors: the number of people who visit a site.
  - Total (includes multiple visits by the same user) or unique (different people) during a specified time frame
  - Unidentified (anonymous) or identified (registered or customer)
  - Unique (each visitor is counted only once during a specified time period)
- Behavior on the site
  - Number of page views
  - Session time
  - Path through the site
  - Shopping cart abandonment
  - Entry page (many visitors do not enter through the home page)
  - Exit page (the last page a user viewed before leaving the site)
  - Bounce rate (percentage of sessions where only one page was viewed).

And there are many others. You should be aware that there is no clear dividing line between traffic and audience measures, but traffic always implies general information about site activity while audience always implies information about the demographics and behaviors of visitors to the site.

In addition, there are measures of marketing campaign effectiveness:
Campaign measures provide data about the effectiveness of marketing efforts.

- By communications channel: email, mail, mobile apps, online banners, and so on
- By offer: free shipping versus 25 percent off, for example
- Search effectiveness by keyword

And, again, many others.

Campaign measures have the ability to integrate measures about social media and offline activity (e.g., direct mail), or activity off the website (e.g., search keywords). Results are shown in terms of metrics like page views, number of visitors, number of unique visitors, and sales revenue. For multichannel marketers, the ability to see reports that cover all types of marketing activities across all their channels is essential.

In order to be meaningful, all these measures must be taken during a specified period of time. That leads to an almost endless set of metrics that can be produced, depending on the needs of the marketer. Some common metrics are as follows:

- Average number of visits per day
- Number of page views per month
- Average visitor session length last month
- Number of visitors for each hour of the day
- Paid search results for the most recent seven-day period

And so it goes—almost infinitely.

Choosing the Right Metrics

Choosing the right metrics is essential, but it is not easy. Digital executive and author Ben Yoskovitz puts it well when he says:

> Remember: analytics is about measuring progress towards goals. It's not about endless reports. It's not about numbers that go constantly 'up and to the right' to impress the press, investors or anyone else. Good analytics is about speeding up and making better decisions, and developing key insights that become cornerstones of your company, large or small.[11]

To answer the question of "how to choose" let's first think about the customer journey and how metrics are needed to follow customers through each stage of their journey. Figure 5.6 shows basic steps in the customer journey and metrics that might accompany each. Remember that, as we discussed in Chapter 4, the customer journey is often more complex than this. Remember also that it is important to map the actual customer journey for specific products instead of simply relying on a hypothetical purchase process. With those *caveats* in mind we can use this simple journey model to tackle the question of how to choose metrics.

When measuring awareness, notice that the first two types of awareness metrics (number of impressions and reach and frequency) shown come directly from traditional advertising. That is, we count how many times someone saw the webpage (i.e., number of impressions), how often they were seen (i.e., frequency), and where they were seen (i.e., reach). First website visits and branded search—searches that use your brand name—are web specific. In the next box—the consideration stage—inbound contacts and brand perceptions (measured by some type of marketing research) have traditional advertising roots. Conversely, subscriptions, repeat site visits, and social media comments are web specific. All of the sample metrics listed for purchase (the term "conversion" is often used, especially in B2B) and for loyalty are traditional marketing measures of accomplishment.

These examples help set the stage but they don't answer the "how to choose" question. There is only one answer: matching marketing objectives to marketing metrics. Figure 5.7 shows

Figure 5.6   Sample Metrics for the Stages of Customer Journey

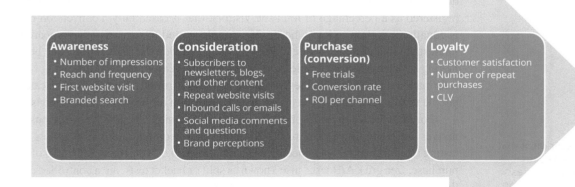

Awareness
- Number of impressions
- Reach and frequency
- First website visit
- Branded search

Consideration
- Subscribers to newsletters, blogs, and other content
- Repeat website visits
- Inbound calls or emails
- Social media comments and questions
- Brand perceptions

Purchase (conversion)
- Free trials
- Conversion rate
- ROI per channel

Loyalty
- Customer satisfaction
- Number of repeat purchases
- CLV

Figure 5.7 Matching Marketing Campaign Objectives to Program Metrics Source: © Cengage Learning 2013

Sample Campaign Objective	Corresponding Metrics
Increase Number of Email Captures by 5% in Q1	Number of unique visitors Referral source Length of visit Number of unique visitors to registration page • Number of completed registrations • Number of incomplete registrations • Last form box completed
Reactivate 10,000 Lapsed Customers in Q4	Number of emails sent • Reactivation message A/B Number of click-throughs A/B Bounces from reactivation landing page Number of incentive offers accepted A/B
Convert 2,000 Newsletter Recipients to New Customers in Last Six Months of FY	Number of emails sent Monday/Friday • Product offer A/B/C Number of click-throughs for each newsletter link Number of sales • By newsletter edition • By product Value of average sale by product Bounces from offer page A/B/C Heat map of offer page A/B/C

three typical marketing campaign objectives and some of the metrics that might be used to measure them. The objectives are SMART—that is, they are specific, measurable, achievable, realistic, and they have a time frame. We discuss SMART objectives in the context of website development in Chapter 6. Later in this chapter, we will present an example using KPIs, which is another approach to establishing metrics that measure business success.

Take, for example, the first objective listed; to increase the number of registrants for an email newsletter in the first quarter of the fiscal year. How many people come to the site and how many continue on to the registration page are clearly important. Where they come from (the referral source) is likely to reveal important data for planning future programs. Would you hypothesize that the longer a visitor remains on the site, the more likely they are to register for the newsletter before leaving? Probably. Take a careful look at the drill down to specifics about activity on the registration page. It is important to know how many registered as a percentage of total site visitors; that is essentially a conversion measure. It is equally important to know how many people started to register—they apparently were interested—but did not complete. Why did they abandon the registration page before completing it? The last box completed may suggest the reason. Did the following box ask for information that the potential registrant did not want to reveal? That is often the case. If many people terminated registration at that point, a redesign of the registration page is in order.

A/B Testing is a controlled experiment that helps optimize web pages. The digital marketer creates two (or more) communication pieces (i.e., email, promotion, landing page) and presents one communication to one group and the other communication to the other group. The marketer then compares the results using the proper statistical test to determine which one works best.

For both the reactivation objective and the conversion objective, it is obvious that alternatives are being tested. The reactivation objective requires multiple A/B tests as well as testing the different types of incentives being offered (i.e., 10 percent off vs. $5 off your first purchase, free gift). A/B tests, also known as split or bucket tests, are a controlled experiment that helps optimize web content. The experiment typically has two or more groups of content that are being compared. The marketer will randomize which groups received each piece of content and then run the proper statistical test to determine which piece of content succeeded.

Additionally, the conversion objective differs in that the metrics it's following--people who read the company's free newsletter—and is trying to convert them to being paying customers. You might see this with the number of free newsletters who then ask their subscribers to subscribe to their Patreon or Substack accounts so that they can make money from their followers. A conversion campaign identifies metrics that drill down on what offers work to convert readers to paying customers.

There is a logic to each set of metrics beyond just arriving at a measure of campaign success. In each case, the metrics begin with a baseline of activity and drill down to the specifics that measure campaign success. In each case, the objectives guide the choice of metrics. *Mapping metrics to objectives in a clear and explicit manner is the only way to bring order to the mind-numbing array of metrics choices.*

Using Google Analytics and Segmenting Visitors

There are many good analytics platforms; many of them offer at least part of their functionality for free. Why single out Google Analytics? Exact numbers are hard to come by, but it is estimated that 40 million sites use Google Analytics[12]. Is the heavy usage because Google Analytics is free? While that certainly does not hurt, Google Analytics provides robust analytics that many users need. Google gives good explanations of how to use it, and a small industry of marketing services firms and consultants offer assistance.

A good piece of advice for most new users is to start small, with a free platform, and determine what is really needed in terms of metrics, reporting, and access by various individuals within the firm. It will be obvious when the business outgrows the free platform and needs a paid metrics provider.

Posing and Answering a Question in Google Analytics

The platform provides the website owner with a dashboard and many options for accessing more detailed metrics. While some hosting providers or ecommerce and blog software platforms provide some metrics, they are not very flexible or detailed. It is easy for a website owner to connect to Google Analytics to get more detailed metrics.

Figure 5.8 shows the dashboard in our example—of Google's Merchandise Store with the GA4 platform. As of July 1, 2023, all of Google's platforms migrated from Universal Analytics (UA) to GA4. The main reason for migrating from UA to GA4 is because of more accurate reporting. In UA, Google had a hard time de-duplicating (deduping) the same user who visited the page many times. In GA4, the main advantage is that each user's ID is monitored across all reports and web pages. In sum, it helps reports more accurate, real-time data. Google provides all users access to two of their ecommerce stores so that users

Figure 5.8 Dashboard for G4 Google Analytics Merchandise Store Source: Google, Inc., https://analytics.google.com/analytics/web/

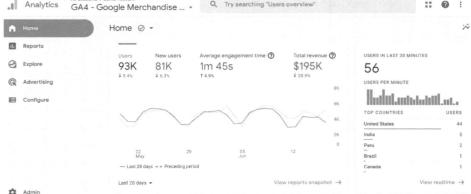

can "play" with the Google Analytics pages. The first site is Google's merchandise store where the company sells Google-branded products (https://shop.googlemerchandisestore .com/) and the second is their Flood It! game (https://flood-it.app/), where users can play a Google-created game on both an app or on a desktop. To access these analytics, users can click on https://support.google.com/analytics/answer/6367342 to access the demo accounts.

The overview on the dashboard shows some of the basic metrics we have just discussed (e.g., the number of visits and page views). The page has generated revenue of US $194,000 in 28 days. Not bad for a side hustle! We can also see that the average engagement time is 1 minute 45 seconds. Google's GA4 does not report bounce rates anymore. They report engagement rates to see how long people are on the site and engaging with it. Engagement sessions are often a more accurate depiction of how the user is interacting with the website. For instance, if a user clicks on a news article and reads it within 45 seconds, then clicks off of the page, the interaction was successful. They read their article and they accomplished what they meant to do. However, the old way that Google used to calculate the interaction was to consider it part of the bounce rate because the user did not go anywhere else within the website.

Continuing on through the dashboard, we might want to see how people are learning about the site, also known as acquisition. In Figure 5.9, we see that organic searches (meaning people coming to the site from a search engine) and CPC (cost per click, paid advertising which is also known as pay-per-click (PPC)) rank highly. Note that the number one area of acquisition is marked as "none." This means that Google was not able to determine where the user came from. This happens more often than not, particularly as more people use incognito browsers (browsers that block cookies) for privacy reasons.

Segmentation and Conversion Metrics

Virtually all analytics platforms, including Google Analytics, provide the opportunity to segment data to uncover the most and least profitable market segments and to provide data about what marketing approaches work best with the most profitable segments. The primary difference between segmentation of digital data and traditional market segmentation is that behavioral data is available to the digital marketer. Conventional digital marketing wisdom is that behavioral segmentation is more likely to reveal segment profitability, although conventional segmentation criteria like gender or geography may be necessary to understand how to reach segments.

Figure 5.9   **GA4 Acquisition Overview** Source: Google, Inc., http://www.google.com /analytics.

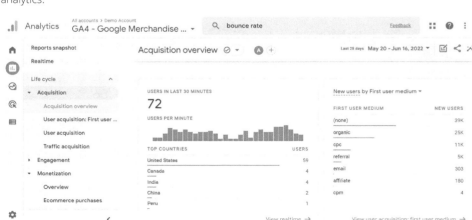

With that in mind, let us look at a few of the types of segmentation and conversion analytics that are available from WebTrends, an analytics platform designed primarily for the enterprise user.

WebTrends offers what it calls "predefined segments" like new versus returning visitors and new versus repeat buyers. They are predefined because the coding and report formats have already been set up and are therefore quick and easy to use. The example that begins with Figure 5.10 focuses on new versus returning visitors. While you look at it, you should keep in mind that customers of sophisticated analytics platforms can develop customized segmentation approaches, using variables of their own choice to meet virtually any marketing need.

Figure 5.10 shows the report for an email campaign carried out by hypothetical electronics supplier, Zedesco. For returning visitors, it shows that average revenue per order—an important retailing metric—was highest for returning visitors who were referred by an affiliate network. While that is an important piece of information, the marketer must couple it with the fact that the affiliate network referred fewer visitors than any other referring source. The marketer can also see that the free shipping offer was more productive in terms of the number of orders and average revenue per order than either of the other email campaigns. For the new visitor segment, the free shipping offer was also the most productive. It produced a higher average order size than affiliate referrals for new visitors, which is different from the data for returning visitors. These data, and more that could be accessed by expanding the various lines on the report, provide the marketer with important information for planning future marketing programs of various types.

Figure 5.11 shows an overlay on the home page of Motorcycle Superstore for a one-month period. Beside the link to each of the site's product pages, the report shows the average revenue per order for each order placed after a click-through on that link. In terms of data, it shows a higher average order size for returning buyers than for new buyers. While this might be expected, it provides guidance for the marketer. In terms of metrics presented, New Buyer, Repeat Buyer, and month of September are all segmentation choices; there are also other segmentations and time periods available. The tabs indicate that there are other data sets available for this site, so once again consider the huge number of metrics that can be chosen when evaluating the most profitable elements of a website.

Figure 5.10   New Versus Returning Visitors Segmentation for Zedesco Email Campaign—Report Format

Source: Webtrends, http://product.webtrends.com/WRC/8.7/ResourceCenter/rc/library/pdf/hdig/How_Do_I_Use_WebTrends_for_Audience _Segmentation.pdf

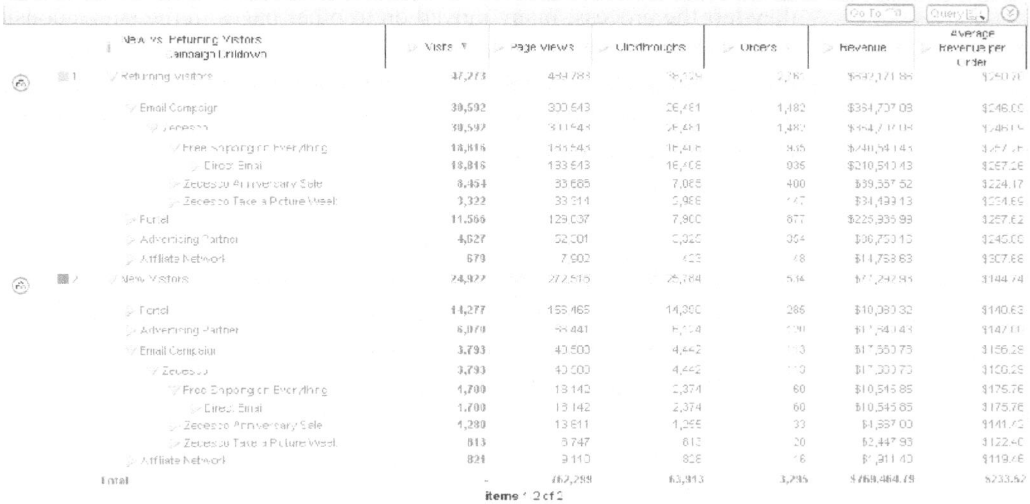

Figure 5.11   New Versus Returning Visitors Segmentation for Web Pages—Overlay (WebTrends SmartView)

Format Source: Webtrends, http://product.webtrends.com/WRC/8.7/ResourceCenter/rc/library/pdf/hdig/How_Do_I_Use_WebTrends_for
_Audience_Segmentation.pdf.

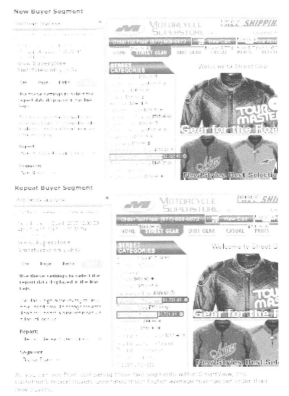

As a final perspective on the metrics commonly available from analytics platforms, consider the conversion funnel in Figure 5.12. This is a graphic representation, complete with data, of the traditional conversion funnel. The steps in the funnel are user-defined; that is, the user specifies which behaviors to show including, for example, viewing a product page and adding an item to the shopping cart.

The left pane shows the point at which visitors entered the process. Most came from sources like search or from various other pages in the site. The right pane shows when they left the process: many moved on to other pages in the site, a considerable number ended their visit instead of adding an item to their cart, and some started the checkout process but did not complete it. About 3 percent did complete a transaction (clicking checkout complete at the bottom of the figure), but what goes on in between is even more informative to the marketer.

Take just one path as an example:

- 38,232 visitors viewed the product page
  - 10,966 added something to their shopping carts
  - 28,264 visitors went somewhere else—many of them went to another Zedesco page; over 5,000 went to other sites
- Of those who added something to their shopping carts, 4,106 started the checkout process
  - 6,529 did not start checkout and went somewhere else—most went to another Zedesco page; 1,539 ended their visit by exiting the Zedesco site

Figure 5.12 **A Conversion Funnel Showing Paths Through the Website** Source: Webtrends, http://product.webtrends.com /WRC/8.7/ResourceCenter/rc/library/pdf/aug/Tracking_Conversion_and_Abandonment_through_Scenario_Analysis.pdf.

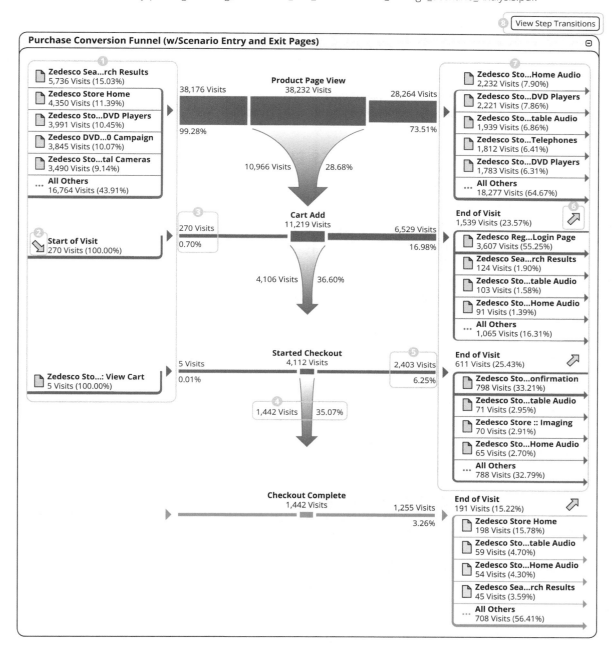

Why did they leave without making a purchase? What can the marketer do to keep them on the site and persuade them to complete a purchase? These are the kind of questions marketers should be asking. If visitors went to another Zedesco page and purchased something there, then it appears they found what they were looking for and metrics provided the answer. If visitors added something to their shopping carts but exited after seeing the shipping charges (more detail than is on this chart, but available from metrics), then shipping charges seem to be a problem. What can the marketer do about this? If people simply looked at the product page and then left the site, where did they go? Keep in mind that information like where the user went might be available with the use of third-party tracking cookies, but not in a first-party program like Google Analytics. If the customer left and went to a competitor site, then we can assume they did not like what they saw on the Zedesco site—which could suggest a product or maybe a pricing problem that should concern the marketer. If they left and went back to search, they did not find the product they were looking for and that may be of less concern to the marketer.

This path analysis and many other views can be very helpful to the marketer trying to understand what is happening on the website. The metrics do not answer all the questions. Sometimes that will require looking at other metrics, as just suggested. Sometimes, it may suggest that marketing research is needed, for example, to find if the product is not viewed as satisfactory by many potential customers. Whatever the situation, *metrics point the way*.

From Metrics to KPIs

Throughout the chapter, we have emphasized the almost infinite number of metrics available to the digital marketer and both the difficulty and the importance of choosing the right ones. One of the undisputed authorities on web metrics is Avinash Kaushik, who is Google's Digital Marketing Evangelist and founder of a firm that offers certification in web analytics. In April 2010, he wrote a blog post called "Metrics 101" that is worth reading in its entirety because the concepts it explains so well have not changed.[13] In it, he distinguishes between a metric, which is simply a number, and a KPI (key performance indicator), which is "a metric that helps you understand how you are doing against your objectives." There are more complex definitions of both concepts, but none that are more helpful to marketers who are attempting to make sense of the metrics issue.

The table in Figure 5.13 is an example from a hypothetical bike company from one of Kaushik's students. The framework includes high-level business objectives, marketing goals, the KPIs that will be reported, and the numerical target for each KPI. The implication is that the KPIs are the result of a conscious decision by marketing managers about what data are essential to the management of the business.

KPI (key performance indicator) a metric that has been identified as an important measure or benchmark of business performance.

Figure 5.13   Web Analytics Template Source: Figure: Bike Company X Web Analytics Framework by Matt Smedley, appearing on Occam's Razor by Avinash Kaushik. Reprinted with permission.

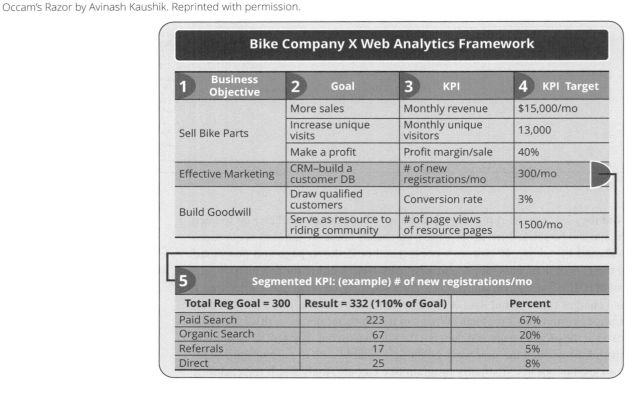

Bike Company X Web Analytics Framework

1 Business Objective	2 Goal	3 KPI	4 KPI Target
Sell Bike Parts	More sales	Monthly revenue	$15,000/mo
	Increase unique visits	Monthly unique visitors	13,000
	Make a profit	Profit margin/sale	40%
Effective Marketing	CRM–build a customer DB	# of new registrations/mo	300/mo
Build Goodwill	Draw qualified customers	Conversion rate	3%
	Serve as resource to riding community	# of page views of resource pages	1500/mo

5 Segmented KPI: (example) # of new registrations/mo		
Total Reg Goal = 300	**Result = 332 (110% of Goal)**	**Percent**
Paid Search	223	67%
Organic Search	67	20%
Referrals	17	5%
Direct	25	8%

Kaushik's comment on his student's work points out another advantage of this type of framework:

> I really liked Matt's presentation for his motor bike company analysis. In less than half a page one could see the complete picture of what the business was solving for and what the expectations were.
>
> Particularly clever I thought was his inclusion of the segmentation in his framework presentation. At a glance for the most important goal for the quarter (build a robust customer database for future marketing) you can see how their campaign strategy worked.[14]

In other words, the choice of KPIs sets a long-term framework for management in controlling the effectiveness of, in this case, the marketing operation. All the KPIs are important, but strategy can single one out for emphasis in one fiscal time period. In this example, Kaushik implies that building the customer database by increasing the number of new registrants was the key focus for the chosen time period. Consequently, the analyst drilled down into the segmentation figure to find out where the most registrants came from. The fact that paid search lead by a huge margin points the way to future strategy.

Kaushik makes another important point in his blog post, "In aggregate, almost all data is useless (like # of Visits)."[15] The actionable data is found by drilling down— to where the visits came from or to the source of the new registrants, for example. Metrics—numbers—alone do not meet marketing and management needs. Only when the metrics are carefully chosen and reported in sufficient detail to guide strategic choices are business needs met.

This is a high-level overview of how businesses use metrics to understand their current operations and to plan for the future. Would you be pleased if we could just stop here and say we have covered the subject? Unfortunately, we have not. There are more issues to consider, but there is good news as well in this picture.

The good news is that social and mobile metrics are being collected by platforms and are available without extra effort. We have not yet shown the integration of video metrics, but that will be covered in a later section.

The good news is very good indeed because some of the metrics marketers needs are readily available. However, in order to understand the performance of mobile apps, social media, and video campaigns, some different sets of metrics are required.

Metrics for Mobile Apps, Social, and Video

Mobile apps, social media, and video all represent unique kinds of communication channels that have different issues from traditional websites. As such, they present unique measurement issues. The three sections that follow will give a brief overview of basic measurement strategies in these spaces.

Mobile App Metrics

As we discuss in other chapters, the main marketing issue for mobile apps is, first, to get customers to *install* them, and second, to get them to *use* them. According to Kissmetrics:

> Mobile app analytics is about converting ad budgets to installs, and installs to repeated app usage and in-app purchases. Ultimately, the objective of a mobile app developer is to evaluate user lifetime value, retention, and the frequency of usage.[16]

Beyond installation and usage, there is no general agreement on the stages of mobile app adoption and retention. This is a set of mobile app metrics that suggests elements of a

Table 5.5   Mobile App Metrics

Installation

- Number of installs
- Source (app store, website, other)
- User characteristics

Engagement

- Number of times accessed in first 24 hours
- In-app session time
- Session intervals
- Consumer data access permissions granted
- Number of screens accessed per session

User Experience

- Screen flow (customer journey through the app)
- App performance (loading time, errors, crashes, and others)

Revenue for Transactional Apps

- Number of paid subscriptions
- In-app purchases

Interest and Intent for Media Apps

- Number of articles read
- Number of pages visited
- Social shared

KPIs for All Types of Apps

- Retention rate
- Customer Lifetime Value (CLV) [17,18,19]

customer journey and recognizes that different kinds of apps may require different metrics. Depending on how the marketer defines the business objectives for the app, revenue, and interest/intent may also be app KPIs. As Table 5.5 indicates, there are a number of metrics that are attributed towards apps.

Persuading customers to install a given app from among the thousands available is no easy task. However, the difficulty of generating installation and trial pales in comparison to generating engagement that leads to repeat use. Statista reports that only 25 percent of apps are used once after its downloaded[20], and 80 percent are deleted within the first 90 days after installation.[21] Clearly, the app must offer real value to customers to get them to use it even a second time. Beyond the app value proposition, the statistics suggest that there should be a major emphasis on user experience (UX). Please note that UX is discussed more in-depth in Chapter 6. Google has published a detailed set of instructions for testing both Android and iOS apps and offers a cloud-based testing laboratory for Android apps. There are other tools and other services that also provide testing capabilities. Marketers should have objectives that include successful app use, retention beyond the three-month time frame, and a satisfactory CLV, and test their apps before introduction to have the greatest probability of meeting their objectives.

As mobile marketing matures, app marketing may acquire a more strategic framework. Perhaps it will be similar to the one developed over several years of effort for SMM.

SMM Metrics

In Chapter 9, we describe the process of developing a social media strategy. Because social media is so different from offline media or traditional digital media, it requires different measurement. The issues of measurement in social media are made more complicated by the fact that many interactions in social media are essentially qualitative in nature. Yes, there are things that can be measured quantitatively, like number of visits to a brand's Instagram profile. However, many of the issues that matter most to marketers in social media are essentially qualitative—the type and quality of engagement with the brand, for example.

Marketers wrestled with these issues for a number of years before settling on the Valid Metrics Framework shown in Table 5.6. While the model is grounded in traditional advertising measurement theory, it captures the activities of SMM and produces metrics that marketers can use to make decisions.

Figure 5.14 uses these stages to categorize some of the most important SMM metrics. There are two things to keep in mind as you look at this figure. First, there are numerous qualitative as well as quantitative metrics. In each stage of SMM there can be numerous qualitative and some quantitative metrics, as indicated in Table 5.3.

Second, the Valid Metrics Framework ends with advocacy, not purchase. That's a significant difference from the familiar purchase behavior model. While there are impact metrics that attempt to capture the role of SMM in a customer purchase, they are not universally accepted. More important, the nature of the model indicates that purchase is not always the expected outcome of a SMM campaign. Marketers must therefore set objectives with care in order to select metrics that genuinely measure what they set out to do.

Table 5.6 Valid Metrics Framework as shown in Zahay, Roberts, Parker, Barker, and Barker, *Social Media Marketing: A Strategic Approach*, 3rd Edition p. 237.

First, some definitions:

a. **Exposure** is the opportunity to see and/or hear a piece of content in any channel. This is the broad definition of exposure. It does not mean that a viewer has paid any attention to or has comprehended any part of the content. It simply means they had the opportunity to do so. Exposure is a term used in advertising.

b. **Engagement** is a term popularized by social media marketers and its exact definition is hotly debated. It is most often measured as some variant of time spent on the piece of content. However, definitions vary widely so you are advised to look for the definition any time you use an engagement statistic.

c. **Influence** is a reasonably intuitive term that describes the ability to affect attitudes and behavior. The topic influence in social media is so important that for a while special tools such as Klout developed to measure it. However, social media influence is hard to measure in one tool because influence is so nuanced. These days, it is far better to develop and measure influence on a particular social media tool.

d. **Impact** is also used in a reasonably common manner: how does a SMM activity affect business results? Specifically, how does it affect the attainment of goals? The impact marketers would most likely to measure is the Return on Promotional Investment (ROPI).

e. **Advocacy** is a term long used in traditional promotion, especially in attempting to understand the effect of word of mouth (WOM). Communications studies have long demonstrated that various topics have identifiable opinion leaders and that these opinion leaders do have an influence on followers. The topic of advocacy has become especially important in SMM where marketers can make specific attempts to locate or create advocates and can measure the extent of their success.

Figure 5.14 Valid Metrics Framework with Metrics Categories, Definitions, and Sample Metrics Source: Zahay, Roberts, Parker, Barker, and Barker, *Social Media Marketing: A Strategic Approach*, 3rd Edition p. 237.

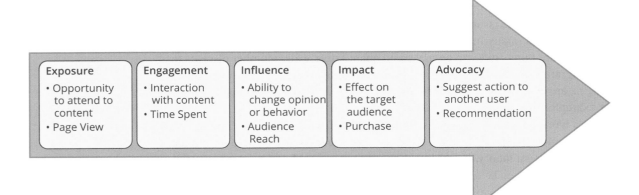

Exposure	Engagement	Influence	Impact	Advocacy
• Opportunity to attend to content • Page View	• Interaction with content • Time Spent	• Ability to change opinion or behavior • Audience Reach	• Effect on the target audience • Purchase	• Suggest action to another user • Recommendation

Consider the SMM campaign of the UN Women's Council, Australia that created the #EmpowerMoves TikTok dance challenge.[22] They chose to work with dance influencer Karla Mura (TikTok handle @karlamura), who choreographed a dance that incorporated multiple self-defense moves such as a release, palm strikes, block, and under-roll. Once the dance challenge caught on, Mura created more videos that broke down how to use each self-defense move in response to an attacker. Figure 5.15 provides an overview of the multiple videos that they created for the campaign.

The campaign was considered a wild success; Figure 5.16 details the analytics of the campaign. The campaign had 130 million video views worldwide with 59 million unique viewers worldwide. The campaign had a total reach of 62 million viewers, they were the third song on the viral TikTok chart (which helped with more views), and they saw an ROI of 4,924 percent. The ROI was calculated by examining all of the time, money and investments it took to create the video. #EmpowerMoves was created to advocate for women's rights and to teach women self-defense moves. They did a great job of advocating for their cause without trying to sell anything. In turn, they raised awareness for the UN Women's Council, educated the public about self-defense moves, and advocated for women's rights without selling anything.

Figure 5.15 UN Women's Council #EmpowerMoves TikTok Dance Challenge Source: https://new.awardshowjury.com /empower-moves/

Figure 5.16   **UN Women's Council #EmpowerMoves Analytics** Source: https://new.awardshowjury.com/empower-moves/

Video Marketing Metrics

The importance of videos, especially video advertising, is discussed in Chapter 10. This section looks exclusively at video content marketing. It excludes the many issues specific to measuring video advertising. The IAB is the primary source for video advertising metrics.[23] Mark Waugh, Global Managing Director, of Newcast puts the situation into context:

> Consumers all around the world are rapidly embracing online video because it offers them a near-limitless array of engrossing content. Some of the keenest users are the young, affluent viewers who are hardest to reach on television. Brands are finding online video a particularly effective way to reach these valuable audiences, not just with advertising, but also with branded content; content that can inform or entertain consumers in a deeper and richer way than is possible with short, interruptive ads.[24]

Like mobile metrics, video metrics are also based on time. For videos to have the greatest marketing impact they must be watched through to the end. Otherwise important content, and probably the call to action, will be missed. Beyond that simple concept there are a seemingly endless number of lists of video metrics, all of which categorize them in different ways, mostly using the same metrics. Table 5.6 shows commonly used video metrics categorized in a way that fits with content strategy issues.

Notice that the final column is user experience, a recurring theme throughout the text. From a metrics perspective, it is important that the user experience metrics are not

Table 5.6   **Frequently Used Video Metrics** Source: https://wistia.com/library/guide-to -video-metrics

Reach	Engagement	Relevance	User Experience
Number of views	Percent of video viewed	Play rate	Bounce rate
Click-through rates	Comments		Time spent on page
Audience characteristics	Social shares		Subscriptions/ Signups
			Conversions

produced by the video itself. They are website metrics that we have already discussed. Each of these website metrics should be improved when videos are part of the content, or the videos are not doing their job. Subscriptions or signups to website content should increase as should the conversion rate, either in terms of purchases or of some other specified conversion objective.

In order for people to have an opportunity to view the video they must first be exposed to it. The video can be embedded on a web page, linked to the page, promoted in an email, or posted to a social media site. Reach, then is measured by the appropriate metric—number of page views for the site or number of views for an Instagram reel, for example. Once a user has been exposed, they make the decision to click the play button or not. Once again, audience characteristics are not collected directly from the video interaction. On social media sites, marketers know the composition of their fan base, although not the exact composition of the specific people who viewed the video. Videos viewed as a result of emails can be linked to the email recipient. If that person has registered with the site and provided personal information, their data can be linked directly to video viewership as a result of the email.

Most marketers would agree that engagement is the primary contribution of video. They are inherently engaging. In Chapter 9, BlendTec's "Will it Blend" videos show that branded videos can be highly engaging. Engagement is most often measured by the percent of the video viewed—total video length to time from hitting the play button to time clicking away from the video. Be careful of a simple measure of engagement; the definitions of what portion of the video must be viewed to constitute engagement differs from platform to platform. Comments and social shares play the same role as in social media metrics—important indicators of how and how much viewers interact with the content. Play rate is a less rigorous metric than percent viewed. It is merely the number of people who clicked the play button and started watching—presumably a sign that the content held some relevance for the viewer.

Some of these metrics are illustrated in Figure 5.17 which features a screenshot from an account YouTube Studio (free software provided by YouTube). The engagement level for this account is quite good. YouTube Studio lists the top videos in the channel as well

Figure 5.17   **YouTube Studio Analytics** Source: https://www.shopify.com/blog/6763696-youtube-analytics-10-ways-to-track-video -performance

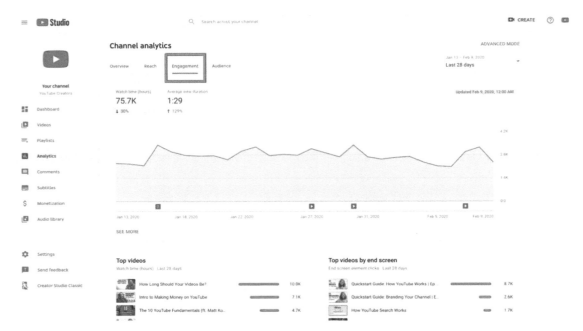

as the engagement for all videos. For instance, the average view duration increased by 129 percent at the time this report was created for a total of 1 minute, 29 seconds. However, the overall watch time for all videos decreased by 30 percent to 75.7k hours. Despite the decrease in engagement, having their videos watched for over 75,000 hours is quite a success! Notice that the average view duration is for about a minute and a half. Be sure your brand name is mentioned early because viewers may never get to your call for action, especially if it is the last piece of content.

The video in Figure 5.18 is a good example of taking an intrinsically boring subject like getting dirty clothes clean and making an engaging branded video of it. It may not be the best video you've ever seen, but considering the subject you may agree that it's pretty good. According to Google:

- The main objective of the YouTube video was brand consideration. Procter & Gamble (P&G) chose view-through rate as their primary KPI for the video.
- Metrics were obtained from YouTube Analytics and they showed Tide's highest-ever VTR and a high Brand Lift score. Brand Lift is a Google score that is obtained from online surveys and search results in the days immediately following the airing of a video.[25]

In the second iteration of the video campaign, P&G retargeted to members of its YouTube channel and to the subscribers to the channels of the creators of the video. The retargeting netted P&G a Cost Per View (CPV) of 50 percent less than its previous campaigns.[26]

Carrying out a video campaign, or any type of digital campaign for that matter, and being rewarded with metrics that show a successful outcome is the goal of any marketer. Unfortunately, there is always one more question: Can the metrics be believed?

Fraudulent Metrics

Marketers must remain vigilant about the quality of metrics data. There is a great deal written about click fraud, which is a big issue in PPC advertising, that is costing advertisers money, hence the high level of interest and prevention attempts. When the problem is with owned content on any platform it is generally referred to as spam.

Figure 5.18   **Identifying KPIs for the Tide Pod Challenge** Source: https://www.thinkwithgoogle.com/marketing-strategies /video/how-identify-right-kpis-online-video/

Tools for Measuring KPIs	Awareness KPIs	Consideration KPIs	Action KPIs
Youtube Analytics Google Analytics Adwords	Views Impressions Unique users	View-through rate Watch time	Clicks Calls Signups Sales
Brand Lift	Awareness lift Ad recall lift	Favorability lift Consideration lift Brand interest lift	Purchase intent lift
Google Consumer Surveys	Answers to custom questions		

Figure 5.19 **Examples of Comment Spam** Source: https://smartblogger.com/comment-spam/.

Submitted on 2015/09/04 at 2:23 pm

The official trailers of the interlude are quite tempting because they reveal a lot about upcoming events.
Download Bucky Larson: Born to Be a Star Movie. An undistinguished low-budget Western,
Buffalo Gun (1961) which he had made for the obscure
Globe in 1958 and which was released in 1961, was his last picture.

Submitted on 2015/09/04 at 11:28 am

Best for soundcloud marketing and social media like Facebook and Instagram also YouTube is blackhaty they
also give's you free trial of 1000 soundcloud plays or likes followers reposts must give it a try 1+ delivery speed
and service quality http://blackhaty.com

Submitted on 2015/09/05 at 9:44 am

Hey very cool website!! Man .. Excellent .. Amazing .. I will bookmark your web site and take the feeds
additionally ... I am happy to search out so many helpful info right here in the publish, we need work out extra
techniques in this regard, thanks for sharing ......

comment spam
abusive practice in which comments are placed on a blog or website, perhaps robotically, for the sole purpose of generating a backlink in an attempt to improve search results.

The most common kind of website spam is comment spam, examples of which are shown in Figure 5.19. The spammers usually post a link with their meaningless, often irrelevant, comment. Either way, the blog is linked to a disreputable site. If you have a low-volume blog you can remove the comments by hand. Blog platforms have filters available—like CAPTCHA—and there are other filters available.

Fake reviews are a big headache for websites. Not surprisingly, Amazon is a huge target for fake reviews as well as Facebook, Google, Yelp, TripAdvisor, and TrustPilot.[27] Amazon itself has taken legal action against the spammers,[28] and there are a number of online tools the consumer can use to detect fake product reviews on Amazon. In an effort to curb fake reviews, the UK's Competition Markets Authority (CMA) can impose fines up to £300,000 for individuals and 10 percent of global turnover (revenue) for businesses that are found guilty of writing fake reviews. The CMA also states that fake reviews influence an extra £900 spend on products and an extra £60 on unwanted subscriptions.[29] In the United States, the Federal Trade Commission (FTC) is in the process of creating a rule that will help combat fake reviews, suppressed negative reviews and sponsored positive reviews.[30] Due to the global nature of the internet, it will be hard for any one country to combat fake reviews for their consumers because people from all over the world can write the reviews. For consumers to see a substantial decrease of fake reviews, there will have to be an iron-clad agreement that is held by most countries, which is unlikely to occur over the next few years.

Summary

The ability to track and measure visitor activities is one of the unique capabilities of the web. If marketers are not using appropriate traffic, audience, and campaign metrics, they are missing out on a major benefit conferred by digital marketing. However, the number of metrics is enormous, and choosing the right ones and applying them to marketing decision making are huge challenges.

There are two different perspectives on the effectiveness of websites and mobile web marketing programs. The user perspective is concerned with the usability of the website itself, which in turn leads to a satisfying user experience, as discussed in Chapter 4.

From the business perspective there are a number of important types of metrics. Site performance metrics are important to the technicians whose job is to keep the site working smoothly but have little direct relevance for marketers. They do, however, impact the performance of marketing programs. Marketers focus on traffic, audience, and campaign metrics in order to provide information about site visitors and to measure marketing campaign effectiveness. Today these metrics are usually obtained from a combination of tagged web pages and cookies placed on user computers that capture data. Internet enterprises, large and small, usually outsource the collection and reporting of these metrics to marketing services firms that have the specialized platforms and consulting expertise required for this demanding endeavor.

The use of traffic, audience, and campaign metrics to gauge effectiveness presupposes that marketers have clear marketing objectives. These objectives may range from provision of information, to customer service, to sale of products. When the objectives are transactional in nature, behavioral measures in the form of traffic and audience metrics are needed. When there are branding objectives, marketing research may be required

to measure the attitudinal variables that are used to assess the effectiveness of branding efforts, both online and offline.

Whether the marketer relies on SMART marketing objectives or the business has identified KPIs, mapping metrics and KPIs to objectives is a key task. Then the marketing analyst must uncover the detailed metrics that point the way to marketing planning and strategy decisions.

One must also keep in mind that apps have a download and use cycle that needs metrics that measure the importance of engagement with and retention of the app. SMM has a Valid Metrics Framework that identifies relevant metrics at each stage of the social media campaign. Video metrics are also time-dependent and many are unique to the video medium.

Measurement on all these platforms must be accomplished in a multichannel environment in which customers interact with various marketing touchpoints over a buying cycle that can last for days or weeks, or even longer. Only if all channels and all touchpoints are monitored can the marketer obtain the desired 360-degree view of the customer that informs decisions that improve business results. That defines the challenge for both the analyst and the user of digital marketing metrics.

Discussion Questions

1. The term "metrics" is commonly used by digital marketers. Explain your understanding of the meaning of the term.

2. True or False: Digital marketers need to decide whether they will conduct measurement from a visitor usability perspective or from a traffic and audience measurement perspective. Defend your answer.

3. True or False: Web developers and the marketer use the same metrics when assessing website effectiveness.

4. What are the uses of tagged web pages and cookies in the collection of website effectiveness data? In what other contexts have you seen tags discussed in this text?

5. What are some of the specific metrics that measure traffic, audiences, and campaigns? Which ones do you think are most important?

6. Why do you think Google Analytics is so popular? Can you think of any other indicators of popularity besides the number of sites and blogs that use it?

7. How should the marketer go about choosing the right metrics to measure website or campaign effectiveness?

8. What role do SMART objectives play in establishing and using metrics?

9. What is the meaning and importance of the term "KPI"?

10. What is the critical difference between website metrics and mobile metrics?

11. Why is it necessary for mobile apps to have a separate set of metrics?

12. Why is it necessary to measure video marketing separately from the website, blog, or social platform on which the video is embedded?

13. What are the chief metrics used to measure video marketing success?

14. True or False. A small website or blog does not have to worry much about fraudulent metrics.

15. Do you believe that most commercial websites are using metrics to improve customer experience and enhance marketing effectiveness? Do you have any personal experiences that support your view?

Endnotes

1. Willem van Zyl, "The Digital Universe – Can You Picture 44ZB of Data?," LinkedIn, accessed May 15, 2023, https://www.linkedin.com/pulse/digital-universe-can-you-picture-44zb-data-willem-van-zyl/.

2. Louie Andre, "53 Important Statistics about How Much Data Is Created Every Day," Financesonline.com, March 14, 2023, https://financesonline.com/how-much-data-is-created-every-day/.

3. Bernard Marr, "What Is Data Democratization? A Super Simple Explanation and the Key Pros and Cons." *Forbes*, October 12, 2022, https://www.forbes.com/sites/bernardmarr/2017/07/24/what-is-data-democratization-a-super-simple-explanation-and-the-key-pros-and-cons/.

4. David Kiron, Pamela Kirk Prentice and Renee Boucher Ferguson, "The Analytics Mandate." *MIT Sloan Management Review*, May 12, 2014, http://sloanreview.mit.edu/projects/analytics-mandate/.

5. Sam Ransbotham, David Kiron and Pamela Kirk Prentice, "Minding the Analytics Gap." *MIT Sloan Management Review*, March 16, 2015, https://sloanreview.mit.edu/article/minding-the-analytics-gap/.

6. Anja Lambrecht and Catherine Tucker, "The 4 Mistakes Most Managers Make with Analytics." *Harvard Business Review*, October 1, 2016, https://hbr.org/2016/07/the-4-mistakes-most-managers-make-with-analytics.

7. Christine Moorman, "The CMO Survey," February 2022, https://cmosurvey.org/wp-content/uploads/2022/02/The_CMO_Survey-Highlights_and_Insights_Report-February_2022.pdf.

8. Anmol Rajpurohit, "Qualitative Analytics: Why Numbers Do Not Tell the Complete Story?" KDnuggets, accessed March 22, 2023, http://www.kdnuggets.com/2014/02/qualitative-analysis-why-numbers-dont-tell-complete-story.html.

9. "What Is Tag Management?: Tag Management 101." Signal, accessed March 22, 2023, http://www.signal.co/resources/tag-management-101.

10. Eric Picard, "Ajax Counting Nightmares." ClickZ, June 5, 2006, https://www.clickz.com/ajax-counting-nightmares/61765/.

11. Dharmesh Shah, "Measuring What Matters: How to Pick a Good Metric." Advice and Insights for Entrepreneurs, March 29, 2013, http://onstartups.com/tabid/3339/bid/96738/Measuring-What-Matters-How-To-Pick-A-Good-Metric.

12. Neil Patel, "11 Ways You Can Improve Your Business with Google Analytics." Neil Patel, July 13, 2020, https://neilpatel.com/blog/11-ways-you-can-improve-your-business-with-google-analytics/.

13. Avinash Kaushik. "Web Analytics 101: Definitions: Goals, Metrics, Kpis, Dimensions, Targets." Occam's Razor by Avinash Kaushik, March 9, 2019, http://www.kaushik.net/avinash/web-analytics-101-definitions-goals-metrics-kpis-dimensions-targets.

14. Avinash Kaushik. "Web Analytics 101"

15. "Neil Patel's Digital Marketing Blog." Neil Patel, Accessed March 22, 2023, https://blog.kissmetrics.com/must-have-mobile-metrics.

16. "Top 12 Key Performance Indicators for Maximizing Mobile App Revenue," *Adweek*, June 11, 2015, http://www.adweek.com/socialtimes/top-12-key-performance-indicators-for-maximizing-mobile-app-revenue/621659.

17. "The 8 Metrics You Should Be Using to Track App Success," Clearbridge Mobile, September 1, 2015, https://clearbridgemobile.com/the-8-metrics-you-should-be-using-to-track-app-success/.

18. "17 Great Mobile App Analytics Strategies To Grow Your App Today." YML, August 24, 2018, http://www.ymedialabs.com/mobile-app-analytics/.

19. YML, ... 00, 0000. http://www.ymedialabs.com/mobile-app-analytics/.

20. L. Ceci, "Mobile Apps That Have Been Used Only Once 2019." *Statista*, July 7, 2021. https://www.statista.com/statistics/271628/percentage-of-apps-used-once-in-the-us/.

21. L. Ceci, "Mobile App User Retention & Churn 2018." *Statista*, July 7, 2021, https://www.statista.com/statistics/384224/monthly-app-launches-churn/.

22. "Empower Moves" Awards, Empower Moves Comments, accessed March 24, 2023, https://new.awardshowjury.com/empower-moves/.

23. Jonathan Barnard, "Online Video Consumption in 2016." *Zenith*, July 31, 2015, https://www.zenithmedia.com/mobile-drive-19-8-increase-online-video-consumption-2016/.

24. "Brand Lift." Google, accessed March 24, 2023, https://www.thinkwithgoogle.com/intl/en-apac/marketing-strategies/video/brand-lift/.

25. "How to Identify the Right Kpis for Online Video: Lessons from Google Brandlab." Google, accessed March 24, 2023, https://www.thinkwithgoogle.com/intl/en-145/marketing-strategies/video/how-identify-right-kpis-online-video-lessons-google-brandlab/.

26. Sean Jackson, "2 Simple Ways to Block 'Floating-Share-Buttons.com' Referral Traffic." Botcrawl, September 11, 2022, http://botcrawl.com/block-floating-share-buttons-referral-traffic.

27. Megan McCluskey, "Fake Reviews: Inside the Fight to Stop Them." *Time*, July 6, 2022, https://time.com/6192933/fake-reviews-regulation/.

28. Catey Hill. "10 Secrets to Uncovering Which Online Reviews Are Fake." *MarketWatch*, December 10, 2018, https://www.marketwatch.com/story/10-secrets-to-uncovering-which-online-reviews-are-fake-2018-09-21.

29. "New Rules to Protect Consumers' Hard-Earned Cash ." GOV.UK, accessed March 24, 2023, https://www.gov.uk/government/news/new-rules-to-protect-consumers-hard-earned-cash.

30. Holly Vedova, and The FTC Office of Technology. "FTC to Explore Rulemaking to Combat Fake Reviews and Other Deceptive Endorsements." Federal Trade Commission, November 8, 2022, https://www.ftc.gov/news-events/news/press-releases/2022/10/ftc-explore-rulemaking-combat-fake-reviews-other-deceptive-endorsements.

Part II | Creating Visibility and Attracting Customers

Chapter 6

Developing and Maintaining Effective Online and Mobile Websites

Learning Objectives

By the time you complete this chapter, you will be able to:

1 Explain the role websites play in the decision-making processes of both B2C and B2B customers.

2 Identify the elements that make a website effective.

3 Explain each step in the website development process.

4 Discuss the concept of usability and its impact on customer experience.

5 Summarize the importance of having an effective mobile presence.

As digital and mobile marketing vie for supremacy, websites have taken on new value and faced new challenges. In the early days of the internet, companies rushed to create a website just to have one. Gradually, the potential of the internet meant a movement from the idea that "everyone must have one," toward carefully crafted objectives, design for user experience (UX), measurement of effectiveness, and the necessity of mobile marketing through websites, apps, or both. Companies want visitors to stay on their sites as long as possible, navigate as many paths as possible, and return again and again, a concept often known as site stickiness. Getting the site to be "sticky" is a complex task involving the graphical design of the website, its content, the degree of personalization and interactivity, and the user's engagement and overall experiences on the website.[1] The marketing aspects of creating and maintaining customer-effective sites will be covered in this chapter. Measurement is the subject of Chapter 5.

The Role of Websites and Mobile Apps

There are three key, but not mutually exclusive, roles a website can play in marketing strategy. A website can be a channel for providing information, a channel for generating sales, a channel for facilitating engaging experiences, or all of the above. Information is key in both B2C and B2B markets. Both B2C and B2B marketers generate sales leads (think about retargeting of display advertising discussed in Chapter 10) and both often make sales on their websites. The order of importance for the two market sectors may be switched, though, with sales often most important in B2C and lead generation most important in B2B. Additionally, some sites offer users the ability to have enriching experiences. These are often sites or apps that typically offer social aspects, entertainment aspects (such as playing a game), or design aspects (such as the ability to create something, like a video or meme).

In the roughly 30-year history of the commercial internet, the use of websites as an "electronic brochure" has faded, and marketers have come to understand—and generally to take advantage of—the reach and interactivity of the internet to meet a variety of marketing objectives. Some of the general objectives of websites include to:

- Increase sales revenue
- Generate sales leads
- Increase the visibility of the enterprise and its offerings
- Advertise products and services
- Act as the focal point for a content marketing strategy
- Aid in brand development
- Interface with brand social media sites
- Provide customer service
- Provide a platform for ecommerce
- Retain and grow customers
- Build an online community
- Provide cost savings, especially in promotion and customer service.

Most firms are looking for tangible returns from their websites, either in cost savings or revenue enhancement, and are also looking for the site to reinforce their company strategy and to work in conjunction with other communications and marketing channels. Smart companies develop specific objectives for their website in terms of the stage of customer development, nurturing prospects until they become loyal customers through a series of targeted communications.

B2C consumers use websites in a wide variety of ways, both informational and transactional. A great deal of data is available about users, and companies like Google (Alphabet) and Facebook (Meta) have aggregated much of it into useful advertising tools that can target users on many levels, including interests (e.g., through search history, sites visited, content interactions), activities (e.g., purchase information), and demographics (e.g., location, gender, age).

What B2B Marketers Expect from Websites

On the B2B side, websites are also a mainstay of information acquisition and product purchase. B2B purchasers want detailed information not only about the products themselves but also about service issues like in-stock availability and delivery issues. What kind of content are they looking for if they need to verify the credibility of a site?

user experience (UX)
a term to describe the usability of a website or a mobile app. Its ultimate goal is to provide user satisfaction at every stage of the digital experience. While it is considered by many to be synonymous with customer experience (CX), some feel that the term UX is not as comprehensive as CX.

stickiness
getting visitors to stay on the site, navigate as many paths as possible, and continue to return to the site.

Outranking every other piece of content by a wide margin is contact information. This suggests that personal relationships and selling are not dead in the digital age. The establishment of a relationship is, however, likely to be based on thorough research before contact is made. Surprisingly the same study found that 51 percent of respondents found detailed contact information lacking on websites—a huge oversight! It also found, as shown in Figure 6.1, that blogs and social media activity, and even videos, do not add much to credibility. That does not mean, however, that B2B buyers do not use this type of content to get the detailed product information they want.

Think back to the B2B buyer journey. The three phases of Awareness, Consideration, and Purchase contain numerous steps, several information channels, and a lot of moving forward, then looping back. Along the way a lot of content is located and consumed, Forrester found that B2B buyers get three pieces of information from outside sources for every one piece of information marketers can deliver through their websites, email, and other channels.[3] B2B agency head Heidi Cohen adds that Google research shows that the average business buyer checks over ten pieces of content before contacting the seller. It's easy to assume that the first direct contact for many buyers will be to visit the website. Website content must recognize that potential customers may already be well into the customer journey. She suggests the following steps:

persona
a way of describing different groups of customers by giving them a unique personality.

1. Know your target audience and create personas (discussed in Chapter 13).
2. Use that knowledge to create the content they want.
3. To draw prospective customers to your site, place your content where they are (Figure 6.2) and where they are most responsive. For example, LinkedIn has become the go-to platform for business users; as such, they are also in a business frame of mind when they are on the site.
4. Break down barriers between marketing and sales. In a multichannel, multiplatform world the two must work together, not work as independent business divisions.
5. Measure results.[4]

Figure 6.1   Using Content to Establish Credibility Source: http://marketingland.com/less-than-20-of-b2b-buyers-say-social-media-blogs-impact-vendor-discovery-process-report-124673

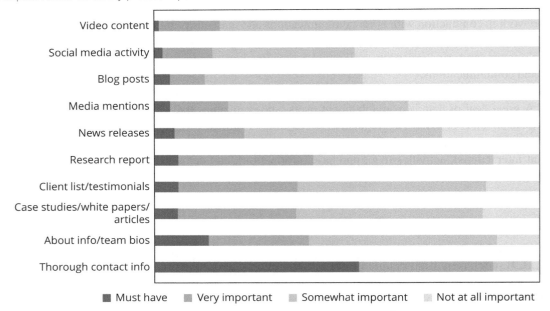

Figure 6.2   Organic Social Media Platform Use B2B – Used in the Past 12 Months Source: https://blog.hootsuite.com/wp-content/uploads/2021/09/B2B-social-media-2.png

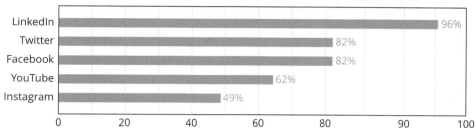

**Organic Social Media Platforms
B2B Content Marketers Used in Last 12 Months**

Platform	%
LinkedIn	96%
Twitter	82%
Facebook	82%
YouTube	62%
Instagram	49%

Other organic social media platforms used in last 12 months: Pinterest (9%); Medium (8%); Quora (4%); Reddit (4%); Snapchat (1%); TikTok (1%); and Other (4%).

Base: B2B content marketers whose organization used organic social media platforms to distribute content in the last 12 months. Aided list; multiple responses permitted.

11th Annual Content Marketing Survey; Content Marketing Institute/MarketingProfs, July 2020

B2C and B2B customers prioritize different types of information on websites. Beyond that, the general principles of designing effective websites hold true in both market spaces. What makes a website effective, and how does the marketer know it is working?

What Makes a Website Effective?

While opinions of websites may differ, there is an overall consensus on what makes a website effective. There are also awards like the Webbys, an annual award for "Internet Excellence,"[5] that can provide inspiration and some guidance. HubSpot maintains a frequently updated list of sites that appeal to marketers for their esthetic and functional qualities.[6] Figure 6.3 shows four examples.

One thing that you cannot see from the static captures is that the websites are consistent throughout. If it has a clean, crisp design, it maintains that theme throughout. If it relies on technology to deliver a spectacular UX, it pulls out all the technology stops. Many of these sites use video and animations to highlight information and gain user attention.

Website design trends are akin to fashion trends. As supermodel and Project Runway cohost Heidi Klum says about fashion, "One day you are in. The next day you are out."[7] The same can be said about website design. Keeping an up-to-date knowledge of website design trends is essential for marketers, and websites should be evaluated regularly to ensure that they are not left behind looking outdated. The Wayback Machine (https://archive.org/web/) offers a powerful and fun way to explore website trends over time. As part of the Internet Archive, the Wayback Machine allows users to "explore more than 682 billion webpages saved over time".[8] The site houses an archive of website snapshots. All you need to do is enter any website address (URL) into the search feature and you will have access to any snapshots stored in the site's expansive database. Larger, more popular sites will have more captures (snapshots) than smaller sites. As illustrated in Figure 6.4, any days highlighted with a circle indicate that there is a capture of the website available for this date. The size of the circle indicates how many captures there are (larger = more) and you can see the timestamps of each capture and select one to view by hovering over any circle.

Figure 6.3 **Examples of Award-Winning Website Designs** Source: HubSpot, Inc.

Figure 6.4 **Internet Archive's Wayback Machine Captures for apple.com** Source: https://web.archive.org/web
/20080201000000*/apple.com

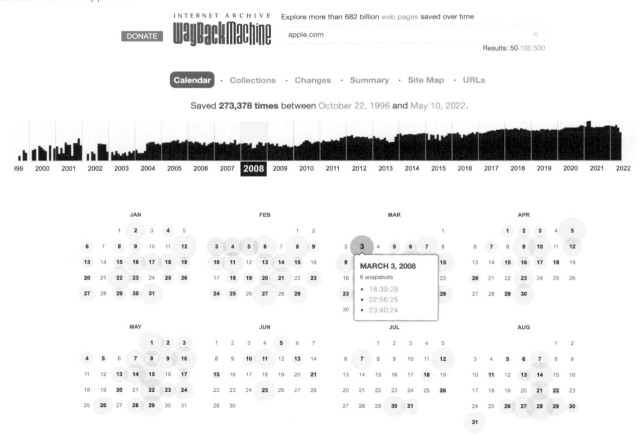

Let's examine Apple.com's design over the years by looking at various snapshots compiled from the Wayback Machine in Figure 6.5. The earliest full snapshot of Apple.com (including images) is from 1997. Here we see the main navigation is on the left-hand side of the screen, which was a common placement for website navigation in the late 1990s to early 2000s. The entire design is very boxy (meaning it is in distinct sections) with few graphics (likely due to the limitations of early internet connectivity). As we move to the year 2000, we see Apple has moved the main navigation to the top of the site in the form of tabs. This positioning and tab-like structure were prevalent on many sites in the early 2000s. Apple has introduced more visuals, with the main photo being front and center, just below the navigation, with less important visuals in boxes directly below it. Apple's design remains relatively similar until 2014, where we see a greater focus on large eye-catching visuals displayed in a grid-like format. Starting in 2018 Apple's design drastically changes. Large images are front and center and stretch along the entire width of the screen. In contrast to earlier designs (especially late 1990s to early 2000s) which were designed so the site fit on the screen without the need to scroll, the site is now designed with scrolling. This difference reflects the changing design needs as users have shifted from visiting the site on a desktop computer to visiting on mobile (phones and tablets).

Take a moment to visit some of your favorite websites and note how they are designed. What are your own personal criteria for effectiveness as you use websites in your daily life? Do you have any special or additional criteria when you are contemplating a purchase from a site? Also, take a look at your favorite sites using the Wayback Machine to see if you can identify trends.

Features for Website Effectiveness

All websites aim to inform their users in a way that helps build brand image and trust. Most also seek to inspire some kind of behavior, such as signing up for an email list so

Figure 6.5 Apple.com's Changing Design 1997–2022 From Archive's Wayback Machine Source: Internet Archive

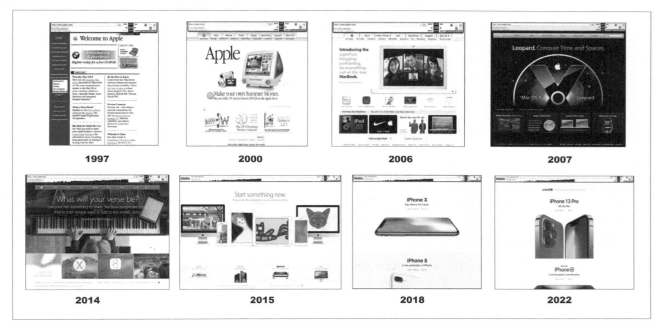

they can receive further information or make a purchase. Ecommerce sites have the special requirement of closing the sale without assistance from any other channel.

In general, sites should have:

- Navigation that is easy to follow and signals to the user where they are within the site and how they got there.
- Images that present products or services in the most compelling way.
- Fast loading times for each page which requires compressing images and other files, among other technical requirements.
- A theme and approach that is appealing to target customers. For instance, a site for a discount retailer would have a different overall look than a site for a purveyor of luxury products.
- A clear privacy policy.
- Follow General Data Protection Regulation (GDPR) compliance for sites targeting European audiences[9] and California Consumer Privacy Act (CCPA) regulations for California residents.[10]
- Easy-to-find contact information and a live chat option using a bot or a person, if possible.
- Easy-to-find addresses for brick-and-mortar establishments.
- Special offers appropriate to the target audience.

Ecommerce sites should also have the following:

- Shopping cart, search bar, and sign-in conveniently placed, usually close to one another.
- The use of filters on sites with a large and varied product array.
- Payment options clearly specified (often contained on the page footer and on the cart and checkout pages).
- A store finder function if the site is for a multichannel retailer.
- A thorough and easy-to-follow return policy.

Think about these effectiveness requirements and the sites shown in Figure 6.3 and ask yourself how marketers know if their sites are effective. We discussed specific website metrics in Chapter 5, but there is a generic answer. *Marketers know that a website works if it is meeting website objectives.* That's why setting objectives is one of the first steps in the website development process, which we now explore.

The Website Development Process

Figure 6.6 summarizes the steps that are essential to the development of an effective website. It begins with the establishment of site objectives, which, in turn, should flow directly from the marketing objectives and the corporate objectives of the enterprise. It goes through six more steps—defining the target market, assessing website development needs, designing the site, conducting usability tests, deploying the site, and measuring site effectiveness and improving the site (refine). Some of the tasks are in marketing's domain; the target market, for instance, and others are in the domain of IT: assessing development needs, for example. Some tasks, such as designing the site structure, require substantial contributions from both departments.

The steps are the same, whether the project is the creation of an entirely new website or whether it is the modification of an existing site. A range of experience and expertise will be required in either instance.

Figure 6.6   The Website Development Process Source: Author-created

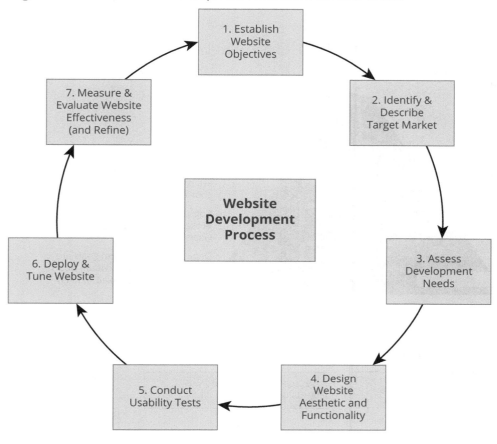

Establishing Website Objectives

The objectives will depend on the nature of the product(s) and what the site is intended to accomplish.[11] There are many possible generic objectives, from brand awareness to ecommerce, as discussed at the beginning of this chapter. The individual enterprise must take these generic objectives and develop them into specific, measurable objectives for the particular website. It is also important for the company to have a clear strategy so that website objectives and target markets can be well delineated.[12]

Figure 6.7a presents the objectives cascade which gives a helpful way for marketers to look at setting their own objectives. Marketing objectives cascade down from corporate objectives, which are strategic and financial in nature. The objectives cascade might look like the examples in Figure 6.7b for one of the several corporate long-term objectives.

Notice that one high-level strategic goal can, and usually does, generate multiple annual goals at lower levels of the organization. Notice also that Figure 6.6a also requires that objectives be SMART—specific, measurable, achievable, realistic, and time-specific.

SMART objectives are essential for success. As we will discuss in Chapter 5, accurate measurement of results cannot take place without SMART objectives. Remember that *marketers can only know that a website works if it is meeting website objectives*. Then add that *marketers can only know if objectives are being met if those objectives are SMART*. Quantitative objectives such as those shown in the cascade example are a start, but they are not fully developed objectives.[13]

In the cascade example, only one corporate strategic objective is shown and that is an internal operating efficiency goal. There would undoubtedly be more and most, if not all, of the others, would be outward-facing. For example, a corporate strategic objective might be to improve ROI by 1 percent per year for each of the next five years.

Figure 6.7a   **How Goals and Objectives Cascade through the Organization** Source: https://www.slideshare.net/RACI101 /raci-overcoming-barriers-to-growth-session-2-51371873

Figure 6.7b   **Examples of an Objectives Cascade**

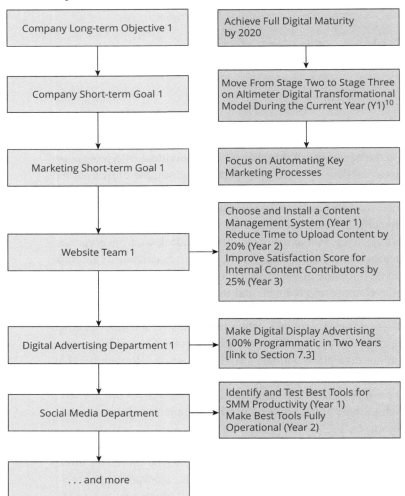

That might lead marketing to adopt an objective of increasing customer retention by 5 percent in each of the next five years, with the cascade to the other departments following.

In establishing objectives, marketers must be keenly aware of their relationship with their target market and its needs and preferences. As a result, a concurrent task is identifying and describing the target market.

Identifying and Describing the Target Market

Marketing is responsible for conveying information about the target market to other participants in the process, in particular, the web designers from the IT department. It is the job of the marketing department to understand how the objectives relate to a specified target market. Marketing is also the location within the firm of detailed knowledge about the needs, attitudes, and shopping behaviors of market segments targeted by the business.

Marketers must share this information with all who are involved in designing and building the site. Think about it. Should a site, say an entertainment-oriented one which is targeted at teenagers, look and interact like an entertainment-oriented site that is targeted at older adults? Likewise, should sites for different audiences have the same functionality? You will undoubtedly agree that it should not and that content, visual appearance, and interaction should all be designed with a specific target market in mind. It is the marketer's job to see that the site is geared to the identified target market by sharing information about the target market with web designers and developers.

The best way to transmit this information within the website development team has proven to be personas. Personas are also discussed in another context in Chapter 13. Figures 6.8a, b, c, and d show one of the personas developed for a website project and how it was used. Penny is a first-time buyer of this brand, a married sales assistant who lives in London. For this project, a total of six personas were developed, each one representing a distinct customer segment.

Figure 6.8   Example of a Buyer Persona (a) First-time Buyer Penny Persona; (b) Storyboard for Penny; (c) Generic Home Page; (d) Home Page Design for the Penny Persona Source: Smart Insights Ltd

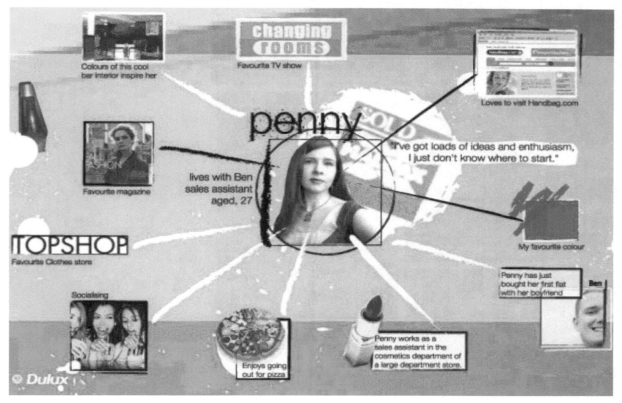

(a)

Figure 6.8   *(Continued)*

Inspire me

Color range

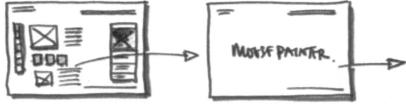

Penny's ideas start to change as she reads the article - rather than just paint the room one color, why not take the advice on the page and try something different?

Penny follows the link through to the colors that she has seen in the article, and sees a link to add them to mousepainter™.

(b)

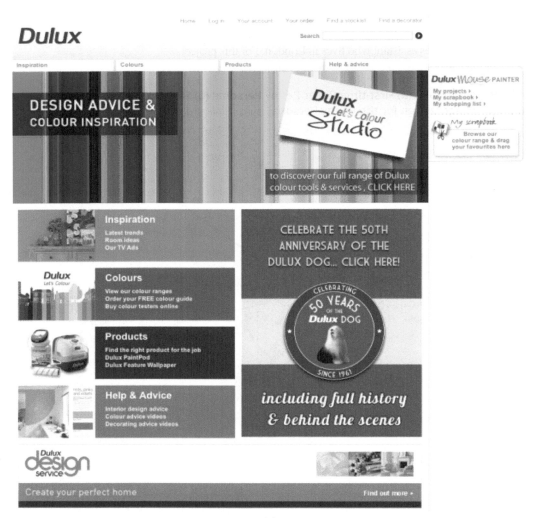

(c)

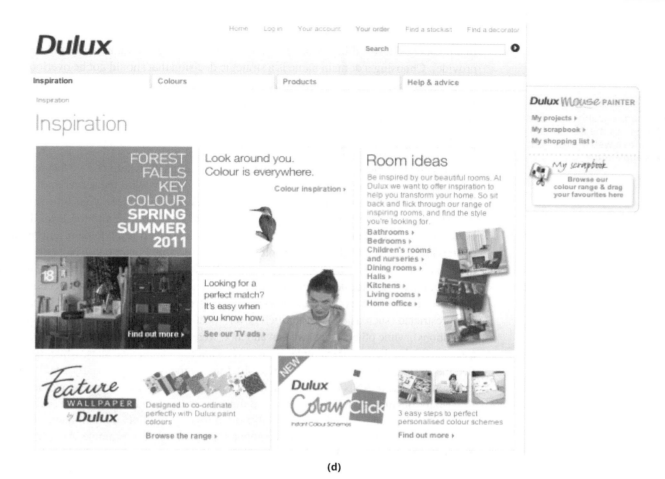

(d)

Notice that the storyboard shown in Figure 6.8b is a technique taken from traditional advertising in which marketing explains to the executors of the website the kind of decision-making process this segment is likely to use and perhaps the emotional states associated with the process. With knowledge about the persona, web designers and programmers can move from the generic home page, shown in Figure 6.8c, to a personalized home page for the persona. It caters to the decisions Penny needs to make when buying paint, giving her useful ideas and information.

A site may be personalized to key segments or not depending on the perceived usefulness of personalization and the time and budget available. Whether there is personalization or not the next step is to design site content and the navigational structure. This step will guarantee optimum accessibility of the content to the target market.

Assessing Development Needs – Registering a Domain Name, Choosing a Hosting Provider, and Website Content Management System

Now that you have clear objectives and have identified your target market, you can assess your development needs. This is an important step since development needs directly impact many technical choices in the website development process. For instance, will you use a Content Management System (CMS) or build a custom site from scratch? If your site is for eCommerce it will need additional features beyond an informational brochure site (such as shopping cart and checkout capabilities).

Purchasing a Domain Name and Website Hosting

In a nutshell, the two things you need to start a website are a domain name and a hosting provider. Choosing a domain name is a strategic decision that should not be overlooked. A domain name represents your company and is the way that users will find your website. Put simply, a domain name is the address of your website. The domain name system (DNS) is managed by the nonprofit organization Internet Corporation for Assigned Names and Numbers (ICANN, https://www.icann.org/). Domain names are simply a human-readable form of an IP address. When you type a URL into a web browser (such as www.apple .com), your web browser uses the domain name to identify where (i.e., what server) to find the corresponding website. Your browser then connects with the server and pulls all the necessary files (e.g., HTML, CSS, images, videos) to display on your browser.

Domains are comprised of two parts, the second-level domain and top-level domain. For example, in the domain sample.com, "sample" is the second-level domain, and "com" is the top-level domain. URLs can also contain subdomains (see Figure 6.9a). Not only do you need to think carefully when choosing a second-level domain, but you also have some flexibility in choosing a top-level domain (TDL). In the early days of the commercial internet, ICANN allowed very few choices for TDLs (such as .com, .net, .org, and .edu). Some TDLs were restricted (such as .gov for verified government sites and .edu for verified educational institutions), while others (such as .com and .net) were not, but still had a specific type of site associated with them. For example, .com was meant for commercial sites, while .org signified the site was a non-profit (see Figure 6.9b). Luckily today, there are nearly 1,500 TDLs to choose from[14] as ICANN opened the ability for people to apply to create new ones in 2012.

Many businesses will choose to use their company name, brand name, or product name for a domain name. Companies also often register multiple domain names to cover an array of products, services, or even company misspellings. For example, Apple currently has apple.com, newton.com, me.com, and airport.com, among others.[15] In most instances, if your preferred name is not available because it is already registered by someone else you are out of luck, so you may have to get creative. For trademarked names, however, this is

domain name
a human-readable form of an IP address. It's the destination you type into a web browser (such as www.apple.com).

Figure 6.9a   **The Anatomy of a Domain.** Source: https://www.ionos.com/digitalguide/domains/domain-administration/what-is-a-subdomain/

Components of a URL with subdomain

| Protocol | Subdomain
Third-Level domain | Domain name
Second-Level domain | TLD
Top-Level domain |

IONOS

Figure 6.9b   **Examples of Different Top Level Domains (TLDs)** Source: Author-created

.com commercial for profit	target.com
.net network resource organizations	alaska.net
.edu Educational organizations	uri.edu
.gov Government organizations	mass.gov
.org Not-for-profit organizations	gsusa.org (Girl Scouts)
.fr/.de /.us/.uk Specific countries	mcdonalds.fr

a different story. A trademark owner may petition to get control of a registered trademark, but the process may not be so straightforward. Sometimes a trademark is registered as a domain name without the knowledge that it is a trademark, while other times people may intentionally register a company name, brand name, or trademark in the hopes of making money by selling the domain name to the business.[16] This is referred to as cybersquatting. Cybersquatting is illegal and there are examples of cases where companies have fought back against cybersquatters. For example, Jennifer Lopez successfully won against a cybersquatter for registering the domain JenniferLopez.biz.[17] It is important to note that to be successful in a cybersquatting case there needs to be evidence of intent to profit. Sometimes people get lucky and have an existing domain name that was registered before a trademark was registered and, in these cases, sought-after domains are purchased by the company. For example, the domain name iphone.com was registered by an individual in 1995 well before Apple decided to create its phone. Apple reportedly paid $1 million to transfer ownership of the domain in 2007.[18] How do you find and register a domain? This is easily done through a domain name registrar such as porkbun.com, google (https://domains.google/), or many others. Go to one of these registrars and search for yourself to see what is available. It is important to note that your domain registrar and hosting provider do not need to be the same.

Once you have a domain name, the next step is to find a website hosting provider. Hosting providers offer server space to host your website. Hosting providers vary in terms of their technical capabilities, price, and speed so it is best to read about current capabilities and do a thorough comparison before committing to one. Some examples of hosting providers include A2hosting, GoDaddy, Dreamhost, and Siteground. Most hosting providers have the same content management system capabilities, a term which we will discuss next, but it is important to check to make sure before committing to one.

Content Management Systems

The majority of modern websites are built using a content management system (CMS). A CMS is a software application that assists in the building and maintenance of your website. Some use WYSIWYG (what you see is what you get) templates that require little to no coding skills, while others may require more coding. The CMS can house your website's digital assets (videos, photos, website) and content. CMSs are ideal for websites where multiple users need access as they offer easy collaboration. In theory, a CMS makes the management and creation of content easier and cheaper since web developers are not needed with each new content addition or change. Some examples of current popular CMS platforms include WordPress (open-source, extended for ecommerce with WooCommerce plugin), Joomla, Drupal, Wix, Bigcommerce, and Shopify.[19]

Designing Website Aesthetic and Functionality

Identifying the necessary content and the appropriate manner of presentation are other tasks in which marketing will take the lead. The content of the site is something that, at first glance, appears quite straightforward. Designing content for the web is both supported and complicated by technology. It is also important to take the requirements of the target market(s) in mind. Identify what is the most important content on the page for each market segment and make sure that it is placed predominantly on the page "above the fold," which is placed at the top of the screen and can be accessed without the need to scroll. This term comes from the pre-digital days when newspapers were the main source of news consumption. Newspapers (then and today) were sold from sidewalk kiosks and because they were folded in half to fit the kiosk potential customers could see the top half of the front page.[20] This made the content in this area extremely important because if it didn't grab the attention of a customer or passerby, then they would not stop and purchase

cybersquatting
the process of registering, selling, or using a domain name with the intent of profiting from the goodwill of others (typically another company's trademark).

content management system (CMS)
software that assists in the building and maintenance of your website, thus allowing people with little or no coding skills to add or edit website content.

WYSIWYG
(what you see is what you get) website editing software that allows content to be created and edited without the need for coding. Content is often entered into a form that resembles its appearance when displayed as a website (as opposed to viewing code).

above the fold
content that appears on a screen without scrolling.

the paper. Moreover, most visitors skim instead of reading word by word. This means that copy should be laid out in short blocks with eye-catching visuals and headings. When the copy is long, the marketer should assume that many visitors will not scroll down far or will not jump to a continuation page and should place key content accordingly.

Technology tools, such as eye-tracking, can offer insights into how to best structure a website's content. A well-sited series of studies conducted by the Poynter Institute, the Estlow Center at the University of Denver, and Eyetools, Inc. uses eye-tracking cameras in an ongoing study to see how consumers read news on websites. The cameras allow the researchers to record with precision the movement of a respondent's eyes on a web page (Figure 6.10a).

Results from the series of studies indicate that in the absence of specific design elements:

- Eyes first land in the upper left of the page, especially if attracted by a headline.
- Users usually look at only the first few words of headlines.
- Respondents tend to look at five headlines on these news pages before clicking.

That information has led to dividing a web page into 16 quadrants, with the upper left being the highest priority for content placement, roughly the middle being the second priority, and roughly the right and bottom being the lowest priority (see Figure 6.10b).[21]

heat maps
visual representations of eye activity on a web page.

The technology has also led to the development of heat maps. The red to orange areas in Figure 6.10c indicate the most activity and the blue to black the least. The upper left-hand corner of the page is often called the "Golden Triangle" because it forms a triangle shape. Others refer to this area as the "F" section since the user's eyes move backward and forward in that triangle area as they examine the content.

Figure 6.10 **(a) An Eye Track Map (b) The Priority Grid (c) A Heat Map** Source: Copyright © The Poynter Institute, http://www.poynterextra.org/eyetrack2004/viewing.htm#1.3, and http://www.poynterextra.org/eyetrack2004/viewing.htm#1.2.

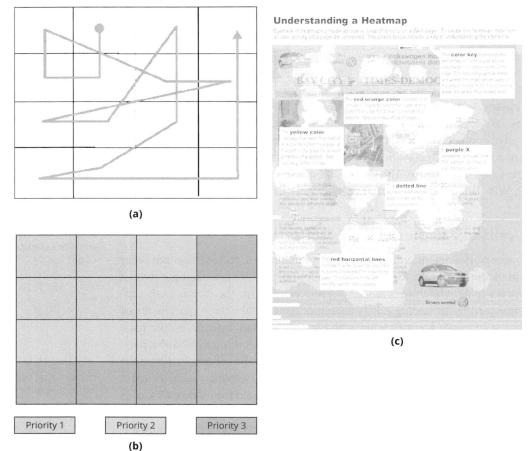

(a)

(b)

Priority 1   Priority 2   Priority 3

(c)

Recent research focusing on the reading of news on tablets shows the ongoing importance of eye-tracking. Researchers from the Poynter Institute found that most readers preferred to hold their tablets vertically and swipe horizontally even though visual content may have been set up in landscape orientation. They also confirmed website findings that people tend to enter a site through a dominant element, often a photograph. Faces in both photos and videos attracted much viewer attention.[22]

Tools that use either eye-tracking or tracking of mouse clicks are a standard part of web design. There are free-standing tools for DIY use like the one at Crazy Egg, which uses mouse clicks to produce heat maps and other website analytics.[23] Many website design and analytics platforms include these tools.

The use of heat maps and the tracking of mouse clicks argue for the importance of well-written and designed content on websites. The more task-oriented the viewer is and the more in a hurry they are, the more likely they will leave because of poor content or poor navigation. It is also important to recognize that visitors enter the site at different times and on different pages—they do not necessarily start on the home page. Content must be relevant, make sense even if it has been archived for a long time, and repeat key points without sounding repetitive. And—of critical importance—visitors must be able to find it easily. This is the job of the content design and the navigation structure.

Designing the Content and Navigational Structures

The first step is to design the content structure or information architecture, which is often done with a sitemap. The implication is that there must be a coherent structure to the content of a site, usually one that is hierarchical in nature. This enables visitors to move around the site in a manner that fits each person's individual need to merely examine summary information or to drill deeper into the site in search of detailed information about a specified topic. At the same time, the site designer or information architect plans a careful and comprehensive structure, they should adhere to a simple premise often referred to as KISS—Keep It Simple Stupid! The end goal of information architecture is to understand how the user expects to find the information presented (their mental model) and design the site to correspond with the way the user thinks about the content. Making a sitemap also ensures that all pages link to one another so users can access them (pages that are not within the sitemap are referred to as "orphan pages"). The level of depth of the website can also be visualized with a sitemap. One way of implementing the KISS rule is to try to see that the visitor is never more than three mouse clicks away from desired information.

sitemap
a visualized structural plan for the organization of a website's pages and how they relate to one another. The term sitemap also refers to an XML document that lists all the pages on the site, which is used by search engines to crawl the site (e.g., https://www.apple.com/sitemap.xml).

There are specific issues to consider when designing a site structure. The main issues and rules of thumb are as follows:

1. **User intent.** Visitors come to the site for a particular reason. Are they primarily searching for information or looking for a transaction, or perhaps both at different stages of the customer journey?

2. **Effective communication.** People scan a website, scrolling quickly through content. Use headings, subheadings, bullets, and "chunk" information in a way that makes it quick and easy for visitors to comprehend.

3. **Readable websafe fonts.** Sans Serif fonts, those that do not have the small lines at the top and bottom of characters, are more readable on the web. Use websafe fonts such as Arial, Helvetica, and Verdana. Websafe fonts are common to all computer users, therefore anyone accessing websites that use these fonts will be able to view them as designed (see https://www.w3schools.com/cssref/css_websafe_fonts.asp for a current list of websafe fonts). Try not to use more than three different fonts and font sizes.

4. Colors. Choose colors carefully to convey the ideas and the emotions you want the visitor to experience. Colors should align with branding.

5. White space. Use white space to give pages a modern, uncluttered look. Effective use of white space also helps direct the user through the site.

6. Visuals. Use images and videos to communicate the message in a way that can be more effective than the best-written copy.

7. Design for ease of use. A good navigation structure with organized layouts that facilitate eye movement is the aim.

8. Fast loading. No matter how much visual content is on your site, it must load quickly. Tools like GTmetrix (https://gtmetrix.com/) and Google's speed page analysis tool (https://pagespeed.web.dev/) are available to help you achieve fast loading.

9. Works on different size screens and different devices.[24] We will discuss designing mobile sites later in the chapter.

10. Accessibility. Websites need to be available to people with physical challenges like impaired vision. Per Title III of the Americans with Disabilities Act (ADA), all websites need to prohibit discrimination "on the basis of disability in the activities of public accommodations."[25] Not having an accessible website can be costly, as seen in the example of the lawsuit filed by the National Federation for the Blind against Target Corporation which Target settled in August 2008 and agreed to pay $6 million in damages.[26]

11. Figures 6.11a and b show two highly recommended steps in developing the navigational structure of a website. The first is to develop a simple graphical flow chart that shows the structure of the site. It shows the home page or parent page, second-level pages (also called "child pages") which are the entry points to major content areas of the site, and the succeeding levels that provide more detailed types of content. Notice that the persona storyboard in Figure 6.8b shows this kind of structure in an informal way. There may be more levels than shown here but going beyond three or four levels creates a complex site that may be difficult for visitors to navigate. Even though the graphical hierarchy appears deceptively simple, it ensures that the connections are logical and it gives an overview of the navigational task that will face visitors. It is a step that must not be overlooked.

wireframe
a blueprint that specifies the layout of pages on a website (similar to a template).

The next step is to develop mockups of pages. A detailed mockup called a wireframe is shown in Figure 6.11b. A wireframe shows the type, placement, and size of each piece of content on each type of page. It also provides notes to guide the technical part of the development process. Wireframes can be developed informally, perhaps on a whiteboard, but there are tools available to make the process faster and easier with tools like HotGloo (shown in Figure 6.11b).

Site Navigation

A website's navigation should be simple and straightforward. It should be set up in a way to guide users through the site's content. Ideally, navigation should answer the questions: Where am I? How did I get here? Where can I go? How can I get back (home)?

Where am I? Simple visual elements on the site's navigation, like underlining, bolding, or changing colors, can communicate to users where they are within the site. An example is shown in Figure 6.12 where the current page the user is viewing is displayed as a different color on the navigation. This is especially helpful in sites with deep content and these are usually done with changes to the code within the CSS (cascading style sheets).

Figure 6.11   **(a) Sample Plan of Website Hierarchy (b) A Wireframing Tool in Action** Sources: (a) © Cengage Learning 2013, (b) http://www.hotgloo.com/

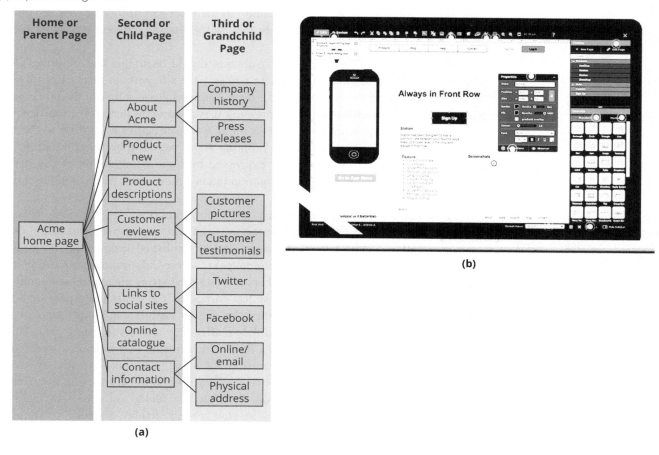

(a)

(b)

Figure 6.12   **Example of Website Navigation Answering the Question "Where am I?" using color.** Source: Otter love

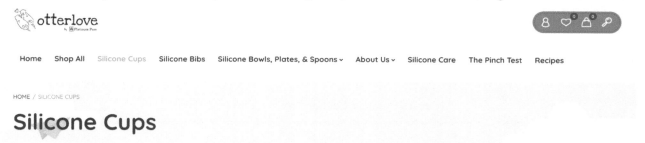

HOME / SILICONE CUPS

Silicone Cups

Natural Grip™ = Perfect Training Cup

We designed our natural grip™ cup to be the perfect training cup for babies and toddlers learning to drink from an open glass. Whether moving from a bottle or a sippy cup, this cup is designed to make the transition as seamless as possible.

100% Pure Platinum Silicone with No Fillers
Like all otterlove products, this cup is made with 100% Platinum Pure™ LFGB Silicone – the purest silicone – with no plastic or fillers.

The unique curvature along our cup's sides allows for a natural fit for a child's hands on

breadcrumbs
navigational aid showing the path that the user has followed.

How did I get here? Taking it one step further, the use of breadcrumbs, a navigational tool near the top of each page showing the path that the visitor has followed to reach this location in the site, allows users the ability to see what part of the site they are on and easily navigate backward. Breadcrumbs look as follows and different styles can also be seen in Figures 6.12 and 6.13.

Where can I go? Navigational structures should be simple and intuitive. Good navigation allows visitors to be able to navigate the site without instructions by following familiar web conventions (like the corporate logo as a link to the home page) or simple logic. Another way of expressing it is to say that the navigation structure should be designed with the visitor in mind, not necessarily according to the way managers and marketers are used to thinking about their corporate information. The navigational structure is commonly expressed by some combination of nav bars at the top of the page, expandable navigation menus, mouseover menus, and text links at the bottom of the page.

website convention
an established design norm that has become ingrained in users' schemas (mental maps)

How can I get back (home)? One of the most important website conventions to follow is to place the site logo at the top left-hand side of the page and that clicking this logo will take you home. This convention, an established design norm, has become so ingrained in user's schemas (mental maps) that research found that "Getting back to the homepage is about six times harder when the logo is placed in the center of a page compared to when it's in the top left corner."[27] It is desirable to provide a link to the home page on every page within the site so visitors can simply start over if the path becomes a bit torturous or if they realize they are on the wrong path. This is typically done by using the logo as a link, which fulfills two functions—providing both branding information and the return to the home page link. As with any image-based navigation, be sure that the visitor can easily identify it as a link by using an alt tag that provides further detail about an image. The alt tag also serves an important function for visitors whose browsers are slow, cannot display graphics, or are using a screen reader for accessibility.

alt tag
a tag (a type of IMG or image tag) that describes the image for people who cannot see it because of browser limitations or physical disabilities or when an image fails to properly display.

Figure 6.13 Example of Website Navigation Answering the Question "How did I get here?" using breadcrumbs.
Source: Saks Fifth Avenue

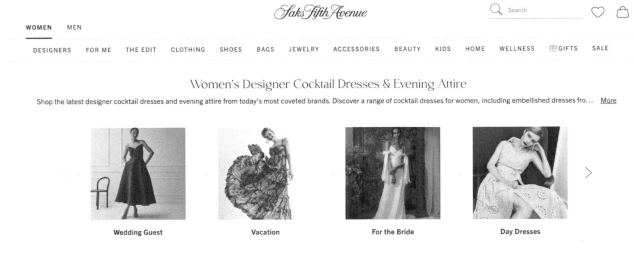

Usability Testing

Usability testing is conducted to see if the site works in a user-friendly fashion according to the expectations of members of the target market. Usability tests are essentially qualitative, and they are performed by marketers interacting with target site users, not by technicians.

usability

the ability of a site to provide a satisfactory user experience.

There are many marketing services and agencies with expertise in usability testing. One such person is Dr. Jakob Nielsen. Now a consultant, he was with the original Bell Labs and IBM before moving to Sun Microsystems where he was the lead usability engineer for the establishment of the first Sun website in 1994. He has been a consultant for many years, doing research on many aspects of usability and being a tireless advocate for the importance of good UX on sites. He advocates testing early and often. In 1998 he founded the Nielsen Norman Group (https://www.nngroup.com/), along with Don Norman, a usability research consulting group that offers insights and reports on usability today.[28]

Stages of Usability Testing

Usability testing can be divided into general categories as follows:

- **Concept testing** is the earliest stage and reflects none of the actual site programming. In testing at this stage, one or more concept boards are shown to respondents who critique it from the perspective of how logical they perceive it to be and how easy they think it would be to use. Concept tests are useful at a very high level to prevent egregious design flaws and to give general guidance to the designers about what customers and prospects expect and what they think about the design concepts presented to them. This type of testing can be done relatively quickly in a focus group setting. Since it requires only the development of concept boards, it is also relatively cheap. Remember that the concept boards are testing the design of major pages on the site and the degree to which these pages communicate the desired corporate image and specific communications objectives, not the communication appeals themselves.

- **Prototype testing** is the second level. At this point in the development process, the site design is complete and at least some parts of the site are functional, but not all content has been added. Testing a prototype affords an opportunity to get reactions to the appearance of the site and to get some information about the degree to which the site structure is consistent with customer expectations. The earlier prototype testing is conducted, the more visual appearance and structure can be changed without increasing the development time and cost of the site. Early testing, however, implies that much functionality is probably not operating and that the test will be somewhat artificial. The marketer must carefully assess the trade-off between early and more complete testing.

- **Full usability testing** indicates that the site has been uploaded to a server and is fully functioning, even though it is not accessible to the public.

The main focus of a usability test is to ask test users to perform tasks that simulate what a visitor would want and expect to do on the site. Various types of tasks are given in a usability test. Typically, users are first asked to simply explore the site for a few minutes. Oftentimes this is done with a "talk aloud" protocol where they freely discuss their choices and ask questions. Next, users are typically given a specific task such as locating a specific product or information on the site. For example, on a home goods site, they may be asked to locate the cheapest blender. Oftentimes users are given a persona profile and instructed to pretend to play the role of that person. They can also be given tasks to follow (based on the persona) and marketers watch the user as they navigate the site. For example, for a university website, a user may be given the persona of a high school student's parent and asked to browse the site in that mindset. They may also be given a specific task, such as "Pretend that your daughter has just been accepted to this school. You are concerned about the school ranking and the tuition costs. Please navigate the site to try to find information about (1) school rankings and (2) tuition." The marketer can test usability by seeing how difficult these tasks are as measured in the number of clicks it takes and the time it takes to complete the tasks along with verbal feedback. Additional usability test tasks can instruct users to answer specific questions about customer service on the site, such as whether the customer could cancel an order after placing it.

Usability Testing and the Pareto Curve

Usability testing should not be considered an option or a luxury. Even the best-designed websites invariably have problems that are quickly detected by users. Even so-called cosmetic problems will produce an inferior user experience.

Pareto curve
a plot of number of occurrences against percent of total; the source of the 80/20 rule.

The need for testing is often questioned on the grounds of both time and expense. Dr. Nielsen makes a strong case for the affordability of user testing by constructing a Pareto curve which shows that over 75 percent of a site's usability problems can be identified with *five user tests and that 100 percent will be found by testing 15 users*.[29] He also states that, with experience, the tests can be completed in two workdays at a cost of less than $1,000 if user recruiting has been outsourced to a commercial marketing research firm.[30] The message should be that eliminating or skimping on usability testing can be detrimental to a site's success. It should be a standard part of the launch of any new website, whether it is completely new or a redesign.

One important decision the marketer will have to make is, at which stage in the development process the usability testing should be done. The earlier it is done, the easier it will be to make fundamental changes. At the same time, the lack of prototype functionality in early-stage testing makes it somewhat artificial. On the other hand, if the functionality is nearing completion, considerable time and money have been invested in the site and it will be harder to make major changes. The issues involved in testing a prototype versus a fully functioning site suggest that several small-scale tests at various mileposts along the way will be more productive than any single larger-scale test. Once the site is launched, usability testing is one of the essential tools for monitoring its ongoing progress and for identifying areas for improvement.

Special Usability Requirements for B2B Sites

All of the requirements for good UX on B2C sites apply to B2B sites as well. However, it is important to remember that the customer journey for B2B may be longer and involves multiple parties in the buying process. That requires some additional considerations to provide good UX for B2B sites. Dr. Nielsen says, "When testing B2B sites, we often hear business customers lament the usability gap between B2B sites and the better-designed consumer sites they use after hours."

Differences in the B2B customer journey and decision-making process should be accommodated by:

- Content that supports long purchase decision processes. The content should focus on solving the problems of business customers, communicate why your product solves problems better than competitors' products, and provide tools to share content with buying team members. Customer success stories are helpful as are various kinds of content including white papers, blogs, and videos.

- Clear information about product integration and compatibility and about regulatory issues. Business purchasers have to know how products will fit into their existing systems and processes and process that they meet the relevant regulatory standards. Images and animations of product use are helpful.

- Content that is relevant to both "Choosers" and "Users." This is another purchasing team issue with one person (the chooser) making the final decision and many users having input into the buying. Users are focused on how products will solve their problems and make their work easier and more productive. Choosers tend to be focused on ROI details such as price, operating costs, and lifespan. They also tend to be the most concerned about regulatory issues.

- Realistic pricing scenarios. B2B pricing can be complex and it must be explained clearly. Careful design, including imagery, is an aid to understanding.

- Design that speaks to different target customer segments without confusing or alienating any of them. Dr. Nielsen explains that the typical B2B approach is to design around audience segments like Small Business and Enterprise Accounts. On the surface, this is being customer-oriented. He explains the problem it can present as follows:

> "Audience-based navigation can cause a myriad of problems if these segments aren't clearly labeled (or if there is any overlap between them). For example, a huge enterprise customer might still have a small team with a specialized (and localized) need closely matches that of small business customer. Whenever using visitor segments in navigation, ensure that they are clearly defined (i.e., define the number of employees for a small business versus a large business), and that they are mutually exclusive."[31]

One way to deal with the issue of multiple target segments with different needs and purchasing behavior is the use of filters. This isn't technology, just good design as shown in Figure 6.14. American Express has credit cards and services specifically designed for consumers (Figure 6.14a) and businesses (Figure 6.14b). Both are clearly shown

Figure 6.14   The American Express Home Page with Distinctions between User Segments (a) The American Express Home Page Showing Personal Options; (b) The American Express Home Page Showing Business Options; (c) The American Express Home Page Showing Card Options Organized by Segment Type Source: American Express

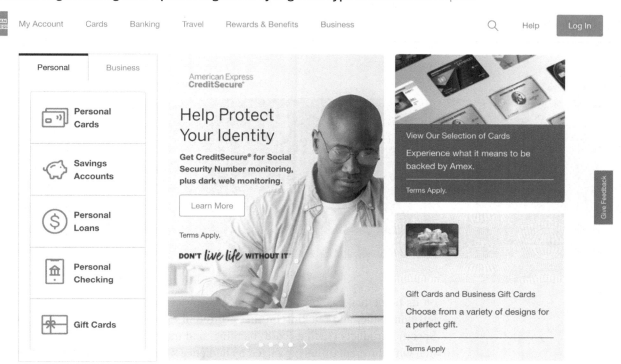

(a)

Figure 6.14 (*Continued*)

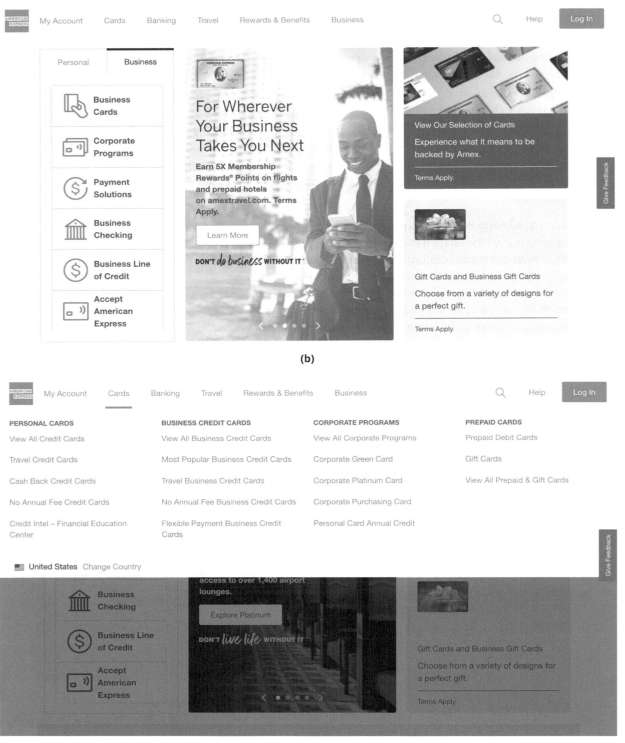

(b)

(c)

on its home page as visitors have the option to choose "Personal" or "Business" on the left-hand side, and clicking on these different tabs provides different targeted options. Specific products (such as card, banking, and travel) are outlined along the top navigation with different offers organized by audience segment appearing when they are clicked (Figure 6.14c). It's clear, well structured, and makes it hard for visitors to lose their way.

Deploying and Tuning the Website

This stage is essentially a technical one. The site itself should be fine-tuned, compressing images to make them load faster, checking links, and in general making sure that the site works as quickly and smoothly as possible. It is then ready to be uploaded to a host server (a computer that manages requests from browsers and returns HTML pages from the website in response to those requests) on the internet. Uploading requires working closely with the hosting service to ensure that the site meets all its technical requirements. The host will deal with technical issues like load balancing and distributing content for faster access, but the site performance must be continually monitored in-house.

Measuring, Evaluating, and Improving Website Effectiveness

Technical monitoring will be conducted by the IT department. Marketing is responsible for measuring and evaluating *the business effectiveness* of the site, a topic discussed in detail in Chapter 5. The evaluation metrics will provide information that points to areas in which it is possible to refine and improve site effectiveness. Possible improvements that surface as a result of site evaluation range from infrequently accessed pages to abandoned shopping carts to navigation paths that indicate difficulty in locating content. Looking for ways to continuously improve your site should be the norm for websites. If improvements can be made without radically revising the site, they should be implemented immediately. When the burden of proof generated by the evaluation metrics and various kinds of user satisfaction measures warrants it, a full-scale redesign and relaunch of the website should be undertaken.

Looking back over this process, it should be abundantly clear that the initial steps in website development rely heavily on marketing for structure and guidance while technical design, function, and usability concerns tend to predominate in later stages. One of the worst mistakes digital marketers can make is to simply turn the process over to the technical experts and say, "design us a website." The result is almost certain to be a website loaded with technical bells and whistles but without a marketing objective in sight. Yet this is what sometimes happens in companies of all types and sizes.

The entire website development process, then, should focus on the marketing objectives of the site, along with usability and user satisfaction required for the accomplishment of the objectives, while making sure the site is fully accessible to all users. The process should be seen as an iterative one, with usability tests at various stages signaling either the need for more work or readiness to proceed to the next stage.

In addition to being an integral part of website development, usability testing should be done throughout the life of the site on a regular basis to uncover possible problems and to understand opportunities that are suggested by changes in visitor behavior. It should also be done when there is a sign of usability problems—a sudden uptick in the number of people abandoning shopping carts at the payment information page, an increased bounce rate, or people leaving the site because it is taking a long time to load, for example.

Designing Sites for Mobile

We have probably all clicked through to a site on our smartphone or tablet only to find it unreadable—or at least not worth the effort. That is unacceptable today as more visitor traffic moves to mobile. Mobile-friendly sites are also important because they are essential for a high ranking in search results. Remember that not being mobile-friendly is not a viable option today as over 50 percent of site visits are reportedly done on a mobile device.[32]

The same principles apply to any economic activity. Customers want easy-to-use digital experiences with mobile often at the forefront. The technology innovators have already transitioned; marketers must focus on making mobile technology work for technology laggards. In designing sites for mobile customer satisfaction there's a piece of good news. All the basic concepts of designing good sites for the desktop apply in principle. However, that does not mean that it is easy to make a desktop site work on any mobile device—and that is the criterion—on *any* mobile device. The issue leads to two questions:

1. Should we have a mobile website or an app?
2. If a site, should we use responsive or adaptive design?

There are a number of considerations when deciding on which route to follow which we will discuss next.

Stand-Alone versus Responsive versus Adaptive Site Design

responsive site
fluid site design that detects the user's device screen size and automatically adapts to it.

adaptive site
a type of site design in which a different site is created for each user device.

dynamic serving
the ability to serve different site code (HTML, CSS) without changing the URL. The term "adaptive site" is synonymous.

There are three basic options for creating a mobile website—a stand-alone site, a responsive site, or an adaptive site (also referred to as dynamic serving). A stand-alone site, identified by a separate URL (typically a subdomain, such as m.yourbrand.com), is completely separate from the main website. It was a popular early solution to the need for a mobile website. However, visitors are redirected from the website to the mobile site and such redirects are typically time-consuming and interfere with the seamless experience. In addition, a stand-alone site requires extensive maintenance since you have two websites to update. For these reasons using a stand-alone site is not the best or most used option. These mobile stand-alone sites are being replaced by either responsive or adaptive mobile sites.

Both responsive and adaptive sites sense the device on which the user is accessing the site and respond automatically, providing a more seamless user experience. The technological difference is whether the code changes based on screen size (responsive) or whether multiple static layouts are made based on pre-identified breakpoints.

> **Responsive web design** (as shown in Figure 6.15) is comprised of a single design with a fluid layout that adjusts to the screen width of the device, meaning that only one set of page templates needs to be created and maintained.

> **Adaptive web design** (as illustrated in Figure 6.16) uses a completely different set of designs and templates for each device being targeted. As a result, designers will create a desktop version of a website and will then design a separate mobile version (and possibly a separate tablet version also).[33]

As you can gather, adaptive websites are likely to be more costly and more work because you need to make multiple design layouts for each size. Typically, designers making an adaptive site make layouts for six common screen widths: 320, 480, 760, 960, 1200, and 1600 pixels).[34] However, some argue that adaptive design offers a better user experience as the goal is to make sure your site is functional on all mainstream devices.

Figure 6.15   Responsive Website Design Fluidly Adjusts to Fit any Device. Source: Wix Inc.

Figure 6.16   Adaptive Design Snaps into Place by Choosing the Most Fitting Layout Out of a Selection of Fixed Designs. Source: Wix Inc.

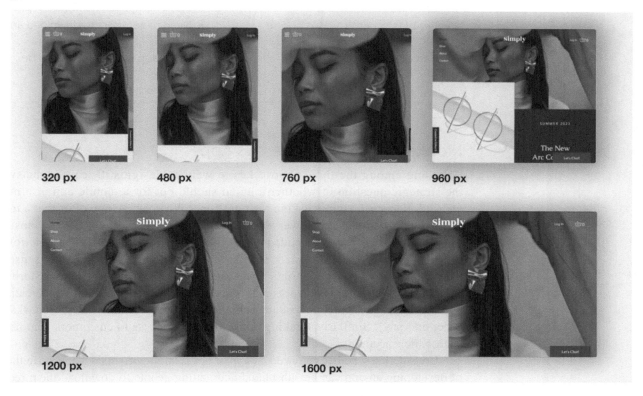

There are several pros and cons for each type of design which are briefly laid out below.[35]

Pros	Cons
Adaptive Design	
• It provides a good user experience to individuals on any device. • Users usually have a specific way they prefer to interact with a website. Their intentions are different if they are doing it on a mobile device compared to a computer, this is considered with adaptive design.	• Typically, more costly to develop an adaptive site. • Creating an adaptive web design is not a simple process. • It involves creating a lot of layouts for different displays (typically six break points). • Google prefers responsive sites
Responsive Design	
• Is fluid to fit any device. • Can be completed faster, will cost less, and is easier to maintain. • Devices with HTML5 are able to continue to display content even if the connection to the internet is lost.	• Navigation can be negatively affected. Images may also be resized too small or large. • It is difficult to run a responsive website on an older web browser because they do not support the media queries needed to provide data about the dimensions of the screen.
Mobile Apps	
• Added interactivity features • Additional features not available on a website can add value • Ideal for frequently repeated or routine tasks • Enables access to core phone functions • Can increase loyalty	• Most costly • Different versions needed for different phones and operating systems (ios vs android, etc.) • More complex development process • Need to get users to download and install • Need app store approval to be approved • Updates needed

Mobile-Friendly Sites versus Apps

Choosing among the three approaches to website design still leaves unanswered the strategic question of whether a brand should opt for a mobile app or a mobile website. For most, simply asking the question, "What can an app offer that a mobile site can't?" is enough to answer whether an app is needed or not. For the most part, mobile apps are not recommended unless they offer specific benefits or functionality that a site can't offer. For instance, Starbucks' mobile app makes perfect sense as it allows users a way to pay, order, and access and use loyalty programs. Starbucks' customers also tend to visit stores multiple times per week (often daily) so creating an app makes sense so customers can easily access their accounts to do core tasks (like order and pay). Similarly, banking apps offer easy access to customers who need to access their accounts.

Considering whether you need an app or not is an important decision since the cost of developing an app can be substantial and getting people to download them requires additional marketing effort.

What are the requirements for a good app? They include the following:

- The brand has a clear app strategy. Is it a customer retention app? Does it offer features for tasks like payment or ordering?

- It is helpful if the task cannot be performed as well on the mobile web as on an app. For instance, if a person wants to summon a cab while standing on an urban sidewalk, doing so from an app should be easier than locating the mobile website and summoning the cab from there.

- The target audience is heavily mobile and becoming more so every day.[36,37]

- When interactivity is essential, as in a game.

- When personalization is necessary, as in a financial services app.

- When functionality is to be built into the application, as in click to call to order a pizza.

- When the functions need to be accessible without internet access.

Designing a Mobile Website

The final question, then, is "what are the additional considerations that apply to designing sites for the mobile web beyond the ones that provide good UX on the internet?" Keep in mind that these are also the issues you want to consider when doing your own evaluation of how well a mobile site is functioning.

Google has a detailed white paper that discusses criteria for good mobile site design. The criteria are based on usability tests they performed with 119 mobile users. They uncovered 25 criteria, which were divided into five major categories:

1. Homepage and site navigation
2. Site search
3. Commerce and conversions
4. Form entry
5. Usability and ensuring that the site renders properly for the device.

If you think through that list, you can probably remember instances where each factor has hindered your ability to have a good experience on a mobile site. Each one needs to be carefully considered when a mobile site is being developed or fine-tuned. Google says:

> The common thread in all sections is that mobile users tend to be very goal-oriented—they expect to be able to get what they need from a mobile site easily, immediately, and on their own terms. Ensure success by designing with their context and needs in mind without sacrificing richness of content.[38]

HubSpot continues with factors that need to be considered when optimizing a mobile site:

- A simple, probably Sans Serif font, at least 12 pixels in size
- Touch-friendly navigation and calls to action
- Keep code as minimalist as possible to speed site loading
- All images sized to the device; none unnecessarily large
- Make sure videos load properly
- Keep forms short.[39]

There are more technical issues, but just as for an internet site it is important for the marketer to establish the appropriate requirements and ask the right questions, then let the web designers do their work.

Summary

This chapter sets forth a marketing perspective on building and maintaining websites without understating the effort and expertise needed for successful technical design, programming, and implementation. Marketers are primarily responsible for the initial stages of website and mobile site development in which objectives are established, the target market is identified and described to all participants, and the information architecture and navigational structure of the site are laid out. Web personas are usually developed by marketers and are a good way to understand customers and how they might interact with the site, especially if used in conjunction with usability testing.

Marketers are also responsible for working closely with technical professionals during actual site development and closely monitoring the site for UX and consistency with business and marketing objectives. To ensure UX usability testing is essential during site development and to uncover problems on a regular basis thereafter.

In today's world, the website may play many roles and be used by marketers for everything from getting sales leads to developing online communities. In addition, customers shop across multiple channels and increasingly rely on the web for product research as well as purchasing. Mobile sites and apps are playing an increasing role in the early purchase journey stages with purchasing increasing, but more slowly.

Having a mobile-friendly site is no longer optional. The choice is between stand-alone, responsive, and adaptive sites with responsive finding the most favor at present. Mobile sites must display properly on all devices or they do not meet the criteria for mobile-friendly. Marketers must also decide whether to create a mobile app.

The same overall process and the same criteria for creating user satisfaction apply to both desktop and mobile sites. There are additional criteria for satisfying experience on the mobile web or with mobile apps. Customers move back and forth between devices, so it is critical that all the criteria be met to create a seamlessly satisfying experience which is the marketer's goal.

Discussion Questions

1. True or False: A website development team will be made up of IT specialists and marketers. Take a position on this statement and be prepared to defend your answer.

2. True or False: It is imperative that marketers play the leading role in all stages of the website development process. Take a position on this statement and be prepared to defend your answer.

3. What are the steps involved in developing a website? What should be the marketer's role in each step?

4. True or False: SMART goals are nice but not essential. Take a position on this statement and be prepared to defend your answer.

5. Discuss the role of personas in creating a website and consider whether one persona or multiple personas are generally required.

6. Website accessibility is important and necessary for all websites.

7. True or False: Marketers must develop their own criteria to determine whether a site is mobile-friendly or not.

8. What are key reasons why it is important to have a mobile-friendly site?

9. Why do you think stand-alone mobile sites are losing favor?

10. What are responsive and adaptive designs? How are they alike and how do they differ?

11. What are some of the reasons to develop a mobile app?

12. True or False: All businesses must have a mobile app.

Endnotes

1. "5 Ways to Increase Stickiness with Web Design," Purely Branded | Cleveland Web Design and Development, October 24, 2012, http://www.purelybranded.com/insights/5-ways-to-increase-stickiness-with-web-design/.

2. Joe Henderson, "CX vs. UX: What's the Difference?: Customer vs User Experience," UserTesting, accessed March 8, 2023, https://www.usertesting.com/blog/cx-vs-ux.

3. Lori Wizdo, "Buyer Behavior Helps B2B Marketers Guide the Buyer's Journey," Forrester, accessed March 8, 2023, https://www.forrester.com/blogs/author/lori_wizdo/.

4. Heidi Cohen, "How the 2015 B2B Purchase Decision Process Has Changed," Heidi Cohen, December 8, 2016, http://heidicohen.com/2015-b2b-purchase-decision-process/.

5. "Home," The Webby Awards, accessed March 8, 2023, https://www.webbyawards.com/.

6. Austin Knight, "37 Of the Best Website Designs to Inspire You in 2022," HubSpot Blog (HubSpot, August 25, 2022), https://blog.hubspot.com/marketing/best-website-designs-list.

7. "Project Runway Quotes," accessed March 8, 2023, https://www.imdb.com/title/tt0437741/quotes.

8. Internet archive: Wayback Machine, accessed March 8, 2023, https://archive.org/web/.

9. "General Data Protection Regulation (GDPR) Compliance Guidelines," GDPR.eu, accessed March 8, 2023, https://gdpr.eu/.

10. "California Consumer Privacy Act (CCPA)," State of California-Department of Justice-Office of the Attorney General, February 15, 2023, https://oag.ca.gov/privacy/ccpa.

11. Andrew Kucheriavy, "Best Examples of Website Goals and Objectives," Intechnic (December 2, 2019), https://www.intechnic.com/blog/best-examples-of-website-goals-and-objectives/.

12. Brian Solis with Jaimy Szymanski, "Six Stages of Digital Transformation," http://www.altimetergroup.com/pdf/reports/Six-Stages-of-Digital-Transformation-Altimeter.pdf.

13. Andrew Kucheriavy, "Best Examples of Website Goals and Objectives," Intechnic (December 2, 2019), https://www.intechnic.com/blog/best-examples-of-website-goals-and-objectives/.

14. "TLD DNSSEC Report," ICANN DNS Engineering, accessed March 8, 2023, https://www.dns.icann.org/services/tld-report/.

15. James Iles, "Top 10 Domains Owned by Apple in 2022: Apple.com, Next.com, and More...," James Names, January 19, 2022, https://jamesnames.com/2021/02/top-10-domains-owned-by-apple-in-2021-apple-com-next-com-and-more/.

16. Nolo, "Cybersquatting: What It Is and What Can Be Done about It," www.nolo.com, *Nolo* (April 3, 2013), https://www.nolo.com/legal-encyclopedia/cybersquatting-what-what-can-be-29778.html.

17. "Cybersquatting Examples: Everything You Need to Know," UpCounsel, accessed March 8, 2023, https://www.upcounsel.com/cybersquatting-examples.

18. Yoni Heisler, "Wipo Orders That Ipods.com Domain Be Transferred over to Apple," *Network World* (August 1, 2011), https://www.networkworld.com/article/2220308/wipo-orders-that-ipods-com-domain-be-transferred-over-to-apple.html.

19. "15 Best and Most Popular CMS Platforms in 2023 (Compared)," *WPBeginner*, January 1, 2023, https://www.wpbeginner.com/showcase/best-cms-platforms-compared/.

20. Sharon Hurley Hall et al., "17 Stunning Examples of above the Fold Content to Hook Your Visitors," OptinMonster, January 18, 2021, https://optinmonster.com/11-examples-of-superb-above-the-fold-content/.

21. Steve Outing, "Eyetrack III: What News Websites Look like through Readers' Eyes," *Poynter*, September 1, 2015, http://www.poynter.org/2004/eyetrack-iii-what-news-websites-look-like-through-readers-eyes/24963/.

22. Sara Dickenson Quinn, "New Poynter Eyetrack Research Reveals How People Read News on Tablets," *Poynter*, November 24, 2014, http://www.poynter.org/2012/new-poynter-eyetrack-research-reveals-how-people-read-news-on-tablets/191875/.

23. "Crazy Egg Website - Optimization: Heatmaps, Recordings, Surveys & A/B Testing," Crazy Egg, accessed March 8, 2023, https://www.crazyegg.com/.

24. Sofia Woods, "10 Top Principles of Effective Web Design," Shortie Designs, February 14, 2019, http://shortiedesigns.com/2014/03/10-top-principles-effective-web-design/.

25. "All You Should Know about Web Accessibility Laws in the United States 2021," *Rev* (August 11, 2022), https://www.rev.com/blog/web-accessibility-laws-in-the-u-s.

26. "A Cautionary Tale of Inaccessibility: Target Corporation," W3C Web Accessibility Initiative (WAI), accessed March 8, 2023, https://www.w3.org/WAI/business-case/archive/target-case-study.

27. Kathryn Whitenton, "Centered Logos Hurt Website Navigation," Nielsen Norman Group, accessed March 8, 2023, https://www.nngroup.com/articles/centered-logos/.

28. "History of Nielsen Norman Group: UX Training, Consulting, & Research," Nielsen Norman Group, accessed March 8, 2023, https://www.nngroup.com/about/history/.

29. Jakob Nielsen, "Why You Only Need to Test with 5 Users," Nielsen Norman Group, accessed March 8, 2023, https://www.nngroup.com/articles/why-you-only-need-to-test-with-5-users/.

30. Jakob Nielsen, "When to Outsource the Recruiting of Test Users," Nielsen Norman Group, accessed March 8, 2023, https://www.nngroup.com/articles/when-to-outsource-recruiting-test-users/.

31. Page Laubheimer, "B2B Vs. B2C Websites: Key UX Differences," Nielsen Norman Group, accessed March 8, 2023, https://www.nngroup.com/articles/b2b-vs-b2c/.

32. Tiago Bianchi, "Global Mobile Traffic 2022," *Statista*, January 30, 2023, https://www.statista.com/statistics/277125/share-of-website-traffic-coming-from-mobile-devices/.

33. Graham Charlton, "What Is Adaptive Web Design (AWD) and When Should You Use It?," Econsultancy, May 28, 2014, https://econsultancy.com/blog/64914-what-is-adaptive-web-design-awd-and-when-should-you-use-it/.

34. "Responsive Design vs. Adaptive Design: What's the Best Choice for Designers?," Studio by UXPin, December 23, 2022, https://www.uxpin.com/studio/blog/responsive-vs-adaptive-design-whats-best-choice-designers/.

35. "Adaptive vs. Responsive Website Design: Best Comparison Guide," Fireart Studio, January 3, 2022, https://fireart.studio/blog/adaptive-vs-responsive-website-design-best-comparison-guide/.

36. Rank Fishkin, "Mobile Web vs Mobile Apps: Where Should You Invest Your Marketing?," Moz, accessed March 8, 2023, https://moz.com/blog/mobile-web-mobile-apps-invest-marketing-whiteboard-friday.

37. Ken Lin, "The 4 Key Beliefs of Mobile-First Companies | Inc.com," accessed March 8, 2023, https://www.inc.com/ken-lin/the-4-key-beliefs-of-mobile-first-companies.html.

38. "Principles of Mobile Site Design: Delight Users and Drive Conversions," Google, March 2016, https://www.thinkwithgoogle.com/marketing-strategies/app-and-mobile/principles-mobile-site-design-delight-users-drive-conversions/.

39. "The Marketer's Guide to Mobile," HubSpot, accessed March 8, 2023, http://offers.hubspot.com/mobile-friendly.

Chapter 7

Search Engine Marketing

Learning Objectives

By the time you complete this chapter, you will be able to:

1 Summarize the reasons why search marketing is so important.

2 Explain what is meant by the term Search Engine Marketing (SEM).

3 Explain how the process of organic search or Search Engine Optimization (SEO) depends on keywords and title tags.

4 Explain the technical process behind a search query.

5 Discuss the basic process of optimizing a website for organic search.

6 Explain how search and social media work together.

There are multiple customer acquisition techniques used by marketers in integrated programs spanning both advertising techniques and media. In this chapter, we discuss an acquisition technique that has enjoyed explosive growth and has become an integral part of how we work in digital marketing—search marketing. Search marketing is in a sense a true outgrowth of the direct marketing roots of digital marketing discussed in Chapter 1 because it allows us to be in front of the customer at the exact moment they are researching a product or service or considering a purchase. Although we may not know exactly who the customer is at the point they see an organization or firm listed on the results of a search, the company knows what they are interested in at that moment. If we can encourage them to learn more about us or make a purchase, we then have the opportunity to acquire them as a customer, to collect specific information about them, and develop a long-term relationship.

The Growing Impact of Search

Search has proven to be one of the key drivers in the growth of digital marketing. When the Pew Internet & American Life Project asked American consumers in 2004 about their use of search engines—websites that work to help users to find the things they wanted to find on the internet—32 percent said they "couldn't live without them."[1] At that time, the average internet user performed 33 searches per month, a total of 3.9 billion searches on the 25 most popular search engines. To put this information in perspective, Google currently processes over 100,000 searches per second or 6 billion search inquiries per day or 2.5 trillion searches per year, and growing.[2]

However they are quoted, the statistics above underline the fact that the trend toward search engine usage and dependence has continued at a breakneck speed. Overall attitudes toward search are positive. The following information also puts that usage in perspective:

- Ninety-eight percent of all internet users use a conventional search engine at least once a month.[3]

- Seventy-one percent of B2B clients start product research with search engines.[4]

- Eighty-one percent of retail shoppers conduct online research before buying

- Google accounts for 78 percent of desktop and 89 percent of mobile search traffic. (https://99firms.com/blog/search-engine-statistics/)

- Ninety-nine percent of 18- to 29-year-olds in the United States are internet users, making it the age group with the highest level of internet penetration in the country. Seventy-five percent of adults over 65 years of age say they use the internet also.

- Internet usage by age is clear, but usage by gender, ethnicity, and other demographic characteristics is a little less clear. Men (78 percent) slightly outpace women (75 percent). Internet usage by ethnicity shows that Whites (78 percent) are pretty similar to Latinos (75 percent), with both exceeding usage among African Americans (68 percent). Not surprisingly, internet usage increases with education and income.[5]

Around the world, 63 percent of people say they trust "search engines" for news and information.[6]

Results are so positive that it appears that desktop search volumes peaked in 2013 and that nearly 60 percent of all searches are now performed on mobile devices.[7] However, the mobile search market only represents about a third of the revenue of desktop search, as users continue to make larger ticket purchases during the week and when they are on their desktops. Mobile users typically look to search engines for information about products but may make purchases on their desktop. We can expect those trends to reverse as mobile purchasing becomes easier and mobile ads more relevant.[8]

Web users continue to look for information on specific topics, maps and directions, news and current events, general information, shopping, and entertainment—in other words, just about everything! Millions of searches every day encompass a wide range of subject matter. Search has radically transformed fields such as healthcare and real estate, with patients walking into their doctor's office armed with information and home buyers depending on real estate search sites and virtual tours to limit their possibilities before they even set foot in a home for a real-world tour. No wonder marketers have found opportunities for marketing through search engines on the web medium and now on mobile devices.

Marketers are also using search engine marketing for just about everything. Web marketers use search for branding, online sales, lead generation for both manufacturers and dealers, driving traffic to websites, and simply to provide content. As Figure 7.1 illustrates, search spending has been steadily growing with worldwide search spend expected to exceed $250 billion by 2026. Statista estimates search spending for the United States alone in 2022 to be over $100 billion:[9]

- Ad spending in the Search Advertising segment is projected to reach US$116.50 billion in 2022.

- Ad spending is expected to show an annual growth rate (CAGR 2022–2027) of 11.87 percent, resulting in a projected market volume of US$204.10 billion by 2027.

Figure 7.1 Search Marketing Ad Spending Shows Continued Growth Source: Statista, Inc.

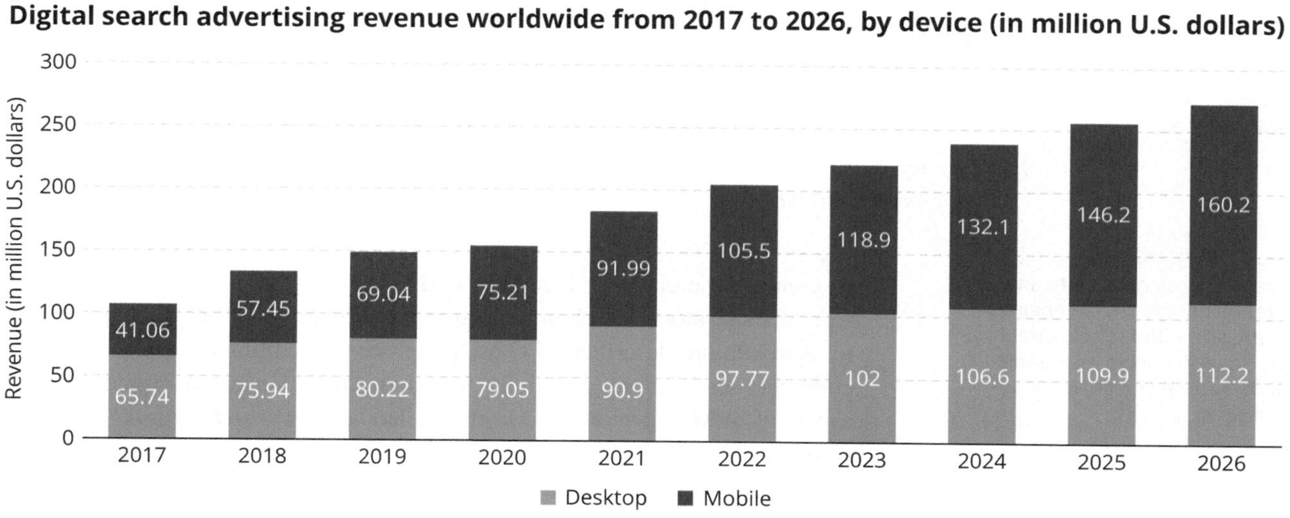

Digital search advertising revenue worldwide from 2017 to 2026, by device (in million U.S. dollars)

Year	Desktop	Mobile
2017	65.74	41.06
2018	75.94	57.45
2019	80.22	69.04
2020	79.05	75.21
2021	90.9	91.99
2022	97.77	105.5
2023	102	118.9
2024	106.6	132.1
2025	109.9	146.2
2026	112.2	160.2

Revenue (in million U.S. dollars)

■ Desktop ■ Mobile

- In global comparison, most ad spending will be generated in the United States (US$116.50 billion in 2022).
- In the Search Advertising segment, US$132.50 billion of total ad spending will be generated through mobile in 2027.
- The average ad spending per internet user in the Search Advertising segment is projected to amount to US$379.10 billion in 2022.

Search is still a formidable industry, with the biggest SEO challenge for marketers being measuring the ROI of search efforts.[10]

The above information illustrates the importance of search in digital marketing today. However, the world of search is broader than just a search engine that helps users find the things they want to find on the internet, important though they are. Search includes several types of search engines, including desktop-only search, specialty search, and another major category, directories, which are aids in finding internet websites. Directories and classified advertising sites like craigslist and Angi (formerly Angie's List) still play a role in how consumers find information online.

Directories create a list of sites that are usually arranged by category, and each directory has a search function. Directories emerged early in the history of the internet. For example, Yahoo! began as a directory in which Jerry Yang and Paul Filo listed their favorite websites. The essence of a directory is that it offers both free basic listings and paid enhanced listings that allow any local business to add business details, including photos and a link to their website, to their basic listing.[11]

Directories can also be compiled from other sources. The Open Directory Project by DMOZ is free and describes itself as "the largest, most comprehensive human-edited directory of the web. It is constructed and maintained by a vast, global community of volunteer editors."[12] Online directories seem to be overtaking their offline counterparts in many market sectors, ranging from finding former high school classmates to locating business services. However, directories have declined in importance in terms of SEM with the rise of search engines. In reality, the most important aspect of being able to be found on the internet is to be indexed by the major search engines, which can require submitting the website to these engines. Like directories, search engines have both a paid aspect and a free aspect.

search engine
website that works to help users find the things they want to find on the internet.

directory
an aid in finding internet websites; a list of sites are usually arranged by category, an aid in finding internet websites; a list of sites are usually arranged by category, and the directory has a search function.

Search Engine Marketing

The entire process of getting listed on search engines so consumers can find a company online is called search engine marketing (SEM). The Search Engine Marketing Association (now part of the Digital Analytics Association) popularized the definition of SEM as "a form of internet marketing that seeks to promote websites by increasing their visibility in search engine result pages."[13] There are two basic aspects of SEM:

search engine marketing (SEM)
process of getting listed on search engines.

search engine optimization (SEO)
process of designing a site and its content whereby search engines find the site without being paid to do so; also known as organic search, natural search, or algorithmic search.

- Search engine optimization (SEO) refers to the process of designing a site and its content whereby search engines find the site without being paid to do so. The former stand-alone search organization SEMPO (now part of the Digital Analytics Association) described SEO as "the process of editing a website's content and code in order to improve visibility within one or more search engines." The free aspect of SEM known as SEO is also called *natural search*, *organic search*, and sometimes *algorithmic search*.

- **Paid search, also known as Pay-per-Click (PPC)**, advertising, involves "ads targeted to keyword search results on search engines, through programs such as Google Ads sometimes referred to as Pay-per-Click (PPC) advertising and Cost-per-Click (CPC) advertising."[14] The paid aspect of SEM is also called paid search (PPC) and is based on an advertising model where firms seeking to rank high in specific search categories will bid on certain terms or "keywords" in the hopes of a lucrative search ranking. A lucrative ranking is one that makes money for the firm and is not necessarily the number one or two spot on the page. Sometimes a number two or three spot will be just as profitable for the firm. Paid search will be covered in more depth in Chapters 8 and 10.

paid search (PPC)
the paid aspect of SEM based on an advertising model where firms seeking to rank high in specific search categories will bid on certain terms or "keywords" in the hopes of a lucrative ad ranking; also known as PPC (pay-per-click).

In the paid aspect, most search engines' success at bidding and creating relevant ads still determines ad placement, and in the natural search aspect, other factors are taken into account. While both paid and natural search are important, natural search brings in the majority of website visitors (anywhere from 60 to 80 percent depending on the estimates) and is the "most commonly used resource to navigate websites." Paid search advertising growth continues, if at a slower rate than previous years, and is evolving beyond text-only ads as a SERP (search engine results page) would typically not plural as a definition. include additional content like videos, images, shopping, and maps.[15] It is referrals and not ads that drive traffic. Referrals and social media are also playing an increasing role in helping users find websites.[16] The reason is that users want to trust the source that is recommending the site, and organic search results or referrals from a friend or an often-used social media site are the most trusted ways to find information on the web.

SERP (search engine results page)
a list of results displayed to users from their query.

Table 7.1 compares the advantages and disadvantages of the two types of SEM. Although SEO requires no out-of-pocket costs to pay for ad placement, there is a cost in terms of time to effectively design a site to optimize it for natural search. It is also difficult to predict search ranking with SEO and may take several months for the results of the efforts to be noted on search engines. PPC provides immediate results and allows the user to limit spending to a daily budget, but PPC campaigns also must be monitored on a daily (or hourly) basis because it is easy to lose a top search ranking if another firm outbids your firm in terms of keywords. Also, the impact of SEO if monitored properly, while it takes longer to set up and implement, can have a long-term effect versus the short-term effect of PPC programs, which last only for the duration of the ad campaign. (Please note we are referring to search results as "search results" or "search ranking." The specific term "page rank" refers to a mathematical algorithm named after Google cofounder Larry Page to indicate how important a page is on the web.)

page rank
a mathematical algorithm named after Google cofounder Larry Page to indicate how important a page is on the web; used as a metric when evaluating websites.

Table 7.1 Comparison of SEM Techniques: SEO versus PPC

	Advantages	Disadvantages
SEO (Natural or Organic Search)	Better response since majority of clicks are organic More return traffic Lower cost Long-term marketing solution Brand recognition and loyalty	Results are not immediate Ranking is difficult to predict Initial time investment and time is major cost Takes time for results to be displayed
Paid Search (PPC, Pay-per-Click)	Immediate results based on bidding system in which there are charges for clicks received Daily budget can be limited Gives definite search volume Easy to change focus Unlimited keywords Ability to test (keywords, ad copy, landing pages, etc.)	Easy to lose ranking or spot Daily budget can be expensive depending on keywords Unqualified clicks

Organic Search Building Blocks

Keywords are search terms, words, or phrases, selected by the user when making a search in a search engine.

The term "keyword" can be confusing in itself because it can refer to but is not limited to the following items:

- Search terms, words, or phrases, inputted by the user when making a search in a search engine
- Terms that are bid on in a PPC system in a browser such as Google or shopping site such as Amazon

Early search engines relied heavily on the "on-page" factors of web pages, that is, the content of the site. This included the actual words on the webpage and also relied heavily on meta tags, like the keyword meta tag. The keywords meta tag was developed for websites to help search engines index them for relevant topics, but since this tag was controlled by the site owner, it quickly became abused as marketers could stuff often irrelevant keywords that were not even related to the site. This abuse inspired Google's cofounders to develop Google. Google revolutionized search by being the first search engine to consider "off-page" factors, such as the links pointing to a web page. In the now seminal paper authored while Ph.D. students at Stanford University, "The Anatomy of a Large-Scale Hypertextual Web Search Engine," Google cofounders Larry Page and Sergey Brin explained their rationale for a new search engine.

Akin to the process of citations for academic papers, Page and Brin argued that links from other websites act as a signal that can be used to measure the importance and quality of another website. They also argue for the importance of anchor text (the words that are hyperlinked) and the proximity of words to one another. In their paper, they give the example of a user searching for "Bill Clinton" (the sitting U.S. president at the time of the paper's writing). They note that "we have seen a major search engine return a page containing only "Bill Clinton Sucks" and picture from a "Bill Clinton" query… If a user issues a query like "Bill Clinton" they should get reasonable results since there is an enormous amount of high quality information available on this topic."[17] They then go on to show

keywords
(or keyword) terms, words, or phrases that are selected by the user when making a search in a search engine; also refers to terms that are bid on in a PPC system.

Google's results for "Bill Clinton" which are much more relevant results, including the Whitehouse.gov website. In addition to the number of links coming to a site, the paper argues that the quality of those links should also be considered. In a nutshell, it not only matters how many sites are linking to you, but the reputation of those linking sites is also important.

Because the keywords meta tag was so often abused, in 2009, both Google and Yahoo! began disregarding the keywords meta tag in 2009,[18] and other search engines also no longer use it. Today, major search engines, particularly Google, are now concerned with customer "intent" in search and whether the page is a good fit for the search query used. The fear with meta tags is that they may be manipulated and may not refer to anything close to the content that the site actually contains. However, meta tags like "description" and "title" tags are important from a user experience perspective as these are often used by search engines when displaying the results to users. This is important since the content of these tags determines whether a user clicks on your site's link. When tags, like the description tag, are left empty or not present in the HTML code, search engines fill them in with their choice of content from your website, often the first available text, which may not optimally reflect the page's content.

How Search Engines Work

Search engines are the focus of attention in SEM because they are the heart of the search process. Search engines have the ability to organize and make accessible the vast amount of information available on the web.

When a user enters a query, the search engine looks for information on the web and returns a list of results known as a search engine results page (SERP). These results are in the form of suggested web pages, images, videos, maps, or other types of files. Increasingly, they include results from the user's social contacts, as discussed later in the chapter. The inclusion of search results from multiple content sources such as videos, images, news, maps, books, and websites into one set of research results is called universal search.

First, the user initiates a query that goes to the search engine's web server. The web server then sends the query typically to an index server, which stores information on previously categorized pages of websites as a best fit to certain keywords. To index all this information, search engines use spiders or "robots," which are programs that "crawl" the web and follow every link or piece of data that they see and bring this information back to be stored. The content of each page—words extracted from the titles, headings, or special fields (meta tags)—is then analyzed to varying degrees to determine how they should be indexed. (Site content, inbound and outbound links, and other information are also used, which we discuss later in this chapter.)

Meta tags or meta elements are parts of HTML code within the *header* portion of a website. (You can see the HTML code, including the header data, on any website by viewing its source by right-clicking on a webpage and selecting "View Source" or through the web browser menu. Figure 7.2 shows an example of HTML code for title, description, and robot meta tags in the header section of a fictional website for pink purses. Below the

universal search
the inclusion of search results from multiple content sources such as videos, images, news, maps, books, and websites into one set of research results.

index server
stores the information index, which has categorized websites as the best fit for certain keywords.

spiders
programs that "crawl" the web and follow every link or piece of data that they see and bring this information back to be stored; also known as robots.

meta tag
a section in the HTML header section of a website that can be used to describe the site in more detail, including content and keywords; also known as meta name, or meta element.

Figure 7.2 An example of HTML code for Title, Description, and Robots Meta Tags in the Header Section of a Sample Website for Pink Purses.

```
<head>
<title>Pink Handbag World</title>
<meta name= "description" content= "Pink Handbag World has a huge
selection of stylish, affordable handbags and purses. Get the latest
fashion trends and tips to look your best from Pink Handbag World" />
<meta name= "robots" content='index, follow' />
</head>
```

beginning of the header section is the title tag, a useful tag used by search engines as the text of the link in the SERP, and which we discuss more later in this chapter. Below the title tag are two meta tags; these tags are written as meta name=. The first meta tag is the "description," which often contains a sentence or two describing the site, in this example, it describes the website and is often used by search engines in the SERP. The second is a "robots" meta tag that gives website spiders (crawlers) instructions about how they can crawl and index the site. In this example, the tag indicates that robots are allowed to follow links on the page to discover additional content and index the page (note, search crawlers can also be instructed through the use of a robots.txt file that includes instructions for crawlers about how they can crawl and index the entire site). These are just three tags used by Google and other search engines. More information about additional supported meta tags can be found at https://developers.google.com/search/docs/advanced/crawling/special-tags.

While the search results are almost instantaneous for the user, there are a multitude of processes that occur behind the scenes. Figure 7.3 illustrates the process of a web search as discussed above. The relevant documents are then taken from the search engine's document server based on an appropriate *algorithm*, and then displayed for the user. The word "algorithm" in the context of search does not refer to the process of solving a mathematical problem. A search engine algorithm displays the search engine's "best guess" at which pages are most relevant to the user's search and in which order they should be shown.

Figure 7.4a indicates how the ESPN website looks to spiders. As the spiders move through a site, they are just looking to see what topics are covered and the order in which they are covered. The spiders do not make any particular judgment about the activity. In this case, the spider would pass information back to the index indicating each time the term "ESPN" had been used and on which page.

A "word cloud" of the site shown in Figure 7.4b illustrates the most frequently used terms on the site. In this case, "ESPN," "Sports," and "Olympic" are shown as larger than other terms, which indicates that they are used more often. ESPN is known for its comprehensive sports

title tag
the title the user sees in the bar at the top of the web page and appears as a hyperlink in a search engine results page; also known as the HTML title tag.

search engine algorithm
displays the search engine's "best guess" at which pages are most relevant to the user's search and in which order they should be shown.

Figure 7.3 **The Generic Search Process** Source: Adapted from "The Life Cycle of a Query" from Marketing and Advertising Using Google: Targeting Your Advertising to the Right Audience, Copyright © 2007 Google Inc., p. 12.

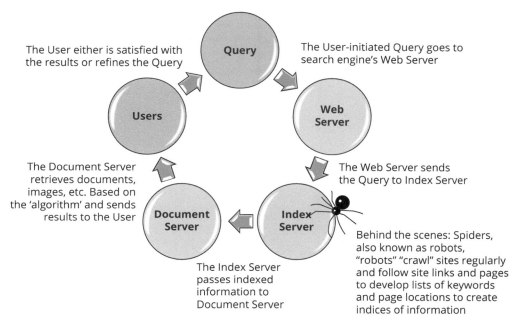

Figure 7.4 (a) Search Engine Spider Simulator and (b) Word Cloud and Keyword Density Chart Source: Webconfs

Page Title Used   META Description Used   META Keywords Used

Enter Captcha To Continue

BJYLR

Spidered content

Spidered Internal Links: 258   Spidered External Links: 119

\#   Link's URL   Link's anchor text   \#   Link's URL   Link's anchor text

Figure 7.4 (b) <u>SEO Tools</u> : <u>Keyword Density</u> Checker - Keyword Cloud

Keyword Cloud

espn worldwide leader sports news scores reached degraded version espncom unsupported internet explorer complete experience upgrade supported browser stockton fighting nate diaz's journey big time mma lochte rio judge orders passports held olympic fantasy wr projections nfl teams power rankings preseason edition christian mccaffrey college football tricky business insurance policies barkley critical team usa's roster construction nba deandre jordan gold trumps title manu's basketball familia usa top world memorable momemts sportsmanship lebron 'my dream' runner fell helped injury biles raisman gymnastics high notes irish ice executive arrested scalping probe rob manfred baseball changing quicker mlb breaking chase scemarios weeks nascar maryse babyface work ethic miz heel today wwe source papelbon pick hours counter strike mania roundup godsent na'vi' win esports asked australian scientist fast human run meter dash bizarre summer olympics endings view stories ventures terms privacy policy safety information your california rights applicable reserved en espantilde;ol undefeated fivethirtyeight fc cricinfo

Keyword Density

Keyword	Count	Density
sports	11	5.5%
olympic	11	5.5%
nba	6	3%
espn	5	2.5%
team	4	2%
nfl	4	2%
college	3	1.5%
football	3	1.5%
power	2	1%
rankings	2	1%
internet	2	1%
time	2	1%
version	2	1%
-	-	---

coverage so the prominence of the term Olympics is not surprising. A keyword density chart is also shown below the word cloud. Keyword density is the percentage of times a particular word is used in comparison to the number of words on a page. The keyword density should not be too large (more than 3 percent), and in this example, 3.16 percent indicates that the site is engaging in keyword practices that might get it in trouble with search engines. However, a density of at least 1 percent was formerly recommended in order to be properly indexed by search engines. Although 1 percent does not seem like a lot of words from one page, it is important not to overload with keywords on the page or try to trick the search engine into indexing and ranking the page a certain way.

As Jayson DeMers noted in *Forbes* online, while keywords and keyword density should not be ignored, it is more important today to place keywords properly on a page and to create longer content that will get the page ranked more highly. The reason is a trend called semantic search, which focuses on the user's intent when searching for something. Users today might say "where can I find cheap pink purses?" or "who makes the best pink purses?" depending on their intent, rather than just searching for "pink purses." The first search would yield results for clearance and discount outlets and the second search would return results for Nordstrom and other outlets that sell designer merchandise, while the second search would bring up information about different purse makers and possibly the process of making purses. A good way to find semantic search results is to look at the 'related searches' section of a relevant search page. Another term used in this context is 'entity,' which refers tot he entire search query and not just a keyword or set of keywords.

One thing is clear, semantic search has changed the game for SEO, as search engines are now programmed to return results based on intent. However, the user is still searching for something and good keyword research is still key. Put the primary keyword for the site in the header tags (H1 and H2), title tags, URL, and the body of the text so search engines know what is important on that page.[19] Marketers should focus on creating valuable content and on the right keywords or set of queries for that product or service first.

However, semantic search is only the beginning of how search has changed recently. Optimizing for search used to be relatively easy in comparison to today. A company needed to find out what keywords customers were searching for and then put those in the pages and wait for the results. Over time, keywords became the phrases we think of in terms of semantic search.

Perform a search today, and the page looks different from a few years ago. Included in a SERP are not only paid ad placements and organic search results but a variety of things that Google thinks will help us with our inquiry. Google wants to provide the best answer that matches the user's search intent. The most common things that are likely to be shown in a search in addition to ads are the related questions, top stories, the knowledge panel, local 3-packs, star reviews, videos, and images.

What this means is that digital marketers need to be aware of how search has changed and be more proactive. When a marketer searches for a particular keyword or phrase for which they wish to be found, they need to respond and take action based on what they see. Below are some examples of the tasks facing the modern digital marketer:

- Related Questions: Marketers need to see what questions are being asked and to answer those questions on their websites.

- Top Stories: If stories are featured in search, the marketer needs to work to get more press coverage for their products and services. If particular blog posts are showing up in search, the marketer needs to reach out to those sources to see if they will cover their product.

- Knowledge Panel: The Knowledge Panel represents Google's best attempt to answer a particular query. Answers come from a knowledge base of entities from answered queries.

keyword density
percentage of times a particular word is used on a website page in comparison to the number of words on that page.

semantic search
focuses on the user's intent when searching for something.

local search

using a local search term in a search query.

- Local 3-packs: Marketers need to fill out all the information for "Google my Business," including address information, to be shown in local search. These are usually the top three businesses that answer that search query in the local area of the person conducting the search.

- Star reviews: If reviews are showing up as important, the marketer needs to direct its customers to the most important review sites.

- Videos and Images: If videos and images are highlighted, the marketer needs to include those items on its web page and make sure they are tagged properly to be indexed for search. Marketers should include descriptions of images in the image alt tags for SEO purposes and also to ensure website accessibility (as discussed in Chapter 6). Alt tags can be viewed easily in most browsers by right-clicking on an image and choosing "inspect." An alt tag should accurately describe a photo to a user for accessibility purposes, but marketers can also choose to include keywords for SEO as long as it is not done in a spammy way. An alt tag is part of the image tag and looks like this: <img alt = "this is a description of a photo" />. Videos can be optimized, so they are accessible and also crawlable by spiders by including a text transcript.

Figure 7.5 illustrates where some of the items we have been discussing show on a typical search page. Ads, related questions, star reviews, images, and videos typically appear on the left. To the right there might be a knowledge panel and a map calling attention to the results of a "3-pack" answer to a query. Organic search results for text ads are rather lost in all of this information, meaning digital marketers need to work to be found in other aspects of the search results.

If the above seems like a lot of work for digital marketers, consider that search results can and do vary dramatically by search engine and by user. For each major search engine, its customers' use must be monitored by the marketer. Of course, search engines know our IP addresses, but a search engine like Google knows a lot about us from our search history.[20] The browser cache and cookies on a single device can affect search results as can previously clicked links, geographic location, and type of device, whether mobile or desktop.[21] All this information is used to make search results more relevant. Those wishing

Figure 7.5 **A Typical Search Page Showing Common Features** Source: Orbit Media Studios

The Seven Most Common SERP Features

to see what their SEO results look like to others should first log out of their Google accounts. Otherwise, information relating to that person will skew the search results.

Most users prefer the search engine that they believe gives them the results they want, with preferences varying depending on the searcher. However, searchers are more likely now to see results that are relevant to them. So, there are pluses to having more relevant search results, although there are some minuses in terms of privacy concerns.

In fact, each search engine has its own algorithm for ranking entries, which is not generally published. The results of a search will vary because of the differing algorithms. In this chapter, we focus primarily on Google because it is the dominant platform. There are a number of search engines with significant market share, as measured by the number of searches conducted both on desktop and mobile devices (see Figure 7.6). However, Google has dominated the search market for many years, and on desktop search has a healthy 65 percent share worldwide and about the same in the United States.[22] These figures are approximately the same whether the user is searching on a desktop or mobile device.

As stated before, search engine marketers try to "guess" or "reverse engineer" the algorithm to get their pages ranked highest in natural search. The entries to the index and the calculations of the algorithms change over time, meaning that site ranks may change just because the way of determining ranking has changed. All the search engine ranking algorithms are different, placing different weights on different characteristics. The exact ranking algorithm of any site is proprietary, although trade sources make educated guesses at the nature of the different algorithms. The meta tag "description," as we have seen, often contains a sentence or two; Google and Microsoft Bing ignore it in ranking the site and focus on the context of the search. However, the meta tag and the title tag do affect how the site is displayed on the search page and are important to searchers in deciding whether to click on a particular page. Some search engines pay attention to the description. This example is just one small indication of the difference in ranking algorithms among different search engines.

Figure 7.6   Search Engine Browser World Wide Market Share, July 2021–July 2022 Source: Statcounter

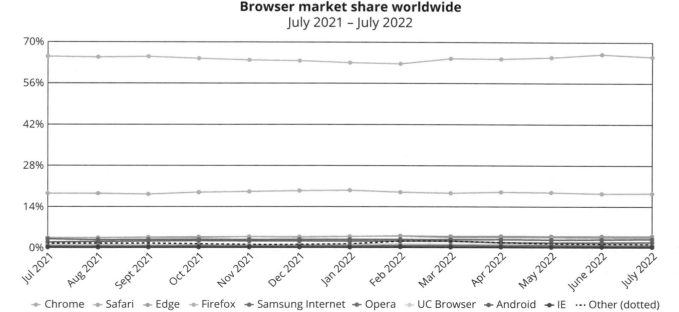

Figure 7.7 **Basic Approach to Search Engine Optimization** Source: https://searchengineland.com/technical-seo-audit-what-to-look-for-385213

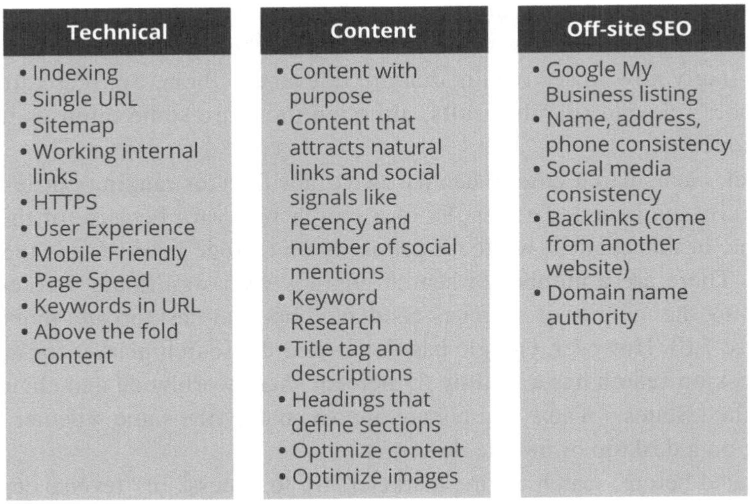

Technical	Content	Off-site SEO
• Indexing • Single URL • Sitemap • Working internal links • HTTPS • User Experience • Mobile Friendly • Page Speed • Keywords in URL • Above the fold Content	• Content with purpose • Content that attracts natural links and social signals like recency and number of social mentions • Keyword Research • Title tag and descriptions • Headings that define sections • Optimize content • Optimize images	• Google My Business listing • Name, address, phone consistency • Social media consistency • Backlinks (come from another website) • Domain name authority

In a series of excellent articles in Search Engine Land, Dave Davis outlines the three factors that website owners need to consider when designing their websites for search. These three factors (shown in Figure 7.7) are as follows:

- Technical
  - Indexing: making sure the site is indexed for search
  - Single URL: the site should point back to a single source
  - Sitemap: aids in navigation
  - Working internal links: links should not be broken or redirect
  - HTTPS (secure site designation)
  - User experience: the number of click-throughs generated by searches to that page and if the user stays on that page
  - Page speed in terms of loading
  - Keywords in URL that match the page
  - Above-the-fold content that is relevant to the search
- Content
  - Purposeful content: content that attracts natural links and social signals, such as the recency of mention and number of social mentions (72 percent of marketers think that content is the most effective SEO technique)[23]
  - Keywords and phrases: should be consistent with the landing page and can aid search (48 percent of marketers favor this method)
  - Meta tags, including the HTML title tag (the title in the bar at the top of the page) and description tag (often the text appearing under the link in a SERP)
  - Headings that define content
  - Optimized content and images: content relates to the subject and has meaning, and images have useful identifying tags and file names and a size that loads quickly

- Off-site SEO
  - Consistency for name, address, and phone number across the web, including (for Google) a complete Google Business Profile listing.
  - Consistency across social media
  - Backlinks: the number of other (legitimate) sites that link to the page
  - Domain name authority

See what marketers think is important at: https://blog.hubspot.com/marketing/seo-metrics-matter-most-leaders. An item that in the past has been considered important for inclusion in the rankings is the location and frequency (density) of keywords on the page. However, search engine optimization has become more complicated than that, particularly with the emphasis on user intent and the user experience. The user intent is what is in the mind of the searcher when they make the initial query, what the user is actually searching for online. The user experience, discussed in Chapter 6, is more narrowly considered in the context of search as how the user progresses on the site after clicking on the displayed search results. For example, if a user clicks on a result for "pink purses" and is directed to a general page for discount purchases for purses, the results from the search will not match their experience and they will quickly exit. The Google search engine in particular takes these experiences into account, particularly on mobile devices.

user intent
what the user is actually searching for online.

Optimizing for Organic Search

Making organic search marketing more difficult is the fact that the search algorithms know quite a bit about users when they are searching and now deliver search results.

From the discussion in the last section, it sounds like it should be relatively easy to get a web page ranked highly on the major search engines. Simply choose the right keywords, stuff the page header and content pages with those keywords, and get ranked accordingly. There are three problems with that reasoning. First, it does not work that way. The search engine algorithms look for items such as undue repetition of keywords, or, even worse, putting keywords on a page in an invisible way, for example, by making them the same color as the background. Second, if the search engines identify the site as an offender in terms of practices deliberately designed to trick them, they can refuse to rank it altogether. This practice is often referred to as "black hat" search.[24] Third, as stated above, the SEO process is more sophisticated now and content-driven.

As the definition of SEO suggests, practitioners try to work within the algorithms of the individual search engines to achieve the best possible ranking for the site or page on that particular search engine so their sites are listed at or near the top in the organic search listings. You may notice a problem here, however. Since the search engine algorithms are not disclosed, practitioners are working from what they believe the algorithms to be, based on their own experience and their own proprietary techniques for studying search engine rankings. This practice is not for amateurs, although nonprofessionals can certainly learn some of the main techniques and practice them.

Therefore, most practitioners of SEO follow the practices suggested here for maximizing their rankings. They start by understanding their target market and their intent in searching, developing keywords to reach that market, and defining and developing the content of their web and mobile pages around those keywords. In addition, it is important to use keywords you think are important in search engines and see if the type of company you are thinking of, yours or a competitor's, is displayed in the search results. For example, the term "dat" can be digital audio tape, a file extension, the Dental Admissions Test, or the Danish Air Transport company.

The SEO Process

A good suggested process for beginning an SEO campaign is as follows:

1. Define the target market.
2. Find out what they search for and why they search.
3. Develop a search strategy: find keywords and phrases.
4. Develop a content strategy to align with the keyword strategy.
5. Redesign the site with those keywords and content in mind.
6. Register the site with search engines.
7. Implement a paid search campaign to complement or inform the organic search campaign (optional).

Starting with the customer and what they are looking for is critical and often overlooked. Sometimes search terms might be obvious and sometimes they might not. For example, there are several spray products based on Cherith Clark and Kirstin Stokes' 2008 book *Monster Spray* that produce an aroma that is supposed to convince young children that this spray eradicates or scares away monsters in their bedrooms at night. However, parents eager to allay their children's fears might not search for "monster spray" but rather search for their intention "my child is afraid of the dark," or "children afraid of the dark," or other related terms.

Even Coca-Cola[25] with its worldwide brand needed help with SEO strategies and worked with an agency to deploy a team that works internationally in 200 countries. By taking its time to select and manage keywords on the site over multiple countries, Coca-Cola's organic search campaign delivers media impressions, traffic, and customer connections, particularly in one of its growing markets, China. The Coca-Cola content marketing strategy relies on "linked" and "liquid" content that can be shared and bring more users to the site.[26] We cover some tools that can help identify relevant keywords to help fuel success later in the chapter.

SEO Tools

Even when conducting an SEO campaign only, a number of tools exist to develop keywords. In addition, it is always a good idea to do market research and ask the customer how they search for your product. Looking at search trends and "hot keywords" with a tool such as Google Trends or the suggested keywords when conducting a search is also a good way to select keywords. In addition, most search engines have keyword finder tools. Paid search sites also have a number of useful tools for free use that can help explore and narrow down keyword selection. One great tool available is the Keyword Tool in Google, which can be used either for free (with a credit card guarantee) or as part of the capabilities of a Google Ads account.[27] It may also be possible to access search volume information but not suggested bid strategies without a credit card. The tool shows how much competition there is for the term and the number of monthly global or local searches (local can be defined for a particular geographic area). The traffic estimator tool can then be used to give the bid estimator a better idea of how many clicks might be expected from that search term and the average CPC, or Cost-per-Click, to the online advertiser. This tool, as well as the concept of CPC, will be discussed in more detail in Chapter 8.

Once the good keyword terms have been identified, the web page can be updated with the appropriate search terms in mind. Search engine optimization is done at the page level as each individual page is indexed by the search engine and has the potential to appear for specific keyword queries. It is a good idea to think of the top five or six terms and their variations for which the company would like to be ranked and to include those terms throughout the content of the site.

SEO Problems

In addition, many companies are unaware of these common problems in organic search that can depress search results, and it is a good idea to make note of them:

1. **Search engine spiders unable to navigate the website:** One problem is that spiders cannot read images. Opening a website entry page with video can be a problem because spiders will not know how to categorize your website. Images in general, even photos, can pose a problem for spiders, and using Alt tags to describe the image can aid in SEO and is also important for website accessibility.

2. **No site map on website:** A detailed and accurate site map provides important assistance to the spiders. Laying out the site in an easy manner means all pages can be crawled and indexed by search engines.

3. **Non-optimized navigation structure:** The spiders need to be able to move through the site, understand the HTML code, and determine how to best index it. Anything that makes it difficult, like extraneous HTML code inserted by some website development tools, impedes their progress.

4. **Diluted link popularity of key category/product pages**. Links are important to ranking. However, they need to be relevant and represent a real relationship to the topic of the main site. The anchor text of the link (the words that are linked on the website) should also accurately describe the content being linked to. This also helps with SEO.

The Google Algorithm(s)

Fixing these problems can improve search rankings. However, improving rankings may take several months after the changes are made for initial results to be seen. Michael Laps outlined these changes on the YoghurtDigital blog as follows:

> Panda (2011): Made it less easy to engage in "black hat" SEO practices and is now part of Google's core algorithm. The algorithm targeted pages with poor quality and duplicate or irrelevant content.
>
> Penguin (2012): Focused on websites that were buying links such as "link farms". Such practices are employed by companies that resort to activity that, while not illegal, may be unethical and artificially raise organic search results. These companies pay to have thousands of links placed on hundreds of sites leading directly to their firm, aiming for search engines to perceive these links as valuable and raise the ranking of the site. Another example that Google perceived as a black hat practice was a firm that provided incentives for colleges and universities (typically perceived as "authority" links by search engines) to link to a particular site.
>
> Hummingbird (2013): Used Penguin but was essentially a new algorithm, which focused on the *intent* behind the search, paying attention to each word in a query rather than keywords.
>
> Pigeon (nickname not given by Google) (2014): Upgraded accuracy and relevance of *local search* results. Especially impacts Google maps.
>
> Mobile Friendly (2015): Gave preference to mobile-friendly pages.[28]

Some of the more recent updates are listed there and are summarized here as follows:

BERT Natural Language Processing Update (2019): Bidirectional Encoder Representations from Transformers (BERT) update helps Google understand queries and webpage content more like how humans do.

Page Update (2021) Uses a new set of metrics: Core Web Vitals; Largest Contentful Paint (LCP) (measures loading performance); First Input Delay (FID) (measures interactivity); Cumulative Layout Shift (CLS) (measures visual stability).

Product Review (2021–2022): gives emphasis on high-quality reviews in rankings.

Those seeking more detailed and timely information on algorithm updates should consult the following website: https://searchengine-land.com/library/google/google-algorithm-updates

In spite of continuous algorithm changes, some easy ways to rank in natural search include the following:

- **The URL or domain name:** The uniform resource locator (URL) itself should be descriptive of the firm and consistent with how a firm wants to be found. Being around for a long time and having a search history will also help.
- **Title tag, also known as the HTML title tag (the title seen in the blue bar at the top of the page):** Many companies ignore the title tag, which should include a company description and the most important search terms or keywords. A good example to follow would be to include the keyword portion first (how the firm wants to be found), followed by the branding portion (firm name or description), and to keep the title page tag short (Google typically displays the first 50–60 characters of a title) so it can be read when it displays on search engines. An example is "University of Texas System | Fourteen Institutions. Unlimited Possibilities." Those looking for schools in the University of Texas System can see that they have many choices when deciding to enroll due to the branding portion of the tag.
- **Domain name authority:** Domain name authority is the extent to which that domain name is considered to be a reputable website in a particular category. One of the most popular calculations of this type is produced by the search engine company Moz. In their calculation, authority comes from good behavior over time and includes the length of time links have pointed to the site and the overall authority of those sites. For example, universities, charities, and governmental agencies are in general considered to have high authority. However, search engines do not use these specific commercial measures of domain name authority in ranking websites. Instead, they use their own internal assessment of domain name authority in determining search rankings and may not use domain name in rankings at all.[29]

The Top Ranking Factors on Google

However, some information seems to indicate that the simpler ways of ranking highly in organic search are no longer the most influential. In fact, it appears that the most important elements of the Google algorithm are content, links, and RankBrain. Content and links are both important and neither one is given precedence, according to Google in a rare interview on the subject in 2016. All three elements are described below and illustrated in Figure 7.8.

Figure 7.8   **Top Three SEO Influences per Google** Source: (1) http://searchengineland
.com/now-know-googles-top-three-search-ranking-factors-245882. (2) https://youtu.be/l8VnZCcl9J4.

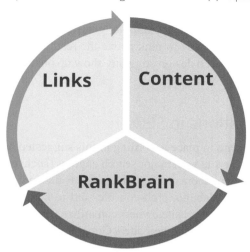

- **Content:** Content includes quality and relevance to the desired search topic as well as the location and frequency (density) of keywords on the page. Certainly, Google places a lot of emphasis on quality content, but it is sometimes hard to determine what is meant by quality. Decide what terms are important and rewrite the page content to reflect those terms. Do not just focus on written content, although this content should contain relevant references to desired keywords. Videos and blogs are likely to improve the search ranking considerably because the search engines look upon these activities favorably, presumably because of the web traffic and links that they produce.

- **Links:** The number of other sites that link to the page, the number of pages the site links to, and their relevancy to keywords and search phrases are most important for the site. Not only the quantity but also the quality of the links is significant for search engines. It is easy to create relevant outbound links from a website and less easy to get sites to link to a site (also known as a backlink). However, backlinks are important to SEO. Authority links as previously mentioned, directory links, real-time links from blogs, and social bookmarking links all increase the chances of a high search ranking. It is estimated that 33 percent of search ranking comes from link activity, including links to blogs and social media.

- **RankBrain** is a component of Google's core algorithm that utilizes machine learning (the ability of machines to teach themselves from data inputs) to determine a user's true intent. While Google does not disclose exactly how RankBrain works, SEO experts believe that the query follows an interpretation model that can apply possible factors like the location of the searcher, personalization, and the words of the query to better understand true intent.[30] Search results will change based on the user and current events. For example, with a sudden event like a tornado, the algorithm will count on content freshness as a much more important signal than backlinks, while for something like the history of Surrealist Art, the algorithm would favor deeper content and backlinks, signaling authority. Machine learning will no doubt play an even bigger part in search in the future as search engine firms seek to match queries to results from a relevance perspective. As such, marketers should think about user intent (as opposed to individual keywords) and incorporate important keywords as phrased in a natural language as they create and review content.

RankBrain
a machine learning query enhancement tool. The tool can match queries to results pages taking into account relevance and the context of the search.

Many other factors can positively influence site ranking, such as technical setup and navigation. Therefore, ranking a site for SEO is challenging and requires constant vigilance, monitoring of key phrases and user intent and attention to detail across all browsers. These efforts can yield results. For example, getting positive reviews on Yelp can get a local air conditioning company to rank above the rest of the pack. Being listed in an influential blog can help a web design company show up on the first, and most important, page of search results.

Other Considerations in SEO

Once the SEO changes are in place according to this suggested process, it is a good idea to request a recrawl of the site with major search engines (such as through Google Search Console). Google offers a plethora of tools and guides available at https://developers.google .com/search/docs/monitor-debug/search-console-start to help marketers with the search engine optimization process. Website owners can utilize Google's Search Console, shown in Figure 7.9, to measure and track their site's Google search performance (https://search .google.com/search-console/welcome). Once linked and verified, site owners can view performance metrics, such as how often pages appear in search and which queries they are appearing for, as well as their average position on the SERP. This information can be used by marketers to identify keywords that can be used for optimization. In addition, the Search Console provides users with diagnostics about their website performance by identifying issues that may affect the site's placement in search. Lastly, the Search Console allows users to upload sitemaps to ensure that the site is fully indexed by Google's crawlers and alert Google about page updates by requesting that Google recrawl the page.

In addition, the main place to register a site is Google because of the large volume of searches, which is done through a request to Google's Search Console (https://developers .google.com/search/docs/crawling-indexing/ask-google-to-recrawl). Not submitting a site does not mean the site will not be indexed—Google and other search engines will likely find it if it is linked from other sites.

Although the information above gives the tried-and-true overview about how to be successful in SEO,[31] there have been many recent changes in the search algorithms (estimates suggest that there are 500 to 600 changes per year).[32] Certain other trends are affecting how websites and mobile sites can maximize their impact in search.

Figure 7.9   **Google Search Console** Source: Cengage Graphic

1. Voice search: As voice search, particularly on mobile devices, increases, RankBrain and semantic search will become more prominent.

2. User experience: This trend means that now search engines are seeing what happens beyond the click. If a person clicks on a site in response to a query, the search engines will look to see if the person got what was needed and stayed on the site or left quickly.

3. Meaningful content length: Formerly, SEO experts would recommend short pages and blog posts. Today, the recommended length for articles is at least 1,200 to 1,500 words because these articles fit better in search, and the average word count on pages has increased to reflect that trend. There are more words and images to rank on the page. As always, use subheadings, bullets, and images to make it easy to move through the pages. Tag images so spiders can index them.

4. Local intent: Local search is more complex than traditional search, with users starting with a general search and then moving along a path that might include directories, customer reviews, and coupons, sometimes taking four or five actions and depending on mobile devices for the results. Generally, less than 40 percent of local searches start with a search engine, so marketers in local businesses such as restaurants must depend on coupons, customer reviews, and local directories in their marketing tactics.

5. Video content and unique images: Search results now include videos and images to which users respond. Creating video and unique image content makes it easier to be found.

6. Mobile optimization: Search engines like Google now make sure that a mobile site is optimized for mobile devices and are more likely to serve that site up in a search if it is.

7. Social content ranking: Search engines are looking for not only your participation on social media but also how much others engage with your posts and other content.

8. Beyond keywords: In the past, SEO experts recommended repeated keywords in the body copy and the headline, and even the meta description. Now, search engines are responding to more than single keywords and looking at related searches. For example, people tend to search for multiple words, i.e., "Mexican restaurants in Austin" and not just Mexican restaurants. Also, search engines are looking for related terms. For a "Fitbit," related terms might be "activity" and "tracker" and "health" and "monitor." A search for activity tracker not only reveals a paid ad but also blogs and magazine articles that rate the various devices. All of this again illustrates the power of content. Applications incorporating AI such as Open AI's GPT (Generative Pre-Training Transformer) technology acquired by Microsoft Bing, also known as ChatGPT, will further assist users in refining their search parameters and provide more relevant and accurate search results.[33]

9. SEO as part of an inbound marketing plan: SEO needs to be seen as pulling users into the brand and should include optimizing landing pages.

Another trend worth mentioning is vertical search, a type of specialty search. By using vertical search, search engine companies hope to reduce extraneous results for users by better guessing user intent. For example, query for 'great white'—the name for an 80s rock band and a shark species—can get very different results on Google compared with an engine that specializes in academic material. In other words, if using an academic search engine, will yield the listings for the shark species, not the rock band. The specialty search engine attempts to narrow the user intent. The user went to the academic search engine with a purpose—or so the search engine assumes.

Vertical search engines can also ask questions more quickly. Shopping search engines, for example, can ask up-front the color, size, and manufacturer of what you want to buy.[34] Some of the other types of search engine are as follows:

- Topical search: such as worldwidescience.org and WebMD
- Industry search: such as business.com and chemindustry.com
- Image search: such as Yandex, Bing Visual Search, and Image Search
- News search: such as NewsNow and onlinenewspapers.com
- Blog search: such as blog-search.com
- Books and articles search: such as Google Scholar
- Social real-time search: such as Twitter Search

It is not hard to see that vertical search engines have sprung up all over the place and are of benefit to mobile users looking for something particular at a given time. There are search engines devoted to travel and others devoted to shopping, as only a few examples. The major search engines also allow for searching on images, videos, and places, among other topics. There are other types of search being introduced into the internet marketspace and as long as vertical search engines can meet the need for relevant search results, the market will continue to grow. For example, YouTube, as a stand-alone company from Google, is the second largest search engine in the world.

How Organic and Paid Search Work Together

Before we move to the discussion of paid search in the next chapter, we would like to discuss the role of paid search in developing an organic search campaign. It is often quite useful to employ a paid search campaign before, after, or during the development of an organic search campaign to determine which keywords should be used to optimize the site for paid search. A paid search campaign can be used to finely target terms for an organic search campaign. In other words, it is useful to use paid search terms where the site is not showing up as strongly in the organic search rankings as was hoped. Equally, once the SEO campaign is successful and showing results, the terms for which the site is ranked the highest naturally can be considered as candidates for paid search. Landing page copy can also be used in paid search ads. In any case, the two campaigns should ideally work together.

iCrossing found a synergy between paid and natural search. If the keywords purchased by paid search were also ranked in natural search, clicks increased by 92 percent, time on the site increased by 39 percent, and orders increased by 45 percent.[35]

It can legitimately be said that "search is search" and that both types of campaign should work together.[36] In the prelaunch phase, the keywords and terms can be used to develop a consistent site message. A consistent message and the intelligent use of keywords and phrases on the site help improve the quality score during the campaign execution phase. During the reporting and analysis phase, the results of each type of search should be compared and paid keywords should be refined based on input from both the paid and organic search campaigns.

The Impact of Mobile Search

It is clear that marketers must learn to optimize their web pages and their search capabilities for the mobile market. The year 2015 was a benchmark year in that more than half of digital ad spending (over $15 billion) in the United States was spent on mobile devices.[37] As was shown earlier, Figure 7.1 highlights the shift to searching on mobile devices with mobile advertising having overtaken desktop in 2021 and predicted to continue to dominate. For a while, Google was highlighting "mobile-friendly sites" as part of its AMP (Accelerated Mobile Pages) project as a way of signaling how important mobile websites were to search. The project rewards in search results those sites which are "responsive" or adaptable to different mobile devices in terms of the user experience. Google will continue to reward mobile sites that are optimized for search.[38] The reason is that more than half of searches take place on mobile devices.[39] In addition, about half of those queries have local intent. Therefore, marketers may need to change their strategies in SEO to accommodate the terms that searchers would use "on the go." Also, specific vertical markets have benefitted from mobile, including restaurants, autos, consumer electronics, finance, insurance, beauty, and personal services, and will continue to do so. Companies such as Groupon that provide searches and special offers related to local markets will also play a role in the expansion of local search, meaning that local and mobile search will continue to grow hand-in-hand for the foreseeable future.

However, the mobile search market will continue to experience growing pains as marketers adjust their marketing techniques to this new medium. The first position in desktop search can receive anywhere from 20 to 30 percent of the total clicks on that search result. Therefore, it is even more important to rank number one in mobile searches. Mobile searchers, while they are searching, are even less likely than desktop searchers to scroll down beyond the first or even the second search position, even if one is displayed. Note that in spite of the increased traffic, conversion rate and average order value are typically still lower from searches from mobile devices than desktop devices, depending on the industry. Consumers may enjoy searching for information on their smartphones but might go to their desktop to purchase. In retail, for example, the desktop conversion rate is 3.7 to 4 percent, while the mobile rate is between 1.25 to 1.34 percent.[40] Tablet conversion rates are typically a little higher. There are a number of explanations for these results, including security concerns on mobile devices, and the benefit of being able to see purchases more clearly on a larger screen. Over time, these discrepancies will narrow as customers become more accustomed to purchasing items they see on a smaller screen.

The Relationship between Search and Social Media

This chapter would not be complete without a few more words about the integration of search and social media. Social media continues to capture the interest of digital marketers for the good reason that consumers are on social media. Figure 7.10 shows the relationship between search and social media. Search marketers are expanding their use of social media by driving inbound links from social media forums, expanding their profiles on social media accounts, and monitoring social media conversations to influence SEO. Marketers want to be where their consumers are and to participate in the conversation to engage and retain those customers. A study by business.com and BtoB Online, written by Dr. Zahay but no longer available online, indicated that the best-performing companies in a survey of 464 business-to-business (B2B) online marketers were using social media to enhance their natural search efforts. Enhancement for these firms was accomplished by expanding their profiles on social media accounts, monitoring social media conversations to influence SEO, and driving inbound links via various social media outlets. Increasing the number of social media followers and

Figure 7.10   How Social Media Supports SEO Source: https://www.semrush.com/blog/social-media-seo/

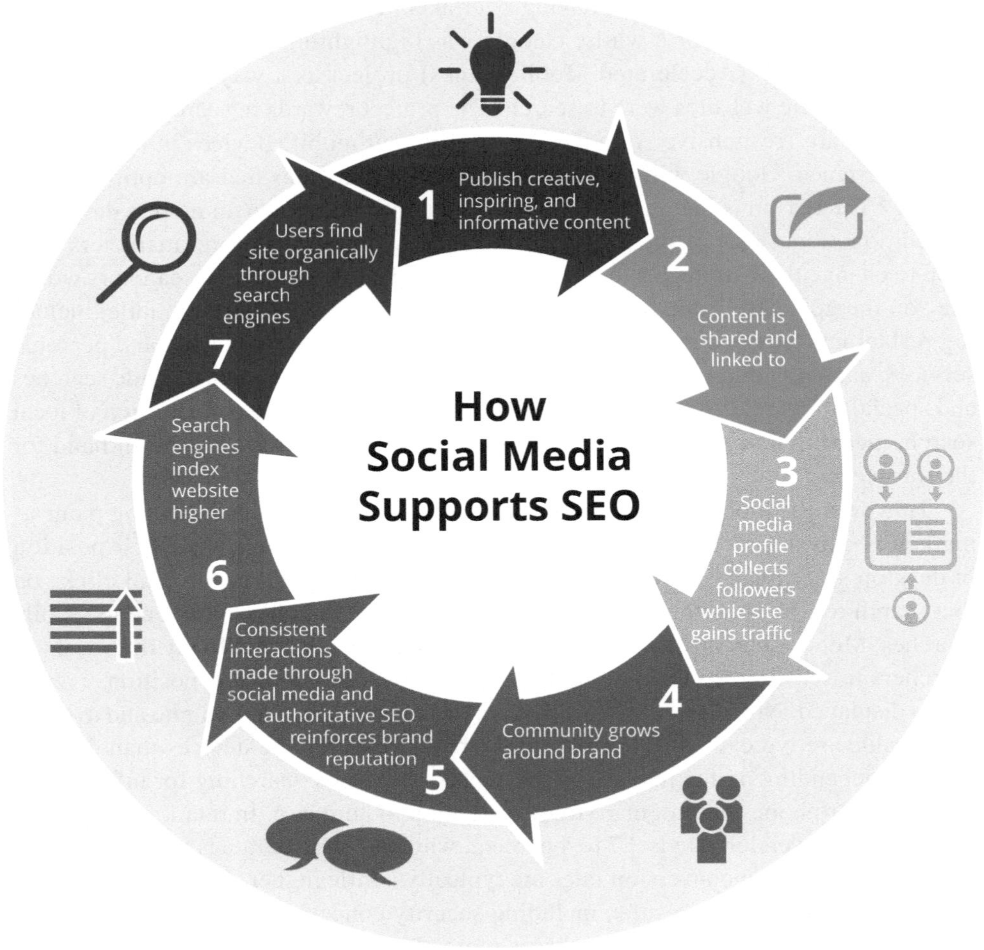

encouraging them to share a company's content in all channels will also impact search rankings. This trend will only continue in years to come.

Monitoring social media conversations is another great way to determine how to pick appropriate keywords to monitor both paid search and SEO. For example, marketers using social media sensing tools such as Radian6 can see what and how customers and prospects are talking about it across the social web and develop search marketing campaigns based on this input. Google's social search capability means that searches conducted while signed into Google will highlight relevant content from social connections, including websites, blogs, images, and other contacts created by or shared by social connections. Web content that has been recommended from relevant sources in other searches will be highlighted. Other search engines have or will have adopted a similar strategy regarding integrating social media "likes" into organic search results. Social media content that has a long life can contribute to brand communities and interactions, causing search engines to index the site even higher and for users to be able to access it more easily. Since marketers know that consumers trust the recommendations of friends more than those of advertisers, the future will bring about an even greater integration between search and social media.

Summary

Search is a key focus of internet marketers at present. Other customer acquisition techniques, however, continue to evolve and remain an important part of the marketer's toolkit. Since the size of the web increases by many pages each day, the importance of search to users, B2C and B2B alike, can hardly be overstated. Because it is important to internet users, marketers and advertisers are close behind. While search has a growing impact and can be confusing for marketers to understand, the basic concept is simple.

Search engines send out spiders or crawlers that look at websites and categorize them to create indices that are used in specific search queries. The marketer needs to think about what words its customers or prospects use when trying to find a product or service, the questions they are likely to ask, and the format in which they would like to receive their answers (i.e., text, audio, or video). There are a number of free tools that can be used to develop these keywords. Relevant keywords can then be used in both organic and paid search. Organic search is sometimes called natural search or algorithmic search, as it depends on algorithms that are developed by commercial search engines to find the most relevant web pages to display as the result of a search query.

In organic search, content, links, and RankBrain contribute most to success, but the savvy marketer needs to pay attention to technical items such as using relevant keywords, group of keywords, or entity in the title bar of a website, and content issues such as the website content, to raise the ranking of the page as the result of a query. Other off-site SEO techniques to optimize the website include links from and to the page and the overall authority the page commands. It is also important that the website be responsive and optimized for mobile search.

The search process as a whole is iterative and is "never done" as the search engines are constantly updating their algorithms and the bidding for keywords changes daily, if not hourly. The field offers a good opportunity for employment and a steady prospect for growth as new aspects of search are developed.

One can expect two levels of change to affect SEM in the years to come. At a granular level, the search engines themselves will continue to tweak their algorithms to provide more relevant results. Search engine marketers will continue to scramble to keep up with those changes and work to be found in response to search entities and not just keywords. At the level of the overall search marketplace, innovations such as vertical, local, social, mobile, and voice search, and others yet unknown will continue to proliferate and impact the ever-changing search landscape.

Discussion Questions

1. Why do you think search has become such an important part of the life of internet users?

2. What options do marketers have when it comes to developing a search marketing strategy?

3. What are the three most impactful elements of a website in terms of optimizing a site for organic search and why are they important?

4. How come the major search engines do not publish their algorithms?

5. Compare the same search results in two separate browsers. Which produces the better results in terms of quality and relevance? Why?

6. Why do paid and natural search work so well together? What about search and social media?

7. How do search strategies differ for mobile devices?

8. Why is local search likely to be important in the future? What other trends are likely in organic search?

Endnotes

1. Ryan Jones, February 28, "Why Search – and Seo – Is Important," *Search Engine Journal*, November 25, 2021, https://www.searchenginejournal.com/seo-guide/why-is-search-important/.

2. Renderforest, "70+ Google Search Statistics to Know in 2021," Renderforest, December 8, 2022, https://www.renderforest.com/blog/google-search-statistics.

3. "Search Engine Statistics 2022," 99firms, January 25, 2023, https://99firms.com/blog/search-engine-statistics/.

4. "Seo Statistics," WebFX, November 28, 2022, https://www.webfx.com/seo/statistics/.

5. Jim Tobin, "Internet Usage by Age, Gender, Race and More," Ignite Social Media, November 4, 2008, https://www.ignitesocialmedia.com/social-media-stats/internet-usage-by-age-gender-race.

6. Adam Epstein, "People Trust Google for Their News More than the Actual News," Quartz (January 18, 2016), https://qz.com/596956/people-trust-google-for-their-news-more-than-the-actual-news/.

7. Greg Sterling, "Report: Nearly 60 Percent of Searches Now from Mobile Devices," Search Engine Land, August 27, 2021, https://searchengineland.com/report-nearly-60-percent-searches-now-mobile-devices-255025.

8. Olga Andrienko, "Serps, Traffic and Trends: Mobile vs. Desktop in 2021 <Study>," Semrush Blog, accessed December 19, 2022, https://www.semrush.com/blog/mobile-vs-desktop.

9. "Search Advertising - U.S.: Statista Market Forecast," *Statista*, accessed December 19, 2022, https://www.statista.com/outlook/dmo/digital-advertising/search-advertising/united-states#ad-spending.

10. Mordy Oberstein, "State of Search: Discover How the Web Changed in 2021," Semrush, April 7, 2022, https://www.semrush.com/blog/state-of-search/.

11. "How to Set up a Local Business Listing <Local SEO>," *Moz*, accessed December 19, 2022, https://moz.com/learn/seo/local-business-listing-components.

12. "DMOZ," DMOZ, accessed December 19, 2022, https://www.dmoz-odp.org/.

13. Iggy Durant, "What Is Sem Marketing?," Peep Strategy, November 7, 2022, https://peepstrategy.com/what-is-sem-marketing/.

14. Mordy Oberstein, "State of Search: Discover How the Web Changed in 2021," Semrush Blog, April 7, 2022, https://www.semrush.com/blog/state-of-search/.

15. "Digital Marketing Snapshot," Skai, October 27, 2022, https://skai.io/digital-marketing-snapshot/.

16. SWEOR, "27 Eye-Opening Website Statistics: Is Your Website Costing You Clients?," January 20, 2022, https://www.sweor.com/firstimpressions.

17. Sergey Brin and Lawrence Page, "The Anatomy of a Large-Scale Hypertextual Web Search Engine," The Anatomy of a Search Engine, accessed January 10, 2023, http://infolab.stanford.edu/~backrub/google.html.

18. Kristi Hines, "Are Meta Keywords a Google Ranking Factor?," *Search Engine Journal*, November 21, 2022, https://www.searchenginejournal.com/ranking-factors/meta-keywords/#close.

19. Neil Patel, "HOW MUCH DO Keywords Still Matter?" Neil Patel, January 24, 2020, https://neilpatel.com/blog/do-keywords-still-matter/.

20. Leo A. Notenboom et al., "If an IP Address Doesn't Do It, Then How Does Google Know My Location?," Ask Leo!, December 19, 2016, https://askleo.com/if-an-ip-address-doesnt-do-it-then-how-does-google-know-my-location/.

21. Mike McEvoy, "7 Reasons Google Search Results Vary Dramatically," Web Presence Solutions - SEO, Marketing, eCommerce Services, December 16, 2022, https://www.webpresencesolutions.net/7-reasons-google-search-results-vary-dramatically/.

22. "Search Advertising - U.S.: Statista Market Forecast," *Statista*, accessed December 19, 2022, https://www.statista.com/outlook/dmo/digital-advertising/search-advertising/united-states#key-players.

23. Ellice, "The 11 Most Important SEO Metrics to Track," Website Guides, Tips & Knowledge, July 19, 2022, https://www.dreamhost.com/blog/most-important-seo-metrics/.

24. Dave Davies, "Seo Tactics Outlined," Beanstalk Internet Marketing | SEO, PPC & SMM Services (Beanstalk Internet Marketing, Inc., May 20, 2021), https://beanstalkim.com/info/tactics/.

25. iCrossing, "46664/Coca-Cola - 'Drinking Global, Thinking Local,'" AdForum, accessed December 19, 2022, https://www.adforum.com/creative-work/ad/player/34479067/drinking-global-thinking-local/46664coca-cola.

26. TheCognitiveMedia, "Coca-Cola Content 2020 Part One," YouTube (January 17, 2023), https://www.youtube.com/watch?v=LerdMmWjU_E.

27. "Use Keyword Planner," Google Ads Help (Google), accessed December 19, 2022, https://support.google.com/google-ads/answer/7337243?hl=en&utm_source=pocket_reader.

28. "Google Algorithm Updates & Changes: A Complete History," *Search Engine Journal*, August 20, 2022, https://www.searchenginejournal.com/google-algorithm-history/.

29. "Domain Authority: What Is It and How Is It Calculated," *Moz*, accessed December 19, 2022, https://moz.com/learn/seo/domain-authority.

30. "Google RankBrain," *Moz*, accessed January 10, 2023, https://moz.com/learn/seo/google-rankbrain.

31. Jami Oetting, "The Ultimate Guide to SEO in 2023," HubSpot Blog (HubSpot, July 18, 2022), https://blog.hubspot.com/marketing/seo.

32. Aleksandra Stefanovic, "Why & How to Track Google Algorithm Updates," Play Media, October 3, 2022, https://play-media.org/how-to-track-google-algorithm-updates.

33. Aaron Holmes, "Microsoft and OpenAI Working on CHATGPT-Powered Bing in Challenge to Google," *The Information,* January 10, 2023), https://www.theinformation.com/articles/microsoft-and-openai-working-on-chatgpt-powered-bing-in-challenge-to-google.

34. Verne Kopytoff, "New Search Engines Narrowing Their Focus / Vertical Sites Cater to Specific Interests like Shopping, Job Hunting, Doing Research," SFGATE (*San Francisco Chronicle*, January 25, 2012), https://www.sfgate.com/business/article/New-search-engines-narrowing-their-focus-2688080.php.

35. Gail Kalinoski, "Study Finds Integrating Paid and Natural Search Significantly Boosts Online Performance," *Total Retail*, April 17, 2007, https://www.mytotalretail.com/article/study-finds-integrating-paid-natural-search-significantly-boosts-online-performance-52643/all/.

36. Jeremy Collins, "Leverage PPC and Seo Together: Ways to Maximize Performance," BrightEdge, accessed December 19, 2022, https://www.brightedge.com/blog/organic-paid-search-together-integration.

37. "Mobile to Account for 70% of Digital Ads by 2026," O'Dwyers PR, accessed December 19, 2022, https://www.odwyerpr.com/story/public/17584/2022-03-02/mobile-account-for-70-digital-ads-by-2026.html.

38. Emil Protalinski, "Google Search Removes 'Mobile-Friendly' Label, Will Start Negatively Ranking Mobile Interstitials in 2017," VentureBeat (August 23, 2016), https://venturebeat.com/2016/08/23/google-search-removes-mobile-friendly-label-will-start-negatively-ranking-mobile-interstitials-in-2017/.

39. Teai, Payman. "57 Important SEO Statistics for 2022," *Respona.* May 5, 2022, https://respona.com/blog/seo-statistics/.

40. Christoff Petro, "Mobile vs Desktop Conversion Rates," GoCardless (November 8, 2021), https://gocardless.com/guides/posts/mobile-vs-desktop-conversion-rates/.

Chapter 8

Paid Search and Social Advertising

Learning Objectives

By the time you complete this chapter, you will be able to:

1 Explain the impact of mobile technology on the search process.

2 Define the paid search process.

3 Define the process of Google Ads responsive display ads.

4 Compare display ad formats used on Google, Meta, and other major social platforms.

5 Explain the nature of a promoted post.

The Growing Impact of Paid Search and Mobile Technology

Search marketing is the heart of the web because it allows advertisers to be in front of the customer at the exact moment when they are researching a product or service or considering purchase. Although we may not know exactly who the customer is at the point when they see our organization or firm listed on the results of a search, we do know what they are interested in at the moment. With 94 percent of all B2B product inquiries beginning with search,[1] and 87 percent of online shoppers searching online before they make a purchase, advertisers know that search is important.[2] In fact, advertisers spend much of their energy on search engine marketing, both paid and organic. As of 2022, the search industry is by itself a $60 billion industry and growing, with job opportunities abounding.[3]

When we consider that in 2021 that the largest tech agencies—Google, Amazon, Meta, and Apple—total net media advertising revenue increased to 45 percent and their share of the online segment increased to 65 percent, you can see how big of an industry mobile advertising is. Figure 8.1 shows how much each tech company contributes to the online revenue stream outside of China. Additionally, as shown in Figure 8.2, spending on ads that are accessible via desktop browsers has decreased significantly over the past few years with mobile ads taking the lead. It is predicted that mobile ad spend will count for 72 percent of market share by 2026.[4]

Figure 8.1   **Global Net Online Advertising Revenue** Source: https://infotechlead.com/digital/online-advertising-forecast-for-google-amazon-meta-and-apple-70428

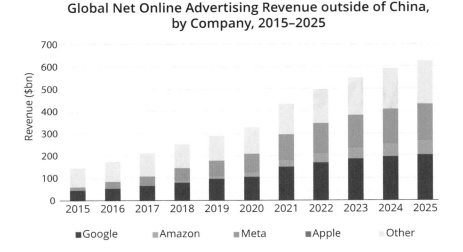

Mobile ads, which are typically more expensive and yield higher revenue, have increased steadily year over year. Clearly, mobile searching and shopping habits have had a dramatic impact on the paid search industry. As digital advertising has increased in its strength, there are several major challenges that are influencing the landscape. First, data privacy is a big hurdle for digital advertisers. In particular, in 2021 when Apple released iOS 14.5, users were able to choose whether or not they wanted to share their mobile activity when not using an app that was tracking them. Citing the economics adage, "there is no such thing as free lunch," this was (and still is) the case for many "free" apps. Many free apps sell user activity and location data to advertisers so that they can make money and to continue to offer the app for "free." For instance, if a customer had a weather app (or dating app) on their phone and agreed to share their data with the app owner, the app owner can then sell the location data and browsing data of the user to advertisers. This is how app developers typically make money-they sell the data to data brokers who then sell the data to advertisers to allow for more personalized,

Figure 8.2   **U.S. Digital Ad Spending by Device, 2017 to 2026** Source: https://www.statista.com/forecasts/459593/digital-advertising-revenue-device-digital-market-outlook-usa

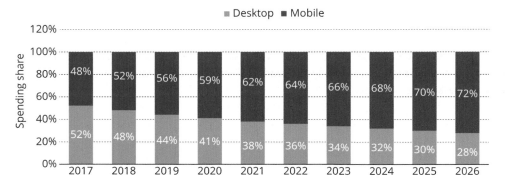

nano-segments for advertising purposes. However, when iOS 14.5 was launched, Apple installed a feature that allowed users to stop sharing their data with app developers when they are not using the app.

Second, which is discussed throughout the book, is the elimination of third-party cookies. Google is set to eliminate third-party cookies by 2024. Third-party cookies help advertisers track users across multiple devices—such as mobile, desktop, apps, etc. By eliminating third-party cookies, it does not matter if users choose to share the data or not, that data will no longer exist. At the time of writing, Google was still testing their solution for advertisers to continue to segment and advertise to particular consumers but no definitive solution was communicated yet.

PPC or Paid Search Defined

So, what exactly is paid search? PPC is defined as "Paid search advertising is a type of digital marketing strategy that allows companies to pay search engines to place their ads higher on relevant search engine results pages (SERPs) with the goal of driving traffic to their site. Pay-per-click—or PPC advertising—is the most common form of paid search."[5] In this section we will focus on Ads as Google has the largest market share of the traditional search engines. Search advertising is growing on social networks, as more and more users spend their time on those networks. Please note that these days ads can take many formats, from a small thumbnail picture to video, to ad text at the top of a Gmail inbox to shopping ads with high-quality images. Other formats are discussed in Chapter 7 and formats unique to paid advertising on social media platforms will be discussed in the last half of this chapter.

Whatever format is used, the paid aspect of SEM is also called paid search (PPC) and is based on an auction model. In this model, firms seeking to rank highly in specific search categories will bid on certain terms or "keywords" in the hopes of a lucrative search ranking. Winning the auction usually means being displayed higher in search results, although search engines will take other factors such as the relevance of the ad into account.

In this section we will focus on creating and placing ads in Google Ads. In 2018, Google rebranded Google Adwords as Google Ads.[6] Sometimes on older sites and YouTube videos, you'll hear the product referred to as Adwords instead of Ads. They're the same thing—just a rebrand! As with other forms of SEM, the objective of using Google Ads is to attract the attention of that specific user when they are actively searching for information about the business's products or services, and bring them to its website. Google tries to find the best "match" based on the search terms used by the customer, and the keywords the advertiser associates with those search queries and the match is not just based on winning the auction.

With well-chosen keywords and appealing ad copy, advertisers can attract consumers who are searching for a specific product or service that they sell. There are three options for bid costs:

1. **Cost-per-click (CPC):** This is how much you pay when someone clicks on your ad.
2. **Cost-per-mille (CPM):** This is how much you pay per 1000 ad impressions.
3. **Cost-per-engagement (CPE):** This is how much you pay when someone responds to your call-to-action (CTA) such as signing up for a list, watching a video, etc. Chapter 1 discussed? CTAs in much more detail.

Google Ads is a cost-effective means of advertising for some businesses and nonprofits. A lucrative ranking is one that makes money for the firm and is not

paid search (PPC)
the paid aspect of SEM based on an advertising model where firms seeking to rank high in specific search categories will bid on certain terms or "keywords" in the hopes of a lucrative ad ranking; also known as PPC (pay-per-click).

necessarily the number one or two spot on the page. Sometimes a number two or three spot will be just as profitable for the firm. Whether or not a spot is profitable depends on the number of clicks, the CPC, and the revenue obtained from the advertisement. However, please note that because consumers are searching on multiple different devices: desktop, phones, tablets, these spots differ by the type of device where the information is being searched. Desktops, in theory, have more room for CPC ads than mobile devices.

Advertisers understandably want the most noticeable position in the results from a customer's search query. Certainly, one of the few top spots on the page is preferred. Google decides on a company's ad position among all its advertisers based on its **Ad Rank**. The ad with the highest Ad Rank gets shown in the top position, and so on.

The Ad Rank depends on the following:

- The bid for each keyword, that is, CPC.
- The **Quality Score**—how relevant an ad and website links are to the person who will see the ad.
- The **Ad Rank Threshold**—a dynamic assessment that calculates the ad quality, ad position, what type of device the user is searching from and where they're located, the search terms used, and related auctions.
- The expected impact from ad extensions and other ad formats. Adding additional information, such as a phone number or links to specific pages is a feature called ad extensions. Adding these features to an ad may impact the attractiveness of an ad to customers.

The **Quality Score** in turn depends on the following:

- Expected click-through rate
- Ad relevance
- Ad extension relevance
- Landing page experience, for example, how long the viewer dwells on the page and website, or "bounces" out quickly.

The matching process starts with a query from someone using the Google search engine. When someone searches for something on the internet, Google tries to match the term the searcher uses with the most relevant terms (keywords) used by Google Ads advertisers. The Ads with the most relevance to that specific query get more prominent placement in the search results. Google determines if there will be an auction for the advertisers' ad placements in the search results, that is, which ad is shown in which order, on which page, and so on.

How does Google determine "relevance" in the Quality Score? That information is a closely guarded secret so that advertisers do not "game" the system, which might result in less relevant ads placed higher in search results. (Google assumes that irrelevant ads annoy users and therefore make them less likely to click on revenue-generating ads.) In general, "relevance" is determined by a combination of the past click-through-rate (CTR), text-matching relevance, cookies, and the associations to the landing page, such as related business partners with strong connections to the search query. Google will downgrade the Quality Score if there are few click-throughs, quick "bounces," indicating little relevance to the searcher, and/or intentional advertiser manipulation of the search result process. As such, it is possible that no ads will appear if Google determines that none would satisfy the viewer's criteria, as evaluated by its Ad Rank, a value used to determine the ad's position. The main components of Ad Rank are bid and Quality Score.

ad extensions
provide additional information with the ad such as a phone number, locations and reviews and can increase the click-through rate.

click-through-rate (CTR)
CTR is the number of clicks that a link receives divided by the number of times it is shown (in an ad, email, etc.).

Advertisers identify keywords they want to bid on and how much they want to spend overall. The keywords are paired with Google Ads the advertisers want displayed. Google then enters the keyword from the advertiser's account it deems most relevant into the auction, with the maximum bid specified, as well as the associated ad. Thus, if an advertiser wants to improve the position of its ad in the search results, it can increase the bid or improve the Quality Score of the ad, or both.[7] As of July 2022, Google has required that all ads in Google Ads use responsive search ads. These types of ads are powered by both the advertiser's word choices and Google's AI. So instead of manually conducting A/B tests, Google helps determine which ad receives the best CTR and shows that ad more often. It's a win–win for the advertising company and Google as they both make money.

Responsive search ads are Google's most flexible format for search ads. For example, each business can create up to fifteen separate headlines and four unique descriptions for each ad group. Each responsive search ads *may* display:

- Three headlines
- Two 90-character descriptions
- Google will rotate through the various combinations of the headlines and descriptions using AI to help determine the best combination.

The Basic Process for Google's Responsive Ads

In the summer of 2022, Google eliminated their "classic" text search ads in favor of moving to responsive search ads instead. This format as shown in Figure 8.3 should look familiar to the readers as it was the dominant form of PPC advertising for many years.

Instead of using the text ads that Google used for years, Google migrated to responsive search ads. The reason for this change is multipronged. First, people's search habits evolved over the years. People use their phones more often to search for an item, and they are more likely than ever to use a voice assistant to help with their searches. Second, the photos in display ads are more likely to encourage people to click on the ad. Text ads have limitations in that people can't "see" what they're clicking. Display ads, on the other hand, allow consumers to visually see the product. However, due to Google's migration to responsive search ads, the type of device will also determine the ads that are shown. In Figure 8.4a you can see an updated example of the search results for "cat food for older cats" on a desktop versus Figure 8.4b with the same search on a mobile phone. You will notice that the ads on a desktop are more display oriented and the text ads appear on the mobile phone.

Figure 8.3   Old Google Text Advertising

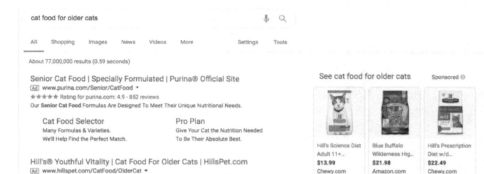

Figure 8.4a–4b **Updated Responsive Ad Search** Source: https://www.google.com/search?q=cat+food+for+older+cats

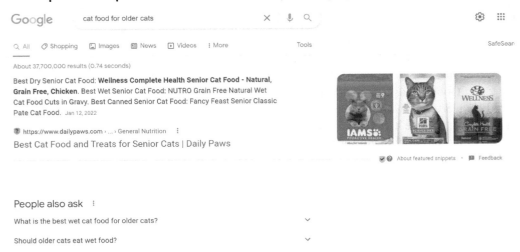

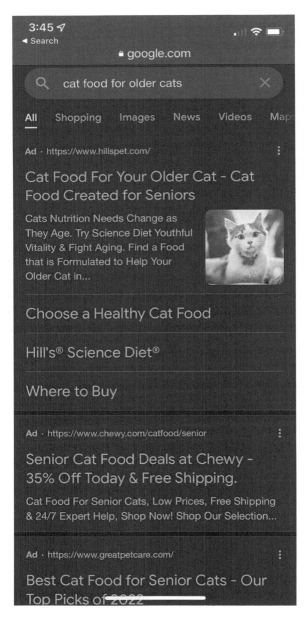

The paid search process is similar in most of the major web browsers and revolves around bidding on keywords that are entered in when a user searches the web. The keywords that are bid on may or may not be the same keywords that are entered into the HTML on the advertiser's website, but there should be a relationship between the website "landing page" and the keyword term bid on in the campaign. The term "keyword" is the same as in organic search, but the purpose is quite different. In paid search, the company or individual engaged in paid search selects a number of keywords, usually at least 20 for each ad that will then be displayed in the paid search results.

Each keyword will have a separate price that is based on its popularity. Some keywords may be priced out of the range of smaller advertisers. Some categories dominated by larger companies, such as auto insurance price quotes or mortgage loan rates, may have keywords on some days that cost over $10 per click. Other categories may, however, appear to be quite cheap and have a minimum bid of 25 cents. On some search engines, the minimum bid will actually be the lowest amount paid. Google, however, may set a higher minimum based on the popularity of the word, and often times the minimum bids suggested in Google Ads is not the final minimum bid in the campaign.

In these sections, we use Google for our paid search examples because the company is the largest search firm and dominates paid search. Display advertising is discussed in detail in Chapter 10. Social media sites and other forms of paid advertising will be covered in the rest of the chapter. Another reason to focus on Google for this paid search section is because the company has a number of programs that benefit undergraduate students hoping to make a career in digital and interactive marketing. One program that Google offers is free certification of their various platforms. At the time of writing, Google offers the following certificates for free:

- Google Ads Search Certification
- Google Ads Display Certification
- Google Ads Measurement Certification
- Google Ads Video Certification
- Shopping Ads Certification
- Google Ads Creative Certification

Certification should help everyone, including students, improve their chances of finding and doing well in a job in paid search.

Google Ads

Google Ads (formerly Google AdWords) is an online platform that enables advertisers to display brief advertising copy to web users. Ads is based on pay-per-click (PPC), or the cost-per-click (CPC) that the advertiser is willing to pay to "win" the top ad placement locations when users enter a search query into Google's search engine. This process is in contrast to SEO strategies discussed earlier in the text that rely solely on the "natural," or "organic" relationships of the search queries to the advertiser's keywords, aside from any bidding process or other forms of paid advertising.

As stated above, Google's platform for placing and managing PPC advertising programs is called Google Ads. When embarking on a paid search campaign, remember that the steps that we listed for organic search are also steps to follow for paid search in terms of first knowing the customer and what they want from a site. These steps are:

1. define the target market,
2. find out what they search for, and then
3. develop a search strategy in terms of keywords and phrases. Good keywords for paid search advertising reflect the products/services that are offered.

While the overall process for a paid search campaign is similar to an organic search strategy, the execution is different. There are more details in a paid search campaign and a more specific process is warranted to achieve good results. A more detailed suggested process for paid search campaigns as used by industry leaders is briefly described as follows and is illustrated in Figure 8.5:

1. Keyword Research: Develop the campaign by selecting appropriate keywords and match criteria and designing ads.
2. Ad Copywriting: Create several key phrases that work best with your target market as well as your call-to-action.
3. Landing Page Development: Ensure that the landing page is prepared to handle people finding the information that you advertised on your site. Also, ensure that it loads quickly.
4. Campaign Setup: Create several ad groups to test which ones work best for your target market(s).
5. Tracking and Testing: Watch results as the campaigns are running and then monitor the results and refine. Use A/B testing to test one ad against another. Use available reporting tools to understand which ads and campaigns were the most successful and try to determine why. Make a note of any changes for the next campaign.

This process is illustrated in more detail in Figure 8.5 and described in much more detail in the following narrative.

Stage 1: Keyword Research

The first step in the research phase is to investigate broad search categories and trends. By using tools such as Google Trends and Alerts and by monitoring search traffic to one's own website using various analytical tools, advertisers get a good idea of where to start in investigating the keywords most appropriate for a paid ad campaign. In Google Ads, Google will also provide recommendations for their responsive ads. Another way to research is to ask customers or other stakeholders how they search for your product and monitor their search patterns. From the information in the investigative phase, the advertiser narrows its keyword search and determines if it can afford to bid on the most appropriate keywords, adjusting its strategy if necessary.

Figure 8.5   Paid Search Process Source: Authors.

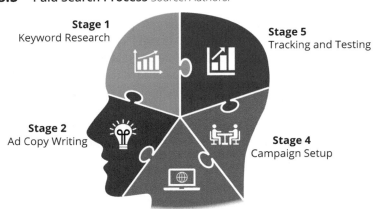

Stage 1
Keyword Research

Stage 5
Tracking and Testing

Stage 2
Ad Copy Writing

Stage 4
Campaign Setup

Stage 3
Landing Page Development

Table 8.1 Types of Keyword Matches

Types of Match Terms	Example
Broad match: reaches widest audience and not in same sequence	**cat food** = raw, freeze-dried, dry (kibble) and wet cat food ads will appear
Phrase match: must be in exact sequence, enclosed in quotes	**"cat food for seniors"** in that order will trigger an ad specifically for senior cats
Exact match: most precise method, enclosed in brackets	**[cat food sensitive stomach]** will trigger an ad but not **cat food kitten**
Negative match: uses a minus sign and prevents ads from appearing	**-raw**, using the negative sign, will exclude words from your search

Stage 2: Ad Copywriting

Next, in the ad copywriting phase of the campaign, the advertiser can make the final selection of keywords to bid on for each ad and each campaign, using tools such as Google's keyword planner or Moz's keyword explorer (https://moz.com/explorer). Keywords that are too expensive or don't have enough traffic will be discarded in favor of others. For matching categories, a broad match includes that keyword idea in any search, including synonyms and related words, whereas a phrase match must include that entire phrase. An exact match will return the search volume for that particular keyword or set of keywords, and a negative match is a term that should not be considered (see Table 8.1). Generally, the broad match will not be the most cost-effective as the ad will show in response to searches that may not be relevant to the product or service. See Figure 8.6 for a visual explanation of the different types of keyword match types and Table 8.1 for a more detailed explanation.

There are various types of campaigns that you can use on Google. At the time of writing, there are five different campaign types:

- Search Campaign
- Display Campaign

broad match
search setting allowing for matching on a wide variation of a keyword or set of keywords.

phrase match
search setting that includes an entire phrase.

exact match
paid search parameter that is set to display to those looking for a particular phase.

negative match
search setting that is the opposite of what is desired; used to avoid paying for unnecessary clicks.

Figure 8.6 Google Match Types

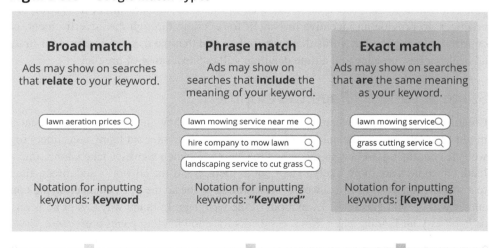

Broad match	Phrase match	Exact match
Ads may show on searches that **relate** to your keyword.	Ads may show on searches that **include** the meaning of your keyword.	Ads may show on searches that **are** the same meaning as your keyword.

lawn aeration prices 🔍

lawn mowing service near me 🔍
hire company to mow lawn 🔍
landscaping service to cut grass 🔍

lawn mowing service 🔍
grass cutting service 🔍

Notation for inputting keywords: **Keyword**

Notation for inputting keywords: **"Keyword"**

Notation for inputting keywords: **[Keyword]**

Loose matching   **Moderate matching**   **Tight matching**

- Shopping Campaign
- Video Campaign
- App Campaign

The **search campaign** allows for text ads using the using the responsive search ads tool built? by Google. Responsive search ads leverage the strength of Google's machine learning by determining the best combination of keywords, description, and phrasing to use in the ad. The **display campaign** allows for ads that are part of Google's Display network. Google's Display network uses Google's partnerships with other sites to advertise on their website. The **shopping campaign** allows for ads that are part of Google's shopping page. These ads show local (and national) retailers who carry the product that is being searched. The **video campaign** allows for text ads that appear on YouTube videos. The **app campaign** also allows for ads that appear in apps that are part of the Google network. Please note that Chapter 10 discusses these different ad types extensively.

Using the Display Network allows the advertiser to choose specific sites on which to display PPC ads. Choice of sites will be based on the product offered and the characteristics of the target market. For "cat food," we might choose animals. Site placement targeting also allows the advertiser to pick specific sites or categories that match specific products and services and to select matching demographic characteristics of those who would want to see an ad. The pricing for site targeting is based on the cost-per-thousand (CPM) impressions. Note that it's cost-per-thousand because "thousand" in Latin numerals is mille, so what looks like should be CPT is actually CPM for "*mille*".

Of course, whether an ad does get served up to users who enter a particular match term is dependent on cost, the actual bid, and the quality of the ad. The idea is to discourage irrelevant advertising and create a "fair playing field" where it is not just the amount of money that is bid that determines whether the ad is served.[8]

The next step of the ad copywriting phase is then to design ads based on different characteristics. A good start is to create multiple ad groups and then test different ads within that group to determine which ones are most effective. Google's responsive search ads will help with identifying the best ads to use, but it is still wise to keep an eye on the different types of ads. An ad group might be cat food, and then different types of advertisements could be created for the different types of cat food within that category, such as dry cat food, canned cat food, dehydrated cat food, raw meat cat food, and so on. The Quality Score will also drop when keywords are not grouped logically together.[9]

When writing any type of ad, remember that an effective ad is persuasive, specific, and concise and distinguishes the firm or not-for-profit from the competition. A good practice is also to include an offer and a call-to-action, standard direct marketing best practices, to provide an incentive or benefit for clicking through the advertisement. Of course, including the keywords that users bid on and that the user is searching for in the ad is also a best practice and a time deadline will create a sense of urgency.

Stage 3: Landing Page Development

Creating a landing page where consumers can go after they click on the ad is critical. It might seem obvious to the marketer how to navigate their site, but many consumers find websites confusing. In fact, as discussed in Chapter 5, when websites take a long time to load, consumers are more likely to exit out of them. So, if the ad works and directs them to a website that does not load well or look similar to the ad they just clicked on, the consumer will … you guessed it … exit out of the webpage. In many ways, your ad is only as good as your landing page. Keys to success for good landing pages are:

1. Loads quickly (about three seconds or less)
2. Contains good visuals (i.e., pictures and text)

cost-per-thousand (CPM)
the amount paid in purchasing advertising; in this case, it means the cost-per-thousand (M is the abbreviation for the Roman numeral for thousand) impressions, or the cost divided by the total number of impressions.

3. Navigates easily

4. Contains the product that is being advertised

Stage 4: Campaign Setup

During the campaign setup phase, advertisers make sure to target their ads and monitor campaigns closely. During launch, another technique advertisers might use for increasing CTR includes using a local search term for ads targeted to geographic areas Google allows for targeting of ads to countries and regions within them. In the United States, regions can be as small as metropolitan areas, allowing PPC ads to be affordable and relevant to local and regional businesses. Facebook allows for more specific geographic targeting, one reason for its recent success.

During launch, advertisers will want to monitor the campaign closely and possibly make use of all the features of ads, for example, showing their ads only at certain days and times (informally known as Day Parting). By making use of the settings available, the ad will only be displayed when potential customers normally look for the product or service. Monitoring budgets on a daily basis is also crucial during this time period. More information on ad campaigns can be found in Chapter 10.

local search
using a local search term in a search query.

Stage 5: Tracking and Testing

The final step after the ad campaign runs is to measure results. Not only can the advertiser measure on a daily basis how much was spent, the number of clicks or impressions, the click-through rate, the CPC, and other key metrics in Google Ads but can also sign up for conversion tracking and measurement. A conversion is any action a visitor takes on your site that is of value, such as a purchase or a request for information. In addition, by using Google Analytics, discussed in Chapter 5, an advertiser can also determine how traffic arrived to the site, whether from search engines or other referral sites, and which keywords have been most effective. Larger and more sophisticated websites rely on other reporting tools such as Hubspot to monitor site traffic, improve conversion rates, and attribute performance to the proper marketing channel.

For PPC analysis, Google Ads and Analytics maintain a high market share among both large and small businesses. There are paid metrics suppliers that offer even more functionality and opportunities for customization and are included in the discussion in Chapter 5. Larger and more sophisticated websites also rely on other reporting tools to monitor site traffic, improve conversion rates, and attribute performance to the proper marketing channel.

Additional Ad Formats

Although the chapter has focused on text ads in Google, there are many additional ad formats as shown in Figure 8.7. The formats include the following:

- Text ads
- Responsive ads that change to fit the space available, for instance, from the desktop version of an ad to the mobile version.
- Image ads that can be either static or interactive.
- App promotions, which are ads specifically to drive app downloads.
- Video ads, which are more engaging to viewers.
- Shopping ads which emphasize product features to encourage purchase on a dedicated shopping page.
- Call-only ads that offer click-to-call functionality.

Figure 8.7 Other Ad Formats Available in Google Ads

Source: https://www.demandcurve.com/blog/types-of-google-ads

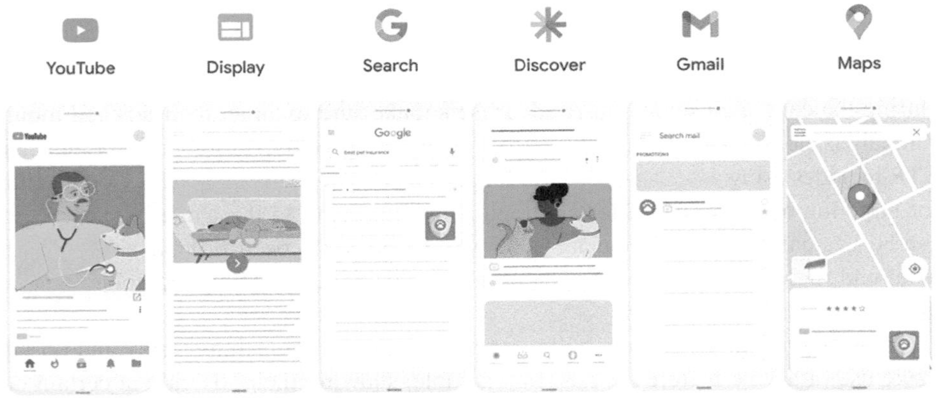

Ad formats should match the objective for a particular paid search ad campaign. For example, a call-only ad is quite effective in a mobile environment for a restaurant owner who knows that potential customers are searching for a restaurant on a mobile device and want to call for information or to make a reservation. All Google Ads can be run on mobile devices as well as on desktop.

While search advertising, especially Google Ads, has been a staple of online marketing for many years, there is another area of paid advertising that is enjoying explosive growth—paid social. That type of advertising will be explored in the next section.

The Emergence of Paid Social Advertising and Google's Display Ads

Advertisers have been taking advantage of *free social media platforms* to listen to and engage with customers almost since their inception. More recently the growing reliance of advertisers on social media intersected with the need of the platforms to monetize their properties. At the intersection sits search advertising and *paid social* advertising formats that are more like the display advertising discussed in Chapter 10. The growth of paid search and the impact of mobile on that advertising sector. The growth of mobile and its impact on digital marketing will be further explored in Chapter 12. In this section, we will focus on paid advertising on social platforms, both desktop and mobile. To illustrate its importance, the Chief Marketing Officer (CMO) Survey of 2022 found both B2C and B2B advertisers making heavy use of the social options as depicted in Figure 8.8. They found the following:

- There was a dip in spending during the COVID-19 pandemic for both B2B and B2C
- A sum of 24 percent of budget is set aside for paid social regarding B2C products compared to 12 percent for B2B product
- Consumer services (i.e., life coaches, fitness plans) exceeds all other sectors in social media spend and is projected to be the leader over the next year or so.

When the subject is specifically paid social media there are two indisputable facts. First, it is growing rapidly. The second is the dominance of Instagram and YouTube as can be seen in Figure 8.9. What is fueling growth of this magnitude? Consider a paid social campaign run by a niche website.

This paid social campaign shows how the social platforms work—and work together—for advertisers. Olivia Rose is a website that offers Black hair tutorials to English- and French-speaking women. It focused on video because its videos were being monetized on Google's AdSense platform. AdSense is a Google platform that allows publishers of

paid social
any type of paid promotion on social media platforms.

AdSense
a way to monetize a website or a blog on Google by showing paid ads.

Figure 8.8   CMO Survey Social Media Spend Source: https://cmosurvey.org/

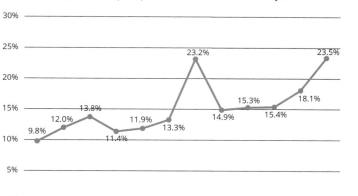

February 2022

Social media spend increased slightly over the past year, but is expected to increase at a much faster pace moving forward

What percent of your marketing budget are you currently spending on social media? And what percent will you spend in the next 12 months? 5 years?

Economic Sector

	Feb-22	Next year
B2B Product	11.6%	14.8%
B2B Services	13.7%	16.9%
B2C Product	23.5%	25.3%
B2C Services	21.5%	23.1%

Insights

Consumer Services exceeds all other industries in its current social media spend (31.2%) and will continue to be a leader in the next 12 months (32.0%) and five years (35.8%). This is likely because these companies are attempting to meet and interact with their consumers where they are spending their time and money (i.e., social media). Companies with <$10M sales revenue also invest heavily (21.5%) and show no sign of stopping (12 months, 25.9%; 5 years, 31.3%).

websites and blogs to display ads on their sites and receive payment when ads are seen or clicked.[10] Using AdSense allowed Olivia Rose to show its videos as ads on other websites and blogs.

The specific objectives of the campaign were to

- Increase the size of their Facebook fan base
- Increase the number of subscribers to their YouTube channel

Figure 8.9   Social Media Marketers' Platform Usage Trends in 2022 Source: https://www.marketingcharts.com/digital/social-media-225913

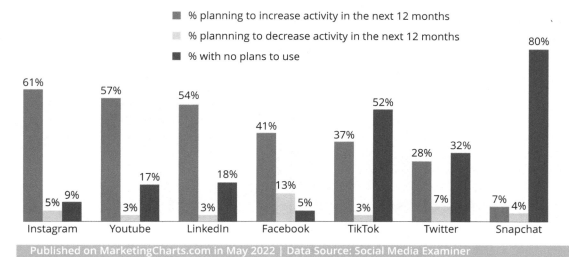

Remaining respondents are maintaining their level of use of the platform | Figures based on a global survey of 2,897 marketers, the majority (64%) of whom work for small business (1-10 employees). Close to two-thirds (63%) focus primarily on B2C marketing and half (50%) are based in the United States.

- Increase subscribers to their blog
- Increase the number of Instagram followers

A still shot of the Facebook ad is shown in Figure 8.10. It ran for 20 seconds, including some text and a CTA, so it could be used on both Facebook and Instagram. As of 2023, Facebook allows videos of up to 240 minutes, but Instagram's maximum length is 120 seconds. By creating an ad that was 20 seconds in length, Olivia Rose was able to advertise on both Instagram and Facebook. They targeted an audience that was female only, 13 to 40 years old, and living in French-speaking countries outside of France such as Guadeloupe and Reunion.

Olivia Rose ran a one-day Sunday trial that was so successful it broadened the campaign specifications by increasing the bid price and extending its reach to English-speaking African and Caribbean countries, the United Kingdom, the United States, and Canada. It ran the broadened campaign for four days with the following results:

- 15,647 new Facebook fans
- 1,784 new YouTube subscribers
- 1,758 new Instagram followers
- 6 new blog subscribers.[11]

The company also reported an increase in engagement with its social media postings and increased inquiries about its products.

This campaign is a good example of how a well-planned and executed social media campaign can produce results. It also gives an initial sense of the large number of paid social options available to advertisers.

While Google and Facebook account for about half of all internet advertising (roughly $250 billion), their dominance has steadily dropped since 2017. As of 2022, Google accounted for 28.8 percent of all paid advertising, and Facebook accounted for 19.6 percent.[12]

promoted posts
regular posts for which the marketer pays a fee to have the post prominently displayed in a feed or on the platform page.

There are two basic formats in paid social advertising—display and promoted posts. Figure 8.11 shows Meta's display ad formats. The table includes Instagram, which is owned by Facebook, and usually incorporates Facebook ad products soon after they are introduced by the parent company. Perhaps that rich assortment of options is one reason it is the fastest-growing of the social media platforms in terms of ad dollars. YouTube, owned by Google, is not included in the table although ads on YouTube are discussed later in the chapter. YouTube concentrates on video advertising, although it does offer one format that it simply calls Display Ads.[13]

Figure 8.10 **The Basic Facebook Video** Source: http://www.marketingsherpa.com/article/case-study/olivia-rose-paid-social-media-growth.

Figure 8.11 Display Ad Formats Offered by Meta

The display formats shown in Figure 8.11 fit into two categories. First, ad formats similar to the ones illustrated in the discussion of Ads in the first part of the chapter—text and links ads. The other seven types of ad formats listed are essentially display ads, sized and otherwise constructed to meet the needs of the viewing device and the objectives of the advertiser. These nine ads make up one general category of paid social ads. Call them display ads for simplicity.

The other category is promoted posts. These are unique to the characteristics of the platform; a promoted post on Facebook is not the same thing as a promoted Tweet. And yes, Facebook does have promoted posts in addition to all the ad formats in Figure 8.11. And Twitter has other ad formats unique to its platform.

In order to make this bewildering array of options as simple as possible, and to keep this chapter from turning into a book, we are going to cover the basic formats in Figure 8.11. Then we are going to select some of the other social media platforms with the most advertising power and highlight non-display ad formats that are either unique to that platform or shared only with similar platforms. That will give a high-level understanding of paid social advertising and resources to further your knowledge about advertising on platforms important to your brand or career aspirations.

Display Ads on Major Social Media Platforms

You will learn more about display ads in Chapter 10. Many of the formats for both desktop and mobile ads remain similar in appearance and the principles of serving ads to targeted audiences remain the same. In other words, the principles of display advertising on websites and social platforms are the same. Different vendors supply services such as ad creation and serving in the different markets, but the principles remain the same.

The bad news is that different terminology is used in different markets, even sometimes on different platforms. Some of those occurrences will be mentioned here, but the advertiser must exercise caution. Part of the due diligence required for running an ad campaign anywhere on the web is to read the format specifications in order to understand what can and cannot be done with a given format. The IAB establishes ad formats for the industry. For paid social ads advertisers will also need to look at the format descriptions on the platform's site because some formats are specific to that platform. Yes, it's complicated, but the information the advertiser needs is easily accessible.

Since Facebook (owned by Meta) offers more display formats than any other platform, so we are going to use Facebook as the primary example. The examples in this section are from the Meta Ads Guide publication. It has detailed specifications for each ad format and shows images of each https://www.facebook.com/business/ads/ad-formats. It also contains the ad formats for Instagram, owned by Facebook, as you can see in Figure 8.11. On Facebook's business page, you will find video tutorials on many aspects of Facebook advertising, including measuring results. On that page, you will find a link to How Facebook Ads Work which has a number of tutorials including audience targeting and Facebook Ad Auction Basics.

There are many good posts that describe Instagram ads that work well, and the advertiser can get excellent ideas from them. However, it is essential that you consult the platform itself before trying to create your own ad. Advertising on social media sites is in a constant state of evolution and the ad format that worked yesterday might have changed today. The platform itself is the only place you can count on getting information that is up to date. Even so, the Meta Ads Guide carries a warning that recent changes may not show up for a time. Announcements generally appear first on the Meta blog.

Text and Links Ads on Meta and Google

Notice that in Figure 8.12 the term "Sponsored" is clearly visible in order to meet FTC guidelines "Advertisement" and "Promoted" are also acceptable identifiers as is #ad. On platforms that allow the user to create their own ads, this is handled automatically.

Now for perhaps the best news of all. On each one of the Ads Guide pages, there is a Create Ad button like the one in Figure 8.13 It takes you to a page that corresponds to the ad objective and format you are looking at. If the advertiser already has an Ads account it shows the account settings and allows access to items like photos that have been used before. If the advertiser is satisfied with the existing Audience definition in the settings, just continue on. But first, consider once again the objectives of the specific campaign. If the objective is to reach loyal Facebook fans with a particular message, a narrowly drawn audience like fans who live in a particular geographical area or fans who have a specific set of interests may be indicated. Facebook is popular among advertisers for its ability to reach precisely defined target markets by location, demographics, interests, and behaviors.

Figure 8.12   **Facebook Sponsored Ad Example** Source: https://www.facebook.com/

Figure 8.13   **Meta Ad Types for Desktop and Mobile** Source: https://www.facebook.com/business/ads-guide

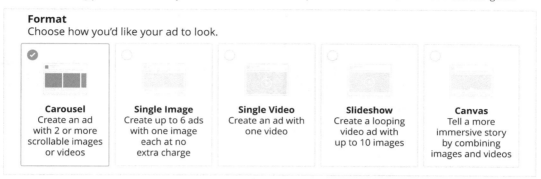

Facebook also has a huge reach as its user numbers indicate. That makes it useful for running broadly targeted campaigns in order to build the brand's fan community on the platform.

Once the audience has been specified go on to Placements to identify the sites chosen to reach it. Many large publishers such as the *New York Times*, National Geographic, and BuzzFeed as well as many gaming apps display Facebook ads. The advertiser may wish to use Automatic Placements until it is clear which publisher sites work well. Next, set the Budget and Schedule. Then go on to create the ad by selecting the format (including images and video), choosing media, and entering text. Facebook provides a lot of suggestions that is useful to the beginner. However, examine them carefully. The audience settings may not be what is needed for this campaign.

Ads are launched on the schedule that was set and advertisers receive results on the account dashboard. Consider that this process gives more good news—it is exactly the set of steps shown in Figure 8.5—Keyword Research → Ad Copywriting → Landing Page Development → Campaign Set up → Tracking and Testing. Remember also what the advertisers at Olivia Rose did; they performed a one-day trial, analyzed those results, and revised what became a very successful result based on the data.

When advertising on Google, video ads are shown across the various YouTube ad types as well as websites on Google Video Partners (GVP). Google has partnered with various websites and apps to increase their reach. For instance, have you ever noticed that many news articles contain a video ad? That publisher probably partnered with YouTube and is part of YouTube's video partner network. The different types of ads that YouTube allows are:

- Skippable in-stream
- Non-skippable in-stream
- In-feed
- Bumper
- Outstream
- Masthead

YouTube's ad types are created to work with various types of devices such as a desktop, phone, tablet, etc. The first type of video ads are in-feed ads. These ads are ones that YouTubers are used to seeing at the beginning and middle of a video. Some ads are skippable and others are not. Skippable ads do not have a maximum length, though YouTube recommends that they should not exceed three minutes. Non-skippable ads can range between 15 to 20 seconds. The second type of video ads are in-feed ads. These types of ads appear in the YouTuber's recommended and home pages. Discovery ads are another form of in-feed ads, and they appear as the sponsored ads that appear in YouTube's home feed. The third type are bumper ads. These types of ads are for highly targeted people based on their interests and demographics. They are six-second videos that play either before, during or after a video. They differ from In-stream videos because they are limited to the six-second time limit and are shown to specific target markets.

Figure 8.14   Example of YouTube Masthead Ad Type

A newer type of video ad that YouTube rolled out in 2019 is the masthead (shown in Figure 8.14). These types of ads can only be purchased on a reservation basis with a Google sales representative. These are the ads that are typically on the first quarter page of the YouTube Home page. They play without sound for 30 seconds. These ads are the most prominent and are displayed in YouTube's TV network as well. Finally, the outstream ads are best for mobile users. They are shown as mobile-only and utilize GVP. Sometimes they appear as banner ads, or as native, and in-feed ads. It depends on how the GVP sets up the ads on their website.

Google has many options for creating ads within these basic categories. Some allow the advertiser to serve personalized content to the viewer or to set up the ad for remarketing and there are many others.[14]

Promoted Posts and Other Social Media Ad Options

As noted in the previous section, both Meta and Google offer promoted posts options—Meta on its own platform,[15] and Google on YouTube.[16] In both cases the advertiser can promote directly from the post page, specify the audience, and set a budget, which can be as low as $5 per day. Performance metrics are provided by the platform.

All the social media platforms we are discussing in this section have some type of promoted post offering and most other prominent platforms do also. Many promoted posts show in the user's main feed with a label like Sponsored or Promoted, but they blend in like other types of native advertising. They can also show at the top of the feed or in the right column, depending on the format of the platform. Some examples of promoted post and other offerings include the following:

- **Instagram.** Accounts with a business profile get access to Insights about the performance of their posts and the ability to promote posts.[17]
- YouTube. Any video on YouTube can be used to create a promoted post. Table 8.2 shows the different types of promoted posts in YouTube.
- **Twitter.** On Twitter ordinary Tweets can be promoted by any user. The tool to create them is Quick Promote.[18] Twitter also offers Promoted Accounts, which put the user's account at the top of the list to be recommended for other users to follow. Promoted Trends puts the user's ad at the top of Twitter's Trending Topics box.
  - Twitter also offers Twitter cards, which are essentially business cards for the user's tweets that include a link to a web page. The cards are available in a number of objectives-based formats.[19]
- **LinkedIn.** Sponsored Content on LinkedIn is represented by sponsored posts with targeting and tracking options.[20] LinkedIn also allows the user to upload email addresses to his or her account, which is useful in the lead nurturing and conversion process.[21]

Table 8.2 YouTube Ad Types Source: https://support.google.com/youtube/answer/2375464

	Skippable in-stream	In-feed	Non-skippable in-stream	Bumper	Outstream
Selling point:	Users can skip so you are only charged for views	Shows to highly engaged users in the discovery and searching phase	Users can't skip so they view your whole message	Quick message that can't be skipped to raise awareness or reinforce other ads.	Raise awareness to users outside of Google when they are browsing their favorite sites
Where does it serve?	YouTube videos, GVP	YouTube Homefeed, YouTube Search	YouTube videos, GVP	YouTube videos, GVP	GVP
Max video length?	No max length (less than 3 mins recommended)	No max length	15–20 seconds	6 seconds	No max length
Views reported in Google Ads?	Yes	Yes	No	No	Yes
Can increment public view count?	Yes (videos less than 10 seconds will not)	Yes	No	No	Yes
Can remarket to viewers?	Yes	Yes	No	No	Yes

- **Pinterest.** Business accounts on Pinterest can promote pins for wobjectives of awareness, engagement, or website traffic. Currently Pins can only be promoted directly from the Pinterest board, so content must be pinned before starting the three-step promotion process.[22]
- **Snapchat.** The conventional promoted post doesn't work with Snaps that disappear within 10 seconds. Instead they offer Snap Ads that appear between user stories and Snap filters that are overlays on Snaps. Snap Ads are not skippable for six-seconds but can run as long as three minutes. Additionally, they also offer sponsored filters that range from an image overlay (#getoutthevote) to augmented reality (AR) for pics (e.g., Try on a wristwatch).[23]
- **TikTok.** Promoted posts on TikTok are actual TikTok videos that appear as an ad in users' feeds. Users will receive more datapoints about their post such as number of views, number of link clicks, number of likes and shares, etc. This tool is an excellent way for more people to learn about your TikTok channel.[24]

There is a pattern here that you can look for in other platforms. Platforms first try to monetize "native content" on their platform, whether it be a Facebook post or a Pinterest Pin. Then, as understanding of the platform's strengths builds in both the platform itself and in its advertisers, the platform begins to offer additional advertising opportunities suited to the nature of the platform. This continuing expansion of advertising opportunities is the reason we continue warning that advertisers must stay abreast of the ad offerings on platforms that work for their target market segment. It is still early days in the world of paid social ads, however, and promoted content is still the main offering of many of the large platforms.

Native Advertising on Facebook and Google

In Chapter 12, we describe native advertising as advertising that matches the format, tone, and function of the publication or channel. That description fits traditional publisher sites but its meaning has become massively confused in social media. Let's try to make a bit of sense out of the confusion to help the advertiser in his or her ongoing search for what works best.

First, Meta (meaning Facebook *and* Instagram) and Google. The Meta Audience Network offers a native ad unit for mobile app ads. It features a series of templates that allow the app owner to design advertising options that blend with the app design and still meet the requirements of designating it as an advertisement. *Notice that this is an option for selling ads on the app, not for placing ads on behalf of the app.* The ads can contain either images or video and include a CTA. The Meta Advertising Network then serves content provided by an advertiser into the template to create an ad on the app. The network also provides targeting options. You can see examples on the Meta link.

Google accepts ads for its own sites and for the Google Display Network. Its native ad format is offered through Double Click and therefore, like Meta, *it provides an opportunity for publishers to sell ads on their sites.* Ads can appear on desktop and mobile websites and on mobile apps. Google uses two native ad templates, a content ad template, and an app install template. You can see examples of both on the link. The publisher configures the template to be used. Ad Exchange then requests bids for the advertising and serves the ad content of the winning bidder. As you can see, Google's process is similar to that of Facebook's.

Remember that any YouTube video can be promoted and thereby become an ad and that video ads can also be created on the YouTube platform. These ads also seem to be, by definition, native because of the unique nature of the platform. In 2015, YouTube introduced TrueView cards. These are interactive overlays that appear on the right side of the video as seen in Figure 8.15a and b. The viewer can click on the cards, in which case the advertiser is charged. If a viewer does not click to expand the cards, the advertiser is charged only if the viewer watches the video ad all the way through.[25] This type of video advertising moves one step closer to social commerce.

It is worthwhile to distinguish between sponsored content and native advertising in traditional digital media and the use of native advertising on social media platforms where it is

social commerce
using social media platforms to assist in or to conduct ecommerce activities.

Figure 8.15a   **Youtube Video Ad with Interactive Cards on Desktop** Source: https:// invideo.io/blog/youtube-cards/

Night Time Routine w/ Lie Detector

916,525 views · Nov 14, 2019

Figure 8.15b   Youtube Video Ad with Interactive Cards on Mobile

Source: http://www.wordstream.com/blog/ws/2015/04/08/trueview-ads.

a monetization option, not a promotional one. One content marketing expert points out that native advertising is any type of advertising that mimics the format of the site on which it is placed while sponsored content is one specific type of native advertising.[26] Promoted posts on social platforms are clearly a type of sponsored content while native advertising on social platforms is a way of attracting advertising dollars to publisher sites. It is inherently confusing!

Choosing the Right Platform(s)

How is the advertiser to make sense of all the paid search and social options? Once again, the answer is given in Figure 8.5—in a word, research! There are two basic questions: where is your target audience to be found, and what is their intent? For example, if your audience is found on Google searching for products or DIY advice, then Google Ads is an obvious choice because you can advertise in Google's search results as well as on YouTube.

It is important to identify platforms where members of the audience are spending time and engaging with content. Platforms that stimulate attention and engagement are highly desirable, sometimes even more so than platforms selected just because of their size. Then the advertiser's own objectives come into play.

Some examples are as follows:

- With over 450 million business and professional users in 200 countries LinkedIn is the leader in reach for that broad community.[27] It has good ratings on its effectiveness for content marketing and paid social from B2B advertisers,[28] adding to its leadership role. It has many targeting options and, in addition to sponsored content and display ads, it offers Sponsored InMail for direct message access to targeted users.[29]

- Is the target market the coveted Millennials segment? If so, the advertiser may wish to consider Instagram, TikTok, or Snapchat . If the target audience is teenagers, as of 2021, 65 percent of teens report using Snapchat and/or TikTok as their main social platform.[30]

  - Remember, though, that numbers are not the only criterion for inclusion of a platform in a paid social campaign. YouTube is the second most visited website in the world (after Google). They have over two billion visitors. The demographics of YouTube users tends to skew younger. In 2021, 95 percent of those between 18 and 29 in the US report using YouTube and 49 percent of those 65+ use YouTube.[31]

- Is the target market made up of highly educated young men who are not successfully reached by traditional media, even traditional digital media? Consider Reddit which is variously considered a major news source and a remarkably weird place on the internet. They have over 450 million visitors monthly. Its audience is 64 percent male who skew a bit younger—over 24 percent are Gen Z. Reddit is organized into conversational threads called Subreddits. There are over 2.8 million Subreddits and over 45 million visitors per day.[32] The goldmine has proved difficult for advertisers, however, because Redditors are notoriously allergic to advertising, attacking posts that even smack of promotional intent. Reddit does offer sponsored posts. It is also offering something called Promoted User Posts in which a post that has gone viral, after receiving permission from the user who wrote the post, can be offered to the brand for sponsorship.[33]

- Is the target market comprised of women, especially women who shop? If so, the marketer should consider Pinterest. Of its 450 million registered users, 76 percent are women and are mostly Millennials (29 percent of total). They use Pinterest as a discovery engine for products to buy. Eighty percent of weekly users report that they found a new product by using Pinterest. Another surprising statistic is that Pinterest users are likely to spend two times more than shoppers on other platforms.[34]

- TikTok is an excellent platform if you are trying to connect with a younger demographic. During Q1 2022, TikTok generated $821 million in consumer spending. It has over 1 billion monthly active users with the vast majority coming from the United States. Additionally, over 54 percent of users are women. Bytedance, the parent company of TikTok generated over $38.6 billion in ad revenue during 2021. As one of the key homes to influencers, over 55 percent of users report purchasing a brand or product after they saw it on TikTok.[35]

If research is the key to choosing the right platforms for a campaign—and it indisputably is—there are two more important pieces of advice. First, multiple platforms will be necessary to reach the target audience with sufficient frequency and impact. Whenever possible choose platforms for which content can easily be repurposed. Second, having chosen platforms and created content, TEST, TEST, TEST. Many platforms like Google have testing options built into their ad creation process. Initial testing should identify the platforms and content that works best. Testing other campaigns as they are executed allows the marketer to try other platforms that offer interesting features or focus on other types of content. Remember to test new features on the best-performing platforms. This kind of testing is the lifeblood of all good digital marketing, and it is essential to bring order into the vast array of choices open to the marketer in paid search and social.

Summary

Search is a key focus of internet advertisers at present and will continue to play an important role. In paid search, the advertiser bids on relevant keywords to get its advertisements displayed at the top or near the top of the paid advertisements. The bidding processes can be complicated, and there are many tools to help determine which keywords to bid on and how much to pay. Paid social also uses a bidding process for paid ads but placements are more limited, generally in the main feed or to its right. Paid social is already mobile-first territory and the number of ads displayed is limited.

There are five basic steps in the search and social advertising process

Keyword Research → Ad Copywriting →
Landing Page Development → Campaign Set up →
Tracking and Testing

The keyword research step is largely about precisely defining the target audience and identifying the keyword bidding terms and the advertising appeal that will resonate with them. In the ad copywriting step actual ads are created according to the specifications of the platform, bidding terms are selected, and budgets are set. Next, ensuring that the landing page loads quickly and easily from both a mobile and desktop browser are paramount. Then, the campaign is set up and launched, either as a full-scale campaign—or better—as a test. Finally, tracking and testing your ads—at least daily—is essential and, depending on results, campaigns may be refined while they are ongoing. All platforms offer account dashboards that offer metrics, usually in real-time, and graphics that assist in the reporting process. Analytics platforms like Google Analytics are useful in this process and there are numerous digital agencies that offer monitoring and reporting services.

Paid search offers just two basic formats, links and text, with Google having recently rolled out Expanded Text ads. Facebook is far and away the leader in paid social advertising and it offers additional display formats in addition to links and text. In addition, social platforms offer promoted posts. Meta and Google also offer what is called native advertising, although it is a monetization option, not a promotional one. Other platforms offer advertising options unique to their own formats. The bewildering array of formats requires that advertisers retain focus on their own objectives and target audiences in order to make best platform and format choices. It also demands that advertisers continually test and refine their paid search and social advertising programs.

One can expect two levels of change that will affect paid search and social in the years to come. First, mobile advertising will continue to grow and dominate paid search as it already does paid social. Second, advertising formats will continue to adapt to user search and shopping patterns. Most assuredly, the paid search and social landscape will become more, not less, complicated over the coming years. In this chapter we have carefully pointed out that the resources advertisers need to understand paid search and social advertising—and to create and to execute their own ad campaigns if that is their choice—are readily available on the platforms with good advice available from experts all over the web.

Discussion Questions

1. Compare two searches, one of desktop and one on a mobile device, using two search engines. Which produces the better results in terms of quality and relevance? Why?

2. How do the ads differ above in terms of how they are displayed? Which do you like better and why?

3. How do search strategies differ for mobile devices from the customer point of view?

4. Why is mobile search likely to be even more important in the future? What other trends are likely in the future for paid search?

5. What is the effect of the different types of ad formats on how advertisers conduct paid search campaigns?

6. Do you see paid social advertising as a useful or even a necessary element of many digital advertising campaigns? Why or why not?

7. How are display ads on social media platforms both similar to and different from display ads found on traditional digital sites?

8. What do you understand a promoted post to be? Are promoted posts the same on all platforms?

9. Explain the statement, "Any YouTube video can be an ad."

10. Do you agree or disagree with this statement? Ads on social media platforms have many of the characteristics of native advertising.

11. What are some of the elements of a paid social advertising campaign that could usefully be tested?

12. The process of developing paid search and paid social ads is quite different. Explain why you agree or disagree.

Endnotes

1. Lauren Kaye. "94 Percent of B2B Buyers Research Online for Purchase Decisions." Brafton, July 4, 2022, http://www.brafton.com/news/94-percent-b2b-buyers-research-online-purchase-decisions/.

2. Dan Alaimo. "87% Of Shoppers Now Begin Product Searches Online." Retail Dive, August 15, 2018, https://www.retaildive.com/news/87-of-shoppers-now-begin-product-searches-online/530139/.

3. "Paid Search—Reports, Statistics & Marketing Trends." Insider Intelligence, accessed April 5, 2023, https://www.emarketer.com/topics/topic/paid-search.

4. Statista Research Department. "Digital Market Outlook: U.S. Digital Advertising Spending Share by Device 2026." *Statista*, January 10, 2023, https://www.statista.com/forecasts/459593/digital-advertising-revenue-device-digital-market-outlook-usa.

5. "What Is Paid Search? Marketing & Advertising Strategies." Sprinklr, accessed April 5, 2023, https://www.sprinklr.com/cxm/paid-search.

6. Tran, Tony. "A Beginner's Guide to Using Google Ads (Previously Google Adwords)." Social Media Marketing & Management Dashboard, December 20, 2022, https://blog.hootsuite.com/google-ads/.

7. "Evaluate and Optimize Your Bids." Google Ads Help. Google, accessed April 5, 2023, https://support.google.com/google-ads/answer/7085711.

8. "Evaluate and Optimize Your Bids." Google Ads Help.

9. "About Quality Score." Google Ads Help. Google, accessed April 5, 2023, https://support.google.com/google-ads/answer/6167118.

10. "Evaluate and Optimize Your Bids." Google Ads Help.

11. Scott McDaniel. "Inbound Marketing: How a Paid Social Media Campaign Drew in 1,000 New YouTube Subscribers in Just Four Days." MarketingSherpa, January 7, 2016, https://www.marketingsherpa.com/article/case-study/olivia-rose-paid-social-media-growth.

12. Thomas Germain. "Duopoly Done: Google and Meta Take in Less than 50% of Online Ad Money." Gizmodo, December 21, 2022, https://gizmodo.com/google-facebook-duopoly-half-online-ads-amazon-apple-1849920325.

13. "How Ads Work on YouTube." YouTube, January 29, 2019, https://www.youtube.com/watch?v=WPR9PCoeqog.

14. "Create Display Ads for Dynamic Remarketing." Google Ads Help. Google, accessed April 6, 2023, https://support.google.com/google-ads/answer/3265299?hl=en.

15. "Give your Business Story a Boost." Facebook, accessed April 6, 2023, https://www.facebook.com/business/pages/boost-post.

16. "Online Video Advertising Campaigns—Youtube Advertising." YouTube, accessed April 6, 2023, https://www.youtube.com/yt/advertise/.

17. "New and Updated Professional Tools for Businesses on Instagram." Instagram for Business, December 20, 2019, https://business.instagram.com/blog/new-and-updated-tools-for-businesses/.

18. "What Are Promoted Ads?" Twitter, accessed April 6, 2023, https://business.twitter.com/en/help/overview/what-are-promoted-tweets.html.

19. "Advertising." Twitter, accessed April 6, 2023, https://business.twitter.com/en/advertising.html.

20. "Native ADS—Sponsored Content: LinkedIn Marketing Solutions," accessed April 6, 2023, https://business.linkedin.com/marketing-solutions/native-advertising.

21. "Importing and Inviting Your Email Contacts: Linkedin Help," accessed April 6, 2023, https://www.linkedin.com/help/linkedin/answer/4214/importing-and-inviting-your-email-contacts.

22. "Advertising on Pinterest: Pinterest Business." Pinterest, accessed April 6, 2023, https://business.pinterest.com/en/promoted-pins.

23. "7 Best Snapchat Augmented Reality Lenses in April 2023," Catchar, accessed April 6, 2023, https://catchar.io/snapchat-ar-lenses.

24. "Use Promote to Grow Your TikTok Audience | TikTok Help Center," accessed April 6, 2023, https://support.tiktok.com/en/using-tiktok/growing-your-audience/use-promote-to-grow-your-tiktok-audience.

25. Tim Peterson. "YouTube Makes Skippable TrueView Ads More Interactive—and More Lucrative." *Ad Age*, April 8, 2015, http://adage.com/article/digital/youtube-adds-interactive-cards-skippable-trueview-ads/297953/.

26. Joe Lazer. "Ask a Content Strategist: What's the Difference between Sponsored Content and Native Advertising?" Contently, February 25, 2020, https://contently.com/strategist/2016/04/20/ask-content-guy-whats-difference-sponsored-content-native-advertising.

27. Craig Smith. "220 Amazing Linkedin Statistics and Facts." DMR, March 9, 2023, http://expandedramblings.com/index.php/by-the-numbers-a-few-important-linkedin-stats.

28. "B2B Content Marketing: 2016 Benchmarks, Budgets, and Trends—North America," "Content Marketing Institute," accessed April 6, 2023, https://contentmarketinginstitute.com/wp-content/uploads/2015/09/2016_B2B_Report_Final.pdf.

29. "Targeting Options for Linkedin Advertisements: Linkedin Help," accessed April 6, 2023, https://www.linkedin.com/help/linkedin/answer/722/targeting-options-and-best-practices-for-linkedin-advertisements.

30. S. Dixon. "Preferred Social Networks of U.S. Teens 2021." *Statista*, October 17, 2022, https://www.statista.com/statistics/250172/social-network-usage-of-us-teens-and-young-adults.

31. Flori Needle. "YouTube Demographics & Data to Know in 2023" HubSpot Blog. HubSpot, August 5, 2022, https://blog.hubspot.com/marketing/youtube-demographics.

32. Pamela Bump. "24 Reddit Stats and Facts to Know in 2022." HubSpot Blog. HubSpot, October 18, 2022, https://blog.hubspot.com/marketing/reddit-stats.

33. Andrew Hutchinson. "Reddit Looking to Open up Advertising Opportunities via Sponsored Posts." Social Media Today, July 30, 2016, http://www.socialmediatoday.com/social-networks/reddit-looking-open-advertising-opportunities-sponsored-posts.

34. Chloe West. "24 Must-Know Pinterest Stats for Marketers in 2023." Sprout Social, March 29, 2023, https://sproutsocial.com/insights/pinterest-statistics/.

35. Chloe West. "27 Tiktok Stats Marketers Need to Know in 2023." Sprout Social, March 29, 2023, https://sproutsocial.com/insights/tiktok-stats/.

Chapter 9

Social Media Marketing as a Cornerstone of Strategy

Learning Objectives

By the time you complete this chapter, you will be able to:

1 Explain the P.O.S.T. methodology for social media marketing.

2 Describe the five consumer motivations for using social media (5Cs).

3 Identify different social media objectives.

4 Explain what a social media influencer is.

5 Summarize how social media algorithms work.

6 Describe the issues involved in building a successful social media team.

Social media marketing (SMM) is no longer a curiosity or trend. It is an established element of marketing strategy. Social media is so much a part of the daily lives of people around the globe that most businesses cannot avoid using it. Every second, people across the globe—both at home and work—log on to social platforms on desktop or mobile devices. Figure 9.1 provides the monthly active users across different platforms as of January 2022.[1] This global dataset shows that the most popular social media platform at this time is Facebook with 2.9 billion active users, followed by YouTube (2.6 billion active users), WhatsApp (2 billion active users), and Instagram (1.5 billion active users). Figure 9.1b shows the leading social networks ranked by brand awareness in the United States.[2] Comparing these two figures, you can notice some similarities and some differences. In both worldwide usage and United States awareness, Facebook and YouTube take the lead; however, TikTok, Twitter, Snapchat, and Pinterest all appear to be quite popular in the United States, but much less so when considering the rest of the world. Marketers should take note of these differences and take into account differences across countries when planning social media campaigns. Another interesting note is that mobile messaging apps, like Weixin/WeChat and Facebook Messenger, are quite popular across the globe, signaling that not only is social media growing rapidly, but it is shifting to mobile and to messaging and chat apps.

Figure 9.1a   Most Popular Social Networks Worldwide as of January 2022, Ranked by Number of Monthly
Active Users Source: https://www.statista.com/statistics/272014/global-social-networks-ranked-by-number-of-users/

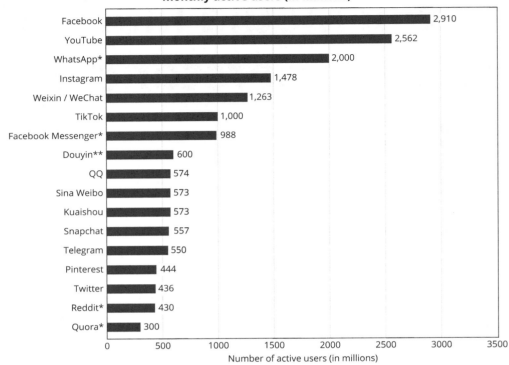

Most popular social networks worldwide as of January 2022, ranked by number of monthly active users (in millions)

Figure 9.1b   Leading Social Networks Ranked by Brand Awareness in the United States in 2022 Source: https://www
.statista.com/statistics/1307244/most-well-known-social-networks-in-the-united-states/

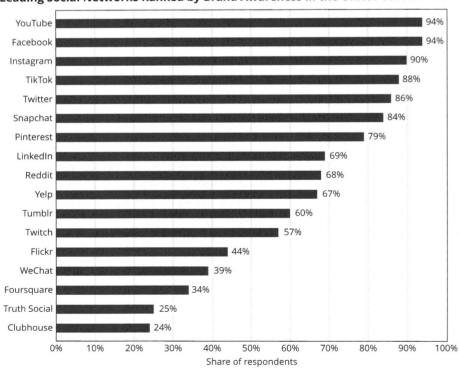

Leading Social Networks Ranked by Brand Awareness in the United States in 2022

How Marketers Can Strategically Use Social Media—The P.O.S.T. Methodology

There is an old advertising maxim that says marketers should "follow the eyeballs." In other words, where their customers go for information and entertainment, marketers must follow. That necessity has prompted an explosion in the use of social media by marketers, both B2C and B2B. This new practice has presented both opportunities and challenges for marketers and for the brands and companies that employ them.

There's no shortage of books, blogs, and articles touting "the best way" to develop an SMM strategy. One of the earliest attempts to identify guidelines for an effective social media strategy comes from the book *Groundswell by* Josh Bernoff and Charlene Li.[3] The P.O.S.T. methodology introduced in the book remains effective today.[4] As shown in Figure 9.2, P.O.S.T. is an acronym that stands for People, Objectives, Strategy, and Technology. P.O.S.T. requires that marketers begin their social media strategy by focusing on people first and foremost. Marketers can only design effective social media strategies if they truly understand their target audience. They must carefully evaluate how their objectives match their customers' needs, how their customers think, and their customers behave. Only after you understand people (your customers) and have identified your objectives can you identify specific strategies (tactics) and the specific technologies you will use to execute your SMM plan.

People

People are the core of social media. Without them, a social platform has little value. It's crucial to know who your target audience is, or your content will go unnoticed. As noted in other chapters, including Chapter 6 in reference to website design, creating a persona that describes your audience based on factors such as gender, age, demographic, income, education, wants, needs, and others, is always beneficial. The same is true for social media. As you are probably aware, social media platforms vary in the types of users

Figure 9.2   The POST Methodology from *Groundswell by* Josh Bernoff and Charlene Li Source: © Cengage

P	People Assess your customer's social activities
O	Objectives Decide what you want to accomplish
S	Strategy Plan for how relationships with customers will change
T	Technology Decide which social technologies to use

that are attracted to the platform. Figure 9.3 offers a comparison of some of the top social media platforms in terms of demographics.

In addition to demographics, understanding why your audience uses social media is also key; so, asking the question, "What's in it for them?" can be quite helpful. Too often businesses focus on their business objectives and end up pushing messages to social media users. This failure can make social media users feel as though it is simply another sales channel, and they will be unlikely to engage with the brand's content. Figure 9.4 provides a simple framework for thinking about consumer motivations to use social media. Inspired by the 4Ps framework taught in many introductory marketing classes, this framework can be used as a guide to create effective social media plans. Marketers should identify at least one C in the framework when planning social media content and campaigns. Social media activities can tap into more than one consumer motivation, and the more motivations (Cs) you include, the more success you will have. The 5Cs are Consume, Connect, Control, Compete, and Create. A detailed discussion of each motivation with examples is presented later.

Figure 9.3   **Comparing Social Media Platforms** Source: https://www.wordstream.com/wp-content/uploads/2022/02/best
-social-media-marketing-platforms-comparison-chart-ws.png

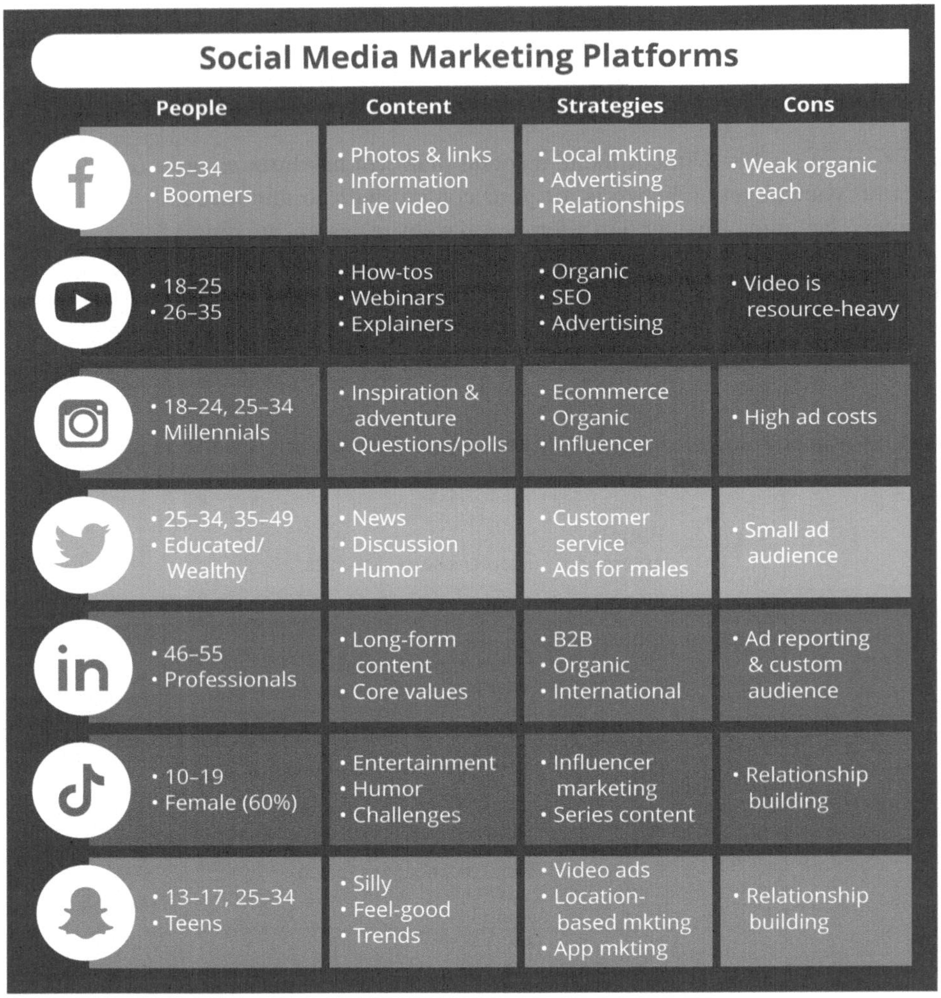

Social Media Marketing Platforms

	People	Content	Strategies	Cons
facebook	• 25–34 • Boomers	• Photos & links • Information • Live video	• Local mkting • Advertising • Relationships	• Weak organic reach
YouTube	• 18–25 • 26–35	• How-tos • Webinars • Explainers	• Organic • SEO • Advertising	• Video is resource-heavy
Instagram	• 18–24, 25–34 • Millennials	• Inspiration & adventure • Questions/polls	• Ecommerce • Organic • Influencer	• High ad costs
Twitter	• 25–34, 35–49 • Educated/ Wealthy	• News • Discussion • Humor	• Customer service • Ads for males	• Small ad audience
LinkedIn	• 46–55 • Professionals	• Long-form content • Core values	• B2B • Organic • International	• Ad reporting & custom audience
TikTok	• 10–19 • Female (60%)	• Entertainment • Humor • Challenges	• Influencer marketing • Series content	• Relationship building
Snapchat	• 13–17, 25–34 • Teens	• Silly • Feel-good • Trends	• Video ads • Location-based mkting • App mkting	• Relationship building

Figure 9.4 The 5Cs of Consumer Motivations for Using Social Media Source: Dr. Lauren Labrecque

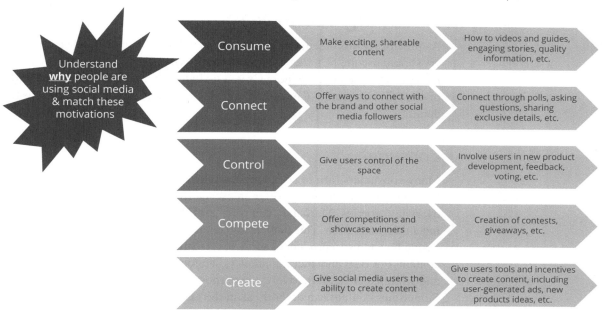

Objectives

Once you understand your audience and have considered motivations, the next step in the P.O.S.T methodology is to identify your Objectives, ask yourself, "What do you want to achieve for your brand?" There are several objectives marketers can choose, including generating awareness, strengthening relationships and build community, search engine optimization (SEO), customer support and reputation management, research, and increasing employee productivity. Each of these is discussed in more detail later in this chapter.

Strategy

Now that you have identified your **objectives**, you can think back to how they align with your social media audience. It is important to refer back to the **"people"** portion of the methodology to consider how you can create content that can fulfill your **objectives** while also meeting your audiences' motivations (the 5Cs).

Technology/Tools

Lastly, only after you clearly understand people, as well as having identified your **objectives** and **strategy**, is it finally time to select the **technology** and tools that you need. Here marketers can identify the platforms where target users are most active and consider how they align best with their **objectives**. At this final stage, you can plan out the specifics of your content. As you can see, the four aspects of the P.O.S.T. methodology do not follow a single straight line but reference back to one another. The important takeaway with this methodology is that **people** are at the forefront of any successful social media strategy, while the **technology** itself is the least important piece of the puzzle. Often marketers may be tempted to jump to the next "new and shiny" platform or trend—doing so without keeping user motivations (**people**) at the forefront, followed by the **objectives**, is ill-advised.

People: The 5cs of Consumer Motivations for Using Social Media

As previously discussed, when planning social media content and campaigns, marketers should use the 5Cs framework to plan activities that tap into at least one consumer motivation. In theory, the more Cs you include, the more successful you will be. Each of the 5Cs (Consume, Connect, Control, Compete, and Create) is discussed next in detail.

Consume

Many consumers turn to social media to learn new information or for entertainment. For some, social media can offer an escape from boredom or offer a distraction from everyday worries. Marketers can offer useful, engaging, and entertaining content to meet this motivation. This content can come in the form of information, such as showcasing how to use a product or service, offering recipes, how-tos, or other instructional content. For B2B audiences, marketers can focus on creating high-quality infographics and whitepapers. Alternatively, the purpose of the content can be simply to entertain. Sometimes content can do both, as in the classic case of Blendtec's "Will it Blend?" social strategy. In its early days, Tom Dickson, the inventor of Blendtec, would test the power of the blenders with nonfood items such as wood boards. This product testing inspired Blendtec to create the "Will it Blend?" video series where Tom takes typically nonedible objects such as glowsticks, BIC lighters, and even iPhones and attempts to blend them using their ultra-powered blender (as shown in Figure 9.5). The content is entertaining and informative at the same time. If a blender can blend an iPhone, one can assume it will easily blend food items. While the Blendtec team chose initial items, later items were selected from social media users' suggestions. This proved to be a great success. In fact, one of their most popular fan-requested videos, blending an iPhone, has amassed nearly 13 million views.[5]

Figure 9.5   **Will it Blend? iPhone** Source: YouTube, LLC

Social media platforms' technological capabilities and userbase drive the types of content marketers can create.[6] Platforms such as TikTok, YouTube, and Instagram rely heavily on video content, while written content such as news stories tend to dominate for platforms like Twitter and Facebook. Visually dominant platforms like Pinterest and Instagram are ideal places for informational content such as "How To" guides, recipes, and infographics.

Connect

At its core, social media is about making connections. In the early days of social media, platforms were not dominated by brands. Instead, they offered a place for friends and family to connect with one another. In fact, Facebook did not allow brands on the platform during its first three years.[7] The motivation to connect can be tapped by creating spaces or campaigns that facilitate users to connect with one another or connect with the brand. Simply asking questions to audiences is a simple way to facilitate connections and start a conversation. Remember, digital marketing efforts should not be viewed as one-to-many communications where a brand broadcasts a message to consumers. Instead, messaging should facilitate two-way interactions. This is what "connect" is all about. Sharing exclusive details and offers is another way to connect with users to provide them with meaningful offers that are not given to everyone. Marketers can also solicit customer photos and stories to connect with consumers in more profound ways.

Oreo's #oreoscope campaign offers a great example of designing campaigns to meet consumers' need to connect. For this Twitter-based campaign (as shown in Figure 9.6), Oreo tapped into people's love of astrology and horoscopes by offering fans to get a personalized "Oreoscope" after analyzing their most recent tweets. People love customized content because it makes them feel like they are getting one-on-one attention from their favorite brands. While the number of unique "Oreoscopes" was limited and not uniquely created for each person, receiving a personal reading still felt special, fun, and sharable. Adding to the benefits, Oreo offered people an easy way to share the results with their

Figure 9.6a   Oreo's #OREOscope Campaign on Twitter Taps Fans Motivation to Connect Source: Twitter, Inc.

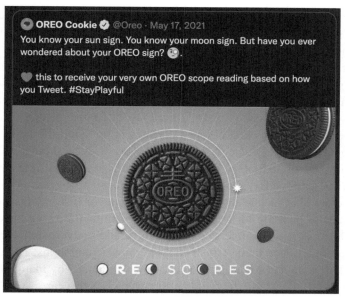

Figure 9.6b **An Example of #OREOscope Results** Source: Twitter, Inc.

own networks, which allowed them to connect with others beyond the brand. Personalized results and content from the results of a quiz or analysis of account data give people an opportunity to connect with other Twitter users while spreading awareness about the sponsoring brand in the process.

Control

Taking it one step further, marketers may structure campaigns to give users some control by soliciting feedback and involving them in new product development. Voting on new product colors and styles is a straightforward method of doing this. Marketers can even allow fans to co-create products and advertisements. There are many examples of large campaigns that tap into the consumer motivation to control, thus allowing fans to co-create new products and advertising for the brands. Mountain Dew's "Dewmocracy" and Lay's "Do Us a Flavor" campaigns are prime examples of social media campaigns that allowed consumers to "control" the brand by creating new products. Mountain Dew's campaigns were so successful that they ran three campaigns in the United States (2007, 2009, and 2016) and multiple campaigns outside the United States.[8] Lay's campaign also found great success not only in terms of buzz generated but in sales as the winning chip flavor (Cheesy Garlic Bread) saw an 8 percent sales increase for Lay's in the three months following the competition.[9] Likewise, Doritos gave consumers control of the brand's advertising by allowing fans to create their own ads in their "Crash the Superbowl" campaigns. The brand ran this contest for ten years and found great success, as evidenced by many of the winning ads being ranked among the best of the Superbowl each year.[10] All three of these examples (Mountain Dew, Lays, and Doritos) also used the consumer motivation to compete, which is described next.

Compete

Social media offers a place where consumers (fans) can compete. On a simple level, brands can devise simple contests, like giveaways where fans can win products or other rewards for doing simple actions like liking a post, commenting, sharing, or answering a question. Often contests like these can be used to create awareness and also provide insights to marketers, two objectives we will discuss later. Marketers can also showcase winners, adding another "reward" to compete. As previously mentioned in the "control" section, large-scale campaigns like those conducted by Doritos, Mountain Dew, and Lays also meet the consumer motivation to compete since they are built around competition. Legos Ideas also leverages the motivation to compete by allowing fans to submit ideas and win prizes. Fans can complete weekly challenges, enter contests, and submit product ideas. In addition to using their creativity (which taps the motivation to create), fans also vote to support entries adding another level of competition. Figure 9.7 shows some examples of fan submissions with high support from other Lego Ideas users.

A smaller-scale example of a brand harnessing the motivation to compete is from the German supermarket chain Lidl. The brand hosts competitions, including a "Funsize Design Contest" where fans were invited to create new characters for their "fun-sized" vegetable products for children. To enter the contest, consumers simply draw a new character and give it a name. Can you think of some examples of brands harnessing the motivation to compete?

Figure 9.7   Lego Ideas Tapping into the Motivation to Compete Source: LEGO

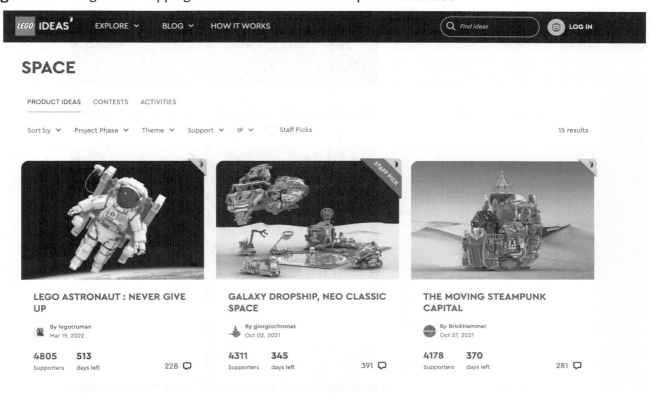

Create

Many social media users love to create content, so campaigns that put user-generated content at the forefront tap into this motivation. Beyond initiating the call to create content around a specific topic, brands can facilitate content creation by giving users tools to do it, such as providing special branded logos, stickers, and frames. A great example of a social media campaign that used the motivation to create is the Getty Museum Challenge. The Los Angeles-based art museum decided to tap into the creativity of its fanbase during the start of the COVID-19 lockdown in March 2020. The museum leveraged multiple social media platforms, including Twitter, Instagram, and Facebook, and challenged fans to recreate their favorite works of art using objects and people in their homes. Some examples of users' answers to this call for creativity are highlighted in Figure 9.8. This simple campaign not only tapped into the motivation to create but arguably tapped into other motivations as well. For example, people connected with both the museum as well as other fans who answered the challenge, which was hugely impactful during a time when people lacked connection from being at home during COVID-19 lockdowns. This campaign also somewhat taps the motivation to control, which again was important since many shared feelings of a lack of control during this stressful and uncertain time. As previously noted, many successful social media campaigns don't just tap into one motivation; those that can meet multiple motivations are likely to be more successful.

Another example that showcases the need to create is Procter & Gamble's Distance-Dance Campaign. Again set during the initial COVID-19 lockdowns in March 2020, P&G asked people to "Stay at home and keep your distance with the #DistanceDance! Tag @charlidamelio and #DistanceDance in YOUR very own video." The brand also incentivized content creation by donating to Feeding America and Matthew 25: Ministries for the first 3 million videos. The campaign was arguably a success as it massed over 18.1 billion views on TikTok.[11]

Figure 9.8a The Getty Museum's Challenge Call on Twitter Source: Twitter, Inc.

Figure 9.8b   Examples from the #gettymuseumchallenge on Instagram Source: Instagram

Objectives

Once you understand your audience and have considered their motivations, the next step in the P.O.S.T. methodology is to identify your objectives. Ask yourself, what do you want to achieve for your brand? There are myriad objectives that social media can have, as outlined in Figure 9.9. Each objective will use different key performance indicators (KPIs) to evaluate success, so at this stage you should also identify the KPIs you will use for each objective. For example, if your objective is to grow a community on Facebook, KPIs may include the number of followers and engagement metrics (such as likes, and comments). Targets (such as gaining 5,000 followers over 3 months) can also be set for your KPIs. Among the most common objectives is generating awareness. Viral campaigns, like Blendtec's "Will it Blend?", follow this objective. Relevant KPIs for an awareness objective may include measures such as number of views, number of shares, and number of new site visitors. Of course, the specific KPI is dependent on the platforms used.

Generate Awareness

Brands can gain awareness by communicating with audiences across three types of media—owned, earned, and paid (outlined in Figure 9.10). Owned and earned media are free, while paid is not. Owned media refers to the content that a business creates and controls. A business's Facebook profile, its website, and its Instagram profile are all examples of owned media. Marketers have complete control over what is posted and when. They can also choose to put customer-created content on its site, like website reviews and testimonials, or even pull content from social media. Like all the rest of social media, owned media

owned media
content that a business owns and controls, such as its website and social media profiles.

Figure 9.9   Social Media Objectives Source: © Cengage

is not truly free. It requires human effort and ingenuity to listen and respond. Marketers need to be aware of how social media algorithms work to optimize the chances that their content will be seen and interacted with. We discuss these algorithms in more detail later in this chapter.

Earned media refers to content that others create about a business. Product reviews or Instagram posts about a product are examples of earned media. Earned media is often the result of doing both paid and owned media well. A great Super Bowl ad is discussed, viewed, and retweeted many times. That's what the brand is counting on when it pays those exorbitant prices for an ad on game day. In fact, in recent years, an entire advertising

social media algorithm
a set of mathematical rules that specify how social media content is presented to users.

earned media
buzz in both social and traditional media that is generated by users (not from the brand or company directly).

Figure 9.10   Types of Media Source: https://www.oneupweb.com/blog/a-look-at-earned-owned-paid-media/

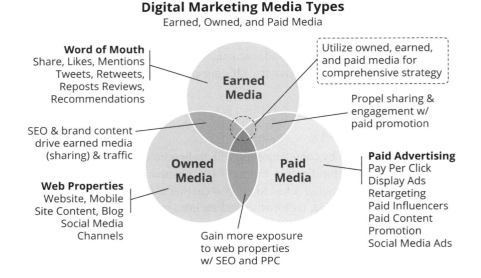

industry has grown up around the practice of creating buzz for Super Bowl ads—and many other types of promotions. The whole idea of creating buzz is to get the product, ad, event, and so on, to be discussed among family and friends or online. Many marketers regard earned media as the most valuable because it carries with it the authenticity and trustworthiness of the publisher (the person talking about the brand) and more people trust peers more than brands. It is also the hardest and most time-consuming to generate.

Lastly, paid media refers to content that marketers pay to place in front of an audience. Businesses can use a social media platform's advertising platform to target potential customers with content, such as sponsored posts on Instagram. Paid media may also take the form of sponsorships with celebrities or influencers in exchange for products or monetary compensation. Paid media in traditional print and broadcast channels still has an important role to play. It can provide great audience reach and as much frequency as the marketer desires and can pay for. It is accessible on a national or local level and can be implemented quickly. Marketers feel comfortable with paid media because they are in control of content as well as all the elements of execution.

paid media
traditional advertising on any channel, traditional or social, that requires payment for placement

frequency
the number of times a person is exposed to a promotional message

Increased awareness can also generate sales (or leads for B2B companies). In recent years, many social media platforms have been adding the ability to complete a purchase without having to leave the platform. For instance, Instagram offers Instagram Shopping where brands can set up the ability for users to make direct purchases through the platform. Brands leveraging this feature can tag products in their posts for direct purchase and host a shop on their profile. According to Instagram shopping statistics, 90 percent of users follow at least one business on the platform and 44 percent of Instagram users are shopping weekly on the platform,[12] making this a good option for brands who want to sell directly on the platform.

Strengthen Relationships & Build Community

Social media creates a perfect environment for both individuals and brands to connect with one another to form and strengthen relationships, and even build communities. The word "community" is often used loosely to refer to like-minded people who congregate somewhere to interact. A brand community is something more limited and precise. Muniz and O'Guinn have advanced a universally accepted definition:

> A brand community is a specialized, non-geographically bound community, based on a structured set of social relations among admirers of a brand.[13] These consumers are drawn together by a common interest in, and commitment to, the brand and a social desire to bond with like-minded others. New modes of computer-mediated communication facilitate and flavor communal communication.[14]

brand community
a group of like-minded people who share interests grouping around a brand on the internet to communicate with one another and the brand.

Building a brand community is not an activity to be undertaken lightly. It takes time, resources, and experience to be successful. If a marketer is extremely lucky, there is an existing brand community that can be gently coopted by the corporation. Such was the case with the Harley Owners Group (HOGs) who, as early as the 1920s, banded together in the physical world to enjoy motorcycle rides together. Harley Davidson recognized its value and assigned executives to go along on the rides long before the internet. The internet gave them an opportunity to "support" the HOGs with a web page. The page facilitated many subtle marketing activities, including support of local chapters and women's activities. The brand community is also alive and well on social media platforms like Facebook and Twitter with many local HOG groups also active.

Whenever you look, there are numerous posts from members and some from local chapters, promoting events. There are, however, few comments from page administrators (i.e., corporate social media marketers). Members keep the community alive. That is truly a vibrant brand community. It started with an experiential product that owners were passionate about, and that is why there have been HOG groups from the brand's early days.

This physical world relationship gave Harley Davidson a rich history on which to build a modern virtual community to promote the real-life experience.

In addition to creating a community around a specific brand, marketers may also opt to create or engage with a community around a certain topic. For instance, brands that sell products for babies may engage with parenting communities by offering content to support new parents such as infographics about baby milestones, healthy recipes for different age groups, or simply offer general support. Whether the focus is on a specific brand, a general activity, or a lifestyle, using social media to build a community can offer long-lasting connections with customers, especially when brands plan their interaction around the 5Cs (consume, control, connect, compete, and create).

SEO Benefits of Social Media

Different social media platforms play different roles in SEO. Content from some platforms, like Pinterest, Twitter, and YouTube, are indexed by major search engines and, therefore, can be great awareness-generating tools. Other social media platforms, such as Facebook, are not indexed by search engines and therefore will not appear on the search engine results page. There is still SEO value in this content though. Links provide some benefits to boost the search engine's assessment of a website's content through backlinks and increasing website activity, which can strengthen the position in the search engine results pages.

Customer Support & Reputation Management

Social media has also become a customer service channel and many customers will reach out to brands on social media before doing so via more traditional forms of contact, such as email or phone. Today customers expect businesses to respond quickly so it is important for businesses to monitor for customer questions. KPIs related to customer service may include response times and response rates.

Moreover, social media offers an opportunity to monitor what is being said about your business (for better or worse). In addition to asking questions, consumers often take to social media to both praise and make complaints about brands. By actively monitoring social media, marketers can quickly respond to complaints before they become larger emergencies. Oftentimes brands fail to recognize that consumers may be talking negatively about them outside of their owned channels, such as the brand's Facebook profile. Social media listening tools like Meltwater (https://www.meltwater.com/), Salesforce Social Studio (https://socialstudio.radian6.com/), and DataEQ (https://dataeq.com/) can effectively monitor for mentions of your brand or its offers across multiple social media channels. With active monitoring, brands can address upset consumers proactively before any social media storms occur.

social media crisis
a large event on social platforms that negatively impacts a brand's reputation. Also referred to as a social media storm.

There are many examples where brands have faced a social media crisis. A social media crisis refers to an event on a social media platform that negatively impacts a brand's reputation. A crisis is not one customer complaining, but something that creates a storm of negative responses that may even lead to some angry customers calling for a boycott. These storms can occur in response to many things, including questionable advertising (such as JCPenney's teapot ad), new product launches (such as Walmart's launch of its Juneteenth ice cream), in response to bad employee behavior, or in response to a brand's own social post media post (such as Burger King's "Women belong in the kitchen" tweet on International Women's Day, as seen in Figure 9.11). No matter the cause, it is important for brands to monitor and respond empathetically. What do you think about Burger King's response?

Having a social media response plan in place for such incidents is important, especially for large brands that have multiple employees monitoring and responding to social media.

Figure 9.11a **Burger King's Initial "Women belong in the kitchen" Tweet on International Women's Day** Source: USA TODAY (NEWSPAPER)

Burger King ✔
@BurgerKingUK

Women belong in the kitchen.

1:01 AM · 3/8/21 · Twitter Web App

163K Retweets **171K** Quote Tweets **666K** Likes

This Tweet has been deleted.

Figure 9.11b **Burger King's Response** Source: USA TODAY (NEWSPAPER)

Burger King ✔ @BurgerKingUK · Mar 8, 2021
We hear you. We got our initial tweet wrong and we're sorry. Our aim was to draw attention to the fact that only 20% of professional chefs in UK kitchens are women and to help change that by awarding culinary scholarships. We will do better next time.

Burger King ✔
@BurgerKingUK

We decided to delete the original tweet after our apology. It was brought to our attention that there were abusive comments in the thread and we don't want to leave the space open for that.

5:41 PM · Mar 8, 2021

♡ 17.2K   Reply   Copy link

Read 2.9K replies

This allows for a unified and consistent response. Figure 9.12 provides an example of a social media response plan in the form of a flow chart to help employees make decisions about how to best respond to both positive and negative comments.

Using Social Media for Research

In addition to monitoring social media for customer service and reputation management, social media listening tools (as previously mentioned) may be used for research purposes. Companies can use social media as a market research tool to gather insights about trends in consumer behavior, identify ways to improve products, and even discover new uses for products. This can be done using social media listening tools such as Meltwater and Salesforce Social Studio that gather and organize social media data based on keywords or hashtags. For example, iRobot, the company that makes the Roomba robotic vacuum cleaner, may analyze customer comments for their brand name or for generic words such as "robot vacuum" or "hands-free vacuum" to identify common issues customers face with these products (like robots getting stuck or having too small dirt collection bins) and make alterations to their products to address these issues. The brand may also use this data to communicate how to best use their product—for instance, offer tips on how to make sure the robot doesn't get stuck or educate consumers about the superiority of their product (i.e., Roombas have special technology that makes them less likely to get stuck compared to competitors). Roomba may also find that people like to name their robot vacuums and

Figure 9.12 Example of a Social Media Response Plan for a Community Bank Source: https://www.figrow.com/blog/6-steps-to-creating-a-perfect-credit-union-social-media-response-plan

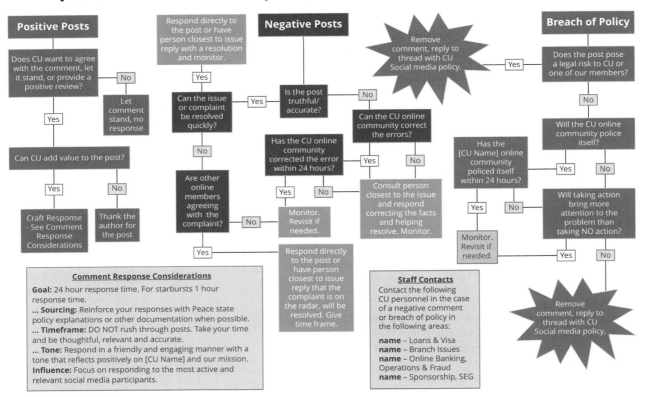

add stickers or accessories to make them look like a pet. This information can be used as a basis for advertising that can connect with consumers.

Beyond social media listening tools, businesses can also create their own communities or idea forums for research purposes. This was discussed in more detail in the "control" section of our 5Cs discussion about Lego Ideas (https://ideas.lego.com/). Another good example of this is Starbucks' My Starbucks Ideas platform. Launched in 2011, the site collected ideas concerning its menu, its experience, and community from anyone willing to share. It worked like this, customers would submit an idea and others could vote to support the idea, which allowed Starbucks to gauge interest. In its first year, it generated over 70,000 ideas directly from consumers. Although closed in 2018, the site led to hundreds of innovations. As shown in Figure 9.13, 277 ideas were launched in its initial five years alone (2008–2012), including free wifi, free birthday treats, and many new flavor ideas.

Increase Employee Productivity

Effective use of social media in the workplace is an important issue that goes beyond marketing. Social media use can turn employees into advocates. It can also provide tools to make the workplace more collaborative and efficient. Numerous software platforms support increased business productivity. Hands-down the most popular in recent years has been Slack. It describes itself as "real-time messaging, archiving, and search for modern teams."[15] It is business collaboration software but it feels like social media. By putting many activities into a single app, employees can communicate without ever leaving the app. Slack was founded in February 2014. Less than two years later it had 1.7 million users with 480,000 paid accounts.[16] By 2019 it had over 10 million active daily users[17] and was acquired by Salesforce in 2021.[18]

Figure 9.13   MyStarbucksIdea.com 5-Year Results Source: http://www.starbucksmelody.com/2017/05/31/starbucks-nixes -mystarbucksidea-community-can-still-submit-ideas/

In sum, the keys to a successful social media presence are planning, persistence, and patience. Oftentimes results on social media take time, especially if your objective is to build community. Marketers need to have a consistent and steady plan. Planning tools, such as content calendars, and social media management services such as Hootsuite may help marketers execute effective social media strategies.

Social Media Influencers

Successful Influencer Marketing

According to eMarketer, influencer marketing is becoming pervasive among brand marketers with platforms like YouTube, Instagram, Snapchat, and TikTok making it easier and more effective. A 2021 global survey of marketing agencies and brands by Statista found that 38 percent of respondents say they invested 10 to 20 percent of their marketing budget for influencer marketing with 11 percent reporting more than 40 percent of their budget being spent on influence marketing activities.[19] Statista also reports from a 2021 survey of worldwide internet users that 43 percent followed some type of social media influencer.[20] Influencers are particularly helpful in activities like content promotion, new product launches, events, and corporate communications. They are also useful in creating search visibility.[21]

To be successful at influencer marketing, it is necessary to:

- Know your audience. Each audience has its own set of influencers and it is important to identify the right one and be able to engage their services. A marketing influencer on LinkedIn will be a different person from a makeup influencer for teen-aged girls on YouTube who will be different from an influencer for young mothers on Instagram. There are numerous free tools to help marketers locate the relevant influencers including influence.co (https://influence.co/) and Intellifluence (https://intellifluence.com/).

influencer marketing
using people who are regarded as authorities in their field (or celebrities) to help distribute brand content.

- Be authentic. This aligns a bit with the point above. Picking the right influencer is integral for the brand. In addition to having the right audience, the influencer's posts should be authentic and not appear forced by the brand. Marketers need to be flexible and allow the influencer some control while ensuring the content is also true to the brand.

- Set clear goals. An influencer campaign is just that—a promotional campaign. Is the goal to create awareness for a new product, to encourage professionals to attend a conference, or one of many other possibilities? Without a goal, the campaign will not have a clear direction and it is impossible to measure its success.

- Identify success metrics. This is the subject of Chapter 5. Without defining and capturing the correct measures a marketer cannot demonstrate the success of any SMM campaign—or any digital campaign for that matter. And a marketer who cannot demonstrate success for the current campaign will have difficulty getting a budget for the next campaign.[22]

- It is also important to recognize that the Federal Trade Commission (FTC) regulates the conditions for disclosure of relationships between marketers and influencers. If marketers do not follow the specific guideline for disclosure in social media[23] they risk enforcement action, including fines.[24]

Social Media Algorithms

You have likely heard the term social media algorithm before but may have never considered how they work. Simply put, a social media algorithm is a set of mathematical rules that specify how social media content is presented to users. These algorithms dictate how both organic (owned) and paid content are ranked and placed within a user's feed. Why do these algorithms exist? They are an attempt by the platforms to keep users happy by showing them the most relevant content. In theory, if a user is consistently seeing the content they are most interested in at the top of their news feed, then they will be happy and continue to use the platform (and not move on to another one). They are controversial, however. Some users have reported content not being seen when it should be or favoring less relevant content.[25] Marketers also have expressed concern that these algorithms give their organic posts less reach and therefore push marketers to spend money on paid social media. Additionally, each social media platform has its unique algorithm, and they are always changing, so marketers constantly have to keep informed of changes across the various platforms they use. The good news is that these algorithms tend to use very similar signals and rules to sort content. As shown in Figure 9.14, there are four main ranking signals for these algorithms—the relationships between users, timeliness of posts, content type, and engagement.

From the components summarized in Figure 9.14, it's apparent that marketers can rise to the top of users' feeds by consistently posting engaging content to users. The purpose of these algorithms is to sort content according to how likely the user is to engage with it. Therefore, you are more likely to see content from users you are connected and frequently engage with.

It's not just one-on-one engagement that matters; even if a user hasn't engaged with the poster frequently, overall engagement from other similar users can signal relevance and push content to the top. This highlights the importance of following the 5Cs framework for creating engaging content.

Newer content is also favored, so it is helpful for marketers to consider their social media analytics or third-party reports that highlight when social media users are most active on the platform. This component also highlights the need for a content calendar, like the one shown in Figure 9.15, to help marketers plan a constant stream of content. In addition to self-created content calendars, social media management tools offered by companies like Hootsuite and Trello can be effective for content planning.

Figure 9.14 Social Media Algorithms Source: © Cengage

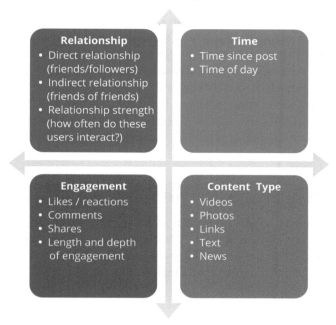

Social Media Algorithms

Relationship
- Direct relationship (friends/followers)
- Indirect relationship (friends of friends)
- Relationship strength (how often do these users interact?)

Time
- Time since post
- Time of day

Engagement
- Likes / reactions
- Comments
- Shares
- Length and depth of engagement

Content Type
- Videos
- Photos
- Links
- Text
- News

Figure 9.15 Social Media Content Calendar Source: https://offers.hubspot.com/social-media-content-calendar

						Key:
						Holiday
						Campaign
						Ebook
	[Insert Month + Year]					Webinar
						Blog Post
						SlideShare
						Product Launch
						Experiment
						Other
Sunday	Monday	Tuesday	Wednesday	Thursday	Friday	Saturday
		New Product Launching		Holiday SlideShare Holiday Blog Post		
	Holiday Campaign	Holiday Campaign	Holiday Campaign	Holiday Campaign	Holiday Campaign	
Sunday	Monday	Tuesday	Wednesday	Thursday	Friday	Saturday
		Social Media Ebook Social Media Blog Post				
	Holiday Campaign	Holiday Campaign	Holiday Campaign	Holiday Campaign	Holiday Campaign	
Sunday	Monday	Tuesday	Wednesday	Thursday	Friday	Saturday
				Holiday		
	Holiday Campaign	Holiday Campaign	Holiday Campaign	Holiday Campaign		
Sunday	Monday	Tuesday	Wednesday	Thursday	Friday	Saturday
		Facebook Experiment	Facebook Experiment	Facebook Experiment		
Sunday	Monday	Tuesday	Wednesday	Thursday	Friday	Saturday
		Social Media Webinar				

Lastly, the type of content is taken into consideration. Social media algorithms analyze the types of content that users tend to interact with more and favor this content. For instance, most algorithms tend to favor video posts over static content like text and photos. Some algorithms also consider hashtags to gauge relevancy, and they are important for discovery and when you want content to be searchable. Analyzing your own social media analytics can yield insights into the most effective content types and popular hashtags. Third-party tools, such as Ritetag (https://ritetag.com/) also offer marketers the ability to conduct hashtag research to identify new and effective hashtags for their target market. Lastly, some social media sites, including Pinterest[26] and Facebook, consider the credibility and quality of links. For instance, in 2020, Facebook began to evaluate the credibility and quality of news articles in response to backlash around its role in the spread of misinformation.[27]

Embedding SMM in the Organization

Skepticism has almost always been a key challenge for marketers who wish to make SMM an integral part of their strategy. Oftentimes top managers are not convinced of the benefits and, therefore reluctant to provide necessary budgets. While reasons vary, there appear to be two that are especially important:

1. Marketers have found it difficult to document ROI in a way that convinces management.
2. Many top managers are not frequent users of social media and doubt its value.

Demonstrating ROI for SMM campaigns takes some time and effort, but it can be done. Throughout this chapter, you have seen examples of success measures for campaigns, some even being able to link increased sales to social media efforts. There are many useful discussions of how to compute SMM ROI that are beyond the scope of this text, but the two most important issues are:

1. All SMM campaigns must have clearly defined objectives and KPIs. Most often, the KPIs will be behavioral—clicks, likes, and shares, for instance— although they can include an impact on sales.
2. Campaign results must be carefully tracked to measure the achievements for each objective.

UTM parameter:
short pieces of code added to links to help identify and track the campaign performance.

Campaign tracking can easily be done using UTM parameters. UTM parameters are pieces of code that can be added to any link, including links shared in your social media posts (or any marketing campaign). The acronym UTM stands for Urchin Tracking Module, as they were introduced by Google Analytics' predecessor Urchin and are supported by Google Analytics and other web analytics software. They are customizable and allow marketers to track clicks and traffic from a specific social media post or campaign. For example, the link below is a fictitious link for an Instagram post about Dr. Labrecque's color research.

> https://www.uri.edu/?utm_source=instagram&utm_medium=paid_social
> &utm_campaign=color_marketing_labrecque&utm_content=video_ad&utm
> _term=color_research

The UTM parameters provide the following information: the link, which included a video, was posted on a paid campaign called "Color Marketing Labrecque" targeting the term "color research." Google Analytics requires the first three UTM parameters (source, medium, and campaign), while the other two are optional. The parameters are separated by "&" symbols, and they begin after the "?". The table below, adapted from Hootsuite, gives examples of the five parameters.[28]

Campaign source		
This indicates the social network, search engine, newsletter name, or other specific source driving the traffic.		
Examples:	**UTM code:**	**Sample code:**
Facebook, Twitter, blog, newsletter, etc.	utm_source	utm_source=facebook
Campaign medium		
This tracks the type of channel driving the traffic: organic social, paid social, email, and so on.		
Examples:	**UTM code:**	**Sample code:**
cpc, organic_social	utm_medium	utm_medium=paid_social
Campaign name		
Give each campaign a name so you can keep track of your efforts. This could be the product name, a contest name, a code to identify a specific sale or promotion, an influencer ID, or a tagline.		
Examples:	**UTM code:**	**Sample code:**
summer_sale, free_trial	utm_campaign	utm_campaign=summer_sale
Campaign term		
Use this UTM tag to track paid keywords or key phrases.		
Examples:	**UTM code:**	**Sample code:**
newyork_cupcakes, vegan_cookies, valentines_gifts	utm_term	utm_term
Campaign content		
This parameter allows you to track different ads within a campaign.		
Examples:	**UTM code:**	**Sample code:**
video_ad, text_ad, blue_banner, green_banner	utm_content	utm_content=video_ad

Source: https://blog.hootsuite.com/how-to-use-utm-parameters/

Building a Successful Social Media Team

One of the requirements for a high level of SMM effectiveness is a strong social media team. Most businesses of any size that are serious about social media will find it necessary to have a social media team whether it is solely focused on social media or whether it shares other marketing responsibilities. Finding the right people and organizing them for effectiveness is therefore of paramount importance.

There are several roles that must be filled in a social media team. They include the following:

- Social media manager
- Content creators, including SEO and platform optimization specialists
- Community management

- Campaign management and promotion. Campaign promotion often includes paid promotions as well as PR and perhaps events
- Analytics and strategy. This may include not only analysts but people who are familiar with testing a variety of campaign elements as discussed in Chapter 5.

This suggests that teams will have a number of members who must work well and creatively together so choosing the right people, not just the right skills, is important.[29]

One example of an effective social media team is JetBlue. It is a standout in social media customer service. Head of the Social Media and Customer-Commitment team Laurie Meacham says, "JetBlue's social media goal is for a truly organic experience—people talking to people." To make that happen JetBlue team members are trained to be their own authentic selves, being willing to engage with customers and doing so in the language of the customers. They are building a network of customer relationships that is a strong foundation for the good and the bad of everyday air travel.[30]

Despite all the success stories in this chapter, it is difficult for SMM to gain traction in a firm without the support of top management, particularly the CEO. It is even better if the CEO provides leadership in the field of social media.

Bringing Top Management into the Social Business Fold

A study by BrandFog uncovered key benefits of top management involvement in social media. They are as follows:

1. Social media involvement makes better leaders. They create transparency for the brand and build connections with customers, employees, and other stakeholders.
2. Their engagement in social media builds brand trust. It helps build brand awareness and trust in the brand by communicating its mission, values, and purpose.
3. Social media is modern PR for top managers. Social media engagement helps establish them as industry leaders who have credibility with the public and the media. It may help prevent reputational crises, and if an event does occur, it provides a trusted channel for communicating to transmit facts and preserve brand reputation.[31]

There is a widespread belief that pressure will continue to grow for top managers to have a constructive social media presence. How can you lead if you do not understand important aspects of your business?

All in all, the concept of the social business—whose employees are engaged from top to bottom levels, who build strong customer relationships through communication, and who have a trusted public presence—is a vision that will propel much corporate and personal transformation in the years to come.

Summary

Well-informed marketers—large and small, B2C and B2B—are finding success in the social media space. In order to thrive, going forward, most businesses will have to incorporate elements of SMM into their marketing communications mix. If customers are in social space—and they are as the statistics in this chapter show—marketers must be there also. Marketers find that good SMM engages visitors and encourages them to participate in campaigns and co-create content by understanding their motivations (as discussed with the 5Cs). Influencers can be a powerful force in well-designed campaigns that can bring social media success.

Marketers are using social media to reach many different objectives, including awareness, strengthening relationships & building community, SEO, customer support & reputation management, research, and increasing employee productivity.

No matter the objective, marketers must identify KPIs to measure success. To optimize reach and engagement, marketers must also understand social media algorithms and keep up-to-date with changes.

Businesses of all kinds are using social media in the workplace. In some firms, CEOs and other top executives are part of the social media activity. They find ways to engage and motivate employees and customers and identify tools that increase productivity.

There are also important metrics that are used to evaluate the effectiveness of social media. It is important to link social media campaigns to actual sales results and ROI whenever possible, but that is often difficult. UTM parameters can help achieve this. It is essential for all SMM campaigns to have clearly defined objectives and to track and analyze the campaign results. This will produce valuable insights for future campaigns.

Businesses need a solid social media team with an explicit, if not a total, focus on social media. The team must have the necessary skills to carry out the social media strategy and work well together in an environment that often requires real-time responses. It is helpful if top managers are part of this activity. Top management involvement enhances the brand and engages employees.

Discussion Questions

1. Why do you think social media platforms have grown so quickly in countries all over the world?

2. What are the benefits of using SMM for brands and businesses?

3. What is the P.O.S.T methodology?

4. What are some consumer motivations for using social media?

5. How are businesses using social media?

6. Define own, earned, and paid media. Which do you think is the most effective and why?

7. How can brands benefit from a brand community?

8. What is influencer marketing?

9. What are social media algorithms?

10. Discuss the different signals that algorithms use to rank social media post relevancy.

11. What are some examples of social media engagement beyond the ones discussed in the chapter?

12. What is necessary to build a good social media team?

13. Why do you think some managers are resistant to the idea of engaging in SMM? What could you do or say to convince your reluctant boss that SMM could be a good idea in a specific business setting?

Endnotes

1. S. Dixon, "Biggest Social Media Platforms 2023," *Statista*, February 14, 2023, https://www.statista.com/statistics/272014/global-social-networks-ranked-by-number-of-users/.

2. Alexander Kunst, "Social Media Brand Awareness KPI Ranking U.S. 2022," *Statista*, January 2, 2023, https://www.statista.com/statistics/1307244/most-well-known-social-networks-in-the-united-states/.

3. Charlene Li and Josh Bernoff. *Groundswell: Winning in a World Transformed by Social Technologies.* Harvard Business Press, 2011.

4. Jim Tobin, "No Longer Young and Sexy, Post Methodology Just Works," Ignite Social Media, April 14, 2016, https://www.ignitesocialmedia.com/social-media-strategy/no-longer-young-and-sexy-post-methodology-just-works/.

5. "Will It Blend? – iPhone," July 10, 2007, https://www.youtube.com/watch?v=qg1ckCkm8YI.

6. Lauren I. Labrecque, Jonas Vor Dem Esche, Charla Mathwick, Thomas P. Novak, and Charles F. Hofacker. "Consumer Power: Evolution in the Digital Age." *Journal of Interactive Marketing* 27, no. 4 (2013): 257–269.

7. Deborah Sweeney, "How Has Facebook Changed for Business through the Years and What Have We Learned?," *Social Media Today*, May 4, 2015, https://www.socialmediatoday.com/marketing/2015-05-04/how-has-facebook-changed-business-through-years-and-what-have-we-learned.

8. "Dewmocracy," Mountain Dew Wiki, accessed March 9, 2023, https://mountaindew.fandom.com/wiki/DEWmocracy.

9. Kat Franklin, "Lay's Increases Sales by Asking Customers to 'Do Us a Flavor,'" Digital Innovation and Transformation, accessed March 9, 2023, https://digital.hbs.edu/platform-digit/submission/lays-increases-sales-by-asking-customers-to-do-us-a-flavor/.

10. "Doritos Crash The Superbowl Case Study," Doritos Crash the SuperBowl Case Study, accessed March 9, 2023, https://paperzz.com/doc/7621781/doritos-crash-the-superbowl-case-study.

11. "#Distancedance," TikTok, accessed March 9, 2023, https://www.tiktok.com/tag/distancedance.

12. "How Many People Use Instagram Shopping in 2023?," EarthWeb, October 19, 2022, https://earthweb.com/how-many-people-use-instagram-shopping/.

13. Albert M. Muniz, Jr. and Thomas C. O'Guinn, (2001). "Brand Community." *Journal of Consumer Research* 27, no. 4 (2001): 412–432.

14. Thomas C. O'Guinn and Albert Muniz, Jr., "Collective Brand Relationships," in *Handbook of Brand Relations*, eds. Joseph Priester, Deborah MacInnis, and C. W. Park (N.Y. Society for Consumer Psychology and M.E. Sharp), p. 19.

15. "Slack Is Your Digital HQ," Slack, accessed March 9, 2023, https://slack.com/.

16. Jeff Bercovici, "Slack is Out Company of the Year. Here's Why Everybody's Talking About It," accessed March 9, 2023, http://www.inc.com/magazine/201512/jeff-bercovici/slack-company-of-the-year-2015.html

17. "With 10+ Million Daily Active Users, Slack Is Where More Work Happens Every Day, All over the World," Slack, accessed March 9, 2023, https://slack.com/blog/news/slack-has-10-million-daily-active-users#.

18. "Salesforce Completes Acquisition of Slack," Slack, accessed March 9, 2023, https://slack.com/blog/news/salesforce-completes-acquisition-of-slack.

19. Valentina Dencheva, "Influencer Share of Marketing Budgets 2022," *Statista*, January 6, 2023, https://www.statista.com/statistics/268641/share-of-marketing-budgets-spent-on-digital-worldwide/.

20. Valentina Dencheva, "Effectiveness of Influencers Worldwide 2021," *Statista*, January 6, 2023, https://www.statista.com/statistics/1275239/effectiveness-influencers-worldwide/.

21. "Influencer Marketing 2022: Industry Stats; Market Research," *Insider Intelligence*, March 15, 2022, http://www.emarketer.com/Article/Influencer-Marketing-Rapidly-Gaining-Popularity-Among-Brand-Marketers/1013563.

22. "Izea - We Are Influencer Marketing," IZEA - We Are Influencer Marketing, accessed March 9, 2023, https://www.tapinfluence.com/the-ultimate-influencer-marketing-guide/.

23. Stephanie T. Nguyen, "The FTC's Endorsement Guides: What People Are Asking," Federal Trade Commission, August 27, 2020, https://www.ftc.gov/tips-advice/business-center/guidance/ftcs-endorsement-guides-what-people-are-asking.

24. Martin Beck, "FTC Puts Social Media Marketers on Notice with Updated Disclosure Guidelines," MarTech, May 4, 2022, http://marketingland.com/ftc-puts-social-media-marketers-on-notice-with-updated-disclosure-guidelines-132017.

25. Alexis C. Madrigal, "How YouTube's Algorithm Really Works," *The Atlantic* (Atlantic Media Company, November 8, 2018), https://www.theatlantic.com/technology/archive/2018/11/how-youtubes-algorithm-really-works/575212/.

26. Clodagh O'Brien, "How Do Social Media Algorithms Work?," Digital Marketing Institute (Digital Marketing Institute, January 18, 2023), https://digitalmarketinginstitute.com/blog/how-do-social-media-algorithms-work.

27. Christina Newberry, "2023 Facebook Algorithm: How to Get Your Content Seen," Social Media Marketing & Management Dashboard, February 22, 2023, https://blog.hootsuite.com/facebook-algorithm/.

28. Christina Newberry, "How to Use UTM Parameters to Track Social Media Success," Social Media Marketing & Management Dashboard, May 3, 2021, https://blog.hootsuite.com/how-to-use-utm-parameters/.

29. Lauren Cover, "Bring It in: How to Build an All-Star Social Media Team," Sprout Social, April 19, 2022, https://sproutsocial.com/insights/social-media-team/.

30. Jason Keath, "The Secret to Jetblue's Awesome Social Engagement," Social Fresh, accessed March 9, 2023, https://www.socialfresh.com/the-secret-to-jetblues-awesome-social-engagement/.

31. "1. Social CEOS Make Better Leaders 2. Social CEO Engagement ... Brandfog," accessed March 9, 2023, https://www.brandfog.com/CEOSocialMediaSurvey/BRANDfog_2014_CEO_Survey.pdf.

Chapter 10

Display and Mobile Advertising for Customer Acquisition

Learning Objectives

By the time you complete this chapter, you will be able to:

1 List the major customer acquisition techniques, including online and offline.

2 Discuss the different ad formats and payment models used in digital display advertising.

3 Explain how ad serving is used for digital advertising.

4 Discuss different types of targeting techniques used for digital advertising.

5 Explain the privacy concerns and regulations affecting digital advertising.

6 Summarize the reasons for the growing importance of mobile advertising.

7 Explain how publicity and affiliate marketing can be used as acquisition tools.

8 Discuss the importance of Integrated Marketing Communications (IMC).

In Chapter 1, we defined the four basic marketing strategy objectives: customer acquisition, conversion, retention, and value growth. The concept of customer lifetime value (CLV), by which the marketer measures customer value, is discussed in Chapter 4. Conversion to a loyal customer and customer retention are very important marketing objectives discussed in Chapters 13 and 14. Still, while trite, it is also true that the marketer must acquire a customer before creating loyalty and retention. It is also important to note that a steady stream of new customers is necessary to fuel growth in most organizations.

This chapter focuses on specific digital marketing tools that are most often used in customer acquisition strategy. There are other acquisition tools, most importantly search engine and social media marketing, which are discussed in previous Chapters (7, 8, and 9). Throughout these chapters, it is important to realize that virtually any of the digital marketing tools can be used in an acquisition program, but some of them are especially well suited to acquisition efforts.

Examples also imply that there is more than one definition of *customer acquisition*. Simply put, *acquisition* can be defined as "making the first purchase." However, it can also be defined as getting the customer to engage in a behavior that permits further contact—signing up for a newsletter, for example. For the social media marketer, *acquisition* may be defined as getting additional fans or followers on a social media profile page.

Digital Customer Acquisition Techniques

While there are numerous ways to acquire new customers in B2C and B2B markets, they can best be described by the channels shown in Figure 10.1. The figure shows the channels as digital, offline, or programs that could take place online or offline. The channels and the tools available through each are better used in combination with one another, as discussed throughout this text. There is no one "best channel" to be used independently of all others.

To better understand the complex issues of developing an effective media mix for acquisition, it is necessary to understand the strengths and weaknesses of each channel. In this chapter, we focus our discussion on display advertising. In other chapters, we discuss email promotions, search engine marketing (SEM), and social media marketing (SMM). In so doing, we will keep in mind that any of these techniques can and should be used in concert with traditional offline advertising and promotion channels. Examples will illustrate media mixes, including various digital and offline channels and tools.

Figure 10.1 Channels for Acquisition of New Customers Source: © 2018 Cengage Learning

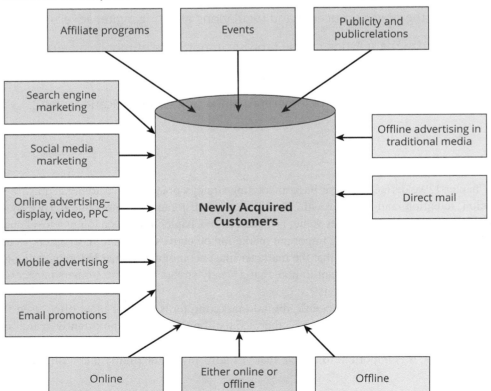

Digital Display Advertising

Display Advertising

Display ads, also referred to as *banner ads*, are a type of digital advertising that are primarily visual and include a URL that links to a website where a customer can learn more about a product or service, or make a purchase. In addition to visual content, such as images and video, it may include text, sound, and motion. Most display ads are formatted to contain a headline and body text, with visuals being the focus. Brand names and logos should be prominently displayed for the ad to link the message with the brand. These statements are true whether the display ad is offline, in a print magazine, for example, or online, displayed on a website or a mobile site.

Digital advertising has proven cost-effective and continues to be a top acquisition channel for marketers. It is expected to remain the bulk of marketing spend throughout 2026, as shown in Figure 10.2. Display ads are typically rectangular or square but can take on various formats, which we will discuss next.

display ads
a type of digital advertisement that combines text and visuals (images and video) with a URL that links to a website where a customer can learn more about or buy products and services. Also referred to as banner ads.

Figure 10.2 **Digital Advertising Spend Worldwide 2021–2026** Source: Based on eMarketer, March 2022.

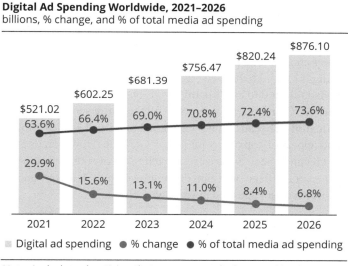

Digital Ad Spending Worldwide, 2021–2026
billions, % change, and % of total media ad spending

Year	Digital ad spending	% of total media ad spending	% change
2021	$521.02	63.6%	29.9%
2022	$602.25	66.4%	15.6%
2023	$681.39	69.0%	13.1%
2024	$756.47	70.8%	11.0%
2025	$820.24	72.4%	8.4%
2026	$876.10	73.6%	6.8%

■ Digital ad spending ● % change ● % of total media ad spending

Note: includes advertising that appears on desktop and laptop computers as well as mobile phones, tablets, and other internet-connected devices, and includes all the various formats of advertising on those platforms

Digital Display Advertising Formats

The number of digital display formats is limited only by the imagination of web designers and marketers and perhaps by the size of screens. This would lead to chaos even if digital advertising space was purchased manually for each ad, but it becomes impossible when most ad placement is done with technology (that will be discussed later in this chapter). We will discuss three broad aspects:

- Static display ads (banner ads)
- Rich media ads
- Video ads

The Internet Advertising Bureau (IAB), which comprises over 700 media and technology companies responsible for the majority of online advertising,[1] is the custodian of industry standards for digital formats. Because the number of possible display formats is so large, they have developed a set of standards that member companies have agreed to support.[2] Fixed-size display formats included in the Ad Unit Portfolio are illustrated in Figure 10.3. Some have names that describe their shape and positioning, such as *leaderboard* (a horizontal ad at the top of the page), *skyscraper* (a vertical ad that usually shows up in a sidebar or menu), and *square*.[3]

The IAB guide also contains standards for other types of ads (non-fixed size), including mobile ads. It specifies other agreed-upon criteria such as maximum size, load time, and sound requirements.

The most recent IAB ad formats have been revised for HTML5 standards (the most recent HTML version) to allow for greater interactivity. Rich media enables many kinds of technology and interaction in display ads. Google's Display Network unit is one of the largest ad servers (to be discussed later in the chapter). According to Google, rich media is an ad with advanced features like video, audio, or other elements that encourage viewers to interact and engage with the content. While text ads sell with words, and display ads sell with pictures, rich media ads offer more ways to involve an audience with an ad by expanding, floating, or having some other motion.[4] Google specifically focuses on two major types of rich media formats—expanding and interstitial—but also discusses many possibilities to add interactivity through dynamic creatives.[5]

An expanding ad starts as a standard banner ad size in a slot they've been served in. However, when a user interacts with the ad in some way (such as hovering over the ad or clicking the ad), the ad grows larger and expands out of the ad slot. A push-down ad is a type of expanding creative that pushes down the content of a webpage when the creative expands—making it look like the web page is pushed out of the way for the ad to fit. An interstitial ad, also referred to as a floating ad, is an ad that appears to float on top of the content on a desktop. On mobile, it appears to fill the entire screen. This type of ad format allows a lot of flexibility because it isn't assigned to a fixed ad slot allowing it to be any shape or size and appear on top of any publisher's content. However, one drawback of this type of ad is that it can be seen as invasive since it takes over the entire screen. Expanding creatives expand over the page or in-app content by default, but you can also enable them to push content down on a page (see push-down below).

rich media
combination of text, images, video, and other interactive elements in a digital ad.

expanding ad
an ad that first appears as a standard banner ad that grows larger and extends out of the ad slot when a user interacts with the ad in some way (such as hovering over the ad or clicking the ad).

push-down ad
a type of expanding ad that appears to push down the content of a webpage when the ad expands.

interstitial
an ad that appears to float on top of the content on a desktop. On a mobile, it appears to fill the entire screen. Also referred to as a floating ad.

Figure 10.3   **IAB New Standard Ad Unit Portfolio for Fixed Display Ads** Source: https://www.iab.com/wp-content/uploads/2019/04/IABNewAdPortfolio_LW_FixedSizeSpec.pdf

Fixed Size Ad Specifications			

The following fixed size ad units are recommended as part of the new ad portfolio. These have been recommended based on Attitudes and Usage Study to determine which of the ad units, contribute to the majority of revenue and are sufficient to advertise across multiple screen sizes.

Ad unit Name	Fixed Size (px)*	Max. K-Weight (kB)	
		Initial Load	Subload
Billboard	970 x 250	250	500
Smartphone Banner	300 x 50 or 320 x 50	50	100
Leaderboard	728 x 90	150	300
Super Leaderboard/ Pushdown	970 x 90	200	400
Portrait	300 x 1050	250	500
Skyscraper	160 x 600	150	300
Medium Rectangle	300 x 250	150	300
20 x 60	120 x 60	50	100
Mobile Phone Interstitial	640 x 1136 or 750 x 1334 or 1080 x 1920	300	600
Feature Phone Small Banner	120 x 20	5	N/A
Feature Phone Medium Banner	168 x 28	5	N/A
Feature Phone Large Banner	216 x 36	5	N/A

Consider the number of viewer actions that are possible in the rich media ad shown in Figures 10.4a and b. The square banner ad shows no obvious interactivity, not even a call-to-action, but when the viewer clicks on the square, they are sent to the leaderboard where the game is accessed. To play, viewers click on the "Expand" button and are taken to another version of the leaderboard, which has a QR code. When a QR code reader is aimed at the ad, the game shows on the screen. To play it, viewers must verify that they are over 21 years of age and install it on their phones. This ad and game are part of the Heineken Legends campaign, which primarily aims to show on TV and YouTube. The campaign has won both praise for its creativity and criticism for its "legends" being paid actors.

Display ads appear on social platforms like Facebook, Instagram, and LinkedIn. Each platform has its own standards for display advertising, but the process of creating a good ad does not differ—it simply requires creativity. Creativity has always been a keystone of good advertising. In comparison to traditional offline advertising, digital has allowed more ways to execute your creative idea. There are tools to help, such as tools to assist in the designing or optimization of your ad for specific channels or platforms. But creativity is still important, as all these ads show, especially perhaps, the interactive ones. Creativity is still the product of human minds, not technology, and we can

Figure 10.4a   A Simple Square Banner with Rich Media Promoting a Game
Source: Google LLC

(a)

Figure 10.4b   A Leaderboard Ad that Can be Expanded to Install and Play the **Game** Source: Google LLC

(b)

expect it to remain just that. Constant Contact offers some tips on designing effective display ads, including:

- Use eye-catching images to break through the clutter
- Use animation to overcome banner-blindness
- Offer a discount, free download, or free trial
- Spotlight your product (let a strong product speak for itself- keep both the visual and the call-to-action clean and clear)
- Inspire urgency by highlighting a limited-time promotion or product availability
- Offer a statistic. Instead of simply claiming to be "the best" or "better," justify it with hard numbers, choosing to focus on a common user concern. For example, "we're 22 times faster than the leading competitor" or "2-second average download speed"
- Offer a solution to a customer's want or need[6]

This section on display advertising just skims the surface of the number of online advertising formats available. There are many other specific formats in the categories we have discussed, and more are being developed almost daily. It is matched in the number of available options only by the number of target market segments that can be reached in the digital environment. Now we briefly discuss ad payment models.

Payment Models

Cost per Action (CPA)
an advertising payment model where advertisers are charged for actions other than clicks, such as moving a cursor over an ad, filling out a form, liking a social media post, etc.

CPM and CPC are the most common payment methods for digital ads. In CPM (cost per thousand), an advertiser is charged a rate for every 1,000 views (the M stands for Mille, which is the Latin word for 1,000). In CPC (Cost per Click) an advertiser is only charged when a user clicks on an ad. Other user actions, like moving a cursor over an ad, filling out a form, or liking a social media post, are also ways to set up an ad payment model. These are generally referred to as Cost per Action (CPA) or CPE (Cost per Engagement). Lastly, some may also charge a flat fee for placement, which is common when doing a roadblock campaign where one marketer takes over the entire page or on smaller, niche sites.

Now that we have a better understanding of the types of ad options and payment models available to marketers, we next need to understand how these ads get delivered (or placed) on website content.

Digital Ad Serving

You saw the first-ever display ad during our discussion of business models in Chapter 3 (refer to Figure 3.7). This small banner ad with the words "Have you ever clicked your mouse right here? You will," sponsored by AT&T, was the first documented digital ad. In the early days of the commercial internet, ads were placed directly in slots on websites, and each viewer who came to the site would see the same ad. The million-dollar homepage, shown in Figure 10.5, is an artifact of the days of this type of ad buying. Created in 2005 by Alex Tew, a British student, the site (www.MillionDollarHomepage.com) was nothing more than a 1000 × 1000 canvas of blank pixels where advertisers could pay for a slot at the cost of $1 per pixel. The webpage garnered $1,037,100 (the last 1,000 pixels were auctioned off for $38,100) and still exists today, although many links are no longer working.[7]

Thankfully, digital advertising has come a long way since the million-dollar homepage. Ads today are not added by hand to a website (i.e., hard coded into the site). Instead,

Figure 10.5   **The Million-Dollar Homepage** Source: http://www.milliondollarhomepage.com/

they are dynamically served onto web pages using ad servers. Simply put, ad servers function to store ad content and serve them on websites. Ad serving is an important activity of third-party marketing firms that match an advertiser's need for targeted ad placement with a publisher's need for revenue-generating ads on its site. An ad server can be defined as "the ad technology that enables the management, serving, and tracking of an ad or internal promotion on one's digital properties."[8] Ad servers can be local (e.g., run by a content publisher to serve ads to their websites) or run by a third party. Ad servers decide, often in real-time, the best ad to serve based on relevance, targeting, budgets, and revenue goals.

ad serving
technology that places and tracks ads on digital properties (websites, mobile apps, etc.).

Ad servers have many benefits. Instead of an advertiser having to send ad content to different publishers, ad servers offer a centralized way to store and send it. Ad servers also offer different techniques for optimal serving (placement). These techniques include *roadblocks* where one advertiser takes over all or the majority of the ad space on a publisher's page. Other serving options may include the ability for *exclusivity,* where an ad server ensures that no direct competitors' ads are seen alongside a specific advertiser.

Ad servers can track users across websites using cookies or IP addresses, which can offer advertisers benefits in terms of targeting and optimization. For instance, advertisers can limit the number of times a person sees a specific ad, which is called "*frequency capping*" or "*impression capping.*" Here an advertiser may not want to overload a user with an ad, so by setting a cap, the ad server will not show the ad again to the same user once the cap has been met. Other server settings include *sequencing*, which involves showing ads in a particular order to a user. This is especially important when a story is told through a series of ads in a campaign and therefore ads are designed to be seen in a specific order. While all these benefits sound great, marketers need to be aware of new regulations, such as those in the *General Data Protection Regulations* (discussed later in this chapter), that prohibit technology that uses PII (Personally Identifying Information) to identify users—including the use of IP addresses and cookies. We'll talk more about how ad servers can target users later.

An ad server can be thought of as the technology that runs the digital advertising ecosystem. It stores, manages, and places advertisements on the publisher's website. But how do ads get placed across different websites? There are a few options, including working directly with the publisher. Booking ad space directly with a publisher works very much the same as in traditional advertising. A marketer may know a specific site that they want their ads to appear on, and some sites offer the ability to set up advertising directly. Although many marketers opt to use ad networks and ad exchanges to facilitate the buying and placement of ads across multiple sites. An ad network is a company that brings together advertisers and publishers. Simply put, an ad network is an online platform that acts as an intermediary between advertisers and publishers. They sell the online space to advertisers and then deliver the ads to the sites that display them. While offering a similar function, an ad exchange differs mainly in that it is not an intermediary. That is, it allows advertisers and publishers to sell and place ad inventory directly. A more detailed comparison of ad networks and ad exchanges is outlined in Table 10.1.

ad network
a platform that collects ad inventory from publishers and sells it to advertisers. It acts as an intermediary between advertisers and publishers.

ad exchange
a digital marketplace where advertisers and publishers purchase and sell ad inventory directly in an auction setting.

Table 10.1   A Comparison of Ad Networks vs Ad Exchanges Source: adapted from https://smartyads.com/blog/ad-network -vs-ad-exchange-not-the-same-thing/ and https://www.spiceworks.com/marketing/programmatic-advertising/articles/ad-network-vs-ad-exchange -key-differences-and-similarities/

	Ad Network	Ad Exchange
How it Works	Acts as an **intermediary** between publishers and advertisers.	Acts as an **open ad marketplace** offering direct access for both publishers and advertisers.
Essence	A company.	Technological platform for media buying.
Key Characteristic	The platform offers specific categories of ads pre-segmented for serving to particular audiences.	The marketplace offers an open pool of various inventory.
Transparency	Advertisers don't know which websites serve their ads. Publishers don't know what companies buy their inventory.	Advertisers know what publishers they buy inventory from and vice versa. Pages on which ads are served sometimes can be tracked too. Some ad exchanges allow advertisers to see competitors' bids.
Quality of Inventory	Offers mostly first-tier inventory, often sold for the first time.	Offers all available inventory, including remnants (good quality inventory is oftentimes already purchased by ad networks for reselling).
Campaign Optimization	Takes time to implement.	Can be conducted on-the-go. Changes reflect in real-time.
Pricing	The inventory cost remains stable, as it's determined by an ad network.	The inventory cost fluctuates, as it's based on the bids coming from advertisers during a real-time bidding auction.
Pros for Advertiser	Prices are higher because they're determined individually, so advertisers often overpay.	Advertisers define the price by themselves.
Pros for Publisher	Publishers have less control over inventory optimization and pricing.	More control over the value of each impression.
Examples	Google's AdSense, Yahoo Publisher Network, Bing Ads.	SmartyAds, Yahoo Right Media, AppNexus.

Advertising networks emerged as a result of the explosion of the digital advertising industry in the late 1990s and early 2000s by offering a solution to aggregate the ad space supply (publishers) and match it with ad demand (advertisers), simplifying the ad buying process. However, this solution wasn't perfect, as publishers were often left with unsold inventory (space) that they had to sell at lower prices. Advertisers also found ineffectiveness because many had to use multiple ad networks to reach all their desired audiences. This added some complexities and inefficiencies that led to reduced control over the campaign—such as ads reaching the same audience more than once because they were served on multiple networks.[9] This fostered the development of new technologies leading to the development of programmatic advertising on ad exchanges. According to IBM,

> "Programmatic advertising is the automated bidding and placement of ads on a given platform. Traditional ad placement involves a long, tedious process of negotiations, bidding, contracts, and requests for proposals. Programmatic, on the other hand, streamlines the process into mere seconds. How? Through the use of machine learning and AI to handle the sale and placement of digital ads.
>
> More specifically, programmatic advertising uses historical traffic data and online targeting methods to put these ads in front of people who are the most likely to want to see them, which helps to improve conversions and ROI for your business."[10]

When you stop to think about the fact that it is important to serve the best ad from *both* the website's and the advertiser's point of view, the complexity begins to become obvious. When you consider that the entire process (the decision of which ad to display, the retrieval of the ad from inventory, and sending the ad to the appropriate site) is done all while the site content is loading (often in a matter of milliseconds) another layer is added to the complexity. Even though complex, this example represents the basic situation. If the advertiser wishes to use more complex targeting techniques, the question of which ad to serve to which viewer on which site becomes even more daunting, explaining why most sites of any size use ad-serving technology of some kind.

Programmatic advertising uses real-time bidding on ad exchanges to optimize the buying and selling process. Real-time bidding means that ads are bought and sold by a nearly instantaneous auction, much like stocks on a stock exchange. Ad exchanges are the online marketplaces in which these exchanges take place, offering all types of advertising, including display (banner), native, video, mobile, and in-app advertising options. Programmatic advertising relies on demand-side platforms (DSPs), supply-side platforms (SSPs), Ad Exchanges, and data management platforms (DMPs) to function. Simply put, publishers use SSPs to sell their ad spaces, while advertisers use DSPs to bid for the ad space. The ad exchange brings the two sides together. DMPs store and analyze user data to get a better understanding of website visitors for publishers and ensure that the purchased ads are aimed at the right demographic for advertisers. This system is illustrated in Figure 10.6.

programmatic advertising
automating the advertising buying process through machine learning and AI.

real-time bidding
ads are bought and sold instantaneously through electronic exchanges.

demand-side platform (DSPs)
software that connects advertisers to multiple ad exchanges to buy or bid for the inventory provided by the publishers through programmatic advertising.

supply-side platform (SSPs)
software used to sell a publisher's ad inventory through programmatic advertising.

data management platform (DMPs)
platforms that collect data and integrate with DSP so that the advertisers can target the appropriate audience and improve the efficiency of their ad campaigns.

Figure 10.6   **How Programmatic Advertising Works** Source: https://www.technolush.com/blog/how-does-programmatic
-advertising-works

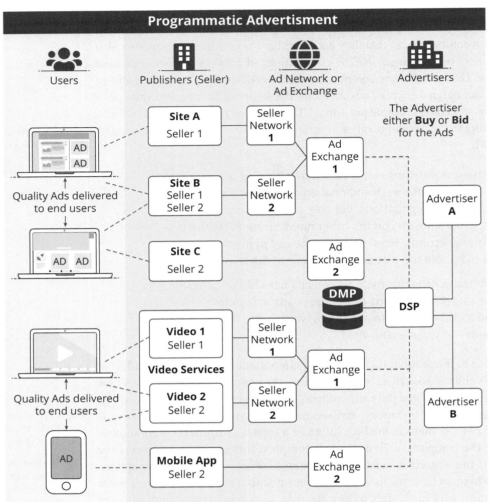

Audience Targeting

Now that we have a better idea about how ad-serving technology works, we now discuss
the ways in which advertisers can target who sees their ads.

Contextual Targeting

Contextual targeting matches ads based on the context of the website content. The matching
is done by considering the content of the site by analyzing the site's content and audience,
which can be done by analyzing keywords and identifying topics. Other variables, like
language and location, can also be considered. For example, an ad for diapers might be
placed on a parenting website, or an ad for baking sheets may be placed on a recipe site (or
a specific page with a cookie recipe). Contextual advertising was popular in the early days
of the internet but grew less so as advertisers began to use cookies for behavioral targeting.
However, contextual advertising is increasing in popularity as new regulations are limiting
the use of third-party cookies (which we will discuss more in detail later).[11]

behavioral targeting
presenting relevant content, such
as ads, based on users' previous
activities.

Behavioral Targeting

In the offline world, marketers have to ask customers to self-report what they do, which
can have elements of unreliability. In the online world, marketers and third-party data

collection services can collect data about what people do—what sites they visit, what pages on the site they visited, how long they spend on sites and pages, purchases, and much more. There are variations in the ways advertising networks carry out the process, but the three basic types of behavioral targeting are:

1. Targeting identified users (people who have registered on a website, for example)
2. Targeting unidentified users by using cookies
3. Targeting with predictive models

Targeting Identified Users

Targeting identified users is straightforward for the marketer and observable to the customer. When customers visit Amazon, for example, they are encouraged to log in to the site. When they do, several Amazon services become available—the wish list, 1-Click ordering, and recommendations among them. The wish list and 1-Click ordering are set up by the customers. It is obvious to even the casual observer that the recommendations are based on previous purchases. Amazon encourages customers to provide additional data to improve the recommendations. Amazon is more open about what it does and how it does it than many sites,[12] but this type of targeting on the site is visible and does not arouse a lot of concern among most users.

Targeting Unidentified Users

Targeting anonymous users is an issue that does raise privacy concerns and we discuss this later in this section. In this section, we discuss how it works. Figure 10.7 presents an understandable view.

cookies
a few lines of code that a website or advertising network places on a user's computer to store data about the user's activities on the site. Cookies can be classified as either first-party or third-party depending on how they are used.

Figure 10.7 **How Behavioral Targeting of Anonymous Users Works** Source: © Cengage Learning 2013

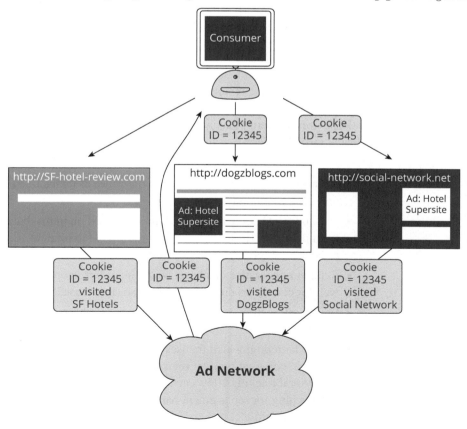

This type of targeting is done by advertising networks and is made available to advertisers who use the network. The hypothetical situation set up in Figure 10.7 shows an unidentified (not signed in) user visiting a website that has information about hotels in San Francisco. The user's activity suggests intended behavior, and a cookie is set on the visitor's browser. A cookie is a piece of code that can track visitor activity that can last for a single web session or longer. In Figure 10.7, the cookie is simply used to track the visitor on other websites and to display an ad for a hotel supersite (a client of the advertising network) on both a site about dogs and on a social media site.

Cookies have been around since the dawn of the internet. Recently a new type of user tracking has come into vogue—the hashed email. While cookies only work on the web, a hashed email can work on any channel. For instance, it can track a user via the app on their mobile device, making it a very useful adjunct to the standard cookie. Hashed emails have benefits over cookies, including that they can allow tracking across multiple devices, can be used in mobile apps, and allow for multi-browser tracking.

Hashing an email address is a simple process. An email address is run through a hash algorithm (a cryptographic tool) to produce a 32, 40, or 64-character unique identifier that cannot be reversed. This becomes a data point in the person's record in a marketing database. It allows the marketer to track the user on any device or platform where they are signed in with their email address.[13] Hashed emails are one option that marketers are considering when in response to the waning support of the use of third-party cookies, which is discussed later in this chapter.

The ad networks collect huge amounts of behavioral data and mine the data to find patterns of behavior that constitute market segments. The hypothetical user in Figure 10.7 could be a "frequent traveler" or perhaps an "adventure traveler," which are fairly generic segments, although the targeting they represent is still valuable to the marketer. The network can drill down into the data to find microsegments, "architectural history traveler" or "garden traveler," for example. The ad networks configure the segment to be targeted for each individual advertiser, so you do not find much detail on their sites about the segments they offer. Collecting and using data like this also implies placing cookies that persist over a period of time, not cookies that are set for a single user session. Tracking a user over time also allows retargeting of a visitor who has left a site (one that sells shoes, for example) without making a purchase. All the shoe sites would like to reach that person. You see the results of retargeting on other sites you visit virtually every time you search for a product or service online.

Behavioral targeting has gone far beyond simple visitor behavior—data points like websites visited, types of products examined, coupons downloaded, and so forth. Many third-party databases vastly expand behavioral targeting options.[14] They include:

- Values targeting, which the agency describes as being able to reach people based on enduring human values.
- Cut-and-paste content sharing, which is based on items that readers cut and paste from publisher sites. This content produces search keyword suggestions, as well as behavioral profile data.
- Retailer cooperative database, which identifies people who are shopping on the web for certain products. This database can be used for retargeting.
- Search retargeting, which is the ability to purchase display advertising based on search activity.
- Owner targeting, which focuses advertising based on ownership. Direct marketers have long used product registrations, for example, to confirm ownership. Behavioral tracking allows activities such as looking at online owner's manuals or searching for replacement parts for a product to be included in the database as evidence of product ownership.

hashed email
a compliment and alternative to third-party cookies that applies a hash algorithm (a cryptographic tool) to produce a 32-, 40-, or 64-character unique identifier to identify, track, and target users.

retargeting
ads are displayed based on the user's recent online behaviors.

For anything beyond simple behavioral targeting by user activities, as shown in Figure 10.8, marketers turn to predictive models to construct audiences that meet their specific needs.

Targeting with Predictive Models

Behavioral targeting often makes use of the kind of predictive modeling described in Chapter 1. Predictive modeling has long been a staple of direct marketing and can be described in the context of segmenting mailing lists, the forerunner of online behavioral targeting. In predictive modeling, the company starts with a profile of high-value customers and then builds a model that can identify other users who have similar characteristics, a "lookalike audience." The marketer targets this lookalike audience since these people are similar to their high-value customers and therefore are likely to convert. Targeting lookalike audiences is an option on social media platforms, like Meta. Let's look at an example.

Figure 10.8   A Predictive Model for Private Online College Enrollment Source: http://www.tru-signal.com/wp-content/uploads/2014/11/TruSignal-Online_College.pdf

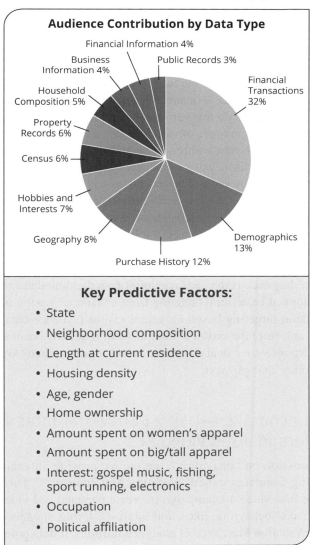

Audience Contribution by Data Type

- Financial Information 4%
- Business Information 4%
- Public Records 3%
- Household Composition 5%
- Property Records 6%
- Census 6%
- Hobbies and Interests 7%
- Geography 8%
- Purchase History 12%
- Demographics 13%
- Financial Transactions 32%

Key Predictive Factors:

- State
- Neighborhood composition
- Length at current residence
- Housing density
- Age, gender
- Home ownership
- Amount spent on women's apparel
- Amount spent on big/tall apparel
- Interest: gospel music, fishing, sport running, electronics
- Occupation
- Political affiliation

Figure 10.8 shows the outcome of this kind of predictive modeling exercise. The client was a private online college that had been using PPC and affiliate marketing to acquire new students. The cost of leads (to be discussed in Chapter 13) was acceptable. However, not enough people registered, and the cost per enrolled student was unacceptably high. They added paid search, organic search, and simple behavioral targeting to their acquisition media mix. That helped, but it still did not produce enough students who would enroll and persist.

The college turned to an agency that uses both traditional marketing data and big data to build predictive models. The college knew who its high-value students were. Presumably, these are students who took numerous courses and perhaps completed programs of study. The college was able to provide a profile of these high-value students to the agency so it could build a model that would identify other people who have the same characteristics ("look like") as the current high-value students. These prospects will have a higher probability of becoming high-value students than other viewers of the college's ads.

The data used for this model included 12 types of offline data that contained thousands of attributes for each individual case used to build the model. Online data for these cases was drawn from a database comprised of 220 million U.S. adults with more than 640 million cookie profiles, 720 million hashed emails, and 300 million mobile IDs. This massive data set was fed into a scoring model with the results seen in Figure 10.8. The Key Predictive Factors are the variables that contributed most to the variance in the regression-type model. They included several variables related to location and others that helped identify prospects by gender-specific traits, occupation, and political affiliation.

Looking at the pie chart you see that three broad types of variables contributed over 50 percent of the variance—financial transactions, demographics, and purchase history. It is common for only a few variables to contribute most to this type of modeling. However, the other eight types of variables give useful information, especially for identifying media channels that will reach the highest-scoring prospects.

Targeted display advertising was used in a campaign to reach these prospects. Results were carefully tracked and showed a 32 percent higher enrollment rate with a cost 21 percent lower than the campaign target. Moreover, 84 percent of the leads from this new campaign converted within seven days of an inquiry about the college.

Predictive modeling is a demanding discipline, but it is not unusual to see significant results like these. The amount of data used in this model also reminds one of the old "looking for a needle in the haystack" saying. In this case, the needle is a high-value prospect, and the haystack is the vast amount of data that inundates marketers today.

When you look at behavioral targeting from a marketer's point of view, the desirability of precision targeting based on actual visitor behavior data seems obvious. When you look at it from the visitor's point of view, it quickly becomes clear that a lot of digital firms know a great deal about users. Is that good or bad? We discuss privacy concerns and policy changes next.

Vacation Matchmaker—Using Behavioral Targeting to Create Personalized Video Ads

To end our discussion on behavioral targeting we provide an example of a digital video advertising campaign called "Vacation Matchmaker."[15] This award-winning campaign is the first video ad campaign to create personalized videos edited in real time to match users' behaviors, likes, and interests. Using Spongecell's dynamic ad technology, the Vacation Matchmaker analyzed millions of data points about the user as the page loaded and then scanned hundreds of prerecorded video clips about Tennessee tourism to find the clips to perfectly match the user's interest. These clips are then stitched together into a short, personalized video ad to entice the user to plan a visit to Tennessee. The videos directed users to Tennessee's tourism website, where they were invited to explore the attractions featured in each scene in their video or choose from hundreds more attractions to create their ideal vacation itinerary. Users were also encouraged to share their itineraries on social media to inspire other travelers.

Let's say a user is interested in history, rock climbing, and country music (interests identified from search behavior, website visit data, and social media activity). Vacation Matchmaker then presents the user with a video highlighting historical sites from the civil war, like the Chickamauga & Chattanooga National Military Park, rock climbing in Sunset Park, and finally scenes from live music venues in downtown Chattanooga. Pretty neat idea, isn't it? Instead of showing viewers potential attractions that may not interest them, these dynamic videos were much more likely to catch viewers' attention and result in more qualified leads. The results did not disappoint. The four-week campaign resulted in 332,889 hours of video exposure, a CTR three times the industry average, and a 46 percent increase in Tennessee tourism's website traffic. Moreover, 93 percent of people surveyed said the ads inspired them to plan a vacation to Tennessee in the next year, and 17,442 people shared itineraries shared on social media.[16] See Figure 10.9 for a campaign summary.

Figure 10.9   Vacation Matchmaker Advertising Campaign Source: CDN

Privacy Concerns and Regulations

First-Party Vs. Third-Party Cookies

The internet was conceived to be a place of anonymity—meaning that websites would not know *who* visited them, only that *someone* visited them. Initially, there was no need for a website to recognize that a person had visited before, but as the internet grew and websites started to offer products and services for sale, the need to identify users became apparent. Netscape, a web browser launched in 1994, created a solution.[17] They developed *cookies* as an integral part of the ecommerce experience. Cookies allowed shopping carts to remember what a customer added to the cart even if the customer had not registered to the site. Cookies are small text files that contain a unique identifier and are stored in a user's browser. Imagine shopping on a retailer's website, like Target.com. You spend 30 minutes browsing the site, adding 10 items to your shopping cart. You realize it's time for your next class, so you close your computer (or put away your phone) and go to class. After class, you return to Target.com to make your purchase only to find that your shopping cart is empty, and you need to find those 10 products all over again. Cookies solved this problem.

Cookies were originally designed to only identify a user to the same website that created the cookie. Since cookies have a unique identifier to a specific website, websites could identify repeat visitors. This type of cookie (one only used by the website that created it) is referred to as first-party cookies, and they are integral in website analytic programs like Google Analytics. Seeing the potential to personalize and target users across websites, advertisers found a way to share cookies across websites. Using embedded references that point to other websites to share cookie information across websites is referred to as third-party cookies. As Lou Montulli, inventor of the cookie, recounts:

> "A problem that I missed during the Cookie design phase was an interaction between cookies and embedded content within a webpage. Webpages start as a single HTML document on one server. That one HTML document contains references to other resources loaded to display the site the user sees. Images, videos, more text, and plug-ins are all references within an HTML document, and any of those resources can be loaded from anywhere in the world. This referencing technique is one of the things that make the Web so amazingly powerful. When Web Cookies are combined with embedded references that point to other websites they are called "3rd party cookies" and they represent a new way in which users can be tracked across multiple websites."[18]

first-party cookies
small text files stored in the user's browser that are created by a website when a user visits. First-party cookies are designed only to be used by the website that created them (not shared across websites).

third-party cookies
using embedded references that point to other websites to share cookie information across websites.

Figure 10.10 outlines the major differences between first-party and third-party cookies. For years, advertisers have relied on third-party cookies for tracking and targeting users; however, users' privacy concerns have forced both companies and lawmakers to reconsider how cookies can be used. Mozilla and Apple stopped using them in 2019, and in January 2020, Google announced plans to eliminate third-party cookies, creating panic among many digital advertisers.[19] Google has postponed its plans, saying it will now phase out the use of third-party cookies in 2024,[20] leaving advertisers with a bit more time to find a solution. Potential alternatives include a Universal ID that users have control over, more focus on contextual advertising, and increased first-party data collection.[21]

Companies are not the only ones who are leading change in this area. Many lawmakers have also enacted new legislation to safeguard consumer privacy. The *General Data Protection Regulations (GDPR)* are privacy and security laws put into effect in the European Union (EU) in 2018. They are some of the toughest and strictest privacy regulations in the world. The law imposes obligations to anyone targeting or collecting data on EU citizens, including American companies doing business in the EU.

Figure 10.10   First-party Vs. Third-Party Cookies Source: https://termly.io/resources/articles/first-party-cookies-vs-third-party-cookies/

	First-party cookies	**Third-party cookies**
Who made the cookies?	They come from the webpage publisher. Can be JavaScript code or part of the website's server.	Ad servers and other servers load them onto your browser. They do not come from the main website you visited.
Where are the cookies used?	Only work on the website that made the code.	Accessible on any website that loads a third-party server's code.
Who can read the cookie?	Only the original website can read them.	Anyone with the correct program can read them.
When can the cookie be read?	Only when the original user is actively on the original website can they be read.	Users can read them at any time.
What does my browser do with them?	Supported by all browsers. Browsers give users tools to reject cookies.	Once supported by all browsers. However, browsers are increasingly blocking them or providing ways around them.

Companies that violate the GDPR's privacy and security standards may be subject to harsh fines, with penalties reaching tens of millions of euros.[22]

The state of California also passed digital privacy-focused legislation named the *California Consumer Privacy Act (CCPA),* giving California residents more control over their online information: "This landmark law secures new privacy rights for California consumers, including:

- *The right to know about the personal information a business collects about them and how it is used and shared;*
- *The right to delete personal information collected from them (with some exceptions);*
- *The right to opt out of the sale of their personal information; and*
- *The right to non-discrimination for exercising their CCPA rights."*[23]

As privacy becomes an increasingly important issue for consumers, marketers must be vigilant to stay knowledgeable about laws regulating the collection and use of consumer data.

Mobile Advertising

No discussion of contemporary digital advertising would be complete without mention of mobile display advertising. Figure 10.11 shows that estimates for mobile advertising have outpaced desktop spending. Like desktop, mobile advertising is available in different formats, including banners, rich media (expanding, floating, etc.), video, and native. Most advertising networks, like Google Ads, allow for buying different formats (desktop and mobile) within the space and may resize ads to fit the placement. Desktop and mobile ads are similar in many ways. Still, it is important to consider a few additional elements for mobile advertising to avoid a negative consumer experience and accidental clicks. Some best practices for mobile ads include:

- Avoid placing banners near any element that requires user input that can lead to accidental clicks
- Placing ads on an active game screen

Figure 10.11 Growth of Mobile Spending vs. Desktop Ad Spending Source: CNBC

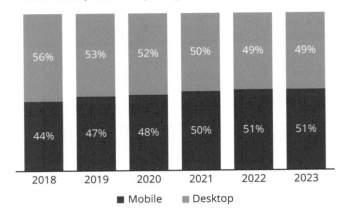

Mobile Set To Outpace Desktop Ad Spending By 2022

Global desktop/mobile ad spending distribution forecast by platform

- Placing ads in a scrollable element or making them not visible
- Placing ads on top of an app's content, which can be frustrating and drive accidental clicks
- Putting more than one banner ad on the same screen can be overwhelming and cause a bad user experience

According to Pollfish, 85 percent of respondents have accidentally clicked on a mobile banner ad, and 67 percent believed that the app creator misled users (such as misplacing elements in an app) in order to make users click on a banner ad.[24]

Mobile Advertising Using Location

One tremendous benefit of mobile advertising is the ability to use technology to identify users' locations and send targeted and personalized ads directly to them. Figures 10.12a and b show ways in which such localized targeting can work. The Rogers Centre is a multi-purpose sports and event stadium in downtown Toronto. In Figure 10.12a, a geo-fence or virtual perimeter has been drawn around the center. That enables the marketer to target all mobile users who pass through the space. If the Toronto Blue Jays are playing at the center, that might attract a set of advertisers who wanted to reach sports fans. If Disney on Ice is playing, there it would suggest advertisers of family oriented products. That is powerful targeting.

Figure 10.12b shows how hyperlocal advertising can work in a different way. In mobile advertising contextual refers to the specific characteristic of the defined geographical area including types of locations, demographics, and other census data. In Figure 10.12b the map shows a green space near York University. The space contains a bridle path and that is the title given to the defined area. You can see how this would interest advertisers who are trying to reach the student population or advertisers of recreational products who want to reach a population enjoying an outing. Messages that reflect the context in which people receive them also represent powerful targeting.

Local businesses can, of course, develop their own local advertising campaigns and numerous mobile agencies provide advertising platforms at affordable prices. Small local businesses can also place their ads on apps where localized content is already being presented like Yelp and the Weather Channel.

geo-fence

using geolocation technology such as GPS or RFID to establish a geographical area that can be defined by a virtual perimeter.

Figure 10.12 a. Geofencing b. Contextual Local Targeting Source:marketingland.com

Additional Acquisition Techniques

Other acquisition techniques can take place either on or offline. Event-driven marketing, affiliate programs, and digital public relations are the most used. Events and experiential marketing are discussed in Chapter 4 as part of the customer experience. We will end with a discussion of affiliate marketing and online press releases.

Affiliate Programs

We discuss affiliate programs as a digital business model in Chapter 3. Since many prospects who enter a website from an affiliate listing may be new customers, affiliate programs qualify as a customer acquisition technique. Marketers like affiliate marketing because it is a relatively low-cost activity. It can largely be automated, and affiliates are paid based on performance. Note that low-cost, however, does not necessarily mean high revenue.

> **affiliate programs**
> programs that offer incentives to partner websites, wherein a website agrees to post a link to a transactional site in return for a commission on sales made as a direct result of the link.

Affiliate programs follow the 80/20 rule: about 80 percent of the affiliates are low volume, and 20 percent produce significant volume, meaning only a small number of the affiliates produce the most click-throughs and profitable sales. Consequently, affiliate programs need to be actively managed. Networks have grown up to serve the affiliate marketing sector by finding appropriate affiliates for merchants and publishers and relevant sites for small businesses who wish to participate in affiliate marketing. There are also marketing services firms that will assume the management of an affiliate system. The rise of blogs and social media marketing has also increased affiliate marketing, as many social media influencers use this for revenue generation. If you search for virtually any subject that includes the term "affiliate marketing," you will see many "make money fast and easy" sites and ads. That should be a *caveat emptor* signal to anyone trying to enter the business.

There are, however, interesting new businesses that are affiliate programs. Several of them operate in the space that is known as fintech (financial technology). Two examples are:

- Nerdwallet—is an American firm that offers links to dozens of products in financial sectors, including banking, credit cards, insurance, loans, and more, and advice that aims to help the user choose the best product for their circumstances. Nerdwallet describes the nature of their affiliate program as:

> The Nerds strive to provide consumers with transparency, and in that spirit, we would like to share how we make money. Some financial institutions with products on our site may pay us a referral fee when customers get approved for specific products.

> When you click to apply for those products through our site, we may receive compensation from the company that issues that product. This compensation enables us to maintain our growing database of financial products, many of which we don't receive compensation for. It also helps us support our Nerds who research and stay up-to-date on the latest news and offerings for you.[25]

- BankBazaar—is an Indian company that was started to take advantage of the fact that penetration of many financial services is low in India and most users patronize brick-and-mortar establishments. Much of the population is online through their smartphones but do not have credit cards and, therefore, cannot shop online. The company was founded to take advantage of the opportunities this presents.[26]

Giving customers in India and nearby countries mobile access is key to the company's business. BankBazaar offers a robust mobile app (Figure 10.13) and

Figure 10.13 **The BankBazaar Mobile App** Source: Bank Bazaar

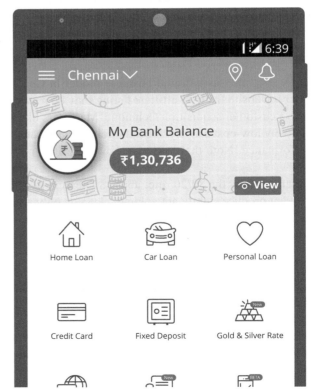

offers at least one third-party app on its site to assist customers with financial calculations. The app features links to information about personal finance, and they have an active blog.

Like other affiliate models, they offer customers and direct them to the financial service website. If customers enroll, they make a commission, which could be based on something like the size of the loan. At this early stage in its corporate life, the company also builds and maintains websites for Indian financial services companies. However, it is the affiliate revenue on which it is apparently banking its future.[27]

Generating Publicity

Although public relations is a communications discipline separate from marketing, the two must work closely together. Staging events, arranging product placement in films and TV, and issuing press releases are all tools that the public relations professional uses to generate unpaid media attention for products, services, and causes. Of those, the issuance of press releases appears to have been most changed by the internet.

public relations
strategic communications that manage an organization's or brand's public image and reputation through tools such as press releases, product placements, and events.

Writing press releases and distributing them to the firm's media list or through a newswire service is the stock in the public relations trade. It has always been important to write press releases well, keeping in mind the interests of the target media, and to distribute them in a timely fashion to journalists who are likely to pick them up and use them to write an article or even write a feature article around the subject of the press release. The issue has always been that journalists are deluged with press releases. This problem has only increased with the internet, and drawing their attention to a particular one is difficult.

Making press releases visible to journalists on the internet—optimizing press releases— assumes more importance in this environment. In addition to writing the press release well, optimization requires the use of search marketing tools, including:

- Selecting relevant keywords.
- Using the keyword or phrase in the title of the release and in the various tags that identify the content to search engines.
- Tagging images for identification by search engines.
- Using three anchor links: one to the home page, one to the product page, and one to the most relevant blog post.

The optimized press release[28] is posted with its URL on the business's website to facilitate search. The releases are tagged with keywords, and the content is optimized for search, both topics covered in Chapter 7. In addition, most businesses use an internet press service to distribute their releases to the most extensive possible set of relevant journalists, who will generally have all the information they need to write articles or posts without having to contact the marketer and wait for a reply.

- In addition to being optimized for search, press releases should also contain rich media, including images and videos, providing journalists with engaging content such as traditional elements like text and contact information plus rich media elements, including links to images and videos. Other links encourage writers to post their content to bookmarking and news sites. These postings add to the reach of the content and may also increase the search ranking since they represent incoming links (discussed in Chapter 7).

All these channels and techniques are important in customer acquisition. However, nothing works if the target audience does not see it. We end the chapter with a discussion on the importance of integrated communications for reaching target audiences.

Integrated Marketing Communications for Reach and Impact

The digital age has not changed another key fact. No single medium or channel of communication is enough to reach a given market segment. Examples throughout this chapter have shown that multiple channels are necessary to provide reach and do so in a way that is impactful to all audience members. That will require integrating online and offline media into coherent, sequenced marketing campaigns for the foreseeable future. Coca-Cola has become an expert in integrated marketing campaigns through many years of experience in many offline and online channels.[29] Admittedly, most of Coca-Cola's advertising is reminder advertising, not customer acquisition. However, it uses display and other components in various media channels.

Coca-Cola is also a master of individual campaigns under the overarching umbrella of a brand theme. Since the beginning of 2016, the brand campaign has been "Taste the Feeling" with initial TV ads (also posted on YouTube, of course) which convey the emotion of the Coca-Cola experience.[30]

The worldwide success of the "Share a Coke" campaign, which started in Australia and rolled out to other countries based on initial success, is one such example (Figure 10.14). The Australia launch featured a digital outdoor billboard with Coca-Cola users' names occupying a major square in Sydney. The campaign quickly spawned videos all over the world.[31] It was gradually rolled out to countries around the globe. In the United States, it was supported by television advertising.[32] The campaign is credited with increasing soft drink sales by 2 percent in the United States alone.[33]

The campaign's primary goal was to connect and engage with young people personally and emotionally. Facebook and other social media are credited for much of the campaign's success.[34]

Figure 10.14   **Examples of Share a Coke Campaign on Instagram** Source: https://medium.com/user-generated-content-marketing/best-ugc-campaigns-to-get-inspired-from-2020-updated-518c3d9f11ae

One Coca-Cola executive pointed out that:

- The results were phenomenal because Coca-Cola encouraged consumers to spread the word about the campaign on social media using the #shareacoke hashtag.

- More than 500,000 photos were shared using the #shareacoke hashtag.

- Consumers created and shared more than 6 million virtual Coca-Cola bottles by September 2014.

- Coca-Cola gained 25 million Facebook followers as a result of the campaign[35] and the hashtag is still being used today across social media platforms.

All the evidence suggests that digital advertising in general, and mobile in particular, will continue to grow in popularity and impact. However, marketers cannot afford to ignore other digital channels, nor should they ignore the traditional communications channels. Acquiring new customers requires a broad reach. That requires an integrated marketing communications mix to expose target audiences to the acquisition marketing message.

Summary

As the internet has matured and its ability to perform as a branding channel has been recognized, online advertising has become an increasingly important digital marketing tool, as evidenced by its growing role in the marketing budget. This budget is still dominated by search marketing expenditures (direct response), but display advertising and, more recently, advertising on social and mobile networks continue to grow. The growth is primarily because of their reach and their effectiveness in branding, especially as new digital advertising formats are developed to engage the viewer more effectively. Each of these digital marketing tools contributes to brand development and, at the same time, operates as an effective customer acquisition mechanism.

Numerous formats can be used for online display ads. Static banner ads have lost popularity to rich media ads, which attract attention and deliver compelling messages. Most online ads are placed on websites by an ad-serving network. The system tries to balance the site's requirements with the advertiser's requirements. The site wishes to sell as many spaces as it has available on its site at the best possible rates. The advertiser wishes to reach the defined target audience with the right frequency at the lowest possible cost. Ads can be served directly to large sites or within networks of sites brought into an alliance for that purpose. Programmatic advertising automates identifying target markets and purchasing the ad space. Real-time bidding carries this out in nanoseconds so the visitor can be targeted with ads that match current activity like search for a specific product.

As technology and databases improve, it becomes possible to target ads more precisely. Behavioral targeting can be based on a user activity profile, either an anonymous web user or an identified user. It can also be based on more complex predictive models. Using any of these targeting approaches, the visitor is followed through the site, and ads can be served based on the visitor's segment membership without regard to the content being viewed at any given time. Third-party cookies allow the site to follow visitors outside of the site so they can be served relevant ads on other websites. Advanced targeting requires compiling and using consumer data, often without the consumer being aware that the data are being collected. Importantly, marketers need to be knowledgeable about new consumer privacy laws, such as GDPR and CCPA, that govern the tracking and use of consumer data.

In recent years, a new advertising opportunity has arisen due to the time spent on social platforms and mobile networks. The same display advertising formats and targeting options apply to social and mobile sites. The reach of social platforms like Facebook is vast and the targeted advertising opportunities they offer make them attractive to marketers. Similarly, the amount of time spent on mobile networks and the ability to engage visitors through video and games make mobile advertising the fastest-growing display segment. The growth of mobile display advertising is enhanced by the ability of apps to display advertisements. In addition to online advertising, other customer acquisition techniques include affiliate marketing and publicity.

Display advertising and other customer acquisition techniques must be part of an Integrated Marketing Communications strategy that includes both digital and offline marketing efforts. In a multichannel world, no single advertising technique can be effective. Marketing effectiveness requires judicious use of techniques that are appropriate to the target user and the nature of the campaign.

Discussion Questions

1. Identify the main customer acquisition tools.

2. What is online display advertising, and how does it relate to offline advertising?

3. What is an online ad format? Why must marketers be familiar with the formats and understand what creating an online ad requires?

4. Why are new ad formats continually being developed? What benefits does this offer the marketer? Do any of the formats presented in this chapter have any potential downsides?

5. What is ad serving, and how does it relate to targeting an ad to the correct target audience?

6. Why is ad serving an improvement over just placing an advertisement on a web page and leaving it there?

7. Explain what programmatic advertising is and why it is an essential tool for both the digital publisher and the digital advertiser. What capability does real-time bidding add?

8. Behavioral advertising is especially important for digital marketing. Explain why and give a hypothetical example, perhaps based on your own experience.

9. How do cookies and hashed emails facilitate audience targeting? Do you see any ethical problems in the use of these technologies?

10. What are cookies? Describe the differences between first-party and third-party cookies.

11. Why do you think mobile advertising is growing at such a fast pace?

12. Discuss whether or not generating publicity is one of the few marketing communications activities that has not changed much due to the internet.

13. Do affiliate programs tend to attract many websites or blogs that can generate a large volume of traffic that results in sales? Why or why not?

14. What is IMC, and why is it important to marketers and advertisers?

Endnotes

1. "About IAB," IAB, February 1, 2023, https://www.iab.com/our-story/.
2. "About IAB," IAB, February 1, 2023, https://www.iab.com/our-story/.
3. Megan Smith, "Banner Ads 101: Basics and Best Practices," Constant Contact, November 9, 2022, https://www.constantcontact.com/blog/banner-ad/.
4. "Build an HTML5 Creative-Studio Help," Google (Google), accessed February 11, 2023, https://support.google.com/richmedia/answer/2672542.
5. "What Is Rich Media?-Studio Help," Google (Google), accessed February 11, 2023, https://support.google.com/richmedia/answer/2417545.
6. Megan Smith, "Banner Ads 101: Basics and Best Practices," Constant Contact, November 9, 2022, https://www.constantcontact.com/blog/banner-ad/.
7. John Bowers, "A Million Squandered: The 'Million Dollar Homepage' as a Decaying Digital Artifact," Library Innovation Lab, July 21, 2017, https://lil.law.harvard.edu/blog/2017/07/21/a-million-squandered-the-million-dollar-homepage-as-a-decaying-digital-artifact/.
8. "What is an ad server? the definitive guide for 2022," accessed February 11, 2023, https://www.kevel.com/blog/what-is-an-ad-server/.
9. Sarbashree Mallik, "Ad Exchange vs. Ad Network: What's The Real Difference?," AdSparc, June 9, 2022, https://adsparc.com/ad-exchange-vs-ad-network/.
10. "What Is Programmatic Advertising?: IBM Watson Advertising Thought Leadership," What Is Programmatic Advertising? | IBM Watson Advertising Thought Leadership, accessed February 11, 2023, https://www.ibm.com/watson-advertising/thought-leadership/what-is-programmatic-advertising.
11. "What Is Contextual Targeting?," What Is Contextual Targeting?, October 13, 2022, https://insights.digitalmediasolutions.com/articles/what-is-contextual-targeting.
12. "GP," Amazon (Goettsche Partners, 2011), http://www.amazon.com/gp/help/customer/display.html?nodeId=468496.

13. Suryanarayan Pal, "How Does a Hashed Email Address Benefit Email Marketers?," Mailmodo (June 21, 2022), https://www.mailmodo.com/guides/hashed-email-address/.
14. Jim Nichols, "5 New (and Powerful) Targeting Methods," accessed February 11, 2023, http://www.imediaconnection.com/articles/ported-articles/red-dot-articles/2011/jun/5-new-and-powerful-targeting-methods/
15. Justin Lake, "Vacation Matchmaker," accessed February 21, 2023, http://justinthewords.com/tennessee
16. "National State Tourism Directors Mercury Awards Digital Campaign; Tennessee Department of Tourist Development," accessed February 21, 2023, https://ustravel.secure-platform.com/a/gallery/rounds/3/details/1803
17. Nicolai Safai, "Cookies: A Basic Form of Data Persistence," Medium (Make School, September 7, 2018), https://medium.com/make-school/cookies-a-basic-form-of-data-persistence-f3b576eaf122.
18. "The Reasoning behind Web Cookies," The reasoning behind Web Cookies, accessed February 12, 2023, https://montulli.blogspot.com/2013/05/the-reasoning-behind-web-cookies.html.
19. James Avery, "Where Will Our Data Go When Cookies Disappear?," TechCrunch, January 4, 2022, https://techcrunch.com/2022/01/04/where-will-our-data-go-when-cookies-disappear/.
20. Anthony Chavez, "Expanding Testing for the Privacy Sandbox for the Web," Google (July 27, 2022), https://blog.google/products/chrome/update-testing-privacy-sandbox-web/.
21. D. Thomas, "Third-Party Cookie Alternatives-4 Top Choices," Claravine, January 26, 2023, https://www.claravine.com/2021/06/25/third-party-cookie-alternatives-4-top-contenders/.
22. "What Is GDPR, the EU's New Data Protection Law?," GDPR.eu, May 26, 2022, https://gdpr.eu/what-is-gdpr/.
23. "California Consumer Privacy Act (CCPA)," State of California - Department of Justice - Office of the Attorney General, January 20, 2023, https://www.oag.ca.gov/privacy/ccpa.
24. By Andreas Vourkos, "Mobile AD Formats Lab #3-Banner Ads DOS and Don'ts," Pollfish, January 7, 2020, https://www.pollfish.com/blog/app-monetization/mobile-ad-formats-lab-3%E2%80%8A-%E2%80%8Abanner-ads-dos-donts/.
25. NerdWallet, "How We Make Money," NerdWallet, accessed February 12, 2023, https://www.nerdwallet.com/blog/how-we-make-money/.
26. Catherine Shu, "India's BankBazaar Raises $60M Series C Led by Amazon," TechCrunch, July 3, 2015, http://techcrunch.com/2015/07/02/bankbazaar/.
27. "What Is Bankbazaar's Business Model ?. How Does It Generate Revenue and Is It Profitable ? If Not, Then by When Is the Estimated Time to ...," Quora, accessed February 12, 2023, https://www.quora.com/What-is-Bankbazaars-business-model-How-does-it-generate-revenue-and-is-it-profitable-If-not-then-by-when-is-the-estimated-time-to-profits.
28. PR Newswire Association LLC, "Maximize Social Sharing with Your Press Release," Maximize Social Sharing with Your Press Release, June 28, 2018, https://www.prnewswire.com/news-releases/maximize-social-sharing-with-your-press-release-300137514.html.
29. Gregory Stringer, "Case Study: Coca Cola Integrated Marketing Communications," LinkedIn, March 11, 2015, https://www.linkedin.com/pulse/case-study-coca-cola-integrated-marketing-gregory-stringer.
30. Will Heilpern, "Coca-Cola Just Launched a Massive New Ad Campaign to Change the Conversation around Sugary Drinks," *Business Insider*, accessed February 12, 2023, http://www.businessinsider.com/coca-colas-taste-the-feeling-campaign-2016-1.
31. Jay Moye, "Share a Coke: The Groundbreaking Campaign from 'Down Under,'" accessed February 12, 2023, https://www.coca-colacompany.com/au/news/share-a-coke-how-the-groundbreaking-campaign-got-its-start-down-under.
32. "Coca-Cola TV Spot, 'Share a Coke' Song by Trimountaine," iSpot.tv | Realtime TV Advertising Performance Measurement, accessed February 12, 2023, https://www.ispot.tv/ad/7y_C/coca-cola-share-a-coke-song-by-trimountaine.
33. "3 Marketing Lessons from the 'Share a Coke' Campaign," http://www.mayecreate.com/2015/05/3-marketing-lessons-from-the-share-a-coke-campaign/
34. Casey Neal, "The Britton Blog," Britton Marketing & Design Group, September 4, 2019, https://www.brittonmdg.com/blog/.
35. "3 Marketing Lessons from the "Share a Coke" Campaign," http://www.mayecreate.com/2015/05/3-marketing-lessons-from-the-share-a-coke-campaign/

Part III | Maintaining and Strengthening Relationships

Chapter 11

Email Marketing to Build Consumer and Business Relationships

Learning Objectives

By the time you complete this chapter, you will be able to:

1 Discuss reasons for the growing importance of email marketing.

2 Describe the various levels of permission.

3 List the steps involved in developing an email marketing campaign.

4 Learn the basics of email design.

5 Recognize key provisions of email marketing laws in the United States and worldwide.

6 List the future trends in email marketing.

The Importance of Email marketing

Despite what many people born in the early 2000s might believe, email is vital when influencing purchases. People do open their emails and buy things. As seen in Figure 11.1, 44 percent of people state that a general email influences their purchase intent more than any other form of communication, including text messages, social media, influencers, etc. Additionally, consumers are more likely to open an email from a brand they know than they are to open a text, direct mail, or social media message.[1] Thus, despite what type of preconceived notion one might have that "no one reads email anymore," the fact is that email is still the dominant promotional technique that generates sales leads, engages customers continuously, and informs customers about your brand.

Email as a promotional activity has exploded in recent years, and most forecasters believe that its growth is likely to continue for the foreseeable future. A report by the CMO survey showed that in 2022, 68 percent of CMOs surveyed increased their spending on email marketing.[2] Why this continued growth from what has been termed the "granddaddy" or "workhorse" of internet marketing channels? After all, email started many years ago and today's focus tends to be on new media like social and mobile marketing. In the 1970s, the first email program was developed through ARPANET and was instrumental in developing the protocols to help send email messages from computer to computer.

Figure 11.1 Customers' Top Purchase Influencers Source: https://www.marketingcharts .com/brand-related/brand-loyalty-226116

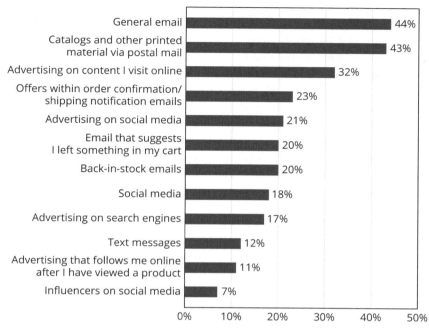

"Which of the following marketing efforts influence your decision to make online purchases?"

Influencer	Percentage
General email	44%
Catalogs and other printed material via postal mail	43%
Advertising on content I visit online	32%
Offers within order confirmation/shipping notification emails	23%
Advertising on social media	21%
Email that suggests I left something in my cart	20%
Back-in-stock emails	20%
Social media	18%
Advertising on search engines	17%
Text messages	12%
Advertising that follows me online after I have viewed a product	11%
Influencers on social media	7%

With the popularization and commercialization of the internet, email caught on quickly as a way to communicate directly with prospective customers.

Email was one of the first technologies to take off on the internet. Despite its early presence and the emergence of other media, the tool is not going away. Email marketing continues to be one of the strongest marketing channels in terms of return on investment (ROI). According to Constant Contact, every dollar spent on email marketing offers a return of $36.[3] With numbers like these, email cannot be considered an out-of-date tool.

Many people start their day with email and 60 percent of customers check their email on their mobile devices.[4] It is obvious that email plays a critical role in consumers' lives. Email offers marketers a fast, flexible, and highly controllable format. Email is essentially direct mail on steroids because not only is the customer contacted directly, but also different offers and methods of engagement can be tested to find the most effective means of communication. A deep understanding of the nature of offline mail promotions is also useful to the email marketer because of the relationship between the two media channels. In both direct mail and email, the marketer needs a solid offer and time deadline, and an attention-getting device (think envelope versus subject line). In both cases, measurement is critical to gauge success.

Even better, email direct marketing offers several advantages to traditional direct mail marketing and was initially positioned as a cost-effective alternative to direct mail. Emails can be developed quickly, tested, and revised on the fly based on almost immediate feedback, and can reach many internet users in a short time. Compared to other types of internet promotions, email is cheap on a per-customer contact basis. Although email response rates differ widely by application and industry, email still has a strong ROI. Forrester estimates that emails are so cost-effective that they can drive ROI two or three times higher than other forms of direct marketing, resulting in a continued increase in email spending.[5] However, the wise marketer should note that email is not the ONLY solution.

email marketing
the process of developing customer relationships through offers and communications contained in email messages.

Direct marketing is still quite an effective promotional channel. The promotional channel that works best is often context-dependent. Email typically works best for brands that the consumer has a relationship with, direct marketing tends to work best for brands the consumer does not know, and email and direct mail are about even when it comes to brands the consumer is aware of but does not have a relationship with. Text messages and social media—while still important—do not influence consumers as much as email and direct mail. See Figure 11.2 for more details.

Additionally, email can be used by any marketer—B2C, B2B, or nonprofit—who has an acceptable way to acquire an email list of potential customers. Email, like direct marketing, is also highly measurable and database-driven (see Chapter 1). Email marketing systems also offer a good way to tap into data from other internal and external systems to create meaningful and relevant communications for customers.

Email has proven to be a more powerful retention tool than an acquisition tool (see Chapter 10). Increasing customer engagement often tops the list of marketing goals and email is seen as the ideal retention tool. The reason email is so effective is that marketers have lists of existing customers to use, a "house" list of customers most likely to purchase again.

Email marketing has evolved into a sophisticated tool for customer engagement. The trend toward a true one-to-one marketing channel is closer to becoming a reality with changes in marketing technology, including email marketing, CRM tools, and integrating text messaging/SMS. Figure 11.3 identifies some of the key features of when a firm should use text messaging versus when they should use email. Text messages tend to allow for easier two-way communication and app integration, whereas emails allow for the use of multiple images to reinforce the brand's message.

The cornerstone of a good email marketing campaign is the concept of permission. Targeted emails to those customers who want to hear from a company are going to get a higher response rate than a list of customers that are not familiar with a product or service. Although it is possible to conduct an email marketing campaign to unknown prospects, it is not a recommended practice. Seth Godin's book, *Permission Marketing*, outlined the concept of permission that holds true today. Customers want to interact with companies, but on their terms and in their time frame. This is also known as customer journey mapping.

Figure 11.2   Consumers' Preferred Communication Channel as of 2022
Source: https://www.marketingcharts.com/cross-media-and-traditional/direct-mail-226611.

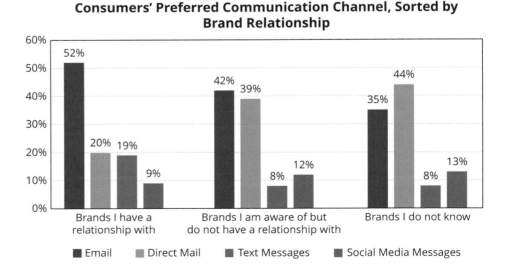

Figure 11.3   Differences Between SMS and Email Marketing Source: https://simpletexting.com/email-vs-sms-marketing/

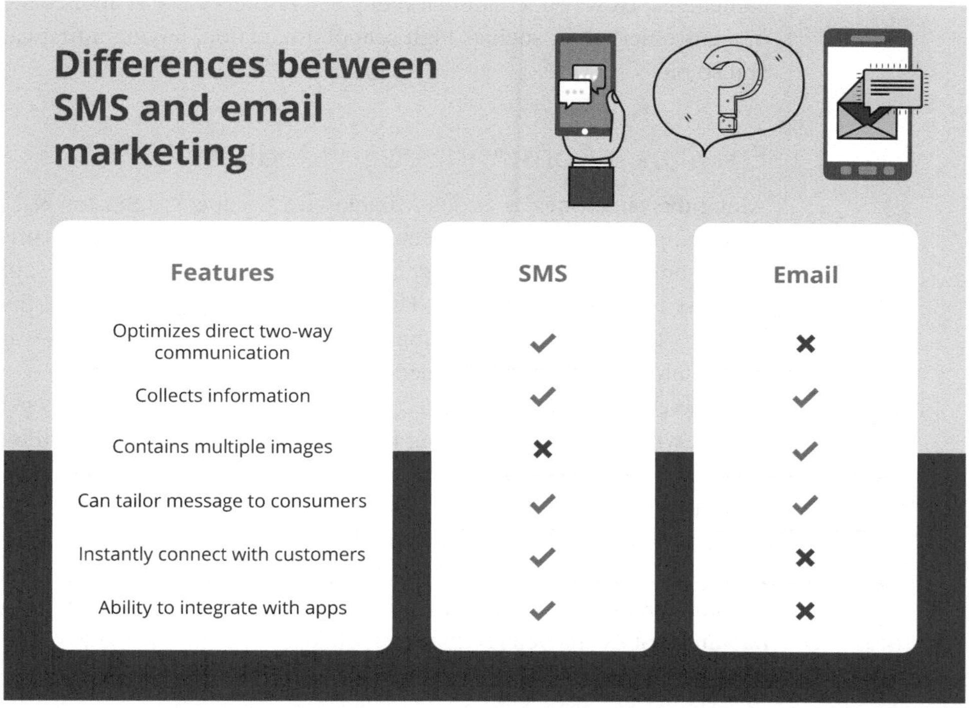

Some transactions take a longer lead time for the customer to feel comfortable purchasing, so multiple emails are necessary.

Just as one would not (hopefully) propose marriage on a first date or accept such a proposal, consumers want to see that they are doing business with the right type of company for them before revealing personal information and permitting companies to use that information. Academic research supports the use of Permission Email Marketing (PEM). A recent study indicated that PEM positively influences the experience of shopping online and thus can benefit marketers.[6]

Scotts Miracle-Gro Company

Email is also ideally suited to event marketing campaigns, as discussed in Chapter 6.

The Scotts Miracle-Gro Company, known for its lawn and garden expertise and the Miracle-Gro product, started a lawn care update email program in the spring of 2000 and now has over a million and a half subscribers. The company uses over 355 unique geo-demographic variations of its newsletter for a variety of purposes, customizing it for the customer. The content of these updates is based on the consumer's grass type, zip code (which indicates climate zone), and possible weed and insect problems that might abound at a particular time of year. Imagine getting an email telling you it is now time to treat the lawn for grubs! A customer living in an area where grubs are a concern would be grateful.

Email marketers have integrated their campaigns with direct mail for years. As social media has become more widely used, another opportunity for engagement has developed. In this case, Scotts Miracle-Gro Company also invites its Facebook friends to opt-in for emails, incorporating social media and developing an integrated campaign strategy. The "events" noted in this case could be, for example, times of the year for planting seeds, fertilizing, and providing other lawn care services. These event-type emails nurture the customer relationship each step of the way.

This type of approach is just one example of how email works with event marketing campaigns. However, email marketing can just as easily be applied to other major events in a customer's life, such as high school graduation, buying a first car, entering college, and so on.

Email as a Communication Medium

Along the same lines as Scotts Miracle-Gro Company, Johnston & Murphy, a high-end shoe company, has highly segmented its customer base and provides offers that are relevant to the consumer based on age, gender, interests, and past purchases, increasing open and response rates, as well as sales. Therefore, despite being one of the first communications channels to "take hold" in the marketplace, email remains a vital way for businesses to communicate with their customers.

Social media can help better with reaching new customers to get them in the sales funnel, whereas email marketing is better once the customer is willing to initiate a relationship with the company. Please see Figure 11.4 for further detail.

Customers, for their part, are very active in the email space. Email is so prevalent that most people check email every 37 minutes.[7] According to the same study, that results in 28 percent of the workday being devoted to reading and answering email. Additionally, a study conducted by Statista found that in 2017 there were 269 billion emails sent *per day* and that by the year 2025 there will be 376.4 billion emails sent per day. See Figure 11.5 for more detail.

However, nearly 85 percent of emails received by consumers are *spam*.[8] This figure accounts for emails that get caught in spam filters and do not reach the recipient. Spam is considered unsolicited email. Consumers typically report higher open rates for permission-based emails and see the value in signing up for relevant commercial messages. While the latter is good news for marketers, the existence of spam provides an ongoing problem.

However, despite the negative perception that much of email is spam, consumers do value messages from commercial sources and have become more sophisticated in dealing with spam. Spam filters block many unwanted messages and consumers can manage which messages they wish to receive. Many marketers have come to rely on email marketing as a cost-effective tool, not necessarily for customer acquisition, but for customer development and retention. For instance, when examining the click rates of different types of email automation programs, Bluecore, a digital marketing company, finds that welcome

spam
unwanted email communication.

Figure 11.4 **Integrating Email and Social Media** Source: https://hypeauditor.com /blog/how-to-integrate-email-marketing-with-your-social-media-strategy/

Figure 11.5 Number of Emails Received Per Day Source: https://www.statista.com/statistics/456500/daily-number-of
-e-mails-worldwide

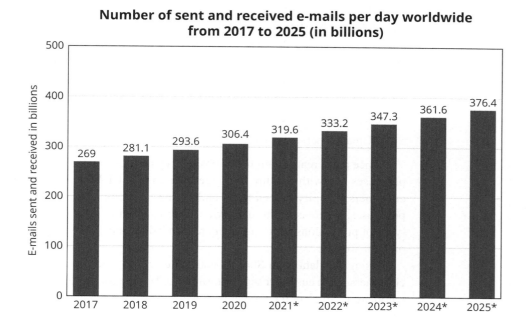

Number of sent and received e-mails per day worldwide from 2017 to 2025 (in billions)

emails receive an 11.27 percent open rate in comparison to a 5.26 percent open rate for an abandoned search. While these are automated emails, they are not considered spam because the customer opted-in to receive these emails from the company. Figure 11.6 details the various types of email click rates.

Not only is email usage growing, but also email marketing performance results are strong. While click-through rates (CTR) in general have been declining and are hovering at about 2.4 percent in North America and Europe,[9] savvy marketers realize that click-through rates can be triple that of the general rate with the use of techniques such as messages triggered by specific customer actions or events, as discussed below.[10]

click-through rates (CTR)
number of clicks divided by the number of opens.

Figure 11.6 Email Click Rates for Automated Email Campaigns Source: https://www.marketingcharts.com/industries
/retail-and-e-commerce-226629

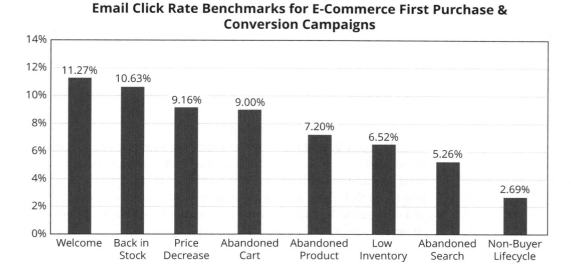

Email Click Rate Benchmarks for E-Commerce First Purchase & Conversion Campaigns

Levels of Permission Marketing

Magnolia Bakery: A Case Study on Permission Marketing

Famed Magnolia Bakery started in New York City in 1996. As their prestige and brand awareness grew over the years, they opted to create a direct-to-consumer portion of their business in addition to their brick-and-mortar stores.[11] But since they were mostly known for their brick-and-mortar bakeries they needed to expand their online presence so that they could reach more potential customers. They had two main goals as follows:

1. Acquire new customers
2. Create a personalized experience for each customer

Once they created their new website, they partnered with Shopify to handle customer purchases and with Sailthru to merge their current CRM with their data on new online customers. Shopify helped them understand the who, what, when, and how much for purchases, whereas Sailthru allowed them to monitor who was opening emails, what types of promotions their customers responded to, and who was spending time browsing on their website.

Using the data from Shopify and Sailthru, Magnolia created multiple segments of customers. Each customer segment was placed on a separate customer journey using email automation. Some of the segments were new customers, abandoned carts, and identifying product preferences for existing customers (i.e., someone always buys the same cake on March 12). Additional insights were invested to discover high-value customers, repeat purchasers, deal seekers, and gift-givers so that they could cater their journey map differently dependent upon each behavior. They knew that deal seekers would react differently to an email campaign than a gift-giver and they mapped out the paths that made the most logical sense based on their past purchases.

As a way to widen their customer base, they also launched a paid social media campaign. New customers were offered a 10 percent discount and entered into a raffle for a birthday giveaway (e.g., cake, party bowl, and a cupcake assortment) in exchange for their email address. Figure 11.7 illustrates an example of one of their paid social media campaigns. They also collected their patrons' cell phone numbers so that they could experiment with text messaging strategies as well as future social media strategies.

By engaging with their customers through multiple marketing touchpoints (i.e., brick-and-mortar, email, social media, and text messaging) they saw that email subscribers were more engaged with the brand and spent 35 percent more time on Magnolia's website browsing than non-subscribers. Additionally, Magnolia's personalized email strategy increased their conversion rates by 39 percent. And Adam Davis, Media and Marketing Manager at Magnolia Bakery notes, "On the days we sent emails we saw a six to eight percent revenue lift. By making our strategy more thoughtful, we've uncovered email as a gem for our business."

Modern-day email campaigns that seek to gain more subscribers by using permission marketing must think through the various facets that consumers will consider based on their customer journey. By having consumers engage in a raffle with highly prized items from their bakery, Magnolia Bakery was able to entice consumers to trade their email address in return for a slot in the raffle.

Magnolia Bakery illustrates an important principle of email marketing—the issue of permission marketing. Magnolia has multiple ways that they ask customers for their email address: through online purchases that are gathered through Shopify, by a pop-up on their main webpage that offers a 10 percent discount on their first purchase, and through raffles that are promoted through social media, among others. Figure 11.8 shows an example of Magnolia Bakery's pop-up promotion. Magnolia states in fine print that in exchange for the email the customer is granting Magnolia permission to send

permission marketing
refers to gaining the customers' agreement to market it in a certain way.

Figure 11.7   **Magnolia Birthday Giveaway on Social Media** Source: Property of Cengage

the customer recurring marketing emails. Permission-based marketing is the preferred way of obtaining emails, particularly in email messaging, as opposed to purchasing lists of emails from third-party vendors. Firms have the option of purchasing emails for sales leads, but purchased email lists typically do not generate the level of engagement with the company like permission-based marketing emails.

Figure 11.8   **Magnolia Pop-up Email** Source: Property of Cengage

The first issue relating to permissions is that of spam. Unsolicited email is referred to as "spam," but it is not because the food product SPAM is unliked. Instead, the origins are from a Monty Python skit on SPAM in which it is offered on the menu of a restaurant many times (see Figure 11.9). The waitress' continued use of the word "spam" to describe the menu items made the word become annoying. (Watch the original Monty Python video online to get an idea of how really annoying spam can be.)

No responsible marketer uses or sanctions the use of spam. Ever. Period. And as stated earlier, permission-based marketing is the only responsible way to conduct email marketing campaigns.

Direct marketers have been sending unsolicited mailings for many years. Many, if not most, consumers do not like it. However, unsolicited physical mail does not appear to arouse the same level of ire in consumers that spam email does. It seems that consumers regard spam email as more intrusive than mail. Either way, it is clear that reputable marketers do not want to be identified with spam in the minds of the consuming public.

In order not to be considered a spammer, the marketer must obtain permission from the customer or prospect before sending email. There are four levels of permission:

opt-out

taking an action to prevent the receipt of further communications, usually unchecking a box on a registration form.

1. Opt-out means that the visitor *did not* refuse to receive further communications from the marketer. This is an improvement over spam, but it does not represent a high level of commitment on the part of the visitor. Usually, there is just a check box that needs to be unchecked to opt out.

   Opt-out email addresses are often collected via online registration forms or other methods, even face-to-face. The point is to make consumers take some explicit action in order *not* to receive further communications. The theory behind opt-out seems to be that people may not bother to take the action, or be unaware that they could take it, and will therefore, almost by default, become members of the list. This is often operationalized by an already-checked box saying in effect, "Please send me email." Even if the choice is made to pre-check the box, the accompanying statement must be clear about what the visitor is agreeing to. The statement should be unambiguous and it should be located in a visible place. Under the U.S. CAN-SPAM law (described in detail at the end of this chapter), all emails must have a clear option to unsubscribe.

Figure 11.9   Monty Python SPAM Skit Source: Python (Monty) Pictures.

Opt-out represents, at best, passive agreement to receiving email, but at present, it represents the minimum acceptable standard. Opt-in is the preferred method by many marketers and observers of the field.

2. Opt-in means that visitors have actively chosen to receive further communications, usually by checking a box on a registration form. It represents active acquiescence, if not enthusiasm, about receiving future communications from the marketer. Consequently, members of opt-in lists should be more receptive to messages.

3. Double opt-in is a technique by which visitors agree to receive further communications, probably by checking an opt-in box on a site, and are then sent an email asking them to confirm their consent by replying to the email. The visitor has taken two actions, first indicating a willingness to accept email, then actively confirming it by replying to the confirmation. This response should indicate an interested, potentially well-qualified prospect.

4. Confirmed opt-in is somewhere in between opt-in and double opt-in. Visitors actively acquiesce to receiving email, again probably by checking a box. They are then sent a follow-up email confirming the permission, but no reply is required.

An easy way to remember the difference between opt-in and opt-out is that in opt-in, you must check the box and in opt-out, you must uncheck the box or perform some action.

The opt-in/opt-out controversy is in part the traditional direct marketing issue of fewer, better-quality leads versus more leads of lower quality. Marketers are often wise to choose quality over quantity in lead situations. As with direct mail, the list is critical in maximizing response rate. The differences in the email context have to do with both the economics and the relationships with potential customers. The cost of incremental email is virtually zero, arguing for larger lists, even if they are less qualified. The annoyance factor is so high, however, that there is a strong argument for high-quality opt-in lists of prospects who are genuinely willing to receive marketer-generated communications.

The one gray area is when the marketer has an email list that was obtained without use of specific opt-in or opt-out authorization by the consumer. These lists should be converted to either opt-in or opt-out by means of one carefully constructed email to confirm participation, perhaps including the use of incentives. There are relatively few email lists like this which were collected in the early days of the internet before the permission-based protocol became something of an accepted standard. The existence of a small number of lists in this category should not be taken as an excuse for spam by other marketers. Today when email lists are rented from a list broker, the marketer does not get the emails. Rather, the list broker who owns the permission-based list sends out the emails and the marketer only gets the addresses and other personal information if there is a response, such as an order or inquiry. Once the person or business on the list moves from a customer to a prospect and the relationship is developed, then the marketer gets information about that person or company. As in direct marketing, the "house" list is most effective, which incents the marketer to provide the best offer possible to be able to gather a new inquiry or order and, hopefully, an ongoing customer.

Both the emails in Figure 11.10 are the result of a new registration on a site. Staples replied to a new registration with a welcoming sales message that linked to promotional areas on the site.

Many other marketers will also ask for the customer's mobile phone number so that they can send them text messages. Integrating texting and email is essential for the modern marketer.[12] Due to the sheer volume of email messages that consumers receive throughout the day, some email messages can get lost. However, integrating an email and

opt-in
actively choosing to receive further communications, usually by checking a box on a registration form.

double opt-in
a technique by which visitors agree to receive further communications but must perform two actions, usually checking an opt-in box on a site, and then responding positively to a sent email asking for confirmation.

confirmed opt-in
somewhere in between opt-in and double opt-in; the visitor actively acquiesces to receiving email, again probably by another email confirmation.

Figure 11.10 (a) Welcome Email from Staples; (b) Weekly Featured Products Email Source: Staples the Office Superstore, LLC.

(a)   (b)

text campaign for certain types of messages helps engage the customer. There are several types of messages that a marketer will want to consider sending via text, such as:

1. **Triggered Texts.** Examples can include product shipment dates, due dates for bills, suspicious account log-ins, and two-factor authentication passwords.
2. **Transactional Texts.** Examples can include password resets, bill payments, and new account creations.
3. **Promotional Texts.** Examples can include sending customers timely promotional deals, rewards deals, new product alerts, and back-in-stock announcements.

Developing a Strategic Email Marketing Campaign

The Peppers and Rogers Group, whose expertise is in relationship marketing, summarizes the email marketing process as it moves from analysis to action (see Figure 11.11). Their process involves four steps:

- **Gather customer data.** This includes contact information, physical address or email address, or both. The transactional data from the company's own files also includes purchase history and a record of all customer interactions. It also includes the types of information (offers) they wish to receive, their preferences for receiving it (frequency and communications channel), and their privacy preferences.
- **Derive customer insight.** Using the different types of information that have been captured about the customer, begin to understand what the customer needs and values. The most valuable type of understanding is what should come next in the purchase cycle—an extended warranty program for a recently purchased appliance, for example.
- **Suggest proactive action.** This is the point at which the process moves from analysis to action. Email programs are developed, executed, and refined based on the results of the programs themselves, captured in the customer database.
- **Evaluate response.** In this step, program metrics are collected and analyzed to refine existing programs and suggest new strategies. Different approaches and

Figure 11.11   The Basics of Email Marketing

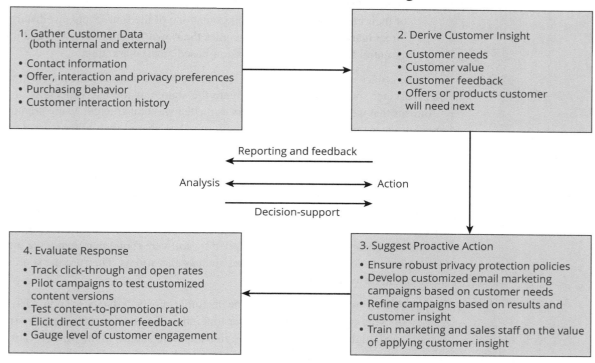

Customer Insight Drives Email Marketing Action

1. Gather Customer Data
   (both internal and external)
   - Contact information
   - Offer, interaction and privacy preferences
   - Purchasing behavior
   - Customer interaction history

2. Derive Customer Insight
   - Customer needs
   - Customer value
   - Customer feedback
   - Offers or products customer will need next

Reporting and feedback

Analysis ⟷ Action

Decision-support

4. Evaluate Response
   - Track click-through and open rates
   - Pilot campaigns to test customized content versions
   - Test content-to-promotion ratio
   - Elicit direct customer feedback
   - Gauge level of customer engagement

3. Suggest Proactive Action
   - Ensure robust privacy protection policies
   - Develop customized email marketing campaigns based on customer needs
   - Refine campaigns based on results and customer insight
   - Train marketing and sales staff on the value of applying customer insight

High-impact email marketing relies on leveraging customer insights throughout the email marketing campaign lifecycle. By applying customer-focused approaches to email marketing, companies can better generate the positive customer experiences driven by long-term, loyal relationships.

content should be tested to see which perform better. It is also good to encourage direct feedback from recipients to further understand likes, dislikes, and desires.

Peppers and Rogers present an overview of the process that applies whether email is being used for acquisition of prospects or relationship marketing to customers. Let us now turn briefly to a detailed set of steps for developing an email campaign, which also applies to either acquisition or retention settings (see Table 11.1).

Table 11.1   Steps in Developing an Email Marketing Campaign
Source: © Cengage Learning 2013.

1. Build or obtain an email list
   a. Build a permission-based list
   b. Rent email lists
2. Profile and segment the list
3. Establish a communications schedule
4. Develop specific program objectives
5. Write compelling copy
6. Structure your email to be received and opened
7. Create links to further information
8. Make it easy for viewers to take action
9. Test and revise the email
10. Measure results
11. Integrate learning into next email program

- **Build or obtain an email list.** Like Rome, email lists are not built in a day, and list development needs to be an ongoing process, one begun well in advance of an actual email campaign. Marketers who wish to be welcome in the inboxes of their customers obtain permission at one of the four levels just discussed. In direct marketing terms, this becomes their own "email house list" and it is an essential foundation for permission-based email marketing.

If it is necessary to rent email lists—and there are a considerable number available—the marketer should carefully investigate the source of the list, especially any privacy promises that were made to consumers as the list was constructed. Many privacy policies make it clear that lists will "from time to time" be shared with other marketers deemed acceptable to the list owner. When this is the case, both marketers are clearly within their legal rights. However, that does not mean that the consumer will be thrilled about receiving email from a company with whom they may have no relationship.

Lists for acquisition programs should be rented with care, from reputable list management agencies. Although lists are available for less, good lists will run from $100 to $400 per thousand (known as CPM), with established, performing lists closer to the higher end. Extremely cheap lists have been compiled by software (bots) that search the internet and snatch email addresses in public places such as chat rooms. They are the source of spam and should be avoided at all costs.

- **Profile or segment the list.** The customer/prospect database should have data, the volume of which grows over time, that allows a descriptive profile (middle-aged, high-income golfer living in an upscale suburb in the Midwest) or segmentation analysis that produces typical demographic (high-income two-worker family with school-aged children) or lifestyle segments (patron of the arts). We return to the subject of segmenting the database as an element of relationship marketing strategy in Chapter 11.

It is essential to know what communications to address to which segments of the list to get the best response.

- **Establish a communications schedule.** The ease of sending email makes it tempting to send email whenever the firm feels like it. With the exception of important "breaking news" types of notifications, which should be rare, the organization should establish a mailing schedule and stick to it. Better yet, it should ask the subscriber for their preferences when they sign up. Then the marketer will send content that is relevant to the subscriber on the schedule they dictated. That is the way to make email welcome in the inbox.

- **Identify the target segment and communications objectives.** Each mailing should have its own specified target segment and specific objectives. Simply sending the same message to an entire list will not often be effective. Perhaps the business marketer is announcing a new product to users of that product line. The marketer of consumer credit cards may be delivering an offer of credit card protection insurance to new cardholders. The nonprofit marketer may wish to invite large donors and prospects to a special event showcasing the successes of the organization. The objective and the target segment must be a good fit and the single campaign must fit into the overall communications and marketing strategies. Specify the action you want the recipient to take. You may, for instance, give the prospective large donor the option of calling a special phone number or visiting a special landing page to respond to the invitation.

- **Write compelling copy.** Email copy should be only as long as is necessary to convince the recipient to take the desired action. Often this action will be to click through on a link to go to a particular page on the website, known as a landing page or microsite specific to that campaign. The target pages should be carefully examined to make sure they are consistent with the objectives and message of the email campaign. Writing short copy that persuades is not an easy task.

- **Structure your email to be received and opened.** In their effort to control spam, ISPs have set up filters in an attempt to remove the offenders. In the process, they capture many messages from legitimate marketers. The "from" header and the "subject" header are both important in this respect. The source must be clear and the subject descriptive.

- **Create links to further information.** One of the beauties of email, whether text or HTML, is that links to more detailed information, usually on the website, are easy. Copy has to be written around the concept of linking. The website and/or landing page must be examined to ensure that it is ready to receive visitors from the email.

- **Make it easy for readers to take action.** Marketers need to specify what it is they want recipients to do after the recipients click through to the site. Do they want the recipients to send for additional information? If so, create an email link, or better, a form that requests a small amount of information about the requester. Is the objective to persuade recipients to donate to a charitable cause? If so, the links to material on the site need to make the case for the contribution, with multiple opportunities to click through to the form that accepts the donor's information.

- **Test and revise the email.** Emails can and should be tested. Important things to test include the preheader, subject line, and the offer. A test can be mailed to only a selected segment of the target list using an A/B test. Testing is a powerful tool, and it should not be overlooked.

- **Measure results.** Email service providers supply the most common metrics—delivered, opened, and clicked-through are typical. Marketers can get more detailed results by creating special landing pages to receive click-throughs and then tracking them through the site. Results will also include maintenance issues like bounce-backs and unsubscribes. Detailed reporting is usually available with most email service providers.

- **Integrate learning into the next email program.** Most organizations today will find themselves doing another email campaign rather quickly. An ongoing challenge is how to use the results of one campaign to make the next one better. Some companies have developed formal programs for doing so, a subject that is covered in Chapter 5.

This list appears to be a rather formidable series of steps. However, the seasoned email marketer, with the support of a well-maintained database and suppliers of the necessary services, can develop and launch an email campaign in days, if not hours. The speed, the relatively low cost, and the ability to target and measure will only fuel marketers' interest in effective email marketing.

Designing an Effective Email Campaign

There are many types of emails, such as email newsletters, new product announcements, general marketing and advertising, alerts and reminders, and market research emails—all of which need to be designed according to the objective for each. Since email marketing has its roots in direct marketing, an email for promotions and discounting—which is the majority of emails that companies send out—should follow the basic rules of direct marketing. In other words, the email should have a clearly defined offer or call-to-action, with a time deadline, and should also use good web design principles as discussed in Chapter 6.

In addition, there are basic elements of design that are unique to emails themselves. These design elements are summarized in Table 11.2. A good promotional email includes a preheader (a short text blurb; the part of the email that displays after the subject line and is above the text or HTML of the email) and can include many items. Successful

Table 11.2 **Promotional Email Checklist** Source: © Cengage Learning 2013.

Email Element	Recommended Approach
Preheader	Link to online version of email, reminder of relationship, restates offer
Subject line	Short, include brand, call-to-action, urgency
Offer or call-to-action	Specific, clear, and meaningful
Time deadline, sense of urgency	Not only what the customer should do, but by when?
Web design principles	Above the fold, golden triangle
CAN-SPAM	Include reply-to and unsubscribe, and otherwise be compliant
Viral marketing	Include forward-to-a-friend as well as social media links
Social media	Integrate with popular sites on social media

preheaders restate and reinforce the offer provided, link to the online version of the email if the receiver cannot view the email, and perhaps include a short reminder of the relationship or an option to view on a mobile device.[13]

Although the preheader is important, the email subject line is often the determining factor in *open rates*. There is much debate over the email subject line and what is most compelling since what works most effectively depends on the product, the offer, and the customer. What works for B2C might not work in B2B marketing. In general, the subject line should be short, less than fifty characters, which is usually the number of characters displayed on an email system and generates a higher open rate. The email subject line should also include as much as possible the reason for the email, including a brief summary of the offer.

The email itself should clearly state the offer—and only including one offer is best. Sometimes you might see emails that try to cram in a lot of information and refer to several different offers with different time frames. Studies have shown that people get fatigued by multiple messages in the same email and tend to click through less as more competing messages are provided. The offer should include the time deadline, that is, when the offer expires and by when the action is expected. The email should also use good web design principles, including the most important information (e.g., the offer) appearing in the "golden triangle," the upper left triangle area where the user's eye spends most of its time. Another good web design principle to apply to email design is "above the fold." Above the fold is a simple concept adapted from newspaper publishing which suggests that the reader's eye is going to concentrate above the fold of a newspaper, which, in this case, is the area above where their web browser cuts off the email. Where the fold falls depends on the physical size of the monitor used, the resolution that the screen has been set to, and the type of browser used. As Figure 11.12 illustrates, the information available can vary greatly based on these criteria. It is a good idea to test emails on multiple web browsers before sending to ensure readability and clarity. Mobile marketing campaigns also mean that emails must be designed to be read and responded to on smaller screens on various devices.

Good promotional emails are also CAN-SPAM compliant and clearly state that the message is advertising or promotional in nature; they have a valid reply-to address and street address listed; and a valid opt-out or unsubscribe feature. (We will discuss CAN-SPAM more at the end of this chapter.)

Finally, a good promotional email takes advantage of word-of-mouth marketing and social media, including a forward-to-a-friend feature and the ability to post on the consumers'

open rates

number of opens divided by number of emails delivered (sent minus bounces).

Figure 11.12   **Above the Fold Viewing Dimensions** Source: © Cengage Learning 2013.

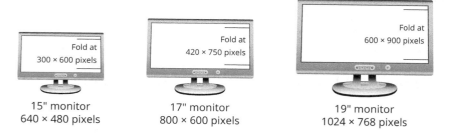

15" monitor
640 × 480 pixels

17" monitor
800 × 600 pixels

19" monitor
1024 × 768 pixels

social media accounts (which accounts depends on the consumers and where they "hang out" in social media).

Although we have focused on promotional emails, the design of other types of emails can be equally important. *Transactional emails* can be an overlooked source of marketing. *Welcome emails* typically have a higher open rate than traditional emails and can be used to up-sell and cross-sell as well as to leverage social media marketing. All these emails can benefit from the viral and social aspects of email marketing.

Figure 11.13 illustrates an email received by one of the authors that is a good example of all the elements discussed in this section. It makes good use of the preheader, provides

Figure 11.13   **Shein Welcome Email** Source: SHEIN

the offer in the golden triangle space, and has pertinent information above the fold. This email also has social media integration and is CAN-SPAM compliant, although it is missing a clear time deadline in the text of the email.

Figure 11.14 clearly shows an email offer of free shipping that expires in a certain time frame. It is simple in design and does not provide too many competing messages. Not all promotional emails illustrate the principles mentioned here. It could be that companies not using these principles are testing different approaches or it could be that they need to

Figure 11.14 **Hu Email Offer with Time Deadline** Source: Hu Products LLC

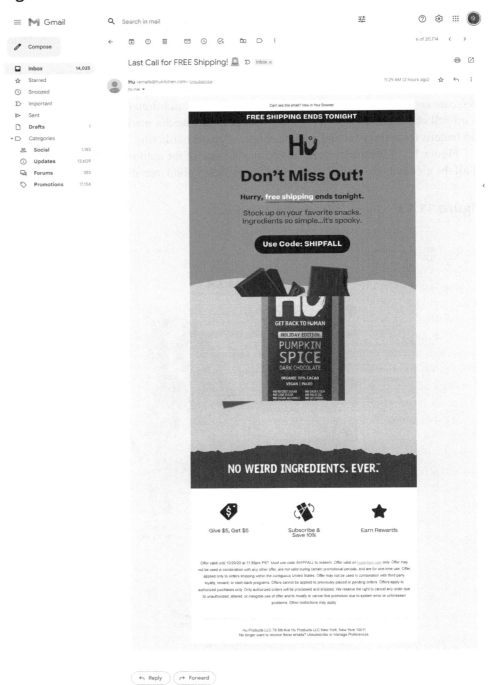

hire people who have taken an internet marketing course to help them with their email design. In any case, marketers will continue to test different approaches to determine what generates the best response.

Using Email Service Providers to Send Emails

There are a number of different choices in sending emails, but with any type of volume, it is usually wise to use an email service provider. An email service provider does several things for its customers, including helping with the design. First, though, most standard email packages have limits on the number of recipients for an email in an effort to avoid spam filters, so most email service providers can help figure out what will trigger a spam filter and get emails delivered. For example, the tried and true direct marketing offering of "free," which historically has delivered the highest response to direct mail campaigns, will trigger a spam filter at some ISPs.

Other benefits of using a service company for email include help in tracking and measurement, easy integration with a company's internal database and other software programs such as salesforce.com, and other marketing campaigns.

One of the key benefits of using an email service provider is usually the ability to integrate with a current database of customers and their transaction history. Integration with the database means that emails can be personalized to individuals and offers can be customized based on the data and interests of that particular customer. Dynamic content management is what allows Scotts Miracle-Gro Company to send out over 300 versions of its emails or Johnston & Murphy to customize its product offerings in its promotional emails. The content and greeting change per email, making it more personal and less like spam. When used wisely, dynamic content can increase the chances emails will be opened and responded to by the target consumer. Table 11.3 provides a summary of what an email service provider can do for a company.

Another major concern is timing—what time of day to send emails and on what date. The answer depends on the customer base. The best way to determine when people will answer emails is to test a few different days and times, using some common sense about the habits of the customers. In general, for business customers, Monday mornings and Friday afternoons are bad times to send email, with Tuesday mornings or afternoons often being preferred as people have gone through their inboxes the previous day. For consumer messages, weekends and evenings are preferred, but again, this timing depends on the targeted consumer and the product or service offered. Services like Mail Chimp will analyze the company's emails and provide suggestions for the best time to send email. Shockingly, the firm Tidio recommends that companies send emails between 3 AM and 7 AM as seen in Figure 11.15. During the COVID-19 pandemic, more customers started working from home and had more flexible work hours. Companies found that more customers began opening emails late at night (or earlier in the morning) than they were previously.[14]

dynamic content
ability to change greeting and other content dynamically based on to whom the email is addressed.

Table 11.3   Advantages of Email Service Providers

Help get emails delivered through ISPs
Aid in tracking, measurement
Provide database integration
Manage content dynamically
Integrate with social marketing, other campaigns

Figure 11.15 **Email Engagement Throughout the Day** Source: https://www.tidio.com/blog/best-time-to-send-email/

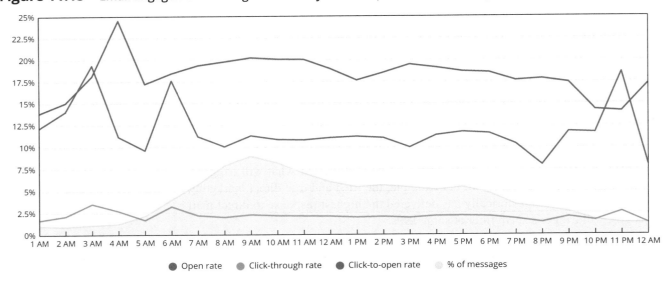

In addition, conventional wisdom in the area indicates that email programs that delivered less than one message a month experienced a higher bounce rate than programs with at least a daily delivery. So more frequent email can mean better delivery prospects because lists are more likely to be updated and consumers are expecting regular communications.

bounce rate
number of bounces divided by number of emails sent.

Email Campaign Dashboard Metrics

One of the biggest benefits of using an email service provider is the ability to track metrics such as click-through and open rates, and compare metrics across different offers (known as A/B testing from the direct marketing world). Email service providers (ESP) allow users to send email campaigns to a list of subscribers. ESPs make it much easier to tell which emails were effective. Figure 11.16 depicts an example analytics dashboard that uses MailChimp's data for multiple campaigns.

email service providers
allow users to send email campaigns to a list of subscribers.

As you can see, multiple campaigns are being analyzed at once. Because there are often multiple segments of customers receiving a separate customer journey email message, this dashboard allows the marketing manager to see how all of their customer segments reacted. It's possible that the messages differed by promotional discounts, messages about new products, regional differences, etc. For instance, over 200,000 emails were sent, and the open rate averaged 54 percent across campaigns. Campaign 6 had the most customers that opened the email, whereas Campaign 2 had the least number of opens. There is also a section that shows how many customers opted out of receiving email messages by clicking on "unsubscribe." This dashboard examines email open rates by unique open rates by campaign. The reason why marketing managers want to examine the overall open rate versus the unique open rates is because each time an email is opened it counts toward the total count of opens. By examining the unique open rates, the marketing manager can see how many unique visitors are opening the email. There are times when emails are initially skimmed—not read thoroughly—and at a later point in the day the customer opens the email again to read it more thoroughly. This dashboard provides an insight into how often customers are opening the email multiple times. The metrics are discussed in more depth below.

Figure 11.16 **MailChimp Email Dashboard** Source: https://www.zoho.com/analytics/mailchimp-advanced-analytics.html

Understanding the Basics of Email Dashboard Analytics

In the email dashboard, as depicted in Figure 11.17, we can see that of the emails sent, there was an overall 32.1 percent open rate, 10.3 percent click-through rate, 26 percent click-to-open rate, 10.1 percent unsubscribe rate, 8.2 percent hard bounce rate, and 12.76 percent soft bounce rate. Depending upon the ESP used (i.e., MailChimp, HubSpot, Constant Contact), their email analytics dashboard will look different from what is shown. Many of the ESPs also partner with third-party vendors to help make the company's dashboards customizable so that the marketing manager can view the company's specific KPI (key performance indicators). For instance, companies like Ubiq, Dasheroo, TapClicks, and Cyfe partner with ESPs to make customized dashboards for their clients.

To get a better understanding of the numbers in the dashboard, let us assume that the company emailed 8,000 subscribers. The total open rate tells us how many people opened the email. This is an okay metric but should be used for directional purposes when determining if the email was part of a successful campaign. How many times have you accidentally clicked on an email on your phone that you didn't mean to open? The open rate keeps counting—even for accidental opens. The click-through rate (CTR) calculates the number of clicks that an external link embedded in an email receives. It is a slightly better metric than the open rate, but it can be rather noisy. The CTR typically adds more noise (e.g., extra data that throws off the calculation of how well your campaign did) because it includes all clicks to the external links embedded in the email such as firewalls opening the links to check for malware, people forwarding the email to someone who clicks on the link, someone opening the email once on their desktop then again on their phone, etc. The CTR metric gets messy quickly.

The more accurate metric that will tell you how your email is performing is the click-to-open rate (CTOR).[15] The CTOR calculates the unique clicks that an email receives.

click-through rate
calculates the total number of clicks that an external link embedded in an email receives.

click-to-open rate
calculates number of unique clicks that an external link embedded in an email receives.

Figure 11.17   Email KPI Dashboard Source: https://ubiq.co/analytics-blog/top-5-email-marketing-kpi-metrics-email-marketers/

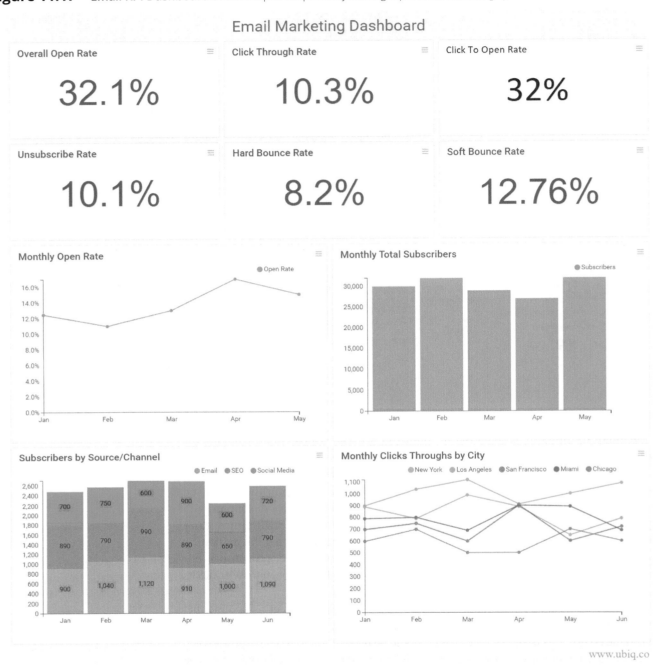

For instance, if you send a newsletter with multiple external links, your subscribers are likely to click on your email multiple times and on multiple devices to read your content. The CTR metric keeps tally of each click, which results in an inflated count. However, the CTOR considers who is clicking on the content as opposed to how many times it's being opened. Many digital marketing managers prefer to use the CTOR because it provides a more holistic view of how many people responded to the call-to-action in the email campaign (i.e., 30 percent discount, click on survey link). The CTR and CTOR are both good metrics to use, but keep in mind that they tell different stories. The CTR is a good metric to review to get a sense of email engagement because it takes into consideration the total number of times the subscriber interacted with the email. Alternatively, the CTOR is a good metric to use when the digital marketing manager wants to get a sense of how many people are interacting with the email campaign.

How to Calculate Open Rate, Click-Through Rate, Click-to-Open Rate

Using the example from 11.16, assume that the company emailed 8,000 subscribers and on average, 2,570 of these subscribers open the newsletter. Of those 2,570 subscribers who open the newsletter, about 825 click on an external link within the newsletter. The equations for each are listed below.

OPEN RATE: (2570 / 8000) * 100 = 32.1%
CTR: (825 / 8000) * 100 = 10.3%
CTOR: (825 / 2570) * 100 = 32%

Unsubscribes, Hard Versus Soft Bounce Rates

Moreover, the additional metrics that digital marketing managers keep track of in email campaigns surround the number of people that did not want or did not receive the email. For instance, in Figure 11.14 we see that the unsubscribe rate is 10.1 percent. The unsubscribe rate is the number of people who wish to unsubscribe from the company's marketing emails. If the email was sent to 8,000 people, that means that 808 people (8,000 * .101 = 808)unsubscribed from the company's email list. This number should cause quite a bit of concern to the digital marketing manager because that is a lot of people! Additionally, the hard bounce rate means the email address is bad or truly undeliverable, whereas the soft bounce rate means the email could not be delivered at that particular time, perhaps because of a system problem. In this particular example, this email list was rather poor.

Figure 11.18 illustrates activity over time on the MailChimp platform and we can see that this email was opened primarily within three days of delivery. In fact, most activity occurred within 24 hours of delivery, down from 48 hours just a few short years ago. This figure illustrates again that fast email response rates are critical in developing effective programs. If something does not work, a marketer can try another offer, list, or design to get the desired response from the customer and provide the information the customer needs.

unsubscribe rate
number of people who unsubscribe from the company's marketing emails.

hard bounce rate
when an email is undeliverable, usually due to a bad email address.

soft bounce rate
temporarily undeliverable, usually due to a system problem.

Figure 11.18   **Open Rates Decline after 24 Hours** Source: Mail Chimp.

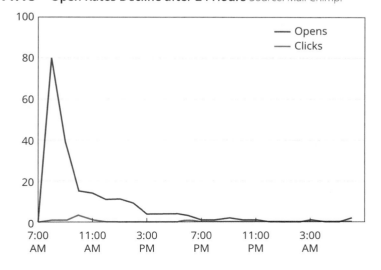

Targeting, Personalization, and Customization

As we discuss email marketing as a whole, we enter another semantic thicket: the differentiation between targeting, personalization, and customization. These three important terms are used often, in many contexts, with many shades of meaning—different authors often give different definitions.[16] The distinction between "personalization" and "customization" is especially fuzzy, with some authors using them interchangeably and some attempting to give more precise meanings. For the purpose of our discussion in the remainder of this chapter, we will give the terms the following meanings, which help tease out the specific ways in which marketers can use these techniques. These definitions were presented in previous chapters and they are still applicable:

- **Targeting** refers to directing marketing communications to individuals or businesses that have been identified as valid prospects for acquisition or retention for the good or service. Targeting can be visible, as when a marketer sends an email newsletter with personalized content to a customer who has permitted this type of communication. It can be invisible to the receiver, as when targeted ads are served onto a website without the visitor's explicit knowledge.

- **Personalization** involves the creation of specialized content for a prospect with a known profile by choosing from an array of existing content modules. In addition to the email newsletter just described, personalization occurs when a visitor registers on a website like Reddit and creates a list of personalized "subreddits" by choosing relevant content from extensive lists presented by the site.

- **Customization** is the creation of new content, services, or even products based on the needs and wants of an individual customer—either business or consumer. Internet marketers like Nike by You are offering the ability to customize products. Others like iTunes are offering customers the ability to customize their own user experience.

Note that this terminology defines customization rather tightly, calling into question the way in which the term is often used by internet marketers. Even so, there is still a gray area in which goods or services are configured to customers' orders from a standardized set of components or services. This type of customization is represented by manufacturing processes allowing for customized computers such as that pioneered by Dell and Nike By You as discussed in Chapter 4 and has been called "mass customization" in discussions in both the academic and trade press.[17]

With few exceptions, internet marketers are not engaging in customization at this level, and we can therefore center our discussion on targeting and personalization. In so doing, we are not missing any important marketing issues since the processes used to identify and reach prospective customers with offers for truly customized products are the same as the ones used to identify customers in order to target them with personalized content.

In fact, email personalization does appear to be related to increased email response rates. Campaign Monitor states that just using the recipient's name in an email subject line can increase response rate by 26 percent.[18] However, with this kind of claim it is important to understand that open and click-through rates are also dependent upon other factors. Open rates vary depending on the type of industry, a factor that can affect the influence of personalization.

The use of personalization in marketing is found to be compelling. Some research by White, Zahay, Thorbjornsen, and Shavitt[19] indicates that although personalization can yield higher response rates, consumers do not react well to highly personalized messages that are given too soon in the relationship. Too much personalization is usually considered creepy. For example, in 2019, the company Mother's Lounge purchased a "bad" direct mail list and sent cards with coupons to congratulate women on their pregnancies.[20]

The problem was that most of the women on the list were not pregnant and were "creeped out" that a company was targeting them for something highly personal.

When a marketing campaign is too personal, the consumer develops a response called "reactance" where the fit between the offer in the message and consumers' personal characteristics is not explicitly justified by firms. In other words, if Magnolia Bakery were to send an email based on highly personalized information (i.e., they knew the consumer's age before it was disclosed), it might turn customers off and decrease response. However, starting the consumer relationship with a 10 percent promotional discount is not viewed as threatening and is a better place to start the relationship. Figure 11.19 lists several benchmarks by industry type regarding email open rates. Notice that, in general, the open rates are relatively low. Working to increase open rates is often a top priority for an email marketer.

Figure 11.19   2022 Email Benchmarks by Industry Source: https://www.campaignmonitor .com/resources/guides/email-marketing-benchmarks/

Industry	Open Rates	Click-Through Rates	Click-To-Open Rates	Unsubscribe Rates
Advertising & Marketing	20.5%	1.8%	9.0%	0.2%
Agriculture, Forestry, Fishing, Hunting	27.3%	3.4%	12.5%	0.3%
Consumer Packaged Goods	20%	1.9%	11.1%	0.1%
Education	28.5%	4.4%	15.7%	0.2%
Financial Services	27.1%	2.4%	10.1%	0.2%
Restaurant, Food & Beverage	18.5%	2.0%	10.5%	0.1%
Government & Politics	19.4%	2.8%	14.3%	0.1%
Healthcare Services	23.7%	3.0%	13.4%	0.3%
IT/Tech/Software	22.7%	2.0%	9.8%	0.2%
Logistics & Wholesale	23.4%	2.0%	11.7%	0.3%
Media, Entertainment, Publishing	23.9%	2.9%	12.4%	0.1%
Nonprofit	26.6%	2.7%	10.2%	0.2%
Other	19.9%	2.6%	13.2%	0.3%
Professional Services	19.3%	2.1%	11.1%	0.2%
Real Estate, Design, Construction	21.7%	3.6%	17.2%	0.2%
Retail	17.1%	0.7%	5.8%	0.1%
Travel, Hospitality, Leisure	20.2%	1.4%	8.7%	0.2%
Wellness & Fitness	19.2%	1.2%	6.0%	0.4%
Average Totals	**21.5%** (+3.5%)	**2.3%** (−0.3%)	**10.5%** (−3.6%)	**0.1%** (−)

Email inboxes are crammed with spam, emails of dubious value to the recipient, and a small number of communications that are welcome and that have a good chance of inciting to action. There is an approach marketers can follow to give their emails the best chance of being opened and acted upon. These principles are often called the three "Golden Rs of Email Marketing."[21] They are as follows:

- **Relevance.** All content should be applicable to the recipient's needs and life-style. Content that is not relevant will not motivate the recipient to take action and it may tarnish the brand of the communicator.

- **Respect.** Relevant content cannot be generated without in-depth information about the recipient. In order to get the information and keep the trust of the recipient, the sender of emails must guard data against unwarranted or frivolous use.

- **Recipient control.** Go beyond simply obtaining permission to communicate with the recipient. Make the recipient an active partner in deciding what content they want to receive and how often they want to receive it. That gives the content a much better chance of being seen as valuable.

Following these three Rs will not only give the emails the best possible chance of success but it will also, over time, contribute to the creation of a brand that is trusted by the members of its target market.

Present and Future Email Marketing Laws

CAN-SPAM Act
the U.S. law regulating advertising and promotional emails.

Because email is open to abuse by spammers, phishers, and others who seek to dupe the unwary, legislation (in the United States the CAN-SPAM Act) was passed in an attempt to curb the worst abuses. *Phishing* is the process of using emails to obtain or "fish" for a consumer's personal information, usually financial. An example of a phishing email is shown in Figure 11.20. The subject line says that it is from Amazon.com

Figure 11.20 **What Is Wrong?** Source: © Cengage Learning 2013.

Subject line: Private Message from Amazon.com Accounts Management

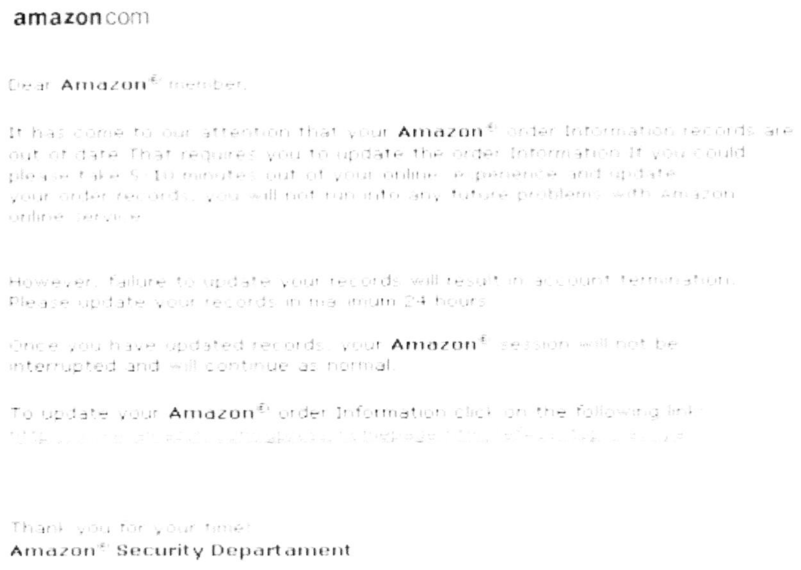

amazon.com

Dear Amazon® member,

It has come to our attention that your Amazon® order information records are out of date. That requires you to update the order information. If you could please take 5-10 minutes out of your online experience and update your order records, you will not run into any future problems with amazon online service.

However, failure to update your records will result in account termination. Please update your records in the mturn 24 hours.

Once you have updated records, your Amazon® session will not be interrupted and will continue as normal.

To update your Amazon® order information click on the following link.

Thank you for your time.
Amazon® Security Departament

accounts management and the text asks for the recipient's personal bank account information. When receiving emails that look suspicious, see if the emails are compliant with the CAN-SPAM Act, as discussed later. If there is a valid reply-to address, a valid street address, and an unsubscribe provision, the email is less likely to be a "phishing" expedition.

The law, officially named "Controlling the Assault of Non-Solicited Pornography and Marketing Act," was passed in 2003 by the U.S. Congress in an attempt to curb unsolicited and, especially, offensive email. Although it does not use the terms, it distinguishes between acquisition mailings by marketers and relationship mailings. Relationship mailings, or in the terms of the Federal Trade Commission (FTC), "a transactional or relationship message," are emails that facilitate a transaction or update an existing customer. As long as the content is not false or misleading, these emails are generally exempt from the provisions of CAN-SPAM. Acquisition or promotional mailings as we have been discussing here, however, come under the provisions of the law. It is wise to pay attention to the law since every separate email in violation of the law can be subject to a penalty of $16,000.[22]

According to the FTC website, the main provisions of the law are as follows:

- **It bans false or misleading header information.** Your email's "From," "To," and routing information—including the originating domain name and email address—must be accurate and identify the person who initiated the email.

- **It prohibits deceptive subject lines.** The subject line cannot mislead the recipient about the contents or subject matter of the message.

- **It requires that email give recipients an opt-out method.** You must provide a return email address or another internet-based response mechanism that allows a recipient to ask you not to send future email messages to that email address, and you must honor the requests. You may create a "menu" of choices to allow a recipient to opt out of certain types of messages, but you must include the option to end any commercial messages from the sender.

- **Any opt-out mechanism you offer must be able to process opt-out requests for at least 30 days after you send your commercial email.** When you receive an opt-out request, the law gives you ten business days to stop sending email to the requestor's email address. You cannot help another entity send email to that address, or have another entity send email on your behalf to that address. Finally, it is illegal for you to sell or transfer the email addresses of people who choose not to receive your email, even in the form of a mailing list, unless you transfer the addresses so another entity can comply with the law.

- **It requires that commercial email be identified as an advertisement and include the sender's valid physical postal address.** Your message must contain clear and conspicuous notice that the message is an advertisement or solicitation and that the recipient can opt out of receiving more commercial email from you. It also must include your valid physical postal address.

Commercial email service providers as we have discussed help marketers abide by the provisions of the law. Most of them seem straightforward, but some are difficult to implement if the marketer has a large list. This is especially true of the requirements for removing "unsubscribes" from the marketer's own list as well as those of any affiliates who may have been given access. If the list is to be rented, the unsubscribes must be meticulously purged from the rental list. Software that automates this process is desirable since errors must be avoided.

There are other practices specified as unacceptable in the FTC implementation guidelines. Most are practices not used by reputable marketers. These practices include harvesting of email addresses from other websites or a so-called "dictionary attack" in which the spammer uses computer algorithms to create email addresses and they change the letters in succession: for example, a.email@gmail.com; b.email@gmail.com; c.email@gmail.com.

Advocates of permission marketing argue that the requirements of the CAN-SPAM Act and other email marketing laws are simply good business practice. In fact, many of them would argue that they represent the minimal acceptable levels, not best practices. Some level of opt-in is considered more effective than opt-out. Many would go a step further, arguing that segmentation and personalization of content is a requirement for effectiveness. Permission marketers speak disparagingly of "blast" emails that are sent to all members of a list, regardless of the relevance of the content.

Privacy Laws and Their Effects on Email Marketing Worldwide

As data privacy concerns abound, various countries are passing laws to protect their consumers from nefarious businesses who seek to sell consumer data without the consumer's consent. These privacy laws influence the types of information that are required to be displayed in an email as well as dictating the level of consent required to send the email. Additionally, digital marketing serves a global audience. It is quite possible that many customers on a company's email list will be in various countries. The way some of these laws are written, particularly Europe's General Data Protection Regulation (GDPR), the citizen of the country is protected regardless of the country where they live. For instance, if a customer is an Italian citizen that lives in Buffalo, NY, GDPR protects them and any company that has their data can be fined for not complying with GDPR terms.

A key question that is guiding data privacy legislation is "who owns the data." GDPR was passed in 2018 as a way to give consumers ownership of their data back. The United States also has numerous state privacy laws that have either passed or are about to be passed. As of early 2023, the following states have their own privacy laws: California (known as the California Consumer Privacy Act- CCPA), Colorado, Connecticut, Virginia, and Utah.[23] Sixteen other states have their own bills written that will be voted on soon. These states are Hawaii, Indiana, Iowa, Kentucky, Maryland, Massachusetts, Minnesota, New Hampshire, New Jersey, New York, Oklahoma, Oregon, Tennessee, Texas, Vermont, and Washington. Please see Figure 11.21 to see a list of the state bills that are being debated.

To get a sense of what laws apply when sending emails, Figure 11.22 is helpful to get a sense of the major international laws that influence email marketing as well as the fines that are applied if the company violates the law. For instance, if a company violates GDPR compliance, they are subject to a fine of up to €20 million. According to the Italian Data Protection Act, if a company does not comply with the regulations of data transfer, the marketing manager can even be imprisoned![24]

Because there are so many laws to keep track of—and with more being implemented monthly—how can a modern marketing manager stay compliant? Modern ESPs will guide their clients toward ensuring that their emails comply with these ongoing

Figure 11.21   **U.S. State Privacy Legislation Tracker 2023** Source: https://iapp.org/media/pdf/resource_center/State_Comp_Privacy _Law_Chart.pdf

State	Legislative Process	Statute/Bill (Hyperlinks)	Common Name	Right to access	Right to correct	Right to delete	Right to opt out of certain processing	Right to portability	Right to opt out of sales	Right to opt in for sensitive data processing	Right against automated decision making	Private right of action	Opt-in default (requirement age)	Notice/transparency requirement	Risk assessments	Prohibition on discrimination (exercising rights)	Purpose/processing limitation
Laws Signed (To Date)																	
California		CCPA	California Consumer Privacy Act (2018; effective Jan. 1, 2020)	X		X		X	X			L	16	X			X
		Proposition 24	California Privacy Rights Act (2020; fully operative Jan. 1, 2023)	X	X	X	S	X	X		X	L	16	X	X	X	X
Colorado		SB 190	Colorado Privacy Act (2021; effective July 1, 2023)	X	X	X	P	X	X	X	X~		S/13	X	X	X	X
Connecticut		SB 6	Connecticut Data Privacy Act (2022; effective July 1, 2023)	X	X	X	P	X	X	X	X~		S/13	X	X	X	X
Virginia		SB 1392	Virginia Consumer Data Protection Act (2021; effective Jan. 1, 2023)	X	X	X	P	X	X	X	X~		S/13	X	X	X	X
Utah		SB 227	Utah Consumer Privacy Act (2022; effective Dec. 31, 2023)	X		X	P	X	X				13	X		X	
Active Bills																	
Hawaii		SB 974	Consumer Data Protection Act	X	X	X	P	X	X	X	X~		S/13	X	X	X	X
		SB 1110	Consumer Data Protection Act (C)	X	X	X	P	X	X	X	X~	X	S/13	X	X	X	X
		HB 1497		X	X	X	P	X	X	X	X~	X	S/13	X	X	X	X
Iowa		SSB 1071	(C)	X		X	P	X	X	X	X~		S/13	X		X	X
		HSB 12		X		X	P	X	X	X	X~		S/13	X		X	X
Indiana		SB 0005		X	X	X	P	X	X	X	X~		S/13	X	X	X	X
		HB 1554		X	X	X	P	X	X	X	X~		S/13	X	X	X	X
Kentucky		SB 15	Kentucky Consumer Protection Data Act	X		X	P	X	X		X~		S/13	X		X	X
Maryland		SB 698	Online and Biometric Data Privacy Act (C)	X	X	X	P	X	X	X	X~	L	S/13	X	X	X	X
		HB 807		X	X	X	P	X	X	X	X~	L	S/13	X	X	X	X
Massachusetts		HD 2281	Massachusetts Data Privacy Protection Act (C)	X	X	X	P	X	X			X	S/17	X	X	X	X
		SD 745		X	X	X	P	X	X			X	S/17	X	X	X	X
		HD 3263	Massachusetts Information Privacy and Security Act (C)	X	X	X	P	X	X	X	X~	L	S/13	X	X	X	X
		SD 1971		X	X	X	P	X	X	X	X~	L	S/13	X	X	X	X
		HD 3245	Internet Bill of Rights	X	X	X	P	X				X	16	X	X	X	X
Minnesota		HB 1367		X		X		X	X			X	13	X		X	X
		SB 950							IN		X	X	X		X		X
New Hampshire		SB 255		X	X	X	X	X	X	X	X~		S/13	X	X	X	X
New Jersey		A 505	New Jersey Disclosure and Accountability Transparency Act	X	X	X	X	X			X	X~	X		X		X	X
New York		SB 3162								X		X	13	X		X	
		A 3593		X	X	X	IN	X			X~	X		X	X	X	X
		A 3308	Digital Fairness Act (C)	X		X	IN	X	IN		X~		ALL	X		X	X
		S 2277		X		X	IN	X	IN		X~		ALL	X		X	X
		SB 365	New York Privacy Act	X	X	X	P	X	X	X	X	X		X		X	X
		A 2587	New York Data Protection Act	X		X								X		X	X
Oklahoma		HB 1030	Oklahoma Computer Data Privacy Act	X		X			X		X~			X		X	X
Oregon		SB 619		X	X	X	P	X	X	X	X~	X	S/13	X	X	X	X
Tennessee		SB 73	Tennessee Information Protection Act (C)	X	X	X	P	X	X	X	X~		S/13	X	X	X	X
		HB 1181		X	X	X	P	X	X	X	X~		S/13	X	X	X	X
Texas		HB 1844	Texas Data Privacy and Security Act	X	X	X	P	X	X	X	X~		S/13	X	X	X	X
Vermont		HB 121					P	X									X
Washington		HB 1616	People's Privacy Act (C)	X	X	X	IN	X	IN			X	S/13	X	X	X	X
		SB 5643		X	X	X	IN	X	IN			X	S/13	X	X	X	X

Figure 11.22 Email Laws Around the World Source: https://www.codetwo.com/guides/legally-compliant-emails

and updated laws. Figure 11.23 shows an example of an email that is compliant with international data laws. You will notice the similarity between this email format and the email format that is compliant with the CAN-SPAM Act. The key is to ensure the email campaign has the following information:

1. **Accurate header information:** the "From" line must clearly identify who the sender is. Spoofing—adding in a fake name—is not allowed.

2. **Avoid misleading subject lines:** The subject line should indicate what is in the email body.

3. **Full contact information:** The company that is sending the email must disclose the company name, phone number, email address, and postal address.

4. **Company identification:** The company must provide as much information about the company as possible such as license number, registered trade name, etc.

5. **Unsubscribe link:** This allows email recipients to opt out of receiving future emails from the email sender. Some countries require compliance with unsubscribing within ten business days.

6. **Confidentiality disclaimers:** This reduces the risk of privacy of confidentiality breaches.

Figure 11.23 **Example of Data Privacy Compliant Email** Source: Code Two

U.S. Federal-Level Privacy Legislation and Bilateral
Data Trade Agreements
==

The U.S. federal government has been working on writing a federal-level data privacy bill for many years. While several bills have been proposed, no law has been codified yet. Creating a federal-level privacy law reduces the likelihood that companies will have to comply with fifty different privacy standards—each of which would differ at the state level. The proposed American Data Privacy and Protection Act covers several areas of data privacy:[25]

- Consumer/individual privacy
- Health privacy
- Financial privacy
- Children's and educational privacy
- FTC authority and enforcement
- Government restrictions and obligations

If this bill is passed into law, regulation will most likely not be more stringent than the CAN-SPAM Act has already outlined. However, one additional area that is being legislated for is artificial intelligence. With the emergence of ChatGPT and other AI content creators, legislating AI will impact email marketers. Additionally, AI is often used to sift through the data to provide insights on the ESP dashboard. It is not clear when this legislation will pass, but email marketers will have to stay tuned to see how they are affected.

Additionally, in March of 2022, the United States and European Union (EU) formed the U.S.-EU Trans-Atlantic Data Privacy Framework (TADP Framework) as a bilateral trade agreement.[26] GDPR prevented data from being sent over to the United States without informing and receiving consent from the consumer whose data was being analyzed. For large multinational companies like Microsoft, Google, and Meta, this was a severe restriction in the way they conducted business. The EU views data privacy and the protection of personal data to be a fundamental right of its citizens. The United States has been selective on what data it protects and what it considers private (i.e., HIPAA protects healthcare data, FERPA protects student data). The TADP Framework was generated to ensure that data can move between the EU and the United States without any legal problems. TADP enables organizations based in the EU and/or United States to legally share information that includes customer or employee data, marketing information, fraudulent payments, proprietary algorithms, and competitive innovations without the fear of violating a European data privacy law.

The Vibrant Future of Email Marketing

Email marketing continues to be a valuable tool in the marketer's arsenal because of the high ROI, the ability to target and segment customers directly, and the ability to measure results. Some current trends are making email even more relevant today:

1. **Personalization.** Personalization will continue to improve as marketers use more than name and address. The next frontier of personalization will be truly one-to-one email marketing campaigns. AI can help add the name into the subject line, embedded in the design of the email. People open and react to email messages that are tailored to them.[27]

2. **Relevant segmentation.** Not only personalization but targeting content to highly segmented lists will continue to improve the success rate and the reliability of email marketing. Although many marketers are using segmented campaigns, having AI help create nano-segments is even more helpful. Consumers, particularly American consumers, prefer to be treated as individuals as opposed to being grouped together based on particular demographics.[28] The intersectionality of demographics is where AI-assisted segments can help. For instance, old-school demographics used to segment consumers into age, race, and gender. However, through the use of data analytics, email marketers can group people according to how they interact with the firm (i.e., use the store app, visit the store in-person, social media usage), their past purchases, and their engagement level. This sophisticated level of grouping people helps personalize their customer experience.

3. **Interactive email.** A type of technology that is still being tested is one that would allow for video content to be embedded in the email, in-email instant messaging, as well as embedding user-generated content (from reviews or social media posts) into emails that are relevant to the receiver.[29]

4. **Determining the ideal open time for each customer.** While many ESPs will indicate the best time to email a campaign, determining the ideal open time at

the individual level is on the rise. With the help of AI and a sophisticated ESP, each customer will be sent their email campaign depending on the times they most likely interact with the brand.[30]

5. **Machine learning and artificial intelligence.** Email will be brought to the next level as more ESPs adopt AI to help their clients produce the best-worded and most profitable email campaigns. Machine learning is a type of artificial intelligence and is the software code that is used to help the AI continually learn. As machine learning is incorporated into more software programs, email marketers will continue to gain more knowledge about their customers and their preferences.

6. **More customized email automation routines.** Email automation is used to nurture a customer while on a customer journey. As AI is integrated into the ESPs, there will be more customization of the types of emails that can help a customer along in their journey. Currently, marketers spend time mapping out the different types of customers and their journeys, but an AI-assisted automation tool will have a better sense of when the emails should get sent (how many days apart) as well as the content that they should contain.

Summary

The marketer's list of customer retention techniques is rich, varied, and growing. The challenge is to use the correct ones for the correct objective at the correct time and to do so in a fully integrated online and offline communications program. Emails can be used in conjunction with other communications channels such as direct mail and social media for powerful results.

Email marketing for customer retention offers several legitimate benefits. Not only can marketers contact consumers in a timely and more cost-effective fashion than other response mechanisms, but response is almost immediate, and offers and campaigns can be altered to increase response rate. Permission is the key to effective email marketing since email is marketing's version of a two-edged sword. Email has genuine benefits when used as part of an integrated permission marketing program. However, the volume of spam threatens to drown the efforts of legitimate marketers. Governments around the globe are attempting to stem the tide of spam.

The secret to effective email marketing, as with all direct techniques, is a good list, and in this case, permission-based lists are superior. Levels of permission range from opt-out to opt-in to double opt-in. Generally, a form of opt-in permission is considered to be most consistent with good email marketing practices. Good lists help decrease the bounce rate and increase click-through rates. Emails need to be designed with good web design principles in mind, compelling subject lines and offers, and need to take into account in their design the limitations of the computer screen on which they will be received.

Marketers need to offer the consumer the right to opt out or unsubscribe at any time, provide a physical address on their email and a valid reply-to email address, and otherwise comply with good email marketing practices as outlined in the CAN-SPAM provisions. Good campaign planning is critical to success and the ability to measure many aspects of response can allow the marketer to adjust the campaign accordingly in short order. Used properly, with a concern for relevance, respect, and recipient control, email can be a highly effective marketing tool. Increasing sophistication in marketing technology, including personalization, and email automation will ensure that emails will continue to be relevant, timely, and worth opening.

Discussion Questions

1. Why is email still a strong tool for internet marketers?

2. What is meant by permission marketing? Do you think it is an important concept to email marketers and if so why?

3. Think about email communications from marketers, perhaps some that you receive yourself. What makes them interesting and worth your time to open and

read? Do you ever take any action as a result of the emails? Why or why not?

4. What are the main benefits of using an email service provider? Say you are the head of a student organization and you need to regularly contact members, would you consider using an email service provider if the cost were within your budget? Why or why not?

5. What aspects of promotional email design would you take into account if you were designing an email to

invite students to a student organization meeting? Where would you put the most important information? What would be your call-to-action?

6. From your perspective, which of the newer privacy laws is likely to be the most influential on email marketing? Why is that?

7. What emerging trends in email marketing will be the most significant in the future?

Endnotes

1. JC Lupis, "3 Points about Consumers and Direct Mail," Marketing Charts, August 5, 2022, https://www.marketingcharts.com/cross-media-and-traditional/direct-mail-226611.

2. Christine Moorman, "Marketing in a Post-Covid ERA: The CMO Survey - September 2022," YouTube (September 13, 2022), https://www.youtube.com/watch?v=Nwcosu6ssPo&t=2s&ab_channel=DukeUniversity-TheFuquaSchoolofBusiness.

3. Jake Link, "10 Email Marketing Statistics You Need to Know (Updated 2021)," Constant Contact, December 13, 2022, https://www.constantcontact.com/blog/email-marketing-statistics.

4. Link, Jake.

5. Forrester, U.S. Email Marketing Forecast, 2009–2014.

6. Vaughan Reimers, Chih-Wei Chao, and Sarah Gorman, "Permission Email Marketing and Its Influence on Online Shopping," *Asia Pacific Journal of Marketing and Logistics* 28, no. 2 (March 2016), https://doi.org/10.1108/apjml-03-2015-0037.

7. Rebecca Knight, Ron Friedman, and Caroline Webb, "How to Spend Way Less Time on Email Every Day," *Harvard Business Review*, October 29, 2020, https://hbr.org/2019/01/how-to-spend-way-less-time-on-email-every-day.

8. "What's on the Other Side of Your Inbox - 20 Spam Statistics for 2022." Dataprot, accessed February 14, 2023, https://dataprot.net/statistics/spam-statistics/.

9. Dave Chaffey, "Average Email Open Rates for 2022 [Email Marketing Stats]." Smart Insights, January 23, 2023, https://www.smartinsights.com/email-marketing/email-communications-strategy/statistics-sources-for-email-marketing.

10. "What's on the Other Side of Your Inbox - 20 Spam Statistics for 2022."

11. Kevin Mogyoros et al., "Marketing Automation Case Studies: Email Marketing Case Studies," Sailthru, December 6, 2022, https://www.sailthru.com/customers.

12. Martin, Casey. "7 Tips for Integrating SMS into Your Email Marketing Campaigns." SparkPost, January 8, 2022. https://www.sparkpost.com/blog/5-tips-integrating-sms-email-marketing-campaigns.

13. "Lyris." Aurea Software, February 4, 2021, http://www.lyris.com/Email-marketing/535-Email-Preheaders-Work-So-Make-Them-Work-For-You.

14. Gosia, Szaniawska-Schiavo, "Best Time to Send Emails: What Fresh Studies & Practice Tell Us." Tidio, December 21, 2022. https://www.tidio.com/blog/best-time-to-send-email/.

15. "Email Click-through Rate: What You Need to Know to Succeed." CXL, August 29, 2022, https://cxl.com/guides/click-through-rate/email.

16. For a discussion of competing definitions see, "Is It Personalization or Customization?" Don Peppers and Martha Rogers, *Inside 1 to 1*, June 20, 2000, http://www.marketing1to1.com.

17. "The Four Faces of Mass Customization James H. Gilmore and B. Joseph Pine II, *Harvard Business Review* (January/February 1997), 91–101," *Journal of Product Innovation Management* 15, no. 2 (1998): 191-193, https://doi.org/10.1016/s0737-6782(98)90099-6.

18. "The Ultimate Guide to Personalized Email for Every Marketer." Campaign Monitor, December 22, 2021, https://www.campaignmonitor.com/resources/guides/personalized-email/.

19. Tiffany Barnett White et al., "Getting Too Personal: Reactance to Highly Personalized Email Solicitations," *Marketing Letters* 19, no. 1 (January 2007): 39–50, https://doi.org/10.1007/s11002-007-9027-9.

20. "'Questionable' Pregnancy Marketing Scheme Targets Women–Even If They're Not Pregnant." *CBS News*. CBS Interactive, November 6, 2019. https://www.cbsnews.com/news/pregnancy-marketing-questionable -scheme-targets-women-raises-privacy-concerns/.

21. Based on a concept suggested by Bill Nussey, *The Quiet Revolution in Email Marketing* (New York: iUniverse, Inc., 2004).

22. Alex Gaynor, "Can-SPAM Act: A Compliance Guide for Business." Federal Trade Commission, February 3, 2023, https://www.ftc.gov/tips-advice/business-center/guidance/can-spam-act-compliance-guide-business.

23. International Association of Privacy Professionals, accessed February 14, 2023, https://iapp.org/media/pdf /resource_center/State_Comp_Privacy_Law_Chart.pdf.

24. "Keeping Your Emails Legally Compliant: Infographic." www.codetwo.com, October 14, 2019, https://www .codetwo.com/guides/legally-compliant-emails.

25. Müge Fazlioglu, "U.S. Federal Privacy Legislation Tracker," accessed February 14, 2023, https://iapp.org /resources/article/us-federal-privacy-legislation-tracker/.

26. "U.S.-EU Trans-Atlantic Data Privacy Framework-Congress," accessed February 14, 2023, https://crsreports .congress.gov/product/pdf/IF/IF11613.

27. "The Future of Email Marketing: Data and Personalization." Business News Daily, accessed February 14, 2023, https://www.businessnewsdaily.com/7315-future-of-email-marketing.html.

28. "Our Choices May Be Making Us More Individualistic." ScienceDaily, September 30, 2021, https://www .sciencedaily.com/releases/2021/09/210930104832.htm.

29. "The Future of Email Marketing: Data and Personalization."

30. "The Future of Email Marketing: Data and Personalization."

Chapter 12

Content Marketing

Learning Objectives

By the time you complete this chapter you will be able to:

1 List reasons why content marketing is used more than traditional advertising.

2 Describe the definition of content marketing.

3 Summarize issues involved in content distribution.

4 Describe the content marketing strategy process.

5 List the benefits of using native advertising.

6 Explain the role of storytelling in content marketing.

7 Explain how technology will influence content marketing in the future.

Content Marketing Is More Than Entertaining Digital Content

Marketing expert Seth Godin is often quoted as having said, "Content marketing is the only marketing left."[1] And Godin adds, "Marketing is no longer about the stuff that you make, it is about the stories you tell."[2]

A similar refrain is heard from advertisers and their critics alike when they say that traditional advertising as we know it is dead. The web has totally upended the way marketers are expected to communicate with their target audiences. Professor Jennifer Rowley has a good comparison of the characteristics of traditional media and online media shown in Table 12.1.

The comparison makes it clear that information is the primary characteristic of online channels while push and image best characterize traditional media. People are tired of promotional content; they want information that helps them improve the quality of their lives. The number of communications channels has exploded and many of them give the smaller business an opportunity to be heard at an acceptable cost. The emphasis on information in digital channels and the importance of community building there means that transparency and trust are indispensable if content marketing is to achieve its goals.

In the roughly 25 years since Seth Godin made his famous statement content marketing has evolved. Instead of quantity of content, quality is more highly valued. Highly targeted distribution channels are expected. Above all, the entire content effort is driven by behavioral data from the web and marketing research that sheds light on the purchase journey. Creating an always-on content strategy that measures up to these standards and more is the subject of this chapter.

content marketing
strategic approach to creating
and distributing content.

Table 12.1 Comparison of Traditional and Online Media Channels Source: JOURNAL OF MARKETING MANAGEMENT, 2008, Vol. 24, No. 5–6, pp. 517–540. ISSN0267-257X print /ISSN1472-1376 online © Westburn Publishers Ltd.

	Traditional media	Online
Space	Expensive commodity	Cheap, unlimited
Time	Expensive commodity for marketers	Expensive commodity for users
Image creation	Image is everything Information is secondary	Information is everything Image is secondary
Communication	Push, one-way	Pull, interactive
Call to action	Incentives	Information (incentives)
Audience	Mass	Targeted
Links to further information	Indirect	Direct/embedded
Investment in design	High	Low, allows change
Interactivity	Low	Ranges across a spectrum from low to two-way dialogue

The history of content marketing dates back hundreds of years. Content marketing provides value to the consumer without directly selling the product to them. The earliest forms of content marketing date back to 1895 when Deere and Company began publishing *The Furrow* as a way to promote their John Deere brand. The Furrow, still in print today and read by millions across the globe, discusses current agricultural technologies as well as business trends.[3] The magazine sought to solve problems for the readers, build trust, and gain a following for the brand. It worked! Current examples of offline content marketing are AARP's (formerly known as the American Association of Retired People) way of connecting to their members who publish the *AARP Bulletin* and the *AARP Magazine.* As of 2021, the *AARP Bulletin* and *AARP magazine* are circulated to approximately 23 million people in the United States. These magazines are not overtly selling AARP to the readers, but they are providing a service by curating knowledge and disseminating it to their readers. Another example is Costco's magazine titled, *Costco Connection* which, as of 2021, was distributed to roughly 16 million people in the United States.[4] Both are examples of modern-day offline content marketing techniques that provide value to their members by telling stories, sharing insights about the industry and transferring knowledge to their members (aka followers).

What Exactly Is Content Marketing?

There is little agreement on what exactly content marketing IS and what it IS NOT. According to the Content Marketing Institute:

> Content marketing is the strategic marketing approach of creating and distributing valuable, relevant, and consistent content to attract and acquire a clearly-defined audience—with the objective of driving profitable customer action.[5]

Their definition highlights the fact that content marketing is part of overall marketing strategy. As such, content must be created with a specific, clearly-defined target audience in mind. The content must be useful to them—must resonate in their lives—and it must motivate them to take the actions the marketer calls for. That is good; isn't it enough? No, in order to accomplish the content marketing task, marketers need a content strategy. Here is a good definition that clarifies the difference:

> Content strategy deals with the planning aspects of managing content throughout its lifecycle, and includes aligning content to business goals, analysis, and modeling, and influences the development, production, presentation, evaluation, measurement, and sunsetting of content, including governance.[6]

In other words, content marketing is not just a bunch of people writing, filming, or otherwise creating content that they find interesting. It is an activity that is aligned with marketing and digital marketing strategy and carefully tracked and evaluated. That still leaves two interesting terms in the definition.

Sunsetting is obvious but not easy. Marketing content is not usually developed with an end date in mind. For example, if the content is the promotion of a branded marketing event, the promotion needs to have an end date—the date the event begins. However, good content marketing will transform the communications, both formal and informal, at the event into "evergreen" marketing content. Content should be so good and so relevant that is valuable for a considerable period of time—hence, "evergreen." At some point, however, specific points are no longer valid or, overall, the content is too old to be useful and, as such, reflects poorly on the brand. Who decides to take down that content? When? How? Sunsetting requires policy guidelines that specify these matters.

Governance is also a familiar term that has specific meaning when it comes to content marketing. Another definition:

> digital governance is 'a discipline that focuses on establishing clear accountability for digital strategy, policy, and standards.' In other words, digital governance gives organizations a way to manage content-related decisions that does not involve the seat of anyone's pants.[7]

Good governance, in content marketing or any other organizational activity, identifies the people or teams that make decisions. Decision-makers then need to get out of the way and let people do their jobs. Governance is not micromanagement, nor does it stifle innovation or creativity. One writer has a wonderful analogy:

> A small digital team, like a jazz ensemble, can get away with making things up as it goes along. A large team, on the other hand, needs to operate like a symphony orchestra … Improvising doesn't scale. A large team needs to follow standards just as an orchestra needs to follow sheet music.[8]

Content marketing represents a different way of thinking about marketing. One term that is used to describe that is "*always on*." In the early days of content marketing it was often said that "the marketing campaign is dead." Campaigns have a beginning and an end, while content has an indefinite life span. As content marketing has matured brands have learned to treat the two separately, with content marketing as an ongoing, permanent activity—always on. Marketing campaigns are used as highlights—a new product introduction or an appeal to a new market segment for example.

Just as content marketing itself has evolved, content marketing activities within an organization mature. We will return to that issue as we discuss content marketing strategy. First, however, let's take a quick look at the growing role and importance of content marketing.

There has been much discussion over what "counts" as content marketing over the years. A helpful tool titled the "Content Marketing Matrix" created by Dave Chaffey at Smart Insights finds that content typically falls into a 2 × 2 matrix: purchase intent × engagement as seen in Figure 12.1.

As you can see in the upper left corner of the matrix, the goal is to *entertain* consumers by creating awareness with products that have an emotional undertone (i.e., dating websites, fitness plans, etc.), the content that fits best is interactive, with quizzes, viral videos, competitions, etc. This will likely get consumers to think about the brand in a more unified manner because they are invested in learning more about it. In comparison, in the lower left corner of the matrix, the goal is to *educate* consumers. With this type of content, firms want to create awareness with products that are more rational (i.e., investment trends as they relate to the economy). These types of topics work better with infographics, guides, and trend reports.

Furthermore, as you can see in the upper right corner of the matrix, sometimes the goal is to *inspire* consumers. This is when the company is trying to encourage an emotional purchase (i.e., anti-aging skincare products, impulse items). Celebrity endorsement in content marketing is turning commonplace in social media. Some of the more successful campaigns include musician Travis Scott teaming up with McDonald's to create "The Travis Scott" meal (a medium Sprite, a quarter pounder with bacon, and fries with barbecue sauce).[9] Or Shaquille O'Neal teaming up with Papa John's to create the Shaq-a-Roni pizza.[10] When this topic occurs, the firm should consider adopting celebrity endorsements, celebrity cameos, and community forums to help create buzz. Finally, in

Figure 12.1 **Content Marketing Matrix** Source: Chaffey, Dave. "The Content Marketing Matrix." Smart Insights, November 4, 2022. https://www.smartinsights.com/content-management/content-marketing-strategy/the-content-marketing-matrix-new-infographic/.

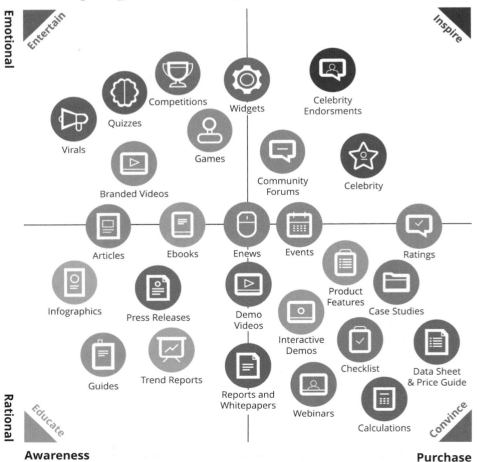

the lower right corner of the matrix, when the goal is to *convince* consumers to purchase a rational product (i.e., life coaching services, insurance, etc.) running a webinar, creating checklists, calculators, etc. are more helpful content pieces.

Who Uses Content Marketing—What and How Much?

A 2022 study by HubSpot showed that[11]:

- 90% of marketers are using content marketing.
- 66% of marketers expect their budget to increase for more content marketing.
- Over 60% note that they consider their content successful by measuring their sales conversions.
- Primary goals for content marketing are: brand awareness, increasing sales, and increasing engagement.
- Successful content marketing achieves: brand awareness, building credibility and trust, and educating audiences.
- The top challenges with content marketing are: creating content that generates leads, finding ideas for new content, and creating content that receives high levels of online engagement.
- Google's search algorithms are trying to transcend text to images, voice/podcasts, and videos.
- Video is the number one format marketers used in their content strategy in 2021.
- The top four formats marketers leverage in their content strategy are videos, blogs, images, and infographics.
- The top technologies B2B organizations use to supplement content marketing are analytics tools, social media publishing, and email marketing software.
- The top three owned media content distribution channels for B2B marketers are a personal website, blog, and email newsletter.

Does it surprise you to see B2B marketers spending more on most aspects of their content marketing? Business marketers have a pressing need to inform their customers and prospects, and content marketing is the answer. B2C markets are increasingly realizing the need to inform their customers but they use more expensive—and entertaining—tools.

B2B and B2C content marketers have somewhat different objectives. Top objectives for B2B marketers are:

- Lead generation
- Sales
- Lead nurturing
- Brand awareness

  B2C content marketers prioritize

- Retention and loyalty
- Engagement.

The differences are less in final objective—sales—than in approach; lead generation and conversion in B2B and direct attempts at conversion in B2C. The longer sales cycle in B2B is another explanation for the slightly higher usage of content marketing in B2B. Considering the different purchase journeys, you might expect to find the content that works for B2B versus B2C marketers is also somewhat different.

Among the questions Joe Pulizzi of the Content Marketing Institute and Ann Handley of Marketing Profs ask in their annual benchmarking survey is what types of content marketers use. Are you surprised that social media is at the top of the list for B2B? Case studies and blogs rank high in usage; B2B customers are looking for detailed, product-specific information and these are two good tactics to convey it. So are e-newsletters and in-person events.

The importance of content marketing in B2B is documented in a highly-cited research article by Professors Geraint Holliman and Jennifer Rowley. The authors offer a definition of B2B content marketing that reinforces the importance of achieving business goals:

> B2B digital content marketing involves creating, distributing and sharing relevant, compelling, and timely content to engage customers at the appropriate point in their buying consideration processes, such that it encourages them to convert to a business-building outcome.[12]

They also point out that most discussions of B2B content marketing focus on unpaid content, although there are important types of paid B2B content. When they add social digital content to the framework it becomes an important way of understanding B2B content. Figure 12.2a outlines the types of content in the B2B space. Figure 12.2b outlines the effectiveness of content in the B2B space.

The picture that is emerging is that of a complex, labor-intensive process. What is required to establish and perpetuate an always-on content marketing strategy?

The Content Marketing Strategy Process

An underlying theme of this book is that marketers need strategies and plans to guide their efforts. Otherwise, there would be no effective marketing—just marketing chaos. That is just as true for content marketing as for any other sub-discipline of marketing. However, the discussion frequently becomes confusing because people do not clearly distinguish between content marketing strategy and content strategy. Content strategy is a broader activity and, as such, may be one foundation for content marketing strategy. Exhibit 12.1 pinpoints the origin of content strategy in web development, gives a working definition, and lists the characteristics of good content.

The distinction is important. The remainder of this chapter will concentrate on content marketing strategy, which is a key job of today's marketing professionals.

Figure 12.2a   **Types of Content Used in B2B** Source: http://contentmarketinginstitute .com/wp-content/uploads/2015/09/2016_B2B_Report_Final.pdf.

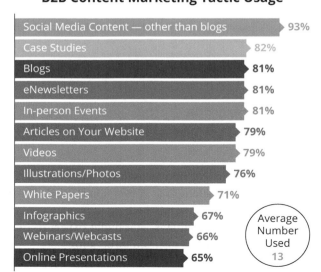

B2B Content Marketing Tactic Usage

Tactic	Usage
Social Media Content — other than blogs	93%
Case Studies	82%
Blogs	81%
eNewsletters	81%
In-person Events	81%
Articles on Your Website	79%
Videos	79%
Illustrations/Photos	76%
White Papers	71%
Infographics	67%
Webinars/Webcasts	66%
Online Presentations	65%

Average Number Used 13

Figure 12.2b **Effectiveness of Types of B2B Content** Source: http://contentmarketin ginstitute.com/wp-content/uploads/2015/09/2016_B2B_Report_Final.pdf.

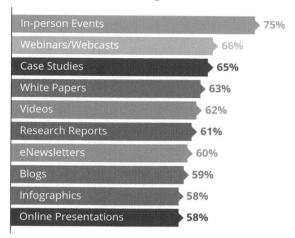

Effectiveness Ratings for B2B Tactics

In-person Events	75%
Webinars/Webcasts	66%
Case Studies	65%
White Papers	63%
Videos	62%
Research Reports	61%
eNewsletters	60%
Blogs	59%
Infographics	58%
Online Presentations	58%

Exhibit 12.1 describes content marketing strategy as an ongoing process, never a static document. The world in which marketers create content is constantly changing. The context in which users consume that content is constantly changing. The technology by which the content is distributed is constantly changing. In the midst of all this, marketers must create, refine, evaluate, and further refine the content that tells the brand story. That requires the guidance of a documented content strategy. Content marketing is still in the early days and the CMI benchmark studies found that less than 40 percent of marketers had a documented (i.e., written) strategy while just under 50 percent had a verbal-only content marketing strategy.[13,14] Figure 12.3 illustrates the types of B2C content that often work best. The reader should note, though, that content creation is often context-dependent. For instance, a sneaker company will create different types of content than a record label.

Exhibit 12.1 Content Strategy

There is a distinction between content strategy and content marketing strategy but discussions often do not make that clear.

Content strategy is an integral part of website design, defining how an organization's content shapes user experience with the brand. It often is used in reference to other kinds of digital communications, but it originated with website developers.

Author Erin Kissane says that the golden rule of content is to *"Publish content that is right for the user and for the business."*

Then Kissane goes on to explain the nature of content strategy:

"There's really only one central principle of good content: it should be appropriate for your business, for your users, and for its context. Appropriate in its delivery, in its style and structure, and above all in its substance. Content strategy is the practice of determining what each of those things means for your project—and how to get there from where you are now."

Content that is right is:

- Right for the user and the user's content—what are the user's goals, what is the user doing, thinking, and feeling?
- Right for the business and its objectives
- Useful in achieving the goals of both viewer and business
- Reflects how users think and talk about the subject
- Clear and easy to understand
- Consistent in presentation
- Concise
- Supported by information and data
- Updated as necessary.

Adapted from http://alistapart.com/article/a -checklist-for-content-work

Figure 12.3 Effectiveness of B2C Content Types Source: http://contentmarketinginstitute.com/wpcontent/uploads/2015/10/2016_B2C_Research_Final.pdf.

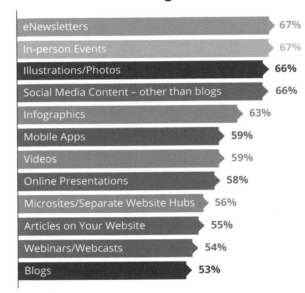

Effectiveness Ratings for B2C Tactics

eNewsletters	67%
In-person Events	67%
Illustrations/Photos	66%
Social Media Content – other than blogs	66%
Infographics	63%
Mobile Apps	59%
Videos	59%
Online Presentations	58%
Microsites/Separate Website Hubs	56%
Articles on Your Website	55%
Webinars/Webcasts	54%
Blogs	53%

One way to think about content strategy is to use the Reach, Act, Convert, Engage (RACE) principle as depicted below in Figure 12.4. Additionally, Figure 12.5 illustrates the overall big picture of content strategy. The RACE principle helps the digital marketer think through the steps of the content strategy process. Using the RACE method helps content creators to make sure that they are thinking about their topic comprehensively. Many marketers think it is easy to create content, and to an extent it is easy to make content,

Figure 12.4 The RACE Framework for Content Marketing Source: https://www.smartinsights.com/content-management/content-marketing-strategy/the-content-marketing-matrix-new-infographic/

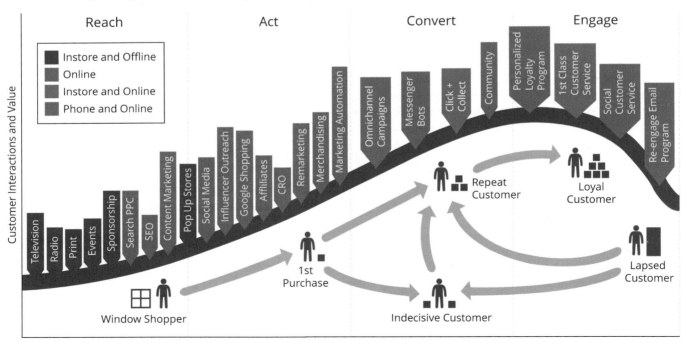

Figure 12.5 The Content Marketing Strategy Process

but making content that connects to the audience is much more difficult. The following framework helps content creators think through the process.

So, a lot of marketers believe they have a content strategy; it just isn't written down. Is that dangerous for an essential marketing activity?

Creating Content

The first step in the strategy process is to create content. There are several ways of looking at the content marketers have available.

Sources of Content

There are three basic ways in which marketers obtain content. Marketing teams can:

- Create the content themselves, which is labor-intensive but hopefully produces high-quality, relevant content.
- Curate content, which is basically locating good content from other publishers and publishing all or part of it with an explanation to your audience about its relevance.
- Purchase syndicated content, a traditional publishing model in which content from a recognized source is republished, usually for a fee. There are several networks that specialize in syndicating marketing content.[15]

curate
to select and prepare content from other sources for publication.

syndicated
content from another source published under license.

Despite laws governing digital content marketers need guidelines and best practices for curating content. Figure 12.6 offers a roadmap for curating a blog post.

Notice that the new title is a search issue; do not confuse the new post with the original one. The new image is more a copyright issue; images are a problem, and it is better to use one whose origin and permission requirements are known. Obviously, the writer is going to link to the original post, but the majority of the text is commentary which links the original ideas to those of the writer's blog and puts them in context for their audience. A really good quote is essential both for the readability of the post and for search results. (The curated post will of course follow all the other requirements for effective SEM including use of keywords and tagging.) Finally, there should be a call to action. Notice that the call-to-action (CTA) in this post is the download of an ebook, which should be related to the subject of the curated post if it is to be effective.

Figure 12.6 Best Practices for a Curated Blog Post Source: Curata

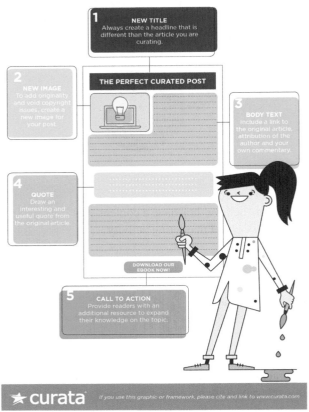

There are two things in Figure 12.6 that good content marketers do automatically. The Curata logo is part of the image, so it is captured along with the image when someone else uses it. They also have a "please cite us" statement which is a reminder to be polite along with the implication that their content is available for public use.

Hootsuite points out that effective social media marketing (SMM) requires a substantial amount of outside content and recommends a Rule of Thirds:

- One-third of content should directly promote your business.
- One-third of content should share content of thought leaders and like-minded businesses in your industry.
- One-third should be brand-building content.

Hootsuite makes content curation a formal part of its content marketing. Each week it does a blog post "This Week in Social" and sends an email newsletter to subscribers with the best blog posts of the week.[16]

If curated content sounds like a lot of work, it is. However, it is considerably less work than thinking of a great idea and writing from scratch. If you choose well, the curated content is likely to be effective in helping you meet business goals. It also may help you make content with influencers and thought leaders if you do the curation in a professional manner.[17] Marketing platforms like Hootsuite are helpful to prepare the best-curated content.

Types of Content

Basic content types are shown in Figure 12.7 as a pyramid. The large foundation of the pyramid is made up of high frequency/low effort types of content while the top is made up of in-depth publications that provide detailed customer assistance. B2C and B2B marketers use somewhat different mixes of content types in spite of the differences in effort.

The core content at the top level of the pyramid is made up of the insights and research your brand has developed. More importantly, it must embody the mission and values of the business. "Where Marketers Go to Grow," for example, provides the core concepts and a great many specific ideas for content at the lower levels. For instance, research reports provide almost limitless content opportunities ranging from videos and slide shows to infographics and blog posts. Blog posts often have "tweet this" boxes with some of their better quotes. Even pdf research reports can have "tweet this," which is a powerful way to make content shareable.

The middle three rows of the pyramid, the derivative assets, are directly derived from the core content. They allow for more focused, more frequent, and perhaps more targeted pieces of content. They also lend themselves to visual images and videos that many users find more engaging than lengthy text. They improve reach as well as frequency because the basic content can be repurposed for a variety of channels—a blog with an embedded video which is then posted to YouTube or an infographic that is constructed from the data in a long set of slides. Content marketing has a voracious appetite, and successful repurposing for various channels is essential.

The high-volume promotional content at the bottom comes, in many cases, directly from the levels above but it also provides many other marketing opportunities as we learned

Figure 12.7   **Types of Content by Effort and Frequency** http://www.curata.com/assets /sales/Curata_Content%20Marketing%20Pyramid_v01.pdf.

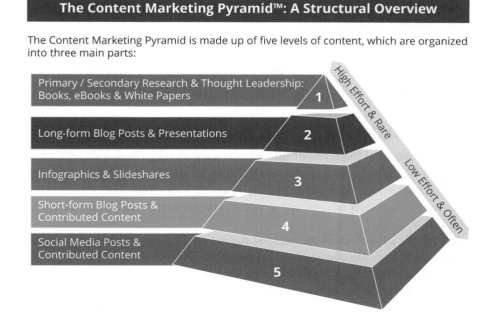

in Chapter 5. It can be timely, appeal to emotion or humor, and is the best type of content for humanizing the brand in the eyes of its target audience. All that is very good—as long as it stays on mission as defined by the values and the message themes of the core content.

Another important way of looking at content uses stages in the customer purchase process and an emotional/rational continuum to classify content. The matrix in Figure 12.1 has stages of the purchase process across the horizontal axis and emotional/rational content on the vertical axis. It then identifies the marketing role of the content in each quadrant:

- To *entertain* is an emotional, early purchase stage activity. It aims to reach potential customers and create awareness. It includes traditional marketing activities such as brand advertising and interactive ones such as games.

- It also lists viral content. The marketer should be aware that when a piece of content goes viral it is much more a case of luck than of skill. There are many lists of viral content and most of the content is not branded content. In 2022, the most viral moments were the Amber Heard vs. Johnny Depp defamation suit trial, Queen Elizabeth II's death, and Will Smith smacking Chris Rock at the Oscars.[18] Marketers would be wise to set their objectives in terms of shareable content, not viral. Some digital publishers have gotten very good at that. BuzzFeed is one; one analysis showed that 65 percent of its viral articles are its famous listicles.[19] You might recognize listicles as the types of articles that state, "Top 7 Reasons How You Waste Time When You Brush Your Teeth." These titles appear like "clickbait" but they are content that appeals to consumers and are easy to share. Other publishers have become good at shareability such as the Huffington Post, which published a large-scale study of the subject.[20]

- To *persuade* is an emotional, late purchase stage activity. In that quadrant, you see celebrity (or influencer) endorsements and the very powerful customer reviews.

- To *educate* is a rational, early purchase stage activity. The chart lists webinars and guides. An important addition would be informative videos. Google is reported to have found that 55 percent of consumers use video in their pre-purchase research.[21]

- To *convert* a visitor to a customer is a rational, late-stage activity. As such this quadrant contains informative content such as demos and testimonials. This quadrant might have included videos also, especially the DIY type popularized by brands from home improvement stores to makeup.

There are some popular types of content that are in the middle between emotional and rational that run from blogs to case studies.

The marketer truly has a dizzying array of content from which to choose. That is why it is so important to be guided by the core mission and values of the brand. With those firmly in mind, the marketer can develop a content strategy and plan and learn from the advice about specific kinds of content that is plentiful on the web.

Identify and Develop the Target Audience

Marketers know well the types of information used to segment and target customers: demographics, lifestyles, and media use. The bare statistics—although readily available from online behavioral data and marketing research both online and offline—are cold. Consequently, marketers have turned to buyer personas to put flesh on the bare bones of the statistics.

In Figure 12.8 you meet the persona named "Kyle Fisher." Fisher is a marketing manager who struggles to find good content writers. When you read the persona, you should, indeed, feel that you have met this consumer. That is the purpose of the persona—not only to make a hypothetical person feel real but to give life to an entire target market segment.

Figure 12.8 **A B2C Buyer Persona** Source: https://digitalmediaintelligence.com/buyer-persona-examples/

Kyle Fisher - Potential Drake Motors Small SUV Buyer

Personal Profile
Kyle is a 42-year-old and owner of a late model Ford Escape.

He's an active father of two, still plays team sports and is always connected to friends and family through the internet and his mobile phone.

Kyle is looking for a vehicle that offers outstanding fuel economy since he commutes approximately 90 miles round trip each day.

He's also considering the Ford Escape Hybrid, Toyota Highlander, the Honda CR-V and the Ford Flex.

He uses a variety of review and third party print research sites in addition to dealer catalogs.

Background
• 42-year-old caucasian male
• Father of two
• Plays drop in hockey 3 mornings a week
• Uses vehicle daily for commuting, picking up kids from sports, weekend coaching and vacations
• Drives long distances and puts 20,000 miles on vehicle every year

Attributes
• Upper Middle class
• Smartphone and laptop user
• Influenced by online reviews, heavy user of print
• iPod and Smartphone user
• Spends time reading in social media researching, but less time contributing

El Nariz/Shutterstock.com

"I want a vehicle with outstanding fuel economy, smart features and enough space for me and my family."

Kyle's Product-Content Needs
• Information supporting fuel economy
• Photos and video that highlight vehicle's technology and styling features
• Guidance, education and reassurance that the brand can be trusted
• Competitive comparisons to his current vehicle
• Ability to gather and share information easily

From Existing Assets
• Running Footage
• Still Photography
• Build Your Own Material
• Catalog Images
• Longform video
• 'Other' Images

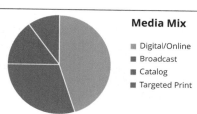

Media Mix
■ Digital/Online
■ Broadcast
■ Catalog
■ Targeted Print

Developing a buyer persona is not an exercise in creative writing, however. It is an exercise in gathering the right data, drawing insights from the data, and creating a believable human story around it. A word of caution—much of the content you will find on personas deals with B2B personas. That is an important topic to which we will return in Chapter 13. The process described for B2B personas is similar to that for B2C but it has more steps, some of which are irrelevant to the B2C case, and that can throw you off if you are not careful. Learn from the B2B process, but be wary of the differences.

The steps in developing a B2C customer persona are as follows:

- Develop the personal profile. The data is likely to be available in the business's marketing database or its metrics program—Google Analytics or another.

- Give the person a relevant but hypothetical name that doesn't produce any predispositions about the person.

- Include a photo.

- Financial status and preferred payment methods. There is a substantial amount of secondary data available on the finances of various cohorts of generational groups, one of which your persona should fit into.

- Describe "a day in the life."

- Describe the hopes and dreams of the persona.

- Also describe worries and fears.

- Explain how the persona interacts with and uses technology.

- Provide a social media profile.
- What information the persona finds influential.
- What are the current brands used?
- Add a quote that sums up the persona.[22]

Various tools can help you build a persona. One tool to note is HubSpot's persona builder (https://www.hubspot.com/make-my-persona) which walks the user through various questions to help build a persona. Keep in mind that the purpose of writing a persona is so that the proper target audience is reached. For instance, if you are creating an email campaign that targets folks 65+ as well as another email that targets folks who are 18–24, the consumers who are 65+ will not respond in the same way as those who are 18–24. As an example, think about your grandparents or someone who is of grandparent age (i.e., most often someone who is 55+). They are most likely NOT going to buy concert tickets to see the next Bad Bunny performance. They are not excluded from attending the next Bad Bunny concert or even buying a ticket, but a smart marketer should probably not spend money on trying to recruit them to attend the concert. On the other hand, thinking through an email campaign that targets 18–24-year-olds who are located near cities where Bad Bunny is touring makes more sense. Personas help marketers walk through these questions before they start a campaign and can help save a lot of time, money, and frustration.

The persona in Figure 12.8 covers most of these topics but not all. It may have been done from a persona template that was designed specifically for automobile purchases. That would make it more focused than the broader template just described.

Once a persona has been developed to characterize the nature of the target market the work of audience development begins.

audience development
creating a loyal following for branded content.

The term audience development represents another seismic shift in the post-advertising era. The advertising model is to reach people with promotions and convince them to buy. The audience development model is to create a community of people who are loyal subscribers to the brand's content. The term has long been used in nonprofit marketing, for obvious reasons, and has been popularized by content marketers. One manifestation of this approach is the creation of email lists discussed in Chapter 11, "Developing an Email Campaign." Creating an email list requires that people first become aware of the brand and its content, then opt-in to join the list and, over the long run, find the emails relevant and interesting enough to continue with the subscription. Email lists are a powerful marketing tool—if used in the proper manner to facilitate an ongoing relationship with the customer.

Just as in traditional advertising, the goal of the early stages of audience development is to reach as many people as possible—with content, not promotional messages. The content must be persuasive enough to get them to take action—to join an online community, to subscribe to an email list, or increasingly to permit push messaging. The content must be engaging and relevant to the early stages of the purchase journey. Is that enough? Probably not. Even well-known brands with a great story to tell, like Red Bull, need promotional help to build their audience.

As the customer begins to move through the purchase journey a nurturing approach is required. Customer Journey mapping, which is discussed in much more detail in Chapter 4, walks marketers through the steps to ensure that the customer's experience is nurtured along the way through the use of various types of emails and social media posts.

Select and Optimize Distribution Platforms

Figure 12.9 gives an overview of the content *distribution* process that illustrates what we have just described. It shows a basic set of platforms including the brand hub: either

Figure 12.9 **Native and Sponsored Content on Platforms** Source: https://contently
.com/strategist/2015/12/17/state-of-content-marketing-2016/.

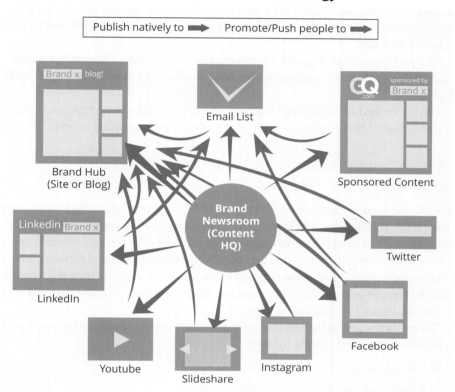

a website or a blog. It includes email, sponsored content on what could be thousands of
websites, blogs, and other properties, and several social media platforms.

There are several important ideas in this graphic. The first is that most of the content
is designed to drive people to the brand hub (purple arrows—the arrows pointing from
each platform to the brand hub/blog) where they can take some action such as purchasing a product. The green arrows indicate the converse perspective. The green arrows
point from the brand newsroom towards each platform. In that process, there is another
term used—call it native content. That means publishing content in a format that is
appropriate for that channel, tweeting a link to an Instagram video, for example. That
is also called repurposing of content. "Native" is an important term and we will return
to it later in the chapter.

Choosing platforms and sites on which to distribute content is not easy, even when
guided by a strong audience definition, because there are so many options to choose
from. Choosing the best set of channels with which to reach your target audience is the
optimization step.

The advice centers around beginning with the brand's owned channels. Most brands
have a website and a blog and a few social media channels including perhaps a Facebook
page, Twitter account, and a YouTube channel. Red Bull lists nine video channels on its
YouTube page along with a TV channel for first-run films and videos. A brand can have
a great deal of owned media, but it takes a great deal of effort, money, and usually a lot of

native content
a paid advertising format where
the content matches the content
of the media where it appears.

help from user-generated content to keep multiple channels viable. It also takes a large audience to make them worthwhile.

Then work on getting as much earned content as you can with reasonable effort and cost. That leaves paid content to fill out the picture—to be sure that the content is reaching the target audience. Paid channels provide a great deal of control and work quickly, more reasons why paid placements have become an essential part of content marketing strategy.

The process of selecting and optimizing platforms for distribution has a huge role in audience development and marketers need to carefully match channel to audience persona.

Having created and distributed relevant content to identified target audience segments, marketers must then measure the success of their content marketing efforts.

Monitor Conversations and Evaluate Content Marketing Effectiveness

We discussed the importance of monitoring social media conversations for content and tone in Chapter 5. It is important to listen to the conversations that surround brand content to gain insights about what can make content more effective. Marketers also need to monitor their content for amplification—the degree to which content is shared by users. There are social media tools to measure sharing and it is a feature of many metrics platforms. How much the content is shared tells the marketer a lot about how effective it is, but it is not the only important type of content metric.

There is a fair amount of agreement among content marketers about the four key types of content metrics. They are as follows:

- Consumption
  - How many people are consuming content?
  - Which channel?
  - How frequent and how in-depth is their content consumption?
- Sharing
  - Which items are being shared?
  - By whom and how often?
  - How and where are they sharing?
- Lead generation
  - How is content supporting lead generation and nurturing?
- Sales
  - Is content driving sales and revenue?
  - Is there appropriate content at all stages of the customer journey to support customers and move them through the journey?[23]

Google Analytics, which was discussed in detail in Chapter 5, has metrics that will answer most of these questions and many content platforms and services provide their own insights. When monitoring content marketing effectiveness, it is important to remember that it is not the number of visitors that is critically important; it is the amount of time spent—the extent to which visitors actively engage with the content— that is important. Marketers are fond of quoting a statistic that says that 55 percent of website visitors stay no longer than 15 seconds. Whether that is true of your brand hub or not—and metrics can provide your own specific figure—the more time you can get visitors to spend with your content, the more likely it is to have an impact.[24] The ability to measure content marketing effectiveness should not be taken as a given.

Measuring the ROI on content marketing is difficult and many marketers admit that they do not do it well. In one study 79 percent of marketers agreed with the statement, "My team makes awesome content that our audience loves," but only 18 percent of those same marketers agreed with the statement, "We have a clear understanding of the ROI our content delivers."[25] Is that a bit of a disconnect? Another study found that while 50 percent of marketers rated their ability to measure ROI from paid search as being good, only 17 percent said that their ability to measure ROI from content marketing was good.[26]

The CMI Benchmark Study quoted earlier in the chapter asks what may be a better question, at least at this early stage of content marketing development. They asked, "In your organization, is it clear what an effective or successful content marketing program looks like?" That allows marketing teams to establish content marketing objectives and identify metrics that measure their accomplishment, not just rely on financial ROI.

Measuring the effectiveness of content marketing is not a one-size-fits-all process. Where it starts is clear, however. It starts with clear content marketing objectives, includes careful traffic of the metrics that measure those objectives, and results in insights that improve the content marketing program.

It may be that engagement is the most important concept in defining what is meant by content marketing success. However, before we tackle that important but rather slippery subject, we need to take a look at a concept that does not fit neatly either into content marketing or into advertising. Wherever it fits, native advertising is rapidly growing in importance.

Native Advertising—Promotion That Looks Like Content

In our discussion of audience development we emphasized that paid promotion is necessary to get content noticed by new audience members because growth from new internet users has essentially disappeared. To put it bluntly, there are the same number of users, and more content is being created, so the competition for eyeballs becomes fiercer every day. And we all know that most people don't think too highly of paid advertising of any kind on any channel.

Enter native advertising. Native content was mentioned when we discussed advertising-supported business models and in the discussion of publishing to content platforms. What exactly is native advertising? The definition of the Native Advertising Institute is:

> Native advertising is paid advertising where the ad matches the form, feel, and function of the content of the media on which it appears.[27]

That's clear, but the use of the term native content can muddy the waters. A definition of native content is:

> A piece of content that has been commissioned or paid to be placed on an external website with the view that the content fits and the form and function of where it exists.[28]

The author points out that what makes a piece of content native is:

- It fits the content style of the publisher.
- It is created or curated for that publisher's target audience.
- It is on an external website, not the brand's own.

That makes the two terms almost synonymous, just leaving the possibility that native content could be an unpaid placement. To be clear what we are discussing we will stick to the term native advertising in this section.

You see native ads on many sites today, especially the most trafficked ones. However, you may not be especially conscious of seeing them. That is exactly the point; they blend in with the other content. However, native ads must be clearly labeled as advertising whether the reader pays attention or not. The FTC released guidelines on native advertising in 2015 and it can charge advertisers with deceptive advertising if they violate them.[29]

Gentlemen's Quarterly (GQ) is a publication that has worked to create a comfortable environment for native advertising. This is how Wil Harris, digital head at the magazine's parent company, Conde Nast, describes it:

> the site offers the same set of tools, the same kind of integration, and the same placement for native advertising as it does for editorial content. This means content that is created in collaboration with its commercial partners can show up in related articles, on the front page, in the story stream, and on social media in exactly the same way as its editorial content does.

"If we are creating content with commercial partners it should be accessible in the same way that all our other content is created. This new version of the GQ website puts commercial and editorial content on complete parity," said Harris.[30]

But as of 2022, consumers are savvy in detecting native advertising. They don't necessarily trust it, but they still want the information. Pictured below in Figure 12.10a and 12.10b are two examples of native advertising by Adobe who wrote an article about virtual reality (VR) shopping. It focuses on Adobe's interaction with VR without being too "salesy."

Figure 12.10a **Adobe ad is displayed next to other NYT stories** Source: AdEspresso LLC

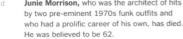

A History of Race and Racism, in 24 Chapters
A decade-by-decade history of race and racism in America, compiled by a National Book Award Winner.

John Legend Can't Say Times Are Normal
The singer and actor on the "La La Land" controversy, forms of resistance and playing the role of Frederick Douglass.

Maria Callas, From Reality to Runway
One of Italian fashion's most enduring icons is having a moment, almost 40 years after her death.

but when a former scientist took to an obscure blog **to accuse his former boss of mishandling data,** he ignited a furor over climate change.

21h **The Waldorf Astoria hotel** in Manhattan will close indefinitely for renovations next month. The salad that bears its name will live on as a staple of American menus.

1d **Junie Morrison,** who was the architect of hits by two pre-eminent 1970s funk outfits and who had a prolific career of his own, has died. He was believed to be 62.

Send Feedback

FROM OUR ADVERTISERS

TIFFANY & CO.
Hacking the Art World
How art has adapted to the internet.

ADOBE
Shopping Goes Virtual
Virtual reality will change how you shop.

ROYAL CARIBBEAN
Vacation Off the Beaten Path
Bobsled and jump waterfalls on your next Caribbean

VANGUARD
Where Do You Stack Up?
Discover if your peers are already saving for retirement.

ADP
Creating a Stronger Workforce
The work of this anthropologist can affect US

Figure 12.10b Adobe is shown as the sponsor of the article in the NYT about VR shopping Source: AdEspresso LLC

Using Content to Engage Readers—Storytelling and More

The concept of engagement with content is both important and frustrating. Marketers want viewers to pay attention to their content and to react to it in some way. It is about as far as agreement goes; there is simply no agreed-upon definition of engagement. One school of thought believes that engagement means that the reader takes some action, from liking a post to purchasing a product. The other believes that engagement means building stronger emotional ties with the product or brand. You can see the divide here between sales goals and branding goals.

AOL conducted a study in eight different countries and found the motivations for engaging with content shown in Figure 12.11. They called them "content moments" and pointed out that some motives seemed more suited to certain channels. For instance, "entertain" seems tailor-made for video while "update socially" seems intended for social media content. The research also showed that motives for engagement had different prominence in different markets.

There is no single answer to the question of how to get viewers to engage with content. It is, however, clear that marketers must set their own engagement objectives in light of their overall marketing strategy and measure the achievement of those objectives. That opens another can of worms because there is endless argument over which metrics best measure engagement. Again, there is a partial answer; it is usually necessary to use multiple metrics to get a clear picture of content engagement. We discussed the measurement of engagement in Chapter 5.

In this section we will focus on the issue of creating engaging content, which is central to our discussion of content marketing strategy. That should be reasonably straightforward, but it is not. A search for "create engaging marketing content" returns over 57 million results. Many of them are interesting and give good advice. However, a remarkable number

Figure 12.11 What Motivates Consumers to Engage with Online Content Source: http://www.marketingcharts.com /online/what-motivates-consumers-to-engage-with-online-content-70543/.

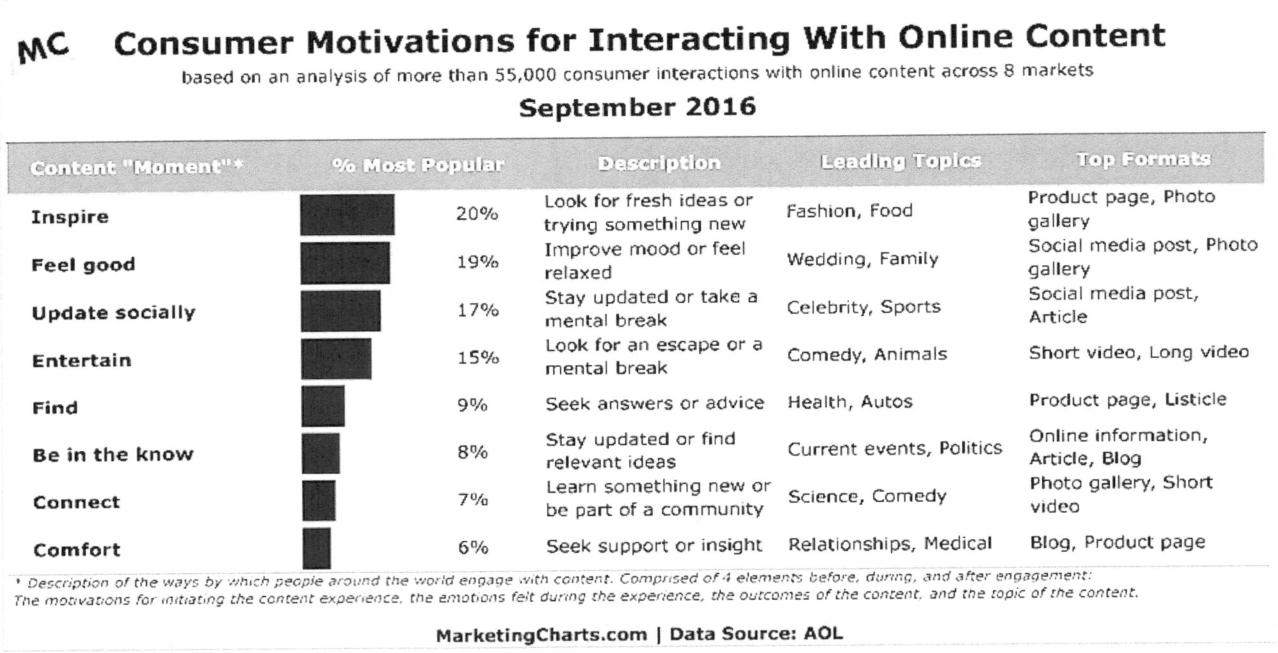

MC **Consumer Motivations for Interacting With Online Content**

based on an analysis of more than 55,000 consumer interactions with online content across 8 markets

September 2016

Content "Moment"*	% Most Popular	Description	Leading Topics	Top Formats
Inspire	20%	Look for fresh ideas or trying something new	Fashion, Food	Product page, Photo gallery
Feel good	19%	Improve mood or feel relaxed	Wedding, Family	Social media post, Photo gallery
Update socially	17%	Stay updated or take a mental break	Celebrity, Sports	Social media post, Article
Entertain	15%	Look for an escape or a mental break	Comedy, Animals	Short video, Long video
Find	9%	Seek answers or advice	Health, Autos	Product page, Listicle
Be in the know	8%	Stay updated or find relevant ideas	Current events, Politics	Online information, Article, Blog
Connect	7%	Learn something new or be part of a community	Science, Comedy	Photo gallery, Short video
Comfort	6%	Seek support or insight	Relationships, Medical	Blog, Product page

* Description of the ways by which people around the world engage with content. Comprised of 4 elements before, during, and after engagement: The motivations for initiating the content experience, the emotions felt during the experience, the outcomes of the content, and the topic of the content.

MarketingCharts.com | Data Source: AOL

of them give the advice "have a content marketing strategy, develop audience personas, and create relevant content for the audience." That is good advice and it is what we have discussed in this chapter. However, when you bring that advice down to the granular level of a single piece of content that grabs the attention of the reader and causes some reaction, it is useless.

We shall therefore combine two approaches to present a workable method for creating engaging content. They are as follows:

1. Storytelling is at the heart of good content marketing. Many marketers agree with this statement and Neil Patel and Ritika Puri of Quick Sprout built an infographic that covers many of the issues. In it they say:

   Contrary to popular belief, brand storytelling is not about your company. It's about your customers and the value that they get when engaging with your product or service. The most powerful brand stories are the ones that prioritize customers as the stars. Think of your company as a supporting character.[31]

2. Brand stories are all around the alert content marketer. Consultant Heidi Cohen has concrete suggestions for how to find those stories. Cohen says you find stories in your company in several places:

   • Your company—its heritage, "a day in the life," its community outreach, and more.

   • Your products—special history or product lore, famous people associated with them, unique product features, special uses, and more.

   • Your brand—what is special about the brand, its logo, its story over time, the causes it supports, its mascot, and more.

- Your employees—who are they, what are their relationships to your products, what are their associations with causes and community activities, and more.[32]

In Kindra Hall's book, *Stories that Stick*, there is The Four-Story Cheat Sheet that helps businesses create multiple stories for multiple audiences.

	Value Story	Founder Story	Purpose Story	Customer Story
Purpose	More effective sales and marketing	Increased confidence in investors, partners, and employees	Team, organization alignment	Sales and marketing, fostering excellence
Primary Audience	Prospect/Customer	Stakeholders	Employees, teams	Prospect/Customer
Who Should Tell It	Marketers and sales-people	Entrepreneurs	Leaders, executives, ad managers	Customers and companies

Source: Excerpt from p.207 Kindra Hall (2019) Stories That Stick, HarperCollins Leadership.

Hall also breaks down the four components of a great story. A great story must contain:

1. Identifiable characters
2. Authentic emotion
3. A significant moment
4. Specific details

Example of a bad business story from Square, a point-of-sale credit/debit card reader:

> Our story starts with you.
> Square was established to give every business owner an easier way to take credit cards. We've grown our commitment since, offering a complete suite of business tools and equitable loans that give every eligible business with a dream access to funding. From side gigs to sports stadiums, we're helping power businesses to succeed on their own terms.
> Source: https://squareup.com/us/en/why-square

Note that there are no identifiable characters, authentic emotions, significant moments, or specific details. In comparison, here is an example of a good business story from La Brea bakery (who make some of the best bread in the world):

> Our Story
> When the pastry chefs at Campanile Restaurant in Los Angeles could not find artisan bread good enough for the restaurant, they spent a year crafting the perfect recipe, creating bread with a caramelized, golden crust, soft inside and rustic appearance. The signature recipe resulted in such delicious artisan bread that they opened La Brea Bakery on La Brea Avenue. When there were people lined up outside the bakery every morning, and the bread sold out by 11 a.m., they knew they had a hit.

Note that you can identify the characters (the chefs), the emotion (frustration to satisfaction), the significant moment (when the bread was sold out by 11 a.m.), and specific details (can't you just taste that baguette in your mouth?!).

Consumers love stories. We, as marketers, have to learn how to tell them. People are more open to new ideas when they are told in the form of a story.

Technology and the Future of Content Marketing

In the continuing quest for viewer engagement, content marketing seems certain to add more elements of technology over the months and years to come. This is just a sampling of technology-enhanced content marketing:

- The *New York Times* has introduced a native ad format different from the Adobe ads featured earlier. The Flex Frame Everywhere is intended to replace the banner ad, which is losing popularity, especially among mobile advertisers. The *Times* says "it is a horizontal, large format, cross-device, responsive unit which appears in-stream alongside editorial content."[33] It can contain video, 360-degree images, 360-degree video, slideshows, static images, and other formats specified by the advertiser. Brand Studio technology, along with that of advertising platform Double Click, allow advertisers to configure their own ads on the NYT site.

- *Adweek* identifies VR as the "next great storytelling canvas."[34] Philanthropist Bill Gates posted a VR video of a trip to South Africa on his blog. He says:

  > In this video, you will hear the stories of young women living with HIV. Sit beside me as I drive from the leafy suburbs of Johannesburg to the dusty township of Soweto. Feel what it's like to be in the center of a stomping gumboot dancing troupe. And be inspired by the power of South Africa's youth, who will drive the next generation of innovations to create a future free of AIDS.[35]

- Canva (canva.com) has been a revolutionary resource for content creators. Canva is an online resource that is much easier to use than Photoshop or Illustrator. It creates inexpensive access to templates that look like they were designed by a design team.

- Artificial Intelligence (AI) like ChatGPT is infiltrating all aspects of our personal and professional life. That includes content marketing. AI is...

  - helping writers choose engaging subject lines.[36]

  - helping digital marketers individualize their customer journey by personalizing their emails.

  - Optimizing send times because it knows when each person is more likely to open their email.

- OpenAI (openai.com) created DALL-E, which utilizes the deep learning modules of ChatGPT.

Note that DALL-E is a spin on Dalí, as in the artist Salvador Dalí. Deep learning modules are a different type of AI because they can process images. DALL-E allows a user to type in a command and the AI creates an image in response. DALL-E can create a completely new image from a prompt such as "Draw me an airplane in the shape of a fish." It can also adjust an original image. For instance, with the prompt, "make a Coca-Cola can blue," DALL-E can generate an image of a blue Coca-Cola can in multiple ways. The debate about the fairness of art in the Creative Commons (art that can be reproduced for free) is up for debate and most likely legislation. Using AI to help generate images in seconds as opposed to using a graphic designer is welcomed as a cost and time savings among content creators.

- Topic Clusters and Pillar Pages are hugely influential to a company's search results.[37] Google consistently shifts their SEO algorithm to determine if a webpage is an authority on a topic. Companies want Google (and other search engines) to consider their webpage as an authority. As such, creating great content and choosing the best keywords are important, but not as important as ensuring that a website contains pillar pages and topic clusters. Spending time to update a pillar page with topic clusters on the company's website will ensure that Google keeps their results on (hopefully) the first search page. Figure 12.12 illustrates how a pillar page and cluster topic is designed.

    - Pillar pages are webpages that provide an extremely thorough overview of a topic. They are typically about 5,000 to 10,000 words long. The content is written broadly and linked to a topic cluster that is written in more detail. It is something that is broad enough that it can support about ten or more mini-blog posts. Sites like www.answerthepublic.com, and www.semrush.com can inform the content creator of topics and keywords that are being searched.

    - Topic Clusters are webpages that support the pillar page. They are written in more detail about a specific topic. They are a group of interlinked posts that connect to the pillar page.[38]

A working example of a pillar page versus a topic cluster is how HubSpot writes posts about Instagram Marketing Strategies.[39] Their pillar page is written very broadly about Instagram Marketing Strategies and their topic clusters are:

- In-depth posts about setting goals for Instagram usage
- Determining the target audience
- Conducting a competitive analysis
- Configuring an editorial calendar
- Building a consistent brand on Instagram
- Growing an Instagram follower base.

That just skims the surface of technology use in content marketing. Marketers will continue to find good ways to use the technology we now have as well as to discover new technologies to help them develop and execute their content marketing strategies.

Figure 12.12 Illustration of Pillar Pages and Topic Cluster Design Source: https://blog.hubspot.com/marketing/what-is-a-pillar-page

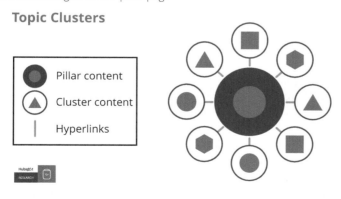

Summary

If traditional advertising is not yet dead, it has certainly been devalued in the minds of customers and marketers alike. Content marketing has taken over center stage for most B2C, B2B, and nonprofit marketers. Good content marketing focuses on being valuable and relevant to its carefully defined target audience, not on product-focused sales communications. In addition, good content is "always on." It is available to the potential customer whenever, wherever, and on whichever device they desire it.

The creation of successful content marketing is not a randomly creative act. Good content marketing is driven by a strategy that involves, first, creating or curating content, then identifying and developing loyal audiences for the content, followed by optimized distribution of content in multiple channels, and finally evaluation of the content strategy effectiveness that provides insights for future content marketing. As part of this process, buyer personas are developed to give all those concerned with content marketing a deep understanding of audience segments.

Native advertising is not the same as content marketing, nor is it traditional advertising. It is a rapidly growing type of marketing communication that places content that has no overt advertising intent into publications that can reach the target audience with content that is engaging and relevant.

There is a growing body of evidence to suggest that storytelling is not only a type of content that audiences find engaging. It is also effective in creating brand attitudes and in inciting action. Storytelling in marketing borrows structure and techniques from types of creative writing that include plays and short stories.

Storytelling and other types of marketing content are beginning to be impacted by technologies like VR and AI. It is likely that content marketing will take increasing advantage of technology going forward to engage and delight audiences.

Discussion Questions

1. Discuss the reasons for the emergence of content marketing as a major force in marketing and give your own opinion of whether it is likely to continue to grow or, at some point, to go into decline.

2. What are some of the major differences between traditional media communications channels and digital channels?

3. Can you see a reason why B2B marketers may make even more use of content marketing than B2C marketers do?

4. Discuss the nature and importance of the four elements of content marketing strategy.

5. Discuss the three basic ways of obtaining marketing content. Which do you think is the most valuable to the brand? Which requires the most effort? The least?

6. What is the meaning of "audience development"? Why is it different from the selection of a target audience in an advertising campaign?

7. Explain in your own words why buyer personas are considered essential in content marketing strategy.

8. Why are paid channels a necessary addition to owned and earned in most content marketing strategies today?

9. What are the four categories of content marketing metrics? Why is each one important?

10. What do you think marketers mean when they talk about engagement with their audience members?

11. Do you agree that storytelling is at the heart of good content marketing? Why or why not?

12. Do you have personal opinions about which communications channels are best for storytelling about brands and product categories with which you are involved?

13. Have you seen examples of the use of technology in either native advertising or content marketing? If so, bring a good one to class.

14. In the end, what makes a piece of content valuable to the viewer?

15. Is it fair that artists who posted their art on the Creative Commons are having their art used by AI and are no longer receiving credit for their work? Work in the Creative Commons is free to use, but the artist requires an acknowledgment that the work is theirs.

Endnotes

1. "Seth Godin, 'Content Marketing Is the Only Marketing Left' and 10 New Marketing Lessons," Content Marketing Institute, accessed March 8, 2023, https://contentmarketinginstitute.com/articles/seth-godin-cont/.

2. Heidi Cohen. "Seth Godin: 7 Truths at the Heart of Marketing (& How to Use Them)." Heidi Cohen, December 14, 2011, http://heidicohen.com/seth-godin-7-truths-at-the-heart-of-marketing-how-to-use-them.

3. Alan Lo, "From 1895 and beyond: John Deere's 'The Furrow' and Why Content Marketing Is Still Relevant Today." Growth Advisory Toronto, April 26, 2021, https://www.stratwell.ca/john-deere-the-furrow-content-marketing/.

4. "AAM: Total Circulation for Magazine Media," accessed February 14, 2023, https://abcas3.auditedmedia.com/ecirc/magtitlesearch.asp.

5. "Getting Started." Content Marketing Institute, accessed February 14, 2023, https://contentmarketinginstitute.com/getting-started/.

6. "Rahel Anne Bailie | the Content Wrangler," accessed February 14, 2023, https://www.thecontentwrangler.com/author/rahelab.

7. Marcia Riefer Johnston, "Digital Governance Basics for Content Marketers." Content Marketing Institute, accessed February 14, 2023, http://contentmarketinginstitute.com/2015/11/basics-digital-governance.

8. Marcia Riefer Johnston, Content Marketing Institute.

9. Jaya Saxena, "Travis Scott Made How Much from His McDonald's Deal?!" Eater, December 4, 2020, https://www.eater.com/22152480/travis-scott-forbes-30-under-30-mcdonalds-meal-deal.

10. Mindy Weinstein, "10 Examples of Social Media Celebrity Endorsements That Paid off Big Time." Search Engine Journal, September 16, 2021, https://www.searchenginejournal.com/social-celebrity-endorsements/415568/.

11. Kirsty Daniel, "The State of Content Marketing in 2022 <Stats & Trends to Watch>." HubSpot Blog. HubSpot, April 12, 2022, https://blog.hubspot.com/marketing/state-of-content-marketing-infographic.

12. Geraint Holliman, and Jennifer Rowley. "Business to Business Digital Content Marketing: Marketers' Perceptions of Best Practice." *Journal of Research in Interactive Marketing* 8, no. 4 (2014): 269–293.

13. "2016 Benchmarks, Budgets, and Trends—North America." Accessed February 15, 2023, https://contentmarketinginstitute.com/wp-content/uploads/2015/10/2016_B2C_Research_Final.pdf.

14. B2B Content Marketing: 2016 Benchmarks, Budgets and Trends—North America.

15. "A Guide to Content Syndication Networks for Bloggers." QuickSprout, January 1, 2019, https://www.quicksprout.com/the-complete-guide-to-building-your-blog-audience-chapter-8/.

16. Michelle Martin, "The Complete Guide to Content Curation in 2023: Tools, Tips, Ideas" Social Media Marketing & Management Dashboard, February 23, 2022, https://blog.hootsuite.com/beginners-guide-to-content-curation/.

17. Neil Patel, "How to Do Curated Content Right: A Step-by-Step Guide." QuickSprout, November 11, 2015, https://www.quicksprout.com/2015/11/11/how-to-do-curated-content-right-a-step-by-step-guide.

18. Moises Mendez, II. "The Top 10 Viral Moments from 2022." *Time*, December 12, 2022, https://time.com/6240488/most-viral-moments-2022/.

19. Eric Brantner, "The Science behind Buzzfeed's Viral Content." Social Media Today, September 7, 2016, https://www.socialmediatoday.com/marketing/science-behind-buzzfeeds-viral-content.

20. "International Association of Privacy Professionals." Accessed February 14, 2023, https://iapp.org/media/pdf/resource_center/State_Comp_Privacy_Law_Chart.pdf.

21. Roger Montti, "Google Research: 55% of Consumers Use Videos for Purchase Decisions." Search Engine Journal, September 3, 2019, https://www.searchenginejournal.com/youtube-shopping-influence/323503/.

22. Elizabeth Earin et al., "A Step-by-Step Guide for Creating a B2C Buyer Persona." Iterative Marketing, March 22, 2016, http://iterativemarketing.net/step-step-guide-creating-b2c-buyer-persona/.

23. Andy Crestodina, "A Guide for Content Marketing Metrics: The 37 Most (and Least) Useful Metrics." Orbit Media Studios, September 28, 2018, https://www.orbitmedia.com/blog/content-marketing-metrics-to-track/.

24. Andy Crestodina, Orbit Media Studios.

25. JC Lupis, "Minority of Content Marketers Say They Know Their Content Production Costs." Marketing Charts, July 5, 2017, http://www.marketingcharts.com/online/minority-of-content-marketers-say-they-know-their-content-production-costs-66471.

26. JC Lupis, "Which Digital Channels Are Marketers Most Confident in Measuring for Roi?" Marketing Charts, July 5, 2017, http://www.marketingcharts.com/online/which-digital-channels-are-marketers-most-confident-in-measuring-for-roi-67300.

27. Anders Engberg Vinderslev, "What Is the Definition of Native Advertising?" Native Advertising Blog by the Native Advertising Institute. Brand Movers, January 22, 2020, https://blog.nativeadvertisinginstitute.com/what-is-definition-native-advertising.

28. Ben Young, "Definition of Native Content: Nudge." Nudge, get customer insights with ease, May 10, 2021, http://giveitanudge.com/definition-of-native-content/.

29. Will Critchlow, "A Checklist for Native Advertising: How to Comply with the FTC's New Rules." *Moz,* accessed February 15, 2023, https://moz.com/blog/checklist-for-native-advertising.

30. Jessica Goodfellow, "GQ's Native Ad Offering 'Taking Inspiration' from Buzzfeed as It Puts Commercial and Editorial Content on 'Complete Parity.'" The Drum. March 24, 2016, http://www.thedrum.com/news/2016/03/24/gq-s-native-ad-offering-taking-inspiration-buzzfeed-it-puts-commercial-and-editorial.

31. Lars Lofgren, "Lars Lofgren." QuickSprout, April 22, 2019, https://www.quicksprout.com/the-beginners-guide-to-online-marketing-chapter-3.

32. Heidi Cohen. "Brand Storytelling: 30 Ideas That Will Make Your Business Memorable." Heidi Cohen, October 17, 2017, http://heidicohen.com/how-to-find-stories-for-your-brand-within-your-organization.

33. "The Times Works to Transform Digital Display Ad Business with Launch of Flex Frame Everywhere." *The New York Times Company*, October 5, 2016, http://www.nytco.com/times-works-to-transform-digital-display-ad-business-with-launch-of-flex-frame-everywhere.

34. Gian LaVecchia, "Virtual Reality Is Becoming the next Great Storytelling Canvas." *Adweek*, August 8, 2016, http://www.adweek.com/news/advertising-branding/virtual-reality-becoming-next-great-storytelling-canvas-172797.

35. Bill Gates, "South Africa: Virtually There." gatesnotes.com, September 13, 2016, https://www.gatesnotes.com/Health/South-Africa-Virtually-There.

36. Mike Kaput, "Artificial Intelligence in Email Marketing." Marketing AI Institute. Marketing AI Institute, July 27, 2022, https://www.marketingaiinstitute.com/blog/ai-in-email-marketing.

37. "Your Guide to Pillar Pages and Topic Clusters: Clariant Creative Agency." Clariant Creative Agency, LLC. Accessed February 27, 2023, https://www.clariantcreative.com/guide-to-pillar-pages-and-topic-clusters.

38. Sophia Bernazzani, "What Is a Pillar Page? (and Why It Matters for Your Seo Strategy)." HubSpot Blog. HubSpot, January 13, 2022, https://blog.hubspot.com/marketing/what-is-a-pillar-page.

39. HubSpot. "Instagram Marketing: The Ultimate Guide." HubSpot. Accessed February 27, 2023, https://www.hubspot.com/instagram-marketing.

Chapter 13

Demand Generation and Conversion in B2B Markets

Learning Objectives

By the time you complete this chapter, you will be able to:

1 Explain the relationship between conversion and demand generation.

2 Summarize the relationship between the B2B buy cycle and the customer journey.

3 Explain how the internet, and search in particular, has changed the B2B buying process.

4 List the functions of a marketing automation system.

5 Explain the steps of the sales lead generation and qualification process.

6 Explain how the buying group concept will change B2B marketing.

7 Explain the organizational challenges in moving toward account-based management.

Demand Generation and Customer Conversion

As background to the important concept of customer conversion in B2B markets, it is important to reexamine the core marketing strategies discussed in Chapter 1. This framework suggests that all marketing strategies fall into one of the four following generic categories:

1. Acquisition
2. Conversion
3. Retention
4. Value growth

This book has previously discussed a number of digital marketing tools that can be used for customer acquisition. Some, like display advertising and search marketing, are primarily used for acquisition.

Email marketing is primarily used for customer retention. Social media marketing falls in between, with its value for acquisition or retention depending on platform and marketer objectives.

Customer conversion is the second of the generic activities. Conversion and the processes leading up to conversion will be the focus of this chapter in terms of its end result. In its broadest sense, conversion is generally equated with making the first sale to a particular customer. This is a good place to start, but this chapter will show that conversion is a more complex process. Conversion is not a simple activity with a clear beginning and an equally clear termination. It is more like a river, with many tributaries entering it, that eventually empties into the sea—in this case, a customer database. This entire process of getting to conversion is today known as demand generation. Conversion is the ultimate goal of demand generation, the desired action by the *prospect*, or unqualified lead, but there are many steps along the way. Conversion also does not stop when the prospect becomes a customer, as continuous feedback helps refine the actions the marketer takes each step of the way. In the process of this discussion, we will also distinguish between the three terms that are often loosely used, which are "demand generation," "inbound marketing," and "lead generation," and understand them in the context. However, before delving into the demand generation process, it is important to note some recent changes to the B2B (business-to-business) buy cycle and what is important in that cycle.

Demand and lead generation are the two most commonly used terms in B2B marketing today. While lead generation as an activity can stand alone, demand generation as a process includes lead generation. The demand generation process drives awareness and interest in a company's products and services, starting with attractive content and ending with a desired action, or conversion and associated metrics.

Lead generation as the second step in the demand generation process also drives interest or inquiry into products or services. The goal is the collection of qualified connections to build initial relationships with prospects so we can nurture them until they are closed as customers.[1]

demand generation
entire process of developing customer demand for a product or service.

The B2B Buy Cycle and the Customer Journey

Since the discipline of B2B marketing is concerned with the flow of the buying process from prospect to loyal customer, demand generation is a natural way to organize this process. Another aspect of this flow of B2B marketing is the concept of the buy cycle. Looking at Figure 13.1, it is immediately evident that the concept known as the buy cycle or buying cycle is a restatement of the consumer decision process familiar to all students of marketing. Whether using the term "B2B" or the older descriptor, industrial, it is the set of stages business buyers go through as they make a purchase. Using business marketing terminology, the process is as follows:

buy cycle
process a customer goes through in deciding to make a purchase.

- **Needs awareness**, in which the potential purchaser recognizes the need for a product or service to meet the needs of a specific business activity
- **Research**, in which the potential purchaser investigates products and vendors
- **Consideration and comparison**, in which the potential purchaser studies potential vendors and their products, arriving at a shortlist from which the purchase will be made
- **Procurement**, in which the actual purchase transaction is completed.

Both the length and the number of people involved in the business purchasing process complicate the task of the marketer. These factors also enhance the importance of

Figure 13.1   **The B2B (Industrial) Buy Cycle** Source: Marketing Maven Blog: "The Industrial Buy Cycle: Part 1," February 4, 2010, GlobalSpec. Reprinted with permission.

lead generation and management in order to understand who the information researcher (gatekeeper) for the business buying center is and to access the current stage of the buying process.

In addition to the buy cycle, today we often speak of the buying process as the buyer's journey[2] and seek to map the buyer's path through that journey as part of the demand generation process. Therefore, it is useful to ask the following questions in the buyer's journey:

buyer's journey
the customer's specific path taken in the buying process.

Who is making the purchase? A majority of B2B purchase decisions are made by a group, not by a single person. That phenomenon has long been[3] called the buying center or the decision-making unit.

buying center
a group of people in an organization who make decisions for high-value and/or risky purchases.

Why and what outcome is desired? What is the buyer's pain point and desired outcome, and what is their perception of the value of the product or service?

When is the purchase being made? The length of the purchase cycle increases as the price and the risk inherent in the purchase go up.

What content can answer the buyer's question? Is an infographic enough or will a whitepaper better answer the question? The answer depends on the buyer and the stage in the buy cycle.

Where does the buyer seek the information? As shown in Figure 13.2, there are many sources for B2B purchase decisions, including blogs, webinars, and industry events. Where the buyer seeks information can determine the marketer's actions.

From the above discussion and Figure 13.2, it is clear that the purchasing process is changing for B2B customers. Not only do those in the buying center or buy center rely now on search, social media, and other content in making their decision, but also another hard fact is that quite often, much of the purchase decision has been made by the time the salesperson walks in the door. The reason for this change is that the buyer is doing much of their own research and is less dependent on the sales force as a source of information. Sources such as Adobe Marketo Engage and Forrester Research all indicate that much of the purchase decision will have been made by the time the salesperson actually contacts the customer. HubSpot estimates that more than a full 1 million sales jobs have been lost in the process of this change as the role of the salesperson changes to a more consultative selling orientation and there is less of a need for "order takers" in the sales force.[4]

Figure 13.2 The Changing Purchase Process for B2B Means Salesperson Comes Later in Process Source: Zahay, Debra, Don Schultz, and Archana Kumar (2015), "Reimagining Branding for the New B2B Digital Marketplace," Journal of Brand Strategy, 3(4), pp. 357–372.

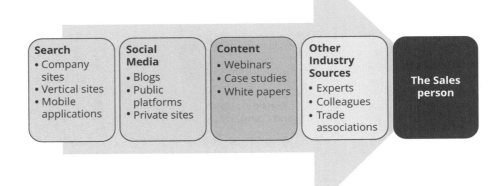

The Changing Behavior of the B2B Buyer

This changing process means that search marketing and being able to generate good quality content to attract potential buyers is more important than ever to B2B marketers. Generating high-quality sales leads has traditionally been perceived as the greatest challenge by B2B marketers and we will discuss the lead generation process shortly. A large volume of leads was considered important, but much less so than *high-quality* leads. While business marketers need to be concerned with high-quality leads, changes in the B2B marketing process have shifted the emphasis of how leads are obtained.

The Importance of Search in B2B Marketing

The change is that now most B2B buyers start their purchase process with search and rely heavily on social media and other online content for research before making a purchase decision. As stated above, buyers rely on the salesperson much later in the process and to a lesser extent (see Figure 13.2). In fact, it is suggested that 85 percent of the purchase decision has been made before the buyer ever sees or contacts a salesperson.[5] According to a state of B2B Procurement Study, 94 percent of B2B purchasers performed research online.[6] Their search activity was as follows:

- Seventy-seven percent use Google Search.
- Eighty-four percent consult business websites.
- Thirty-four percent rely on third-party websites.
- Forty-one percent refer to user reviews.

Therefore, B2B marketers must concentrate on being found in searches, both mobile and desktop, and having a strong presence on social media platforms. This shift in the purchase process means that branding is more critical than ever, as evidenced by the concerns of B2B marketers in a survey by B2B International, summarized in Figure 13.3. In that survey, brand/marketing communication is seen as the top challenge by 46 percent of B2B marketers surveyed, whereas concerns involving the sales function (finding top talent) were only listed as a top marketing challenge by 3 percent of those surveyed. Retaining customers and increasing brand awareness were the two items that increased

Figure 13.3   Top Ten Business Challenges Demonstrate Shift in Focus Away from Pure Lead Generation

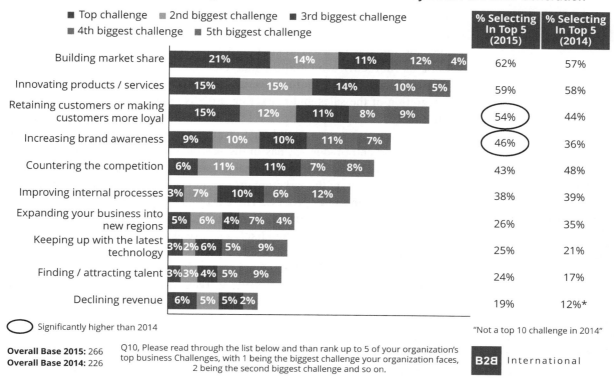

	% Selecting In Top 5 (2015)	% Selecting In Top 5 (2014)
Building market share	62%	57%
Innovating products / services	59%	58%
Retaining customers or making customers more loyal	54%	44%
Increasing brand awareness	46%	36%
Countering the competition	43%	48%
Improving internal processes	38%	39%
Expanding your business into new regions	26%	35%
Keeping up with the latest technology	25%	21%
Finding / attracting talent	24%	17%
Declining revenue	19%	12%*

⬛ Top challenge   ⬛ 2nd biggest challenge   ⬛ 3rd biggest challenge
⬛ 4th biggest challenge   ⬛ 5th biggest challenge

⬭ Significantly higher than 2014

"Not a top 10 challenge in 2014"

Overall Base 2015: 266
Overall Base 2014: 226

Q10, Please read through the list below and than rank up to 5 of your organization's top business Challenges, with 1 being the biggest challenge your organization faces, 2 being the second biggest challenge and so on.

B2B International

significantly, reinforcing the need for a solid demand generation process starting with content marketing as described in this chapter.

While B2B marketers will continue to have a goal of the generation of high-quality sales leads, priorities are shifting. Among overall business challenges, retaining customers and increasing brand awareness are seen as in the top five by half of the participants in this study, as illustrated in Figure 13.3. With branding becoming more important, so is content, as it is one way to tell the brand story. Some samples of brand-reinforcing content channels such as email and social media are illustrated in Figure 13.4. In addition, B2B Marketers are focused on hiring new talent, integrating their data sources, and continuing to digitize their processes and use artificial intelligence in their processes.[7]

Figure 13.4   Content Channels to Reinforce the Brand Image

Content Channels
- Social Media
- Website
- Email
- Video
- Blog
- Mobile
- Search
- Others

Brand Strategy and Brand Story

How Sales and Marketing Must Work Together

Because of these technological changes noted above, increasingly, the sales and marketing functions are seen as a holistic system, tied together by marketing automation systems, such as Oracle Eloqua or Adobe Marketo Engage (referred to also in this book as Marketo), which allow marketers to manage and track customer interactions and leads and measure the results. HubSpot calls this process "Smarketing," an integration of the sales and marketing process to convert and retain customers more efficiently. Marketo says that the sales funnel, which usually shows the process of leading the customer through brand awareness to conversion and then retention and cross-selling and up-selling, has in the past had a gap between brand awareness and conversion by the sales team. The sales team has typically had most of the interface with the customer, with marketing providing leads that were seen as poor quality and not relevant to the sales process. The B2B Sales Funnel has changed to emphasize a more important role in marketing in nurturing leads through the process. It is marketing that decides if a prospect is more likely to move along the demand generation process to convert if they are offered a chance to view a webinar after downloading a whitepaper or receive an informational email, as seen in Figure 13.5.

From the marketing point of view, Marketo says that the corresponding gap in the marketing sales funnel between brand awareness and conversion can be filled by the processes of lead nurturing (developing relationships with customers before conversion), scoring, routing, and management, as shown in Figure 13.6. Armed with better-qualified leads and prospects that are more likely to buy, the sales team can not only close the sale faster but also concentrate on post-sale retention, and cross- and up-sale activities. In this new perspective, marketing takes a leadership role in the sales process and is no longer seen as an ancillary and sometimes unnecessary function that is focused on mass messages and intuitive decision making, hence the origin of the term "Smarketing," where sales and

cross-selling
selling a different, related product to an existing customer.

up-selling
upgrading an existing customer's account by selling more expensive products or packages in an attempt to increase the revenue value of that customer.

lead nurturing
developing relationships with customers before conversion.

Figure 13.5 **The B2B Industrial Sales Funnel Then and Now** Source: Zahay, Debra, Don Schultz, and Archana Kumar (2015), "Reimagining Branding for the New B2B Digital Marketplace," Journal of Brand Strategy, 3(4), pp. 357–372; and https://stevepatrizi.com/2012 /10/23/the-new-marketing-sales-funnel/.

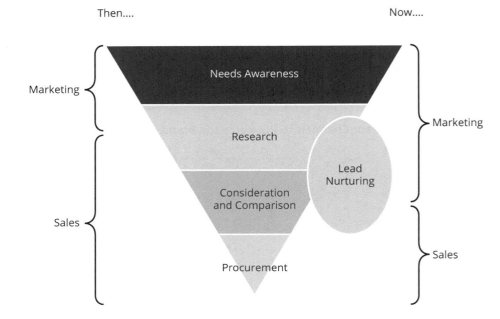

Figure 13.6   Filling the Gap between Lead Generation, Sales, and Customer
Retention Source: https://business.adobe.com/blog/basics/lead-generation

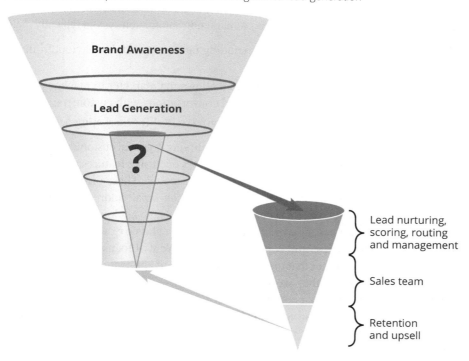

marketing work together. Figure 13.7 illustrates the Marketo view of the transformation of marketing that has accompanied the transformation of the sales process. Marketing's mission is now to represent the customer's view and see that the company is found in search, to use customer intelligence for the best message targeting, and also to focus on customer relationships quickly, using the best customer information possible.

Figure 13.7   The Transformation of Marketing with the Rise of Demand
Generation Source: https://business.adobe.com/blog/basics/lead-generation

Automation Systems Fill the Gap

This gap between marketing and sales to make both functions more effective is quite often filled by a marketing automation system. A marketing automation system typically includes

marketing automation system
marketing interaction management system including a database, engagement engine, and analytics component.

1. a centralized marketing database including interactions and behaviors from prospects and customers;
2. an engagement marketing "engine" that allows the marketer to manage and automate the process of interaction and conversations with customers; and
3. an analytics tool to test, measure, and optimize ROI for marketing activities.

For example, BMW has long been good at identifying potential customers and nurturing them. Its U.S. home page shown in Figure 13.8 offers exclusive features and the ability to "build your own" car to people who sign up for an account. These offers of information and special functions encourage people to provide their email address along with other personal information to complete account registration. Have no doubt that BMW will be in touch once a prospect has registered! This activity is a classic example of the use of the lead process in both business and consumer markets. We will focus on B2B applications in this chapter, but remember that there are also important applications in B2C (business-to-consumer) markets, and they work in the same way.

BMW might next send an email reminder to a customer who had recently been on the website looking for new car information or place an ad on a website that the consumer visits next. A marketing automation system would be able to "automate" that process and track conversion, whether the prospect actually purchased something from the site, and the exact conversion path.[8] In fact, visitors to the HubSpot or Adobes Marketo Engage sites seeking to learn about marketing topics in this chapter will not have to wait long before seeing a pop-up that tries to capture personal information and email for continued contact and communication.

Figure 13.8 **The BMW USA Home Page** Source: BMW https://www.bmwusa.com/home.html

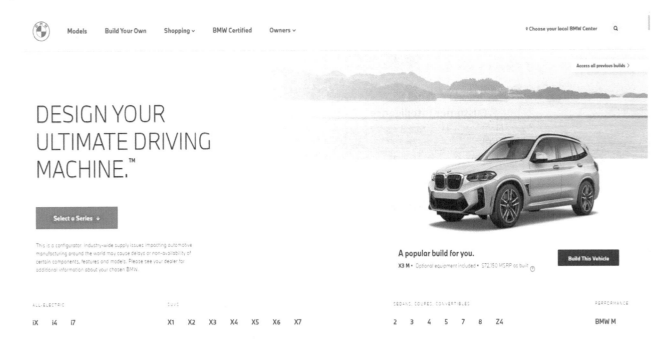

The B2B Process Today: Demand Generation

While leads will continue to be a focus of B2B marketing efforts, in recent years, as stated above, the term demand generation has entered the marketing lexicon as a way to organize and understand customer interaction processes. Demand generation is the process of stimulating demand and creating excitement for a product or service.[9] The idea behind demand generation is to manage, as much as possible, the process of acquisition, conversion, retention, and value growth. Demand generation begins with good content creation to attract leads. Leads are then nurtured and qualified and converted to customers, as shown in Figure 13.9. There is a "pull" aspect to this prospect which is known as inbound marketing and consists of attracting customers based on quality content and then converting them. The "push" aspect is known as lead generation and nurturing and, in this activity, marketers reach out directly to potential leads and nurture them through the sales process to conversion. After conversion, a good demand generation process involves using metrics to analyze what went well and what needed improvement through a feedback process. What this conceptualization suggests is that much of the material in this text represents demand generation activities, whether in a B2B or B2C context. However, before we go further into the lead generation and conversion processes, we will explore first the concept of content marketing in a B2B context.

Demand Generation Step One: Content Creation and Content Marketing in B2B Markets

We discussed content marketing in detail in Chapter 8 as a strategic process to attract and retain a clearly defined target market for a brand for the purpose of profitable customer actions. B2B marketers have always done a certain amount of content marketing. Informative content in traditional B2B marketing is generally described as "collateral material." This process includes things like brochures or other "leave behinds" that salespeople use as part of the personal selling process. Collateral material has been almost an afterthought as compared to advertising and the strength of the sales force's presence in B2B markets and even less emphasized in B2C markets. However, the shift in the B2B buying process has raised the importance of collateral material and any type of relevant content about the brand and its products and services. Focusing on the concept of content marketing shifts the focus from traditional advertising, in offline or online media, to marketing that depends on marketer- and customer-created content that is either informative, entertaining, or both.

content marketing
creating and distributing content across the web that users find valuable and relevant, driving visitors to the website.

Figure 13.9 **Demand Generation Process Begins with Good Content and Ends with Analysis**

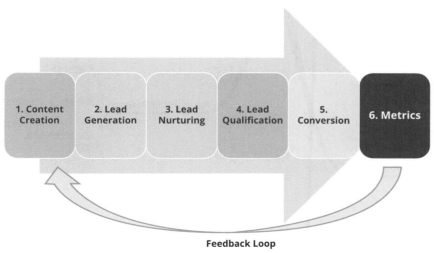

1. Content Creation
2. Lead Generation
3. Lead Nurturing
4. Lead Qualification
5. Conversion
6. Metrics

Feedback Loop

Many types of content are appropriate for the web. The infographic seen in Figure 13.10 characterizes the types of content, both online and offline, that can be used in lead generation. Content does not have to be completely original every time. Content can be repurposed across channels. This repurposing can mean something very simple, such as posting a video on YouTube as well as on the corporate website. Repurposing can also take more effort—using corporate material to develop a webinar, for example. Corporate content can be optimized for search in whatever channel it exists. For instance, corporations might establish YouTube channels to group their content and make it easier to locate. In addition, an individual YouTube video can be tagged to make it easier to find. Businesses can also reach out to customers in other ways on social media, as discussed in Chapter 5. Social media encourages the creation of content by customers, which can be a huge asset to the content-creation effort. Any platform like a blog that encourages customer comments also creates an opportunity for customers to co-create the content.

Notice the many different types of content in this figure represented by these channels. No single firm can or should use all these techniques to repurpose content and distribute it across the web. It makes sense that companies start with only a few options that make sense for them and make it easy to repurpose important content (a feed from a Facebook page to a Twitter account, for example). The marketer should test efforts and solicit

Figure 13.10 Online and Offline Lead Generation Channels Source: https://www.markempa.com/lead_generation-9/

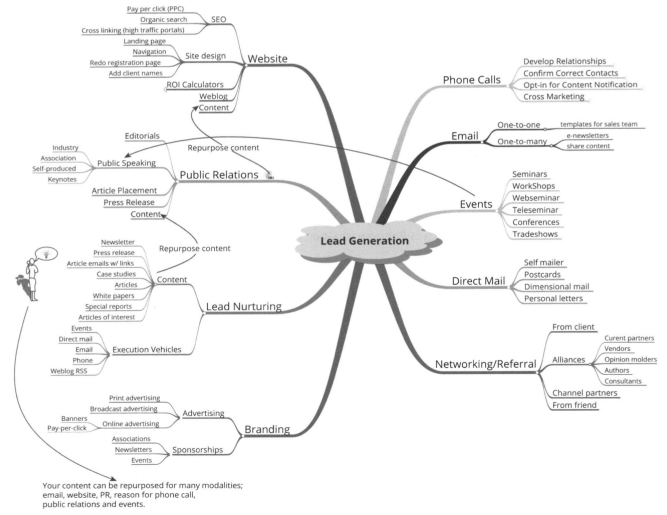

customer feedback and contributions. This testing must all be done in the context of understanding the information needs and media habits of the target audience while producing content that conveys a consistent corporate message.[10] In other words, take a strategic approach to producing and distributing content; it is the essence of being visible on the web. Being visible is the necessary forerunner to attracting people to the corporate website from which they can be identified, nurtured, and eventually converted to customers.

Therefore, content marketing means that marketing is no longer about fluffy or even persuasive advertising messages. Content marketing is a discipline that is about informational content intent on attracting prospects and converting them to customers in the brave new world of digital marketing and demand generation. The goal is to move the prospect through the demand generation process.

Demand Generation Step Two: Lead Generation
What Is Lead Generation?

After content is in place on various channels, the next step is to process the leads that result from content marketing efforts. Traditional offline direct marketers have used the process of sales lead generation and management since the 1950s at least. Over time, the process has taken advantage of customer databases and marketing automation software and has become a highly disciplined and cost-effective marketing technique for the business marketer.[11] The process focuses on getting individuals to self-identify as potential decision makers in the purchase of a product or a service—a sales lead.

lead generation
identifying sales prospects.

Why was this process developed by business marketers? The reason is cost. Business marketers traditionally have large field sales forces that call on customers, which is an expensive process. It is especially costly in the technology and high-ticket industrial spaces where closing a sale may require a year or more and necessitate multiple customer calls from a sales representative supported by engineers and designers. Multiple sales calls by multiple highly paid representatives can add up to an expensive process! This costly process is true even if the customer has a defined need for the product and is ready to purchase.

If the customer is early in the sales cycle—just collecting information for a possible purchase in the indefinite future, for example—personal selling is simply not cost-effective. If personal sales calls represent the only option, the company risks losing contact with a customer who may eventually make a purchase. The other option is to maintain communication in nonpersonal channels—originally by mail, now primarily in interactive channels—until that potential customer is ready to make a purchase decision. It is a simple concept that is surprisingly difficult to implement for reasons that are organizational, not technological.

It is important to understand that sales lead generation and management is a marketing tool that is used for higher-ticket sales with a longer purchase cycle. By now, you may have realized that some consumer purchases also fit that description. The purchase of a car usually fits into that category; so does the purchase of a condo or a house. In consumer behavior terms, these are situations in which the consumer goes through the entire purchase process—triggering cue, information search, selection of alternatives, purchase decision, product use, and information feedback. This type of situation is ideal for identifying someone in the initial stage of the purchase process, communicating as the process unfolds, and making an effort to close the sale when the time is appropriate. All one needs to do is look at the websites of any major automobile brand to see this process in operation. As noted with the BMW example, the prospect will not get far into the site before being required to give an email address in order to proceed. Shortly after registering, behaviorally targeted ads immediately begin to appear based on prior search behavior.

The Lead Generation and Management Process

The first step in the lead generation process is to get a person to self-identify as a potential sales lead. Whatever the channel, this process requires producing and distributing content that induces the reader or viewer to ask for more information. This initial stage is called a **prospect**. In other words, the marketer does not yet know whether that person—the prospect is made by a single person, whether in a B2B or a B2C market—is actually considering a purchase.

The question is not really whether a marketing department can produce leads. Anyone can produce inquiries if the marketing budget is large enough! The question is how to produce a desired quantity of leads that are worth careful qualification and potential distribution to the sales force. Putting the issues of quality and quantity together, lead generation becomes a serious marketing activity.

Now take a look at the actual content of the chart shown in Figure 13.10. Some of the lead generation channels are traditional in nature—telephone calls, direct mail, events (which can be virtual as well as physical), word of mouth (networking), public relations—and the various demand generation activities included under the heading of branding and those characterized as lead nurturing take place typically online. However, all channels have been profoundly affected by the internet. Much of the contact activity that was once done by mail or by phone is now done by email, and offline channels are often used to drive prospects to the corporate website for in-depth information. Events now include activities like webinars. Press releases that are an important part of public relations are now posted on the internet and optimized for search (see Chapter 9).

The connection between corporate events and public appearances by corporate personnel at industry events is a traditional one. The activity of "repurposing content" is not entirely new, but this ungrammatically titled effort has become essential given the endless appetite of the web for relevant new content. The corporate website and its associated corporate blog have become the hub of all this content, which needs to be widely distributed across the web in order to produce the greatest level of awareness and the largest volume of leads.

Despite the importance of online information, marketers cannot just put content on a website and expect people to find it and respond to it in large numbers. People have to find content in places, physical and virtual, that they commonly frequent—which usually does not include corporate websites as a first step. Content distribution that aims to drive traffic to the website can also be described as "inbound marketing."

Inbound Marketing for Lead Generation

The concept of **inbound marketing** introduced discipline in content marketing as a technique for lead generation in the sense that it outlines a clear process for managing content to reinforce a brand image and draw prospects to a web or mobile site. The term has been popularized by marketing services firm HubSpot, although concepts like "interruption marketing" and "permission marketing" were originally used by other marketers. Most notable among users of these terms is marketing expert Seth Godin, who has been preaching the doctrine of permission marketing since the early days of the internet.[12]

It has already been discussed that most potential customers turn to *search* as the first step in the purchase process, even before they consult personal sources (see Chapter 7) or corporate sources of information (see Chapters 5 and 6). This association makes having all content optimized for search a top priority for internet marketers. It is also important to have content in places frequented by potential customers since they generally see corporate websites as a last stop, not a first one.

prospect
an unqualified lead.

inbound marketing
approach that is focused on being visible to potential customers and using the visibility to drive them to a website where they can transact.

HubSpot says succinctly, "Inbound Marketing is marketing focused on getting found by customers"[13] It is not the traditional "marketer talking to customer" approaches, which are also described as "interruption marketing," that might be characterized by intrusive advertising. Instead, inbound marketing involves making content available to customers when and where they want it. Inbound marketing also involves getting customers' permission to push desired content to them through feeds or newsletters of various kinds. As noted above this marketing method has been called permission marketing since the early days of the internet. Students, if interested, can get certified in HubSpot's inbound methodology of Attract, Acquire, Close, and Delight which closely mirrors the Zahay and Roberts approach of Acquisition, Conversion, Retention, and Customer Value Growth.

Cost of Lead Generation

The ultimate question in B2B marketing and in deciding whether to use a sales force or inbound techniques is always, "How much does it/should it cost to generate a sales lead?" The answer, as usual, depends on the nature of the product and the competitive environment in the particular industry. Here are some generalizations. A study of lead generation by HubSpot found that companies that used mostly outbound marketing (e.g., trade shows, telemarketing, and direct mail) incurred an average cost of $346 per lead, whereas companies that used mostly inbound techniques incurred an average cost of $135. Within these figures, there are huge variations by firm and by industry. Compared to the firm's average cost per lead, 63 percent of respondents said that social media and blogs produced leads at a lower-than-average cost. The best-performing outbound media were direct mail and telemarketing, producing leads at 33 percent and 34 percent, respectively, below the firm's average.[14] Again, industry sector and individual company variance is huge, but so are the costs to generate a sales lead, whether qualified or not. The data from LynchpinSEO for 2023 in Figure 13.11 shows a wide variety of average costs per lead in industry, with IT and computer services having the highest cost at $208 per lead and nonprofits having the lowest cost at $31 per lead.

Figure 13.11 Projected Cost per Lead 2023 Varies by Industry Source: https://linchpinseo.com/average-cost-per-lead-by-industry-and-marketing-channel/

Cost per Lead Data by Industry

Industry	Low	High	Average
Financial services	$44	$272	$160
IT, Computer, and technical services	$39	$370	$208
Education	$37	$66	$55
Healthcare and medical	$36	$286	$162
Industrial and manufacturing	$33	$235	$136
Travel and tourism	$29	$182	$106
Retail	$25	$41	$34
Consumer products	$24	$182	$105
Telecom	$24	$64	$45
Marketing agencies	$22	$173	$99
Media and publishing	$21	$191	$108
Nonprofits	$16	$43	$31
Business services	$39	$225	$132

Why the difference in the cost of leads? Think about the average price (more precisely the gross margin) of the two types of sales. In general, financial services will be more expensive and will produce a higher gross margin to cover the costs of lead generation and other marketing activities. The more competition in the field and the higher the return, the higher the cost of a lead.

When the same reasoning is applied to the cost of generating a B2B sales lead, the business marketer can accept a higher cost per lead for a higher return. The large differences in the costs and gross margins of various B2B products mean there will be large variations in lead costs between industry segments in business markets. There will also be differences between inbound and outbound channels.

Purchasing Leads

This discussion of generating sales leads and assessing their cost assumes that the firm, whether B2B or B2C, is generating its own sales leads, alone or with the support of a specialty marketing services firm. Typically, like the direct marketing "house list," the company's own leads will be more effective than purchased leads. However, there are thousands of firms that advertise sales leads at a low cost for virtually any business. On one end are the traditional providers of direct marketing lists, which can loosely be described as sales leads. Hoover[15] and Data Axle USA (formerly InfoUSA)[16] are both traditional purveyors of business databases and lists to the direct marketing—and now the internet marketing—industry, for as little as a few cents per lead. The source of the leads is the business and consumer directories compiled by these firms. These are business leads that are qualified only by industry membership; the "lead" does not necessarily need the marketer's product. While purchased "targeted lists" are still popular among B2B marketers, the marketer's own lists of customers and those who register over the web or click on paid advertisements are usually more likely to result in qualified leads.

Some marketers offer a set of "free leads" for little or nothing as an incentive for purchasing more leads. Many of these leads are of extremely poor quality and have been obtained in questionable ways like hacking. Purchasing sales leads is a "buyer beware" activity! The poorer the initial lead quality, the more it will cost to qualify them and the fewer good leads will come out at the end of the lead funnel.

Demand Generation Step Three: Nurturing Leads

The next step in demand generation is lead nurturing. Business marketers use lead nurturing techniques in part because they achieve results and in part because they have to get used to small numbers. Often, the total market size is rather small, perhaps a few thousand or even a hundred firms. Each sale can be quite large—in the hundreds of thousands or even millions of dollars. Consequently, each sales lead is indeed something to be nurtured.

The Buyer's Journey

Lead nurturing requires a good understanding of the buyer's purchase journey and stage in the buy cycle. Companies use campaign-, industry- or persona-based nurturing "tracks" and deliver content and offer experiences relevant to that track, on average using three "touches" or interactions with each track.[17] Aberdeen's best-in-class companies tended to use a variety of marketing technologies to interface with and nurture leads, including both inbound and outbound telemarketing, as shown in Figure 13.12.

Kaiser Permanente Colorado (KPCO) is a healthcare organization that uses the lead nurturing process to great success. The company is Colorado's largest nonprofit health plan and is consistently rated highly by its customers. KPCO captured leads through targeted

Figure 13.12   Marketing Technology for Lead Nurturing Across Company Type
Source: Aberdeen Group, May 2012

	Best-in-Class	Average	Laggards
Email marketing system	88%	76%	67%
CRM/sales force automation	86%	64%	60%
Web analytics	75%	56%	64%
Marketing automation software suite	63%	40%	36%
Cookie-based website tracking	63%	46%	57%
Outbound telemarketing	63%	44%	29%
Inbound telemarketing	43%	38%	21%
Marketing analytics tools	43%	29%	7%
Marketing automation consultant/services	43%	32%	14%
Content marketing platform	38%	32%	21%
Marketing asset management	29%	13%	7%
Revenue performance management software	29%	9%	7%

landing pages that were driven by telemarketing, email, paid search, and social advertising campaigns. Leads were also sourced from special events, industry associations, or other lead sources. Multichannel marketing programs were used to nurture leads, qualify them, and convert them into customers and messages, which were then segmented appropriately. Based on the point in the buying cycle, the customer could be closed with a quick email or might need a more detailed rate quote. Messaging and content were targeted to the buyer persona as well. The results were an increase in the "win rate" from leads of 3 to 33 percent and $23.4 million in marketing-sourced revenue in 18 months.[18]

Designing and Testing Landing Pages to Nurture Leads

The Kaiser Permanente example illustrates the use of targeted landing pages in the lead nurturing process. The landing page refers to the page customers encounter when they click through from any channel to a business website. A landing page is constructed that is specific to the content or offer in one or more channels. This type of landing page is housed on a server but is not part of the website itself. It allows the marketer to get contact and qualifying information like that in Figure 13.13. Dr. Zahay filled out this form to receive information to help write this book. Although as an educator she is probably not a good prospect for Aberdeen, the company will use her information to make that determination in the demand generation process.

landing page
a web page designed to receive visitors who are coming to the site as a result of a link from another site.

Figure 13.13   A Qualification Form for Information Download Source: Digital Marketing Depot

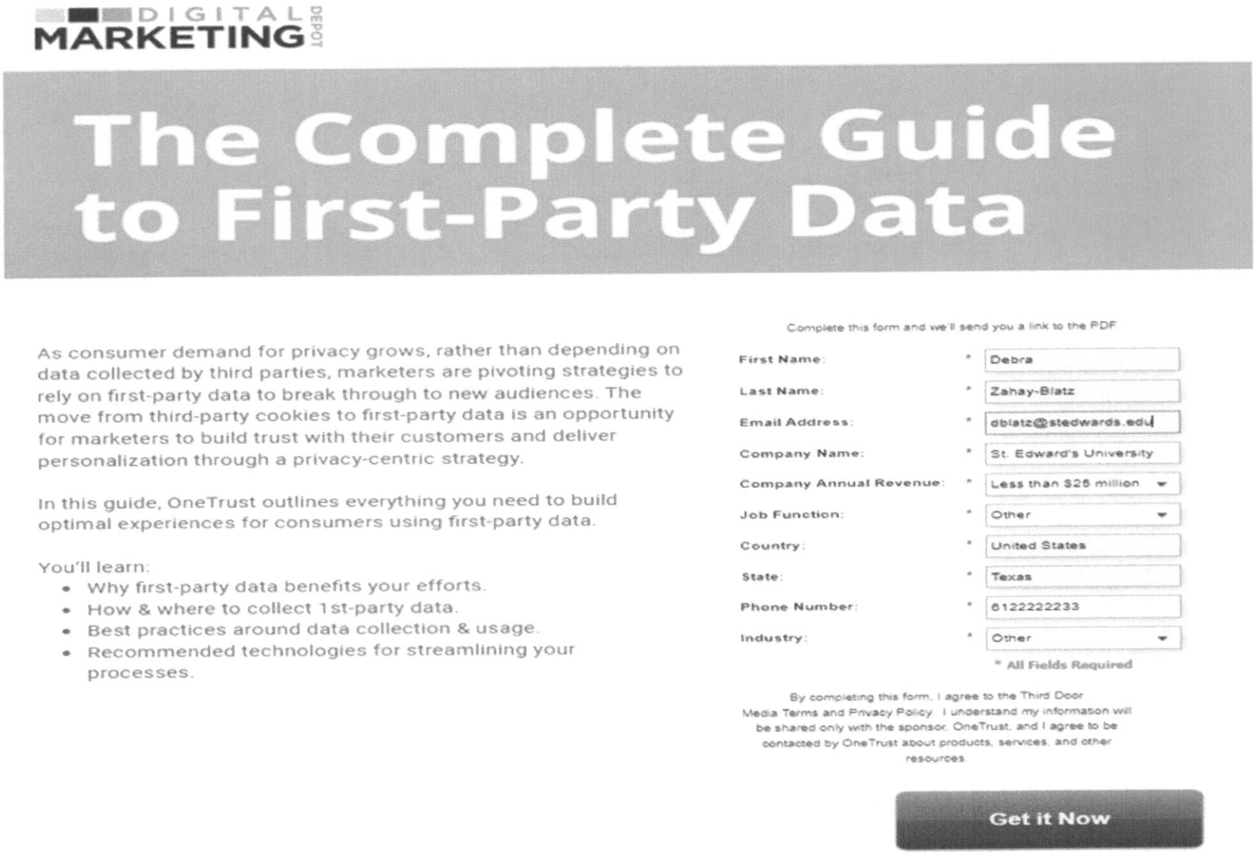

As consumer demand for privacy grows, rather than depending on data collected by third parties, marketers are pivoting strategies to rely on first-party data to break through to new audiences. The move from third-party cookies to first-party data is an opportunity for marketers to build trust with their customers and deliver personalization through a privacy-centric strategy.

In this guide, OneTrust outlines everything you need to build optimal experiences for consumers using first-party data.

You'll learn:
- Why first-party data benefits your efforts.
- How & where to collect 1st-party data.
- Best practices around data collection & usage.
- Recommended technologies for streamlining your processes.

Complete this form and we'll send you a link to the PDF.

First Name: * Debra
Last Name: * Zahay-Blatz
Email Address: * dblatz@stedwards.edu
Company Name: * St. Edward's University
Company Annual Revenue: * Less than $25 million
Job Function: * Other
Country: * United States
State: * Texas
Phone Number: * 6122222233
Industry: * Other

* All Fields Required

By completing this form, I agree to the Third Door Media Terms and Privacy Policy. I understand my information will be shared only with the sponsor, OneTrust, and I agree to be contacted by OneTrust about products, services, and other resources.

Get it Now

This approach is much more useful in the context of lead generation and management and it is the type of landing page we will describe in this section. There is no good reason for simply dumping click-throughs on the corporate home page. There must be a landing page, whether it already exists on the website or whether it must be constructed specifically for the ad or lead generation campaign.

There is a great deal of useful advice on the internet about best practices for guiding the buyer through the buying journey.[19] A key way to support the buyer's journey is to create effective landing pages that make it easy to understand the next steps in the process and give something of value in exchange for any information received. Another key point for firms is to avoid making landing page mistakes, particularly obvious ones such as cases where the landing page goes to the wrong step in the journey, a crowded webpage, or to a product unrelated to the initial search or inquiry.[20] A good summary comes from MarketingExperiments, which, as the name suggests, conducts extensive testing of marketing activities throughout the sales funnel, using the techniques described in Chapter 1. It uses the term "marketing optimization," which has become popular to describe data-driven improvements at any stage of the sales funnel. From its extensive testing experience, it has settled on three criteria for landing pages that work—*simplicity*, *continuity*, and *relevance*.

Figure 13.14 shows the second stage in an optimization process, testing and improving a landing page. The company had already tested and improved the PPC ad for this unidentified business software company, improving the click-through rate by 21 percent.

Figure 13.14 Testing a Landing Page to Optimize Click-Throughs Source: MarketingExperiments. Used with Permission,

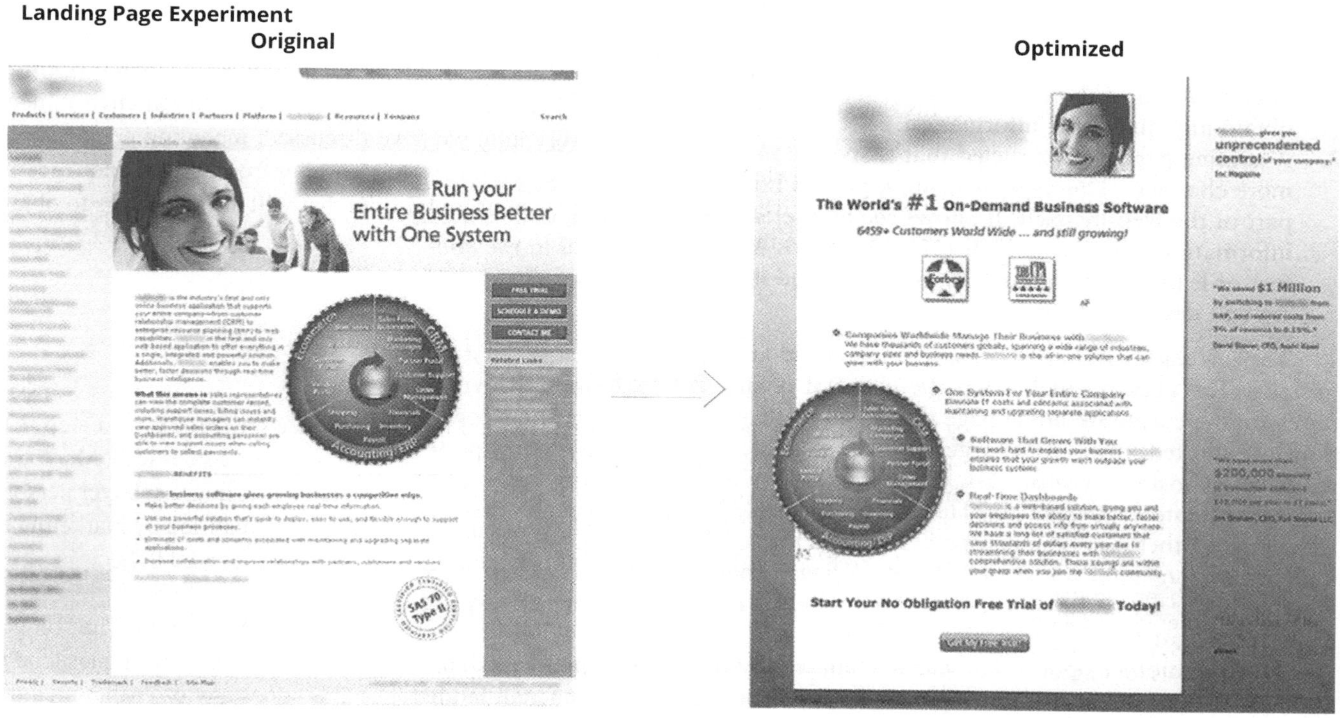

Landing Page Experiment

The company in the second phase made changes to the landing page to increase its simplicity, continuity, and relevance. The changes were as follows:

- To improve the layout by eliminating the left-hand navigation bar and reducing the number of call-to-action buttons to just one. Taking off the website navigation bar from the landing page may seem counterintuitive, but look at it this way; the marketer wants the reader to click on the call-to-action button, following the conversion path the marketer has designed. Clicking on anything else—any one of the links on the navigation bar—interrupts and probably destroys the conversion path. The changes created a *simpler* page.

- To "chunk" the copy into smaller bulleted units. The headline, subhead, and the award symbols directly below the subhead, mirrored the "we're number 1" promise made on the PPC ad, thereby improving the *continuity* from one element of the path to another. MarketingExperiments points out that the information was already there; it just rearranged it.

- To improve the *relevance* of the landing page, it included customer testimonials. Though brief, the testimonials included numbers that demonstrated improved outcomes from use of the software.

Taken together, these changes improved the click-throughs from the landing page to the forms page by 54 percent.

MarketingExperiments also optimized the forms page for this client using both design and messaging that reflected the landing page. The form looked simpler, but it actually asked for the same amount of information. The number of forms submitted increased by 97 percent. That growth was not all the result of the improved form; more people arrived on the landing page and more people clicked through from the landing page. That meant many more people arrived at the forms page where the completion rate improved by just over 7 percent from the original to the optimized form.

An improved landing page helped a great deal in this particular test. However, *it was the optimization of each page as part of a three-step process* that created the final outcome—an improvement of 272 percent in overall conversion. According to Marketing-Experiments, "the optimized path also produced more than four times the monthly profit." This data demonstrates the value of testing in the marketing automation environment. However, it takes knowledge of everything we have discussed, including personas, the buy cycle, knowledge of the customer's journey, and learning from testing and research to create effective paths through the web or mobile site that will allow visitors to obtain the information they need to convert to customers.

Demand Generation Step Four: Qualifying Sales Leads to Create Marketing Qualified Leads

Once a prospect has been generated from an inquiry or other source, the next step is to qualify in order to determine whether the inquiry actually represents a sales lead. Marketing takes the first step in qualifying the leads based on indicated buyer interest, buyer persona fit, or other criteria. The leads that have been scored and further qualified by marketing as worthy to be passed on to sales to check their qualifications are deemed to be Marketing Qualified Lead (MQL).

There are leads at the other end of the qualified/unqualified continuum. The "bingo" cards (many offers on a single response card) that you still see in some magazines tend to produce a large volume of highly unqualified prospects. So does any offer that includes a sizable free gift, especially one that is unrelated to the product itself. Any sources that produce unqualified leads which haven't met the MQL scoring threshold met by the organization will, in turn, produce major marketing expenses as the (few) good are sorted from the (many) bad.

Marketing typically uses scoring models to, as a first step, qualify leads. Lead scoring models tend to be set up and run in marketing automation systems. such as Oracle Eloqua, Salesforce Pardot, and Adobe Marketo Engage. These applications tend to make operations easier, but they do not solve the basic problem. The marketer must ensure that the scoring system genuinely expresses the lead quality, and he must revisit the items and associated scores at frequent intervals to make certain that they still accurately reflect the firm's situation and needs.

Lead scoring requires a model that requires data that includes the following:

- Online activity: Number and frequency of visits to site, multiple visitors from same firm, time spent, clicks on email newsletters, and more (negative: time spent on job openings page)
- Current or previous customer relationship
- Title: role in buying center: Purchasing agent may be a negative, depending on product in question
- Ideal customer profile industry, size of firm, annual revenue, and more.

It should be noted that most of these criteria are not simple "yes/no" questions. It may be sufficient to score them on a simple scale—1 to 3, for example. In that case, a set of categories needs to be developed for items like "number of visits to site: 1 visit in past six months, 3–5 in past six months, 6 or more in past six months." This categorization suggests that the marketer is rescoring leads every six months. It is often better to assign points for each item instead of using a scale. A point system allows the marketer to build in weights for important or negative items. For example, the VP of Procurement title may be heavily weighted positively; whereas a prospect in a region where the firm does not have sales representation may be heavily weighted negatively. A scoring system can

Marketing Qualified Lead (MQL) a lead that has been through scoring and other qualification processes and is ready to be passed on to sales for further qualification.

unqualified leads potential sales leads for which there is no qualifying data beyond membership in a relevant industry.

become much more complex, but it is wise to start as simply as possible and add to the complexity of the scoring only as experience clearly demonstrates the need. Figure 13.15 illustrates a real-life lead scoring form from industry. The scoring model adds points for actions such as viewing a video (+10 points), completing a contact form with a request for a demo (+40 points), or visiting the website multiple times in one day (+5 points). The form takes away points for inactivity (−5 points) or unsubscribing from a newsletter (−10 points). The lead with the above-mentioned activities would have 55 positive points (10 + 40 + 5) minus 15 points (−5+−10) for a total lead "score" of 40 points. Whether this score is good or bad depends on the activity of other leads and what the threshold number of points is for a lead to be considered qualified in this round of analysis by marketing.

Deciding how much information to request from a prospect for lead scoring and qualification requires a delicate balancing act. Think of it in customer relationship terms. There really is no relationship yet, so prospects are reluctant to give up much information. The more information the marketer can get, the less it will cost to identify real leads and qualify them. The minimal amount of information is name and email address.

Figure 13.15   **Lead Scoring Form from Industry Illustrates Complexity of Customer Interactions** Source: Dr. Juli James, St. Edward's University Adjunct Professor, Adobe Marketo Engage Champion.

Website Visits	Score
Viewed Video 75%+	10
Clicks link to Schedule Demo or Talk to Us	5
Multiple Web Visits-One day	5
Form Fill	
Complete Contact Form/Demo Request	40
Decrease Score	
Decrease Score - Inactivity, 1st time	−5
Visited Career Pages	−5
Decrease Score - Inactivity	−10
Unsubscribed from Email	−10
Banner Ad	
Converted - Response	15
Content Syndication	
Downloaded Asset - Response	20
Email Campaign	
Opened	1
Clicked Email (Social link);	2
Clicked Email;	5
Downloaded Asset - Response;	20
Unsubscribed	−10

Events (External Tradeshow)	Score
Invited;	0
Added by Sales;	0
Registered;	10
Scheduled Meeting - Response;	15
Booked Demo - Response;	15
Attended Show;	10
Visited Booth - Response;	15
Attended Seminar Session - Response;	20
Influential Meeting - Response;	40
Attended Demo - Response;	40
Executive Meeting - Response;	40
No Show;	0
Post Show Engagement - Response	25
Google AdWords	
Converted - Response	15

Events (Internal Roadshow)	Score
Invited;	0
Added by Sales;	0
Registered - Response;	10
Scheduled Meeting - Response;	15
Booked Demo - Response;	15
Attended Show - Response;	25
Influential Meeting - Response;	40
Attended Demo - Response;	40
Executive Meeting - Response;	40
No Show;	0
Post Show Engagement - Response	25
LinkedIn	
Converted - Response	15
List Purchase	
Opted- in - Response;	15
Online Advertising	
Converted - Response	15
Paid Search	
Converted - Response	15
Social Media	
Converted - Response	15

Webinar	Score
Registered;	10
Attended - Response;	25
Attended On-demand - Response;	20
Price Request - Response	25
Xing	
Converted - Response	15

How does the marketer know how much information to ask in an information form used in lead scoring and when there is too much information requested? First, testing the response form in various versions helps determine what will optimize response. Second, continually reviewing the metrics for the form to determine how many people start to fill out the form and exit the page before completing it will improve response. It is even better if the analytics allows the marketer to see at which line in the form the visitor stops.

The outcome of lead scoring and qualification is a set of lead categories which then can be distributed to the sales force. The essence of lead distribution is to categorize leads for immediate closing efforts or nurturing them with a view to future closing. There is also a delicate balance between giving salespeople only well-qualified leads that are worthy of their efforts and keeping them supplied with a target number of leads.

Scored leads are usually further qualified based on behavioral characteristics such as customer persona fit and the purchasing scenario before they are passed on to sales. Once further qualification has occurred, a minimum number of categories for lead distribution would be three:

lead distribution
leads that have been through scoring and other qualification processes and are ready to be passed on to sales for further qualification.

1. Leads ready for distribution to sales force (MQLs)
2. Leads for further nurturing
3. Leads to receive no attention at present.

Once MQLs are distributed to the sales force, leads that are to be nurtured might be distributed to a call center or assigned to receive periodic email communications. Some leads might percolate up the system and be candidates for future nurturing. All these nurturing activities can be managed through a marketing automation system. Leads that are to receive no attention at present might be rescored at a later date.

Using Customer Personas

As marketing seeks to further qualify leads beyond the use of lead scoring models, it looks to the concept of customer personas. Every marketing student is familiar with the concept of market segmentation and knows how important it is to select the appropriate target segment for a marketing campaign. The concept of the persona takes the concept one step further. Whether B2C or B2B, a persona puts flesh on the bones of a typical segment profile, which describes a customer (or perhaps a customer firm in B2B) in a series of business demographic, product use, and buying behavior terms. The terms are straightforward quantitative measures: "yearly revenue between $50 and $100 million," for example. A persona weaves a textual description around the set of quantitative data, making it qualitative and humanizing it.

The idea of creating personas is not new, but it has become newly popular in the context of the internet. Personas are helpful to everyone involved with customers, but they are especially helpful with the interface between marketing and IT. It is the job of marketing to select segments around which to develop marketing strategy and to profile those segments for strategy execution. It is the job of IT to design websites and landing pages that reflect the strategy and support the execution. If marketing can give IT a written depiction of a specific customer who represents a specific segment, IT will have a human image to which it can design. Such a specialized strategy should result in a better product from both the marketing and IT standpoint.

In its e-book entitled *Persuasion Architecture Future Now*, a consulting group defines personas as "archetypical fictional characters who represent your buying audience." In describing how this group creates personas for its clients, it goes on to say:

> When we design personas for persuasive systems, we are primarily interested in understanding how they initiate relationships, how they gather information, how they approach the decision-making process, what language they use, and how they prefer to obtain agreement and

closure. These are the principal factors that influence how we choose and connect prospects to content that helps them buy in a manner comfortable to them.[21]

Personas are created based on detailed marketing research—both qualitative and quantitative—and website and other online metrics. Dr. Andrea Wiggins cataloged the steps used in the creation of personas, from collecting initial data to analyzing detailed website reports to the selection of and creation of living personas.[22] Use of personas in website design have been discussed in Chapter 6 and are discussed from a consumer perspective in Chapter 12.

Figure 13.16 is a graphical representation of a customer persona that was developed in the specific context of lead generation and management in a B2B market. It describes a chief marketing officer (CMO). It contains a great deal of detail on what this type of CMO does and how they do it. It includes data that is specific to B2B marketing like goals, motivations, and challenges. It also includes important characteristics for the sales process like key questions and communication preferences.

The questions a marketer needs to answer in order to develop a persona like this are laid out by Jeff Ogden, president of Find New Customers, a B2B lead generation firm. His questions include as follows:

- What pressing issues keep this person up at night?
- What motivates them to take action?

Figure 13.16   **Persona for a CMO** Source: Mkt https://mkt.io/buyer-persona/cmo-chief-marketing-officer/

Chief Marketing Officer

Chineka Francis

As the Chief Marketing Officer (CMO), it's Chineka's job to decide the overall marketing strategy for her organisation. She's responsible for sustainable growth, sales enablement, and financial performance. To do this, she works closely with the CEO or Chief Growth Officer or to set the Key Performance Indicators (KPIs) and marketing metrics that will best drive the growth of the business.

Age	Location	Years of Experience
25 to 34	**Global**	**10+**

Job Seniority	Job Function	Sector/Industry
Director	**Marketing**	**Various**

Goals

- Better tracking of marketing metrics
- Keep up-to-date with the latest industry issues and trends
- Find the best partners and suppliers

Motivations

- Prove the value of marketing within our organisation
- Make the most of the marketing budget
- Gain and maintain a competitive advantage

Questions

- How do we improve our customer experience?
- How can we grow our customer bas‹
- How can we balance short-term revenue with long-term brand growt

Preferred Content

 Articles   ⏵ **Videos**   ✉ **Emails**

 🎙 **Podcasts**   ⏷ Webinars   📊 **Reports**

 🖐 **Social**   📅 Events   Community

Challenges

 Market uncertainty

 Reimagining customer experience

Marketing attribution

- What sources do they turn to for information and daily news?
- How do they go about making business decisions?
- What type of organizations do they belong to and what events do they attend?
- What social networks do they frequent?
- Do they seek advice from colleagues, industry peers, or unbiased third parties?
- What specific words or phrases do they use to describe the problems they are facing? (This is almost always missed!)
- What might prevent them from selecting your company or product?
- What are their content preferences throughout the buying cycle?[23]

Ogden argues that it is important to know the target buyer in as much depth and detail as possible in order to sell effectively, and that a persona is a good example of that kind of knowledge.

Developing Purchasing Scenarios

Another tool marketers use to further qualify leads is the purchasing scenario. The term scenario may be familiar to you from a strategy course. Here are two definitions from the corporate strategy literature:

1. Michael Porter defines a scenario as "an internally consistent view of what the future might turn out to be—not a forecast, but one possible future outcome."
2. Peter Schwartz describes scenario analysis as "a tool for ordering one's perception about alternative future environments in which one's decisions might be played."[24]

Marketers use scenarios to understand the customer purchasing process for uses such as developing a content strategy, understanding how the customer uses the website in making a purchase, and determining if a lead is marching down the path to purchase or just browsing.

The GrokDotCom blog defines a marketing (persuasion) scenario as follows: A scenario consists of persuasive components that lead a visitor segment to participate in a conversion action. Some of these components will be linear; others will be nonlinear. All must be customer focused—based on how each segment approaches the decision to buy—rather than business-focused.[25] Essentially, a scenario is a story abut how a customer goes about purchasing a product.

scenario
essentially a story about how a customer goes about purchasing a product.

Consultant Patricia Seybold, writing about the use of scenarios by her consultancy, describes the kind of revelations marketers can find when they get the customer's perspective on the purchase process. Two of her examples are as follows:

- Monster, the job search website, is an important tool for corporate recruiters. Monster prided itself on providing a large number of qualified candidates for each job that recruiters were trying to fill. What it found was that the large number of candidates it was returning caused the recruiters to spend too much time screening. According to Seybold, "They wanted the best three candidates and they wanted them within 24 hours."
- Merck's Medco consumer prescription management service deals with a long value chain—doctors, insurers, and pharmaceutical companies to name only some. Consumers care about getting their prescriptions refilled quickly and accurately. Other members of Medco's value chain had policies and procedures in place that interfered with or slowed down refilling of prescriptions on the site. By working with the members of the value chain to align refill policies, Medco was able to eliminate 30 percent of pharmacists' and patients' telephone calls that had been coming in to its call center.[26]

In addition, the Irish consultancy iQ Content has an example of a complete scenario written for website design use. It calls it sales call-back (variant 1), which reads as follows

> The Sales Prospect sees an offer on the site that they'd like to avail of but they'd like more information before deciding to buy. There's a link that says you can have a member of the Vodafone customer care team call you about the offer at a time of your choosing. They click that link and because the offer is open only to existing Vodafone customers the system checks to see if they are logged in. They aren't, so they are taken to the login screen. This also offers them the option of registering if they do not have login details already. The Sales Prospect logs in and is taken to the call-back scheduling form. The query title, relating to the specific offer the Sales Prospect expressed interest in, has already been entered on the form by the system and their personal details are already entered in the relevant form fields. The Sales Prospect schedules a call using the form controls and submits the form.[27]

Notice that this scenario works fine if the prospect is a Vodafone customer. What if they are not? One good solution would be a second variant in which there is a different offer for noncustomers and/or a call to action to become a customer. That is a primary benefit of a scenario; it allows the marketer to see what is working or not working and what else may be needed.

To summarize, personas put life into market segment descriptors, and scenarios map out the path to conversion, which can be website-specific or more general in nature. Marketing leads will be classified by persona and marketing will also look at the purchase scenarios of prospects when qualifying leads. If a prospect is on a likely path to conversion, the lead will be deemed more worthy of qualification by the sales force.

Sales Accepted Leads (SALs) and Sales Qualified Leads (SQLs)

The sales department itself usually further qualifies the leads presented by marketing based on its knowledge of the situation, such as the timing of the sale or poor product fit. The leads that pass through this process are known as Sales Qualified Leads (SQLs). Sales will then further qualify the leads making sure that the lead will have sufficient budget, authority, and need to purchase the product in a specific time frame. One of the many qualification frameworks used is known as BANT. BANT stands for the following:

Sales Qualified Leads (SQLs)
a lead that has passed through the BANT process as fully qualified potential customers.

BANT
Budget, Authority, Need, Time; used to qualify sales leads.

B-Budget: Does the prospect have the money to purchase?

A-Authority: Is the prospect the one making the decision?

N-Need: Does the prospect have a defined need?

T-Timing: Is the prospect going to buy now or later?

Leads that meet the BANT qualification are known as SQLs. A moment's reflection suggests that these issues are easily translated into specific questions that can be asked to try to qualify an MQL into an SQL. For instance, "Do you have money in this year's budget to make the purchase?" The prospect will generally know the answers to the qualifying questions and will be willing to provide them. This process saves time for both the marketer and the prospective purchaser. After further research by the sales force, SQLs that are true opportunities are then classified as Sales Accepted Leads (SALs).

This process is illustrated in the traditional Marketo Marketing/Sales Funnel in Figure 13.17. Please note that a Sales Development Rep (SDR) is an outbound sales position that is relied upon heavily for lead qualification in the sales process and helps bridge the gap to turn MQLs into SQLs. The SDR might do much of the BANT qualification before the lead is delivered to the outside sales force. This process is more efficient

Sales Accepted Leads (SALs)
a lead that has been further qualified by sales as close to conversion.

Figure 13.17 Marketo Marketing/Sales Funnel Source: https://nation.marketo.com
/t5/product-documents/long-live-the-funnel/ta-p/249062

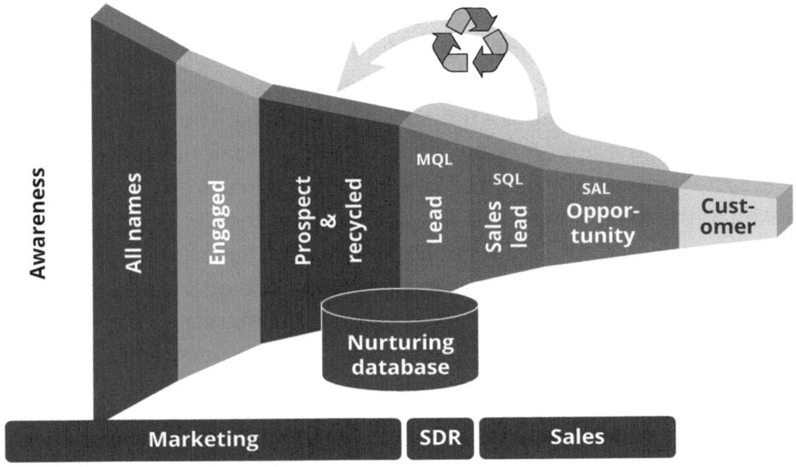

and cost-effective for a company than having highly compensated sales representatives involved in the early stages of lead qualification. All leads are processed through a nurturing database, typically housed in the marketing automation system.

Cost of Lead Qualification

The higher the lead quality, the less it will cost to qualify it; this is the underlying rationale for getting as much information as possible in the prospect process.

David Green, director of best practices at MECLABS, has a hypothetical example of lead qualification, which is drawn from wide experience. The ratio of 70 valid leads per 100, shown in Figure 13.18, is reasonable and can be affected up or down by the desirability of the offer and the amount and intrusiveness of the information requested on the prospect form.

Green assumes that the cost of a sales rep, including salary and fringes, is $200,000, and the rep has 1,960 productive hours available after vacation, training, and so on. If they can make ten qualification calls per hour, that will amount to 19,600 phone calls per year. If they take 4.2 minutes to make a qualification call, it will take a total of 40 hours to qualify all 100 leads. If only the 70 valid leads enter the qualification process, the number

lead qualification
determining whether a prospect has the characteristics necessary to make a purchase.

Figure 13.18 Lowering the Cost of Lead Qualification Source: J. David Green, "2011 Lead Generation Trends and Challenges," p. 20, November 15, 2013. Reprinted with permission of MECLABS.

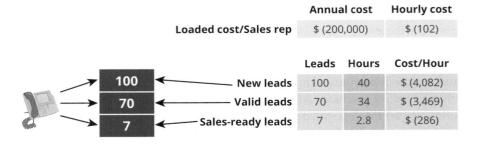

	Annual cost	Hourly cost
Loaded cost/Sales rep	$ (200,000)	$ (102)

		Leads	Hours	Cost/Hour
	New leads	100	40	$ (4,082)
	Valid leads	70	34	$ (3,469)
	Sales-ready leads	7	2.8	$ (286)

Assumes 1,960 hours per year and 19,600 dials.

of hours is reduced to 34. If only sales-ready leads are called, the number of hours is less than 3, reducing the total cost from $4,082 to $286. Thus, the importance of reducing the total cost of a lead is important from a marketing management point of view. Hence the need for the more effective use of marketing automation systems.

However, decreasing qualification costs by acquiring more valid and sales-ready leads is a matter of degree, not of absolutes. It is reasonable to strive for a high proportion of valid leads, but a firm is unlikely to ever get only SALs. In fact, such a scenario would not be desirable. The lead pipeline needs to be kept stocked with leads in various stages of readiness to keep sales stable and sales costs at a minimum. Remember that these figures are hypothetical. Any good marketer tracks the success of individual lead generation programs using metrics like number of leads, cost per lead by medium, and number of qualified leads. Past performance is the best measure of success, not general or hypothetical industry metrics. Prior to the internet, qualification was almost entirely conducted by telephone. It is a process that works, but it is relatively expensive. Today, B2B marketers have other, more cost-effective, options.

Lead Generation and Qualification at EDGAR Online

Lead scoring is an area in which business marketers often seek the assistance of a marketing services firm. Silverpop, now part of the IBM Marketing Cloud, for example, was originally a supplier of email services and developed into a firm that offered lead scoring as part of its marketing automation software.[28]

The experience of financial services firm EDGAR Online with a lead generation and qualification system represents several of the issues and solutions in this area.[29] EDGAR Online's basic problem was one shared by many marketers: EDGAR needed to increase the quality of the leads distributed to the sales force: in other words, to make sure they were indeed sales-ready leads. It began by better promoting its content with whitepapers and newsletters, and by offering free product trials as an incentive. This promotion actually increased the number of leads generated, which could have compounded its problem. Instead, the firm refined its lead scoring criteria and developed a careful, automated lead distribution process.

The EDGAR Online case study recounts the following outcomes:

- Attraction of new customers and better communication with existing ones led to a 400 percent increase in sales leads, with the sales department being happier with the quality.
- The lead scoring system led to five times more qualified leads each month.
- The rate of sales closure was more than double the average for EDGAR Online's industry sector.
- The seven-day free trials for EDGAR Pro resulted in conversion rates in the 40–60 percent range.

This technique makes such good sense that all good B2B marketers do it, right? Sadly, that is not the case. A study by consultancy Aberdeen found only 20 percent of marketers using lead management technology were characterized as "best-in-class," meaning that action was taken on 85 percent of the leads passed from marketing to sales whereas 80 percent of marketers pass on 27 percent or fewer leads that are actionable by sales.[30] A more recent study by LeanData reinforced this trend and illustrated that not much has changed. The study showed fewer than 1 in 5 B2B Marketers (18 percent) felt confident their current lead management system would support 2022 revenue goals.[31] The low effectiveness of these systems is usually the result of an organizational disconnect between marketing and advertising, who distribute the sales leads, and sales, who are responsible for following them up and closing the sale. All too often the MQL process falls into the organizational crack between marketing/advertising and sales and is not followed up effectively. The result is that marketing spends money to generate leads. Sales complains that the leads received are of poor quality. If no one in the organization is responsible for fixing the crack, the organizational return on its marketing and sales investment suffers.

To sum up, the activities leading up to the closing step are of great importance, even though the point of the entire process is to close the sale or conversion.

Demand Generation Step Five: Lead Conversion

Defining Conversion

Traditional direct marketers are responsible for the term "conversion," and its original definition is making the first sale to a prospect—converting the lead to a sale. As the importance of CRM became evident in the 1980s, direct marketers were heard to speak of "converting to a loyal customer." That sounds like exactly what marketers are trying to do, but it begs the question of precise metrics. Is it the second or maybe the third sale? Is it obtaining a growing share of the customer's expenditure on the product in question? It could be either, or both! It could be another performance indicator that is more closely tied to the company's strategy.

While "lead conversion" can generically be defined as closing a sale, it too can be a deceptively simple concept. Conversion in its broadest sense is any desired action, whether it be downloading a whitepaper, registering for a webinar, or subscribing to a newsletter. In terms of the demand generation process and the Marketing/Sales Funnel, conversion is getting the prospect or lead from one stage of the funnel to the next. The conversion rate is the percentage of those leads that make it from one stage of the funnel to the next.

Conversion can often be an overlooked opportunity in B2B demand generation. Omniture, now a part of the Adobe Marketing Cloud for analytics applications, has said that, in general, most organizations spend more time and money promoting their websites through acquisition channels such as search or affiliate marketing than they do optimizing existing conversion rates.

Another important point to note is that there may be multiple "conversion" points in the demand generation process. For example, social media marketers often say they have "converted" a Facebook fan to a sales lead when the fan clicks on a link and provides contact information on the website in return for desired information. From the standpoint of the social media team, it seems to be a conversion, because the team has passed on the responsibility to another group. However, using conversion that way is a loose application of the term. Measurable objectives should be established for each team at each stage of the demand generation process.

Measuring Conversion

In addition to neglecting the conversion process or failing to measure the results, we tend to think of conversion too narrowly as only converting existing site visitors in the "here and now." We often overlook applying marketing fundamentals such as identifying and defining profiles that comprise our larger target audience, developing the right offer and corresponding message, and delivering it to them at the right time in their purchase cycle.

Omniture goes on to say that this is all about relevancy—the right content and offers at the right time—the customer's right time, not the marketer's! It lists seven steps in an optimized conversion process:

1. **Identify Conversion Goals and KPIs**. Key performance indicators (KPIs), which were discussed in more detail in Chapter 5, are internal benchmarks for performance at each stage: number of advertising impressions, number of click-throughs to the site, and number of lead forms completed, for example.

2. **Define and Acquire Target Profiles—Apply the 40/40/20 Rule**. There is a time-honored direct marketing rule that 40 percent of success can be attributed to targeting and another 40 percent to the offer, with 20 percent being attributable to creative execution.

3. **Organize and Optimize Site Structure**. It is important to have a site that makes it easy for visitors to find and purchase what they want.

4. **Develop a Compelling Message**. The importance of the message seems to go without saying, but in this context, it must be a message that is relevant to each specific audience segment.

5. **Place Effective Calls to Action**. Chapters 4 and 8 note that specific and compelling calls to action are a key part of any direct-response effort. That notion applies to conversion as well.

6. **Enhance Shopping Cart and Lead Capture Processes**. A visitor with a product interest has only two positive action options while on the website: he purchases the product at that moment using the shopping cart function; alternatively, he can fill out a form requesting more information or be kept informed via newsletters. (A third option, of course, is to leave without doing either.) It is the job of the marketer to ensure that as few qualified prospects as possible leave the site without taking positive action of some kind.

7. **Test, Measure, and Refine**. Many steps in the conversion process can be tested. We will discuss testing landing pages later in this chapter. Both test results and the metrics produced by the program can and should be used to improve future conversion programs.

These steps also seem to follow a commonsense approach, and they do. However, they only mention the thorny problem of defining exactly what a conversion is so appropriate goals can be set.

In most firms, there are many internal teams involved in various stages of the demand generation process, and each should have its own target to reach for that stage. The "sales funnel" is the concept that previously was commonly used to describe this process. In the sales funnel leads come in at the top and are sifted out at the bottom. Sales is considered a numbers game and if there are enough leads at the top there will be customers at the bottom. The funnel in Figure 13.17 is a marketing perspective on the sales funnel and has some useful additional strategy guidance. The Marketo Marketing/Sales Funnel is on its side and operates from left to right in an intentional manner, leading the prospect through a process that will result in conversion.

The customer is correctly portrayed as the centerpiece of the process with the funnel itself representing the stages of the B2B buying process and the categories in the middle representing the generic stages of lead qualification. All leads from whichever channel go into a central database, which identifies each lead by media source. Each lead should be tracked through to a sale or lack of one. As data throughout the chapter has indicated, leads generated from different sources tend to have different acquisition costs. To further complicate the matter, these leads also tend to have different conversion rates, making the cost per converted lead vastly different from one channel to another. This is an important input into planning future marketing strategies.

Demand Generation Step Six: Metrics

Calculate ROI for Demand Generation

It is obvious from the prior discussion that demand generation is a time-consuming and expensive process. Marketers need to be prepared to demonstrate that it is worth the cost. Marketers will want to calculate not only the return on investment for their efforts but also the returns on each campaign and the maximum cost that can be spent for each lead at various stages of the funnel. Marketing will also want to attribute how much revenue came from its content marketing, lead nurturing, and qualification efforts.

Conversion Paths

For example, we know that visitors take various routes (paths) through a website. One job of the marketer is to ensure that as many of them purchase (convert) as possible. Of course, there is one further complication. Figure 13.19 shows a set of paths through an unrealistically simple video game site that explains the issue.

The complication is that different market segments take different paths through the site. Would you expect the person who comes to a video games site to purchase the latest Star Wars game to take the same path through the site as a person who came to purchase a game but did not know which specific one? Would either one of those segments take the same path as a person who just dropped by the site to see what they stocked? No; these three and other segments would take different paths, and the marketer needs to satisfy the information needs of each and provide a call to action at the appropriate time.

The figure shows that 100 visitors entered the site, and some visitors apparently came to look at games while others came to look at gaming devices. Of the 60 who came to look at games, more (40) went to the Star Wars page than to the PacMan page (20). Of those who went to the Star Wars page, half purchased while the other half was evenly split between leaving the site and going on to the product demonstration page. A majority of those who saw the demonstration purchased the game and the rest exited the site; although it is possible that they could have looped back and looked at another game. The marketer has now accounted for the 40 people who went to the Star Wars page. To account for all 60 who went to the games page, it is necessary to find out what happened to the 20 who went to the PacMan page. Forty went to the devices page and the chart shows that outcome.

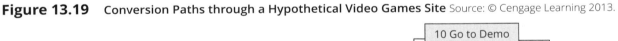

Figure 13.19 Conversion Paths through a Hypothetical Video Games Site Source: © Cengage Learning 2013.

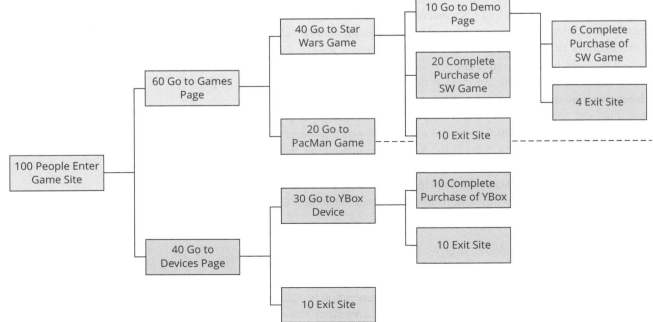

The point is that the marketer has to account for all 100 of the people who came to the site, study the actions of each segment, and locate points where the conversion outcomes might be improved. On a site of any size, this is a monumental task, which can be lessened by concentrating on target segments (some people got here by accident) and on the few target segments that are large enough to be worth the effort of improving outcomes. Still, these measurement efforts constitute a large task. The task is also an important one because this is another instance in which it is cheaper to convert more of the target audience once they reach the site than to engage in acquisition marketing to get more people to the site in the first place. This example illustrates some of the challenges in calculating ROI for specific conversion paths.

That last point actually applies to this entire chapter. It is less expensive in the end to develop great content, generate reasonable quality leads, nurture and qualify them well, and convert a significant portion of them, than it is to engage in endless acquisition campaigns, only to ignore or mismanage the sales leads that are produced.

Beyond Demand Generation: Buying Group Concept

Increasingly, B2B organizations are recognizing the complexity of the buying process and the interchange between customers in what is known as the buying group. According to Gartner a B2B buying group (or buying committee) typically consists of six to ten team members, also known as decision makers as a result of so many members, buying groups and their processes are a key contribution to the longer B2B sales cycle.[32]

Research by Clari, Inc. shows that deals above $250,000 can require as many as 19 external stakeholders to bring the deal to a close. This trend occurs because, in today's world, a complex sale might involve IT, Sales, Operations, Finance, and other areas of the organization. Sellers must be aware of the buying group in their sales efforts.

While similar to the concept of the buying center as mentioned above, the buying group goes beyond a formal decision-making unit to encompass all those who formally or informally may be involved in researching the buying decision.

As Forrester outlines in a report on driving revenue engine performance:

> "Many B2B organizations lack clear insight into their revenue opportunities. Demand processes may still focus on individual leads, even though more than 80% of B2B purchases involve groups of three or more people. They also may fail to recognize multiple selling opportunities within an account."[33]

The idea of the B2B Revenue Waterfall was designed to recognize this complexity. The Waterfall, shown in Figure 13.20, increases the visibility of accounts by shifting the demand process to:

- Focus on buying groups rather than traditional leads
- Recognize multiple selling opportunities per account
- Track opportunities from target accounts to closed revenue
- Account for the unique mix of prospect and customer opportunities that make up B2B revenue goals
- Align marketing, revenue development, and sales to better identify, engage, qualify, and win opportunities.

Although the traditional marketing "waterfall" (if displayed vertically) or horizontal sales funnel, shown in Figure 13.17, focused on specific opportunities for the new B2B revenue,

buying group
(also known as the buying committee) a set of six to 10 team members, also known as decision makers, that are needed to make the purchase decision and to bring the sales cycle to a close.

Figure 13.20   Reach Next-Level Revenue Engine Performance by Switching from Leads to Opportunities Source: Forrester (2022) Driving Growth with the B2B Revenue Waterfall™. https://www.forrester.com/europe/driving-growth-b2b-revenue-waterfall/.

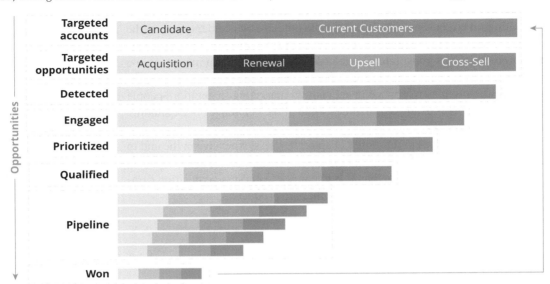

the new waterfall focuses on targeted accounts and opportunities and total revenue generated. This approach relies less on the lead generation and qualification systems that we have outlined and more on treating opportunities as a whole. This approach will undoubtedly dominate B2B digital marketing practices in the future.

The Organizational Approach

The approach described above, therefore, is considered an aspect of Account-Based Marketing (ABM). In ABM, instead of treating leads and prospects individually, the entire organization is treated holistically, and multiple individuals from the same organization are identified. This approach is particularly valuable in high-value accounts or prospects. Multiple key stakeholders are identified and marketing strategies and communications through personalized channels are used to appeal to their specific needs and personalities.[34] Companies such as 6Sense employ artificial intelligence and privacy-compliant solutions to track buying behavior across the internet to determine the stage of the organization in the buyer's journey, how best to communicate with stakeholders, and the timing of these communications.

If the complexity of these efforts leaves students feeling lost, they are not alone! Senior marketing managers recognize the complexity and the fact that it will require an investment in process improvement and marketing automation software to resolve issues in B2B marketing. In addition, ABM requires an organizational approach and is not simply implemented with a software solution. Training and time are both required to change the organization's mindset from just lead qualification to account and opportunity management. Organizations must understand that ABM may take some time, postponing the ROI until sometime in the future.

Even worse, all this complexity occurs in the context of organizational politics in which the leader of each internal team may be trying to maximize their team's performance, even at the expense of performance in other stages of the process. An example would be generating a large number of low-quality leads to meet a short-term goal but not serving the revenue goals of the organization. The organizational context represents a serious management issue that will take time and effort to resolve. Sadly, it is often easier just to ignore the issue of an optimal lead process, or focus just on leads and not look at prospect organizations as a whole. Organizational issues will remain the most significant obstacle to the effective adaptation of demand generation systems and processes within B2B firms.

Summary

As we have seen, the demand generation process is a key element of B2B marketing and is important in certain product categories in B2C marketing. It is a complex process full of sometimes mind-numbing detail. A large part of the challenge in B2B is because market sizes are often small and unit sales can be quite large, making each contact important. The chapter has emphasized throughout that there are many points in the process where marketing strategy or execution can be improved—improvements that can substantially raise revenue, cut marketing costs, or both.

The business buyer goes through a buying cycle process characterized by needs awareness, research, consolidation and consideration of potential vendors, and a purchasing decision. Since this process can take a year or more for a high-risk purchase, business marketers have a major challenge in keeping up with the potential customer's progress, providing the right content at the right time, and attempting to close the sale when the time is right. This leads to a formal process of demand generation (one of the most important activities of the business marketer), which includes content creation, lead generation, lead qualification by both sales and marketing, conversion, and follow-up analysis of relevant metrics. This process is a communications process that is often lengthy and begins with the concept of content marketing, providing the right content at the right time.

In the implementation of this process, many media channels, both online and offline, can be used to generate sales leads. These media include traditional outbound channels such as direct mail and email. Leads are often cheaper when generated by inbound marketing, being visible on the web in a way that draws potential customers to the website for further information. The request

for information can become the beginning of the demand generation process.

Marketing lead qualification may begin with an information form filled out on the website in return for content. The purpose of the information is to determine which state of the buying cycle the prospect is in and what kind of communications are appropriate. As the process goes on, more information is obtained, and when the prospect is deemed ready, the MQL is distributed to internal and/or external sales reps for further qualification by the sales force in terms of an SQL and closing (conversion).

As we have seen, conversion is not a "one size fits all" concept. Each organization is likely to have its own definition and metric for conversion. A well-managed process combines that metric with clear objectives at each stage for each team involved in the lead generation and management process. Demand generation is indeed a complex process that involves many groups within the organization. This complexity makes its implementation and execution problematic in many companies for reasons that are purely organizational, not technological. The move toward ABM and a revenue-oriented waterfall instead of a lead-oriented pipeline only presents more challenges for managers.

In conclusion, there are marketing techniques that can improve the process. These techniques include creating customer personas, building customer journey scenarios, building and optimizing landing pages, and creating clear conversion paths through a web or mobile site, and using artificial intelligence to gain customer insight. This whole process of better understanding customer market segments, developing segment-specific strategies, and testing to optimize the process, can result in major improvements in ROI in the B2B marketing process.

Discussion Questions

1. The chapter states that the discipline of sales lead generation and management was developed by direct marketers and later adapted to the internet. Why do you think direct marketers, and not traditional advertisers, originated the practice of sales lead generation and management?

2. What is the role of search marketing and branding in B2B marketing today?

3. Why do you think B2B marketers consider customer loyalty as one of their most important challenges?

4. Agree or Disagree: The B2B buy cycle has roughly the same steps as the consumer purchase decision process, is carried out in much the same way, and takes about the same length of time. Explain your answer.

5. What is your understanding of content marketing in the demand generation process? How does it differ from the kind of marketing or marketing communications that you are accustomed to?

6. List the six steps in the demand generation process.

7. Identify two or three online and two or three offline channels in which sales leads can be generated. Which channels do you think are likely to be most effective in generating leads? Which are likely to be the most expensive to use?

8. What are MQLs and how are they qualified?

9. What does the sales force do to further qualify leads received from marketing and what is the result?

10. What are some of the issues marketers should consider when trying to make the conversion process on their websites as effective as possible? How can personas and customer journey scenarios be helpful?

11. Why do you think it is hard to come up with a single, concise definition of conversion? Can you give at least two examples of different definitions of conversion and explain why the different definitions are needed?

12. What is the importance of the landing page in a demand generation context?

13. How will the concept of ABM change the B2B Demand generation process?

Endnotes

1. Douglas Karr et al., "Understanding Demand Generation vs Lead Generation," Martech Zone, August 22, 2015, https://martech.zone/demand-generation-vs-lead-generation/.

2. "Understanding and Mapping the B2B Buyer Journey," Qualtrics, April 15, 2022, https://www.qualtrics.com/experience-management/customer/b2b-buyer-journey/.

3. "Understanding the Buy Cycle: Align Your Marketing with Customers' Behavior," "White Papers," GlobalSpec Media Solutions, accessed December 19, 2022, https://www.globalspec.com/advertising/wp/wp_buycycle_maven.

4. Emma Brudner, "1 Million B2B Sales Jobs Will Vanish by 2020 <New Research>," February 1, 2017, https://blog.hubspot.com/marketing/sales-jobs-vanishing

5. Fox Agency, B2B Marketing, "Will you take on the Challenge?," "B2B Marketing Challenge," The 2016 Report, p. 13.

6. Connor Kinnear, "B2B Buyers Do 70% of Their Research Online (via PASSLE)," Passle, September 9, 2019, https://blog.passle.net/post/102fqjl/b2b-buyers-do-70-of-their-research-online.

7. Dayana Mayfield, "These are the Top B2B Marketing Challenges for 2022," December 20, 2021, https://www.drift.com/blog/b2b-marketing-challenges/

8. Alyssa Rimmer, "What is Marketing Automation? A Beginner's Guide," October 20, 2016, https://blog.hubspot.com/insiders/what-is-marketing-automation-a-beginners-guide

9. David Scott, "Demand Generation vs. Lead Generation: What Should You Focus On?," April 28, 2020, https://www.leadiro.com/blog/demand-generation-vs-lead-generation

10. Rick Burnes, "Inbound Marketing & the Next Phase of Marketing on the Web," June 10, 2021, https://blog.hubspot.com/blog/tabid/6307/bid/4416/inbound-marketing-the-next-phase-of-marketing-on-the-web.aspx

11. Roberts, M.L. and Paul D. Berger, Direct Marketing Management, second edition. See Chapter 9, B2B Direct Marketing, New York: Pearson, 1999.

12. Seth's site, accessed December 9, 2022, https://www.sethgodin.com/.

13. Rick Burnes, "Inbound Marketing & the next Phase of Marketing on the Web," HubSpot Blog (HubSpot, June 10, 2021), https://blog.hubspot.com/blog/tabid/6307/bid/4416/inbound-marketing-the-next-phase-of-marketing-on-the-web.aspx#:~:text=Inbound%20Marketing%20is%20marketing%20focused,targeted%20and%20that%20interrupt%20people.

14. Melissa Miller, "20 Fresh Stats about the State of Inbound Marketing in 2012," HubSpot Blog (HubSpot, February 1, 2017), https://blog.hubspot.com/blog/tabid/6307/bid/31550/20-Fresh-Stats-About-the-State-of-Inbound-Marketing-in-2012.aspx.

15. "Accelerate Sales with D&B Hoovers-Dun and Bradstreet," Accelerate Sales with D&B Hoovers-Dun and Bradstreet, accessed December 9, 2022, https://www.dnb.com/products/marketing-sales/dnb-hoovers.html.

16. "Make Finding New Customers Easy with Direct Mail Lists," Data Axle USA, November 14, 2022, https://www.dataaxleusa.com/lists/mailing-lists/.

17. Aberdeen Research Study.

18. "Marketing Success Series: Demand Generation with Kaiser Permanente Colorado," October 7, 2019, https://www.marketo.com/ebooks/marketing-success-series-demand-generation-with-kaiser-permanente-colorado/

19. The LAIRE Team, "How to Reduce Friction in the Sales Process," April 29, 2022, https://www.lairedigital.com/blog/how-to-reduce-friction-in-the-sales-process

20. Neil Patel, "5 Truly Awful Landing Pages You Won't Believe are from Well-Known Companies," December 7, 2010, https://neilpatel.com/blog/5-awful-landing-pages/

21. "Persuasion Architecture Uber Map - 2005-05-08 - Ai-Dealer.com," accessed December 9, 2022, http://www.ai-dealer.com/images/persuasionarchitecture.pdf.

22. Jennifer Havice et al., "How to Create Customer Personas (with Actual, Real-Life Data)," CXL, November 24, 2022, https://cxl.com/blog/creating-customer-personas-using-data-driven-research/.

23. Jeffrey L. Ogden, "Buyer Personas in B2B Lead Generation," accessed December 9, 2022, https://www.youtube.com/watch?v=IcoMvaOFqtM

24. Frank Buytendijk, Toby Hatch, and Pietro Michell, "Scenario-Based Strategy Maps," Kelley School of Business, Indiana University, 2010, p. 337.

25. Web site traffic and conversion factors, accessed March 2, 2023, https://traffic-and-conversion.blogspot.com/2005/05/grokdotcom_111657691989058315.html.

26. Seybold, Patricia, "Get Inside the Lives of Your Customers," May 2001, *Harvard Business Review*, https://hbr.org/2001/05/get-inside-the-lives-of-your-customers.

27. http://iqcontent.com/publications/features/article_77.

28. Griffin LaFleur, "10 Lead Scoring Best Practices to Improve Sales Efficiency," February 17, 2021, https://www.techtarget.com/searchcustomerexperience/tip/10-lead-scoring-best-practices-to-improve-sales-efficiency

29. "EDGAR Online Quadruples Lead Gen Pipeline Results, Raises Bar On Close Rates," September 29, 2008, www.demandgenreport.com., https://www.demandgenreport.com/feed/edgar-online-quadruples-lead-gen-pipeline-results-raises-bar-on-close-rates/

30. Aberdeen.com, accessed January 2, 2023, http://aberdeen.com/research/7603/ra-marketing-lead-management/content.aspx.

31. "The State of B2B Lead Management 2022," Your Resource Center for Everything Sales and Marketing Operations, accessed December 19, 2022, https://learn.leandata.com/ebooks/the-state-of-b2b-lead-management-2022?utm_source=unbounce&utm_medium=lp&utm_campaign=state-of-lead-mgmt-2022.

32. "Hit Your B2B Sales Targets: A Guide to Targeting Buying Groups," INFUSEmedia, February 11, 2023, https://infusemedia.com/insight/6-steps-to-marketing-to-a-b2b-buying-group/#:~:text=According%20to%20Gartner%20(2019)%2C,the%20longer%20B2B%20sales%20cycle.

33. "Driving Growth with the B2B Revenue Waterfall™," Forrester, February 4, 2022, https://www.forrester.com/europe/driving-growth-b2b-revenue-waterfall/.

34. Dr. G. Pavan Kumar and K. Rajasekhar, "Account-based Marketing in B2B Industry," *Journal of Interdisciplinary Cycle Research*, 12(II) (2020): 1154–1161.

Chapter 14

Customer Relationship Development and Retention Marketing

Learning Objectives

By the time you complete this chapter, you will be able to:

1 Discuss the importance of customer lifetime value (CLV) and customer relationship management (CRM) for marketing managers.

2 Describe the difference between transactional and relational marketing.

3 Discuss the development of a CRM strategy.

4 Explain the difference between operational and analytical CRM.

5 Describe the tools for CRM management.

6 Discuss the operational aspects of running a comprehensive CRM.

Why Are CRM and CLV Invaluable to Marketers?

Customer Relationship Management (CRM) has driven leading brands' strategies over the past 20 years.[1] The high customer acquisition cost is one reason for this trend. The original data supporting the relational approach posited that "It costs seven to ten times as much to acquire a new customer as it does to maintain an existing one." The customer acquisition cost argument is still compelling, although more recent studies have placed the figure anywhere from 3 to 30 times![2]

In addition to the high cost of customer acquisition, there are other issues that the adoption of a relational approach could address, alleviate, or possibly resolve:

- The loss of customers in an increasingly competitive marketplace; and the cost to reactivate them.

- Profits can increase by 25 to 85 percent, depending on the industry, by reducing customer defection by even 5 percent.

- Many customers who defect say they were satisfied with their former supplier.

- Extremely satisfied customers are six times more likely to repurchase than somewhat satisfied customers.

- A satisfied customer may tell five people, whereas a dissatisfied customer will tell ten.[3] In today's world of social media, the scale may be amplified when unhappy customers can tell thousands.
- It costs seven to twenty times as much to sell to a new customer as to an existing customer.[4]
- Nine out of ten customers will pay more for a better customer experience (CX).[5]

These data and many more have created two marketing mantras that guide customer-centric marketing programs today:

1. **"Marketing Is Dead."** This is because the consumer decision journey has changed and traditional marketing no longer works. The new marketing is about communities and influencers and getting both customers and influencers involved in marketing activities.

2. **"Customer Experience Trumps Loyalty."** Brand loyalists are still desirable, but the hard truth is that brands can lose even their loyal fans through poor CX. Customer loyalty and marketing loyalty programs are still important, however, as we will discuss later in this chapter.

All this argues for the importance of CRM in all marketing strategies and its preeminence in the strategies of some brands.

The Importance of CLV

The relationship argument relies on the customer lifetime value (CLV) concept to demonstrate the profit impact of relationship strategies. CLV was defined as the monetary value of a customer over time. There are many ways to make these calculations, including sophisticated methods such as discounting cash flows over time. Figure 14.1 documents the importance of relationship maintenance in the online apparel industry. After accounting for acquisition costs, the consultants identify three revenue streams associated with each customer—each one's *base* spending amount, the *growth* of spending as the

Figure 14.1 Components of Customer Lifetime Value for Apparel Purchases Source: Adapted from Bain & Company Mainspring Online Retailing Survey, December 1999. Copyright © 1999 by Bain & Company, Inc. All rights reserved. Reproduced with permission.

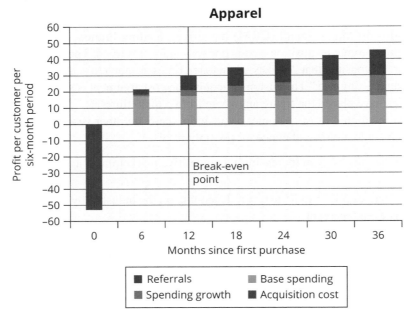

customer persists with the marketer, and the revenue generated by customer *referrals*. In this example, breakeven on acquisition costs occurs after one year; in other industries, it tends to be longer because of higher acquisition costs and/or longer purchase cycles. The general pattern, however, holds across industry sectors in both consumer and business markets. It emphasizes the importance of caring for customers in a way that causes them to return, concentrate more on their purchases with the product or brand, and refer new customers.

Each of the revenue streams contributes CLV as the customer persists. In the case of the apparel industry, the data indicate that:

- The average repeat customer spent 67 percent more in months 31 through 36 of the relationship than in the initial six months.

- An average apparel shopper referred three people to the online retailer's site after the first purchase. After ten purchases, the shopper had referred a total of seven people.

- Loyal online customers would also consider buying other product lines from the online retailer outside the current merchandise offerings, indicating brand development opportunities.

Other CLV studies indicate that loyal customers are more likely to buy across a retailer's merchandise assortment, making them better targets for cross-selling and increasing share-of-wallet. For instance, Amazon claims that they make 35 percent of their revenue by cross-selling products across the platform.[6] The platform consistently cross-sells by using their "other customers have purchased" section of the website powered by the collaborative filtering technology discussed in Chapter 1, as well as suggesting bundles of products such as a toy car with a package of AA batteries. Further, customers who interact with the company or brand on Facebook are likely to be customers already, buy more, and recommend more often after becoming fans.[7] CLV also supports marketers' interest in marketing to Millennials, customers who potentially have a long relationship with a brand.

Although the economics of the relational concept is persuasive, implementing it requires a complete change in how traditional marketers think about and perform their jobs. Modifying this magnitude is always tricky, and such has been the case with relational strategies. To understand the issues, we need to contrast the older transactional model to the relationship model and describe how it is evolving into a focus on the customer journey.

Strategic CRM

Before discussing the process of developing a CRM strategy, it is helpful to understand the changing definition of the familiar acronym.

A Word about Semantics

From its earliest days, CRM has stood for customer relationship management. The discipline focused on acquiring and managing data that provided insights for marketing programs that led to successful customer relationships. In that context, CRM made sense. However, the world has changed in many ways since the advent of data-driven marketing sometime in the mid-1970s. Improved hardware, software, and data storage capabilities materially altered the practice of CRM in the 1980s and 1990s. More recent years have seen the ability of marketers to gather, build, develop, and analyze big data sets of customer information that allow them to track and understand customers on a more detailed level than ever before. Together, these developments allowed marketers to carry out strategies they had previously only envisioned.

big data
unstructured data sets that are so large and complex that traditional data processing is challenged to analyze them.

Significant as these changes have been, they are dwarfed by the impact of social media marketing (SMM). The advent of SMM has allowed marketers to listen to what customers are saying and to engage in real-time dialog with them. Many marketers have adopted the terminology "customer relationship marketing," or sometimes "customer retention marketing," considering that more appropriate to the current environment. Throughout this chapter, CRM should be translated as "customer relationship marketing."

The Elements of CRM

CRM has three essential elements. The *strategic* process identifies CRM goals and objectives within the overall marketing and business objectives framework. The strategy development process is the focus of this section. Later, we will discuss the *operational* or tactical program and analytical elements. Each of the three elements requires different activities and expertise and needs individual attention. However, in practice, they are less distinct and may all be required to carry out a CRM initiative.

The Transactional versus the Relationship Perspective

Consumer marketers in the traditional mass media environment have had no choice except to pursue a transactional (product-centric) approach. These marketers ordinarily did not have direct contact with their customers. Consequently, they could not identify their customers as individuals nor attempt to develop an ongoing relationship with them. The mass media did not facilitate identifying and tracking individual customers and prospects. If there was one, the customer relationship was owned by an intermediary in a distribution channel. These two factors created a powerful barrier to establishing relationships with marketers producing products and services. In addition, the large up-front investment required to build a product-specific customer database could not be justified by the small gross margins provided by many frequently purchased consumer products.

B2B marketers had different but no less severe issues. They typically dealt directly with their customers through field sales forces. Sales representatives felt they owned the customer relationship and were reluctant to provide detailed data to a centralized customer database. Even if that reluctance did not exist, contact with customers often occurred in various units, including field sales, the telephone call center, field service, and technical support. To make the situation even worse, multiple customer contact points existed if the customer purchased items from more than one division or product line within the company. This often confused the company and the customer, who often felt that the brand was not "speaking with one voice." The customer's perception was that the brand did not see them as a valued customer but as a series of isolated problems that the customer was responsible for solving.

What did not usually exist was a data repository which permitted a complete view of the customer relationship with the firm. On the positive side, however, sales reps were often able to recognize customers who were transactional in nature, usually because they were price sensitive. Relationship customers had stronger ties with the firm, perhaps since they required customized products or specialized services. Reps who recognized the difference could, on an individual basis, allocate their time and effort according to the value of the customer relationship.

As long as customer relationship knowledge was the property of individual sales reps, attempts to develop strategic CRM programs floundered. What was lacking was centralized collection and management of customer data that could be analyzed to produce customer insights and translated into strategy. The importance of data was highlighted in a study by

Zahay, Peltier, Schultz, and Griffin. They studied traditional business outcomes data, such as sales and net income, and a type of outcome they called marketing-oriented customer performance. They operationalized the latter as retention rate plus a share-of-wallet, CLV, and return on investment (ROI). In a broad sense, they found that relational data collected at multiple customer marketing touchpoints were more critical than transactional data in predicting both business and marketing performance outcomes.[8] It could be hypothesized that relational data are essential since it is used to develop strategies that affect business outcomes.

Nonprofit organizations also need robust CRM data and strategies. They need to retain and upgrade both members and donors. Some have extensive member databases built from their direct mail and social marketing efforts. Others have little in the way of member data beyond name and address. Some still have members and donors that predate the internet who still have never been asked for addresses or other contact information. Moving to internet-based member retention programs has been difficult for many. However, as more nonprofit organizations become adept at using the internet, and especially as they acquire new prospects or members from web-based contacts, online CRM efforts are becoming a significant part of nonprofit marketing strategies.

Whether in the B2C, B2B, or nonprofit marketplaces, the essentials of the two basic marketing approaches—transactional and relational—do not differ (see Figure 14.2). Traditional transactional marketing is centered on products and single economic exchanges. Marketers engage in one-way communication in the mass media, targeting market segments identified by conventional marketing research. This type of marketing is associated with traditional mass media, but online marketers can also be focused on their products at the expense of their customers.

When the marketing process moves to a relational approach, the focus shifts to customers and their relationship cycle with the organization. Customer needs and expertise in meeting them become key. Communications are targeted to individuals or carefully defined segments and contain personalized content. Goals are focused on growing customer value, not market share. CLV, which incorporates both revenue and cost to serve the customer, becomes a key metric as do customer satisfaction, loyalty, and employee satisfaction. In implementing the CRM strategy, two-way communication in any channel becomes the norm, with project-based marketing research taking a back seat to meaningful, ongoing dialog with the customer. Seamlessly satisfying customer experience becomes the vision that guides all marketing activities and permeates the entire organization.

In recent years, marketers have increasingly found that the relational approach could be improved to ensure lasting customer loyalty. Indeed, the phrase "Marketing is Dead" has become shorthand for a stinging indictment of traditional marketing.[9] Customers today are less influenced by traditional marketing communications, even in relational approaches by favored brands. CEOs are increasingly dissatisfied with their marketing

marketing touchpoint
every time a customer comes into contact with a brand before, during, or after purchase.

transactional marketing
focuses on the individual sale of a product or service. It focuses on short-term goals like customer acquisition and individual sales.

relational marketing
is a facet of customer relationship marketing (CRM) that focuses on customer loyalty and long-term customer engagement.

Figure 14.2   **Product-Centric Versus Customer-Centric Marketing**
Source: Cengage Learning 2013.

Product-Centric vs. Customer-Centric

Product focus	⟶ Customer focus
Transactions	⟶ "Relationships"
Acquiring customers	⟶ Retaining customers
Product profitability	⟶ Customer profitability
Trial and error	⟶ Test, measure, and refine

functions' inability to deliver growth and accountability. Marketers are in the early stages of learning how to harness and use the newer levers of consumer social media influence, especially when an organization's staff doesn't come from the world inhabited by their customers. Somewhat disconcerting to many marketers, consumers' participation on social media gives them as much power to influence buying behavior as their brands or clients.

Add to that the increasing impact of mobile, and marketers face a constantly changing competitive environment that requires a fresh approach, but one that will not lose the insights gained from the past or be unable to tap other valuable resources. The marketer's objective is to become a participant in the customer's environment and build loyalty by communicating brand values that people want to be affiliated with. This is accomplished throughout the many dimensions of the CX process. In part, it is developed using a valuable real-time source of customer information—the digital customer journey as discussed thoroughly in Chapter 4—and delivering the content that the customer values at the appropriate time. That all equates to the seamlessly satisfying CX that marketers strive to achieve—the end goal of CRM.

The B2B Foundations of CRM

While there is much inconsistency in the definition of CRM today, there is little disagreement on how the discipline originated. By the early 1980s, there was growing recognition among business marketers that the cost of a single sales call was spiraling out of control. Figures quoted were typically in the hundreds of dollars for one sales call. Marketers needed a way to make their field sales forces more efficient without risking their ability to grow sales. They turned to sales force automation to offer more cost-effective service to customers while decreasing their overall sales costs. Some of the sales force automation tools are:

sales force automation
business processes, and the software that supports them, permit salespeople to work more effectively both in and out of their offices by providing electronic access to important documents, customer data, and support tools like calendars.

- Sales force productivity tools such as call reporting and checking order and inventory status.
- Direct mail sales lead generation campaigns that included mail fulfillment of product information.
- Telemarketing, often to follow up on the sales leads generated by direct mail.
- Sales and marketing management tools, including sales forecasting and reporting.[10]

In the intervening years, email, text messaging, social media, and other online channels have taken the place of some but not all direct mail as a means of reaching customers. This transition has not decreased the need for automating repetitive, often event-triggered, marketing activities. It has simply increased the number of activities to automate.

This is another information-driven marketing application. In the case of sales force automation, lower-cost media are used to generate (online advertising and events such as webinars and direct mail) and qualify (telemarketing and webinars) sales leads. Field salespeople are given access to a comprehensive customer/prospect database used for sales and marketing management applications. The result should be higher sales, better customer service, and lower costs to the enterprise.

Early systems focused on the sales force, with marketing developing and executing direct mail campaigns, and sophisticated call centers using the customer/prospect database to qualify leads and provide customer service. This has led to the "three-legged stool" concept of CRM portrayed in Figure 14.3. The sales force productivity "leg" has little application in the B2C marketplace, but the concept itself and the marketing and customer service components are entirely applicable. Types of software that support B2B CRM are identified and described in Table 14.1. The term CRM has been adopted to describe relational marketing in B2B and B2C spaces despite the differences just described. It also has the same meaning in the nonprofit space.

From the early beginnings of sales force automation to today's cloud data storage and computing and mobile apps, the purpose has been to make salespeople more productive.

Figure 14.3   The B2B Foundations of Customer Relationship Management

Source: © Cengage Learning 2013

Table 14.1   Software to Support Customer Relationships

Contact Management	Software with multiple modules emulate the salesperson's address book, daily appointment log, and customer files. Key components are contact information, including name, title, address, telephone(s), email, and fax, both work and home; a daily calendar, a tickler (reminder) file, and usually an electronic notepad of some sort. Firms can customize the software to include standard forms such as sales calls and expense reports.
Sales Force Automation	Takes contact management a step forward by integrating various modules and linking them to a central customer database. This lessens the bookkeeping requirements for the field sales force and permits the timely updating and transmission of customer information. For instance, sales leads can be transmitted directly from the central database to the field rep's laptop, allowing immediate follow-up and monitoring by sales management.
CRM	Software that is integrated on an enterprise-wide basis. The objective is to centralize all customer data and to make a 360° (complete) picture of the customer available at each contact point within the firm. Information provision can be highly automated when a telephone number triggers a "screen pop," making the customer record available to the call center representative when the call is answered. Integrated CRM software makes customer and product support data available to any authorized user anywhere in the world. It also incorporates customer touchpoints into a complete view of multiple communication channels. Integration is the precursor to marketing automation.
SaaS or CRM in the Cloud	Cloud computing allows many users to share a robust computing network over the internet. CRM in the cloud means that software, tools, and customer data are all stored on the cloud platform. This allows employees to log in on their browser or a mobile device to access the CRM system from their desk or an app. According to SuperOffice, a CRM software firm, in 2008 only 13 percent of businesses hosted their CRM in the cloud. As of 2022, that number has grown to 87 percent of companies hosting their CRM in the cloud.[11]

360° (complete)
a comprehensive view of the customer, often a profile that interfaces with the firm's customer journey map.

Developing CRM Strategy

There are typically three types of models that are used when determining the most appropriate CRM strategy for a firm to use. The firm's overall goals are what usually determine the model that is used. For instance, the first model is the Identify, Differentiate, Interact, and Customize (IDIC model). This type of model is used to determine what value customers bring to the firm and is very adaptable in B2B and B2C situations.[12] The second model often considered is the Quality Competitive Index Model.[13] This model focuses on customer management rather than customer relationships because its main drivers are customer acquisition, retention, and penetration. The third type of model is called the Value Chain Model and was developed by Michael Porter (who also created Porter's Five Forces). This type of model is used to help companies (1) identify and then (2) prioritize activities that help the company gain a competitive advantage over its competition. Due to the flexibility of the model, this chapter will go into detail on the IDIC model. Many CRM experts agree that the IDIC model captures the essence of CRM due to its customer centricity (see Figure 14.4). The IDIC model is an information-driven one, with every step in the process adding to the customer database that is essential to drive CRM strategy and programs. The steps are:

- **Identify** your customers by an individual or household name and address.
- **Differentiate** customers according to their needs and their actual or potential value.
- **Interact** with customers based on their own needs. From the organization's perspective, the interactions should become more cost-effective. Each interaction should be used as an opportunity to increase the store of data about the individual or household.
- **Customize** some aspects of the organization's dealings with the customer. Things like tailored communications, site personalization, and specialized offers allow the enterprise to recognize the customer as a valued supporter, and present an opportunity to grow the value of the individual customer.

Next, we explore how to differentiate using the "value sieve." The company has to (1) identify the CLV of its customers, then (2) identify the different needs of its customers via segmentation. They have to figure out what similarities there are between the customers. For instance, are there some customers who only shop when there is a promotional sale? Are there others who order from your company each month? Each week? Are there customers who cost your firm a lot of money due to returns, complaints, and missed payments? Once the company has a good understanding of the different segments of customers they have, then the company can differentiate depending on the different needs that each segment might have. Anticipating the needs of the customer before the customer has them generally exceeds customer expectations, which usually increases interaction and retention with the customer.

Figure 14.4 The IDIC Model for CRM Strategy Source: https://www.lucidchart.com/blog/crm-models

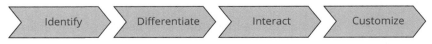

Customer data are the engine that drives CRM strategy forward to an ever-deepening relationship with the customer. However, customers do not have to be differentiated by hand. Companies like 6sense, an AI-powered marketing firm, help firms segment their customers by using predictive analytics.[14] They can identify customers that are in different stages of the buying process and have interacted with the company in multiple mediums, such as the website, email, the company app, etc. Software like 6sense can help companies determine which accounts they should spend more effort on trying to work on. 6sense can provide more guidance for the sales team on which accounts are more engaged and likely to stay with the company and it helps the marketing department craft more programs that encourage customer loyalty.

Other things that CRM strategies help with…

- Lifecycle communications depend on the customer's position in the relationship cycle, from new through very active to ultimate trust in the brand.

- Active management and monitoring of performance, using KPIs throughout.[15]

McKinsey & Company suggest a plan that integrates a digital data map into the CRM/CX orientation, as shown in Figure 14.5. It requires that the marketer:

- Capture customer behavioral pathways and attitudes at each stage of a purchase journey. A customer may seek inspiration about family sports before seeking information about a vacation spot with those activities. A website will likely show a lot of product descriptions and services before price promotions are mentioned only when visitors are closer to buying.

Figure 14.5   **Characteristics of the Digital Shopper Genome** Source: http://www .mckinsey.com/business-functions/marketing-and-sales/our-insights/cracking-the-digital-shopper -genome

Companies should create a complete picture of the customer across a comprehensive set of characteristics.

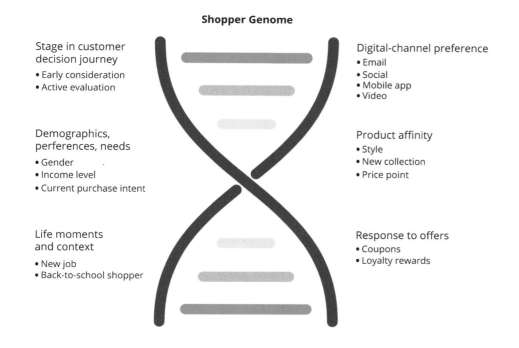

Shopper Genome

Stage in customer decision journey
- Early consideration
- Active evaluation

Demographics, perferences, needs
- Gender
- Income level
- Current purchase intent

Life moments and context
- New job
- Back-to-school shopper

Digital-channel preference
- Email
- Social
- Mobile app
- Video

Product affinity
- Style
- New collection
- Price point

Response to offers
- Coupons
- Loyalty rewards

- Determine each customer's digital brand preference, that is, how a shopper wants to interact with a brand. Many customers use a variety of brand contact media.
- Determine the customer's "key preference indicators" for the brand, indicating the customer's affinity to spend time visiting the site by brand, style, price point, size, etc.
- Understand their response to offers—discounts, loyalty rewards, gifts-with-purchase, etc.
- Identify life moments and context that foretell buying triggers, such as having a child, going to college, and planning a vacation.

Information about demographics, preferences, and needs can be acquired beyond interactions with the company. Data aggregators such as Axiom can append "the usual suspects" of demographics and identify preferences and intent gleaned from customer browsing behavior across networks of hundreds of websites. This allows brands to understand what customers do when not engaging with their brand. It is the added data in the CRM that enables the company to create a seamlessly excellent CX.

Proponents of moving CRM to a customer journey/CX orientation note other important changes required in marketing strategy:

- The organization's technology teams must be involved at every stage of development, analysis, and operations. The "conversation" and tactics needed to design and understand today's CX required systems designed and built to listen, analyze, interact, and deliver the appropriate customer interaction on an increasingly real-time basis.
- Marketers must design systems that actively encourage customers to participate in the relationship, in contrast to using SMM as simply a selling tool. Starbucks uses their Instagram stories to describe their favorite way to drink iced coffee.[16] Stanford Professor Jennifer Aaker calls this having the customer "message in." It's not just a way for the brand to "message out."
- Brands must develop a "just-in-time" orientation to accompany individual customers throughout the CX. A study of 500 CMOs by Accenture found that 87 percent of the more successful companies have employees with specialized analytical skills to develop actionable customer insights versus their peers (36 percent). More successful companies also showed a more remarkable ability to deliver "right time" marketing and showed higher levels of integration between their digital and traditional marketing strategies. This means providing personalized relevant content, not just creating more content.[17]

For example, in late September 2020, Nathan Apodaca, who uses the TikTok handle @420doggface208, was on the way to work when his car broke down. Instead of driving to work, he filmed himself skating on a longboard drinking a bottle of Ocean Spray cranberry juice and singing along to "Dreams" by Fleetwood Mac.[18] This organic co-creation was posted on TikTok by Apodaca and it resonated with so many people that "Dreams" received a 374 percent increase in online sales and an 89 percent increase in streams, which resulted in more royalties for Fleetwood Mac. Ocean Spray also saw a lift in revenue and reported that people "cleared the shelves" of their juice. They responded to the video by purchasing a new truck and filling it with cases of cranberry juice for Apodaca.[19] Neither Ocean Spray nor Fleetwood Mac created the video, but they were able to respond well to Apocaca's video as a way to engage with the customers in a *real*, non-scripted, interaction.

The importance of all these activities, especially active management and monitoring, has been heightened by the potential of SMM in CRM. SMM expands the number of communications touchpoints and makes it imperative to integrate communications across channels.

IMC Case Study: Hulu's Hilarious Animated Hulu Awards (HAHA)

As a way to increase engagement with consumers, Hulu created the HAHA for funny animated shows in 2021 using an IMC approach. Previously, there was no award show for animated content. Their IMC approach to the campaign often serves as a case study of mastery.[20] It promoted Hulu due to the streaming content, but it was also promoted heavily on YouTube and allowed consumers (both subscribers and nonsubscribers) to vote for the awards on Twitter. Additionally, each show that was under consideration for the various awards promoted the HAHA awards to their audience as well.[21] The result was an increase in engagement with Hulu as nonsubscribers were directed to Hulu's webpage and/or their Twitter page to vote. Nonsubscribers were directed to their website where they were met with a free trial promotion.[22] What made their campaign a good example of digital IMC is their use of multiple platforms: Twitter, YouTube, LinkedIn as well as their own streaming platform and their company website. Additionally, because they allowed consumers to vote for the best shows, they engaged with many nonsubscribers. As such, they were able to advertise their brand without a traditional advertisement.[23]

The Customer Lifecycle

The concept of the customer lifecycle (not the product) is illustrated in Figure 14.6. It starts with strategic customer acquisition—acquiring more customers like your

customer lifecycle stages develop the relationship between the customer and the brand.

Figure 14.6   **Mining the Customer Lifecycle** Source: © Cengage Learning 2013

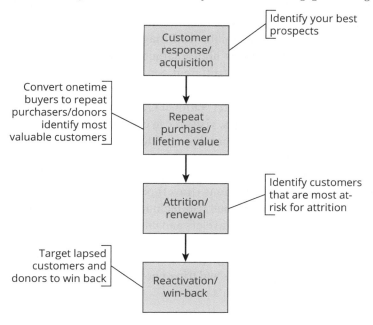

best customers. The next step is conversion, and the concept is specific in stating that conversion means a repeat customer, not a onetime purchaser. The continuing objective is to grow customer value. The other requirement of the relational approach is to identify customers who are at risk of attrition—no longer using the product—and target them for retention or for migration to a different product in the line. A classic consumer example is baby food. When the child grows too old for baby food, attrition from that product class will naturally occur. The wise marketer has a line of toddler foods and snacks in the wings and has the data to know when it is time to market them to a household. Capturing and using that kind of data at the individual household level is the essence of relational marketing.

The attractiveness of the CRM concept quickly became apparent to marketers. After all, they had been preaching the virtues of customer orientation for many years. As a result, marketers of all kinds have taken many different paths in their search for solid and lasting relationships with their customers.

National Geographic

National Geographic is a respected global nonprofit membership organization with many facets to its mission focused on "a passionate belief in the power of science, exploration, and storytelling to change the world."[24] In addition to its research and publications, it manages an extensive travel services division of guided and individually designed tours. The target customers are segmented based on several factors, including interests, family lifecycle, and demographics. The trips include various travel modes (small ship; land and sea), family travel, photo trips and workshops; private jet; active adventures; student expeditions; and small group and private "journeys." This allows customers to engage in various activities complementary to the National Geographic mission (understanding science; exploring cultures of the world; related hobbies like regional foods and sports) throughout their lifetimes.

For example, in the past, a person may have become curious about exploring the natural world through National Geographic publications, television shows, or films. While these venues are still important drivers of customer interest, a general interest in nature may bring today's potential customer to National Geographic's Instagram pages. With over 261 million followers, it is the second largest noncelebrity brand on that platform[25] (just behind Nike) and is the 14th most popular overall.[26] What makes National Geographic so popular on Instagram is that they have multiple sub-accounts and each sub-account is highly targeted for content. For instance, users who follow NatGeo Wild will see different content than NatGeo Travel or NatGeo Adventure.[27]

Much of this effort also supports National Geographic's web page. Here, besides exploring interests in specific topics, visitors can contribute to the website with photos, kids can play games, and learn more through blogs tied into programs and research activities. Other initiatives encourage engagement through storytelling.

National Geographic continues the dialog through a variety of CX touchpoints. The National Geographic Expeditions (travel) page has the usual information about trips, destinations, and facilities, but also includes a section to "get inspired." Here, viewers can see photos from past travelers and understand more about the experts that accompany trips. Given the popularity of its various activities and social platforms, the data provided allows National Geographic to gauge interest in its travel destinations, provides insight into new programs and trip opportunities, and develops communities of users to further the organization's mission.

Figure 14.7a   The National Geographic Instagram Page Source: Cengage

Figure 14.7b   The National Geographic Home Page Source: Cengage

The Processes of CRM—Operational and Analytical

The reason that CRM requires considerable discipline is twofold. First, as emphasized in the preceding section, relationship marketing requires significant changes in marketing. The emphasis must move from promotional campaigns and marketing research projects to the ongoing dialog on multiple platforms, much of which can be captured and stored in a customer database. Second, it must be treated and managed as an ongoing process, not as a series of discrete events. CRM management has often been described as "A Journey with No End." CRM management is the antithesis of how most marketing managers are measured, using short-term metrics, such as market share, sales growth, and customer base expansion. The result is that, for CRM to succeed, changes in organizational thinking and action must go beyond the marketing department to the highest levels of the corporation. This degree of change is not easy and it requires a clear vision of the requirements and potential achievements of CRM.

Successful CRM cannot exist outside the context of the business unit's overall marketing strategy. The economics simply will not work unless the business identifies high-value customers (initially based on marketing research if no database is available), individually or by market segment, targets those customers, and develops marketing strategies and programs that specifically meet their needs. This is genuinely a customer-centric approach; target customers are identified first and the value proposition, encompassing all aspects of the marketing mix, is then developed. It, too, is the antithesis of the traditional marketing model in which products are developed and it becomes the job of the marketing department to market and sell those products.

operational CRM
designing and executing tactical CRM programs based on data items or customer profiles.

analytical CRM
mining the customer data and developing programs or predictive models based on the resulting insights and data discovery.

The customer database is the focal point of both operational CRM and analytical CRM. The database is developed and used to conduct segmentation analysis and develop customer profiles that drive outbound programs like email newsletters and inbound programs like display advertising. Analytical models include CLV and response models that predict response to future marketing programs based on past response to similar programs. As programs are developed and executed, additional data are captured to enrich the database, allow performance measurement of individual programs or customers, and continually refine critical marketing models.

Marketers are beginning to include limited social media behavior in their databases. The data are limited because they must be usable in raw form or quantifiable. This does not include most brand-related conversations on social networks, although they have an essential role in CRM. That will be discussed in the section on Social CRM.

Examples of data from social networks that can be usefully added to the database include:

- In B2B, it is possible to build apps that monitor the social conversations of a specific sales prospect on platforms such as LinkedIn, TikTok, and Facebook. This gives the salesperson valuable information about what the prospect is saying and often allows them to gauge how close the prospect is to a purchase decision. Be aware of three things: First, this is social media listening data. It is ephemeral and not easily quantifiable, but it adds a useful dimension to quantitative prospect information. Second, it involves identifying individual customers in a way that probably would not be acceptable in B2C markets. Third, while this kind of data can contribute to customer qualification, it is likely to be accessed by a desktop or mobile app that lets sales reps follow customers of interest as they interact on social networks, not by entries in the customer database. ChatGPT, by OpenAI, provides numerous promises that AI will analyze this type of unstructured data in a seamless and timely fashion when the final product is released to the public.[28]
- It is difficult to link consumer social network data to identified consumers without violating privacy restrictions. On a small scale, however, social data may be worth adding to consumer profiles. Marketers are always on the lookout for influencers *(opinion leaders)*. There is also identifiable data from sources like top blog listings.
    - For example, if mommy bloggers are strategically crucial to the brand, a list of Top Mommy Bloggers found online[29] could be entered (manually) into the

blog owner's database record. The effort could be worthwhile if the brand needs to reach out to influential mommy bloggers. There are tools for measuring the influence of identified persons on various platforms.

- Still, as the influencer sphere has become more sophisticated, the brand should investigate the influencer's audience.[30]
  - Are they engaged?
  - Who are they?
  - How does the influencer engage with their audience?
  - How many followers do they have?
  - Does your brand make sense in their lives?

Integrating social media data into tactical CRM programs and potentially adding it to the consumer database is a subject of great interest to marketers. However, the privacy challenges are huge, and other countries are increasingly challenging information gathering about customers through digital trials. Various privacy laws such as General Data Protection Regulation (GDPR) in Europe, the California Consumer Protection Act (CCPA), and the (as of writing in 2023) proposed American Data Privacy and Protection Act are helping to define what serves as Personal Identifiable Information and what types of information companies can gather.[31] For now, the best marketing advice for including social media fans and participants in the database is to drive them to the website and persuade them to register, thereby collecting email addresses and other valuable data.[32]

Operational (tactical) CRM program execution emanates from the customer information database. Outbound programs, which could be email promotions, tweets, mobile posts, or marketing programs supported by physical world promotional media such as direct mail, are planned and implemented based on data from the database. One of the disciplines necessary to make CRM work is to compel programs to rely on the database. Often the pressure to get programs out the door causes marketers to want to forgo the front-end analytics and simply blast the entire list. The economics of the internet makes that a seductive argument. It is fast and inexpensive compared to any other channel. However, damage to the relationship can be caused by an onslaught of untargeted, irrelevant marketer-originated communications.

Airlines, for example, know the residential location of their frequent flyers and, if they have mined their data warehouses intelligently, they may have been able to ascertain clear flight patterns for individual customers. Why do airlines contact their frequent fliers with promotional offers that originate in cities where they do not live and do not travel? Has your bank or credit card company recently sent you a promotion for a service or card to which you already subscribe? The cost of sending these messages may not be high, but the longer-term damage to the customer relationship and brand perception may be significant. How can a customer trust a company that appears to know nothing about them, even though they have transacted with that company? As discussed in our email chapter, consumers—by far—prefer personalized emails.

It is essential that inbound programs also depend on the customer database. Telephone call centers and web-based chat rely on the customer database for real-time data that allow representatives to provide seamless service to customers based on knowledge about their dealings with the firm, both past and present. Social media data can be a useful help to that knowledge if it can be made visible to the service rep.

Operational and analytical CRM works from the customer database. CRM strategy development should also be driven by knowledge and insights from the customer database. Strategies that revolve around customer value are the core of CRM. High-value customers are targeted with value propositions developed based on a deep understanding of their needs and behaviors. Care is taken to identify all customers who can be profitably upgraded, whether their current value is high or moderate. Resources are not dissipated on the attraction or even retention of low-value customers.

However, none of these data-driven programs or strategies is viable unless we can selectively reach identified targets with content and messages custom-tailored to each. The internet provides a compelling medium for digital marketers to target customers with personalized content. Increasingly sophisticated technologies can take advantage of a seemingly random event if the brand can respond quickly to unpredictable opportunities or problems. As we've previously made the case, today's digital environment increasingly presents opportunities that come from outside an organization's traditional communication channels.

Targeting and Personalization

Direct marketing, discussed in Chapter 1, provides the foundation concepts for *targeting* the internet. Direct marketers in the physical world have long used mailing or telephone lists as their primary targeting mechanism. Email lists are now available and likely to grow in size and number in the coming years. For the present, however, good lists (translated as opt-in lists) are expensive and short. If the correct rental list is available, it can be helpful to the internet marketer in the acquisition process, although building an opt-in list is recommended.

For retention purposes, however, the issues are different. The process that supports relationship marketing in either the physical or the online worlds is represented in Figure 14.8. The chief difference between the two is that internet marketers can capture more data faster and revise their content on a more frequent, even real-time, basis.

customer profiles

a description of a customer or set of customers that includes demographic, geographic, and psychographic characteristics. A profile could consist of other relevant information, such as buying patterns, creditworthiness, and purchase history.

Targeting in CRM programs is most often accomplished by developing customer profiles and using them to identify either customers who are appropriate to receive a particular offer (the more traditional approach) or customers who represent sufficient value, either as individuals or as a segment, to warrant the development of a unique value proposition (a CLV-based strategy). Customer profiles differ from customer personas because customer profiles identify specific customers who are appropriate to receive

Figure 14.8   **The Targeting and Personalization Process** Source: © Cengage Learning 2013

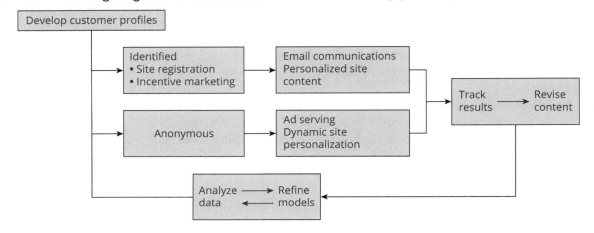

the marketing collateral. Customer personas are a group of hypothetical people that the marketing team uses to help them think through their marketing communications.

There are two types of profiles available to marketers. *Anonymous* profiles are created without knowledge of the identity of the prospective customer. They are developed from clickstream data and perhaps enhanced with other data that belong to the marketer or are purchased from a third-party supplier. First-party cookies, meaning they are used by the company website and are not sold to another site, are the most common way to develop anonymous profiles. A cookie can be used to track movement on the site after the click-through, create a user profile, or manage the serving of ads to the user (see the discussion of behavioral advertising in Chapter 10). A cookie is also set when a user selects personalization options on a web page. However the cookie is set, when the user contacts the website again, the cookie is automatically activated. Generally, a cookie can be read only by the server that sends it and can track activity only on one website, including where visitors come from and where they go as they exit. The user can disable cookies, which may prevent access to some websites. It will also erase any personalization the user has done.[33]

Identified profiles are compiled from data that are explicitly provided by a known prospect. This is often done by asking the visitor to register on a website and provide profile information. Some infomediaries offer incentives in return for customer information which they then sell to marketers. Companies that offer coupons from participating manufacturers over the web are an example of this type of information product.

The fastest way for a firm to build its house list and create its own identified profiles is by registering on the website. This sounds simple, but it has to be done carefully. The process itself must be carefully thought out. And, of course, people must first be attracted to the site using the acquisition techniques described in previous chapters, often by using contests or offering something in exchange for the email (i.e., e-book, discount).

The registration form must be carefully designed for ease and speed of completion, as discussed in Chapter 13 in the context of landing pages. A new registrant may have a negligible existing relationship with the organization and will divulge only minimal information. Techniques that prevent error, like pull-down lists, are desirable. Even so, the form may not be completed unless there is an incentive. The incentive may be tangible, as on the many B2B sites that require visitors to register to receive information of some type, perhaps to download a white paper. It may be intangible, as when the nonprofit offers the ability to "customize our newsletter to reflect your interests." There may be services provided to the registered visitor that are not available to the general public.

Note two things about the common strategy of providing an information incentive. First, the registrant should receive instant gratification, either by clicking on a link to download or by automatic email provision of the report. Making the person wait for something to arrive invalidates many advantages of the internet. If the information comes on a scheduled basis, not on demand, automate the process to send a "thank you" email (for an email newsletter subscription, for example) immediately. Second, this is a classic direct marketing lead generation process.

Consequently, enough information should be gathered to begin to categorize the desirability of the prospect. At the same time, the information should not be so detailed or complex that the visitor does not complete the form. Abandoned forms can be tracked. If there is a consistent point at which the form is being abandoned, it signals a problem with the information gathering that should be corrected immediately.

The basic rule is to gather only the information the marketer needs to make the subsequent communication effective. As the relationship strengthens, more information that is more detailed and more personal can be collected. Like politeness in the physical world, do not presume too much on a brief acquaintance! There should be a relationship program plan from the beginning that specifies the data needed and the customer lifecycle stage in which it will be collected. Without a plan, data collection is just a "fishing expedition" that is unlikely to be valuable to the marketer and is highly likely to be annoying to the customer.

Additionally, the GDPR and the CCPA make it illegal to ask for more personal information than they need. For instance, according to GDPR, brands are not allowed to ask for a consumer's exact birthdate unless it is absolutely necessary. Typically a month, year (i.e., March 1997) designation is enough as the full birthdate (including date) is considered personal information. Additionally, according to GDPR, certain protected information such as religion, political affiliation, and sexual orientation should not be gathered by a marketer. If and when brands violate this rule they can be fined by the GDPR. However, the data collection and the relationship marketing strategy should be flexible and examined at every step for possible improvements. For example, it is possible to shop through Instagram and mobile apps. These developments could make real-time purchases more relevant as target customers engage in their "native" digital environments.

Email Reengagement Campaigns

The average office worker receives about 120 emails per day and generally responds to about 40 per day.[34] That's not including the count on their personal email accounts, which probably receive about the same number of emails. As such, it is not surprising that many consumers clean out their inboxes by unsubscribing to email newsletters and retailers that they no longer want to engage with. According to Hubspot, marketers lose 25 percent of their email list each year due to people changing jobs and changing emails, or people deciding that they are no longer interested in receiving the email, among others.[35]

Companies that manage their database well will notice when their subscribers are no longer opening their emails. According to Campaign Monitor, it costs five times more to acquire a new customer than to re-engage an inactive subscriber.[36] Folks who do not open their emails are at a hazard of lapsing as email subscribers. In an effort to counteract their lapsed email subscription, multiple email vendors recommend running a reengagement campaign. Reengagement campaigns help clean up the email list and can be beneficial for multiple reasons. First, the open rate of the email campaign will improve. When a company sends emails to only the people who want to engage, it is easier to cater messages to each segment. According to Active Trail and to Campaign Monitor, who are marketing companies, there are several strategies a company can use when trying to reengage an inactive subscriber.

1. **A standard reminder email.** This email template reminds customers why they will find value in your product. For instance, maybe the product saves them time or money—a simple reminder of this value is beneficial.
2. **A "We Miss You" email.** This email template often provides customers a discount on the next purchase.
3. **A time-dependent discount email.** This email template reminds customers that a time-dependent email discount is about to expire.

The tone of the email is key. The company rarely knows why the customer stopped reading their emails, and writing the email in a light-hearted way is usually easier to maintain the relationship. Additionally, Marketing Sherpa finds that 2.1 percent of subscribers will go inactive every 30 days. This means that over the year, a company can lose almost one-fifth of their email list.[37] Much of this can be determined by how a company determines that a customer is inactive. Have they not opened an email in a month? Six months? Two years? At what point does the email manager want to purge them from their email list?

Personalized Email and Site Content

One way to keep customers actively engaged is through personalized content curation. Done correctly, email personalization is an important marketing tool. Email is one tool in an outbound marketing program in which the marketer reaches out to customers.

If, however, the marketer chooses the *personalized site content* part of the relationship program, that requires a different type of technology that can identify the customer segment in real-time and make the changes needed to personalize to that segment. There are three basic types of personalized site content in use at present:

1. Rules-based personalization that chooses content based on known characteristics, either from current information or from previous user information stored in cookies. Weather.com provides geographically appropriate content when the visitor enters a Zip code and remembers the Zip code for later use; both Amazon and Netflix have recommendation engines that infer additional product choices from items previously purchased. Rules-based algorithms can be pretty complex and link many characteristics, but the concept is straightforward.

2. User-controlled personalization in which the user chooses the content elements to be displayed. This is often used in opt-in where the subscriber is asked which newsletters they wish to receive or the bargain hunter is asked the product categories for which the user wants to receive offers.

3. Information-driven personalization uses complex profiles and models to assign content instead of straightforward decision rules.

User-controlled personalization remains unchanged until the user decides to modify it. Rules-based personalization can also be relatively static, with rules and associated actions being established in advance and merely executed at the time of the visitor's arrival on the site. Information-driven personalization requires sophisticated quantitative models but can be completed in real-time for an inbound contact or as part of an outbound communication. The software builds a profile almost instantaneously when the visitor hits a site. It can use many types of data, depending on what is available and the level of identification of the visitor—everything from clickstream data to transactional data from the customer database. As the visitor moves around the site, the profile is updated. It also stores information, perhaps in the customer database or on a cookie on the visitor's computer, in preparation for the next visit. Virtually any aspect of site content can be served to the visitor based on the profile—the products to be displayed, incentives to be offered, and characteristics of the offer itself, including price.

CRM and the tools of targeting and personalization all imply a continuous, closed-loop process of data capture, information-driven programs, and knowledge refinement. One additional technique is widely used to increase the momentum and power of relationship marketing. That important technique is the loyalty program.

Customer Loyalty Programs

Loyalty programs are familiar and ubiquitous. Businesses from the corner pizza parlor to the urban department store to the international hotel chain all have loyalty programs. Consumers and business travelers have phones full of loyalty apps. As of 2022, the average American consumer belonged to 16.6 loyalty programs.[38] While loyalty programs are helpful for businesses to encourage repeat purchases, loyalty programs can also serve as a business risk, as well. In 2022, companies spent $22 billion worldwide on loyalty programs.[39] That is one reason why we see loyalty programs constantly reformulating their tiers and reward systems.

Remember, though, that loyalty programs are only a part of CRM strategies. Loyalty programs alone do not represent a strategy. The key issue is that loyalty programs focus on changing behavior and their effects may not last past the reward. Strategic CRM focuses on long-term relationships and brand-building and may have more long-term impact. Despite their potential to have only short-term effectiveness, loyalty programs have become a staple of the marketing strategies of firms like Victoria's Secret, a luxury brand for the discerning female shopper. Victoria's Secret has been recognized as a leader in loyalty programs from the early days of direct mail coupons and catalogs up to the present with its email programs and mobile apps.

The end of an era occurred when Victoria's Secret shut down its famed catalog. The firm tested the elimination of the catalog in several markets for a full year and saw little effect on sales (i.e., catalog vs. no-catalog). It ran the same test in two very significant markets and saw no difference in sales. Notably, when the number of catalogs was reduced by 40 percent, online sales went up by 15 percent. Eliminating the catalog would save at least $125 million each year, which could be better directed to more effective marketing actions—namely its stores and its digital business.[40]

In recent years PlayStation (owned by Sony) has experienced considerable success with digital overall and mobile social in particular. With mobile, they can target customers to ease various pain points, like losing the PlayStation remote. PlayStation maintains 64.5 percent of the gaming market share and one way to their success, aside from creating fun games, is their digital presence. Their most considerable following is on Twitter, with over 27 million followers. In the first two years of its launch, PS5 sold over 20 million units worldwide despite a shortage due to supply chain issues and a semiconductor shortage.[41] See Figure 14.9. When preparing for the launch, Sony used a multifaceted IMC campaign.

Customer acquisition is important, especially for the gaming segment, which has a focused target market with a narrow age and gender range. The primary emphasis is on customer retention and growing customer value. One of the problematic marketing aspects that Sony must contend with is that each time a new console is released they have to market

Figure 14.9 **Sony PlayStation 5 Console** Source: skvalval/Shutterstock.com

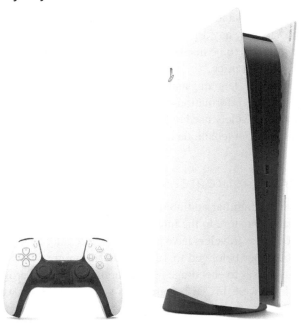

to old *and* new customers. The customer is encouraged to purchase a *new* console and *new* games when PlayStation releases a new console.

In July 2022, PlayStation launched a new loyalty program named PlayStation Stars that appeals explicitly to gamers.[42] This loyalty program is gamified by launching "campaigns" where players must play certain games, solve riddles, and complete tasks each month. In response, the players receive digital rewards, points, and level status. For example, players who wanted to participate in the loyalty challenge in October 2022 had to do the following for The World Warrior's Challenge:

1. Pick a fight to honor 30 years of Hadoukens.
2. Play Street Fighter V, Ultimate Marvel vs. Capcom 3, Mortal Kombat 11, or TEKKEN 7
3. Reward: Novelty Toy Fight Trophy

What makes Playstation's stars loyalty program unique is that it encourages players to *play* their games as opposed to purchasing more. This loyalty program is much more equitable considering that most PS5 games cost $60. By gamifying their loyalty program, they encourage their players to play the games often. That way their customers don't move on to the next game that comes out and forget about their older games.

Aspects Needed When Creating a Comprehensive CRM

The basic concepts of CRM have changed little over the years, but apps and social media are changing the way CRM is executed. Apps and SMM extend reach and customer intimacy and can reach customers wherever they are when they are most likely to be in a frame of mind to buy.

Mobile Apps

As the previous section illustrates, the changes to CRM programs that result from apps are still developing, but they have already had a powerful impact. Todd Wasserman of Mashable says, "Branded apps these days are much more about customer retention than customer acquisition, as they go from something that surprises and delights to something that's expected."[43]

That statement is borne out by statistics about the growth of the app category. According to Forbes, in the first quarter of 2022, consumers downloaded 37 billion apps.[44] Retail apps that carry out the CRM mission are only part of the branded app set.

Up until the COVID-19 pandemic, retailers had a hard time getting customers to download their apps.[45] Customers download a retailer app if there is a quid pro quo. This means that they need to get something in return if they download the app, like racking up points in the McDonald's or Starbucks app, or free shopping in the Victoria's Secret app. Otherwise, consumers often do not see a reason to download the app. Incentives work, but retailer apps are quickly deleted if they do not provide value over time.

Making apps useful appears to be worth the cost and effort. Figure 14.10 shows that users of apps visit the store more often. The one exception in this group of seven apps is Nordstrom. Could it be because it is the one luxury brand in this group of promotional brands? Another study found that 64 percent of customers who used a branded app were more likely to visit the retailer's brick-and-mortar store.[46] So whether it is a retail app or a brand app, they do the CRM job.

There are several requirements for an app that customers will be willing to download and provide personal information:

- It must be useful, giving them benefits like product offers or even entertainment that they like.
- It must provide value, like the coupon offers of retailers from Walmart to Victoria's Secret.
- It must be easy to use.
- It must provide seamlessly excellent customer experience, whether alone or in conjunction with some other marketing message like a direct mail.[47]

Remember that CX trumps loyalty! Marketers should be mindful that although apps are popular and useful, it is not a case of "build it and they will come." Apps represent a marketing communication—and increasingly an eCommerce—program that needs to be targeted and executed with all the care of any other marketing program. It is important to remember that apps are primarily a CRM initiative. Downloading can be done on impulse, but it generally implies brand familiarity and favorability.

Social CRM

Social CRM can be considered a part of SMM, using all the brand's social media platforms, tools, and techniques to support the CRM effort.

The emphasis on Social CRM offers two benefits:

1. It adds useful elements to our understanding of CRM. Traditional CRM involves marketing and public relations, customer service and support, and transactions. Social CRM adds the role of listening to and interacting with the customer and meeting customer service needs in almost real-time.

Figure 14.10 Branded Apps Increase Store Visits Source: http://digiday.com/brands/state-retail-mobile-apps-5-charts/

2. It provides a way to transition programs to platforms like TikTok and Instagram that consumers find engaging. B2B customers can be reached through a thought leadership content strategy on LinkedIn. This extends the CRM effort to platforms that customers use and engage with.

Tools are available to collect and use data from social networks. For instance, Hubspot CRM, and Salesforce Sales Cloud allow for social media CRM integration.[48]

First, companies can utilize Social CRM by creating a social listening program. By finding out when the brand is mentioned online, the brand can get a better sense of who is talking about the brand without tagging the brand. For instance, many companies use social listening on Twitter to see who is complaining (or praising) their brand without tagging them.[49] By responding to the message without being tagged, they are (often) able to initiate a service recovery by having the customer contact their customer service center. Second, brands will want to consolidate social media interactions by using one template. This way they can analyze campaigns in one place. Third, they can incorporate social media data into their existing CRM by learning about the demographics of their customers who are connected on the various social media platforms.[50]

CRM in the Cloud

The supply chain transition to the cloud is similar for CRM or any other business function, for that matter. CRM experts list the business benefits as including:

- Potentially lower costs.
- Improved employee productivity, especially for the field sales force. Cloud-based solutions are available at any location on any device.
- Better data analytics. In addition to integrating all internal data for the CRM system, cloud-based systems can pull in business intelligence data from external systems.
- Tend to be easier and more straightforward for employees to use.
- Easier to increase scale when more capacity is needed.
- Provide a high level of security and reliability.

A small business supplier of cloud-based CRM points out that it makes daunting technology available to small businesses, many of which have avoided installing CRM systems because of the cost and overall hassle. The improvement in marketing results should make it worthwhile, even though the next section indicates that small businesses do not enjoy the same economies of scale with cloud CRM that larger firms do.

The Costs and Failure Rate of CRM Systems Projects

Installing a CRM system is a complex and demanding project in any business, large or small. There are cost comparisons all over the web, but they generally compare various software on a per-seat (translate that as per user) basis. Even looked at that way, costs vary dramatically. But the cost of licensing or purchasing the software is the ultimate issue for management. The problem is Total Cost of Ownership (TCO).

CRMs have evolved over time from being housed on expensive physical servers to being hosted in the cloud. It is estimated that 91 percent of companies with over 10 employees

total cost of ownership (TCO) the purchase price of a product or service plus the indirect costs of operating it through its lifetime.

use a CRM. Additionally, CRMs can help improve sales by 29 percent.[51] According to Statista, as of 2021, the leading CRM platforms by market share are:

- Salesforce Sales Cloud
- Oracle Sales Cloud
- SAP
- Adobe Marketing Cloud
- Microsoft Dynamics 365 for Sales[52]

Notably, as of 2023, there are 1,817 CRM providers in the United States. The industry has seen an annualized growth rate of 15.2 percent from 2018–2023. In 2013, there were just about 300 CRM providers in the United States.[53] What an impressive growth rate! Because there are so many providers, there is a wide range of pricing options ranging from about $12 to $300 per user, per month. As noted in Figure 14.11, the highest rate of adoption is among small businesses that have between 1 and 50 employees. Thus, the total cost of ownership for a CRM in a business with 20 users will range from $2,880 to $72,000 per year.

When marketing managers are trying to determine if it makes sense to spend the money on a CRM or if they should continue to use Excel sheets to keep track of their customers, many of them calculate the ROI of the CRM. Hubspot keeps track of the ROI they provide their customers. As displayed in Figure 14.12, Hubspot indicates that their customers average a 129 percent increase in inbound sales leads (consumers coming to their client's website), a 113 percent increase in website traffic, a 109 percent increase in deal close rate, a 36 percent increase in deals closed and a 37 percent increase in a ticket (for IT issues) close rate.[54]

Aside from Hubspot's reported statistics, it is reported that it generally takes about one year for a business to break even on the cost of implementing a CRM.[55] Additionally, CRMs often increase the customer's experience with the company. Customers want personalization, and they like it when a company keeps record of their order history. It is nearly impossible to maintain all of this information without a CRM. Moreover, 92 percent of companies believe that implementing a CRM allows them to meet their goals of customer centricity.[56]

Figure 14.11 Estimated CRMs Installed Per Year by Company Size

Source: https://pipeline.zoominfo.com/marketing/cost-of-crm-implementation

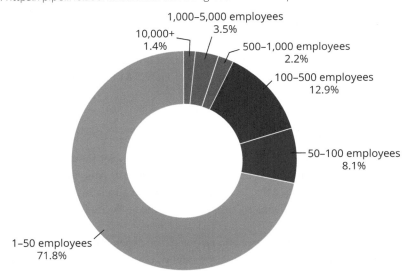

Figure 14.12 **Hubspot CRM ROI Statistic** Source: https://www.hubspot.com/roi

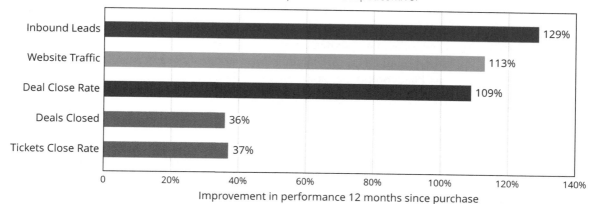

The horizontal axis is labeled: Improvement in performance 12 months since purchase

- Inbound Leads: 129%
- Website Traffic: 113%
- Deal Close Rate: 109%
- Deals Closed: 36%
- Tickets Close Rate: 37%

The CRM Vision—Seamless Customer Experience

The CRM vision is to provide the customer a totally satisfactory experience, through every distribution channel the enterprise employs, by means of any communications channel the customer chooses to use, 24/7/365. In an era of multichannel marketing, that is a tall order indeed!

Figure 14.13 suggests the nature of both the problems and the opportunities. Merchants can offer access to information and transactions through their retail stores, websites, telephone call centers, direct mail and catalogs, self-service kiosks like ATMs, and social networks like Facebook. Field service technicians, the person who repairs your refrigerator at home or copier at work, also represent the enterprise and can, in fact, present up-sell and cross-sell opportunities if they are properly trained and

Figure 14.13 The CRM Vision

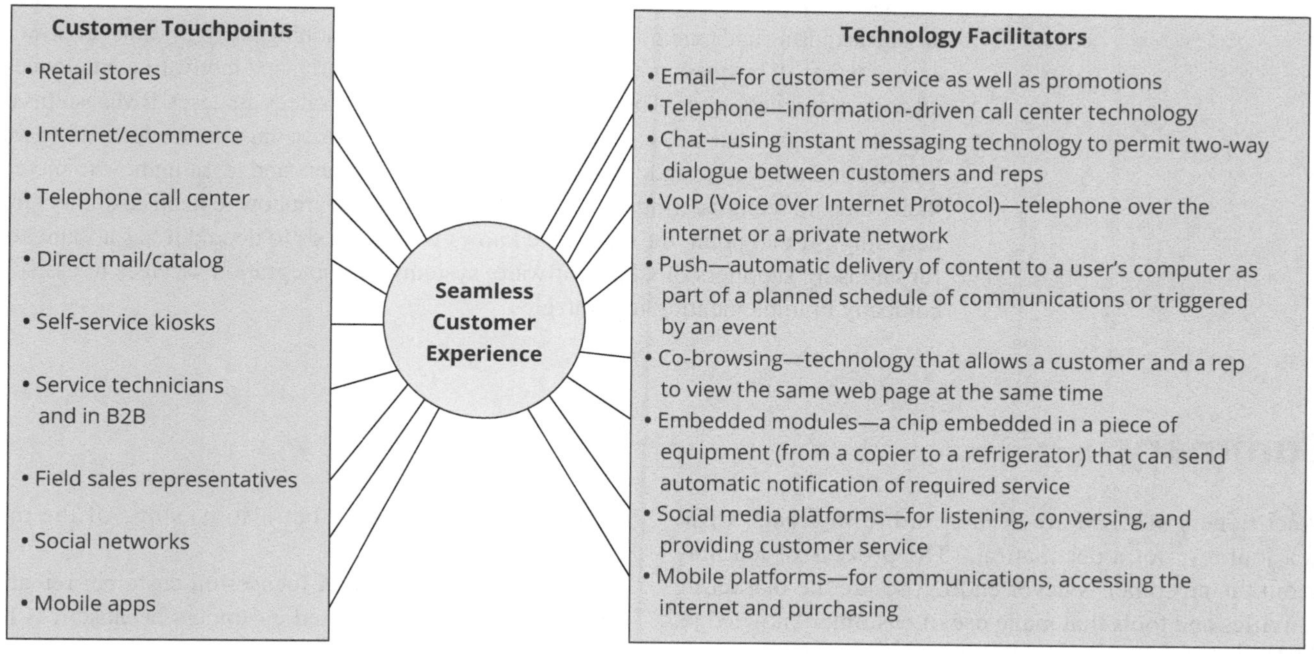

Customer Touchpoints

- Retail stores
- Internet/ecommerce
- Telephone call center
- Direct mail/catalog
- Self-service kiosks
- Service technicians and in B2B
- Field sales representatives
- Social networks
- Mobile apps

Seamless Customer Experience

Technology Facilitators

- Email—for customer service as well as promotions
- Telephone—information-driven call center technology
- Chat—using instant messaging technology to permit two-way dialogue between customers and reps
- VoIP (Voice over Internet Protocol)—telephone over the internet or a private network
- Push—automatic delivery of content to a user's computer as part of a planned schedule of communications or triggered by an event
- Co-browsing—technology that allows a customer and a rep to view the same web page at the same time
- Embedded modules—a chip embedded in a piece of equipment (from a copier to a refrigerator) that can send automatic notification of required service
- Social media platforms—for listening, conversing, and providing customer service
- Mobile platforms—for communications, accessing the internet and purchasing

motivated. B2B marketers also have field sales forces as another important channel. No one marketer, B2B or B2C, is likely to use all these channels of distribution. However, most now offer a set—branch banks, a website, a telephone customer service center, and ATMs, supplemented with occasional direct mail promotions, would be typical for a retail bank, for example. Most nonprofits have mail, telephone, website as well as Facebook page, and personal contacts of various types. An industrial concern would be likely to have a field sales force, a website, printed catalogs, a telephone call center, field service technicians, a blog, and one or more brand communities for customer communication and support. Each of these channels represents a customer touchpoint. Each of these touchpoints provides an opportunity to serve the customer well—through information, transactions, or service. Each customer contact sends a message about the brand—positive or negative. Technology can assist in all these dimensions.

Figure 14.13 also lists the technologies that are in most common use in CRM applications today. The technologies have been discussed in various contexts throughout this text. They all can be applied in B2C, B2B, and nonprofit environments.

The challenge to CRM is that the customer may contact the enterprise at any time, through any of the channels, using any of the available technologies. The marketer's job is to deliver the right product, service, or information—consistently and correctly—no matter when, where, or how the customer makes contact. Further, the product, service, or information should be delivered by the agent—anyone from a call center representative to a field service technician—with whom the customer makes the initial contact. Referring the customer from one person to another in the organization in order to try to get information or settle an issue is the antithesis of "seamless customer experience." The responder on social networks may be an anonymous administrator, but quick and relevant response is essential. It is important to recognize technology as a means to an end, not an end in itself.

Writing in the *Harvard Business Review*, Bain consultants Rigby, Reichheld, and Schefter say, "Executives often mistake the easy promise of CRM software for the hard reality of creating a unique strategy for acquiring, building relationships with, and retaining customers."[57]

Their solutions, as all the perspectives presented in this chapter note, are centered around acquiring and retaining high-value customers, developing the right value proposition, ensuring that all business processes are functioning properly, and motivating employees at all customer touchpoints. These are organizational and strategy issues; CRM systems can support strategies, but they cannot devise them. The enterprise must do the demanding work that goes all the way from identifying high-value customers and learning how to increase their value, to reengineering processes, if necessary, to learn how to keep customers from defecting. At that point, the enterprise knows what it needs to do and it has a foundation for choosing suppliers of CRM software, systems, and integration services to assist the company in implementing its strategies.

Summary

Practitioners of CRM are often heard to say that, "CRM is a journey, not a destination." The process of learning about the customer is never ending; so are the marketing activities and tools that make use of customer knowledge. CRM is not only one of the most important aspects of contemporary marketing, but also it is one of the most challenging.

The discipline of CRM focuses on customer retention and the reactivation of lapsed customers because it is less expensive to maintain existing customers than to acquire new ones. Acquiring the best customers and growing their value is the essence of CRM strategy. CLV is a guiding metric throughout. It requires the business to move from a traditional, product-oriented perspective to one in which the customer is the central focus and the establishment of an ongoing relationship is the overall goal of strategy. Strategy development can be characterized by the steps of identification, differentiation, interaction, and customization. The customer journey is used to establish the types of messages that will be most effective as the customer moves through relationship stages. Ongoing organizational listening to and engaging with customers will cultivate the relationship, with the objective of earning their loyalty and encouraging their participation in delivering positive brand messages in their own communities.

In order to implement either operational or analytical CRM programs on the web, a substantial amount of customer knowledge is necessary. This knowledge is embedded in profiles of individual customers or visitors to the website as part of operational CRM. Profiling is done either anonymously or for identified customers. While anonymous profiling has obvious relevance in the early stages of a potential customer relationship, it also has essential privacy implications that the marketer should not overlook. One way to avoid privacy issues is to develop value-added programs like frequent customer reward plans that deepen relationships over time and lead to a willing revelation of additional information on the part of loyal customers. Identified profiles can be developed when the visitor or customer provides personal information, usually through registration on a site or making a purchase from it. This permits the personalization of content that

can be targeted to identified customers by email or at other touchpoints. This ability to reach identified customers with personalized content is a key reason for marketers to encourage social media followers and mobile app users to register and provide data for the database.

Moving beyond simple profiles, marketers can develop models that target customers whose value can be grown or who are likely to be responsive to a particular offer. Here, proactive marketers will supplement these models with forward-looking research regarding trends and new factors. They need to ask, "What happens if customer interest in this product line decreases?" Think about the impact of "athleisure," the combination of athletic clothing designed for streetwear, on how customers think about their wardrobes. Would a brand see this trend coming if it only relied on what customers were currently purchasing? Are the brand tracking trends outside of their current market offerings by engaging with their customers in Social CRM? Are they using mobile apps to reach their customers when and where they are most receptive?

Marketers have a menu of options in terms of the channels they will use and the technologies they will implement. The CRM vision is to integrate the chosen channels and technologies in such a way that a customer can make contact whenever they please, through that channel the customer prefers, at that particular time (the customer touchpoint), and receive the information or service they desire without delay, errors, or being transferred from one enterprise agent to another. This is the "seamless customer experience." It represents both the opportunity and the challenge facing CRM programs of all types.

Discussion Questions

1. Explain, in your own words, the importance of customer-focused relationship marketing and how it differs from traditional transactional marketing.

2. What is the role of CLV in relationship marketing?

3. CRM is generally considered to have its foundations in three B2B marketing functions. Explain what the functions are and what each contributes to a CRM program.

4. Explain the steps in the Peppers and Rogers model of CRM and the importance of the customer database in the process.

5. Explain what is meant by the customer lifecycle, and how CRM strategies and messages can be crafted for its various stages.

6. Discuss how a focus on the total customer experience (CX) requires an expanded view of a marketer's relationship with its customers. What factors should be considered when developing a profile of a customer?

7. Discuss the differences between operational and analytical CRM and how they make use of the customer database.

8. Explain the difference between a customer profile and a model.

9. True or False: It is easy to include customer data from social networks in the database. Why or why not?

10. Targeting and personalization are different but related CRM concepts. Be prepared to define each, clearly

explaining why they are different from one another and giving an example of each.

11. True or False: Personalization is a simple process of including the recipient's name in the subject line or body of the message. Why or why not?

12. Why have apps become an important part of CRM programs for many companies? Do you believe that apps you use help build relationships with brands? Do you think they stimulate sales?

13. Explain your understanding of Social CRM.

14. What are some of the major reasons that the implementation of large CRM systems may be prone to failure?

15. What do we mean by "seamless customer experience in multiple channels?"

16. Explain why CRM is a process, not a journey with a final destination.

Endnotes

1. Frederick F. Reichheld, *The Loyalty Effect* (Boston, MA: Harvard Business School Press), 1996.

2. Ian Kingwill, "What Is the Cost of Customer Acquisition vs Customer Retention?" LinkedIn, accessed February 18, 2023, https://www.linkedin.com/pulse/what-cost-customer-acquisition-vs-retention-ian-kingwill.

3. Gavin, "Unhappy Customers: Your Greatest Untapped Resource," Customer Thermometer (Gavin https://www.customerthermometer.com/img/, October 27, 2021), https://www.customerthermometer.com/customer-satisfaction/unhappy-customer/.

4. Ian Kingwill, "What Is the Cost of Customer Acquisition vs Customer Retention?"

5. Annette Franz, "Home - Annette Franz: Customer Experience." Annette Franz, June 13, 2022, https://annettefranz.com/.

6. Sarah Bricker Hunt, "What Is Cross-Selling and How Does It Increase Customer Spending?" Constant Contact, March 3, 2021, https://www.constantcontact.com/blog/what-is-cross-selling/.

7. Constant Contact, "10 Quick Facts You Should Know about Consumer Behavior on Twitter," Share and Discover Knowledge on SlideShare, accessed March 9, 2023, https://www.slideshare.net/ConstantContact/10-quick-facts-you-should-know-about-consumer-behavior-on-twitter.

8. Debra Zahay, James Peltier, Don E. Schultz, and Abbie Griffin. "The role of transactional versus relational data in IMC programs: Bringing customer data together." *Journal of Advertising Research* 44, no. 1 (2004): 3–18.

9. Bill Lee, "Marketing Is Dead." *Harvard Business Review*, August 9, 2012. http://www.hbr.org/2012/08/marketing-is-dead.

10. Rowland T. Moriarty and Gordon S Swartz. "Automation to Boost Sales and Marketing." *Harvard Business Review*, August 1, 2014, https://hbr.org/1989/01/automation-to-boost-sales-and-marketing.

11. SuperOffice. "18 CRM Statistics You Need to Know for 2023." 18 CRM Statistics You Need to Know for 2023, October 20, 2022, https://www.superoffice.com/blog/crm-software-statistics/.

12. "4 CRM Models That Boost Customer Loyalty." Lucidchart, November 13, 2020, https://www.lucidchart.com/blog/crm-models.

13. Shruti Thakur, Priya Chetty. "Understanding the Different Elements of the QCI Model." Knowledge Tank, February 18, 2020, https://www.projectguru.in/different-elements-qci-model/.

14. Nick Lafferty. "6Sense Review: Abm Platform Comparisons [2023 Review]." Nick Lafferty. Nick Lafferty | Growth Marketing Expert, October 24, 2022, https://nicklafferty.com/reviews/6sense/.

15. "The CRM Metrics You Should Be Tracking." *Business News Daily*, accessed February 18, 2023, https://www.businessnewsdaily.com/16031-crm-metrics.html.

16. Andrej Csizmadia, "6 Ways You Can Engage with Customers on Social Media Platform." LiveAgent, October 27, 2022, https://www.liveagent.com/blog/engage-with-customers-on-social-media-platform/.

17. Tobi Elkin, "'Just-in-Time,' vs. Mass Marketing, Delivers Higher Marketing ROI," June 7, 2016, www.mediapost.com/publications/article/277421/just-in-time-marketing-delivers-highe.html.

18. TikTok. "Doggface Gives the World a Smile with Juice, a Skateboard, and All the Vibes." Newsroom. TikTok, August 16, 2019, https://newsroom.tiktok.com/en-us/doggface-gives-the-world-a-smile-with-juice-a-skateboard-and-all-the-vibes.

19. Christina Morales, "Millions of Views Later, Nathan Apodaca Keeps the Vibe Going." *The New York Times*, October 8, 2020, https://www.nytimes.com/2020/10/07/us/ocean-spray-buys-car.html.

20. Kayla Carmicheal, "The Best Integrated Marketing Campaigns, According to HubSpot Marketers." HubSpot Blog. (HubSpot, June 17, 2022), https://blog.hubspot.com/marketing/our-favorite-integrated-marketing-examples.

21. "Examples of Effective Integrated Marketing Campaigns." Commit Agency, August 17, 2021, https://commitagency.com/blog/examples-of-effective-integrated-marketing-campaigns/.

22. Jacinda Santora, "What Is an Integrated Marketing Campaign?" Influencer Marketing Hub, August 16, 2022, https://influencermarketinghub.com/integrated-marketing-campaign/.

23. "Services: Full Service Ad Agency." Commit Agency, August 11, 2022, https://commitagency.com/services/.

24. "Press." National Geographic Partners, December 10, 2022, http://press.nationalgeographic.com/about-national-geographic/.

25. "List of Top Brands Ranking." Top 1,000 Instagrammers and Instagram Brand | StarNgage Plus, accessed February 19, 2023, https://starngage.com/plus/en-us/brand/ranking.

26. S. Dixon, "Most Followers on Instagram 2023." *Statista*, January 24, 2023, https://www.statista.com/statistics/421169/most-followers-instagram/.

27. Elena Cucu, "National Geographic's Social Media Strategy: Socialinsider." Socialinsider Blog: Social Media Marketing Insights and Industry Tips, January 6, 2023, https://www.socialinsider.io/blog/national-geographic-social-media-strategy/.

28. "Chatgpt Is a Tipping Point for AI." *Harvard Business Review*, December 14, 2022, https://hbr.org/2022/12/chatgpt-is-a-tipping-point-for-ai.

29. "30+ Best Mom Blogs to Inspire You (2023 Edition)." FirstSiteGuide, December 26, 2022, https://firstsiteguide.com/best-mom-blogs/.

30. "Influencer Marketing Prices: How Much Should You Pay (2023)." Shopify, December 5, 2022, https://www.shopify.com/blog/influencer-pricing.

31. "CCPA VS GDPR: Compliance with Cookiebot CMP." Cookiebot. Accessed February 20, 2023, https://www.cookiebot.com/en/ccpa-vs-gdpr-compliance-with-cookiebot-cmp.

32. Brandon, "How to Build and Nurture Customer Relationships through Social Media." Mailchimp, October 19, 2019, https://mailchimp.com/resources/build-customer-relationships-through-social-media/.

33. "All You Need to Know about Internet Cookies & Your Security," InternetCookies.com, accessed March 9, 2023, http://www.internetcookies.com/.

34. Templafy and Templafy, "How Many Emails Are Sent Every Day? Top Email Statistics for Businesses." Templafy, October 12, 2022, https://www.templafy.com/blog/how-many-emails-are-sent-every-day-top-email-statistics-your-business-needs-to-know.

35. Scott Cohen, "13 Examples of Reengagement Emails for the Subscribers You Miss." HubSpot Blog. (HubSpot, June 11, 2021), https://blog.hubspot.com/marketing/10-examples-of-effective-re-engagement-emails.

36. "How to Create a Re-Engagement Email Template." Campaign Monitor, accessed February 20, 2023, https://www.campaignmonitor.com/resources/knowledge-base/how-to-create-a-re-engagement-email-template/.

37. "How to Create a Reengagement Email Template." Campaign Monitor.

38. J. G. Navarro, "U.S. Loyalty Program Membership 2022." *Statista*, January 6, 2023, https://www.statista.com/statistics/618744/average-number-of-loyalty-programs-us-consumers-belong-to/.

39. Julia Faria, "Topic: Loyalty Programs in the United States." *Statista*, January 6, 2023, https://www.statista.com/topics/7986/loyalty-programs-in-the-us/#dossierKeyfigures.

40. Casey Lewis, "Here's What the Victoria's Secret Catalog Looked like 40 Years Ago." Racked. Racked, July 25, 2016, https://www.racked.com/2016/7/25/12119174/victorias-secret-catalog-rip.

41. "Is the PS5 Sony's Fastest Selling Console Ever?" Android Authority, January 27, 2023, https://www.androidauthority.com/how-many-ps5-sold-3192706/.

42. Marcus Stewart, "Sony Unveils PlayStation Stars, a New Loyalty Program Aimed at Players." Game Informer, accessed February 20, 2023, https://www.gameinformer.com/2022/07/14/sony-unveils-playstation-stars-a-new-loyalty-program-aimed-at-players.

43. Mikhail Gurevich, Dmitry Nosov, and Nikita Krichfalushiy. "Top 5 Branded Apps: Revealing Branded App Success Secrets." Azoft, April 15, 2021, https://www.azoft.com/blog/top-5-branded-apps/.

44. John Koetsier, "Top Apps of 2022 by Installs, Spend, and Active Users: Report." *Forbes*, October 12, 2022, https://www.forbes.com/sites/johnkoetsier/2022/03/23/top-apps-of-2022-by-installs-spend-and-active-users-report/.

45. Anna Hensel, "Why Retailers Are Seeing App Downloads Surge." Modern Retail, May 4, 2022, https://www.modernretail.co/retailers/why-retailers-are-seeing-app-downloads-surge/.

46. "Inmobi Calculating the Value of Apps." Reach Premium In-App Audiences Programmatically, accessed February 20, 2023, https://go.inmobi.com/inmobi-calculating-the-value-of-apps-2022/.

47. "Inmobi Calculating the Value of Apps."

48. "Find the Best Social CRM Software." Best Social CRM Software - 2023 Reviews & Pricing, accessed February 20, 2023, https://www.softwareadvice.com/crm/social-crm-comparison/.

49. Christina Newberry, "Social CRM: What It Is and Why Your Social Strategy Needs It." Social Media Marketing & Management Dashboard, December 20, 2022, https://blog.hootsuite.com/social-crm/.

50. CRM.org., "What Is Social Crm? 10 Best Social Media CRM Tools & Software Platforms." CRM.org, September 27, 2022, https://crm.org/crmland/social-crm.

51. Daniel Ruby, "54+ CRM Statistics Every Business Should Be Aware of in 2023." Demand Sage, January 30, 2023, https://www.demandsage.com/crm-statistics/.

52. Lionel Sujay Vailshery, "CRM Applications Market Share by Vendor 2021." *Statista*, June 13, 2022, https://www.statista.com/statistics/972598/crm-applications-vendors-market-share-worldwide/.

53. "Industry Market Research, Reports, and Statistics." IBISWorld. Accessed February 20, 2023, https://www.ibisworld.com/industry-statistics/number-of-businesses/crm-system-providers-united-states.

54. HubSpot. "Hubspot CRM Platform Roi." HubSpot. Accessed February 20, 2023, https://www.hubspot.com/roi.

55. Daniel Ruby, "54+ CRM Statistics Every Business Should Be Aware of in 2023."

56. Daniel Ruby, "54+ CRM Statistics Every Business Should Be Aware of in 2023."

57. Darrell K. Rigby, Frederick F. Reichheld, and Phil Schefter. "Avoid the four perils of CRM." *Harvard Business Review* 80, no. 2 (2002): 101–6.

Appendix

Comprehensive Class Project

This appendix provides a framework and exercises for a class project in line with the content covered in this book. The project can be adapted to many course formats and ability levels. While this text is most frequently used in undergraduate courses, it can be used in graduate programs and full-semester or accelerated programs. The project can also be facilitated both in person and when teaching online.

The project can be assigned individually, in groups, or as standalone exercises. For projects, it is recommended that students be assessed throughout the process and given feedback to help improve their projects. Instructors can choose to have students work with real businesses either as clients or from secondary research. An alternative is offered here to structure the project around creating a new product or service, allowing students greater freedom and creativity. While real businesses have the advantage of giving students exposure to the "real-life" world of business, there can be drawbacks, such as the availability of client company contact and the time pressure of the academic semester.

Some tips for success for this type of project to help both the instructor and the students include the following:

1. Have a specific contact at each client company who will be responsible for communication with the group. The student group should also assign a leader who will serve as the communication liaison.

2. Choose a client that will communicate with teams about business objectives, customer segments and behavior, and other business-related issues that might not be immediately evident as related to digital marketing.

3. Develop and sign a contract or "scope of work" with the expected deliverable(s) and due dates. This can help keep the project on track.

4. Direct students to complete components as they are introduced throughout the semester (as noted above) and have the instructor provide feedback on each component. This process also helps keep the project on track.

5. Use publicly available information in short-form courses. If working in a six-, seven-, or eight-week module, instead of asking the students to create a new product or service, another option is a product-line extension for an existing company. The Fortune 1000 provides a good list from which students can select companies that will have enough of a web and social media presence so that the students can perform their analysis and make recommendations.

6. Use caution if students choose to work with a local franchise. Their audit and suggestions will be limited because most franchise owners have very limited or no creative control over the website, app, and email marketing campaigns. It is recommended that they choose an independent small business.

This appendix is written under the assumption of a group-based project and includes discussions and assignments for both (1) working with an existing business and (2) creating a new product or service.

Project Option #1 – Working with Existing Businesses as a Real Client Company or from Secondary Research

Assignment #1 – Company Assessment

As a foundation for a digital marketing strategy, students will be asked to conduct research to gain an understanding of their company's business, current marketing efforts, and market analysis. Instructors may choose to find companies for teams to work with or allow students to reach out to potential companies themselves. The project can be structured so that there is one company that all teams work with, versus each team having a unique company. Students can work with a real-life company one-on-one or from publicly available information. In this case, as noted above, a Fortune 1000 company is a good choice to have enough public information.

Students should be instructed to learn more about their companies through their websites, social media sites, and other marketing materials. Students should also be instructed to meet with a representative from their client company at least once for a real-life project. Remember that working with local franchises does not yield the best results. Typically, the corporate office controls their digital strategies.

Students should refer to chapters 1–5 for this assignment.

Students should provide a report with the following information:

Company Profile:

- Name, location, and number of employees. Provide a brief history of the business and describe their business model, pipe, or platform. Include a summary of goods and/or services offered, and the company's value proposition. Library resources such as Standard & Poor's NetAdvantage or D&B Hoovers can often provide this information.
- Report the website URL, along with a description of the website and its purpose. Note the website's age and any other relevant factors.
- Report any social media profiles being used by the company.
- Discuss the company's main distribution channels and subchannels (e.g., the website is the company's main channel for sales, but they also have a small sales team that identifies and contacts potential customers).
- Discuss any customer retention strategies, including email marketing, used by the company.
- Report any additional relevant information.

Market Analysis:

- Who are the company's current and potential customers (this can be obtained through the company interview).
- Who are the company's current and potential competitors (this can be obtained through the company interview and through first-hand research). Library databases such as D&B Hoovers can often provide this insight.
- Provide a brief overview of the industry (key characteristics, competitive/ saturated/mature). Library sources such as Mintel are great for this type of background information.
- Note if there is any seasonality for the goods or services that you or the company have identified.

- Is the company emphasizing one of the generic marketing strategies (acquisition, conversion, retention, and value growth) more than another? What does that mean for how it manages the customer lifecycle?
- How does the company rank relative to its industry in customer service? Is customer service a differentiator for the company?
- Report any other relevant market information.

Objectives

- Describe the company's digital marketing objectives and goals (e.g., increase awareness, engagement, etc.). What are their goals in terms of the generic marketing strategies of acquisition, conversion, retention, and value growth?
- Has the company identified key performance indicators (KPIs) to measure their goals? If so, report and evaluate them. You may also offer additional KPIs. If they do not have KPIs, provide and discuss some suggestions.

Assignment #2 – Website Evaluation

For the second assignment, student teams will evaluate the company's website. Students should refer to chapters 6 and 12 for this assignment.

Website Evaluation (~3 pages)

- Briefly state the website objectives (e.g., sales, customer service)
- Who is the primary audience (can be more than one)? Is there a secondary audience?
- Conduct a persona analysis for the audience (refer to Chapter 6). Does the website design appear to match the needs of this persona?
- Discuss the website's strengths and weaknesses (content, functionality, and aesthetics). Ask questions like: Does the site clearly communicate the value proposition? Is the site easy to navigate? Does the site load properly? Is the site optimized for mobile? Is contact information available and clearly visible? Are there any accessibility issues?
- Students can use website evaluation tools such as Hubspot's Website Grader (https://website.grader.com/), GTmetrix (https://gtmetrix.com/), and Accessibility Checker (https://www.accessibilitychecker.org/)
- Recommendations: Provide simple, actionable, and well-justified advice on your company's future online marketing efforts in relation to their website.
- If possible, provide traffic summary information from Google Analytics or other software.
- If you suggest changes to the site, it is helpful to provide visuals to illustrate.

Content Assessment (~ 2–3 pages)

- Identify the current content that best supports the company's objectives. If you have access to analytics, you can use this to identify content that has high engagement.
- Does it appear that the content matches the needs of the target audience, and is it written in a voice that represents the company and resonates with the target audience?
- If necessary, recommend additional content to support the site's objectives (e.g., gain awareness, support the buying process, increase engagement, and promote return visits).
- Remember to consider user-generated content too, such as reviews, ratings, and comments, if applicable.

Assignment #3 – Search Engine Marketing

For this assignment, student teams will evaluate the company's website. Students should refer to chapters 7 and 8. Students should be instructed to write for the company (not the professor) since many clients may not be familiar with SEO terminology. The recommendations should be actionable, and students should avoid making assumptions about a client's SEO knowledge.

Organic Search (SEO)

Conduct a thorough analysis of the website in regard to SEO. Use HubSpot's website grader (https://website.grader.com/) or other tools to help you. Depending on the size of the site, you may be able to evaluate the entire site or just focus on a few important pages for the bullets below. Remember, recommendations are made for individual pages, not the entire site.

- Are they actively targeting specific keywords?
  - If so, evaluate them (i.e., are they good, or should they consider others?) If not, provide some suggestions. You can use tools like Moz's Keyword Explorer: https://moz.com/explorer.
- Examine the use of Meta Tags (title, description, alt tags, etc.)
  - How are they doing? Are they missing any important tags? Do pages have unique titles and descriptions? Are they high quality and reflective of the content and targeted keywords? Provide concrete examples of how to improve.
  - You can use free tools like ScreamingFrog's SEO Spider tool to help identify issues (https://www.screamingfrog.co.uk/quick-start-guide/). This tool also creates a spreadsheet that contains relevant SEO data for each webpage, including title, descriptions, and alt tags). Figure A.1 provides an example of this output.

Figure A.1 **An Example of Screaming Frog's Crawl Output** Source: https://www.screamingfrog.co.uk/quick-start-guide

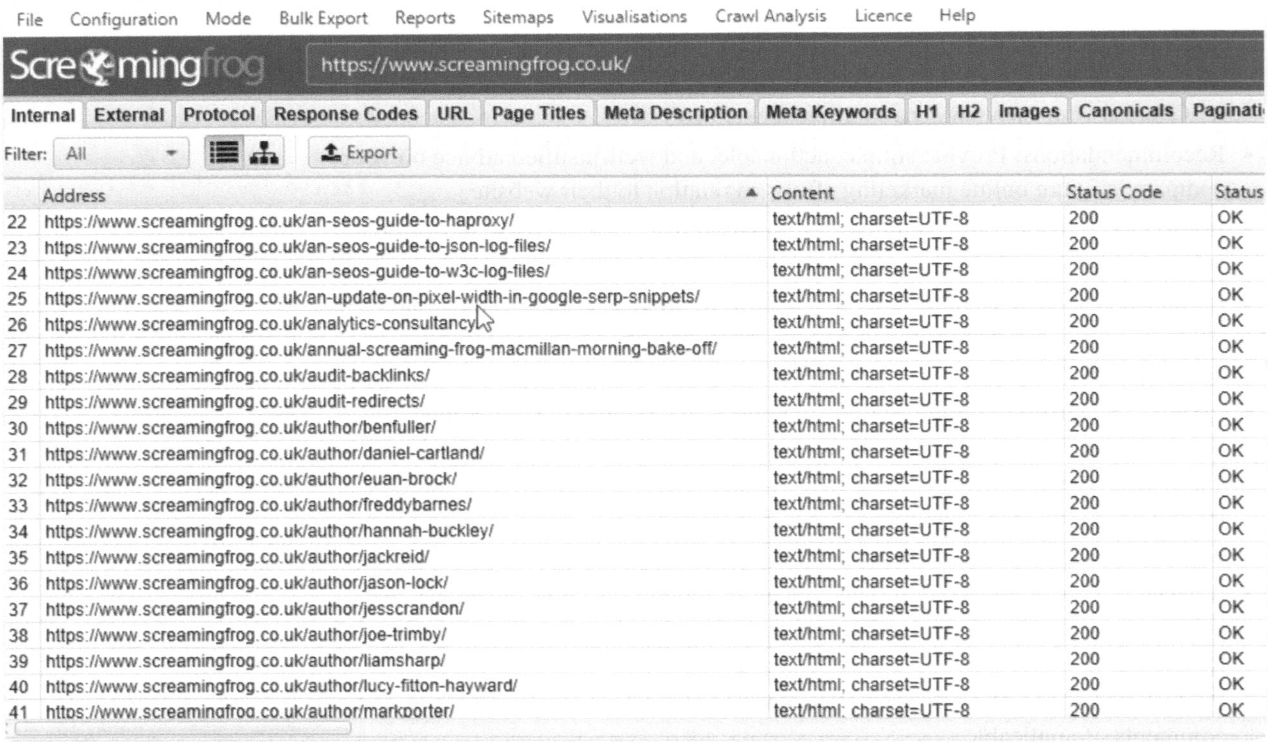

As seen in Figure A.2, the tool also can be used to identify issues, such as missing tags and tags that exceed recommended lengths.

- Examine the site's backlinks using tools like Moz's Link Explorer (https://moz .com/link-explorer). How strong are the current inbound links? Provide suggestions for link building (e.g., high-authority websites that are relevant to the company's business and site content).

Figure A.2 **An Example of Screaming Frog's Errors & Issues Report** Source: https://www.screamingfrog.co.uk/quick-start-guide

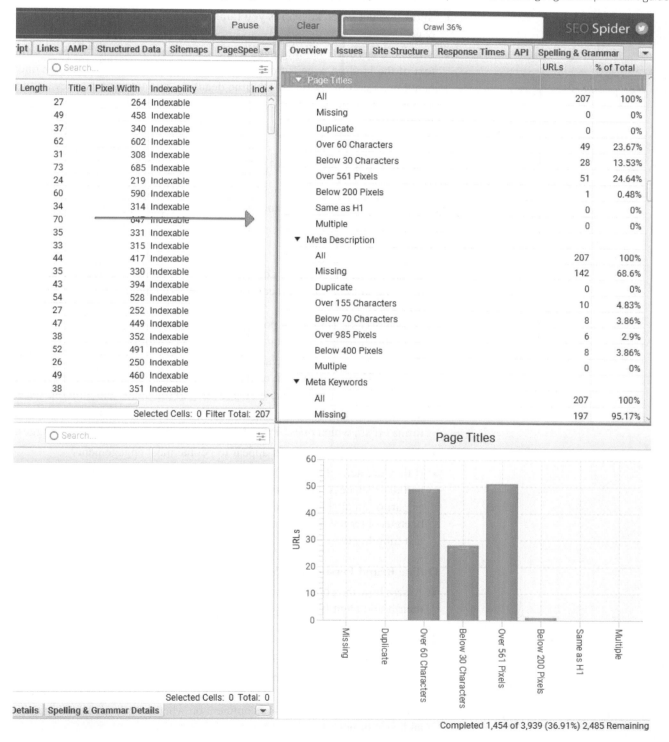

Paid Search

Using what you learned in your course readings and class discussions, you will write three text search ads for your company. Your goal is to create three search ads that would entice prospective customers on search to click on your ad and come to your company's website's landing page, then take an action on your landing page to drive them to the next stage of the funnel.

Using PowerPoint, PowerPoint Online, or Google Slides, create a 3-slide presentation:

- Slide 1: Screenshot of your three ads.
- Slide 2: A list of ten keywords you think are appropriate for the ad and landing page.
- Slide 3: Copy for a landing page and a strong call to action. "Copy" is the text of the landing page for one of your ads. It should include at least one headline, a call to action with a time deadline, and text that is relevant to your selected ad. Indicate which of your three ads you are using to connect to your landing page.

Assignment #4 – Social Media Strategy

For this assignment, student teams will evaluate the company's social media presence. Students should refer to chapters 9 and 8 when completing this assignment.

Social Media Assessment

- Create a table to report the company's social media usage: Include the following for each social media channel: profile name, the number of followers,
  average weekly activity (# posts per week), and average engagement rate (e.g., # of followers who engage/total number of followers).
- Critique the company's social media profiles for completeness and best practices (see Hootsuite guide & reading: https://blog.hootsuite.com/how-to-create-a-social-media-marketing-plan/#Step_5_Set_up_accounts_and_improve_profiles).
- Should the company consider participating in additional social media platforms? If so, which ones? Provide a purpose and rationale for each suggestion.
- What types of posts/content appear to get the most engagement?
- If they are actively using hashtags, report how they have been using them and their success. For example, they may be using #AdventureWithFriends as part of an advertising campaign. Report how many times the hashtag has been used by the brand and its followers over time periods (the last week, last month, etc.)

Online Brand Persona and Voice

- Assess how the company presents itself on social media. Does it align with their brand identity?

Traffic Source Assessment

- If you have access to the company's Google Analytics account, report the monthly website traffic generated by social media.
- If you have access to the company's social media analytics, report audience demographic information and comment on whether they are reaching the right audience or not.

Competitor Analysis

- Conduct a competitor assessment by exploring how two or three competitors are using social media. Create a table with the following: the competitor's name, platform, profile username, number of followers, and strengths and weaknesses.
- Is there anything you can learn anything from the competitors? (i.e., are they doing something that may benefit your company?)

Social Media Objectives

- State the company's social media objectives. For example, increase brand awareness through Twitter, increase followers on Instagram by 20% in 2 months, etc.
- Identify KPIs.

Strategies and Tools

- Discuss strategies for paid, owned, and earned activity. This section can be short but offer some ideas that the company can implement. You may suggest sponsored content or identify influencers to promote a product.
- Does the company use a posting calendar to plan content?
  - What types of topics are covered?
  - Create a sample content calendar for the company or provide suggestions on how to improve their content calendar.
  - Identify key dates, if any, for the company (e.g., holidays to focus on, etc.)

Social Media Roles and Responsibilities

- Who is responsible for managing the account(s)? What is their role and title?

Social Media Crisis Response Plan

- Does the company have one in place? If not, briefly discuss why it is important and offer an example that fits with the company. Refer to chapter 9 and https://sproutso -cial.com/insights/social-media-crisis-plan/ for more detailed examples and steps.

Additional Recommendations

- Provide any additional recommendations as you see fit.

Assignment #5 – Promoted Social Media & Influencers
Promoted Social Media Posts

Using what you learned in your course readings and class discussions, you will create a sample social media post that can be promoted on one of the company's social media channels. Your goal is to create an engaging post to entice prospective customers to click on your post while scrolling their social media feeds. The post can have the objective of getting more social media followers or bringing customers to the company's website.

- Use Canva or another visual tool to create a social media post. Think through if you want to create a story/reel, carousel, or static post. What makes the most sense for your company's product? Ask the company for photos, videos, or other pre-existing assets that you can use.
- Create engaging and relevant text to include with the post.
- Conduct hashtag research to identify at least four relevant hashtags to include with the post.
- Describe suggested targeting, such as age, demographics, and interests.

Social Media Influencers

Identify key influencers that your client's company can reach out to for partnerships. Identify at least five key influencers.

For each influencer, report the following:

- Name
- Channel(s) and profile name(s)
- Reach (number of followers)
- A screenshot of the influencer and or a relevant post by the influencer
- A brief description of why this person is a good fit for your product
- Research the cost of how much the suggested influencers cost. A good place to start is https://influencermarketinghub.com/instagram-money-calculator/ https://influencermarketinghub.com/. Keep in mind that most companies do not have huge advertising budgets.

Assignment #6 – Email Marketing and Customer Retention

Students should refer to chapters 11 and 8. Remember, email is best used as a retention tool for people we already know. Your task is to create an email for your company with the objective of retaining current customers. (If you were sending to a live list of customers or prospects, you would first send a welcome email asking their permission to send future emails, or you would have already gathered permission another way).

The email should have the objective of retaining current customers.

- Define the audience for the email.
- Select the purpose of the email beyond the general objective of retaining current customers. This purpose could be an invitation to a seminar, a contest, or just information about upcoming product enhancements.
- Create a sample email in a product like Mailchimp, which offers a free account, or just create it in Word, PowerPoint, or another design tool.
- Make sure to include a relevant call to action in the email with all the necessary elements such as a time deadline.

Project Option #2 – Developing a New Product or Service

For this option, student teams will come up with a new product or service idea. They will complete a series of assignments to plan the product launch on a crowdfunding site, such as Kickstarter or IndieGoGo, design the website, plan website content, optimize the website for search, and identify the social media platforms and content types for a successful social media strategy.

Assignment #1 – Product Idea & Kickstarter Page

Product Idea

Briefly discuss your product. Include the following:

- What is your product or service's value proposition?
- Identify your business model.
- Discuss the target market (who are the potential customers?). Keep in mind that anyone can buy a product, but smart marketers only spend money to advertise to select groups so they use their budget wisely.

- Identify competitors and compare your idea to them.
- Identify the distribution channels that you will use post crowdfunding (e.g., ecommerce: Amazon.com, Target.com, Walmart.com; brick and mortar stores: small boutiques vs. big box stores). Discuss why you will choose one over another.

Brand Identity

What will you call your brand? Briefly explain your thought process and decision.

- Conduct a thorough online search for your brand name and product to make sure that (1) your idea is not already being done and (2) that the brand name is not already being used.
- Conduct a trademark search to make sure that your product/brand name is trademarked. If it is, choose another that is not: https://www.uspto.gov/trademarks -application-process/search-trademark-database. Figures A.3–A.7 illustrate the steps to complete a simple trademark search for the purpose of this exercise.

Figure A.3   Step 1 for Conducting a Trademark Search

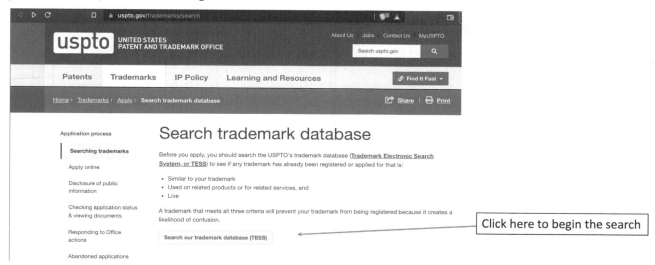

Figure A.4   Step 2 for Conducting a Trademark Search

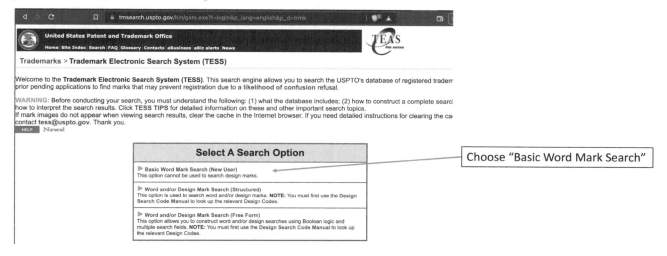

Figure A.5   Step 3 for Conducting a Trademark Search

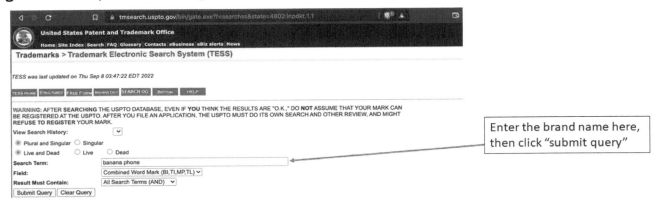

Enter the brand name here, then click "submit query"

Figure A.6   Step 4 for Conducting a Trademark Search

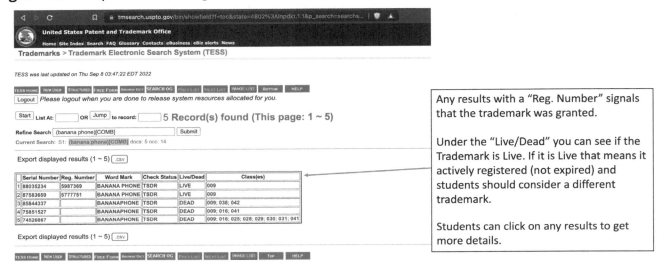

Any results with a "Reg. Number" signals that the trademark was granted.

Under the "Live/Dead" you can see if the Trademark is Live. If it is Live that means it actively registered (not expired) and students should consider a different trademark.

Students can click on any results to get more details.

Figure A.7   Step 5 for Conducting a Trademark Search

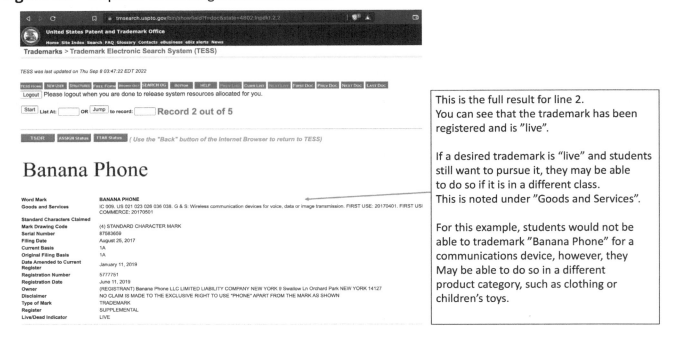

This is the full result for line 2.
You can see that the trademark has been registered and is "live".

If a desired trademark is "live" and students still want to pursue it, they may be able to do so if it is in a different class.
This is noted under "Goods and Services".

For this example, students would not be able to trademark "Banana Phone" for a communications device, however, they May be able to do so in a different product category, such as clothing or children's toys.

Kickstarter Information Page

Go to https://www.kickstarter.com/ and browse through some project pages. Note projects you like and dislike (this does not need to be included in this paper). Browse through the Getting Started Handbook for more detailed information (https://www.kickstarter.com /help/handbook/getting_started?ref=handbook_index)

Provide the following for your product:

- **Project Title** (limit 60 characters)
  This should be catchy and include information about your product.
- **Short blurb** (135 character limit)
  Give people a sense of what you're doing. Skip "Help me" and focus on what you're making.
- **Project Description** (No character limit)
  - Use your project description to share more about what you're raising funds to do and how you plan to pull it off. It's up to you to make the case for your project.
  - Include a description of images or videos that you would use.
- **Goals & Rewards**
  Come up with some goals and rewards. Since we aren't doing any in-depth cost analysis, your recommendations should be based on other projects.

Assignment #2 Website Design

Website

For the second assignment, student teams will plan a website for their new product or service launch. Students should refer to chapters 6 and 12 for this assignment.

Domain Name

Conduct a domain name search using use https://porkbun.com/ or https://domains.google/ and choose one that is available. Note the cost and other domains that are already in use (e.g., you were hoping to register brandx.com, but it was taken, so you will register brandx.net).

Website Objectives & Persona Analysis

- Briefly state the website objectives (e.g., sales, customer service)
- Who is the primary audience? Is there a secondary audience?
- Create a persona for your primary audience (refer to chapter 6). Keep this in mind for designing the website mock-up.

Website Mock-Up

Create a simple but well-thought-out design mock-up for each page of your website.This can be done with a variety of software tools (e.g., Photoshop, PowerPoint, Canva, etc.). At this point, you do not need to write out all of the content—you can simply describe the content for each page and its purpose. This includes visual content too.

Consider including generated content, too (e.g., reviews, ratings, and comments). Make sure to consider site colors, navigation, and other relevant factors.

Assignment #3 Search Engine Marketing Plan

For this assignment, student teams will optimize their website from assignment #2 and plan a paid search campaign. Students should refer to chapters 7 and 8.

Keyword Research

- Step 1: Use tools like Moz's Keyword Explorer (https://moz.com/explorer) to identify target keywords/phrases for each page of your website.
- Step 2: Write a title and a description for each page of the website that integrates your keywords/phrases.
- Step 3: Consider what types of content you should add to the site. This content should provide value to your customers while also attracting others to share and link to your site. Discuss the different types of content you may use (e.g., infographics, photos, videos, recipes, etc.) and the topics that this content will cover.
- Step 4: Consider other sites that would be ideal sites for link building (i.e., sites with authoritative domains that are relevant to your site). Use Moz's Open Site Explorer (https://moz.com/researchtools/ose/) or other link-building tools to identify high-authority sites and high-traffic sites.

Paid Search

You will write three text search ads. Your goal is to create three search ads that would entice prospective customers on search to click on your ad and come to your company's website's landing page, then take an action on your landing page to drive them to the next stage of the funnel.

Using PowerPoint, PowerPoint Online, or Google Slides, create a 3-slide presentation:
- Slide 1: Screenshot of your three ads
- Slide 2: List of ten keywords you think are appropriate for the ad and landing page
- Slide 3: Copy for a landing page and a strong call to action. 'Copy' is the text of the landing page for one of your ads. It should include at least one headline, a call to action with a time deadline, and text that is relevant to your selected ad. Indicate which of your three ads you are using to connect to your landing page.

Assignment #4 Social Media Strategy
Social Media Strategy

For this assignment, student teams will create a social media plan for their new product or service. When completing this assignment, students should refer to chapters 9 and 8.

Social Media Assessment
- Identify which social media channels you will have a presence on. Discuss why you chose these channels over others. For example, if you are creating a new makeup brand, you may choose Instagram and TikTok as your main social media channels because of the visual nature of both of these platforms and audience characteristics and demographics.
- Provide a purpose and rationale for each channel.
- Conduct hashtag research using a free tool such as https://ritetag.com/ to identify relevant hashtags.

Competitor Analysis

- Conduct a competitor assessment by exploring how two or three competitors are using social media. Create a table with the following: the competitor's name, platform, profile username, number of followers, and strengths and weaknesses.
- Is there anything you can learn anything from the competitors, i.e., are they doing something that may benefit your brand?
- Identify the types of content that get the most engagement.

Strategies and Tools

- Discuss strategies for paid, owned, and earned activity. This can be short- but offer some ideas that the company can implement. You may suggest sponsored content or identify influencers to promote a product.

Social Media Influencers

Identify key influencers that you can reach out to for your product launch. Identify at least five key influencers.

For each influencer report the following:

- Name
- Channel(s) and profile name(s)
- Reach (number of followers)
- A screenshot of the influencer and or a relevant post by the influencer
- A brief description of why this person is a good fit for your product
- Research the cost of how much the suggested influencers cost. A good place to start is https://influencermarketinghub.com/instagram-money-calculator/ https://influencermarketinghub.com/. Keep in mind that most companies do not have huge advertising budgets.

Social Media Crisis Response Plan & Content Calendar

Instructors may also consider having students create a social media crisis response plan or content calendar. Refer to Chapter 9 and also https://blog.hootsuite.com/how-to-create-a-social-media-content-calendar/ and https://sproutsocial.com/insights/social-media-crisis-plan/ for more detailed examples and steps.

Glossary

360° (complete)   a comprehensive view of the customer, often a profile that interfaces with the firm's customer journey map.

A

A/B Testing   A controlled experiment that helps optimize web pages. The digital marketer creates two (or more) communication pieces (i.e., email, promotion, landing page) and presents one communication to one group and the other communication to the other group. The marketer then compares the results using the proper statistical test to determine which one works best.

above the fold   content that appears on a screen without scrolling.

ad exchange   a digital marketplace where advertisers and publishers purchase and sell ad inventory directly in an auction setting.

ad extensions   additional information with the ad such as a phone number, locations and reviews and can increase the click-through rate.

ad network   a platform that collects ad inventory from publishers and sells it to advertisers. It acts as an intermediary between advertisers and publishers.

ad serving   technology that places and tracks ads on digital properties (websites, mobile apps, etc.).

adaptive site   a type of site design in which a different site is created for each user device.

AdSense   a way to monetize a website or a blog on Google by showing paid ads.

affiliate programs   programs that offer incentives to partner websites, wherein a website agrees to post a link to a transactional site in return for a commission on sales made as a direct result of the link.

alt tag   a tag (a type of IMG or image tag) that describes the image for people who cannot see it because of browser limitations or physical disabilities or when an image fails to properly display.

analytical CRM   mining the customer data and developing programs or predictive models based on the resulting insights and data discovery.

artificial intelligence (AI)   the ability of a computer to mimic human behaviors.

audience development   creating a loyal following for branded content.

augmented reality (AR)   an enhanced version of reality created by superimposing computer-generated images on top of the user's view of the real world.

affiliate   offers incentives to partner websites, wherein a website agrees to post a link (through an ad or other content) to a transactional site in return for a commission on sales made as a direct result of the link.

B

BANT   Budget, Authority, Need, Time—a process used to qualify sales leads.

behavioral targeting   presenting relevant content, such as ads, based on users' previous activities.

big data   unstructured data sets that are so large and complex that traditional data processing is challenged to analyze them.

Bitcoin   the first cryptocurrency.

blockchain   a shared, immutable ledger that facilitates the process of recording transactions and tracking assets in a business network.

bounce rate   number of bounces divided by number of emails sent.

brand community   a group of like-minded people who share interests grouping around a brand on the internet to communicate with one another and the brand.

breadcrumbs   a navigational aid showing path that the user has followed.

broad match   a search setting allowing for matching on a wide variation of a keyword or set of keywords.

brokers   a business model that brings buyers and sellers together to exchange goods and services, often in exchange for a fee or commission.

business models   the processes by which a business creates value, provides value to its customers, and captures value in the form of profits.

business process management (BPM)   a systematic attempt to make business processes more efficient.

buy cycle   (or buying cycle) the process a customer goes through in deciding to make a purchase.

buyer's journey   the customer's path on the buying process.

buying center   a group of people in an organization who make decisions for high-value and/or risky purchases.

buying group   (also known as the buying committee) a set of six to 10 team members, also known as decision makers, that are needed to make the purchase decision and to bring the sales cycle to a close.

C

call center   a department within an organization that handles telephone sales and/or service.

CAN-SPAM Act   the U.S. law regulating advertising and promotional emails.

channels of distribution   intermediaries through which products and information about transactions move in the course of a single exchange.

click-through-rate (CTR)   the total number of clicks that a link receives divided by the number of times it is shown (in an ad, email, etc.).

click-to-open rate   the number of clicks that an external link embedded in an email receives.

cloud computing   a network of remote servers hosted on the internet, not a local server or computer hard drive, to store data and programs and to process data.

co-creation   business entities or businesses and their customers together to create mutually valuable outcomes.

comment spam   an abusive practice in which comments are placed on a blog or website, perhaps robotically, for the sole purpose of generating a backlink to improve search results.

community model   a type of business model that utilizes the network effects of the internet to connect like-minded individuals and groups.

confirmed opt-in   somewhere in between opt-in and double opt-in; the visitor actively acquiesces to receiving email, again probably by another email confirmation.

content management system (CMS)   software that assists in the building and maintenance of a website, thus allowing people with little or no coding skills to add or edit website content.

content marketing   a strategic approach to creating and distributing content.

conversion   when the customer takes an action desired by the marketer, such as a first purchase or signing up to receive more product information.

cookies   a few lines of code that a website or advertising network places on a user's computer to store data about the user's activities on the site. Cookies can be classified as either first-party or third-party depending on how they are used.

cost-per-thousand (CPM)   the amount paid in purchasing advertising; in this case, it means the

cost-per-thousand (M is the abbreviation for the Roman numeral for thousand) impressions, or the cost divided by the total number of impressions.

Cost per Action (CPA)   an advertising payment model where advertisers are charged for actions other than clicks, such as moving a cursor over an ad, filling out a form, liking a social media post, etc.

customer relationship management (CRM)   (or customer relationship marketing) the process of managing and tracking customer relationships across channels.

cross-selling   selling a different, related product to an existing customer.

crowdfunding   a type of community model that is used to obtain needed resources, including financing, by soliciting from a community instead of traditional funding sources.

cryptocurrency   a decentralized digital currency that utilizes blockchain technology.

curate   to select and prepare content from other sources for publication.

customer journey   a process or sequence that a customer goes through to access or use an offering of a company.

customer lifecycle   stages in the development of the relationship between the customer and the brand.

customer lifetime value (CLV)   the monetary value of a customer over time.

customer profiles   a description of a customer or set of customers that includes demographic, geographic, and psychographic characteristics. A profile could include other relevant information, such as buying patterns, creditworthiness, and purchase history.

customer sentiment   customer response to in their journey that is measured as positive, negative, or neutral.

customer experience (CX)   cumulative experiences across multiple touchpoints and in multiple channels over time.

cybersquatting   the process of registering, selling, or using a domain name with the intent of profiting from the goodwill of others (typically another company's trademark).

D

data   raw, unprocessed facts and numbers. Data mining analytic process and specialized analytic tools used to extract meaning from very large data sets.

data management platform (DMP)   platforms that collect data and integrate with DSP so that the advertisers can target the appropriate audience and improve the efficiency of their ad campaigns.

decentralized applications (dApps)   applications, such as smart contracts, that are developed on blockchains.

demand generation   entire process of developing customer demand for a product or service.

demand-driven supply   a supply chain that operates in response to demand signals from customers.

demand-side platforms (DSP)   software that connects advertisers to multiple ad exchanges to buy or bid for the inventory provided by the publishers through programmatic advertising.

digital disruption   change caused by digital technologies that disrupts ways of thinking and acting.

digital marketing   the use of any digital technology to facilitate the marketing process, with the end goal of customer interaction, engagement, and measurement.

digital transformation   the rapid change in business activities and operations caused by digital disruption.

directory   an aid in finding internet websites; a list of sites are usually arranged by category, an aid in finding internet websites; a list of sites are usually arranged by category, and the directory has a search function.

display ads   a type of digital advertisement that combines text and visuals (images and video) with a URL that links to a website where a customer can learn more about or buy products and services. Also referred to as banner ads.

DNS (Domain Name System)   a database in which human readable domain names are located and translated into Internet Protocol (IP) addresses. The internet's DNS is similar to a phone book and manages the mapping between domain names and IP addresses (numbers).

domain name   a human-readable form of an IP address. It's the destination you type into a web browser (such as www.apple.com).

double opt-in   a technique by which visitors agree to receive further communications but must perform two actions, usually checking an opt-in box on a site, and then responding positively to a sent email asking for confirmation.

dynamic content   the ability to change greeting and other content dynamically based on to whom the email is addressed.

dynamic serving   the ability to serve different site code (HTML, CSS) without changing the URL. The term "adaptive site" is synonymous.

E

earned media   buzz in both social and traditional media that is generated by users (not from the brand or company directly).

ecommerce   buying and selling goods and services online.

EDI (Electronic Data Interchange)   general term used to describe the digitizing of business information like orders and invoices so that they may be communicated electronically between suppliers and customers.

email marketing   the process of developing customer relationships through offers and communications contained in email messages.

email service providers   allows users to send email campaigns to a list of subscribers.

embedded devices   a device, often a microchip, that becomes part of another device, rendering various services, often doing so without human intervention.

ERP (Enterprise Resource Planning)   implementation of processes and software that integrates all aspects of the business from manufacturing resource planning and scheduling through service functions like human resources.

Ethereum   a decentralized blockchain with smart contract functionality. Ether is the native cryptocurrency of the platform.

event marketing   a themed activity that promotes a product, business, or cause.

exact match   a paid search parameter that is set to display to those looking for a particular phrase.

expanding ad   an ad that first appears as a standard banner ad that grows larger and extends out of the ad slot when a user interacts with the ad in some way (such as hovering over the ad or clicking the ad).

experiential marketing   promotional activity that helps consumers understand a product by having direct contact with it.

F

first-party cookies   small text files stored in the user's browser that are created by a website when a user visits. First-party cookies are designed only to be used by the website that created them (not shared across websites).

first-party data   data from a company's own websites and customer data repositories.

frequency   the number of times a person is exposed to a promotional message.

G

gas the fee required to conduct a transaction on Ethereum. These fees are paid to miners who use their computing power to validate blockchain transactions (i.e., those running the computations).

geo-fence using geolocation technology such as GPS or RFID to establish a geographical area that can be defined by a virtual perimeter.

H

hard bounce rate when an email is undeliverable, usually due to a bad email address.

hashed email a compliment and alternative to third-party cookies that applies a hash algorithm (a cryptographic tool) to produce a 32 -, 40 -, or 64-character unique identifier to identify, track, and target users.

heat maps visual representations of eye activity on a web page.

hit any file, including a graphic, that is requested from a server.

I

inbound marketing approach that is focused on being visible to potential customers and using the visibility to drive them to a website where they can transact.

index server where the information index, which has categorized websites as a best fit to certain keywords, is stored.

influencer marketing using people who are regarded as authorities in their field to help distribute brand content.

infomediaries intermediaries in channels of distribution that specialize in the capture, analysis, application, and distribution of information.

Information data that has been processed into more useful forms using techniques that range from simple summary formats to complex statistical routines.

interactive choices based on user actions that allow for response.

Internet of Everything (IoE) the use of technology to bring together people, process, data, and things to make networked connections more relevant and valuable than ever before—turning information into actions that create new capabilities, richer experiences, and unprecedented economic opportunity for businesses, individuals, and countries.

Internet of Things (IoT) network of physical objects embedded with electronics that allow the objects to collect and transfer data.

interstitial an ad that appears to float on top of the content on a desktop. On a mobile, it appears to fill the entire screen. Also referred to as a floating ad.

IP (Internet Protocol) address a number assigned to each device that uses the internet.

K

keyword (or keywords) terms, words, or phrases that are selected by the user when making a search in a search engine; also refers to terms that are bid on in a PPC system.

keyword density percentage of times a particular word is used on a website page in comparison to the number of words on that page.

KPI (key performance indicator) a metric that has been identified as an important measure or benchmark of business performance.

L

landing page a web page designed to receive visitors who are coming to the site as a result of a link from another site.

lead distribution dividing leads into categories based on their purchase readiness stage.

lead generation a process for identifying sales prospects.

lead nurturing in the demand generation process, developing relationships with customers before conversion.

lead qualification a method for determining whether a prospect has the characteristics necessary to make a purchase.

local search using a local search term in a search query.

M

manufacturer direct model bypassing intermediaries such as wholesalers and manufacturers' reps in the channel of distribution; direct from manufacturer to customer.

marketing automation system marketing interaction management system including a database, engagement engine, and analytics component.

Marketing Qualified Lead (MQL) a lead that has been through scoring and other qualification processes and is ready to be passed on to sales for further qualification.

marketing touchpoint every time a customer comes into contact with a brand before, during, or after purchase.

merchant models consist of retailers or wholesalers that offer goods and services online.

meta tag a section in the HTML header section of a website that can be used to describe the site in more detail, including content and keywords; also known as meta name, or meta element.

mixed reality   a combination of the real and virtual worlds to produce a new environment in which objects can interact and humans can interact with them.

N

native advertising   paid media in which content follows the form and function of the site on which it is placed, not traditional advertising formats.

native content   a paid advertising format where the content matches the content of the media where it appears.

negative match   a search setting that is the opposite of what is desired; used to avoid paying for unnecessary clicks.

Net Promoter Score (NPS)   customer satisfaction score calculated based on a single question, "How likely is it that you would recommend <brand> to a friend or colleague".

non-fungible tokens (NFTs)   original digital assets, like artwork, music, or other digital goods, that are created using blockchain.

O

omnichannel   a strategy that delivers personalized and consistent customer experience across multiple channels.

open rates   the number of opens divided by number of emails delivered (sent minus bounces).

operational CRM   designing and executing tactical CRM programs on the basis of data items or customer profiles.

opt-in   actively choosing to receive further communications, usually by checking a box on a registration form.

opt-out   taking an action to prevent the receipt of further communications, usually unchecking a box on a registration form.

oracles   facilitate secure communication between blockchains and off-chain systems (e.g., data providers, IoT devices, payment systems, web APIs, e-signature systems, and other blockchains).

owned media   content that a business owns and controls, such as its website and social media profiles.

P

page rank   a mathematical algorithm named after Google co-founder Larry Page to indicate how important a page is on the web; used as a metric when evaluating websites.

page views   an instance of a webpage being loaded (or reloaded) in a browser; generally measured as a page being delivered to the visitor.

paid media   traditional advertising on any channel, traditional or social, that requires payment for placement.

paid search (PPC)   the paid aspect of SEM based on an advertising model where firms seeking to rank high in specific search categories will bid on certain terms or "keywords" in the hopes of a lucrative ad ranking; also known as PPC (pay-per-click).

paid social   any type of paid promotion on social media platforms.

pareto curve   a plot of number of occurrences against percent of total; the source of the 80/20 rule.

permission marketing   gaining the customer's agreement to market it in a certain way.

persona   a way of describing different groups of customers by giving them a unique personality.

phrase match   a search setting that includes an entire phrase.

pipe   a business model where businesses create value by controlling a linear series of activities—(the classic value-chain mode). The inputs at one end of the chain undergo a series of steps that transform them into a finished product to create value. Value is produced upstream and consumed downstream.

pivot   a quick change from one business model to another. It is usually applied to startups that can make rapid model changes that may be impossible for entrenched business models of large enterprises.

pixel/pixel tag   a small bit of code in the form of a one-pixel transparent GIF that is added to the pages of a website allowing sites to track visitor activity.

platform   a business model where businesses create value by facilitating interactions between external producers and consumers.

pop-up store   (or pop-up shop) a temporary retail store.

predictive analytics   the use of data, statistical algorithms, and machine learning techniques to predict the likelihood of future outcomes or behaviors.

programmatic advertising   automating the advertising buying process through machine learning and AI.

promoted posts   regular posts for which the marketer pays a fee to have the post prominently displayed in a feed or on the platform page.

prospect   an unqualified lead.

public relations   strategic communications that manage an organization's or brand's public image and reputation through tools such as press releases, product placements, and events.

push-down ad   a type of expanding ad that appears to push down the content of a webpage when the ad expands.

R

RankBrain   a machine learning query enhancement tool. The tool can match queries to results pages taking into account relevance and the context of the search.

real-time bidding   ads are bought and sold instantaneously through electronic exchanges.

relational marketing   a facet of customer relationship marketing (CRM) that focuses on customer loyalty and long-term customer engagement.

responsive site   fluid site design that detects the user's device screen size and automatically adapts to it.

retargeting   ads are displayed based on the user's recent online behaviors.

retention   when the customer continues to make purchases.

rich media   combination of text, images, video, and other interactive elements in a digital ad.

S

Sales Accepted Lead (SAL)   a lead that has been further qualified by sales as close to conversion.

sales force automation   business processes, and the software that supports them, that permit salespeople to work more effectively both in and out of their offices by providing electronic access to important documents, customer data, and support tools like calendars.

Sales Qualified Leads (SQL)   a lead that has passed through the BANT process as fully qualified potential customers.

scenario   essentially a story about how a customer goes about purchasing a product.

search engine   a website that works to help users find the things they want to find on the internet.

search engine algorithm   search engine's "best guess" at which pages are most relevant to the user's search and in which order they should be shown.

search engine marketing (SEM)   process of getting listed on search engines.

search engine optimization (SEO)   process of designing a site and its content whereby search engines find the site without being paid to do so; also known as organic search, natural search, or algorithmic search.

semantic search   the user's intent when searching for something.

SERP (Search Engine Results Page)   a list of results displayed to users from their query.

Service-Dominant Logic   the idea that service is the basis of all economic exchange making all firms service providers and all products essentially services.

sessions   group interactions that a user has with your website that occur within a specific time frame. For example, a single user session can contain viewing multiple pages on a website or other events within the site, such as social actions or ecommerce transactions. Many analytics programs also offer a pages-per-session metric, which captures the average number of pages viewed during a session. Sessions are time-based (e.g., expire after 30 minutes of inactivity, such as with Google Analytics).

sitemap   a visualized structural plan for the organization of a website's pages and how they relate to one another. The term sitemap also refers to an XML document that lists all the pages on the site, which is used by search engines to crawl the site (e.g., https://www.apple.com/sitemap.xml).

six-sigma   quality management technique that results in near-perfect products; technically, results that fall within six standard deviations from the mean of a normal distribution.

smart contracts   sets of rules that are written and stored on the blockchain that are automatically executed once the defined conditions in the contract are met.

social commerce   using social media platforms to assist in or to conduct ecommerce activities.

social media algorithm   a set of mathematical rules that specify how social media content is presented to users.

social media crisis   a large event on social platforms that negatively impacts a brand's reputation. Also referred to as a social media storm.

soft bounce rate   when an email is temporarily undeliverable, usually due to a system problem.

Software as a Service (SaaS)   software available on a fee for use basis instead of on a license or purchase basis.

spam   unwanted email communication.

spiders   programs that "crawl" the web and follow every link or piece of data that they see and bring this information back to be stored; also known as robots.

stickiness   getting visitors to stay on the site, navigate as many paths as possible, and continue to return to the site.

subscription   a business model that delivers products, services, and content for a set fee.

supply chain   the downstream portion of the value chain, the channel from suppliers to producers.

supply-side platforms (SSPs)   software used to sell a publisher's ad inventory through programmatic advertising.

syndicated   content from another source published under license.

T

tagged web pages   a technique in which a small image is placed on a web page that tracks data about users' activity on the web page. As an example, Google Analytics uses JavaScript to track a visitor's activity across a website.

third-party cookies   using embedded references that point to other websites to share cookie information across websites.

third-party data   data collected by companies that do not have a direct relationship to a particular firm's customers.

title tag   the title the user sees in the blue bar at the top of the web page; also known as the HTML title tag.

total cost of ownership (TOC)   the purchase price of a product or service plus the indirect costs of operating it through its lifetime.

transactional marketing   focuses on the individual sale of a product or service. It focuses on short-term goals like customer acquisition and individual sales.

U

universal search   the inclusion of search results from multiple content sources such as videos, images, news, maps, books, and websites into one set of research results.

unqualified leads   a potential sales lead for which there is no qualifying data beyond membership in a relevant industry.

unstructured data   data that has no predetermined models or is not organized in a predefined way. Unstructured data is often heavily text but not necessarily all text.

unsubscribe rate   number of people who unsubscribe from the company's marketing emails.

up-selling   to upgrade an existing customer's account by selling more expensive products or packages to increase the revenue value of that customer.

usability   the ability of a site to provide a satisfactory user experience.

user experience (UX)   a term to describe the usability of a website or a mobile app. Its ultimate goal is to provide user satisfaction at every stage of the digital experience. While it is considered by many to be synonymous with customer experience (CX), some feel that the term UX is not as comprehensive as CX.

user intent   what the user is actually searching for online.

utility   business model that delivers services or content on a metered or "pay-as-you-go" basis.

UTM parameter   short pieces of code added to links to help identify and track the campaign performance.

V

value   essentially the usefulness (economic utility) of the product less its price; also known as customer value or customer perceived value.

value chain   an integrated supply chain in which transactions are conducted electronically.

value ecosystem   a way to connect brands and their customers and business partners in a direct, non-linear fashion.

value proposition   a description of the customer value delivered to a specific target market.

virtual reality (VR)   simulation of a three-dimensional image or environment with which the user can interact by using special equipment.

virtual value chain   an integrated value chain that operates exclusively on the internet.

W

website convention   an established design norm that has become ingrained in users' schemas (mental maps).

wireframe   a blueprint that specifies the layout of pages on a website (similar to a template).

WYSIWYG   (what you see is what you get) website editing software that allows content to be created and edited without the need for coding. Content is often entered into a form that resembles its appearance when displayed as a website (as opposed to viewing code).

Z

Zettabytes (ZB)   another iteration of byte; this is multiplication by the 7th power of 1,000 or 10^{21}.

Index